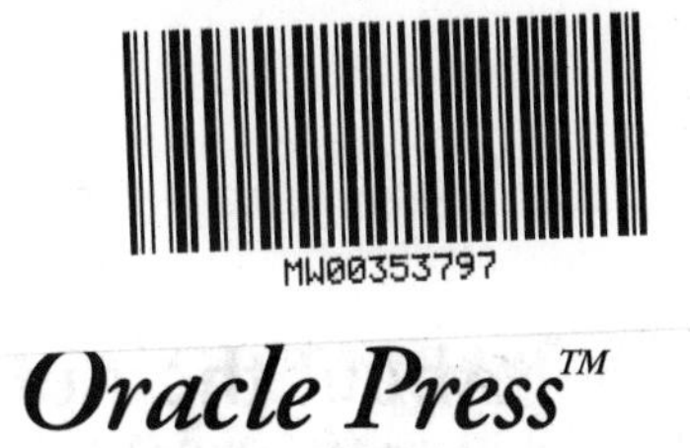

Oracle Press™

PeopleSoft Developer's Guide for PeopleTools & PeopleCode

About the Author

Judi A. Doolittle has a MS in Computer Resource Management from Webster University and a BS from the University of the State of New York. She became an Oracle Certified Professional in 2001. She has worked with databases since 1983 on multiple platforms in multiple database software settings. She spent five years as a Computer Technology Instructor for Central Carolina Technical College. She spent seven years in the corporate world as a Senior Analyst before moving to the University and Government setting working with PeopleSoft. She obtained her first PeopleSoft position with the University of Utah in 2002, where she was trained by a top-notch team of PeopleSoft developers. She currently is the lead for the PeopleSoft Pension team at a National Laboratory. She is the Executive Vice President of the Independent Oracle Users Group (IOUG), and a member of the Fusion Council.

About the Contributing Author

Barbara Sandoval is the Project Lead for PeopleSoft Payroll at a National Laboratory. She holds an MBA from Webster University in Computer Resource Management and a BBA from the University of New Mexico. She has 18 years of experience in Information Technology applications, supporting HR/Payroll/Benefits/Time and Labor systems. For the last five years, she has worked with PeopleSoft applications.

About the Technical Editor

Steve Stein is a 25-year solutions veteran who has a techno-MBA from Drexel University's LeBow School of Business. Currently an associate in the Oracle Business Intelligence practice with Perot Systems Consulting, he also worked as an EPM Product Lead Consultant at PeopleSoft. He is also the webmaster of www.phrug.com for the Quest Greater Philadelphia User Group, is a frequent presenter on PeopleSoft topics to the Oracle and Quest User Group Community, and is the host of the Blogtalkradio podcast "BI dashboard Steve" for visual dashboard design.

Oracle Press™

PeopleSoft Developer's Guide for PeopleTools & PeopleCode

Judi Doolittle

New York Chicago San Francisco
Lisbon London Madrid Mexico City Milan
New Delhi San Juan Seoul Singapore Sydney Toronto

The McGraw·Hill Companies

Cataloging-in-Publication Data is on file with the Library of Congress

PeopleSoft Developer's Guide for PeopleTools & PeopleCode

1 2 3 4 5 6 7 8 9 0 DOC DOC 0 1 9 8

ISBN 978-0-07-149662-9
MHID 0-07-149662-9

Sponsoring Editor
Lisa McClain

Editorial Supervisor
Patty Mon

Project Manager
Vasundhara Sawhney, International Typesetting and Composition

Acquisitions Coordinator
Mandy Canales

Technical Editor
Steve Stein

Copy Editors
Claire Splan
Bob Campbell

Proofreader
Christine Andreasen

Indexer
Claire Splan

Production Supervisor
George Anderson

Composition
International Typesetting and Composition

Illustration
International Typesetting and Composition

Art Director, Cover
Jeff Weeks

Cover Designer
Pattie Lee

This book is dedicated to Blair Wolf, who studies under-appreciated life forms, one of which is me. I love you and thank you for appreciating my uniqueness. And to my best friend Anna Weddington: you have taught me strength and grace—I love you.

—Judi Doolittle

To my husband, James, and my children, Lillian, Victoria, and Nicholas. Love you always and forever.

—Barbara Sandoval

Contents at a Glance

PART IV

Appendixes

Contents

PART IV
Appendixes

Acknowledgments

To the McGraw-Hill team, Lisa McClain and Mandy Canales; there were many times when I was close to giving up—thank you for your patience and understanding. Many thanks to the final leg of the race of the McGraw-Hill team, Patty Mon and Vasundhara Sawhney. To my mentors past and present, especially the teacher and extraordinary businesswoman Pam Patey, who was my most influential teacher at Riverside Community College. To my friend and colleague Stan Yellott, who believed in me when I didn't yet believe in myself. And to Leah Kier—you are truly a remarkable woman, strong, intelligent, and brilliant—thank you for the beginning of my Oracle career.

To my IOUG family and friends—Carol McGury, Ian Abramson, Michael Abbey, Peter Smith, Michelle Malcher, Kent Hinkley, David Teplow, Ari Kaplan, George Trujillo, Andy Flower, Tony Jedlinski, and Steve Lemme—you are truly a source of support in the darkest hours or the best of times: what more could a girl need in a family: And I mustn't forget the incredible staff at Smith-Bucklin: Alexis, Abbey, Julie, Kristine, Stacy, Megan, and Amy.

To my family, my mother Betty Highland, my father Clyde Doolittle, sister Sandy, nieces Debra and Lena, and of course, my favorite cousin Leonard Sletager.

To my team at the University of Utah in Administrative Computing Services: Jane Handy, Lee Stenquist, Joe Taylor, Mike Robinson, Jason Moeller, Able Thompson, Hugh Beyler, Ray Lacanienta, Bill Johnson, Tracy Monson, Tim Richardson, and Garth DeVries. PeopleSoft and PeopleCode are easy for this team, and without their support and mentoring, I would not understand one piece of the code—for that I send a big thank you.

To my team at Sandia, Gary Concannon, leader and mentor: you are truly a pleasure to work for. Sheila Carr, team lead and mentor: you make it easy to be part of the solution. And Jann Levin, team lead and mentor: your business process knowledge is invaluable. And to the worker bees on my team who always go above and beyond—you are a group of highly skilled PeopleSoft professionals:

Leonard Chavez, J.L. Sherer, Peter Keegan, Barbara Sandoval—you have taught me so much—thank you, Kate Rivera, Natasha Garcia, Heidi Welberry, David Baron, Terry Graff, David Bustamonte, Shauna Cromley, Todd Eaton, Bryan Norris, Leslie Gardner, Jason Follingstad, and Otis Stewart. My remarkable team of customers who teach me so much includes: Janey Carroll-Marbach, Gay Hill, Jane Farris, Mark Biggs, Bart Brooks, Marlene Vigil, Linda Stefoin, Rebecca Spires, Dave Medina, Nancy Muller, Ginny Clark, and Mary Romero-Hart.

To those people who helped with the book: Steve Stein, technical editor: without your help and guidance this project would not have been completed. Thank you, Barbara Sandoval—Switzerland, friend and mentor: you wrote three chapters and saved me from drowning. Thanks also to Sue Lampson, Larry Grey, and Chris Heller.

—Judi Doolittle

I would like to thank the many people who helped me contribute to this book. First God: he gave me the talent to succeed and leads me in the right direction. James Sandoval, my best friend and partner, is always supportive and encouraging in whatever I do. Lillian, Victoria, and Nicholas, my children, you were patient, most of the time, while mommy was on the computer. My parents, Joe and Maria Garcia, and my sister, Cindy Garcia, encouraged me to get my education and succeed in life. Judi Doolittle gave me the opportunity to try something new and mentored me along the way. My coworkers at Sandia shared their knowledge and are always there to help. Thanks also to my ex-coworkers at PNM; we learned PeopleSoft together the hard way. Richard Fleming, my first mentor, saw potential in me and gave me the opportunity to excel. Kristina Morris is always there when I need her. To all the people who worked to make this book a success: thank you.

—Barbara Sandoval

Introduction

PeopleSoft is a very powerful application with a lot of information available from Oracle, delivered with the application known as PeopleBooks. Sometimes PeopleBooks is not available when you try to learn PeopleSoft, or it is difficult to understand. This book, *PeopleSoft Developer's Guide for PeopleTools & PeopleCode*, is a starting point for reference material about the common points of understanding that you will need to start your career as a PeopleSoft developer. This book provides you with background information that is important for understanding the way PeopleSoft and PeopleCode work; it provides you with examples to allow for easy understanding of the concepts. The subject of PeopleSoft and PeopleCode is addressed by Oracle in many books, and it is a very large subject. This book does not try to cover the subject in its entirety, which is impossible. Instead, this book is a launch pad of basic theories, concepts, and examples that teach the foundation needed to start working quickly and efficiently in PeopleSoft. With this book you will

- Learn the history of the application
- Learn the basic modules in the HR application
- Learn the architecture of PeopleTools
- Understand the PIA or PeopleSoft Internet architecture
- Learn PeopleTools navigation
  - Application Designer
  - Configuration Manager
  - Fields
  - Records
  - Views

- SQL objects
- Pages
- HTML objects
- Permission lists
- Message catalogs
- How to include items in a project
- Working with derived work records
- PeopleSoft records
- Compare reports

- Learn about PeopleSoft pages
  - Page field properties
  - Page design
  - Levels, scroll bars, and parent/child relationships
  - Grid properties
  - Subpages
  - Menus
- Learn PeopleCode
  - Basic language syntax and structure
  - PeopleCode Editor
  - Events and code placement
  - PeopleCode event summary
  - Errors and warnings
  - Using different errors and warnings for debugging
  - Which is the most useful debugging technique
  - Declaring variables
  - Syntax

- Documentation
- Message catalog
- Message functions
- XLAT fields

- Learn advanced PeopleCode
  - Functions
  - Methods
  - Application packages
  - Modularizing your code
  - Security
  - Testing your application
- Learn about XML Publisher
  - XMLP for PeopleSoft overview
  - XML Publisher security
  - Setting up XML Publisher in PeopleSoft
    - Pages used
    - Global Engine settings
    - Report categories
    - Template design helpers
  - XML Report Publisher
    - Defining reports
    - Templates
    - Output options
    - Security options
    - Bursting options
    - Data sources

        - Subtemplates
        - Template translations
        - Running XML reports
            - Query Report Viewer
            - Publisher Report Repository
    - Output formats in PDF, PS, RTF, HTML
    - Industry-standard templates
    - Using desktop applications
        - Adobe Acrobat
        - MS Word
    - Template Builder add-ins
- Learn SQR
    - The basic language
    - Running from Process Scheduler
    - Creating Excel reports
    - Tips and tricks
- Learn about the Application Engine
    - The basic language
    - Running from Process Scheduler
    - Tips and tricks
- Learn tips and tricks
    - PeopleCode
    - SQL tricks for upgrading
    - The component buffer
- Learn about working with PL/SQL in PeopleSoft
- Learn about working with COBOL, which is not dead yet but a very important language in PeopleSoft

- **Chapter 1: Application Environment** In this chapter you will learn about the application PeopleSoft and its history. After a brief discussion of the modules available you will start to learn about the tools available to you, including PeopleTools and PeopleCode.
- **Chapter 2: PeopleTools** In this chapter you will learn about the architecture that is created behind the scenes in PeopleTools.
- **Chapter 3: PeopleSoft Internet Architecture (PIA)** You'll explore more deeply the architecture that supports PeopleSoft and learn about the PIA, including the PIA structure and why it is important to you as a PeopleSoft developer to understand the PIA.
- **Chapter 4: PeopleTools Basics** In this chapter you will start exploring the tools that are available to you as a PeopleSoft developer. You will learn the basics, how to navigate in Application Designer, how to query, and how to work with Configuration Manager. You will start working with the basic objects, fields, records, views, pages, SQL objects, HTML, permission lists, and message catalogs. You will start to understand the different record types. You will learn what a derived work record is and how to use it to your advantage as a developer.
- **Chapter 5: PeopleSoft Pages** You will take the skills you learned in Chapter 4 and build on them as you learn about the PeopleSoft page, the main canvas in development. You will learn about page field properties, page design, levels, scroll areas, grid properties, subpages, and menus.
- **Chapter 6: PeopleCode** In this chapter you will start to write code. You will learn the basic syntax and structure of the language. You will learn to work with the editor and where to place your code. Events will be discussed in detail so that you can properly place your code to be fired in the right place and in the correct order. This chapter will teach you the basics of writing in the PeopleCode language.
- **Chapter 7: Advanced PeopleCode** This chapter will take the concepts learned in Chapter 6 and build on your skill level. You will learn about functions, methods, application packages, and how to modularize your code. You will learn the most important task of any developer: the skill to be able to test your code.
- **Chapter 8: XML Publisher** In this chapter you will learn about the newest reporting tool to add to your toolkit as a developer. You will see that this language is not the answer to all reports, but it is a powerful resource to have available to you as a developer. In this chapter you will learn how to create XML reports, configure the reports, and create templates.
- **Chapter 9: PeopleSoft Query** One of the options to retrieve data for reports is with the Query Tool. In this chapter you learn to use the Query Tool to retrieve data, write reports, and export into Excel.

- **Chapter 10: Structured Query Language** The mainstay of your reporting tool box is SQR. This chapter explains the basics and how to debug existing SQR reports.
- **Chapter 11: Application Engine** Application Engine is a powerful batch processing language. It allows you to quickly write programs to retrieve data, manipulate it, and process it to and from files. This chapter will teach you how to use this powerful tool.
- **Chapter 12: Tips and Tricks** This chapter is a collection of tips and tricks to use for upgrading, debugging, and better coding. It is a fun and exciting chapter.
- **Appendix A: PL/SQL in PeopleSoft** This appendix discusses how to use PL/SQL in PeopleSoft. Although not all places that have PeopleSoft have Oracle, this appendix shows how PL/SQL is a very valuable addition for shops where the application is run on the Oracle database. Utilize PL/SQL to enable quick and easy processing in your PeopleSoft environment.
- **Appendix B: COBOL in PeopleSoft** COBOL is an integral part of PeopleSoft. Very few sites will develop COBOL applications from scratch. This chapter provides you with the skills necessary to read and understand the legacy programs you may be asked to support as well as the skills to debug newly delivered COBOL from Oracle.
- **Appendix C: References** This appendix lists the references in the text by chapter.

Intended Audience

This book is suitable for the following readers:

- New PeopleSoft developers
- Current and trained developers in PeopleSoft seeking insight on a new subject area, such as XML
- Database administrators who are asked to support PeopleSoft from an application perspective
- End users of PeopleSoft who want to understand the development side of the house better
- Analysts who want to understand better what they are asking from their PeopleSoft developers
- Functional consultants who want to have a greater understanding of the coding side of PeopleSoft
- Project leads and managers responsible for the implementation, upgrade, and customization of PeopleSoft applications
- Computer programmers who want to learn a new skill or language

PART I

Introduction

In 1987 Dave Duffield and Ken Morris founded PeopleSoft. Duffield and Morris set out to develop a non-specific database application based on client/server architecture, and within a year they released the starting point for PeopleSoft's outstanding application suite: PeopleSoft Human Resource Management System (HRMS).

Duffield's background in HRM systems dates to his time as CEO of Integral Systems—the first company to offer DB2-based human resource and accounting systems. He had the idea to change the mainframe versions of Integral System's mainframe HRMS package to client/server architecture, which at the time was very new technology. Duffield also co-founded Information Associates, which specialized in applications for the higher education market; this background eventually led to the development of PeopleSoft's Student Administration application.

Nearly 20 years later in January 2005 Oracle purchased PeopleSoft and PeopleSoft's newly acquired JD Edwards. In a related press release written by Nancy C. Lee and Jim Finn, Oracle stated, "This merger works because we will have more customers, which increases our ability to invest more in applications development and support. We intend to enhance PeopleSoft 8 and develop a PeopleSoft 9 and enhance a JD Edwards 5 and develop a JD Edwards 6. We intend to immediately extend and improve support for existing JD Edwards and PeopleSoft customers worldwide."

Oracle's PeopleSoft application provides the following solution modules:

- Asset Lifecycle Management
- Campus Solutions (Student Administration)
- CRM (Customer Relationship Management)
- EPM (Enterprise Performance Management)
- Enterprise Service Automation (Project Management)
- Financial Management
- Human Capital Management (HCM, the successor to PeopleSoft's HRMS)
- Supplier Relationship Management (Procurement)
- Supply Chain Management
- PeopleSoft Enterprise Tools & Technology (PeopleTools)

As of the writing of this book, the following releases of PeopleSoft are available:

- Oracle's PeopleSoft 8.9 (released in the summer of 2005)
- Oracle's PeopleSoft Enterprise Release 9 (released in the summer of 2006)

This book provides readers with a fundamental PeopleSoft development skill set, paying particular attention to the influence of previous versions on development requirements when moving forward with new technology. In an ideal world all PeopleSoft implementations have been upgraded to the newest release of Oracle's PeopleSoft Enterprise release; however, this book addresses development fundamentals for those of you still at earlier versions. The release that is used in the illustrations and examples is version 8.9.

Oracle Application Lines

Oracle has a vast application line of products including: Oracle E-Business Suite, JD Edwards EnterpriseOne, PeopleSoft Enterprise, JD Edwards World, Siebel, and Oracle Fusion Applications. In the world of applications it becomes difficult at best to decide what is best for a corporation. This book does not address the differences, strengths, and weaknesses between these suites, but is directed toward an audience of developers newly thrust into the PeopleSoft environment. When most people start developing in the Oracle Application arena they have very little training, few books are available, and they are left with co-workers and online developer resources to guide them. It is helpful to understand where the piece of the puzzle that has been put in your lap fits into the overall picture.

Oracle E-Business Suite currently includes 22 products covering many of the functions supplied in the other applications lines. Oracle E-Business Suite includes: Procurement, Contracts, Corporate Performance Management, Customer Data Management, Customer Relationship Management, Financials, Human Recourses Management, Manufacturing, Marketing, Order Management, Product Lifecycle Management, Projects, Sales, Service, Supply Chain Management, Execution and Planning, and Transportation Management.

JD Edwards EnterpriseOne was developed for a small to medium-sized businesses with integrated tools and solutions for that size business, including: Asset Lifecycle Management, Project Management, Customer Relationship Management, Supply Chain Management, Financial Management, Procurement, Human Capital Management, and Tools and Technology.

JD Edwards World was developed to give small businesses the same level of enterprise solutions that previously were available only to larger corporations. JD Edwards World provides: Distribution Management, Human Capital Management, Financial Management, Manufacturing Management, and Home Builder Management.

Seibel is CRM-centric and supports both J2EE and .NET, with solutions tailored to over 20 industries. Details on all Oracle application lines can be reviewed at www.oracle.com.

PeopleSoft Application Modules

PeopleSoft is an Enterprise Resource Planning (ERP) solution. Generally, ERP is broken down into the following business processes:

- Human Resources Management System (HRMS), now known as Human Capital Management (HCM)
- Financial Systems
- Distribution Systems
- Manufacturing Systems

In addition to the ERP core, PeopleSoft also has an excellent Campus Solution that is the number one Student Management system available to colleges and universities. The application world has evolved greatly over the last decade and experienced growth that is unprecedented in any other industry. Oracle PeopleSoft applications offer wonderful solutions to the following Enterprise-level functionality: Campus Solutions, Human Capital Management, Customer Relationship Management, Financial Management, Supply Chain Management, Supplier Relationship Management, and Service Automation. One of the areas PeopleSoft has excelled in is the Human Capital Management (HCM) market. The main focus in this book will be on the HCM modules. One place where integrations are imperative is in the connection of HRMS payroll to the General Ledger. In this basic and required connection the book will address the financial modules and the General Ledger only briefly.

The implementation of a large-scale, Enterprise-level application can take years and is a large and often complex undertaking. This book is not intended to replace PeopleSoft Training, now known as Oracle University training, but is intended to add to or enhance training. Since organization training schedules do not always align with need, it is the authors' hope that this book would assist a new application developer during a significant training void, as well as serve as a reference to experienced PeopleSoft application developers.

Role of the PeopleSoft Developer

What tasks does a PeopleSoft Developer perform and what are the skills that are important to have? One of the important points to understand in the world of application development is the difference between the coder, or developer, and the middleware technology professional. Yes, understanding of the middleware is an important skill, and coding to the web architecture is important, but the two tasks are very different and require different skill levels. This book and the skills that will be discussed are for the person who fulfills the role of PeopleSoft developer in the organization. This person will work closely with the middleware developer, the quality assurance specialist, database analyst, and database administrator. It is important to have good understanding of several of the skills from the other functions. For example, a good PeopleSoft developer is very proficient in SQL (Structured Query Language), PL/SQL or Transact SQL, HTML, XML, Java, and Crystal Reports.

This book assumes a basic knowledge of programming, the math of programming, and fundamental logic. References to other programming languages and SQL will be made, but not completely explained. The reference section of this book provides a list of other books to read to gain a better understanding of the foundations of basic programming and computer science.

PeopleSoft Vanilla and Modifications

There are many reasons to remain with PeopleSoft Vanilla, and many reasons to customize the application. When upgrading or changing PeopleSoft, the authors of this book recommend that no changes be made to PeopleSoft as delivered; any changes should be made by copying the delivered function and saving the copy by a new name. Any modifications to the page, code, query, record, or field should be made in the new copy. Naming conventions should be defined and used to locate all of the modifications quickly and simply within a PeopleSoft project (collection of objects and/or changes). Oracle (PeopleSoft) recommends that the first two letters in the naming convention be the initials of the company. For example, the University of Utah names all changes starting with UU_ (University of Utah). Whatever naming convention is implemented in your organization is acceptable; the important point is to decide on a standard and require everyone in the organization to follow that standard.

It is recommended that all organizations implement PeopleSoft as close to delivered Vanilla as possible. During product upgrades the identification, evaluation, and reapplication of modifications can take considerable time and resources. While PeopleSoft developers rarely have the ability to make the "stay vanilla" decision, they can influence management through recommendations for business process change and through sharing projected short-term development and long-term maintenance costs. Developers can remind management that they made the decision to purchase the application solution at a large cost and to modify the delivered application would void any gain in cost of ownership and add development time and money to the implementation and upgrade project. Extensive modifications can prevent the company from implementing required patches with ease and cause problems with simple tax upgrade modules.

Quality control process and personnel are worthwhile investments as part of the PeopleSoft software support funding. Although PeopleSoft is "self-documenting," talented programmers don't always have a talent for documentation. Developers leave projects only for their successors to discover that change documentation is inadequate and that naming conventions have not been religiously followed. Unidentified changes can wreak havoc with an upgrade, stretching out deliverable timeframes or breaking corporate processes when not properly brought forward into Production. Quality control processes will ensure that naming conventions are followed, documentation is reviewed and adequate, and will verify that the delivered code is maintained and copied prior to the change being implemented.

Hopefully, the organizations the readers are working with have invested in version control software and have a quality process in place. With a good quality control process, version management, and naming conventions, a lot of mistakes that can happen in modifying code can be prevented, upgrades and enhancements can be made manageable, and embarrassing production mistakes avoided. It is surprising even with months of testing what can go wrong when a code change is implemented into Production. Take the time and spend the money to purchase versions control software.

Organization of the PeopleSoft Development Environments

It is the standard in the PeopleSoft development community to use a minimum of four database systems: PeopleSoft Vanilla, Development, Quality, and Production. PeopleSoft Vanilla is retained to assist in determining if hard-to-track bugs were inherent in the delivered code, or are due to a change. Changes can be applied in isolation to the Vanilla environment and analyzed without interference from other changes. After analysis, Vanilla is always restored to the original delivered software. Development is where all customization work and unit testing of changes is performed. Quality closely mirrors Production, and contains only those changes being readied for move to Production through system and customer acceptance testing. Some organizations will also maintain independent Customer Acceptance and/or Training databases, depending on their needs and the number of users directly using the applications, thus increasing the number of database environments to six.

Each shop handles the refresh of the Quality and Development environments on a different schedule, but organizations typically replace the Quality PeopleSoft definitions tables entirely with Production data every couple of weeks. Objects that only exist in Development will remain and not be changed, but if you have the same objects it is important to note that the work that has been done by the developer may be altered and a copy of the Development change may not be recoverable. It is advisable to save off the Development work periodically into a flat file for reference. Production instance data like actual employee personal data, payroll, and other sensitive information may or may not be moved based on the security and authorization in place. Many organizations create test data that is reloaded into the tables after the PeopleSoft objects have been refreshed.

Only when a change to the code has been successfully tested cleanly in Development, Vanilla, and Quality will it move into Production. The move to Production is done only with approval and with a documented trail. With the Quality Assurance process the original code, page, record, and field should be maintained and a copy kept in case a roll-back to the original is required when the project moves to Production.

Proper Testing

Developers should only test and review their code in the Development environment. Although developers might assist in testing in the other environments, the developer who wrote the code should not review or test his work after it leaves the Development environment. The creator is rarely a good judge of the creation's flaws.

Prior to migration of changes into Quality, take the time for peer review by other developers or analysts familiar with PeopleSoft and/or the functionality change request. In addition to identification of bugs or incorrectly performing functionality, logic gaps, usability improvements, and testing risk areas will be pointed out. Many problems can be quickly averted by just having another set of trained eyes review the code and walk through the user interface even if only for a short time or at a high level.

Wherever possible, the customer who requested the change should test the change in the Quality or Customer Acceptance environments to ensure that the function performs as envisioned. As most customers do not know how to test, or how to test thoroughly, a test plan and test scenarios should be provided to them. The test plan should clearly define the function points to test to; even though your customer may understand the request they made for a change, scope change and time can cause a lack of understanding of what should be reviewed. The test plans, scripts, and expected test results can be provided by the developer, but ideally these are developed and maintained as part of the Quality Assurance function. Many organizations retain staff whose sole responsibility is testing; larger or risk-adverse groups will create test departments and facilities that support them. Automated test tools can also be purchased to assist in developing automated scripts to ensure thorough systematic function and regression testing. Any questions and inquiries that come up during this testing can and should be assimilated in Help files, FAQs (Frequently Asked Questions), and customer communications.

PeopleSoft Developer's Guide for PeopleTools and PeopleCode

The intended audience for this book is developers in the Oracle application world of PeopleSoft. This book is a reference guide to provide experienced PeopleSoft developers with new features such as XML, and tips and tricks that have been learned from the authors' years of development experience. The book will utilize sample Oracle databases and sample PeopleSoft applications. There are two separate skill sets required to learn to develop in PeopleSoft and to learn to set up and maintain an application. The focus of the book will be development.

How This Book Is Organized

The book is divided into four parts:

- **Part I, "Introduction"** Contains an overview of the Application Development environment, an explanation of the PeopleTools Development environment, and an overview of the PeopleSoft PIA (PeopleSoft Internet Architecture).
- **Part II, "PeopleTools Development"** Covers PeopleSoft Development, PeopleTools Basics, PeopleSoft Pages, PeopleCode, and Advanced PeopleCode.
- **Part III, "Other Applications"** Covers other tools available for development in PeopleSoft, XML Publisher, Query Tool SQR language, Application Engine, and Tips and Tricks.
- **Part IV, "Appendixes"** Appendix A covers PL/SQL in PeopleSoft, which is available to the groups running PeopleSoft on the Oracle database. Appendix B covers the legacy software COBOL, which is an integral part of PeopleSoft even today. New development doesn't happen often in COBOL, but it is important to know how to support it, read it, and debug it.

How to Use This Book

Throughout the book **bold** will be used to denote a PeopleSoft command or menu navigation command.

Screenshots taken from the sample PeopleSoft Database will be utilized throughout to show the reader how to do a specific task. Code examples will be given to guide through all of the examples of how to code a specific task.

The following naming conventions that will be utilized in the book: all new objects will have the preceding notation of TC_ for Test Company; this is because the sample is used in making up examples. All larger modifications will be stored in a project with the name SCR### with a number noting the change requested by the customer. SQR(s), XML, SQL scripts, and PL/SQL stored procedures will all be named with the SCR project number and each new object will be named to link it back to the original customer request.

Fusion: The Next Generation of Application

The IOUC (International Oracle User Council) has a Fusion Channel available for new information that is released about Fusion. How to have a voice to Oracle in the product that is created and the vehicle to get the customer's opinion to Oracle about customer modifications will be included. There is a very useful SQR available on the web site that documents all of the modifications that have been made in a given system:
http://www.iouc.org/index.php?module=sthtml&op=load&sid=s1_005_fusion.

On the Fusion Channel there are customer surveys and webcasts that feature key Oracle executives answering customer questions. Participation in this group and other user group communities will enhance your ability to keep up with the ever-changing Application environment. It is the authors' hope that the new Application Fusion will bring with it changes and exciting new career opportunities.

CHAPTER 1

Application Environment

his chapter starts you on the path to learn about the PeopleSoft ERP application. This introduction will help you understand how the Human Resource Modules (HRM) are laid out and give you an idea of their functionality. Each organization has a different set of modules, versions, and implementation. This chapter does not try to outline all of the possibilities; it only introduces you, the reader, to one of the several set of modules available. The purpose of this is to give you a starting point to learn to maintain and customize within PeopleSoft. As a reader you can use your company's specifics to learn to develop in the ERP environment.

By using the highly developed HR modules as a starting point, we will be able to readily find examples of the use of PeopleSoft and Fusion Development Tools to accomplish just about every type of processing we want to learn how to do, including online transaction processing, lookup table maintenance, analytics, components, ad-hoc reporting, online lookup, batch reporting, downloads, application integration, workflow, on-demand self-service processing, role-based functionality, row-based security, and more.

Outline of PeopleSoft

The first thing that new developers need to do is make themselves familiar with the look and feel of the PeopleSoft Portal. Sometimes this environment is referred to as the PeopleSoft PIA (PeopleSoft Internet Architecture) because this is the way that PeopleSoft launches itself over the Internet. PeopleSoft launches via the PIA, which is an Internet connection without a client. (For detailed information about the PIA and the configuration, please refer to Chapter 3.) In the simplest terms PeopleSoft deploys without an application on the client. The entire application can be viewed over the Internet with the PeopleSoft Internet Application Server. Connecting with a web browser on a workstation is the most common Internet connectivity to the PeopleSoft application. The PeopleSoft Internet Application Server uses HTML and JavaScript to communicate with the web browser and to connect, you simply navigate to the site just like any other web site.

This book will introduce only one of the key modules delivered by PeopleSoft, the HR modules. The focus of the book is on development, not navigation of the modules. Peoplebooks, which is delivered with PeopleSoft, offers extensive navigation information about each of the modules that your company may have in place.

The Pure Internet Architecture was introduced in version 8.0; prior versions were client-server-based interfaces. Dedication to "pure internet architecture" and "no code on the client" was marketed by PeopleSoft's CEO Craig Conway in the Version 8 release beginning in 2001 as being a differentiator and a credit to the growing importance of the web-based architecture. Today, in addition to PeopleSoft, SAP and Oracle, as well as many other software products, are web standards–compliant and deployable over Internet browsers. Figure 1-1 shows the standard PeopleSoft sign-in page.

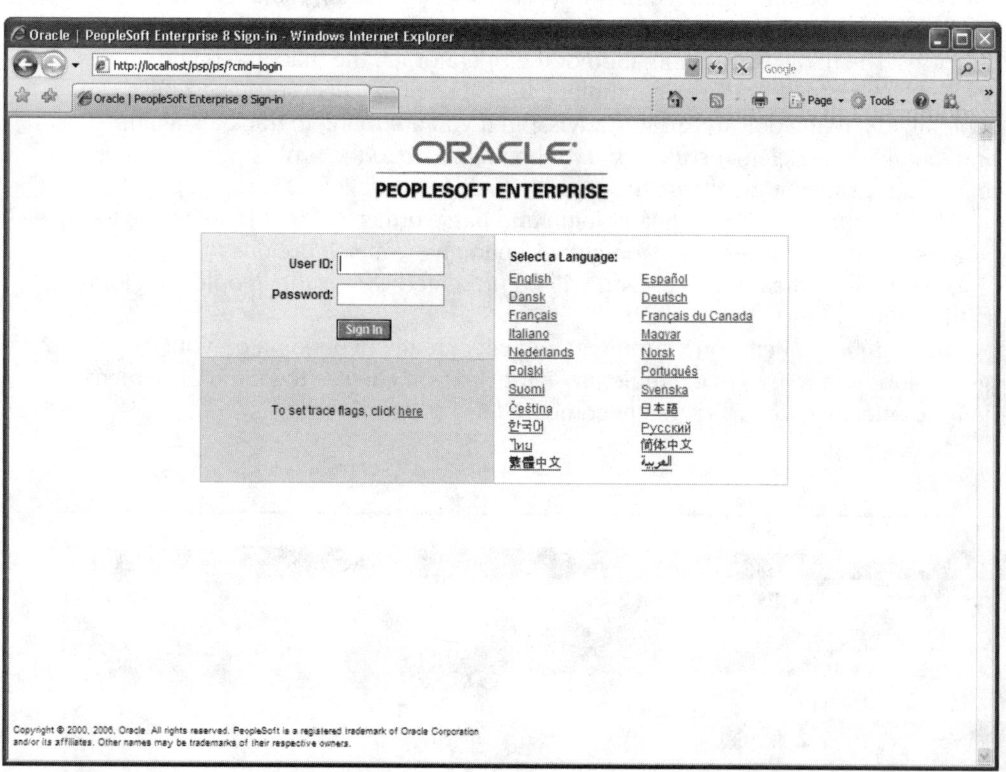

FIGURE 1-1 *Internet login screen*

Signing into the PeopleSoft application is like signing into a secure web application. You enter the URL for your application just like you would if you were going to any web application; you log in with your Oprid and Password. The structure of the URL depends on the company, server names, and the structure of your environments. But you can be assured that you will have a separate URL for each of your environments: Development, Test, Quality, Native, and Production. It is a good practice to create a single HTML web page that has the links to each of your environments on the one page. It makes a nice landing page for your PeopleSoft developers and a one-click solution to quickly understand your URL structure.

One of the nifty features to help with your problems signing-in and any other problems that might pop up for your help desk is to enable SQL trace. With the release of versions 8.0 and higher, the user simply needs to click on the To Set Trace Flags, Click Here link, which leads to a sign-in page that includes the SQL trace settings. Another way to enable trace is to add "&trace=y" to the sign-in URL.

Where do you find the trace file? In versions 8.0 or higher, the trace file is created on the application server in the {PS_HOME}\appserv\{DBNAME}\LOGS directory. The name is a combination of the operator ID, the machine name or IPAddress, and ".tracesql" (for example, JHOTSIN_PSDV1.tracesql). These files can get really big really quickly. So it is advisable if you are trying to track a specific problem that you delete the file first and then navigate to the problem, repeat, and immediately save off the file before it grows to an unmanageable size.

The standard PeopleSoft default login and password is PS/PS. It is advisable to create several other users once you get set up to give yourself options to log in. Once you log in, the first screen you will be presented with is the PeopleSoft Home, as shown in Figure 1-2.

The number of items on your menu will vary greatly depending on your permissions and roles. For example, in Figure 1-3 you can see the number of menu items to select has changed greatly compared to Figure 1-2.

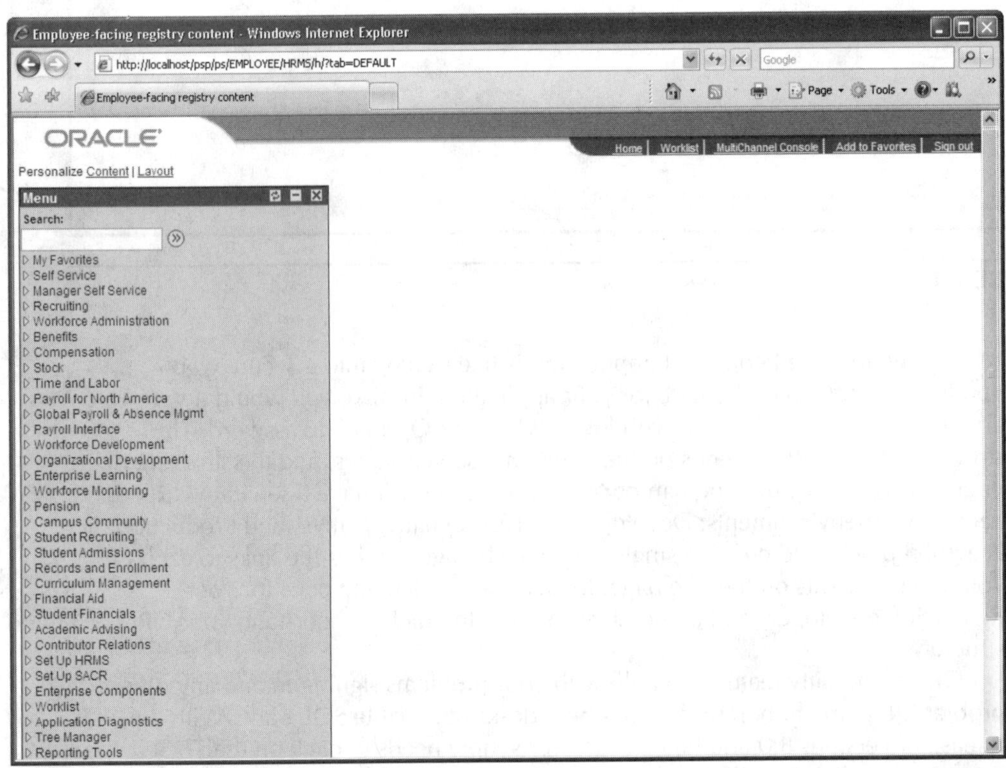

FIGURE 1-2 *PeopleSoft Home*

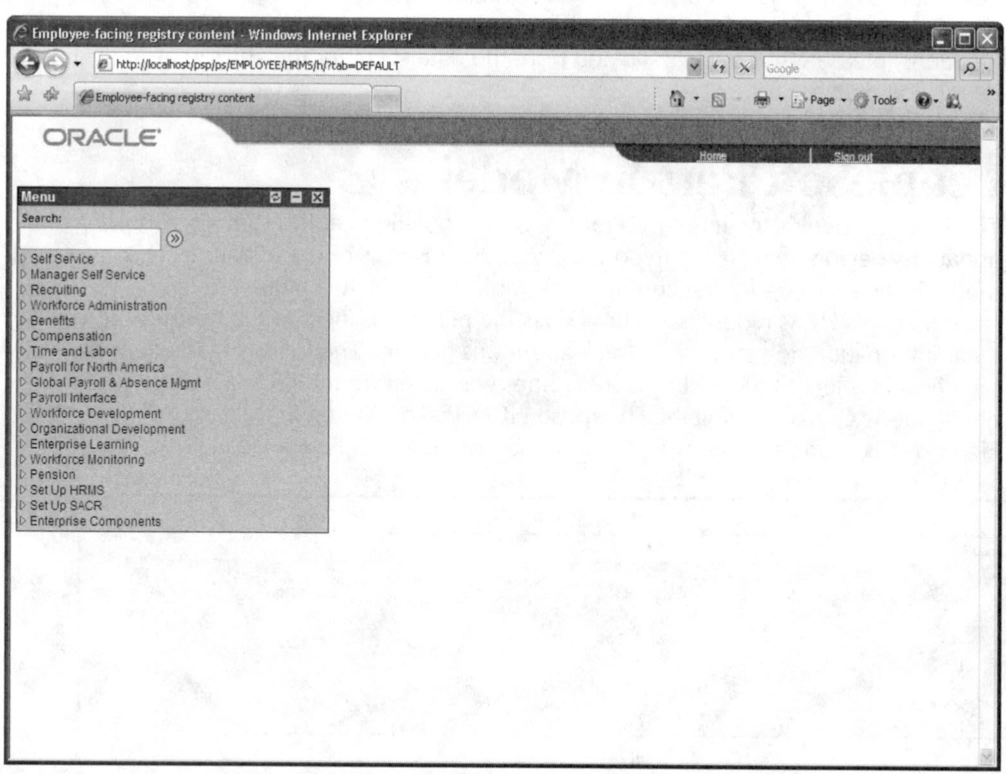

FIGURE 1-3 *PeopleSoft Menus*

HR Modules

Oracle's PeopleSoft Enterprise HRMS allows for the automation of Human Resource tasks that can lead to increased organization productivity. It achieves this by standardizing and automating tasks with a single application. The key to allowing Oracle's PeopleSoft Enterprise HRMS to gain productivity is standardization; in an organization that is deep seeded in tradition and continues to do HR business processes the "way it has always been done," regardless of the application, productivity gain will be lost. Over and over we have seen implementations of PeopleSoft that are so customized that it is difficult to see the original Vanilla application that was purchased to gain productivity. Only once in my career have we had the wonderful experience of working for an organization that chose to change the business processes instead of the software. And the productivity gain was staggering. With the implementation of the vanilla HRMS modules, a business has the potential for rapid return on investment by reducing costs and increasing efficiency. The HRMS module allows for the management of people as an asset. It has features that allow you to add value to traditional HR processes. Most of the descriptions in this chapter are taken from Oracle data sheets, which are available on www.oracle.com. If you need to read more extensively about any of these functions, please visit Oracle's site and print the data sheet for the version of PeopleSoft that you are using.

PeopleSoft Person Model

The Person Model is the term used for the way PeopleSoft captures information about any person who comes in contact with the business or organization. This model is the structure for the core records (tables) that relate a person to the organization's HCM modules. So how does the person connect to the business and what information do you wish to track about this person? The following diagram of the Person Object Model ERD—Core Entities was taken from Oracle's August 2005 publication "Understanding the Enterprise HCM Person Model in Release 8.9." Figure 1-4 is a graphical representation of part of the HCM Person Model.

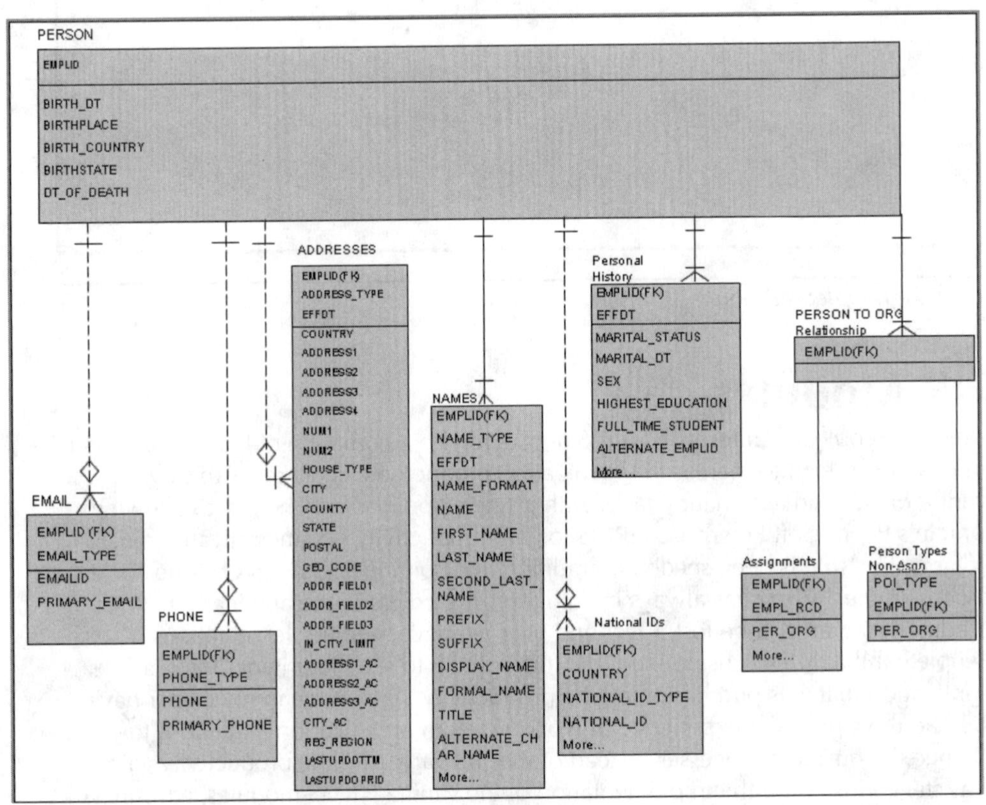

FIGURE 1-4 *HCM Person Model*

The red relationship lines represent required data. To create a PERSON in Oracle's PeopleSoft 8.9, a minimum of one of each of the following records is required:

- PERSON
- PERS_DATA_EFFDT
- NAMES
- One organizational relationship record:
  - The organizational relationship is determined by the sub-type of the JOB.
  - Does the PERSON need a JOB record? If he or she is a worker, then yes, and the assignment record is PER_ORG_ASGN.
  - If the PERSON does not need a JOB record then he or she is a POI, or a person of interest. To relate a POI to the organization, you need a non-assignment type record: PER_POI_TYPE.

The people in the organization are a very important asset and with the Person Model you can model the relationship with your people as it changes over time. With the flexible attributes that are provided with the Person Model, the changing of these attributes allows for different processing depending on the need at the time. For example, an employee in your organization today might have at one time had a relationship as a contingent worker, or person of interest. Only one ID is required to track this person and through this one ID you are able to retrieve a complete history of the person's relationship with your organization. An employee is someone in your organization who has a current JOB record. A contingent worker is someone who provides services under a contract that is non-permanent in nature. You can have POIs with JOB records and POIs without. POIs are not normally part of the HCM model and processing.

HCM Business Processes

HCM Business Processes is where companies can manage all of their Human Resource business processes. It automates paper business processes and frees up Human Resource staff to concentrate on the management of people rather than processes. PeopleSoft has created a standard way of doing Human Resource business processes. From creating standard rules for open enrollment to payroll processing, PeopleSoft has integrated the processes into the application. PeopleSoft allows for the optimization of the recruiting process, the time and pay solutions, management benefits and administration, and reduced administrative costs for the consolidation of the processes and functionality.

Absence Management

PeopleSoft's Enterprise Absence Management allows for an organization to configure the rules around their absence events within the PeopleSoft rule-based system. This creates a single instance of the absence-related data. Employees and managers can use configurable self-service pages to view absences. Managers have the ability to use the pages to authorize, deny, or push back an absence request. Absences can be entered on the Absence page or via the Time and Labor reporting page. Figure 1-5 shows a piece of the Time and Labor module that allows an

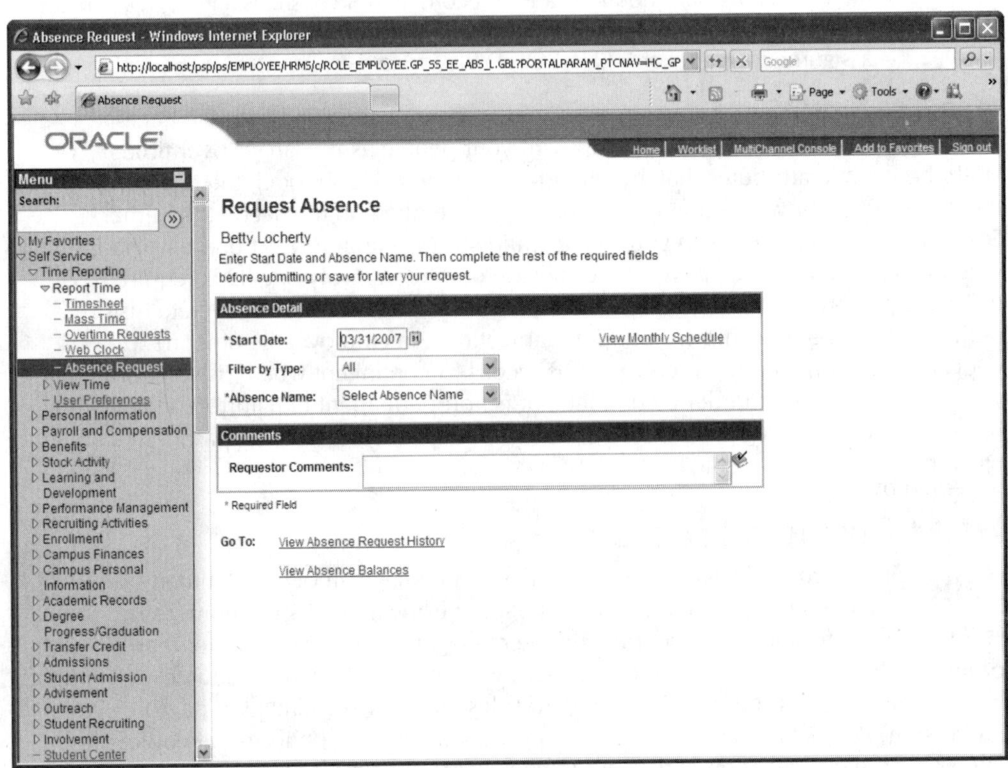

FIGURE 1-5 *Time and Labor module*

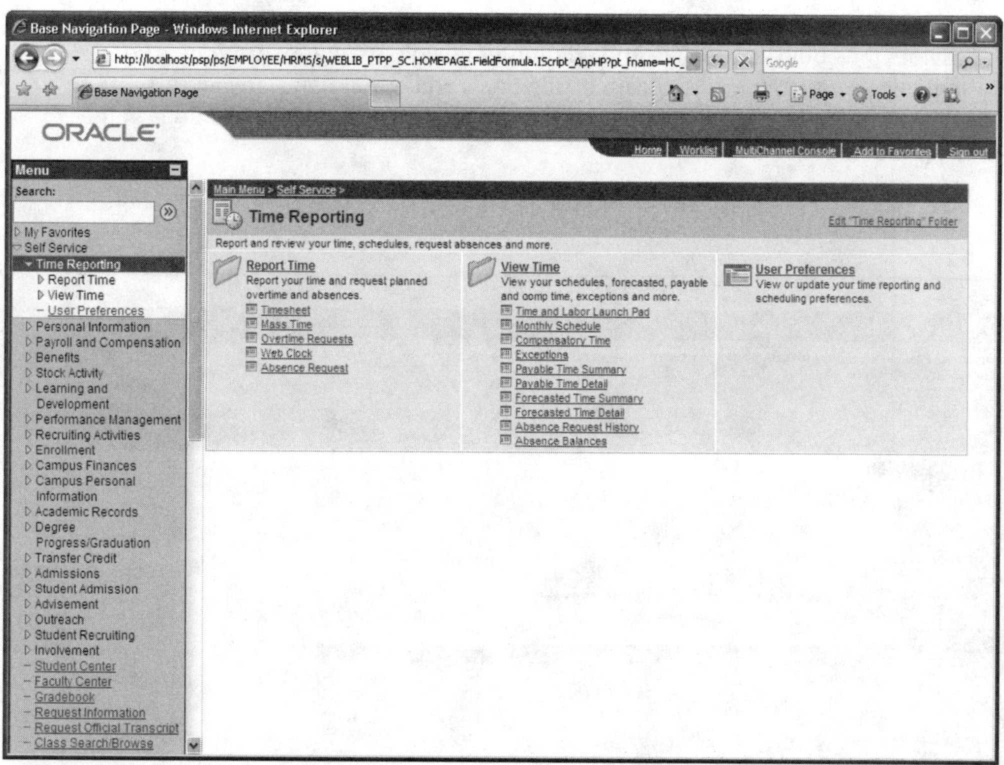

FIGURE 1-6 *Self-service options in Time Reporting module*

employee to submit an absence request. This absence request can then be approved or denied by the manager. Figure 1-6 shows you the self-service options available within the Time Reporting module.

Benefits Administration

Benefits Administration allows you to establish and manage multiple benefits programs, including health and life insurance, savings, leave plans, and dependent care reimbursement. It allows for the definition of the providers, the rates for each provider, beneficiaries for health and life, and the ability to calculate the coverage premiums. You can enroll participants and dependents in a variety of benefit options. It provides the ability to manage and administer flexible spending accounts. The system allows you to track Medicare entitlements and enrollments. In Figure 1-7 you can see a Health Care Summary. Figure 1-8 shows all of the available options in the Benefits module.

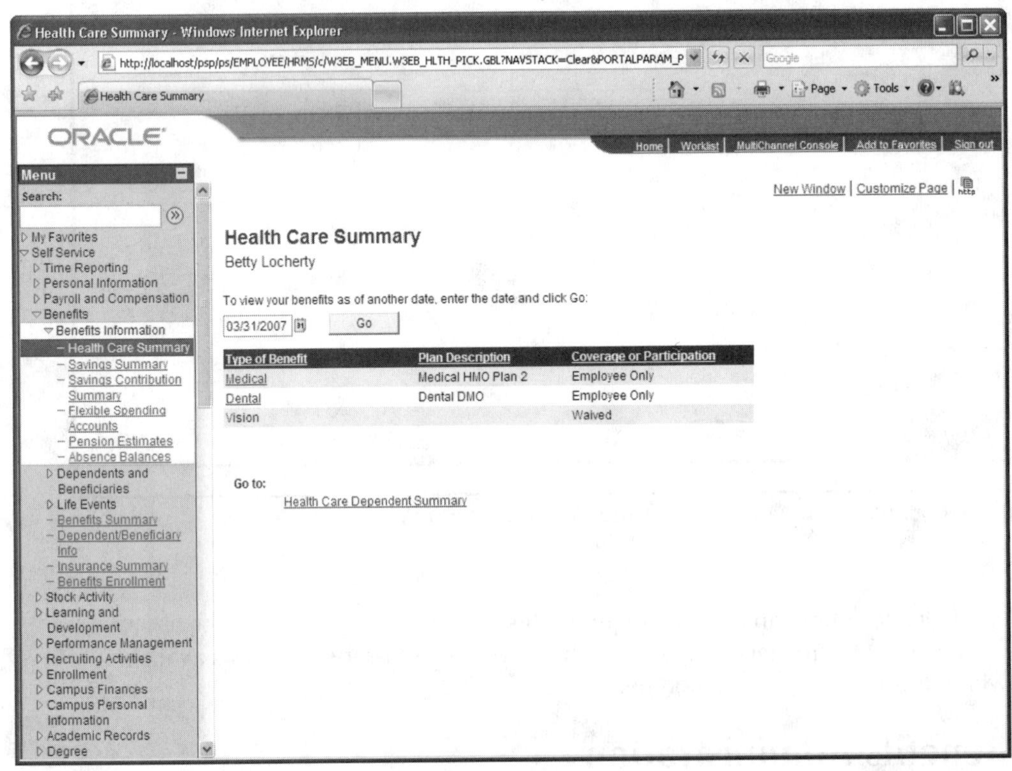

FIGURE 1-7 *Health Care Summary*

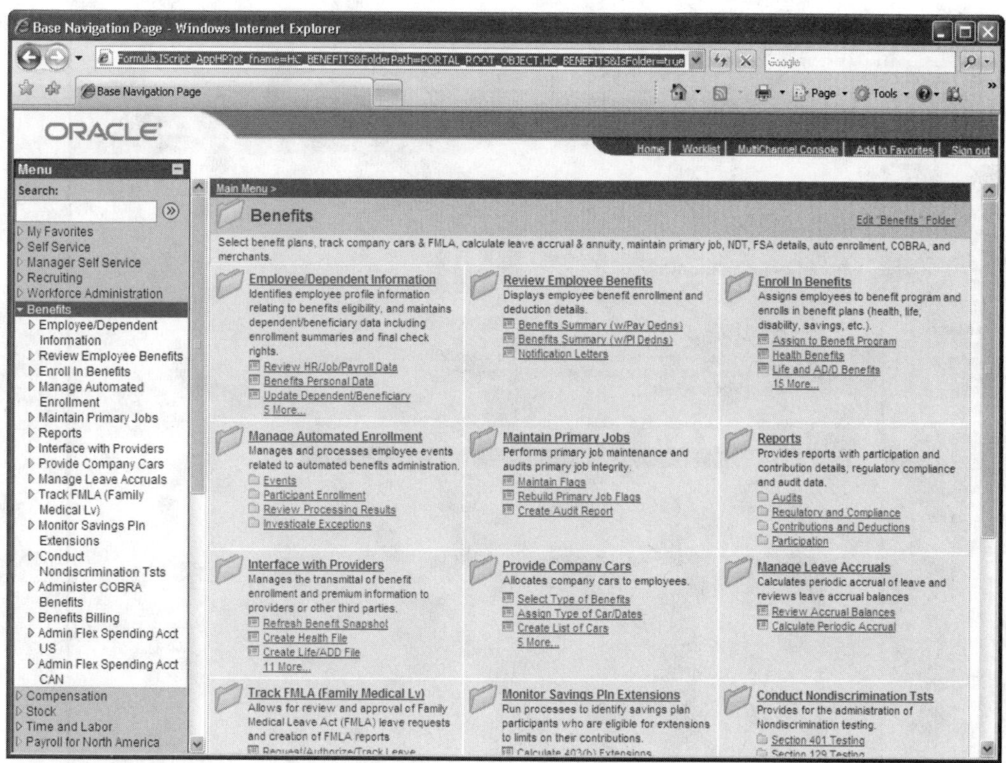

FIGURE 1-8 *Benefits module*

eBenefits

With online capabilities through the self-service options, you can allow employees 24/7 connectivity to your business. It allows for the open enrollment decisions to be done at home with the family. Figure 1-9 shows the look and feel of the online Open Enrollment feature.

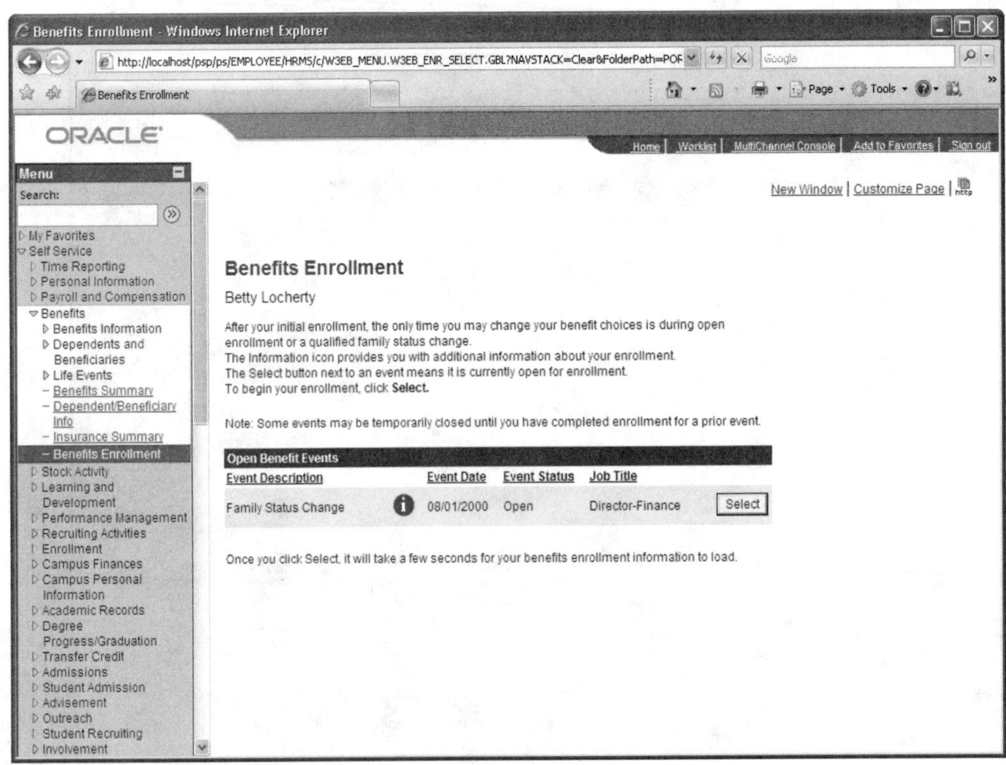

FIGURE 1-9 *Open Enrollment module*

eCompensation

Just like with open enrollment, eCompensation employees can view their pay stubs from home, print them on their printers, and retrieve lost pay slips for any given time period. Figure 1-10 shows what your employees will see when they view their paychecks online.

eCompensation Manager Desktop

The Manager Self-Service links allow for the total management of employees' time, job and personal information, compensation and stock, learning and development,

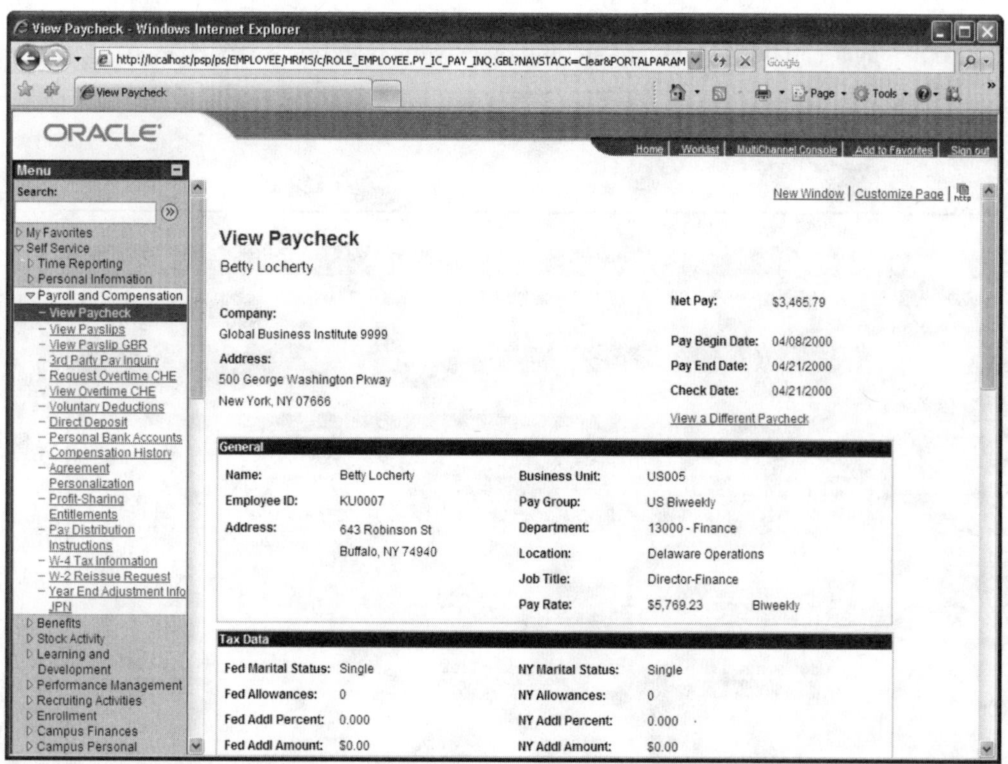

FIGURE 1-10 *Online paycheck*

and performance. Managers can quickly request and apply an ad hoc salary request and process it immediately into the employee's check. The manager can also quickly check the salary budget to make certain the request for the ad hoc change is within the scope of his budget. The manager can review an employee's total compensation and overtime history. The Manager Self-Service links also allow for the one-stop approval of salary changes, stock options, overtime, and budgeted salary changes. Figure 1-11 shows the Compensation and Stock available options. Figure 1-12 shows an employee's compensation history. Figure 1-13 demonstrates how a manager can quickly reward an employee with an ad hoc salary change request, yet remain within his project's budget.

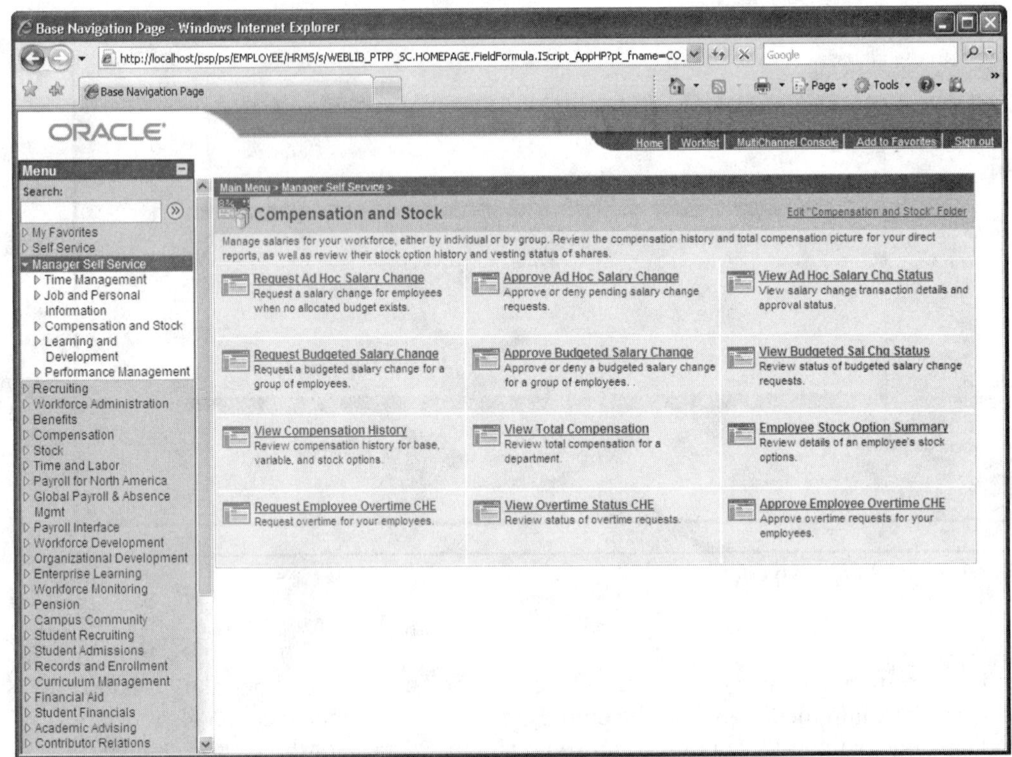

FIGURE 1-11 *Compensation and Stock*

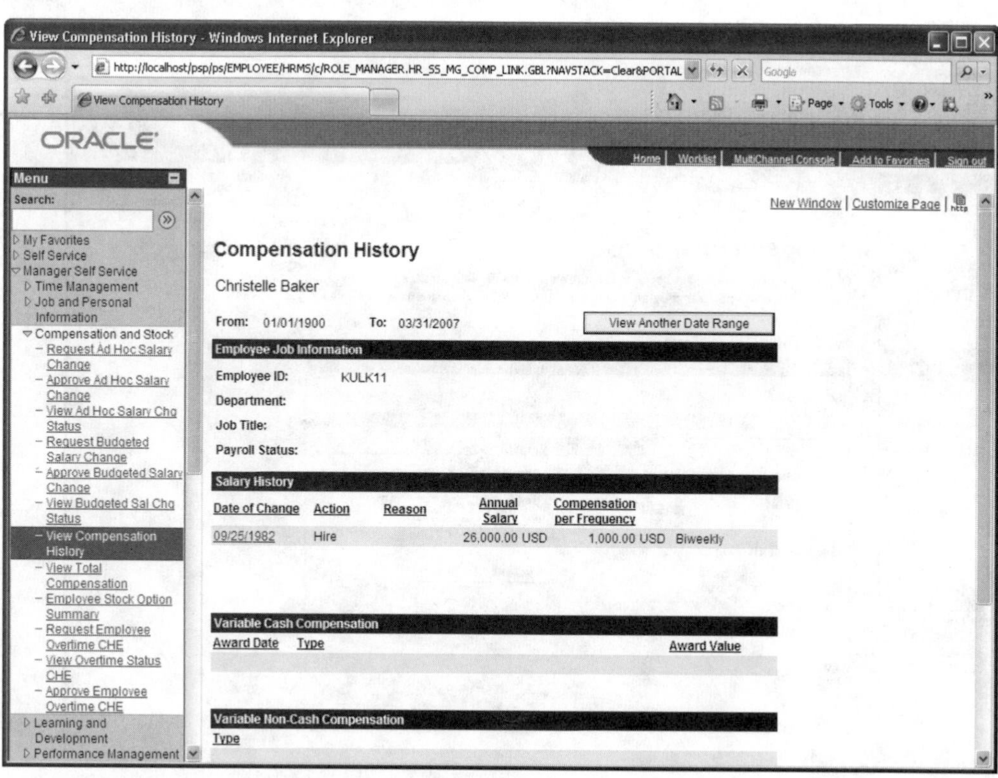

FIGURE 1-12 *Employee Compensation History*

ePay

ePay is seven self-service functions that interface with payroll. ePay allows employees to update, review, add, and delete their own payroll information where it is appropriate. Figure 1-14 shows all of the available options in the Payroll and Compensation modules.

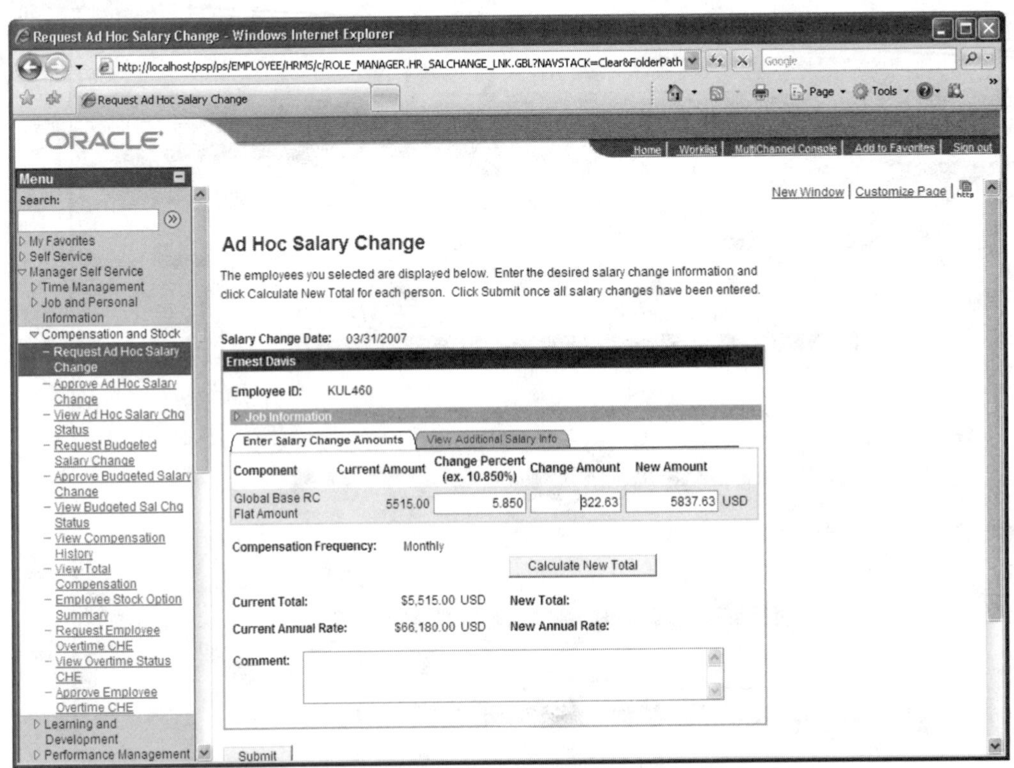

FIGURE 1-13 *Manager Ad Hoc Salary Change Request*

Figure 1-15 displays the ability to enter bank account information and Net Pay distribution information.

With View Payslip, employees can view all of their paycheck information including tax information, benefits deductions, and any voluntary deduction information. Figure 1-16 is a PDF paycheck that can be printed at home by your employees.

With View Paycheck, the check is displayed in PDF format and can be printed at home, saving the company money by eliminating the need to print and distribute paychecks.

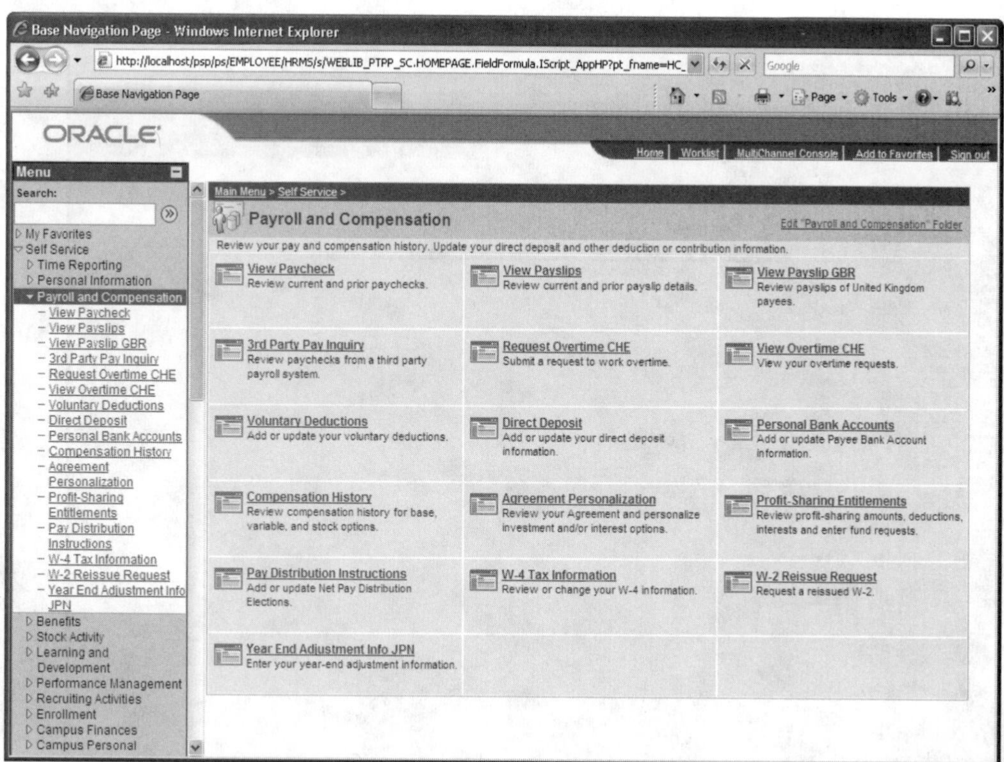

FIGURE 1-14 *Payroll and Compensation modules*

Year-End Processing

With View Year-End Forms, employees have available online processing of W-4 information. They can submit a request that will process and make available the information online or send it to an address. They can also request a reissue of their W-2 information, as shown in Figure 1-17.

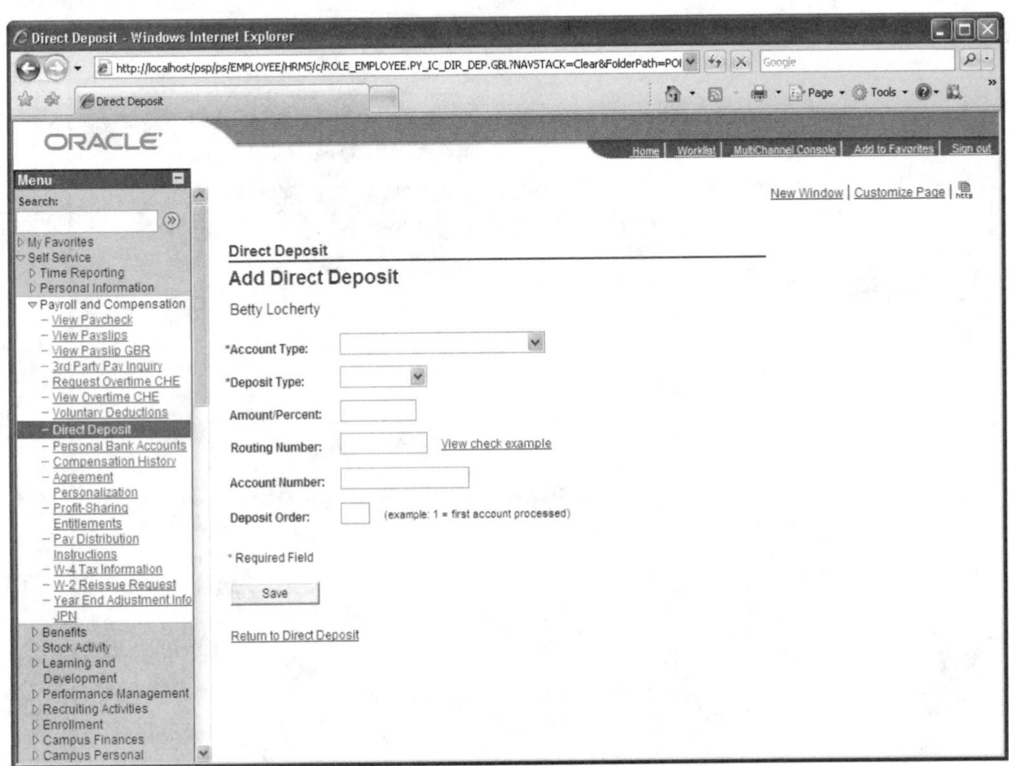

FIGURE 1-15 *Bank account information in Net Pay*

eProfile and eProfile Manager Desktop

This collection of links allows for managers to automate processes that tend to fill up their time. eProfile is a collection of administration functions, change job functions, locations, full-time and part-time status, address updates, telephone updates, and other personal data. Figure 1-18 demonstrates the available options in the Job and Personal Information portal.

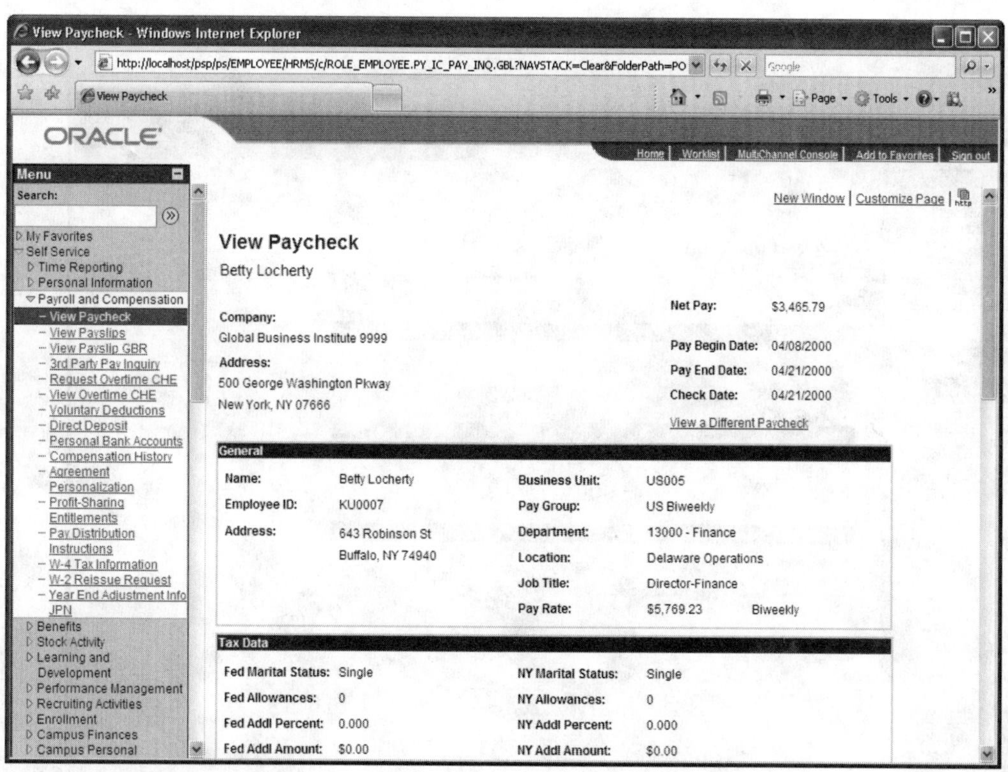

FIGURE 1-16 *Paycheck in PDF format*

It allows for employees to take responsibility for updating basic data on their own. This collection of links allows for people to manage their own life events, such as changing names, addresses, or withholding, and with Open Enrollment it allows for employees to make their own selections. It enables companies to become global and have a workforce virtually anywhere in the world and no one needs to make a

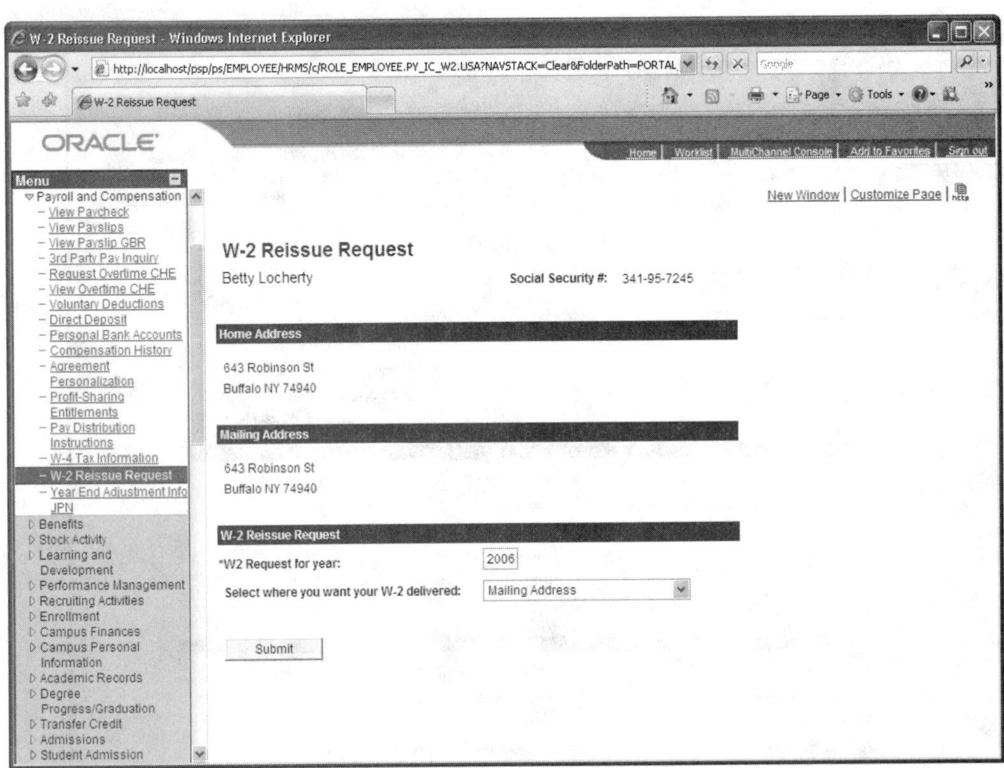

FIGURE 1-17 *Reissue of W-2*

trip to a Human Resource office to make a change to their personal data. Figure 1-19 shows all of the things an employee can be given permission to update on their own; it is up to the company to determine which pieces of information they want to permit employee changes to. Figure 1-20 shows where an employee can update his or her home address. Figure 1-21 is the actual update screen.

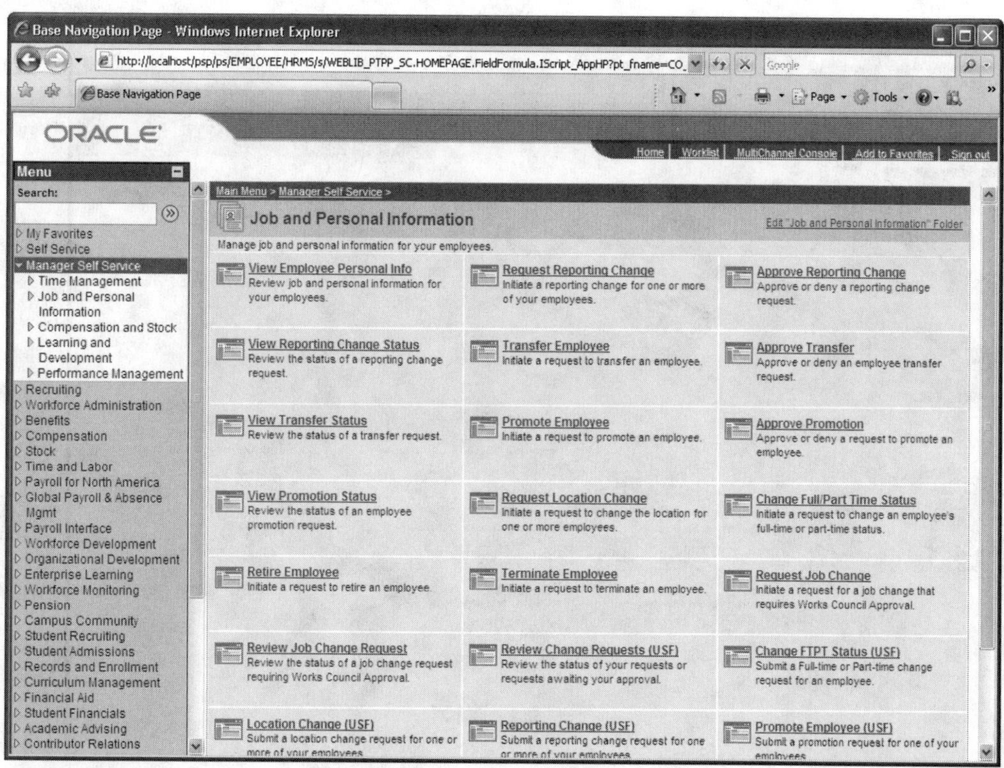

FIGURE 1-18 *Job and Personal Information portal*

Global Payroll

Global Payroll uses a rules-based payroll management system that incorporates accuracy, time controls, and financial controls. It has a single payroll interface with operations in multiple countries using a single database with access worldwide. The rules-based system allows for the country-specific regulations, processes, reports,

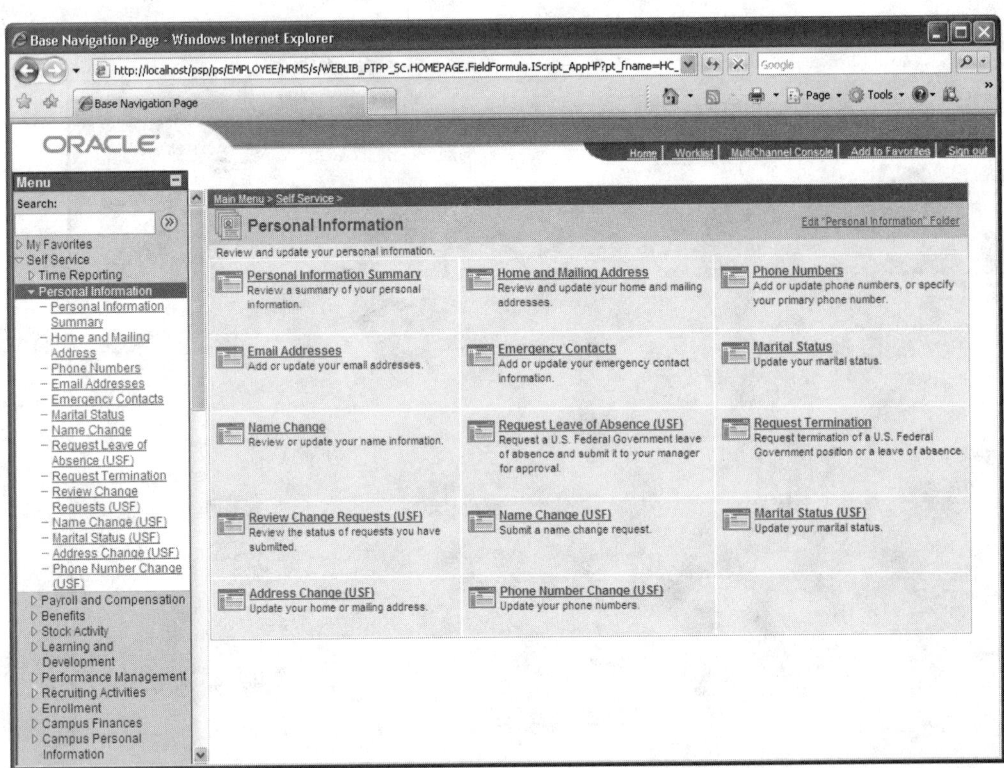

FIGURE 1-19 *Options available for employee update*

self-service, and user-defined rules. An employee's pay can be stated, calculated, and distributed in multiple currencies. The Absence Management module allows for the management of the most common leave types and automates the leave accrual balance process. You can use existing employee HR and payroll data to drive

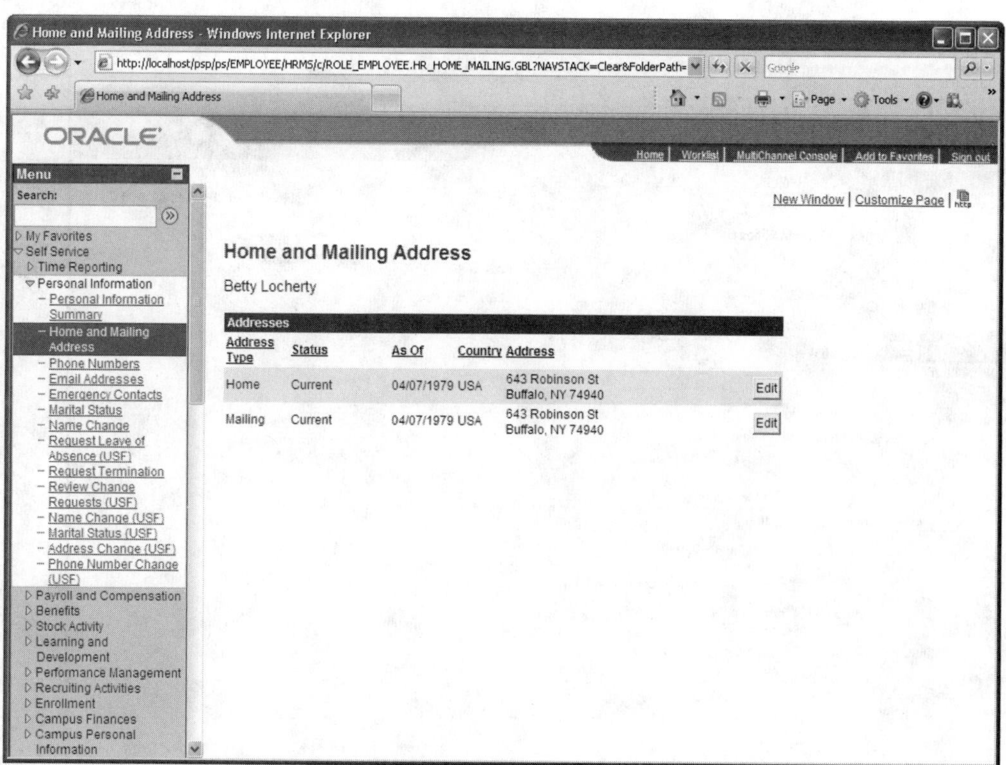

FIGURE 1-20 *Updating a home address*

payroll processing and use delivered business processes across multiple countries. The features common to North American payroll are: arrears processing, retroactivity processing, off-cycle payroll runs, and bank-related information. Figure 1-22 shows the payroll interface.

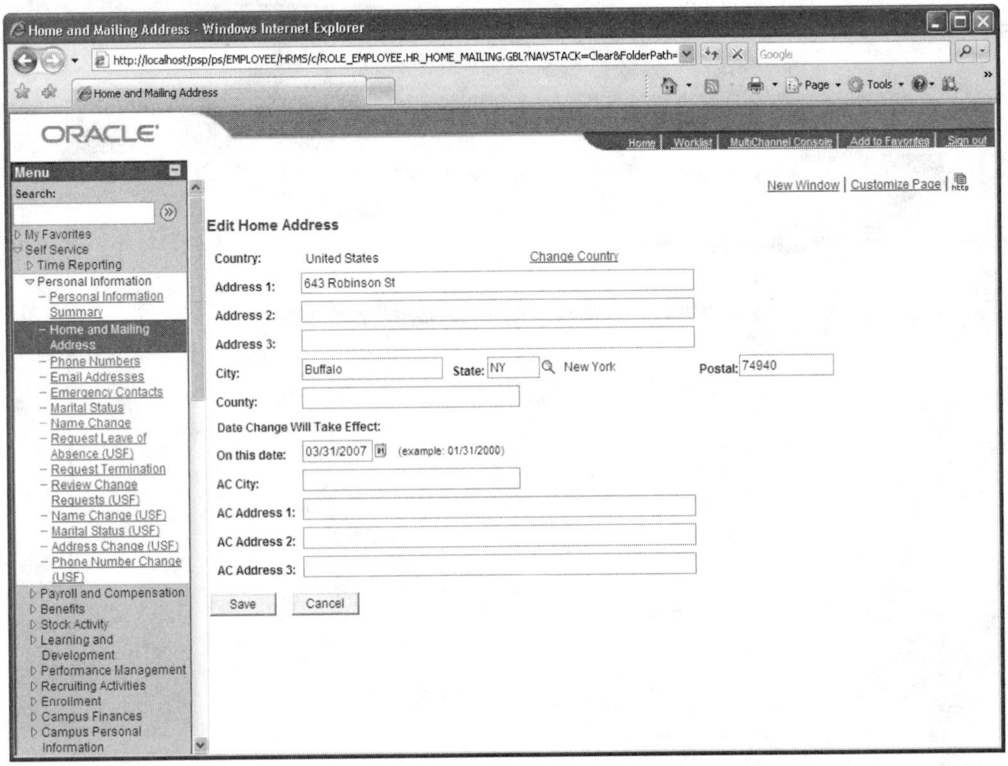

Home and Mailing Address - Windows Internet Explorer

http://localhost/psp/ps/EMPLOYEE/HRMS/c/ROLE_EMPLOYEE.HR_HOME_MAILING.GBL?NAVSTACK=Clear&FolderPath=

ORACLE

Home | Worklist | MultiChannel Console | Add to Favorites | Sign out

Menu
Search:
My Favorites
Self Service
Time Reporting
Personal Information
- Personal Information Summary
- Home and Mailing Address
- Phone Numbers
- Email Addresses
- Emergency Contacts
- Marital Status
- Name Change
- Request Leave of Absence (USF)
- Request Termination
- Review Change Requests (USF)
- Name Change (USF)
- Marital Status (USF)
- Address Change (USF)
- Phone Number Change (USF)
Payroll and Compensation
Benefits
Stock Activity
Learning and Development
Performance Management
Recruiting Activities
Enrollment
Campus Finances
Campus Personal Information

New Window | Customize Page

Edit Home Address

Country: United States Change Country
Address 1: 643 Robinson St
Address 2:
Address 3:
City: Buffalo State: NY New York Postal: 74940
County:
Date Change Will Take Effect:
On this date: 03/31/2007 (example: 01/31/2000)
AC City:
AC Address 1:
AC Address 2:
AC Address 3:

Save Cancel

FIGURE 1-21 *Update screen*

Payroll for North America

Payroll for North America is a set of modules that calculates gross to net earnings and deductions and related taxes. It is integrated with HR, Time and Labor, General Ledger, Projects, Recruiting, and Compensation applications. The flexible interface supports U.S. and Canadian rules, regulations, and processing requirements with regularly scheduled tax updates to keep you in sync with new regulations. The system manages year-end processing, and the preparation for the next year before

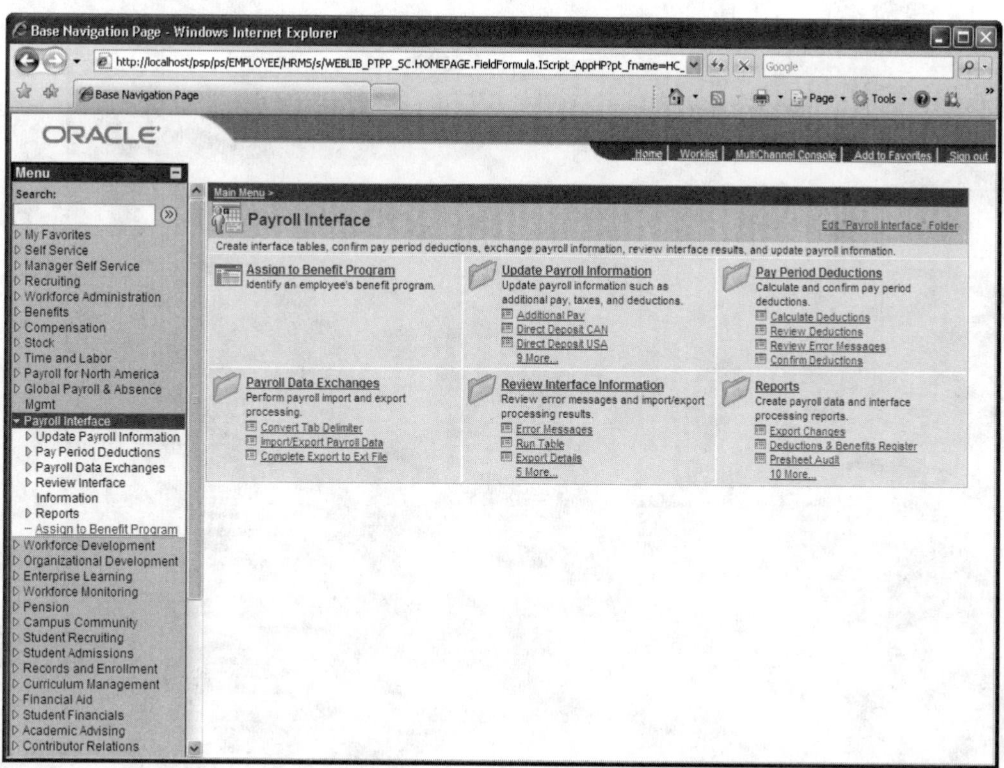

FIGURE 1-22 *Payroll interface*

closing out the books on the current year. Create unlimited earnings and deductions and handle multi-organizational processing, using a Common Paymaster. You can use direct deposit functionality, check printing capabilities, and the complementary ePay to display online check advice. Your company can maintain its own tax filing and record keeping, since PeopleSoft NA calculates federal, state, provincial, and local tax requirements. Figure 1-23 shows the Payroll for North America portal.

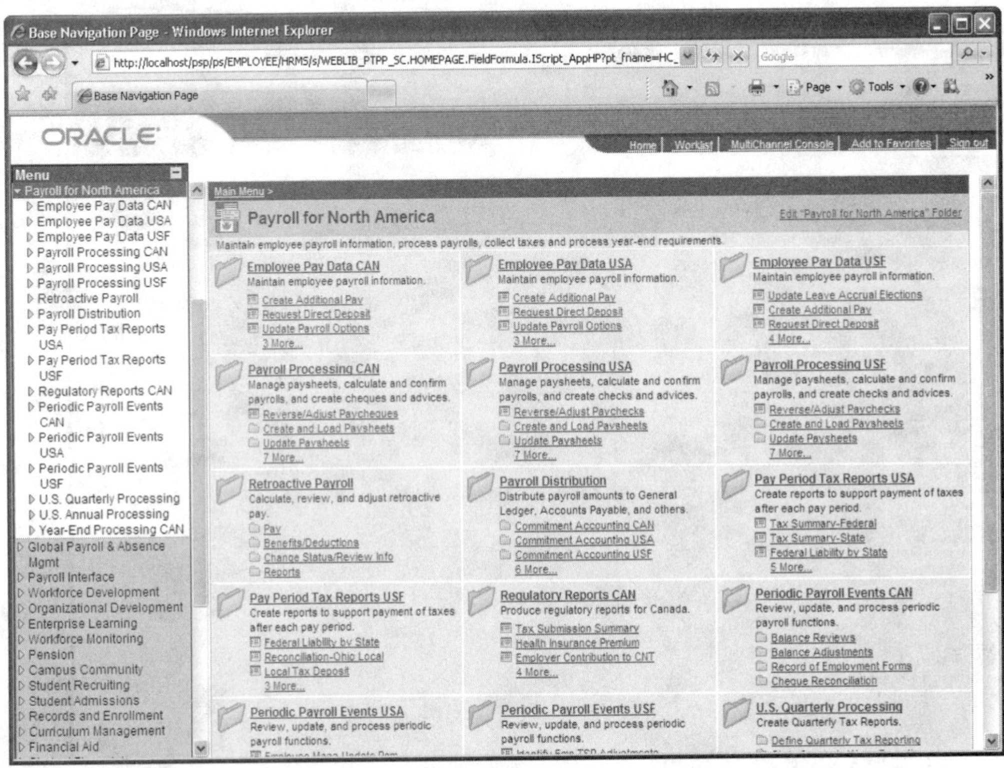

FIGURE 1-23 *Payroll for North America portal*

Payroll Interface

The Payroll Interface allows for the management and exportation of the employee data and related payroll information. You can process multiple payrolls, locally or worldwide, using your defined parameters to exchange employee-level HR and payroll data. Exchange payroll data and interface with benefits, savings plan, 401(k), Thrift Savings Plan (TSP) contribution, W4, and personnel data. Feed payroll data into your PeopleSoft Human Resources system for employees to view and update. Figure 1-24 shows the Payroll Interface.

Payroll Interface for ADP Connection

Oracle's PeopleSoft Payroll Interface for ADP Connection links PeopleSoft HR with ADP payroll services—ADP's Enterprise Payroll Services and ADP's AutoPay utilizing ADP PC/Payroll for Windows. PeopleSoft Payroll Interface for ADP

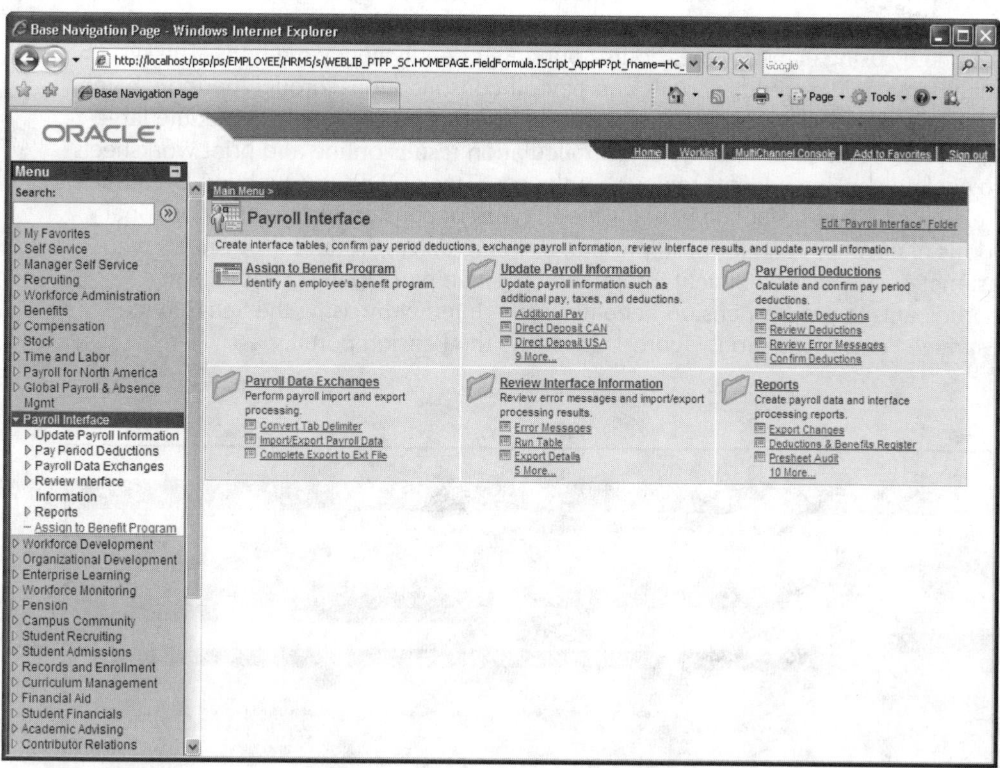

FIGURE 1-24 *Payroll Interface*

Connection increases data accuracy and cuts payroll processing costs by eliminating the need to re-key PeopleSoft Human Resources data into your ADP payroll software.

Pension Administration

Pension Administration enables you to manage multiple, complex, defined-benefit plans. Automate tasks ranging from pension calculations to tracking pension and service credit, create reports, and provide critical information to use when counseling plan participants. The system stores effective-dated employment history to track jobs, employment status, salaried or hourly status, and union affiliation to allow for the movement between pension plans. Access individual historical earnings, hours, and pension contribution data; consolidate data; or keep per-period history. Track all payees (retirees, beneficiaries, and qualified domestic relations order (QDRO) alternate payees) in one database. Use effective-dating to keep a history of plan provisions including grandfathered benefits, early retirement window benefits, minimum benefit formulas, and breaks and bridging in service. Calculate service by using elapsed time, hours counting, or equivalency methods. The system maintains service credit accruals and payroll consolidations through periodic batch updates. Run on-demand calculations for individual employees, or schedule large batch runs for later processing. View calculation results online and print worksheets to explain pension benefits to your employees. Track QDROs (Qualified Domestic Relations Order). Calculate benefits for all types of pension plans; for all optional forms of payment; and for past, present, or future dates. Produce worksheets with estimates and accrued benefit information for plan participants. Enable plan participants to project pension benefits via the Internet by using the Self-Service Estimate Pension function. Figure 1-25 shows the Pension portal.

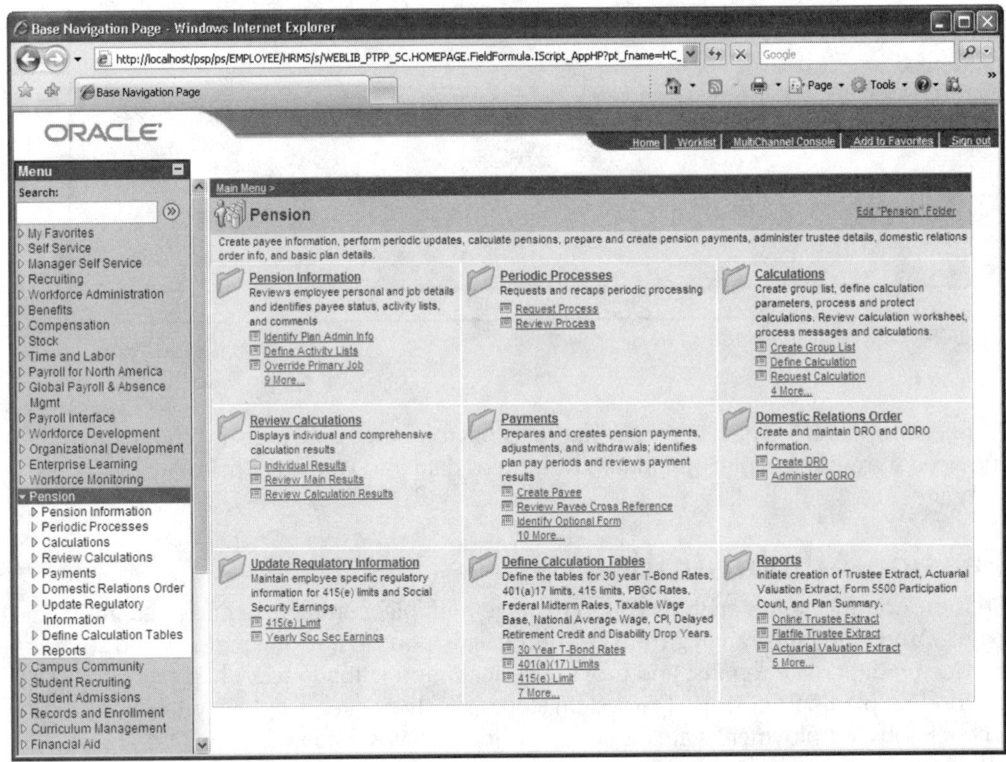

FIGURE 1-25 *Pension portal*

Stock Administration

Stock Administration automates the management of common stock equity plans. The system can manage multiple stock plans, such as incentive stock options (ISOs), nonqualified stock options (NQs), restricted stock awards (RSAs), tandem stock appreciation rights (ISARs and NSARs), and employee stock purchase plans (ESPPs). You can capture online transactions and batch processes for grants, purchases, exercises, repurchases, releases, and sales or dispositions. The system provides employees' detailed and summary information related to their stock transactions, including grants and options, vesting schedules, portfolio valuations, and more. Recipients can also perform portfolio modeling using value and taxation assumptions. Figure 1-26 shows the stock portal.

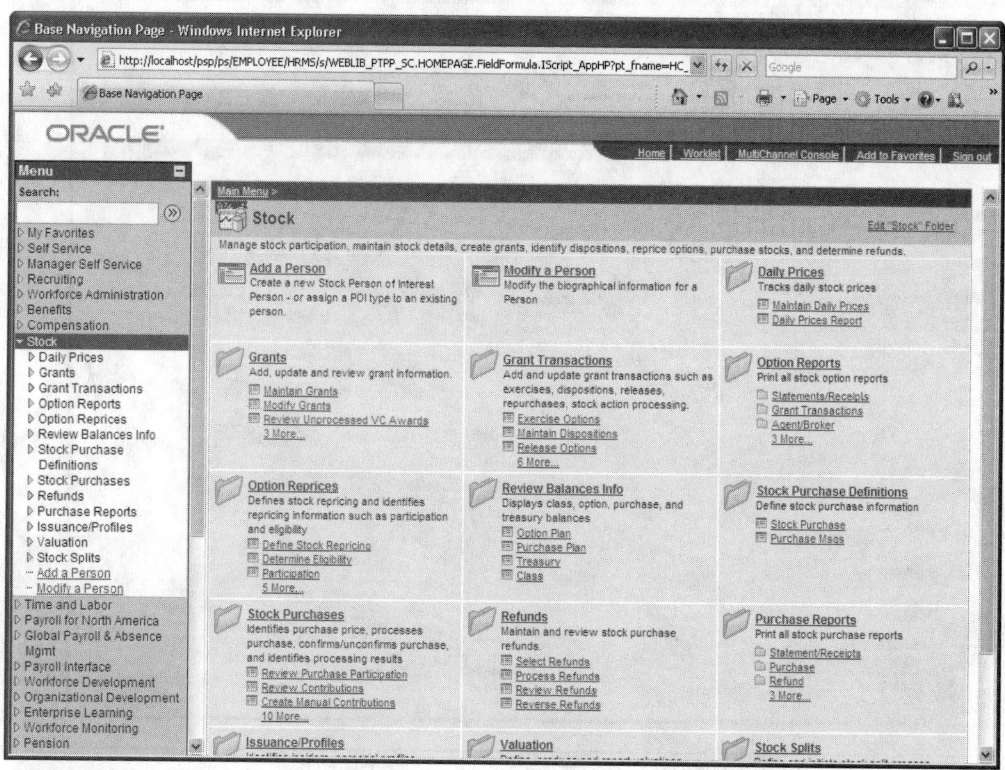

FIGURE 1-26 *Stock portal*

Time and Labor

Time and Labor is a business function module that allows for the connection to payroll, financial and cost accounting, project management, employee benefits, and organizational administration. Employees can enter time, projects, and other related transactions. The system integrates with both PeopleSoft Enterprise Payroll for North America and Global Payroll. Time and Labor exports payable time directly into the pay sheets. The system does online time reporting using pre-populated timesheets. The system provides managers with gathered reported time, scheduled time, exceptions, and results of rules for viewing, editing, and approval. Figure 1-27 shows the Time and Labor portal.

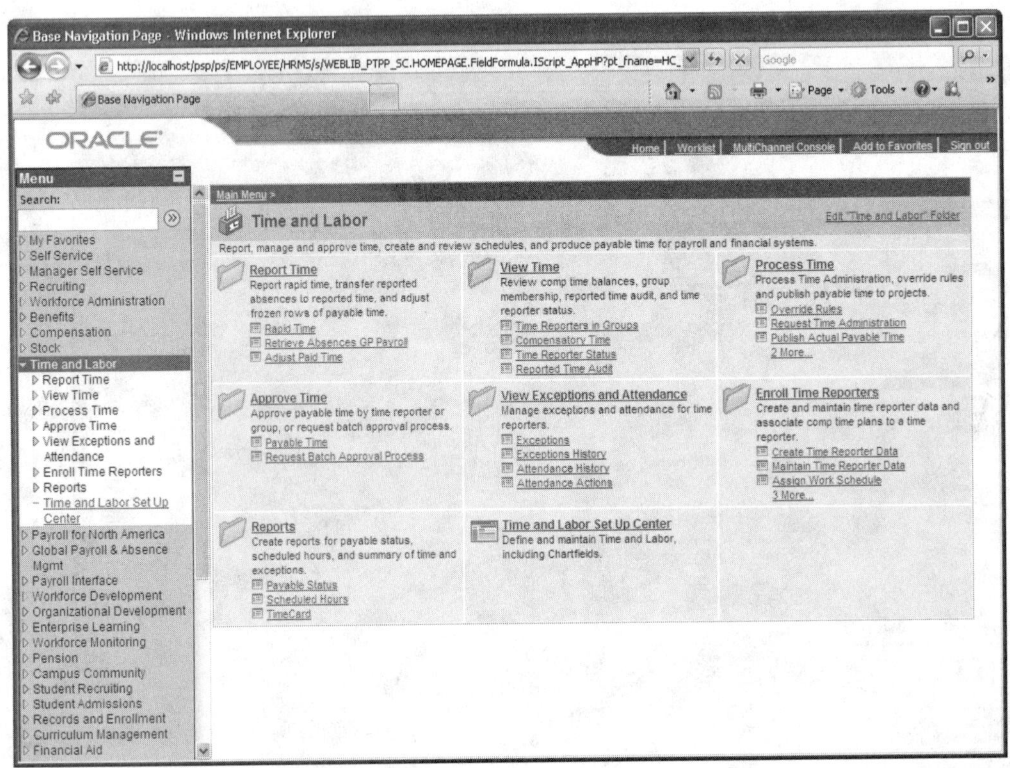

FIGURE 1-27 *Time and Labor portal*

Workforce Scheduling

Workforce Scheduling reports time in many different ways to create complex punch, elapsed, or flexible timecards and the rules that drive them. The system can create flexible schedules for fixed, rotating, or dynamic shifts. Managers can view, approve, and commit time collection with ease for one person or all their direct reports, capturing a myriad of work details in the process. Approve time for direct reports after drilling down to displays of total hours, overtime, and absences. Notifications alert managers to time that is awaiting approval and exceptions that need to be cleared. Automated integration with PeopleSoft Financials sends labor costs to the GL and drives project costing. Figure 1-28 demonstrates the options available for time reporting.

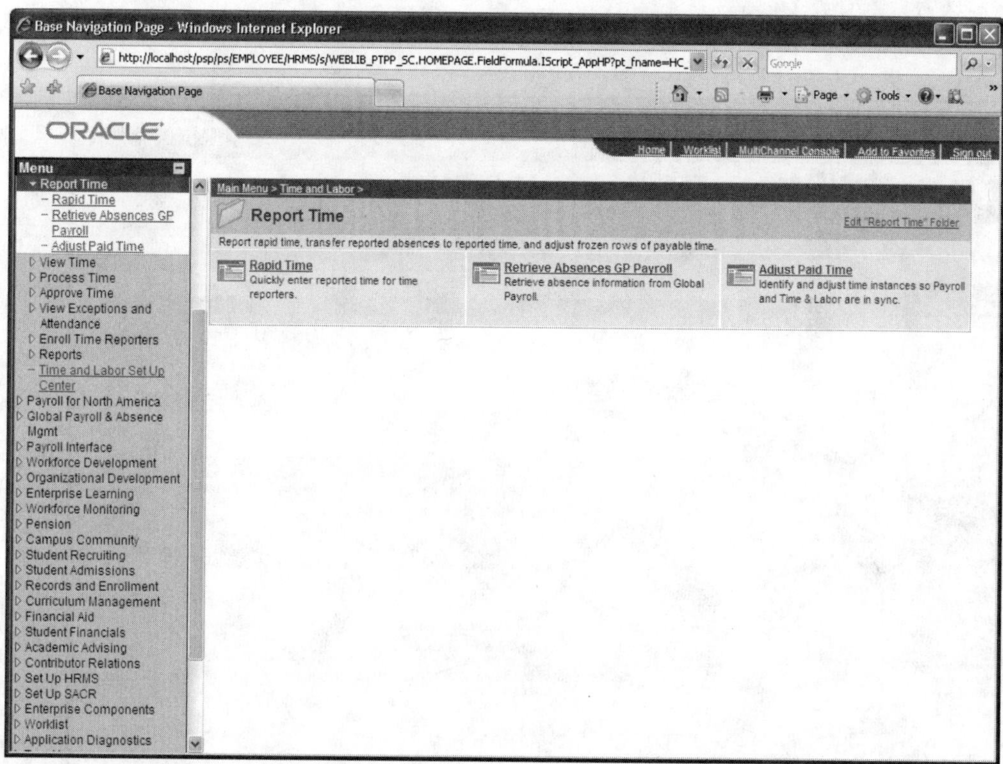

FIGURE 1-28 *Available options for time reporting*

Talent Management

The centralized Profile Management module will deliver enterprise-wide talent management, offering organizations seamless integration of talent management applications. As the foundation for all functional areas of talent management—recruiting, performance management, learning management, analytics, and competency management—Profile Management defines the attributes required for individual and organizational success. Representing a best-in-class architecture, updates to Talent Acquisition Manager, Candidate Gateway, ePerformance, and eDevelopment further extend PeopleSoft Enterprise HCM's robust talent management solution. Figure 1-29 show Talent Acquisition and the options available for recruiting.

Candidate Gateway

Candidate Gateway (formerly known as eRecruit) enables you to advertise your employment opportunities and build relationships with employees and top

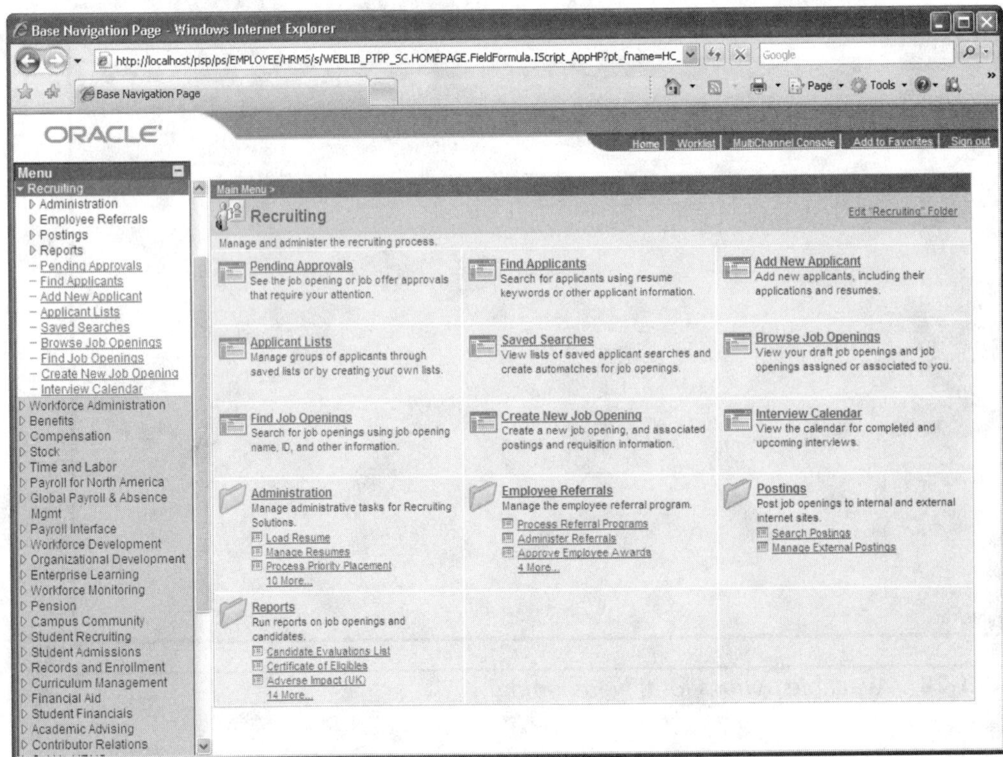

FIGURE 1-29 *Talent Acquisition and the Available Options for Recruiting*

candidates using an online recruiting solution. Candidate Gateway is designed to help candidates search for employment, apply for positions, and track their progress through the recruitment process. Figure 1-30 demonstrates the Candidate Gateway.

eDevelopment

eDevelopment is a self-service solution that supports your employees' personal and professional development. eDevelopment enables employees to create, modify, and view personal profiles reflecting their capabilities and accomplishments. It allows employees to search for jobs that match their own skills and qualifications, or identify and compare various positions of interest to them. eDevelopment provides information to help employees define their next career steps and determine the development steps. It enables employees to review training opportunities and request training enrollment, and enables managers to submit and approve employee profile changes and training requests and review the status of training enrollment approval. Figure 1-31 displays how an employee can actively manage his or her internal career choices.

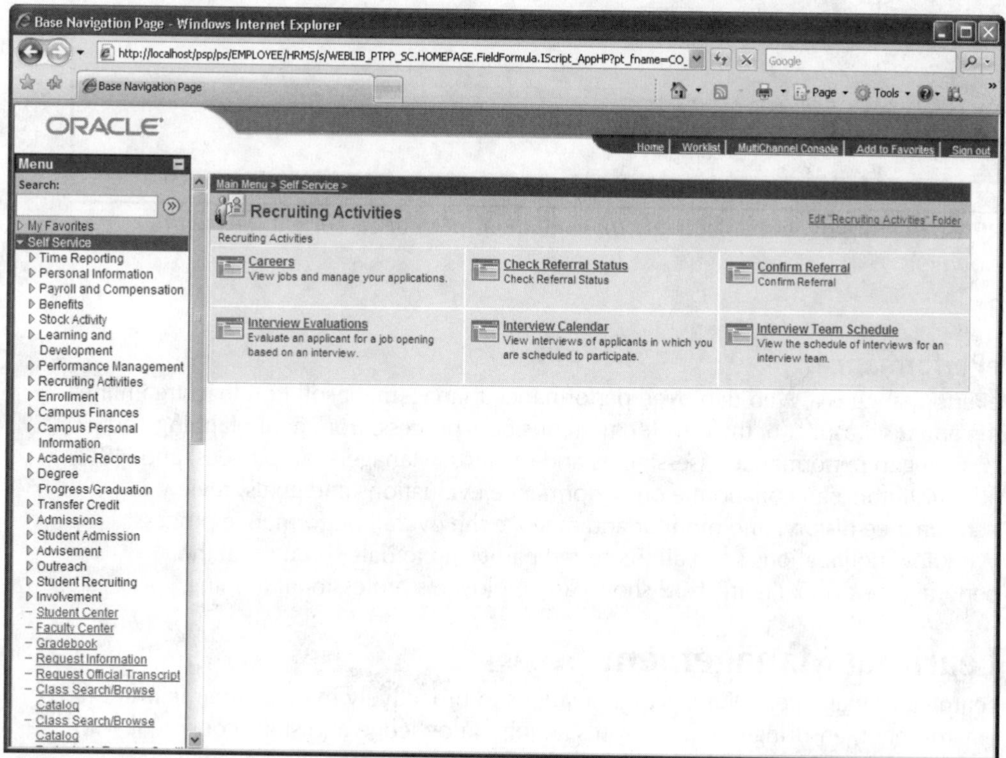

FIGURE 1-30 *Candidate Gateway*

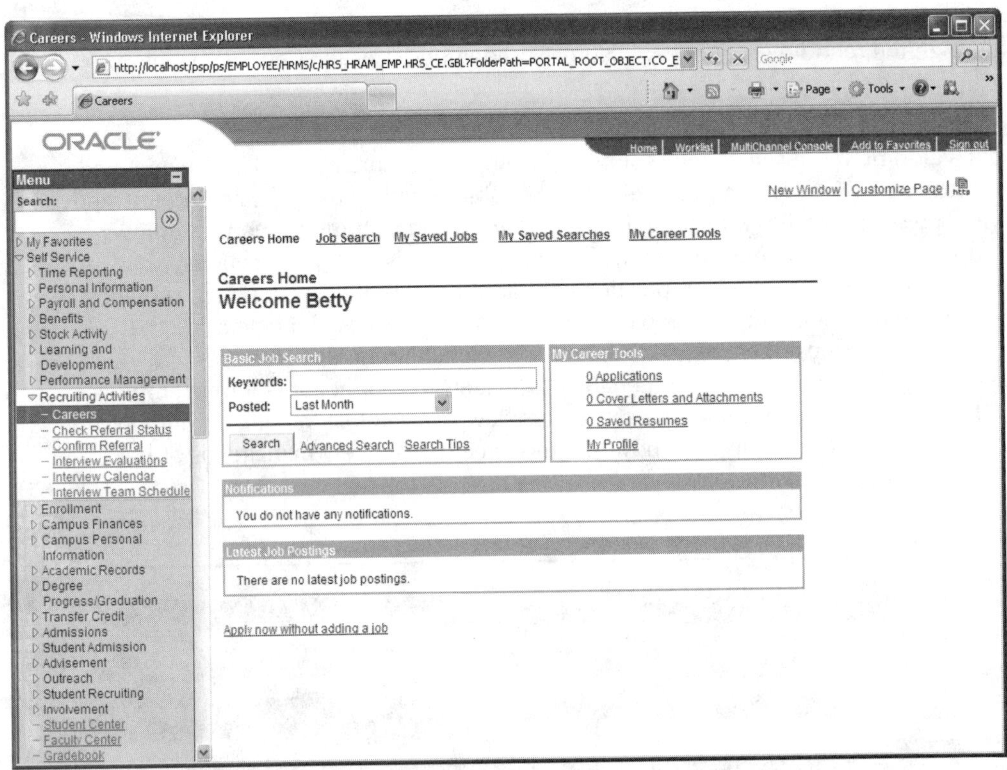

FIGURE 1-31 *Employees can actively manage their internal career choices with eDevelopment*

ePerformance

ePerformance is a Web-deployed performance management solution that streamlines the appraisal aspect of the development business process, from goal planning and coaching to performance assessments and rewards. Managers, employees, and HR administrators can collaborate on performance evaluations and goals, review performance history, and monitor and manage the overall performance process. Workflow notifications keep all interested parties up to date throughout the performance cycle. Figure 1-32 shows an employee's professional training.

Learning Management

Learning Management enables organizations to proactively manage their learning environment, ensuring that employees acquire knowledge and skills consistent with corporate objectives. It helps achieve and maintain regulatory compliance by automating learning delivery, tracking the completion of certifications, and enabling

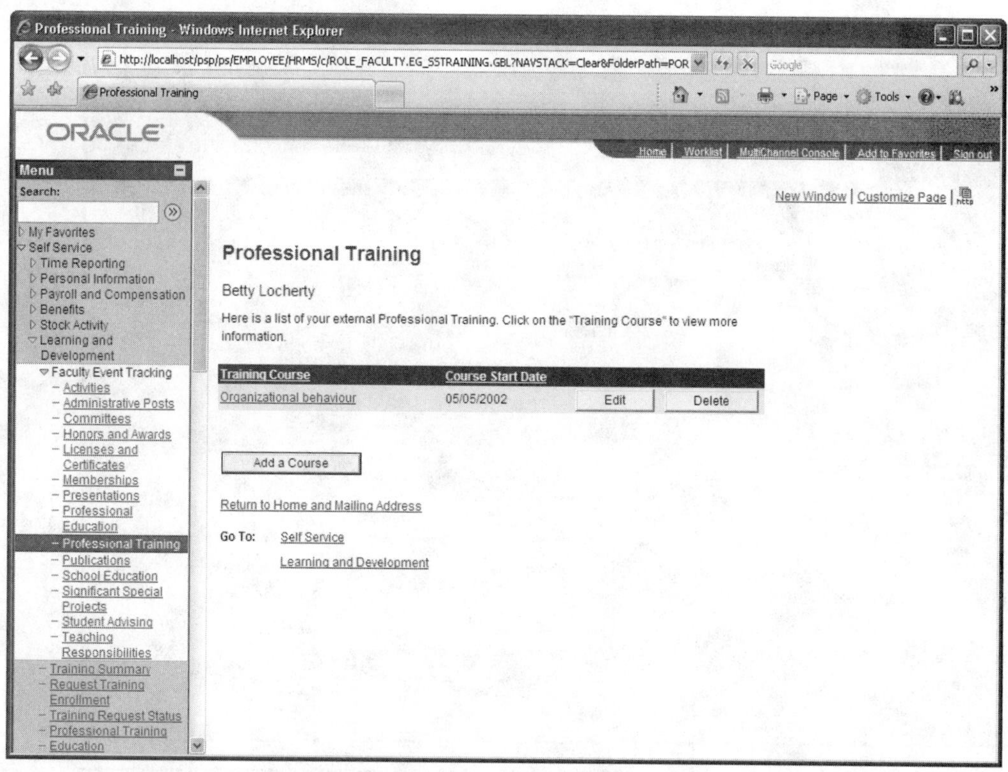

FIGURE 1-32 *Employee's professional training*

the review of standard operating procedures. Businesses can mitigate risk and increase compliance with corporate regulations by ensuring that their organization's policies and procedures are not only disseminated but also understood and adhered to. Figure 1-33 shows the Enterprise Learning portal.

The Learning Management module allows organizations to manage their learning environment, enabling employees to acquire knowledge and skills consistent with corporate objectives. By optimizing your workforce, you can provide a competitive advantage to your customers and partners. The integration of the capabilities of the Learning Management module with the Person Model is an example of the power of the Enterprise Model to eliminate dual entry, and leverage already defined setup of manager-employee relationships.

Services Procurement

Services Procurement allows customers to effectively manage the entire procurement process from request through settlement for all types of services, including deliverable-based services, all while applying service agreement terms and providing visibility

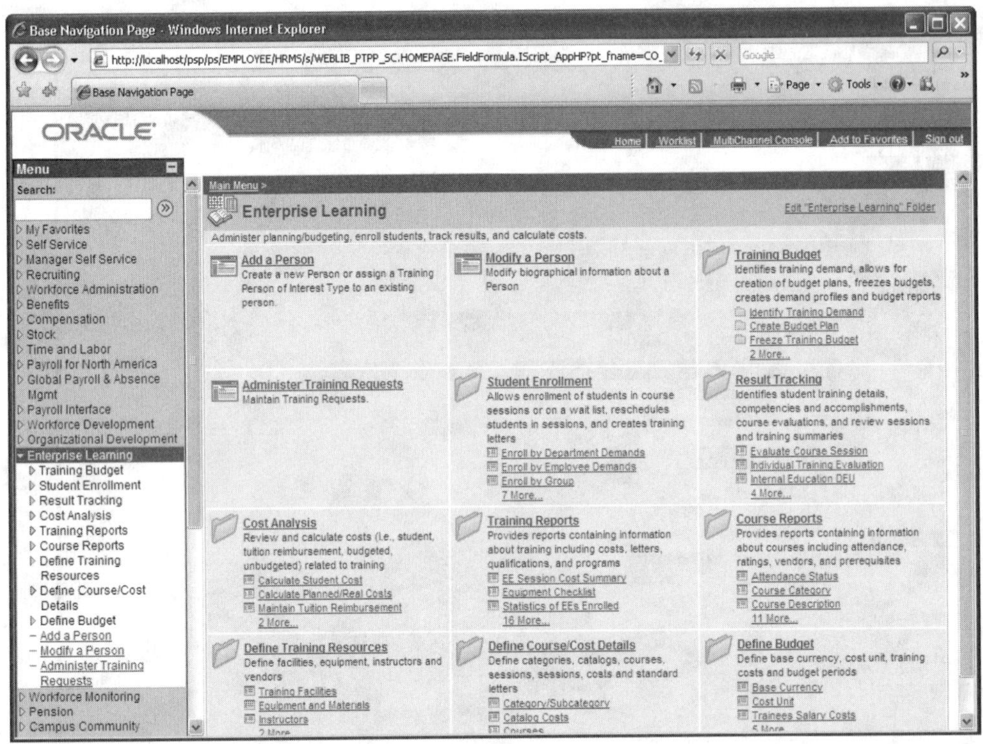

FIGURE 1-33 *Enterprise Learning portal*

into services spend. Automating and tracking services requisitioning are essential to streamlining procurement processes and reducing spending on services. Services Procurement enables customers to maximize preferred supplier savings, reduce cost and services spending, and create visibility into services spending. You can enforce preferred supplier use in every requisition, set policies for services spending approval, automate manual processes, track discounts and make early payments, and oversee the entire services procurement cycle.

Talent Acquisition Manager

Talent Acquisition Manager (formerly eRecruit) is a recruiting solution for candidates, recruiters, and managers. It provides pages for the recruiting process, allowing employees and external candidates to search, view, and apply for jobs online. It has built-in applicant tracking; recruiters and managers can focus on the most important outcome—identifying and hiring talent quickly. Talent Acquisition Manager is designed to expedite the hiring process. Applicants can search for open positions, create "job search agents," submit resumes and attachments online, and track their progress in a secure environment. Managers and recruiters can search an entire applicant pool, including internal talent, by using keyword search. The system has the capability to capture interview results and other notes online to store information in one central location during the selection process. Businesses can prepare and approve job offers according to their pre-defined rules or a one-time creation using the approval design process. The system can be integrated with third-party job search vendors such as Monster. The application can handle resume processing, background and drug tests, and behavioral assessments. Figure 1-34 shows the main menu of the Talent Acquisition Manager application.

Workforce Administration

Workforce Administration helps you conduct in-depth analysis of mid- and long-term workforce requirements to determine which key jobs, competencies, and profiles are essential to fulfilling your organizational strategy. It then links these needs directly to individual employees so you know how your current workforce

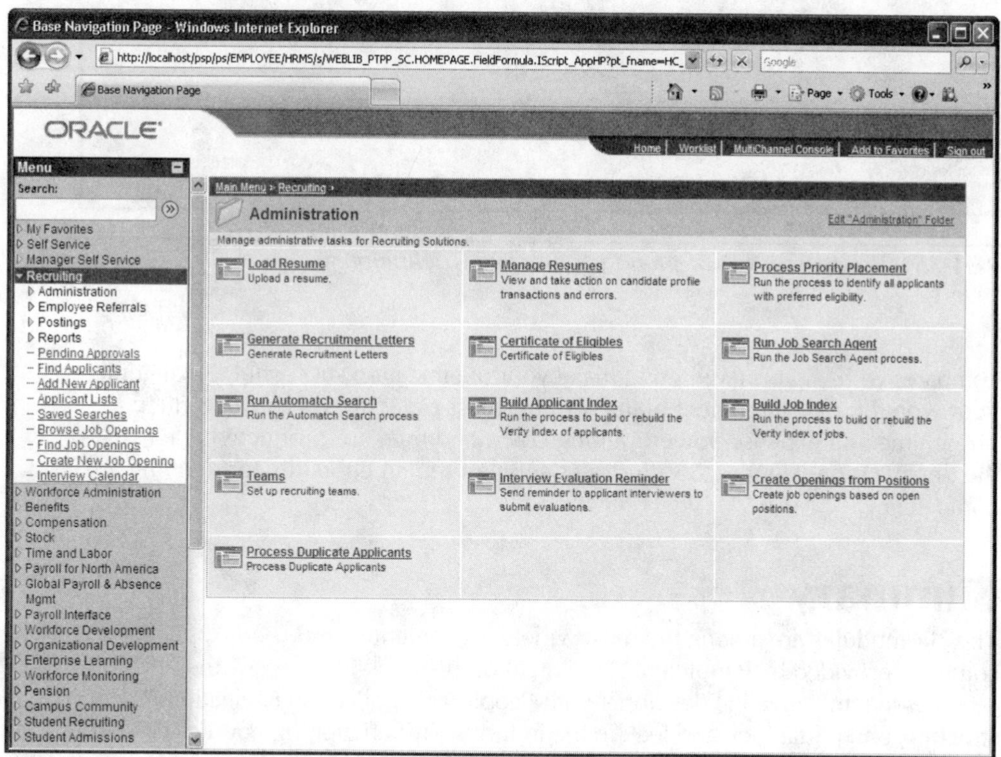

FIGURE 1-34 *Talent Acquisition Manager*

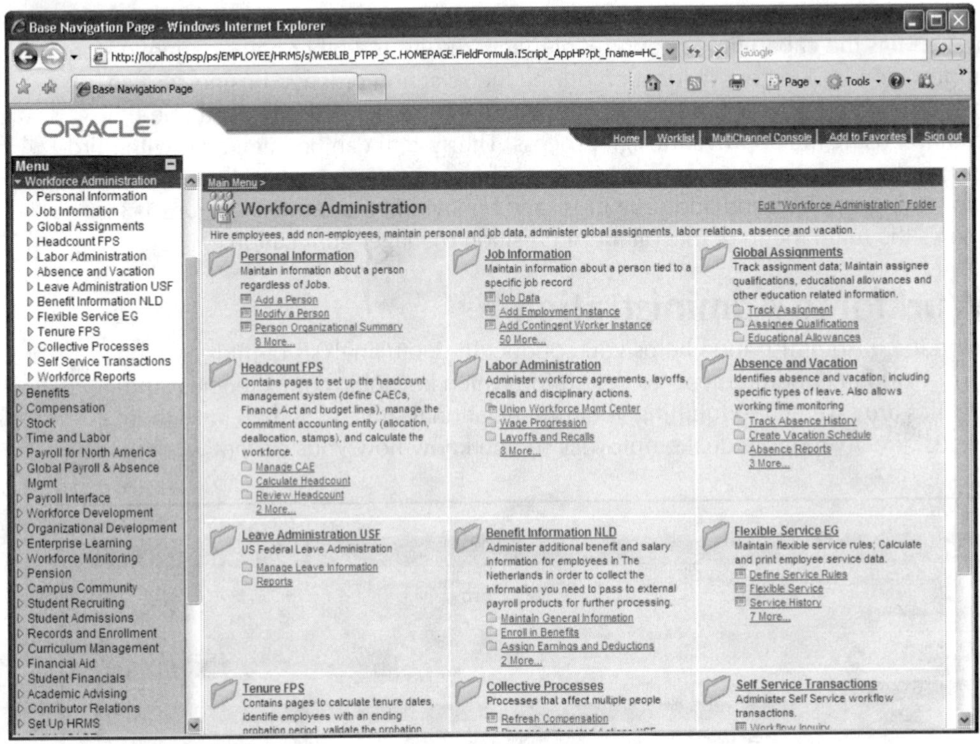

FIGURE 1-35 *Workforce Administration competency definition*

compares with what is required to make your organization successful. By aligning your workforce development plans with business objectives, you can reduce hiring time and expense, lower training costs, and increase productivity across the organization. Figure 1-35 illustrates some of the functionality for defining a competency.

Summary

The HR modules are among the most widely implemented and used Application solutions provided by PeopleSoft. The intent of this book is to review the HR modules to familiarize the developer with PeopleSoft application navigation, menu structure, and portal look and feel. In the industry any variation of modules delivered by PeopleSoft could be implemented. The navigation for these implementations and the look and feel will remain constant.

CHAPTER 2

PeopleTools

n this chapter you will gain an understanding of the configuration of the PeopleSoft Enterprise Application. PeopleSoft is a web-based application that does not require an executable on the client to operate. It uses a configuration of a back-end database with physical database objects such as tables, views, and stored procedures, and a configured metadata that houses the configuration for the PeopleSoft Applications. The metadata includes but is not limited to records, fields, and PeopleCode objects. The database and the metadata repository must be in sync at all times. To code in the metadata in PeopleCode or to configure objects, you utilize the Application Designer development window. PeopleTools, the development set of tools, is coded, created, and developed in Application Designer. With the addition of Oracle Fusion Middleware, more and more development can take place at the Application Server level.

PeopleSoft Development Architecture

PeopleSoft has a highly flexible development environment, with the ability to incorporate business modeling, rules, and tools. It uses the Pure Internet Architecture, with cutting edge toolsets that allow for easy application development and smooth customization. PeopleSoft Enterprise Pure Internet Architecture, introduced with PeopleTools 8, is completely focused on the Internet providing powerful functionality for secure, scalable, Internet-based access and integration.

The Integration Broker allows for XML messaging that offers interoperability via a standard web service. With the Interactive Services Repository, your third-party applications can work with PeopleSoft. The Process Integration Packs can connect PeopleSoft to SAP and Oracle Applications. The portal's open and flexible design makes it easy to link multiple systems and content, resulting in faster portal deployment. Community Portal supports PeopleSoft applications and content, linking up to the other enterprise portals using standards-based communications. PeopleSoft offers some of the best of breed in reporting and analytics. Developers can create new solutions and integrate with the web via XML or use standard structural reporting with SQR. Application Engine offers the best in class for batch processing and the ability to send your results out via e-mail.

Data Architecture

The architecture of PeopleSoft is an Internet-based application with customization taking place on the middle tier with no code being placed on the client. The technology utilizes standard Internet technology and concepts to keep the delivery simple and allow for easy and open flow between systems. By using this type of architecture as the foundation for your application you can have easy access by end-users (customers), with the added feature of ease of integration and customized development.

Internet Connectivity

The Internet architecture is server-based architecture that enables secure end-user connectivity to the application. The connection and technology is standard Internet: HTML, HTTP, XML, and web services.

Web Services

By using Internet technology standards, PeopleSoft delivers a set of server-based technologies that support native web services. These technologies streamline the integration of PeopleSoft with other applications and custom internal systems. Figure 2-1 shows the PeopleSoft Application Architecture. The toolset that provides this integration are:

- Integration Broker
- Application Engine
- Component Interface

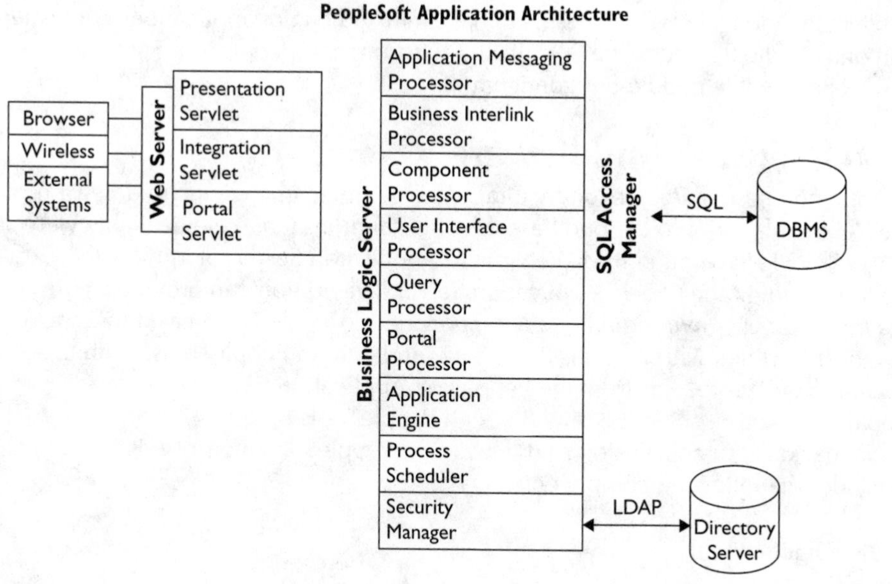

FIGURE 2-1 *PeopleSoft Application Architecture*

Client Access

The client only needs a browser and a URL to connect to the application. Once connected, the customer can process transactions, administer the application, monitor processes, and execute and view reports. In order to do this, the client is not required to download a Java applet or install any local executables. The application does this by using HTML and JavaScript connecting to a web browser to navigate. By handling it this way the PeopleSoft Application can be navigated to as easily and seamlessly as any other web site. By keeping it this simple, the application provides an inexpensive access point as well as a rapid user adoption.

Middle Tier

One of the new features that are currently being offered by Oracle is Fusion Middleware. The new business process functionality that is being offered in the middle tier is amazing. When PeopleSoft was first released the main focus was to keep the middle tier open source and as vendor independent as possible. But with the acquisition of PeopleSoft by Oracle, the options available are now at a completely different level. Middleware brings to the PeopleSoft architecture a standards-based group of products that include J2EE developer tools, integration services, BI (business intelligence), and content management. The umbrella of Fusion Middleware rebrands some technology under the guise of Middleware that is not part of the middle tier. What Fusion promises to bring is support, development, deployment, and management of an SOA Services-oriented architecture. The product does this with a "hot-pluggable" architecture and it allows businesses to have a mixed bag of applications connected with one middle tier including SAP, IBM, Microsoft, and PeopleSoft. Figure 2-2 shows one possible middle-tier configuration.

Oracle Fusion Middleware

With the purchase of PeopleSoft by Oracle the ability to change the middleware suite is possible; prior to the purchase the only solutions that were available were BEA WebLogic Server and IBM WebSphere Application Server. Starting with PeopleTools 8.47 the Oracle Application Server Java Edition can provide a core Java development environment. Key components of Oracle Fusion Middleware have been certified with versions 8.46, 8.47, and 8.48 of PeopleTools. With the separation of PeopleTools from the PeopleSoft Application, you can deploy PeopleSoft Enterprise 8.4, 8.8, and 8.9 with PeopleTools 8.46, 8.47, and 8.48. A special package, Oracle Fusion Middleware for PeopleSoft Enterprise, is available. It includes the following components:

- Oracle Portal
- Oracle BPEL Process Manager

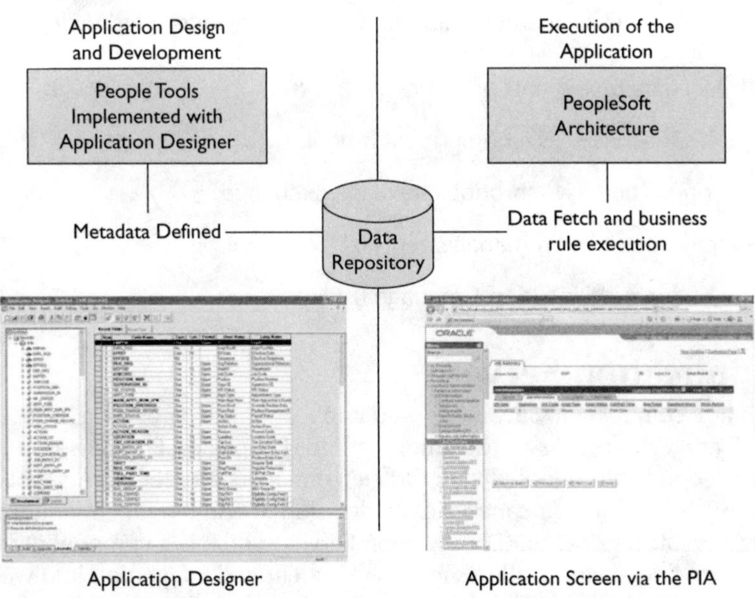

FIGURE 2-2 *Middle-tier configuration*

- Oracle containers for Java
- Oracle Integration B2B
- Oracle Integration BAM
- Oracle Application Server Discoverer
- Oracle Application Server Identity Management (Single Sign-On)
- Oracle Application Server Web Cache

BPEL

Business Process Execution Language (BPEL) is the main component of Service-Oriented Architecture (SOA). It is a standard language created for the execution of web services. It is not this book's intention to teach you how to use BPEL, only to introduce you to key concepts so that when your middleware team members discuss the technology you can understand how it may affect your future as a developer. BPEL was submitted to OASIS in March 2003, and it has gained momentum as a clear standard since. Currently, PeopleSoft uses Workflow technology to integrate and communicate actions to the web tier, but in the future, with the integration of

Seibel standards into the Fusion Architecture, more and more we will see the movement to these (BPEL) standards. Important features to understand include

- XML as a data model and standard
- WSDL/web services as a component model
- Synchronous and asynchronous message exchange
- Hierarchical exception management
- Business Process Execution Language (BPEL)

Web Application Server

You can use any commercially available web application server as long as it supports J2EE and can provide an execution path for PeopleSoft Enterprise architecture. PeopleSoft is bundled with Oracle containers for J2EE, BEA WebLogic, and IBM WebSphere. And you can make the decision to add the functionality and connectivity advantages of Oracle Application Server, which is a component of Oracle's Fusion Middleware. It allows for development and integration into web services, enterprise applications, and portals. The platform is built on J2EE scalable server technology. It is specifically designed to handle the complexities of Oracle grid computing and SOA. Of course, you do not have to use the Oracle Application Server for the middle tier in PeopleSoft. A lot of places still configure it with BEA Tuxedo; this configuration is easier and it is a delivered option with PeopleSoft. BEA Tuxedo is command-line application and is primarily for pinging or bringing the Application Server up and down. It is a simple configuration without many bells and whistles, but it does the job.

Business Logic Server

The PeopleSoft Business Logic Server is key to allowing tens of thousands of concurrent users in the enterprise application at any given time. It does this with a scaleable architecture that provides support for load balancing and failover at this tier. To allow for a quickly scalable application, the enterprise can simply add more application servers to allow for more connections. Multiple instances of the same server processes can be configured to state when the application domain is booted. The Business Logic Server can dynamically spawn incremental server processes to handle more transaction requests. The following services are managed by the Business Logic Server:

- Database Server
- Application Messaging

- User Interface Rendering
- Directory Server Integration
- PS Query Tool
- File Processing
- Process Scheduler
- Database Interaction
- Business Logic

The PeopleSoft Enterprise architecture contains the metadata, the application definitions, and the application data. PeopleTools executed through Application Designer is the development environment and with the interface PeopleTools, you can maintain and access the metadata. The Business Logic Server executes the Business Logic service based on the PeopleSoft metadata.

Web-Based Application

PeopleSoft is a web-based solution, not a web-enabled application. Users can simply enter a URL in the web address bar and go to the PeopleSoft application the same way they would navigate to Amazon or Google. The benefits of having the application configured this way include:

- Platform independence
- Small learning curve for users
- Low bandwidth
- Ease of maintenance and deployment
- Secure access
- Scalable server architecture

PeopleSoft launched on a web platform with a web client that can connect to a web server hosting the PeopleSoft HTML files and Java applets. The web server communication happens currently with a BEA system product, Jolt, which comes bundled with PeopleSoft. How this is configured and what will come bundled with PeopleSoft will gradually change with Oracle's launch of more Fusion Middleware products in the PeopleSoft bundle. Jolt supports web-based client connection and interprets HTML and JavaScript; it acts as an interpreter and takes the HTML and Java applets and relays them into C++ code.

The server architecture can be physical or logical depending on the equipment available. Many configurations are in use currently in business; for example, the development environment and quality environment may be on the same physical Unix server and production may exist on a separate physical machine. In a physical configuration both Jolt Internet Relay (JRLY) and Jolt Relay Adaptor (JRAD) software are required; both products are BEA solutions. Figure 2-3 shows a logical server configuration and Figure 2-4 shows a physical server configuration.

Internet Application Server

The Internet Application Server renders the application interface to the client machine via HTML with light JavaScript, and the web browser presents the application user interface. The browser/server configuration does not require software to be installed, it does not require a client footprint, and it makes deployment very simple. The browser communicates with the web server over a secure HTTP connection and calls to the Presentation Relay Servlet to host the HTML and JavaScript via the browser. The servlet is a very thin layer in the architecture that maps data directly with the HTTP requests to and from the

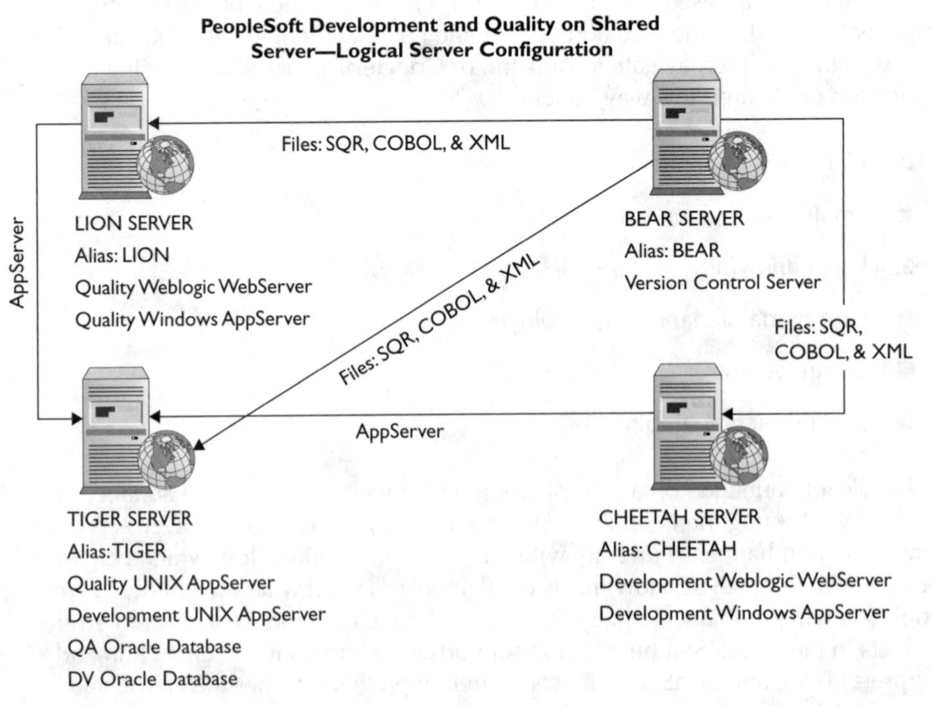

FIGURE 2-3 *Logical server configuration*

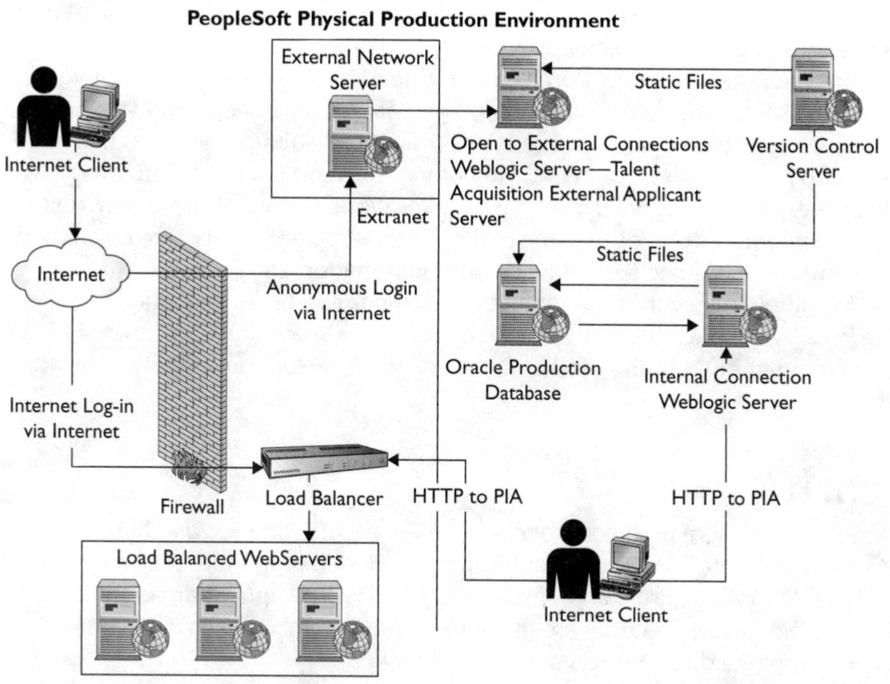

FIGURE 2-4 *Physical server configuration*

application Component Processor and User Interface Generator. The presentation servlet communicates directly with the back-end services via BEA JOLT.

The application utilizes PeopleSoft SQL Access Manager to communicate with the DBMS via native SQL. This feature allows for a sophisticated database connection pooling for efficient access and scalability.

Single Sign-On

The single sign-on features allows for a single unified secure access point. It simplifies user and password management, allowing users to be configured with role-based management. Extending PeopleSoft applications with Oracle Fusion Middleware allows for single sign-on across Oracle Portal and PeopleSoft Enterprise applications even when PeopleSoft is running on BEA/WebSphere, making the overall configuration easy and the end- user experience clean and simple.

Portal

The PeopleSoft Portal technology provides sophisticated features including search, content management, navigation, and home page personalization perfect for

PeopleSoft deployment. PeopleSoft Community Portal technology allows you to utilize the PeopleSoft Community Portal as a central workplace that can be integrated into other enterprise portal technology using web standards WSRP and JSR 168.

The PeopleSoft Community Portal can be extended with Oracle Portal. If your organization is like most in the industry and you are running PeopleSoft for your Human Resource solution and Oracle for your financial solution, you can extend the common portal workspace to include both application interfaces into one landing page. Creating a concentric space makes working with others easier, and total collaboration becomes the name of the game. Oracle Portal is wireless and can be used anywhere it is needed, allowing your information and workforce to be global. Existing PeopleSoft Community Portal screens can be incorporated into Oracle Portal, allowing for a unified access. You can also create a centralized LDAP directory for your organization and customize it to allow for connectivity to legacy systems.

Security

PeopleSoft architecture provides a comprehensive security framework that incorporates authentication and an authorization model. It provides native support for HTTPS, SSL, WS-Security, and others. Any LDAP v3-compliant directory can be used for the application security architecture as the directory server. The configuration of the directory server is shown here:

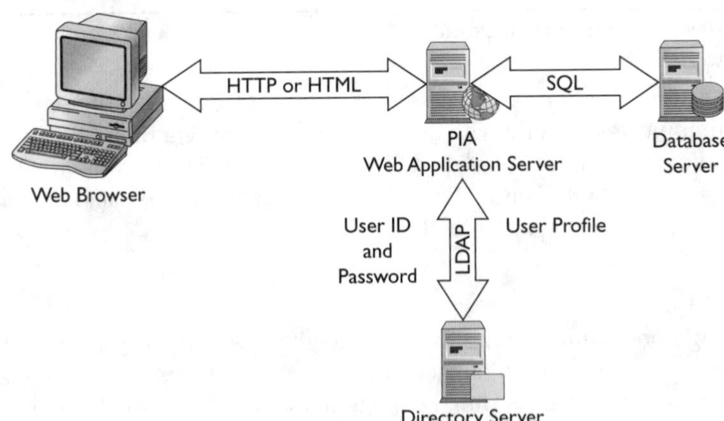

Oracle's PeopleSoft Enterprise Directory Interface enables you to integrate PeopleSoft security with LDAP directories to authenticate directory users. The PeopleSoft Directory Interface allows you to share data that already exists and is maintained in your PeopleSoft HRMS database with your directory.

Integration Broker

The Integration Broker creates the central hub that handles system-to-system integration and becomes the enterprise collaboration backbone. It consists of four parts: Packaged Connectors, Intelligent Routing, Transformation, and Development and Monitoring. Figure 2-5 shows the elements of the Integration Broker, Packaged Connectors or Messaging Gateway, Routing, Transformation, and the Development and Monitoring environment.

Application Messaging

Application Messaging is the messaging architecture for synchronous and asynchronous integration within the PeopleSoft system. It is a feature that allows for the management of messages in a request/reply or in a publish/subscribe paradigm in response to a business event. The messages are rendered in XML format and transmitted over secure HTTP.

Component Interface

With the component interface third-party systems can synchronously invoke PeopleSoft business logic via web services, XML, Java Beans, or XML bindings.

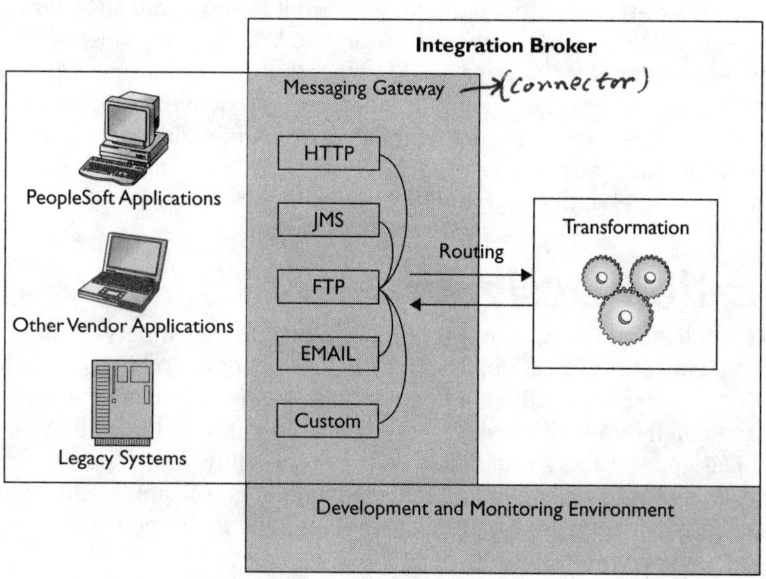

FIGURE 2-5 *Integration Broker*

An external system can invoke PeopleSoft Components via web services or it can invoke the Component Client using COM, Java, or C.

Message Monitor

The Integration Broker provides a Message Monitor to monitor and maintain message-based integration with other systems. It allows you to manage message channels, view the status of a message, view the XML, correct messages, and view the message history.

Application Engine

Application Engine is a turbo-charged script builder that allows you to do file-based integration and handles production-level batch processing. It supports a variety of formats including fixed length, variable length, delimited, and XML.

Metadata

The PeopleSoft Metadata architecture is key to the scalability of PeopleSoft and it is the heart of development within PeopleSoft. PeopleSoft architecture was developed from inception to utilize the metadata as the main configuration point of the database. The metadata has allowed PeopleSoft to maintain its standard of being database independent, and it allowed for the application solution to quickly adapt and move from client-server architecture to an Internet-based application quickly and without a complete re-write of the software. PeopleTools is provided as the development environment for Application Designer that allows for development in the metadata layer and to make changes to the stored and delivered metadata. Application Designer is your window into the PeopleSoft metadata definitions, including: user interface, business rules, data model, business processes, navigation via (portal and structure), and integration definitions.

Application Designer

PeopleTools Application Designer is a tool set provided to developers to allow them to define and change PeopleSoft objects. It is the point of entry to ERP objects and their definition, writing, and coding in PeopleTools; Application Engine; Component Interfaces; and much more, all of which are detailed in Part II of this book. Application Designer creates a direct link via the PIA to allow developers to make changes in a single location that will be reflected via the HTML application over a web browser. The following are the Application Designer components.

Project Workspace

The Project—or Project Workspace, as it is often called—is a container in which the developer can place the objects that are related to making a change to a piece of the ERP application. The Project Workspace organizes and presents the definitions of business objects in logical groups for easier development, adaptation, maintenance, and upgrade.

For example, some development shops choose to manage each and every change to the application with change control software. This is a very good practice and allows for the tracking of changes when the application is upgraded. Using PeopleSoft-provided naming conventions, the change control software then mandates the naming convention of your project. Imagine that your shop is in the process of implementing the change from using Social Security numbers to using a non-descript random EMPLID, a much better unique identifier for employees. Unfortunately, all of the current users of the system are used to having documentation that has Social Security Numbers, and for a variety of reasons need a screen to allow for searching via Social Security Number to obtain the EMPLID. A case would be logged in a tracking software and a project would be created to link back to that number, such as MOD0987 or SCR0987 (MOD = modification, SCR = Service Change Request). A project is then created in Application Designer and all of the objects that would be needed to create this screen—component, menu, page, records, fields, permission lists, roles, etc.—would be added to the project. When testing was complete, it would be easier to move the changed objects at one time from Development to Quality for verification, and with the project acting as a container for all of the changed objects, it provides that ease. It also acts as a change control container. If, when the project was copied from Development to Quality and regression testing was performed, you discovered that the change you made in one area adversely affected several others, the ability to rollback becomes easier with the project because in one container you know all of the objects that were affected and this can help diagnose where the error is occurring. It is imperative as a developer to maintain a balanced level of change control. Do not allow your projects to get to the size where you are changing so much of the application that the purpose of breaking out the focus of the change is lost.

PeopleCode

PeopleCode is the delivered programming language for the PeopleSoft Application. It is a programming language like any other programming language and has only a few specifics that are unique to coding in PeopleSoft. If you are familiar with C++, Visual Basic, COBOL, or Java you will quickly be able to code in PeopleCode with ease. PeopleCode has class and method notations that are exactly like Java. PeopleCode also shares a close relationship with SQL (Structured Query Language); it allows coding directly with metastrings and PeopleCode datatypes resemble SQL. The component processor is the runtime engine that processes the PeopleCode request via a menu or event to the database component and is in control until the database request is complete. The PeopleCode editor enables you to edit and navigate all PeopleCode programs that belong to the same parent definition. PeopleSoft Application Engine is the scripting tool that allows for the creation of batch or online programs that perform high-volume, background processing against your data. PeopleSoft Application Engine consists of two pieces: the designer where the program is defined and the runtime environment.

PeopleSoft Application Engine is a scripting creation tool that allows for a call to PeopleCode, SQL, and actions. Calling actions allows for conditional logic and looping through logic. It also allows for an object-oriented approach to your batch program creation. PeopleSoft Application Engine does not generate SQL or PeopleCode; it only serves as a call to the program interface.

Component Interfaces

A component interface enables exposure of a PeopleSoft component, which is a collection of pages grouped together for a menu or logical business process. The PeopleSoft component allows for synchronous access from another application with PeopleCode, Java, or XML. Component interfaces can be viewed as "black boxes" that encapsulate PeopleSoft data and business processes, and hide the details of the underlying page and data. Component interfaces can be used to integrate PeopleSoft with another PeopleSoft application or with external systems it maps to one, and only one, PeopleSoft component. Record fields on the PeopleSoft component are mapped to the keys and properties of the component interface, then methods are used to find, create, modify, or delete data. Component interface architecture comprises three fundamental elements—components, component interfaces, and the component interface API.

Security Administrator

The Security Administrator provides an interface to manage PeopleSoft Operator IDs. PeopleSoft supports a flexible role-level security model. Users can belong to more than one role, such as Employee, Manager, and Administrator. Each role is associated with a Permission List. The Permission Lists control navigation and access to each page via a component and menu. Figure 2-6 shows the Security Administrator menu in the PeopleSoft Application.

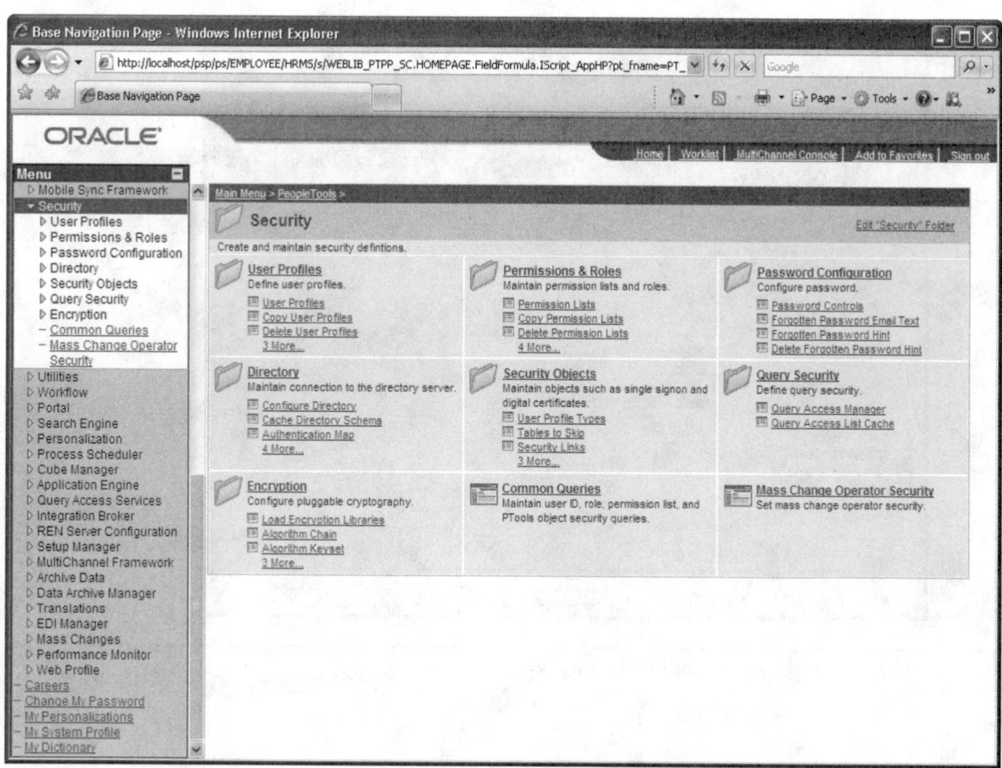

FIGURE 2-6 *Security Administrator menu*

Configuration Manager

The Configuration Manager enables you to administer the settings from one centralized configuration site. The settings are based on how the application was implemented and cannot be changed by the developers who are configuring their clients to make changes and develop in the PeopleSoft environment. They will impact the registry settings on their local machines. Figure 2-7 shows the Startup tab of the Configuration Manager.

On the Startup tab you can configure the Signon Defaults for:

- Database Type
- User ID

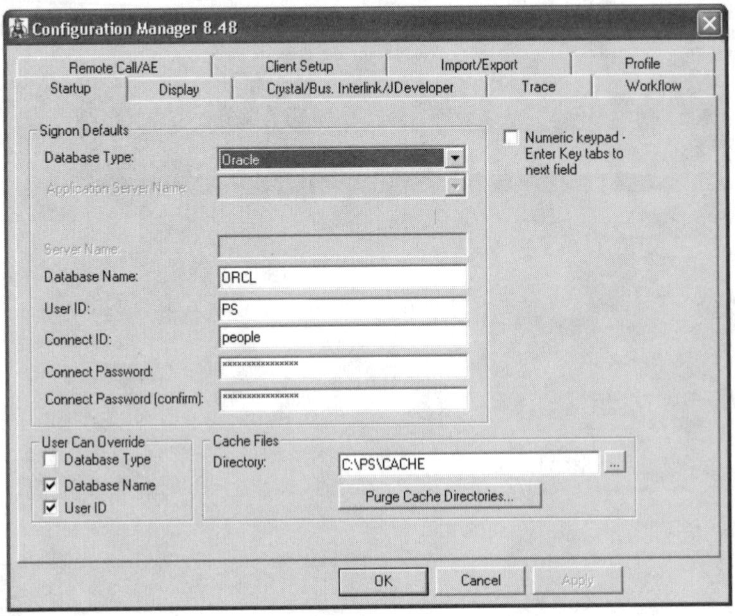

FIGURE 2-7 *Configuration Manager Startup tab*

- Connect ID
- Connect Password

In the lower-left corner of the tab you can toggle options to allow the user to override Database Type, Database Name, and User ID. In the lower-right corner the PeopleSoft cache can be manually purged. The upper-right area of the tab allows you to set the numeric keypad ENTER key to tab to the next field on the screen.

The Display tab, shown in Figure 2-8, is for the modification of the Application Designer set-up and display. Available on this tab are the following settings: Language, Display Size, Font, and toggles for Show Page in Navigator, Highlight Popup Menu Field, Show Database Name, and Business Process Display.

The Crystal/Bus. Interlink/JDeveloper tab shown in Figure 2-9 allows for the configuration of the EXE paths to launch Crystal Reports, set a default Crystal Reports directory, turn tracing on and off, create a default directory for Business Interlink, and configure a JDeveloper Home.

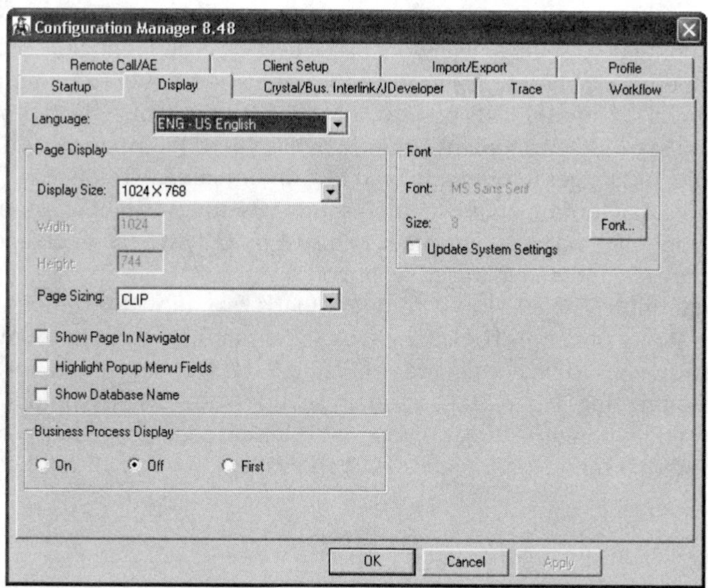

FIGURE 2-8 *Configuration Manager Display tab*

FIGURE 2-9 *Configuration Manager Crystal/Bus. Interlink/JDeveloper tab*

The Trace tab shown in Figure 2-10 allows for debugging during an online session. Several types of tracing can be used and written to the file specified with the most commonly used settings: Network Services, SQL Statement, SQL Statement Variables, Connect, Disconnect, Rollback and Commit, and Row Fetch. Additional tracing that can be set are API calls besides Set Select Buffers (SSBs), Database API-Specific Calls, COBOL Statement Timings, Sybase Bind Information, Sybase Fetch Information, Manager Information, and SQL Informational Trace. It is important to note that turning on any of theses tracing settings can be a resource hog, and it is important that you remember to turn it on only when needed and turn it off immediately after you have traced what you need.

The Configuration Manager has a number of tabs that allow for settings to be made for your set-up of PeopleTools. The tabs shown in the figures to follow allow for these settings to be configured. In Figure 2-10 you have the ability to toggle on and off tracing. Figure 2-11 you can set up Workflow. The important configuration setting here is setting up your SMTP email settings so that Workflow can be configured to send email. Figure 2-12 shows the remote call settings

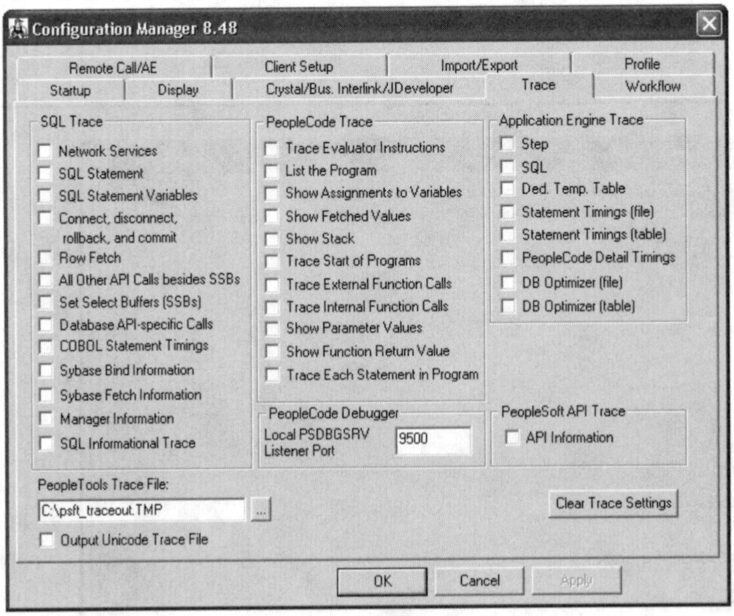

FIGURE 2-10 *Trace tab*

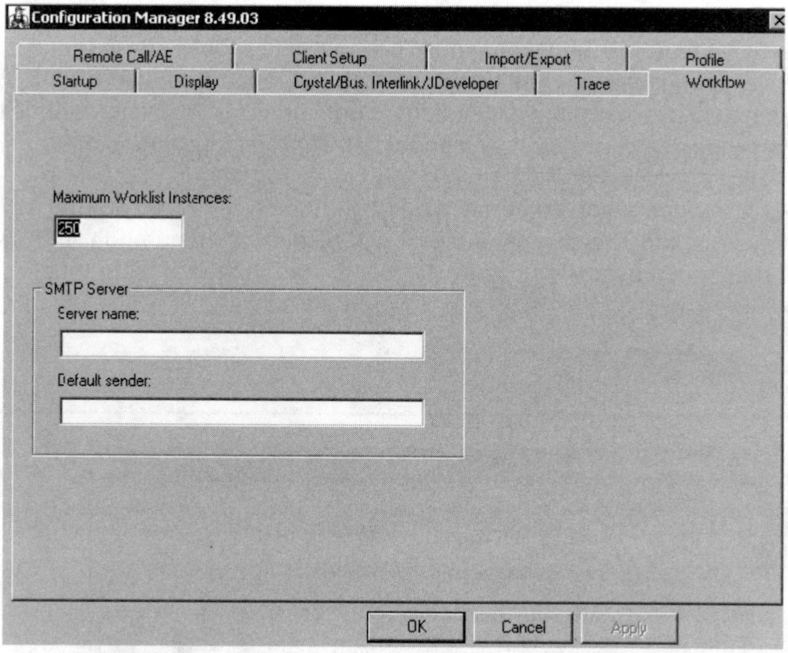

FIGURE 2-11 *Workflow tab*

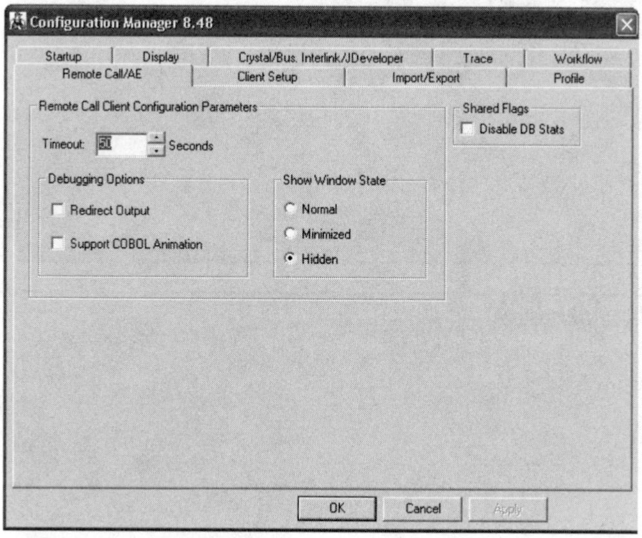

FIGURE 2-12 *Remote Call/AE tab*

for Application Engine. You can set the remote call client configuration parameters here, when it will timeout, if you want to redirect output, turn on support to COBOL Animation, what your Window state should be—Normal, Minimized or Hidden—and whether you want to see the shared flags for DB Statistics. Figure 2-13 shows the Client Setup configurations. You can use this to decide what shortcuts you want to see and what ODBC setups you want to configure. Figure 2-14 is the place where you can set up Import and Export configuration settings. If you configure this it will write settings to your file for export purposes and in the case of import it will read the configuration settings and overwrite them if necessary. Figure 2-15 is the tab in the Configuration Manager where you can create customized profiles.

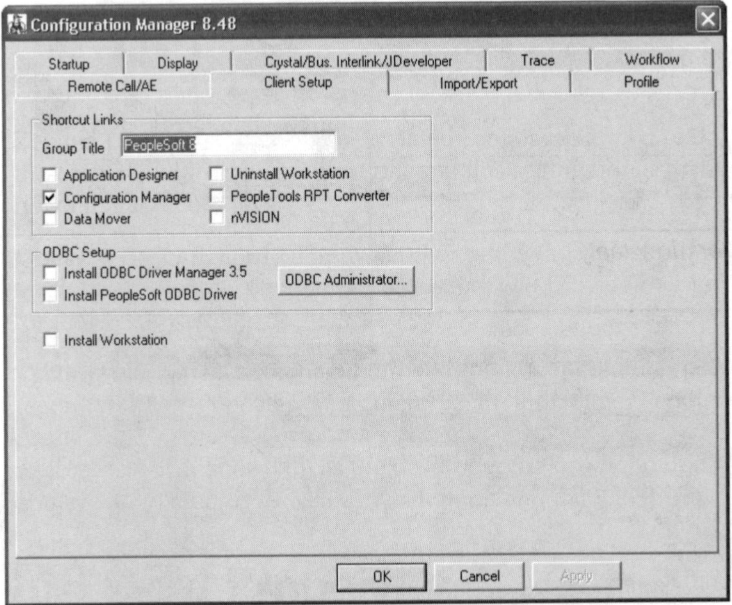

FIGURE 2-13 *Client Setup tab*

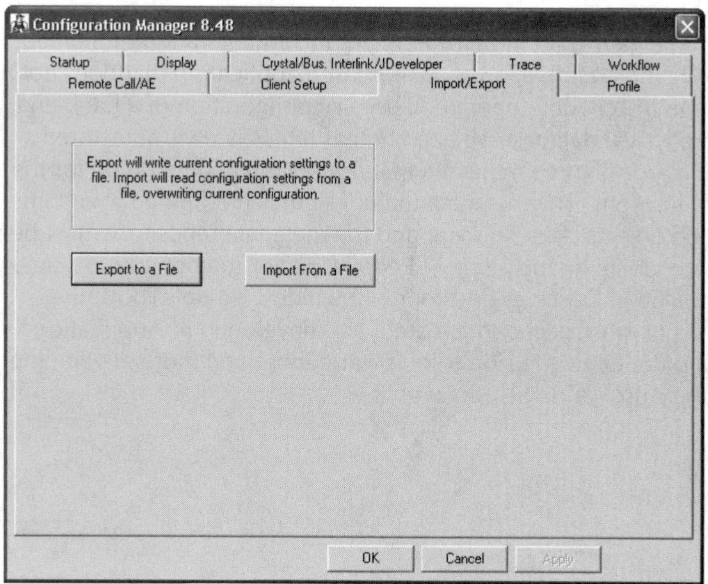

FIGURE 2-14 *Import Export tab*

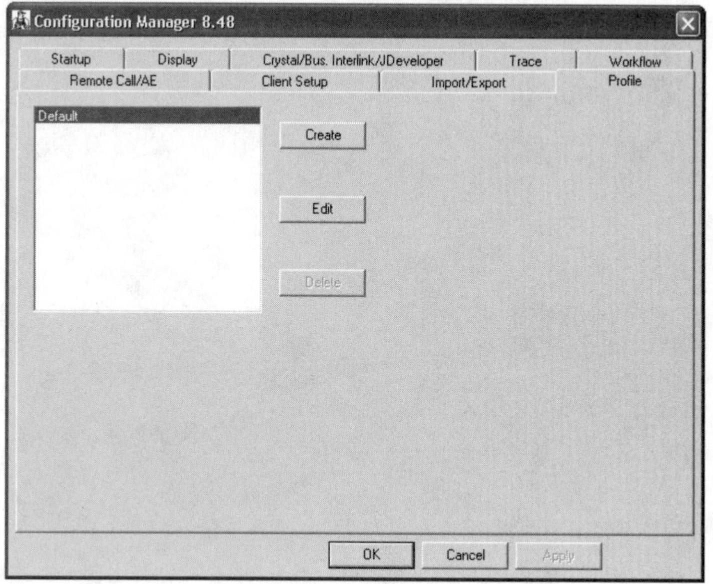

FIGURE 2-15 *Profile tab*

Summary

In this chapter you gained an understanding of the configuration of the PeopleSoft Enterprise Application. PeopleSoft is a web-based application that does not require an executable on the client to operate. It uses a configuration of a back-end database with physical database objects such as tables, views, and stored procedures, and a configured metadata that houses the configuration for the PeopleSoft Applications. The metadata includes but is not limited to records, fields, and PeopleCode objects. The database and the metadata repository must be in sync at all times. To code in the metadata in PeopleCode or to configure objects, you utilize the Application Designer development window. PeopleTools, the development set of tools, is coded, created, and developed in Application Designer. With the addition of Oracle Fusion Middleware, more and more development can take place at the Application Server level.

CHAPTER 3

PeopleSoft Internet Architecture (PIA)

his chapter addresses important architecture configurations that are the foundation of the PeopleSoft Internet Architecture. In this chapter we will discuss the main configuration and the future of the middleware configuration that is currently used by some, but is more a future endeavor for most. When the PIA was first released, it was bleeding-edge technology that led to the integration of the application with the web. The future middleware tier will create a dynamic application that will allow a custom-configured Application Server with pick-and-choose functionality that will be released with the Fusion Application.

PIA Configuration: An Overview

PeopleSoft is a web-based application and has been since the release of PeopleSoft 8.0. The original release was a two-tier application, and with the release of versions 8.8 and higher a web browser became required to access PeopleSoft pages. With a web browser, accessing the PeopleSoft web-based system via the PIA became as simple as typing a URL or clicking a link from a web page. Although the web browser access is easy, the setup isn't; the configuration requires several different types of servers to be up and running for the user to access PeopleSoft from a browser.

This configuration, however, allows users to access PeopleSoft pages with only a browser from their own computers. There is nothing to install on a user's local machine to interface with PeopleSoft—all users need is a browser such as Firefox or Internet Explorer. Programmers have more options for accessing PeopleSoft besides a web browser; they can use an SQL application to access the database; an SQR application; or a PeopleSoft application that accesses all PeopleSoft objects. But once users click or access PeopleSoft via the web browser, they are using the PeopleSoft Internet Architecture to access the database via several other servers.

As you can see in Figure 3-1, three main parts make up the PIA: the Database Server, the Application Server, and the Web Server. Without one of the three, the whole Internet architecture could not exist for PeopleSoft to be used or accessed. These servers deliver the entire PeopleSoft application to the intranet/Internet for companies to access. The PIA allows them to use the PeopleSoft intranet and the Internet to access internal as well as external PeopleSoft applications.

This is what the PIA is all about: there are servers in a series that allow a user to access the data in PeopleSoft for viewing, inserting, deleting, and updating data. The PIA uses protocols like HTTP/HTTPS, Jolt, Tuxedo, and SQL to communicate between the servers, as shown in Figure 3-2, and then communicate back to the browser. The PIA facilitates the user data requests and/or allows data to be sent to the database.

Figure 3-2 and the list in the next section represent the order of the relationships between the servers used to access the PeopleSoft database in either direction. You can see in Figure 3-2 that each server uses different processes/protocols to access each server; for example, the Application Server uses SQL to access the database.

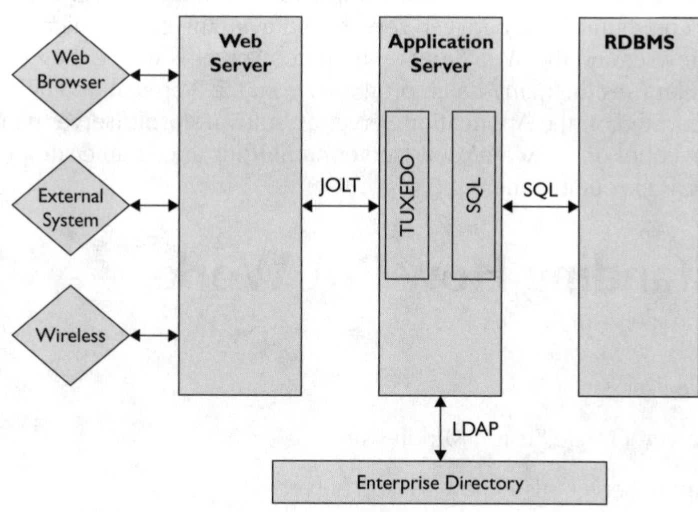

FIGURE 3-1 *A high-level view of the PIA from browser to all servers used by PeopleSoft*

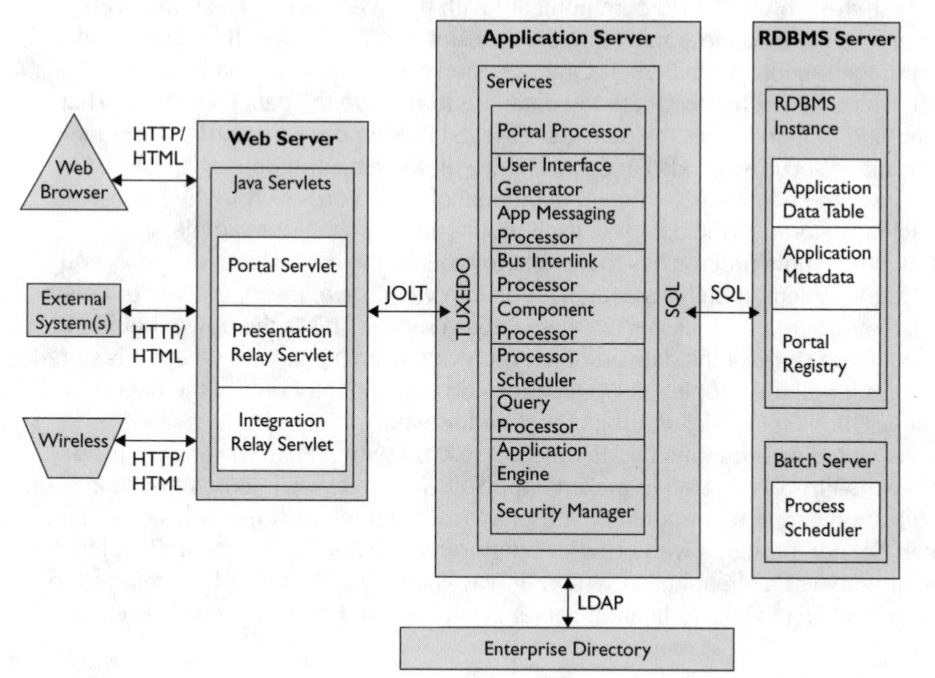

FIGURE 3-2 *A high-level view of the PIA with processes/protocols used by PeopleSoft*

Later on in this chapter we will break down the process for each server even further, examining the communication between servers and even the communication between the browser and the Web Server. The Batch Server is where the PeopleSoft Process Scheduler runs the many batch programs from the Application Engine, SQR, and COBOL. Located on the Application Server at /software/psoft/[server name]/[instance name/cobol or /software/psoft/[server name]/[instance name/sqr are the COBOL and SQR executable files.

Understanding How PIA Works

The major components of the PIA are:

1. Web browser
2. Web Server: Oracle Fusion Middleware
3. Application Server (also know as App Server)
4. Database Server (also know as Database/RDBMS)
5. Batch Server

First, the browser has to communicate with the Web Server. Next, the Web Server has to talk to the Application Server using JOLT (which will be explained later in the section "Web Server: Oracle Fusion Middleware"). Finally, the Application Server has to talk to the database to retrieve the data using SQL. That being said, not only does the data get retrieved but the pages, records, components, menus, and security are also accessed, since all the data and objects are stored in tables within PeopleSoft. So the look and feel of what you see from the browser is all actually stored in the database itself, not as a true page, for example.

But the whole process has to be able to work in the other direction, so as you access the system, it delivers data that you can view, save, insert, update, or delete from the system, in this case from the database server. This is the power behind PIA: the ability to store all the data and then retrieve it from a database where it is stored in tables for all the PeopleSoft Applications on the web. Not only is the data stored in tables, but the PeopleSoft Object is stored as well.

Let's hold on a minute. Did PeopleSoft start off with a PIA? The answer is no. Before the PIA was created to make PeopleSoft work over the Internet, the PeopleSoft Application had to be installed on a user's local machine to communicate with the database, not through a web browser but through the application itself. PeopleSoft at that time was a client-based system. It was known as *two-tier,* which referred to communicating to an Application Server as well as the Database Server. Even in

PeopleSoft 8.3 and all the way until version 8.8, as mentioned in the Chapter 1, the two-tier application could always be run, but starting with version 8.8 you could no longer run in two-tier mode.

PIA actually began in 2000 with PeopleSoft 8, which allowed users to access PeopleSoft applications via the web browser once the three main servers were up and running. PIA is architecture without a client, which means a user can access PeopleSoft with only a web browser—no executable is run on the client side. The client can be any Internet/intranet device that uses the standard Internet technologies such as HTTP, HTML, or XML. Everything is developed and designed to be seen and used from the web browser except the batch process and programming tool.

PIA Servers

Let's give a brief description of the types of servers that make up the PIA. From there we can break down each server into broader terms and processes that each server uses and discuss how all three work together to deliver the web-based PeopleSoft. The servers that make up the PIA are

- Database Server
- Application Server
- Web Server
- Browser—provides the client connectivity

Database Server

Database Server is a computer program that provides the ability to store data in a table (record) format for system PeopleTools and Application tables. This is independent of the process you use to retrieve that data from PeopleSoft. The data should match in both the physical database and the PIA repository; always remember that the physical data is stored in the database. The field EMPLID, for example, will have a different value for each employee, but the field configuration size, length, key settings, indexes will be the same in both the database and the PeopleSoft repository. This applies not only to the data used with the Application itself (in this case the web pages that are rendered by the PIA process to access the data) but also to the actual objects created to store the data within PeopleSoft, known as the metadata records.

Basically, one set of records makes up a PeopleSoft database. When you interface with PeopleSoft, you as a user are only interfacing with one database when you view, change, or update the data. Multi-app servers may connect to a database, but whether you are in a production database or a test database, it is only one database that provides you with data. The various names of the data sources in the database are referred to as a *schema*. Some examples include Production, Quality, Test, Delivered, and Development. Each database may have multiple users and each user may have its own schema. The PeopleSoft schema is built under SYSADM. When you query via SQL you need to know what your Schema name is to know which will allow you to see the physical objects.

The web browser may be Internet Explorer, Firefox, Netscape, or some other browser application. To interface with PeopleSoft, all a user needs is a URL, which the browser uses to locate the Web Server.

The database can use three different types of database software: Oracle, Microsoft, or IBM. All three are different types of relational database management system (RDBMS) products. A *relational database management system* is a data storage system based on Relational Theory, which was introduced into the world of computers in the 1970s. The premise of Relational Theory was to eliminate the large flat-file storage systems of the past. Each time storage was accessed, a record for an individual or customer was stored separately, and the pieces were retrieved with an elaborate file storage pointing system. Relational theorists came along and developed a system in which you can use mathematics to break the pieces up to allow larger amounts of data to be stored. It is important that as a PeopleSoft database developer you have a firm grasp on normalization and relational database design. Many books are available on the topic, but for the purposes of this book, you should understand the theory behind the references to an RDBMS. When you are installing PeopleSoft, you will need to know beforehand the type of database software you are using. Since PeopleSoft will need to be configured to that database platform, PeopleSoft creates and stores a metadata repository based on the database platform in which it is installed:

- Microsoft SQL Server (Only on the Windows OS)
- Oracle
- IBM DB2/UDB

When you are referring to PeopleSoft database, only three types of tables reside inside the schema: System Catalog tables, PeopleTools tables, and Application data tables. Two of these table types, System Catalog and PeopleTools tables, can be referred to as metadata tables; users make use of Application data tables to store the data they need for their processes.

Several types of objects can be defined in the database: tables, indexes, and views defined in the database. The tables or records (in the PeopleSoft metadata) have columns (fields) that can be used by many tables with the same characteristics: data type and length. For example, when you are using the field EMPLID, you are using the characteristics that are set up for the object for each record that is used in PeopleSoft. Tables are made up by fields: the fields have to exist before the records can be created; without fields you cannot have a record (or a table). The table is used to store the data for all three types of records in PeopleSoft. Yes, all three have different jobs inside of PeopleSoft, but all work the same way to store data. Views are records that use SQL objects behind them to retrieve data that already exist in tables. Indexes are used instead of primary and foreign key relationships; indexes are used in PeopleSoft to allow for the quick retrieval of the data via queries as well to establish relationships. A primary and foreign key system commonly known in relational theory is not used in PeopleSoft because the implementation of these types of keys is unique to each software platform, whereas the use of indexes to establish relationships is standard throughout the three platforms and allows for a database-independent applications structure.

System Catalog tables are the tables that store the data about data inside of PeopleSoft. This can be referred to as metadata. The system tables or metadata vary depending on which RDBMS platform is used, but the function for each is the same. This type of record keeps track of all objects inside of that database instance.

The other group of metadata records used by PeopleSoft is the PeopleTools tables. They can be found as PS* without an underscore inside of your PeopleSoft instance. These tables hold the metadata about the PeopleSoft Applications that are installed on the database. The metadata consists of many different type of objects inside of PeopleSoft, including Menus, Components, Pages, and Records. These tables can be retrieved using SQL with an SQL tool. The following SQL statement will retrieve all the PeopleTools records that are used by the PeopleSoft instance:

```
Select * from PSRECDEFN where RECNAME like 'PS%';
```

These records contain the structure that the application uses for each object. The structure is the same for all applications within PeopleSoft. When you install the application, import the data into the PeopleTools tables. One example is the table PSPNLGRPDEFF, which means Panel Group Definition. Whereas PeopleSoft once used Panel Groups, they now refer to this object as a Component. So this table is the record where PeopleSoft stores all the data needed for Components. All Components are used the same way inside of PeopleSoft, which is used to tie Page(s) as an object group to attach to menus so that a user can bring up the pages needed. The pages that use the application Data tables to store and view the data allow the data to be available to other computer programs or computers defined by the client-server model. Another way these pages can be described is as the database engine, where all the system objects, PeopleTools tables, and Application data tables are stored.

Application Server

This server is also known as the App Server, or Application Server. It is the core server in the PeopleSoft Internet Architecture, which communicates between the

Web Server and the Database and even between the Application Designer and the Database. The Application Designer is where the program interfaces are created for the browser and all the objects are created for use with the browser. It is also known as the App Designer. To access the Application Designer you can use PeopleTools. For security reasons only high-level users should have access to this program in PeopleSoft. The App Designer, or Application Designer, is used via a Windows workstation. As discussed in the section "Database Server," the App Designer saves to the PeopleTools records inside of the database. The App server handles the transaction requests and handles the transaction processing, system scaling, and browser requests through the Web Server. This will be explained in the next section. One of the main duties of the App Server is the SQL connection or the Database connection to the database. This is also known as the DB connection. The App Server handles the requests from both the browser and the PeopleTools App Designer.

An application server has server processes, supporting processes, and resource managers that manage and create the connection to the database. Each instance is handled in a separate configuration file, which sets up a separate domain. You can configure one application server to one database or multiple application servers to one database. For example, the Development and Quality environments could be configured to run on the same physical server but be maintained in separate logical instances. In order to configure and connect via a browser, a separate Application Server will need to be configured for each instance: one for Development and one for Quality. PSADMIN, which is located at PS_HOME\appserv, will allow for the configuration of multiple Application Servers. When you configure these multiple Application Servers, separate subdirectories will be created: \PSDV1 and \PSQA1. Each instance establishes a server process and maintains a connection to the PeopleSoft database, with a separate SQL pipeline, which is used to send and receive SQL. From the database side each server process represents a domain and a connected SQL user.

Handlers, listeners, and queues play an important role in the functionality of the Application Server. Handlers include the Workstation Handler (WSH) and the BEA Jolt Server Handler (JSH). Listeners include the Workstation Listener (WSL) and the BEA Jolt Server Listener (JSL). The server process has a service request queue available that it shares with another server of the same type, for example, PSAPPSRV on APPQ, and PSOPTENG on OPTQ. The server processes are the center of the server domain; they maintain SQL processing and transactions against the database while packeting back to the correct DB location. The server process will wait for a service to complete and then return any information to the calling location, such as a browser. While the server process is waiting for a transaction to complete, any other requests will be queued until the completion of the prior service. The minimum configuration of server processes required within a domain includes PSAPPSRV and PSSAMSRV. A request is sent to the application server, and a service name along with a set of parameters is sent, for example, with MgrGetObject. BEA Tuxedo queues the request to a server process and then broadcasts the request to a service that handles that specific type of request. When a server process is booted, it will let the system know the type of service that it handles. To review the connection between services and server processes, look at the PSAPPSRV.UBB file located in \\[tools directory]\appserv\[instance name].

Basic Services include the following:

- **PSAPPSRV** A required service to run any domain. It performs requests to build and load components and provides memory and disk caching for PeopleTools objects on the Application Server.
- **PSQCKSRV** An optional service that processes read-only SQL requests.
- **PSQRYSRV** An optional service that allows running PeopleSoft Query and reduces the load of PSAPPSRV. This will allow developers to access PSQuery in two-tier.
- **PSSAMSRV** A required service that handles the SQL that is processed inside of the Application Designer.
- **PSOPTENG** An optional service that provides optimization services in the Optimization Framework plug-in.

Services required for Application Messaging are:

- PSMSGDSP
- PSMSGHND
- PSPUBDSP
- PSPUBHND
- PSUBDSP
- PSSUBHND

You can administer the Application Server via the command-line interface; the following illustrations show some of the main administrative paths that could be utilized. To utilize the Query Tool via a two-tier system, you use PSQRYSRV. There is also a web browser–based version of PSQuery.

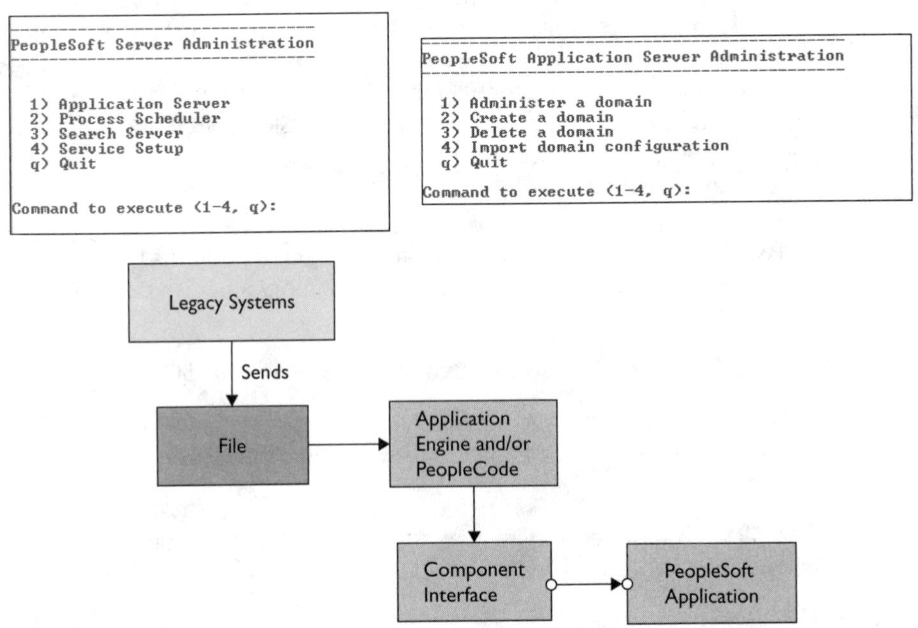

Web Server: Oracle Fusion Middleware

What is currently on our plates as PeopleSoft developers is extending our development platforms from the database level vs. the client level to an entire middle domain. Fusion Middleware developers will be able to develop services that will reside on the web server and be administered as web services; these web services will allow for the incorporation of legacy systems into your PeopleSoft structure. By using exposed events that the legacy systems call and exposing additional events by other systems, it is possible to develop and reuse services that will connect and event-enable the processes into PeopleSoft calls. Fusion Middleware offers a set of capabilities in PeopleSoft to enable, manage, and integrate services and events throughout the application:

- PeopleSoft Integrated Service Repository (ISR) provides Oracle Integration.
- Adapter for PeopleSoft and other tools publish services and events.
- The UDDI registry provides a place to manage all services and events—PeopleSoft and non-PeopleSoft—in one centralized location.

- The Enterprise Service Bus provides a communications backbone across services and events integrating with PeopleSoft Integration Broker.
- Web Services Manager provides the ability to govern policies and security across services.

As you can see in Figure 3-3, Oracle Fusion Middleware brings to the PeopleSoft Application suite a set of standards-based middleware capabilities that allow for a comprehensive technology base in the Application Platform Suite (APS). The toolset aligns with the Gartner Middleware Quadrants: Application Platform Suite, Development Tools, Application Server, Web Service Platform, Enterprise Portal, Business Integration, Identity Management, Web Services Management, ETL Data Integration, and Content Management.

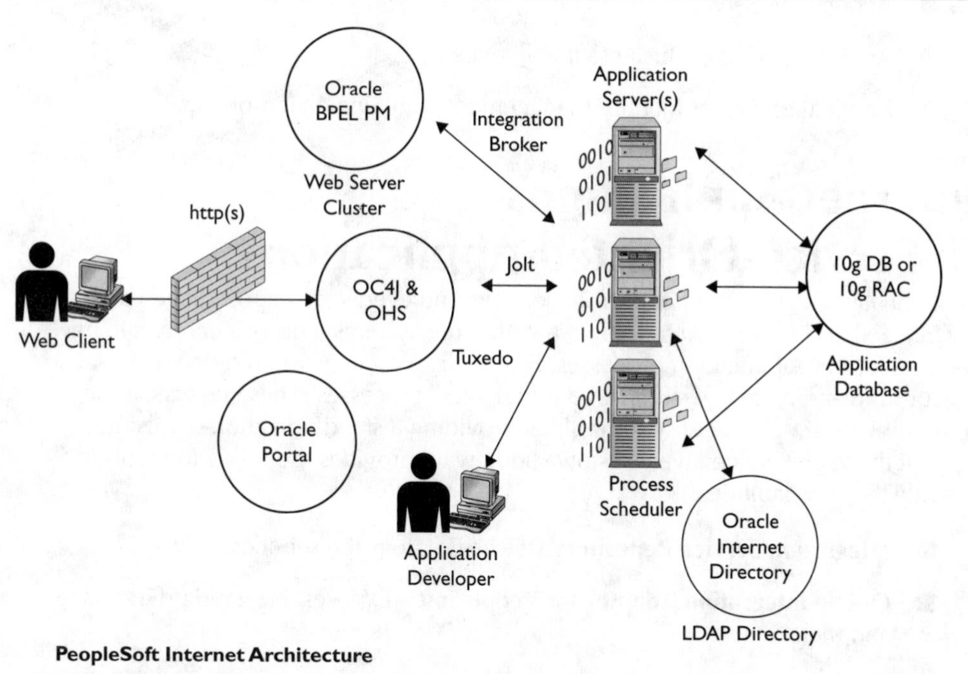

FIGURE 3-3 *The future of PIA, from an Oracle OpenWorld presentation by Jeff Robbins*

Oracle offers a specific Fusion Middleware package for the PeopleSoft Enterprise, which includes:

- SOA Suite (Service Oriented Architecture)
  - Enterprise Service Bus (ESB)
  - BPEL Process Manager
  - Integration BAM
- Integration Adapter for PeopleSoft
- Integration B2B
- Rules Engine
- Enterprise Portal
- Application Server Web Cache
- Application Server Business Intelligence
- Application Server Identity Management with Single Sign-on

Internet Applications to Service-Oriented Applications

With the latest versions of PeopleSoft, services and events are exposed and can be customized and configured to integrate with other systems, and you can create new services for new application processes. Essentially a company could decide to create various service layers for standard business processes. These layers can be re-used by legacy and new systems alike, providing a standardization of business rules at the Web Service layer. Fusion Middleware provides the following tools to provide these capabilities:

- **Integration Service Repository (ISR)** Catalogs the services.
- **Oracle Integration Adaptor for PeopleSoft** Exposes the standard interface and metadata.
- **Enterprise Service Bus** Provides a common communications backbone to the services and events to the PeopleSoft Integration Broker.
- **Web Services Manager** Sets policies and security across the services.

PeopleSoft Integration Service Repository (ISR) is the catalog of services, events, processes, and business models. Currently ISR gives developers access to a catalog of thousands of web services, hundreds of business processes, hundreds of events, and hundreds of business models. With PeopleTools, developers can use UDDI and USIL tools with Oracle BPEL Process Manager to connect to these services without additional adaptors.

PeopleSoft and Oracle Fusion Middleware also provide the Oracle Integration Adaptor for PeopleSoft, which allows for customized development. The Integration Adaptor will allow connections to older versions of PeopleSoft and to other legacy systems. The UDDI service registry, provided by the Oracle Fusion Middleware, allows for the unification of all services and events regardless of their origination, so even if the service or event was not delivered with the prepackaged PeopleSoft, you can publish it with the UDDI.

Fusion Middleware provides an ESB (Enterprise Service Bus); the ESB provides the messaging infrastructure for multiple ways of communication, for example, synchronously (offering an immediate response to a request) or asynchronously (the reply may not come back for days or weeks). ESB can integrate with the Integration Broker and provide a gateway of communication for various communication protocols: HTTP, JMS, POP3, SMTP, and FTP. ESB also allows for communications with older versions of PeopleSoft: 8.4 and 8.1.

To implement an SOA (Service Oriented Architecture) correctly, governance of your services is the top objective; the Oracle Web Services Manager in the Fusion Middleware defines and enforces operation policies that can be layered on top of services. By doing this, you ensure that policies for the services are consistently applied and maintain the integrity of your service-oriented architecture.

Up to this point the discussion has been about the tools that Oracle Fusion Middleware provides to integrate services in a bottom-up approach to enable an SOA. Oracle Fusion Middleware also provides tools that will allow for the integration and development from the top down. The tools that provide the top-down configuration of business process are:

- **BPA Suite (Business Process Architect)** Allows analysts to model and analyze business requirements for business-wide processes based on a process model.
- **BPEL Process Manager (Business Process Execution Language)** Allows for the implementation of enterprise-wide business processes with automated and human workflow steps. It allows for the configuration of business rules and data mappings. It does this with the custom creation of processes and services to integrate with your applications. These applications can be created in a variety of platforms and languages. The only common thread that is required is web service connectivity.
- **BAM (Business Activity Monitoring)** A delivered dashboard that allows for the monitoring of part of the PeopleSoft Application, and services that were created with Oracle BAM and BPEL Process Manager.

The Oracle BPA Suite, which is based on the ARIS tool developed by IDS Sheer, provides business modeling based on industry-standard modeling practices; the tool provides Oracle's modeling standard as well as those set forth by DoDAF, IT City Planning, and Zachman. The Oracle BPA and Oracle BPEL Process Manager share a metadata repository. The integration provides the ability for business analysts and system analysts to collaborate in the creation of business processes. The SOA foundation is outlined in Figure 3-4.

Oracle BPEL Process Manager provides the interface to create, deploy, and manage cross-application business processes that have been developed in BPA or as a web service using the bottom-up approach. It provides support for industry standards such as BPEL, JCA, JMS, Web Services, XML, XPATH, and XSLT. It consumes services from other applications and integrates them in a single tool as a business process that can be launched in your application. It provides a standard platform for security, scalability, and availability. The tool does this with an extensive set of delivered adapters and transformation tools. With the need in organizations to connect PeopleSoft to non-PeopleSoft applications, the BPEL

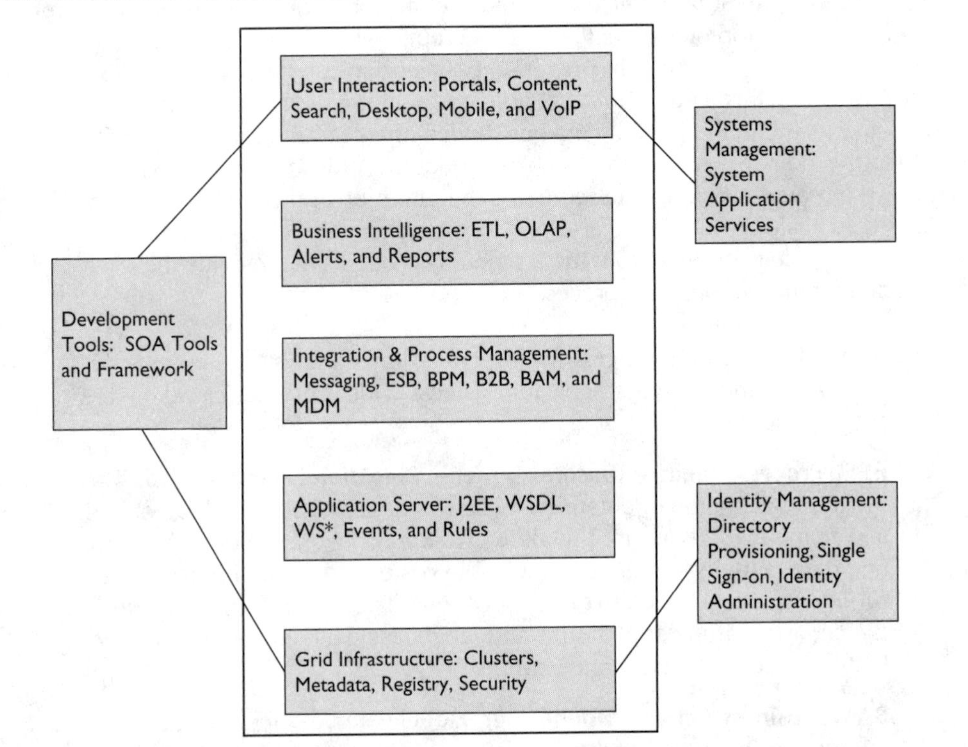

FIGURE 3-4 *BPA overview from Oracle OpenWorld's "Next Generation Business Process Management—With SOA Foundation"*

Process Manager can allow for the extension of processes to enable integration of PeopleSoft with non-PeopleSoft frameworks. It can be integrated with PeopleSoft HCM and/or Oracle Identity Management.

With the latest versions of PeopleSoft, Oracle delivers prebuilt dashboards, with the implementation of Fusion Middleware and the PeopleSoft Application. These dashboards are built using Oracle BAM and BPEL Process Manager. They provide information about the application functionality and real-time framework. You can consume events and transactions that are generated by the PeopleSoft Application and generate real-time visual transactions that can be viewed via a dashboard. The PeopleSoft CRM dashboards provide monitoring of the CRM events and transactions and are delivered with the CRM Module. Oracle provides an initial sets of dashboards:

- **Service dashboard** Shows operational efficiency, service-level adherence, and resolution management.
- **Sales dashboard** Enables visual forecasting, pipeline management, account management, and team performance.
- **Order capture dashboard** Enables revenue management, order processing, and time processing.

Using BAM and BPEL Process Manager, you can build your own dashboards to provide your customers with a visual window to a business process.

Delivered PeopleSoft Components Without Fusion Middleware

You may be a developer working in a shop that hasn't gotten around to integrating Fusion Middleware yet, and you may say, well, all of this Middleware stuff sounds great, but I don't have it. What that means is that you are a developer still working with the standard PeopleSoft PIA and you have not moved to the next generation of Middleware toolsets yet. You can still use XML for reports, manage customized creation of services with the Integration Broker, and avail yourself of all the cutting-edge tools PeopleSoft has delivered for years with the standard PIA configuration. So let's take a look at some of the delivered out-of-the-box solutions that are not part of the Fusion Middleware.

The Integration Broker (introduced with PeopleTools 8.4) is composed of two subsystems: the Integration Engine and the Integration Gateway. The Integration Engine runs on the Application Server, is closely tied to the PeopleSoft Application, and produces messages for the application. The Integration Gateway is a platform that receives and delivers messages passed among systems via the Integration Broker. The Integration Broker provides the ability to create tightly coupled and loosely coupled integrations. With synchronous messaging you can create tightly coupled integrations. *Synchronous messaging* may be defined as a system that expects a response before continuing processing. Loosely coupled transaction processing takes place with asynchronous messaging because with this type of messaging the system continues processing without waiting for a response. Besides messaging, Integration Broker also provides Connector development, which enables the creation and customization of connectors for customized application development. Along with Integration Broker, PeopleSoft provides other integration technologies with Component Interface and Application Engine. You should look closely at the business process before determining the best solution, and you should ask yourself the following questions to help you determine the best solution:

- How much data will be transferred?
- Is the data incoming or outgoing?
- What type of integration does the business require? Real-time? Near-real-time? Or deferred?
- What transaction times are demanded?
- What is the message and data structure?
- What are the technology capabilities of required legacy systems?

The volume of data involved in a transaction is a crucial factor in deciding which communication technology to use. If a large volume of data is to be transferred, the preferred integration techniques are asynchronous messaging and Application Engine. Asynchronous messaging mode allows a large volume of data to be pushed into the subscribing systems. Since this does not wait for a response, it can just publish the information and continue with its own processing.

When you need to transfer a large volume of data in a batch program from an external system into the PeopleSoft Application, writing an Application Engine batch program is the best solution. The Application Engine is often used in combination with the file interface language that is provided with PeopleCode, which you can embed and call from within the Application Engine. A typical business situation is that you need to transfer data from a legacy system into PeopleSoft, and that is most efficiently done with PL/SQL, or an Application Engine program. One of my frequently used Application Engine programs retrieves data from a large data download from Fidelity and places the data in the format needed to display to employees in a PeopleSoft portal. The data is then retrieved via the PeopleCode section of the Application Engine using file manipulation operations and the application is populated using the Component Interface. The menu for the Configuration Gateway—the gateway to portal configuration—is shown here.

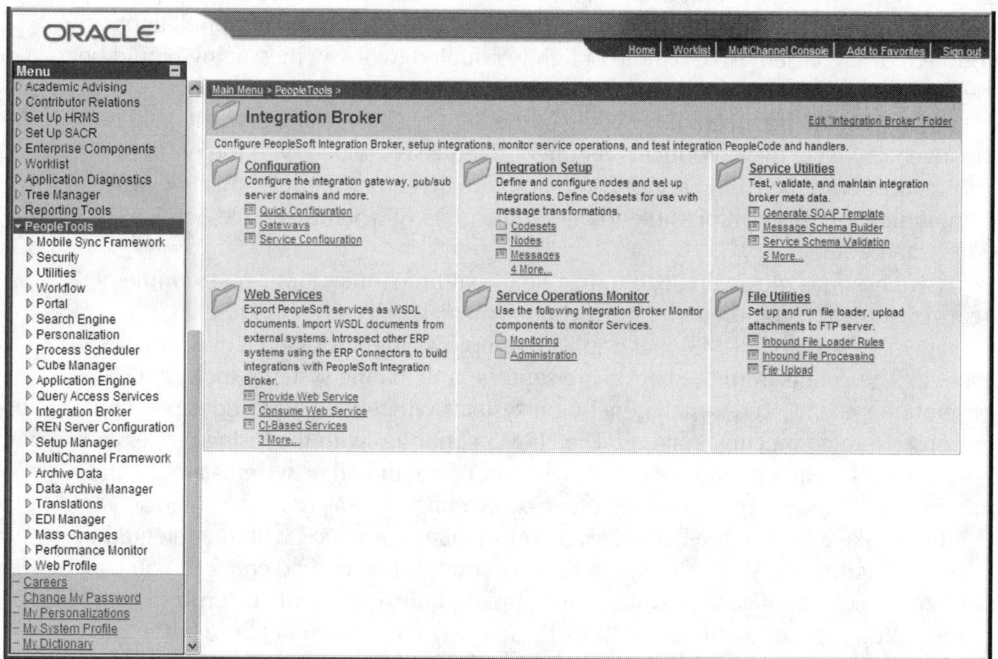

To determine the gateway that should be used, you should look at whether your data is inbound or outbound. Consider the example of customer data being updated between PeopleSoft CRM (Customer Relationship Management) and Financials (FDM). A new customer is added into the FDM; then the information needs to be sent to CRM. The data flow is only one way: outbound from Financials to CRM. In this situation asynchronous messaging would be perfect. With inbound messaging, you can utilize the Component Interface (CI); it has a feature that will use business logic to validate the data prior to saving it off to the database. An example would be using a Component Interface to load leads into the sales module from an Excel spreadsheet. You could also load the Component Interface in combination with asynchronous messaging and the Application Engine, so that outbound data would trigger an Application batch program to load the data via the Component Interface—the Component Interface would validate and load the sales data into the database. If you have a file interface where you have downloaded or produced a flat file, the Application Engine is the best file interface to use within PeopleSoft for this type of integration.

In some cases the integration uses both outbound and inbound messaging. In these cases all three technologies can be used: asynchronous messaging, synchronous messaging, and/or the Application Engine. The choice of which tool (or of all three) is dependent on whether the transaction is loosely coupled, tightly coupled, or file based. An example of tightly coupled two-way messaging would be the Field Service Order module of PeopleSoft CRM messaging as it provides connectivity with the Inventory module of the Supply Chain Management. When the inventory level for a product is required, a request is issued with the product information from the Field Service Module to the Inventory module; this two-way communication makes it possible to determine quickly whether a Field Service order can be filled.

Asynchronous messaging can utilize near-real-time integration. An example of near-real-time integration with asynchronous messaging is a human resource management system (HRMS) that publishes employee details when a new employee is hired. The details from the HRMS are sent to participating systems such as ID generation systems, and e-mail generation systems where the HRMS does need a response from connecting systems. The HRMS continues with the hiring process and proceeds to save the employee details whether or not the other systems are up and running; it will even continue if the other connecting systems produce an error.

If you take a look at the PeopleSoft menus that are provided with the Integration Broker in Figure 3-5, you can see the types of process that can be created. You can see that you can configure the Integration Broker, quickly or with customized settings. You can also configure a specific Gateway for communication. In the Integration menu you can create nodes in which to receive messages and create configuration settings for your services.

The Integration Gateway is a component of PeopleSoft's Integration Broker, which was first introduced in PeopleSoft 8.4. The illustration that follows shows the

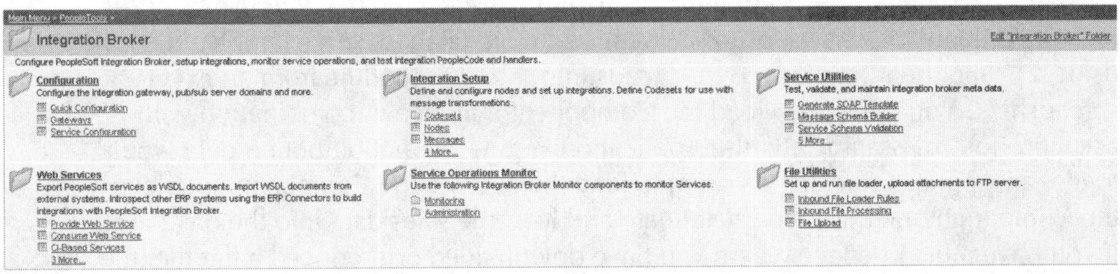

Main Menu > PeopleTools >
Integration Broker
Edit "Integration Broker" Folder
Configure PeopleSoft Integration Broker, setup integrations, monitor service operations, and test integration PeopleCode and handlers.
Configuration
Configure the integration gateway, pub/sub server domains and more.
Quick Configuration
Gateways
Service Configuration
Integration Setup
Define and configure nodes and set up integrations. Define Codesets for use with message transformations.
Codesets
Nodes
Messages
4 More...
Service Utilities
Test, validate, and maintain integration broker meta data.
Generate SOAP Template
Message Schema Builder
Service Schema Validation
5 More...
Web Services
Export PeopleSoft services as WSDL documents. Import WSDL documents from external systems. Introspect other ERP systems using the ERP Connectors to build integrations with PeopleSoft Integration Broker.
Provide Web Service
Consume Web Service
CI-Based Services
3 More...
Service Operations Monitor
Use the following Integration Broker Monitor components to monitor Services.
Monitoring
Administration
File Utilities
Set up and run file loader, upload attachments to FTP server.
Inbound File Loader Rules
Inbound File Processing
File Upload

FIGURE 3-5 *Integration Broker*

PIA Main menu for the Integration Broker. The Integration Broker has several components and services spanning the Web and application server environments.

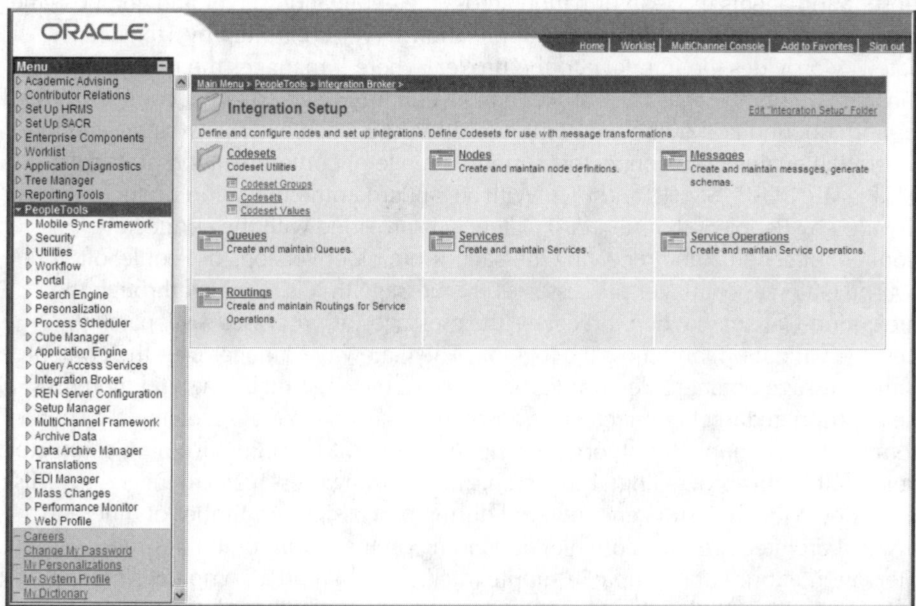

The integration setup menus are shown next. The Integration Broker is an XML-based messaging hub that supports both synchronous and asynchronous messaging.

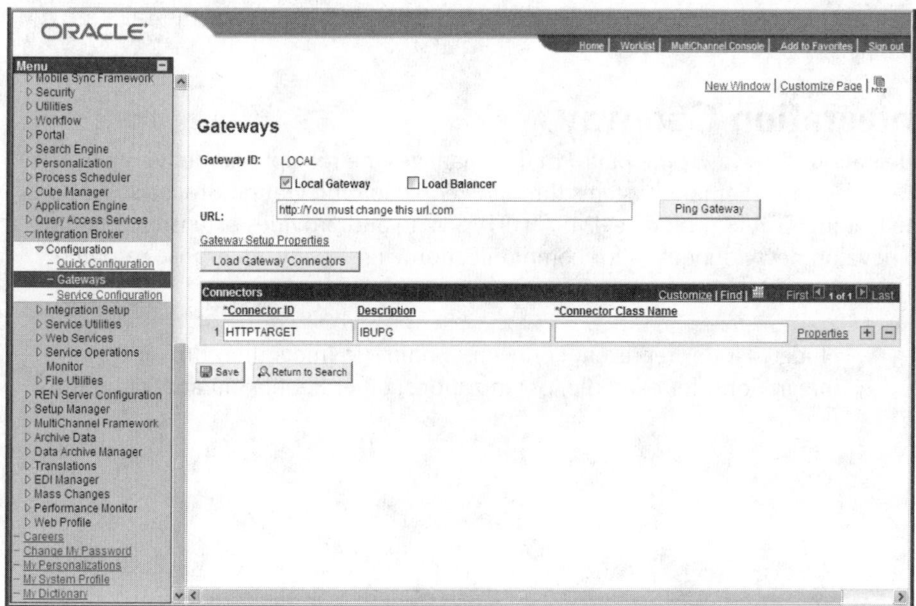

The Gateway resides on the Web server, where it provides inbound and outbound pathways for PeopleSoft applications. The internal publication and subscription agents move information across the application server and compose the Integration Engine; it resides on the application server controlled by Tuxedo. The Gateway provides the interface to the Broker, where it manages the receipt and transmission of messages. The Broker has several listening and target connectors that support inbound and outbound communications between external systems and the integration engine. The connectors support a range of communication protocols: HTTP, JMS, POP3, SMTP, and FTP. With a standard communication protocol that is provided by PeopleSoft, a standard Gateway is provided with the connectors required for sending and receiving messages from older versions of PeopleSoft.

The Gateway Manager processes every message that is received through the Integration Gateway; when it receives the messages, it processes XML parsing, message validation, and message logging. The Gateway Manager uses the content of the message object to determine the intended message recipient, and then uses the appropriate target connector to transmit the message. After receiving a response from the target connector, it forwards the response to the calling listening connector. During all of this processing, the contents of incoming messages are logged to a disk file, along with any errors encountered during processing. A number of different physical architectures are possible, depending on the nature of the desired integration effort. For example, a simple integration behind a company's firewall, may require a single local Integration Gateway. More elaborate integrations across firewall boundaries, LANs, and WANs could very well involve multiple remote Integration Gateway instances and several different listening and target connectors. As such, real-world PeopleSoft integration can get very complex, very quickly. Integration Broker pieces include gateways, nodes, messages, and message channels.

Integration Gateway

Integration Gateway is the platform that manages the receipt and delivery of messages passed among systems through PeopleSoft Integration Broker. It supports the leading TCP/IP protocols (JMS, HTTP, SMTP) and provides extensible interfaces to develop new connectors for communication with legacy, enterprise resource planning, and Internet-based systems.

- **Node** Nodes represent connection points in Integration Broker integrations, for example, organizations, other PeopleSoft applications, or external systems. Nodes can be remote or local and represent customers, business units, suppliers, and/or third-party software systems. Node definitions define the location to or from which the message can be routed; all nodes are considered remote. A node's definition can reference a target connector, indicating the protocol (JMS, HTTP, SMTP) the broker must use in order to reach that node. Each PeopleSoft installation must have one, and only one, default local node.

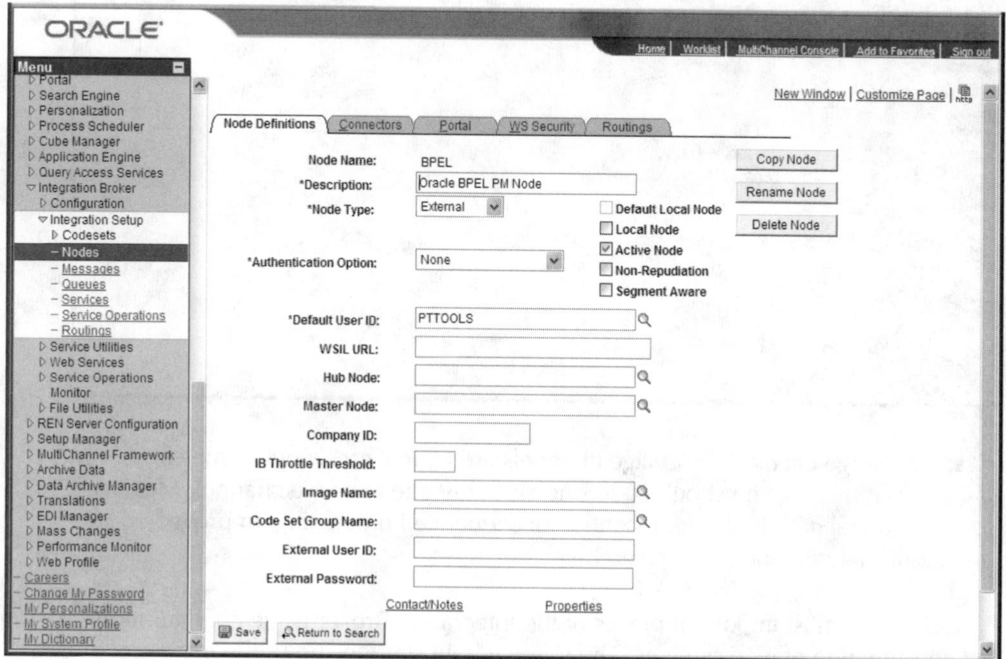

- **Message** Messages are application data that is sent and received through the Integration Broker. Messages can be rowset based, non-rowset based, or containers. Rowset-based messages are hierarchical database information, based on native PeopleSoft records. Non-rowset-based messages are used for other message content or structures, including XML and SOAP.

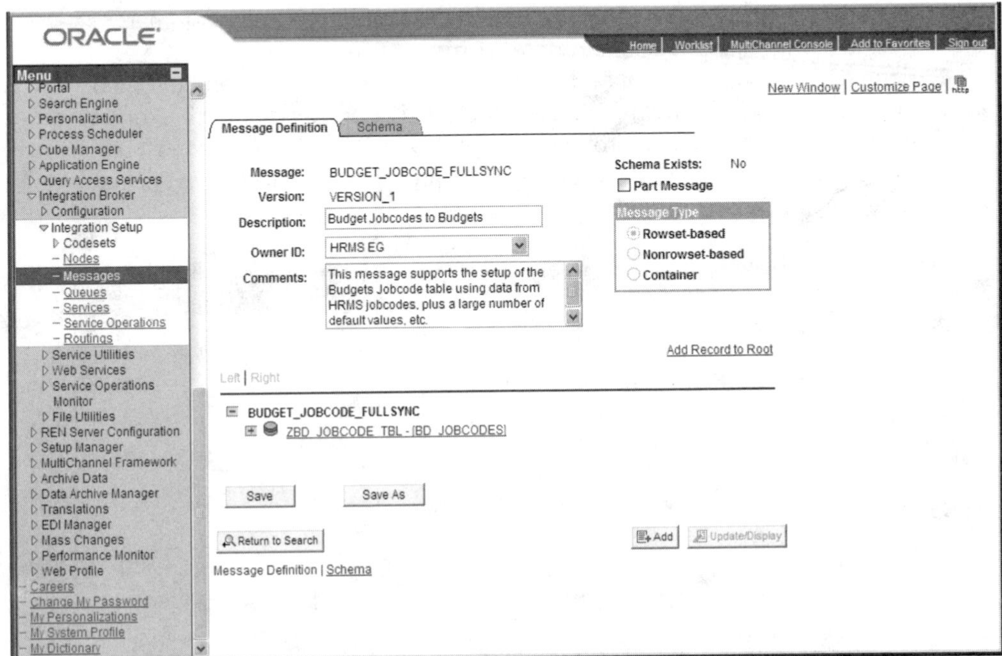

- **Message channel** Message channels are logical groupings of messages. Each message must belong to one and only one message channel. Message channel definitions are essential for sequenced processing, improved throughput, and message archival.

One of the most important pieces of the Integration Broker is the configuration and consumption of web services. The following illustration shows the main menu of the Service Utilities; from this main menu you can go into Service Administration, which allows the creation and deletion of Services, Messages, WSDL, Routings, and Queues. The technology used for web services is WSDL; you can consume WSDL documents from PeopleSoft, and third-party systems allow you to see the service utilities. The Integration Broker will create metadata to integrate the consumed WSDL documents and allow processing and integration.

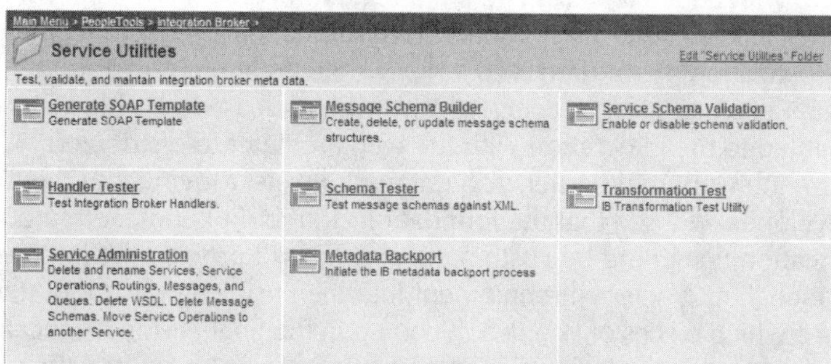

The wizard provided with the Integration Broker allows for the consumption of services.

Consume Web Service Wizard
Step 1 of 8
1 2 3 4 5 6 7 8
Next >
Select WSDL Source
Select the source of the WSDL you would like to consume.
WSDL Sources
UDDI
WSDL URL
WSIL URL
File
Load from File
Legacy WSDL (Prior to 8.48)

Summary

In this chapter several important architecture configurations were discussed. Working with and coding to these levels will be covered in later chapters when Advanced PeopleCode techniques are discussed. Creation of web services and consuming WSDL documents will be outlined in Chapter 8. In the overview of the architecture it is important to understand the basics of the Internet Architecture configuration that led to the standard PeopleSoft Internet Architecture. You should understand that the future is moving to Fusion Middleware configurations with the many layers of possible development structures that will allow for incredible distributed functionality and development. Also, the PeopleSoft concentric PIA is moving forward, with added features like the Integration Broker, which allows for the configuration of Web services connections to incoming and outgoing messages as well as the unitization of standard web languages to create messages and WSDL documents. The PeopleSoft Internet Architecture when released was bleeding-edge technology that led to the integration with the web and later to distributed development on the web, middle-tier, and database levels. Moving into the future, PeopleSoft developers will see that the foundations that built PeopleSoft into a dynamic application that could be custom configured will provide the leading technology stance that Oracle will implement into the Fusion Application. It will be interesting to see which pieces of PeopleSoft end up in the final Fusion Application product. With the advanced technology that PeopleSoft has brought to the Application development community, Fusion is more than likely going to acquire many of the PeopleSoft web development features.

PART II

PeopleTools Development

Part II will take you on a journey through the original PeopleSoft tools. This will provide you, the reader, with the basic skill set required to maintain legacy PeopleSoft systems. This section will also introduce the new tools available in PeopleSoft. These new tools will enable you as a PeopleSoft Developer to spread your wings and do things that your customers have been requesting from you for a long time. It is an exciting time in PeopleSoft development. Read on and re-visit some old friendly tools that you are familiar with. Take a look at the new tools and ways of putting some legacy reports and processes out to pasture.

In the world of PeopleTools development there are many choices that can be made when you look at the specifications for a new feature or bolt-on. Or may be is as simple as creating a report for your customer. What tool are you going to use? How do you make this decision? In Part II we will look at the tools that have been around since the beginning and take a look at some of the new tools that are available to add to your repertoire.

CHAPTER 4

PeopleTools Basics

n this chapter you will begin your journey into PeopleTools. PeopleTools is the main coding tool available in the PeopleSoft development environment. You will learn to navigate, use Application Designer as a development tool, create and save a Project, and understand why you would want to use a Project to store your objects. This chapter will also provide an introduction to records, fields, pages, components, menus, message catalogs, and basic HTML code within PeopleCode. These basics will help you build an understanding that will serve you well in later chapters when we will venture into harder coding techniques.

The main portal to access and code is Application Designer, which is the main development tool available in PeopleSoft. Within Application Designer you can create projects, fields, records, translate values, pages, components, menus, PeopleCode, and HTML. Via the Portal you can also work with objects that can be manipulated using Application Designer, Message Catalogs, and Queries. This chapter will start the basic introduction to the tools, objects, and code that are available through Application Designer.

Application Designer

Application Designer is the main development area in PeopleSoft. It is the primary location of the tools used to design applications and or to change the PeopleSoft-delivered vanilla code. With release 7 of PeopleSoft, the tools for development of the application were integrated into the Application Designer, which becomes your window as the developer to define objects in the metadata. Different terms are used for these items: PeopleSoft objects or PeopleSoft definitions. Well, they are both, you create an object—a PeopleSoft record for example—but until it is defined in both: the metadata and the database, the object does not exist. Just remember that you have both worlds to work in: the PeopleSoft metadata repository and your physical database object that has to be created. And they had better match in every respect; otherwise, the definition and the object will not correspond. The PeopleSoft Internet Architecture (PIA) application contains a collection of related objects that work together for a specific purpose, and object references are tested via the application over an Internet browser.

Development Tools That Have Been Around Since the Beginning

The toolset begins with Application Designer, Security Administrator, the Query Tool, Application Engine, SQR, and the more recently added XML Publisher. With these tools, you can easily create an online application, with components, menus, records, and fields. Once the component, page, and menu are created, security access is assigned to the end users who will be using the component. This toolset has been around since the first release of PeopleSoft, with the use of Application Designer, and PeopleTools, SQR, and PeopleCode. Later releases saw Application Engine and, most recently, XML Publisher.

PeopleCode

PeopleCode is the programming language delivered by PeopleSoft for the customization of the PeopleSoft Application. You code in PeopleCode via the Application Designer. The code can exist on a record, a button, an action, or, possibly, an Application Engine batch program. It is a proprietary language used to do object-oriented coding in PeopleTools. There is a tightly integrated element in the datatypes and metastrings that directly correlates to SQL. There are also elements of dot notation, classes, and methods that give PeopleCode a Java feel.

SQR

Structured Query Report Writer is a PeopleSoft-delivered reporting tool. In industry it is used all too often in place of better and more advanced tools; and with the use of XML on the rise, a lot of SQR reports are going to be benched and replaced by XML reports. This book covers SQR because there are so many reports written in this reporting tool. SQR has a robust report-writing environment with complex procedural logic built in. It is also an easy language to learn and come up to speed quickly with. You can combine database retrieval and row processing. You can even embed PL/SQL in your reports and do complex database manipulation.

Application Engine

Application Engine is a batch processing tool provided via Application Designer in PeopleTools. It resembles a macro shell window that allows for calls to SQL, PeopleCode, or another Application Engine Section. It allows for you to do file extraction, manipulate databases, e-mail results to your staff, and embed PL/SQL within PeopleCode.

Application Engine is different from regular batch programs in that it is not procedural. It focuses on set-based SQL logic and goes to a much deeper level of the underlying application definitions. Describing set-based logic is beyond the scope of this introduction, but suffice to say that set-based logic is more in line with how SQL is supposed to work, but it's not as familiar to developers who have only worked with procedural logic.

To make an already long story short, Application Engine slowly won converts within PeopleSoft, and by the time that PeopleSoft 8 was being developed, Application Engine was adopted by the PeopleTools team. The front end was converted to a regular PeopleTool as part of Application Designer, and the back end was rewritten in C++ and given the ability to run PeopleCode as well as SQL logic.

Why would Application Engine show up as part of Oracle Fusion? There are a couple of reasons. One is that Oracle really doesn't have a good tool for batch development. If you look at existing Oracle applications, you'll notice that batch processing is done by writing raw PL/SQL or Pro*C code—not the most straightforward thing for a typical application developer to do. The other thing about Application Engine that fits well within Oracle is that it is a set-based tool. Most of the processing is pushed to the database, and that plays well to Oracle's strengths. Oracle developers themselves list using Application Engine for batch as number 4 in their top 10 things for PeopleSoft Enterprise customers to do today to get ready for Fusion.

Does it make sense to train current PeopleSoft customers in SQR or in Application Engine? The answer is that both have pros and cons. For starters, there aren't many PeopleSoft applications that don't use both SQR and AppEngine, so you need to have some level of skills in both. I think that CRM is the exception here; I know that CRM has no COBOL, and I think that is true for SQR as well.

SQR also has the advantage of being a little bit more independent of the applications. For example, when you want to write an SQR, all you need is a text editor instead of a proprietary tool like Application Designer. You can also run SQRs in any database, not just a PeopleSoft database. Of course, doing so requires that you license SQR independently of the license that you receive with your PeopleSoft applications, but you could actually do it.

Of course, those pros are also part of the cons of SQR. SQR has *zero* understanding of the underlying applications that it's working with. Trees, effective dating, setids, row-level security, related language records, etc. all have to be coded by hand when you're writing SQR code. Not impossible to do, but it's certainly more costly and error prone to build and maintain it by hand.

Application Engine comes with some cons as well, especially when viewed from a reporting perspective. Aside from being a very PeopleSoft-specific tool, App Engine lacks any kind of built-in output capability. This was the target of the (never finished) PeopleCode Print project, but there's nothing there today.

Meta-SQL

Meta-SQL expands to platform-specific SQL substrings and then causes another function to be called, or substitutes a value. Meta-SQL constructs are used in functions that pass SQL strings, such as the following:

- SQLExec
- Scroll buffer functions (ScrollSelect and its relatives)

- PeopleSoft Application Designer dynamic and SQL views
- Some Rowset class methods (Select, SelectNew, Fill, and so on)
- The SQL class
- PeopleSoft Application Engine programs
- Some Record class methods (Insert, Update, and so on)
- COBOL functions

Not all Meta-SQL can be used by all programs. Some Meta-SQL can be used only in Application Engine programs. Other Meta-SQL can only be used as part of an SQL statement in an SQL or dynamic view. If a Meta-SQL construct, function, or meta-variable is supported in PeopleCode, it is supported in all types of PeopleCode programs, that is, in Application Engine PeopleCode programs (actions), component interface PeopleCode programs, and so on. Even if a Meta-SQL element is used in PeopleCode, you cannot use Meta-SQL like a built-in function. You can, however, use Meta-SQL in the SQLExec function, the Select method, the Fill method, and so on. Note that Meta-SQL is not available in SQR.

"Meta-SQL" is a PeopleSoft extension of SQL that converts to correct SQL code. If you have spent any time looking at PeopleSoft view definitions, you have seen a few of these. They are the pieces that begin with %SQL, and they refer back to SQL Objects, which are pieces of text that store the SQL clauses. It is a easy concept, but it is difficult when you are trying to read it because the nested %SQL clauses require you to have to visually insert the reconstructed SQL text that is missing or replaced by the %SQL parameter. You have the choice of using Meta-SQL or else to use plain old ANSI standard SQL, which is easier to read, but in the context of Application Engine Meta-SQL is invaluable. In view declarations I prefer to use standard SQL, but it is important for you as a PeopleSoft Developer to learn to read both.

COBOL

Going back to the early days of PeopleSoft, there were two main batch tools: COBOL and SQR. Both COBOL and SQR had the benefit of working well across the different platforms that PeopleSoft supported. COBOL also had the benefit of being something that most PeopleSoft developers understood; most of them having come from old mainframe environments. SQR brought a simple, yet powerful, idea to the table: let people write conditional logic as well as output data as part of an SQL statement. Today that's not so strange, but back in the late 1980s and early 1990s, having your printing logic so tightly integrated (some might say "tied") to your SQL was powerful stuff.

The big unspoken question, of course, is why didn't PeopleSoft create some sort of batch/reporting tool as part of PeopleTools? The short answer is that, in the beginning, everyone was too busy just making PeopleTools work for online transactions to even think about some sort of batch/reporting tool.

Although it took more than a decade for Application Engine to get developed and finally moved into PeopleTools, SQR and COBOL didn't really change that much during that time. PeopleSoft bought the source code for SQR.

COBOL was even worse, since PeopleSoft never actually controlled the COBOL compilers in use. Some really big headaches developed because of that. As for the COBOL language, well, it's COBOL.

An early PeopleSoft developer would still feel right at home with the versions of COBOL and SQR that are still in use today. While COBOL and SQR remained static, Application Engine gained in the area of features. It is important as a PeopleSoft Developer to feel comfortable in SQR and COBOL, but the skills areas that will realize growth are Application Engine and XML. Drawing on my discussions on the Fusion Council, I am certain we will see something similar to Application Engine in the Fusion application.

Newer Tools

The newer toolsets include Application Engine, which is an incredible batch processing application; it provides the programmer with a macro type of environment that allows rapid creation of programs that will update tables, import and export files, and even send e-mails. With PeopleTools release version 8.48, Oracle introduced XML Publisher. This added tool allows for the creation of dynamic reports, with the hint from the Oracle PeopleSoft team that XML Publisher will replace and retire SQR.

Fusion Middleware Tools

Oracle Fusion Middleware is a comprehensive middleware family composed of SOA and middleware products, including Oracle Application Server 10g along with related Oracle Application Server products and options such as Oracle Identity Management, Oracle Business Intelligence, Oracle BPEL Process Manager, Oracle Web Services Manager, Oracle Business Activity Monitoring, Oracle COREid Products, Oracle Portal and Oracle Integration, Oracle Data Hubs, Oracle Content Services 10g, Oracle Real Time Collaboration 10g, and Oracle Unified Messaging. When used in conjunction with Oracle Fusion Middleware Enterprise Portal, PeopleTools is designed to serve as a point of access for all enterprise applications. In addition, Web services created from PeopleTools' Service Designer and Integration Broker can be automated and orchestrated via Oracle's Fusion Middleware BPEL Process Manager.

Among other new tools included in the launch is PeopleSoft Change Impact Analyzer, designed to allow customers to study the effect of prospective changes to their applications. Also, XML Publisher is now integrated into PeopleTools, increasing the number of options for customized reports. BPEL provides a standard, process-centric way to integrate disparate systems. Oracle's BPEL Process Manager, a key tool in Oracle Fusion Middleware for delivering service-oriented architecture (SOA), supports the industry-standard BPEL specification backed by Microsoft, IBM, SAP, and BEA, and is widely recognized as an enterprise blueprint for reducing the cost, complexity, and inflexibility of integration projects.

XML Publisher

XML Publisher, called BI Publisher in the Oracle Application world, handles the data formatting and output and has recently been integrated with PS/Query and PeopleCode, which makes it accessible from Application Engine. It's not a big stretch to see how Application Engine could be enhanced to use BI Publisher natively as an output tool and effectively get rid of the need to use SQR at all.

Given that SQR is unlikely to get any further investment from Oracle, and Application Engine is, I would recommend that PeopleSoft customers ensure that they have SQR skills available to them (either from internal resources or from consulting augmentation as necessary), but limit their investment in new SQR development.

How to Navigate

Basic PeopleSoft navigation depends on the modules for which your organization has a license. Some of the navigation and module look and feel were outlined in Chapter 1. The focus of this chapter is how to navigate the development tools. PeopleTools provides the main development and underlying technology for the PeopleSoft modules. The modules are built, maintained, and deployed via Enterprise PeopleTools.

Using Application Designer

Application Designer is the main portal to each of the development tools available in PeopleSoft. This is the place where you can directly develop and update the PeopleSoft metadata. It is a rapid application environment, and Application Designer assists with the upgrade process. It contains the collection of definitions for objects such as fields, records, pages, and components that make up the functionality of the application in PeopleSoft. Within Application Designer you can change and adapt objects through an easy-to-learn process that allows you to define and build your own objects, make definitions, define relationships between the objects and/or definitions, implement and manage security, deploy to the PIA (Internet browser), and test your solution.

The tool Application Designer is an interactive and easy-to-use rapid application development tool. It provides an integrated development environment that allows you to work with several definitions stored in a Project container in one single work area. Application Designer is the main development environment for PeopleSoft. The following are some of the definitions you can build in Application Designer and write to the PeopleSoft metadata:

- Fields
- Records
- Pages
- Components
- Menus
- PeopleCode
- SQL

Projects

Projects are not part of application development or one of the main objects that you will want to have in PeopleSoft—or where you can see a direct correlation to an item that you just coded. Projects are a holding tank that allows you as a developer to store all of the items you have coded in one location. One of the typical ways a shop will develop is to have some type of request tracking software. So, for example, a Project could be an SR or Service Request for a particular enhancement request or a maintenance request. With a Project you can put all of the items that are associated with the change into one SR and name the Project to allow you to have a reference back to the request. The Project will track all of the definitions and their types, but it will not have the definitions. The definitions for the objects will be in the PeopleSoft metadata.

As a developer you are not required to use PeopleSoft Projects, but think of the scenario where you have changed a page, record, field, or component and added a permission list. In this case when you want to move your changes from Development into Testing, you would have to move five things into Testing—and test to make certain they all moved correctly. With a Project you can insert all of the objects into the Project and just do one move—the Project into the Testing platform. This streamlines changes and upgrades in the PeopleSoft environment with the use of Projects.

In Figure 4-1, the left side of the screen is the Project workspace, which shows one object type at a time. You can click the + (plus) sign and expand each of the object types. The Project workspace has two types of views: development and upgrade. In Figure 4-2 you can see the Project Development workspace.

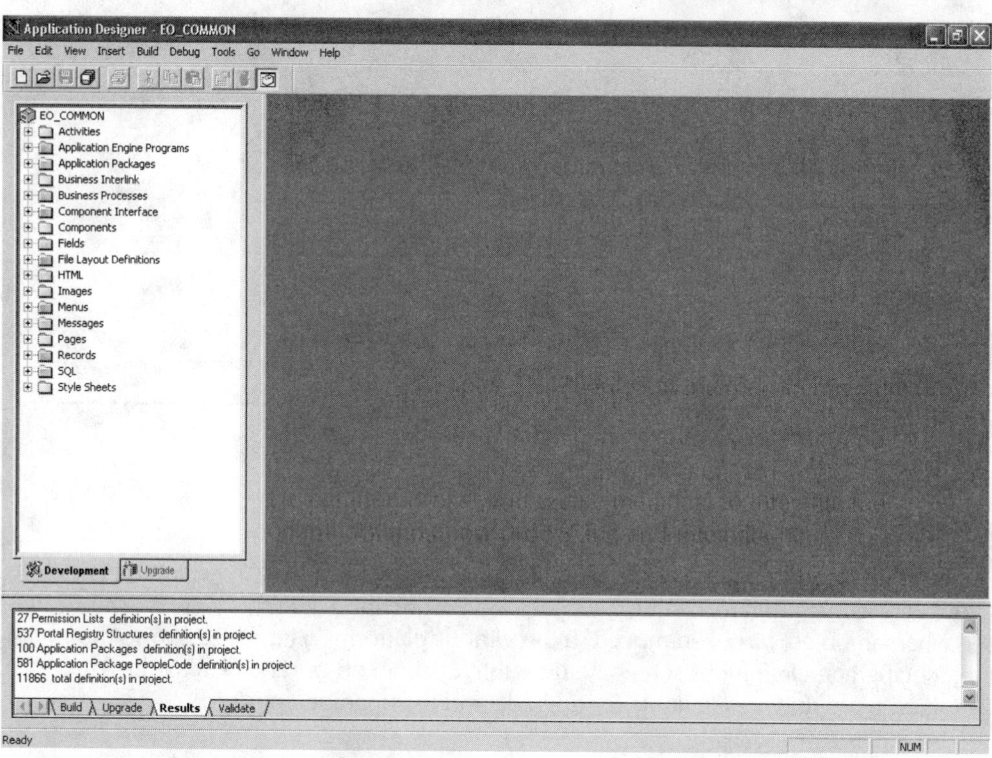

FIGURE 4-1 *Project view*

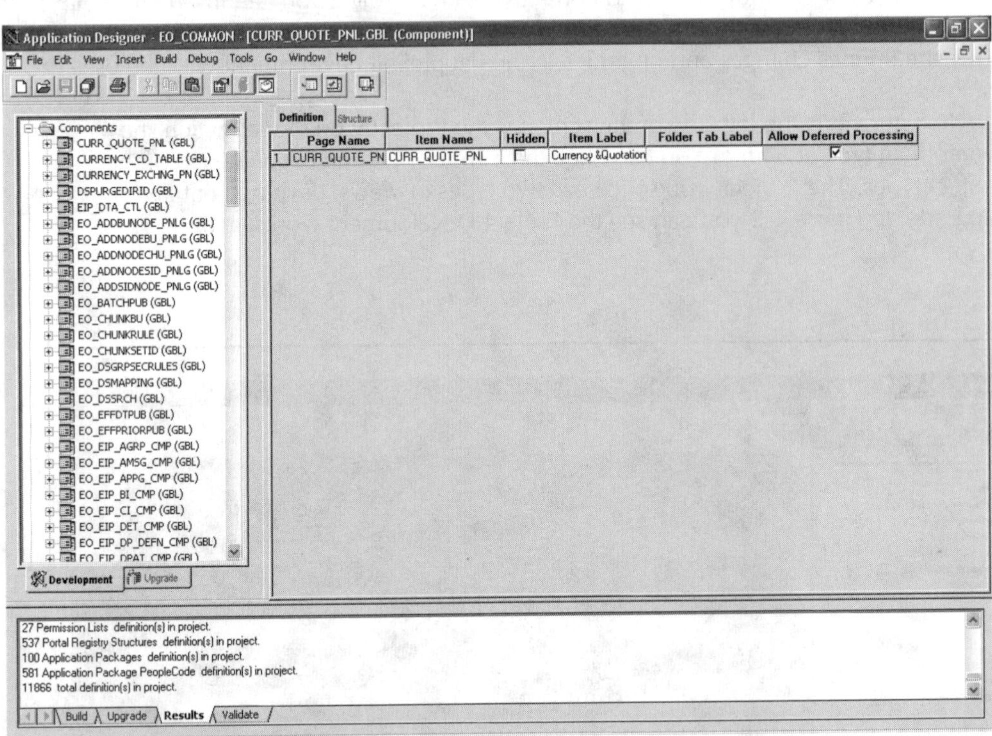

FIGURE 4-2 *Project Development workspace*

Figure 4-3 shows the main functionality of the Project Upgrade view, which is to allow for the migration to Testing, Quality, and Production. With this view you can see when an object has been moved to the various platforms. Figure 4-4 shows the Object Upgrade Definitions screen; you double-click an object and display the definition types that are available for upgrade and the upgrade options.

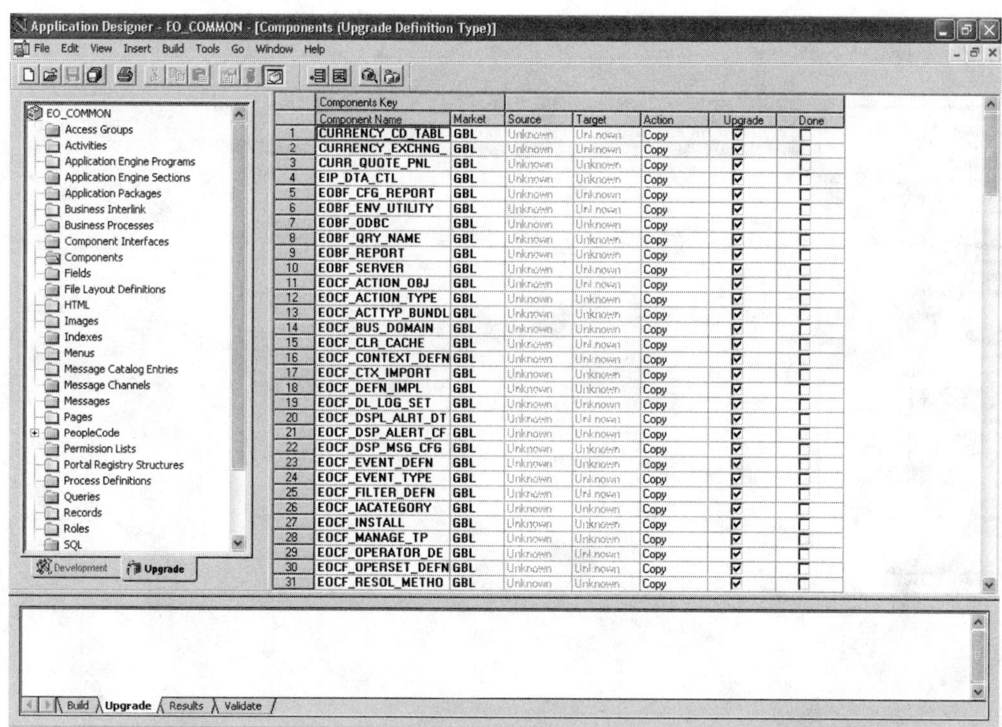

FIGURE 4-3 *Project Upgrade workspace*

Each time you open Application Designer, it will open with a blank Project. In order to save it and use it as the container for your objects, just simply choose File | Save and name the new Project. To add comments to your Project, go to the File | Project Properties menu and add details and comments about your Project; you will see the screen that is shown in Figure 4-5.

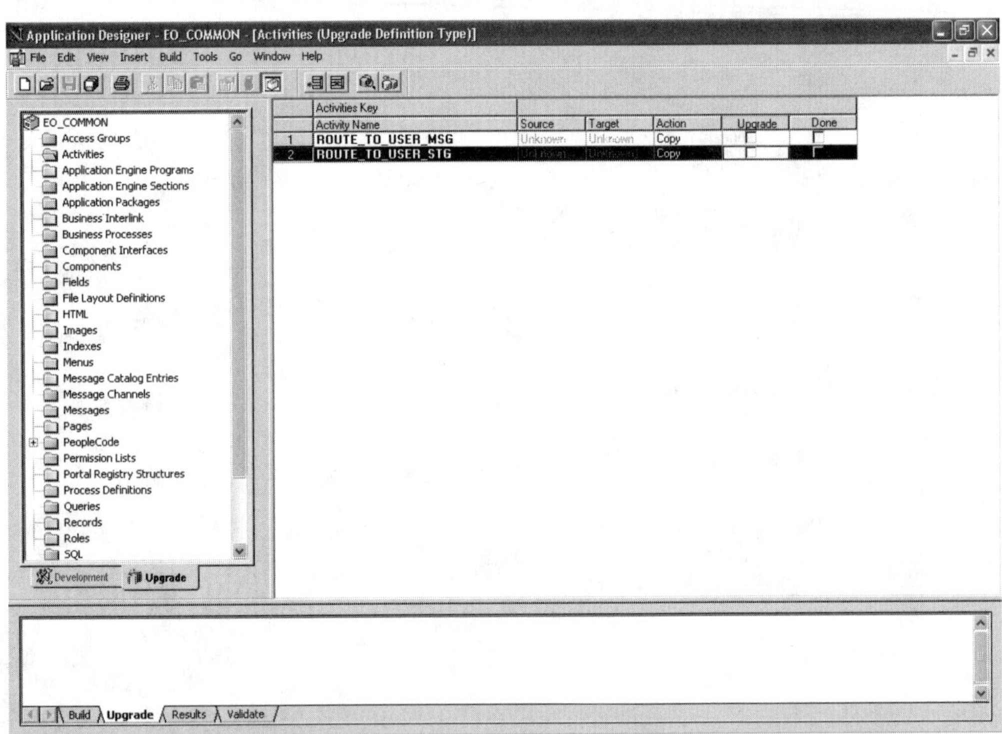

FIGURE 4-4 *Object Upgrade Definitions*

FIGURE 4-5 *Project Properties*

You can insert definitions into your Project or create new objects; see Figure 4-6 for an example of the screen. To create new objects, you go to File | New | and then from the drop-down menu choose the type of object you wish to create. To insert existing objects, choose Insert | Definitions Into The Project or press CTRL-F7.

From the main File menu (Figure 4-7) you can save your Project, add properties to your Project, save your Project with a new name, print your Project, or merge your Project with another. Merging is a nice option that allows you to take two Projects and make one larger or combined Project.

Fields

Fields are the lowest-level definition in PeopleSoft; in general you can think of them as the column definition in your database. They define a single object level. An example would be an EMPLID: the EMPLID field must be defined in the PeopleSoft metadata as well as at the physical database level as a column. When building objects in PeopleSoft, you must always keep in mind that they have to be defined and removed from two places: the physical database level and the metadata repository. In the Application Designer you will define the metadata definition as well as allow the tool to build the SQL that can be submitted to your DBA to build the physical database object. Always be cognizant that the two objects must match in every aspect: size, type, decimal places, and format. If they do not match in every aspect, you will receive an unknown object definition error via the PeopleSoft PIA. Fields have the following attributes:

- Type
- Length

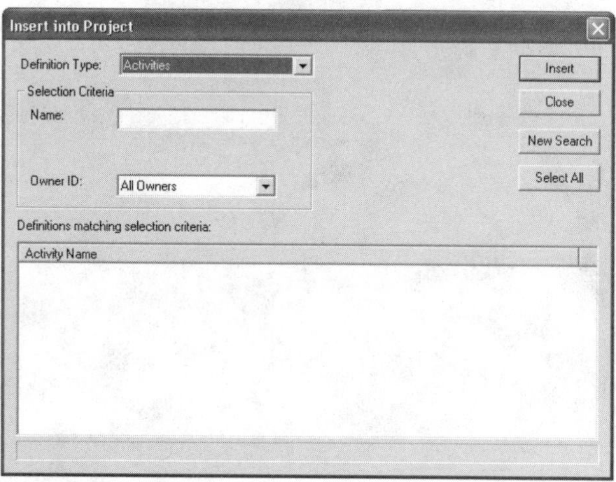

FIGURE 4-6 *Adding definitions into the Project*

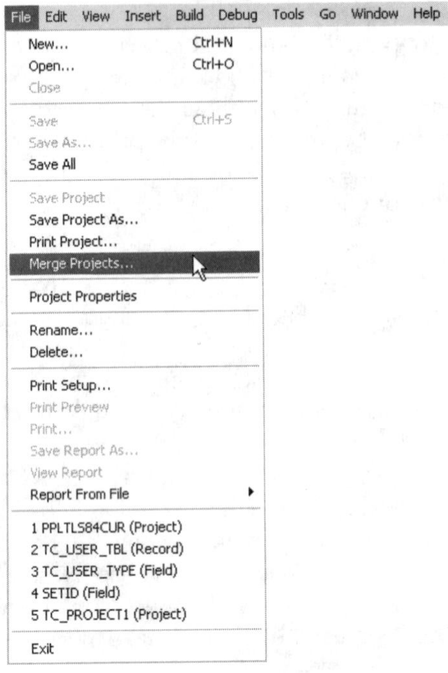

FIGURE 4-7 *File menu*

- Decimal places (if a number type)
- Translation values (optional)
- Long name
- Short name
- Format

Available field types include

- Character
- Long Character
- Number
- Signed Number

- Date
- Time
- Datetime
- Image
- ImageReference
- Attachment

The attributes for fields are stored in the database table PSDBFIELD, which is a metadata catalog table that is populated when a field is created or changed in the PeopleSoft System. When you upgrade, this table is used to compare against for changes it provides you with a list of the changes in a report known as a compare report. The catalog table PSDBFIELDLANG stores the long and short descriptions. It stores these descriptions in multiple languages. If a user of the system has a default language other than English, that user will see the descriptions in his or her default language. To see fields that are used in Record definitions, look at the catalog table PSRECFIELD.

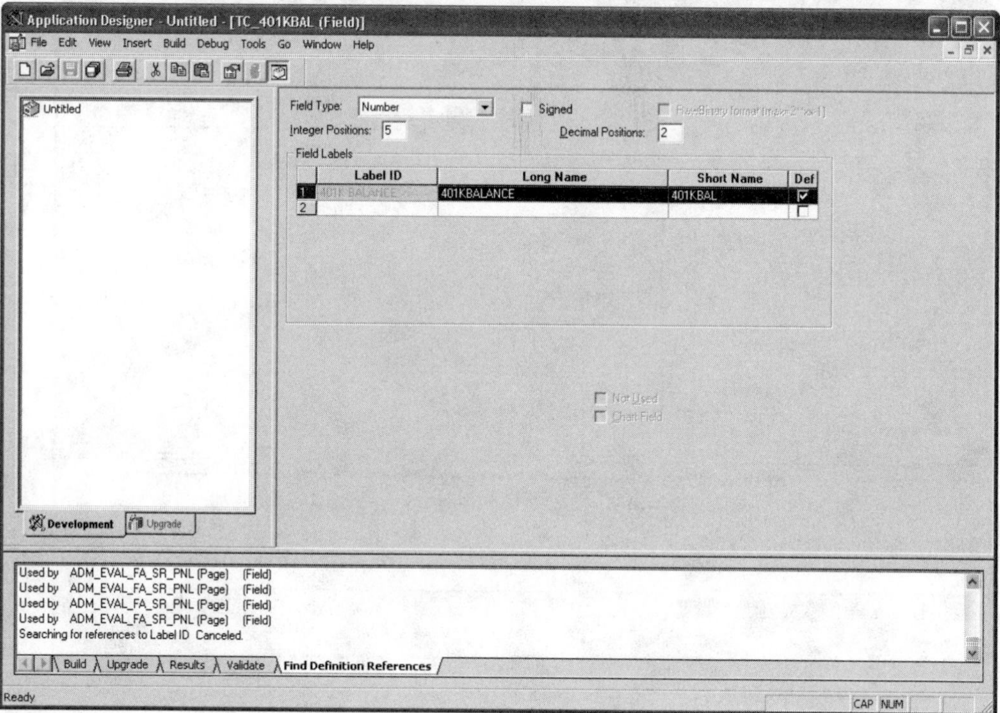

Records

A collection of fields is a record definition. A record can be a table, view, subrecord, derived work record, query view, or dynamic view. Tables and views would exist in both the PeopleSoft metadata and the physical database; the other types of records are only available via the PeopleSoft metadata. Record definitions are stored in the metadata table PSRECDEFN which stores the attributes for the records. It holds the properties of the record definition. These properties are of three types: General Properties, Type Properties, and Use Properties. General Properties describe the record, including the last date and time it was created or updated, as well as the ID of the operator who updated it. Type properties are the definitions used to define the record in the RDBMS: is it a view or a table? Use properties are used for definition of key fields, search fields, list fields, and parent records, to outline a few.

PSRECDEFN holds the previously discussed General, Type, and Use properties as well as the table space name in the SQL Table definition. Each record that is a SQL table and was delivered by PeopleSoft is stored with a prefix of PS_; a table that is created in PeopleTools will be named with the PS_ convention except when the name is defined in the Non-Standard SQL Table Name field in the configuration.

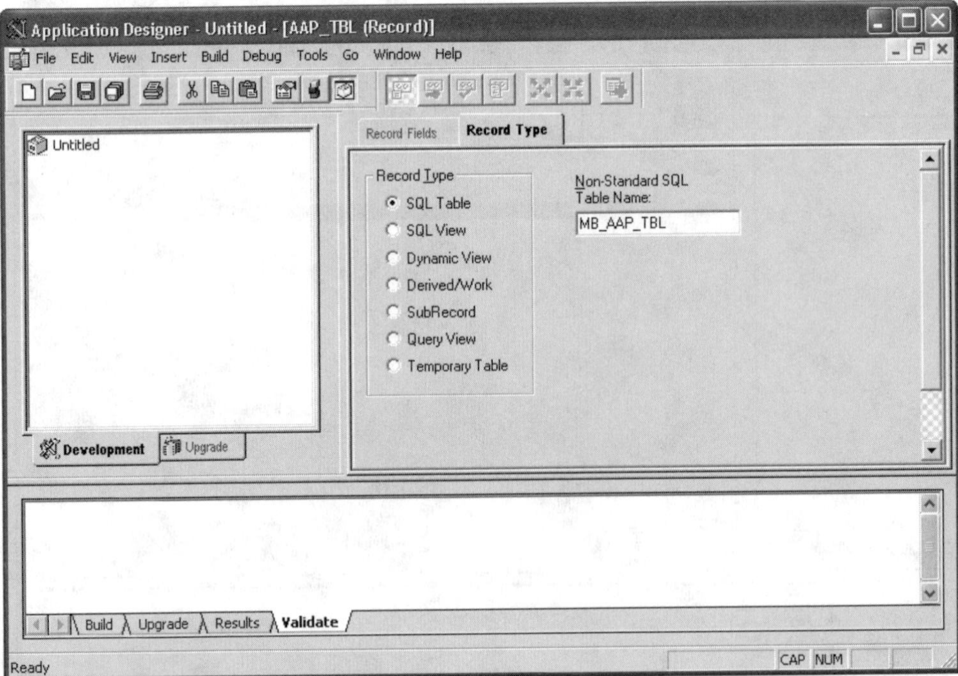

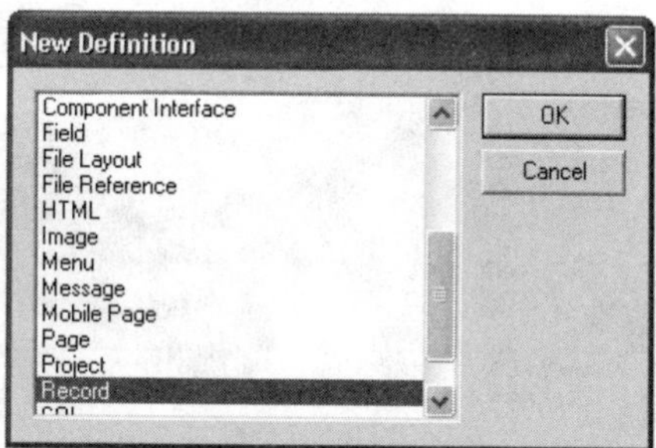

The catalog table that stores the PeopleSoft record definition is PSRECDEFN. SQL tables and views are database objects as well, being defined in both the PeopleSoft metadata and the database.

To create a record definition, you start by opening Application Designer and clicking File | New | Record. Then you insert the fields that you want to have in the record. In the following three illustrations you can see an example of adding a field, how the record definition properties are displayed, and the SQL name of the record.

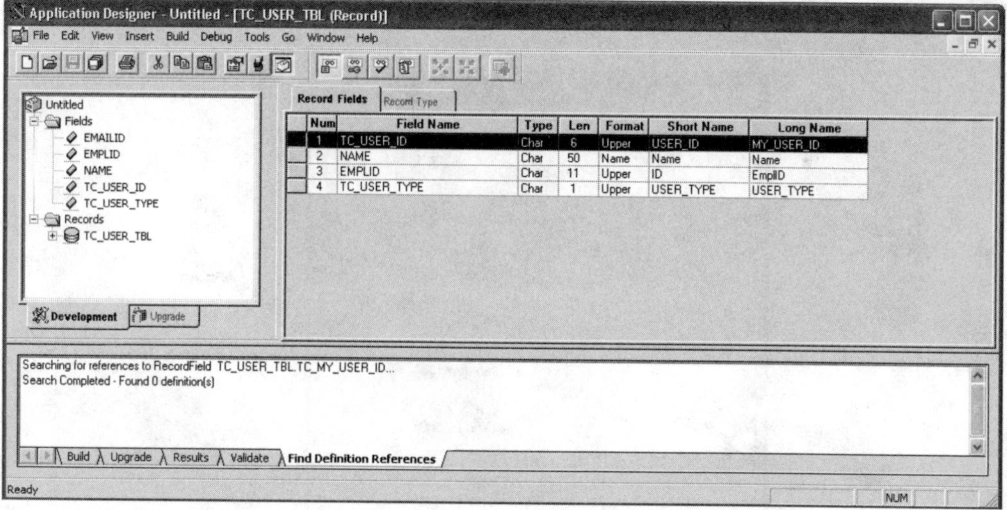

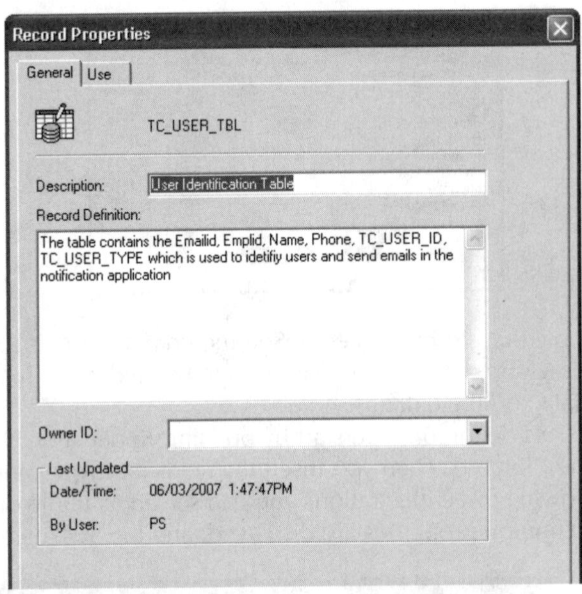

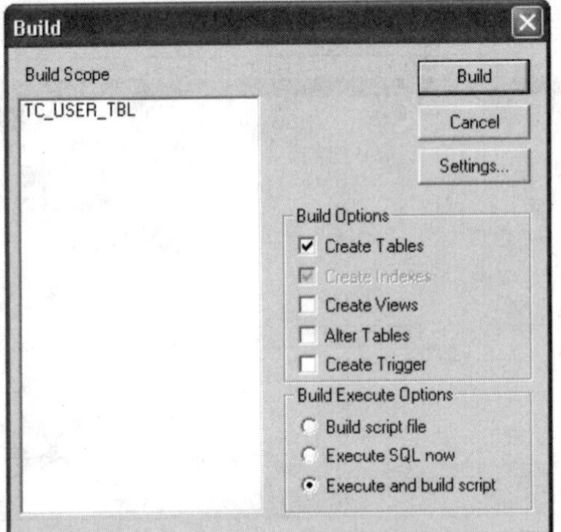

Remember, if you do not want PeopleSoft to use the standard naming convention of PS_, you will need to define a SQL Name in the Record Type property. This override then allows you to define the naming convention for your

SQL objects. In this book we will use the naming convention of TC_ for Test Company. In your organization you create a two-letter abbr be used in the front of each object to follow the long-standing PeopleSo conventions, for instance, PS_ and UU_ for University of Utah. Do not forget that just because you have built an object in the PeopleSoft metadata, that does not mean that it has been built in the database. The next step you have to perform in a customized record creation is the build.

Make certain you check the build log to ensure that the object was created without error. The results from the SQL can be sent to the DBA if you as a developer do not have the permission to create an object in the database where you are trying to build.

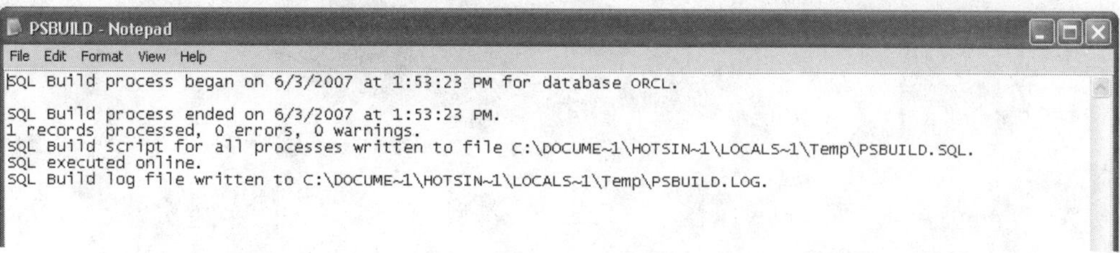

- **Set Control Field** This is the property that is used in a multi-company environment; you can use Set Control Field to share records across company databases. In order to do this, you would have to add SETID to the TC_USER_TBL; the SETID is PeopleSoft delivered. It needs to be defined as the first field in the record definition as a Search Key.

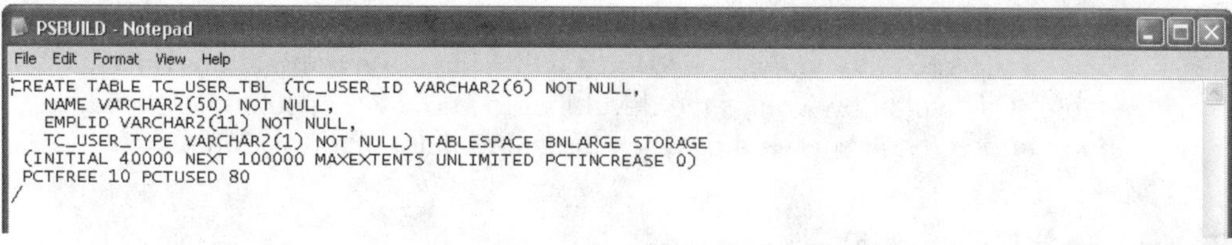

- **Parent Record** Parent/Child definitions and relationships help create automatic joins for use in the PeopleSoft Query Tool. An example is the PERSONAL_DATA relationship to the EMPLOYMENT record. The two have common Search Records that establish the Parent/Child relationship.

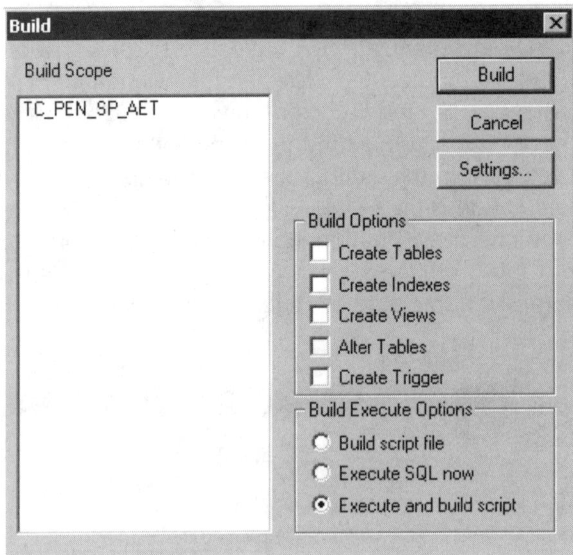

- **Related Language Record** The Related Language Record setting is used in the case of multilingual application, and this setting brings that functionality down to the record level.
- **Query Security Record** This is another setting for the record that is available for PeopleSoft Query. This setting will provide row-level security for the record definition.
- **Record Audit** The audit flag if turned on in the record definition will record all inserts, updates, and deletes in an audit table. PeopleSoft will create a trigger at the database level that will write these transactions off to a table. This will allow you as the developer to know who updated, deleted, and/or added records as well as when (time and date) that was done.

Record Field Properties

PSRECFIELD stores the fields that are contained in the record definition. Each field in a record can have its own properties, translate values, prompt table edits, or yes/no edits set. Each of these attributes is specific to the record definition of the fields. Within the PSRECFIELD table is a column USEEDIT, a 32-bit integer field. The following shows the basic settings:

```
PSRECFIELD.USEEDIT
bit    value  flag
  0        1  Key
  1        2  Duplicate Order Key
  2        4  System Maintained
```

```
  3        8  Audit Field Add
  4       16  Alternate Search Key
  5       32  List Box Item
  6       64  Descending Key
  7      128  Audit Field Change
  8      256  Required
  9      512  Translate Table Edit
 10     1024  Audit Field Delete
 11     2048  Search Key
 12     4096  Reasonable Date
 13     8192  Yes/No Table Edit
 14    16384  Prompt Table Edit
 15    32768  Auto-Update
 16    65536  Identifies field as Field in SubRecord
 17   131072  (Reserved / Not Used)
 18   262144  From Search Field
 19   524288  Through Search Field
```

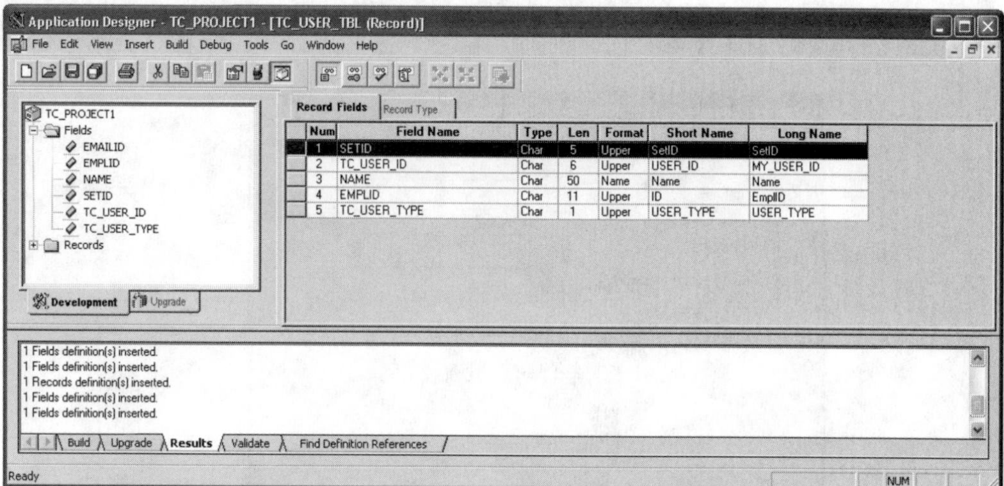

Translate Values

Translate tables allow you to create prompt tables or list boxes that have predefined values for your users to choose from. This will make data entry quicker and more accurate. The data is displayed as an available translate, which is stored similar to an all-purpose data dictionary. The rules for the data that you need to follow when creating a translate table are as follows:

- Field type is Character.
- Field length is 1 to 4 characters.

- Field values consist of a relatively small, static set of values that are not maintained by the user.
- No other fields relate to this field.

If the values you wish to assign are a Y for Yes and an N for No, there is no need to enter them into a translate table. PeopleSoft has created a field for Y and N name PSYESNO. When you select Yes/No for edit, the system will automatically refer to the PSYESNO field in the Translate table. A good example of when to use a translate table would be a gender field. Department ID, for instance, is not a good case for using the translate table because it requires its own prompt table.

The following illustrations show how to create a translate value. First you go to the Field that you would like to set up as a translate value on the record. Then you click on the Properties button, which looks like an index finger pointing to a document. You then see the addition of the value C for the list value of customer; this is how a new value is added in this pop-up box. Finally, you see the new value of customer added as a translate value in the Properties dialog box that shows all the values for this translate value.

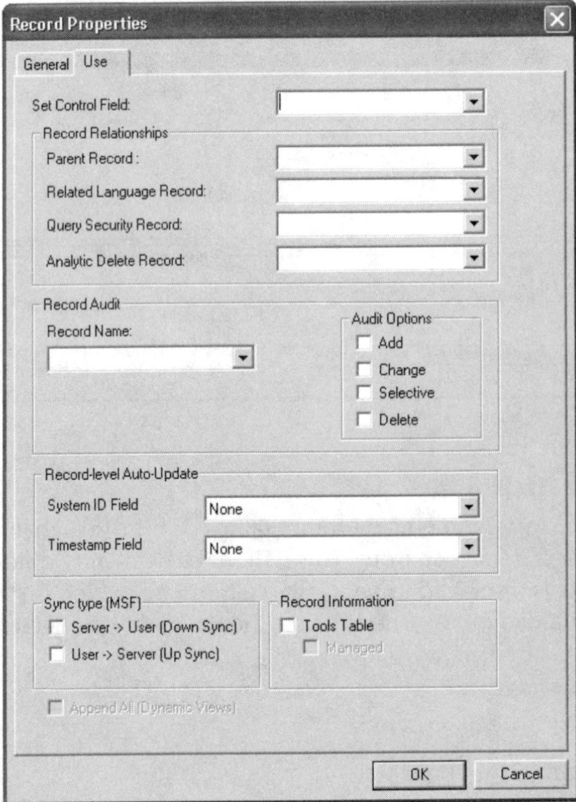

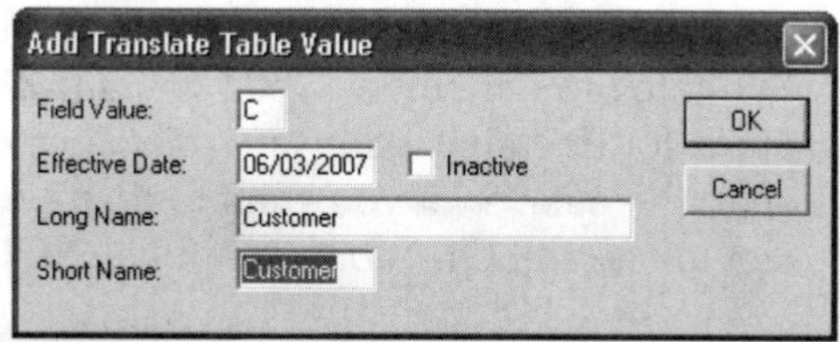

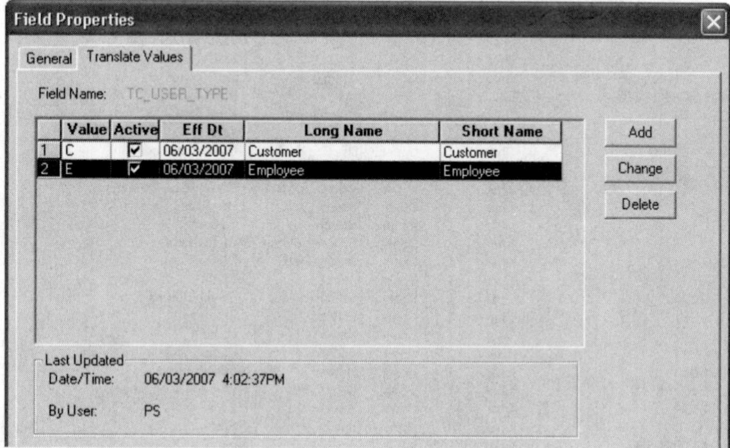

Record Types

Here are guidelines to keep in mind for record definitions: The name length can be 15 characters, with the exception of a Temporary table name, which has a maximum length of 13. The name of a record must always begin with a letter; it can contain underscores, but avoid special characters—they will work in some database environments and not others, so it is best to avoid their use altogether to remain safe.

- **SQL Table** is a regular record in PeopleSoft that is created and stored in both the database and the PeopleSoft metadata. You need to create the record in both places, and unless you have system administrator privileges in your database, you will have to have the DBA create the table or view definition in the database. If you make any changes to the fields, names, types, or sizes, you will need to rebuild the object in both PeopleSoft and the Oracle database.

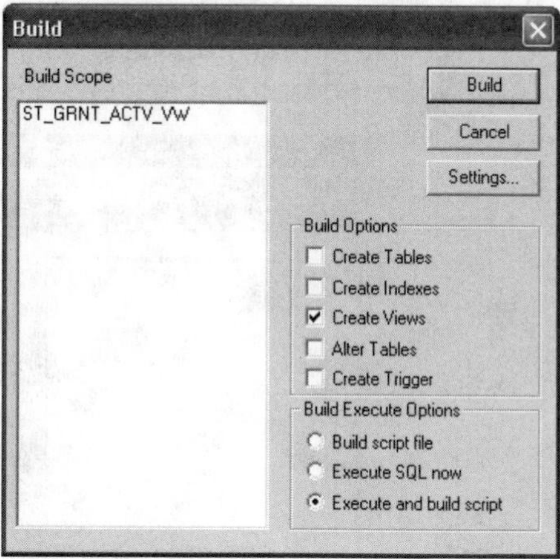

- **SQL View** is a regular view in the Oracle database and the PeopleSoft database. The main thing to remember when you are working with views is that they rarely allow for updating—they are only a view of the data, not the actual connection to the data. So if you want to do more than display the data, you will want to use an SQL Table and not an SQL View.

Record Fields | Record Type

Num	Field Name	Type	Len	Format	Short Name	Long Name
1	ACCT_CD	Char	25	Upper	Code	Code
2	SETID	Char	5	Upper	SetID	SetID
3	EFFDT	Date	10		Eff Date	Effective Date
4	ACCOUNTING_DT	Date	10		Acctg Date	Accounting Date
5	BUSINESS_UNIT	Char	5	Upper	Unit	Business Unit
6	READONLY	Char	1	Upper	Read Only	Read Only
7	TITLE	Char	35	Mixed	Title	Title
8	USE_COMBO_CODE	Char	1	Upper	Use Combo Code	Use Combo Code
9	STOP_FDM_MSG	Char	1	Upper	STOP FDM MSG	Stop Finacials Message
10	USE_VLD_GL_COMBO	Char	1	Upper	Valid GL Combo	Use Valid GL Combinatio
11	USE_SPEED_TYPE	Char	1	Upper	Speed Types	Use Speed Types
12	SRCH_BTN	Char	1	Upper	Search	Search
13	FDM_COMBO_CD	Char	25	Upper	GL Combo Code	GL Combination Code
14	DUMMY_FIELD	Char	1	Upper	Dummy Field	Dummy Field
15	SELECT	Char	1	Upper	Select	Select
16	COMBO_CD_SRCH	Char	1	Upper	Search Options	Search Options
17	GROUP1	Char	1	Upper	Entered	Entered
18	GROUP2	Char	1	Upper	Name	Name
19	GROUP3	Char	1	Upper	Address	Current Address
20	GROUP4	Char	1	Upper	History	Address History
21	CLEAR1_PB	Char	1	Upper	Clear Credit	Clear Incoming Credit Da
22	SEARCH_BTN	Char	1	Upper	Search	Search
23	SPEEDTYPE_KEY	Char	10	Upper	SpeedType	SpeedType Key
24	CHARTFLD_SBR	SRec				
25	SAVEBTN	Char	1	Upper	svaebtn	savebtn
26	CANCEL	Char	1	Upper	Cancel	Cancel
27	CANCELDELETE	Char	1	Mixed	Cancel	Cancel the delete reque
28	RETURN_PB	Char	1	Upper	Return	Return Shipping Line PB
29	OK_BTN	Char	1	Upper	OK	OK
30	OK_BUTTON	Char	1	Upper	OK	OK...

- **A Derived Work Record** is primarily used to store temporary data, data that do not need to be reused. Derived Work Records are also referred to as Derived/Work Records and Work Records. If you wish to look them up in PeopleBooks, please use Work Records. In this book they will be referred to as Derived Work Records. A Derived Work Record is created exactly like a PeopleSoft Record. The difference can be seen in the following illustration, where you see that the record is just defined as a Derived/Work.

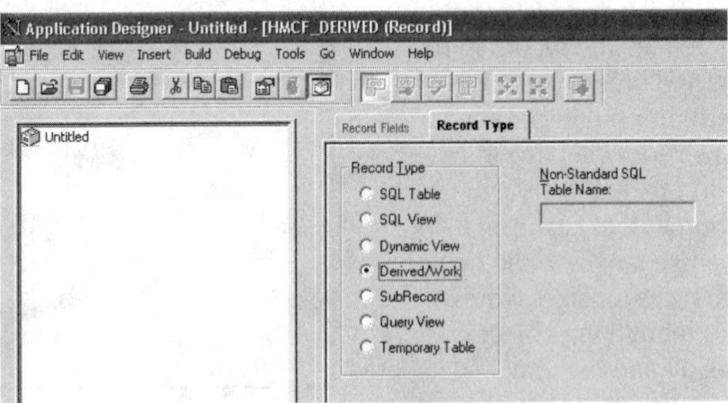

One of the main functionalities of a Derived Work Record is to store totals. Another common use is for buttons, messages, and temporary fields. Derived Work records are only available during your session with the page and are reset anytime the page is re-entered. They can be likened to temporary variables. Because they are defined as a record, confusion about their scope can arise. Keep in mind they are only temporary and if you need the data to be permanent and available after a session, this is not the type of record you want to use. Notice in Figure 4-8 that the record is named ST_LINK_WRK, whereas the record name in Figure 4-9 where information is stored in the record is DERIVED_CO and the naming convention follows the way in which the records are used. In the case of the button it is only a Work Record, and in the case of the information text it is a Derived Record.

- **Subrecord** Is used for SubPages and creates the one-to-many relationship.
- **Dynamic View** Are views that are recreated dynamically with each use.

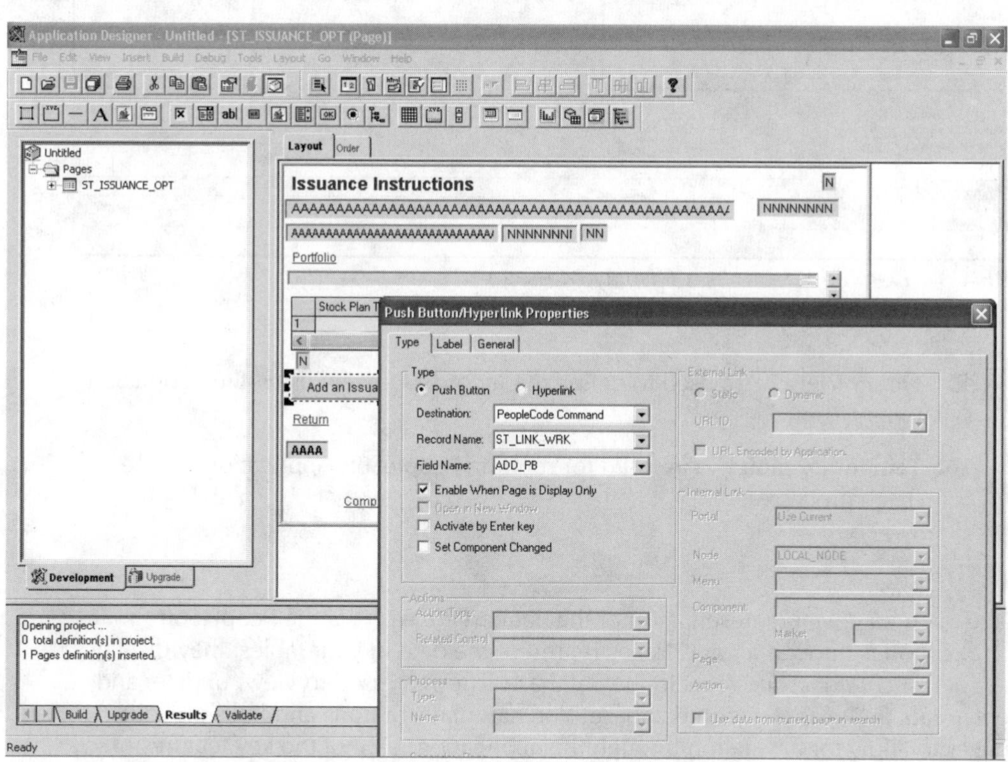

FIGURE 4-8 *Work Record used as a Push Button*

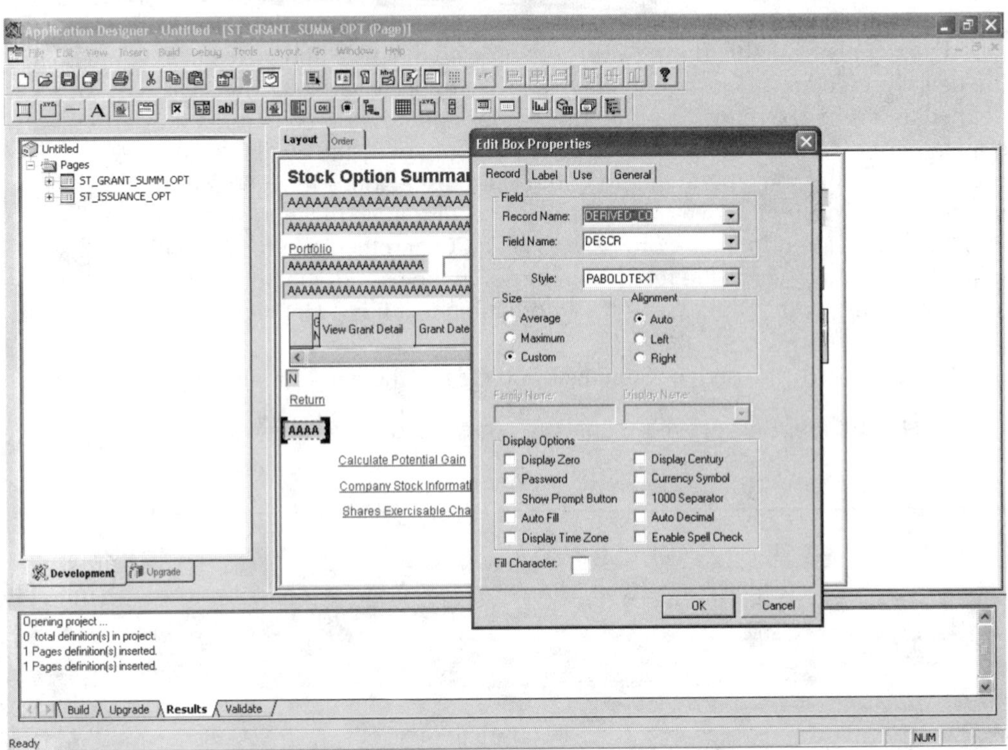

FIGURE 4-9 *Derived Record as a Display Message*

- **Query View** Are used to define the record as a view using the PeopleSoft Query Tool.
- **Temporary tables** Are used for running PeopleSoft Application Engine batch processes.

Pages

The main graphical representation of the data on the web via the PeopleSoft application is through a *page*. Pages represent the data in your tables; they display the fields, columns, and rows in the database. They are used to view, update, and enter data in the application database. You can place buttons and links on your pages to allow for navigation through the application. One of the key features of PeopleSoft is the use of effective dating for the data, and with the use of pages it is important that you understand the use of effective dates and effective sequences. This key feature is how navigation is determined in the PeopleSoft application; it allows for the navigation and the ability to view, edit or, update current, future, or historic data. Take a look at here to see the different types of effective date data.

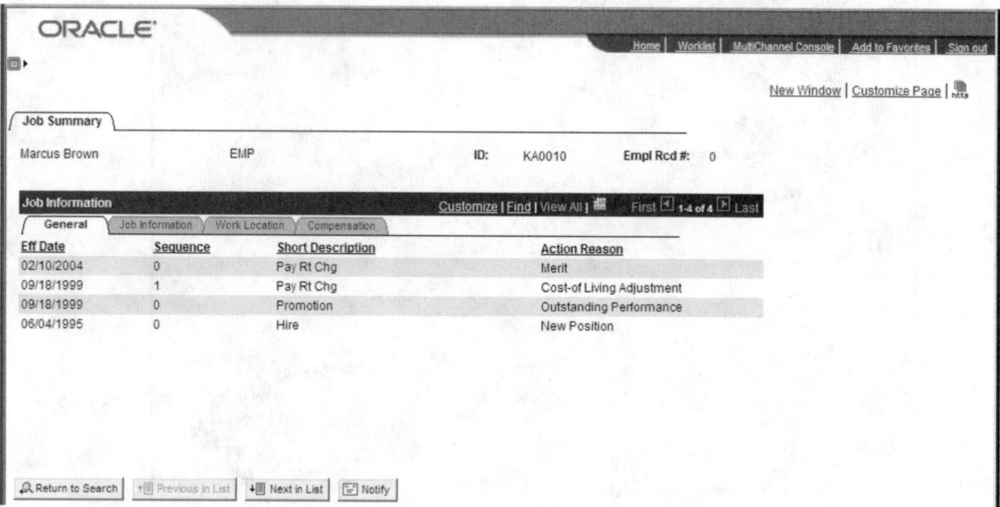

Notice that Marcus Brown has a Job Summary history from 06/04/1995 and with the effective date, we are able to see each of his job changes. Notice also that he has two changes that happen in the same day: on 09/18/1999 he receives a job promotion as well as a pay rate change. This type of activity is handled in conjunction with an effective date and an effective sequence. It is important that the person responsible for entering the data do this type of job action movement on two job records because it allows for effective and efficient reporting. Unfortunately, I have seen all too often cases where the data entry person combines the two actions, promotion and pay raise, on one 09/18/1999 record, and this will cause the developer to lose the ability to easily distinguish that two separate things have occurred.

One of the important elements in your page creation is to determine the mode in which you wish to handle the processing of the data back to the server. It is a difficult balance to strike: the most recent version of the data with the amount of processing power needed to continually swap data back and forth from the Application Server to the Database Server. Most of the PeopleSoft-delivered components run in deferred processing mode; this mode reduces the need for the application to have increased interaction with the server and reduces the number of calls, leading to increased performance. Each trip to the server will refresh the browser page, and too much interaction can lead to screen flicker and slowing down the application. There are two choices for processing modes: deferred mode and interactive mode. Whichever mode you choose for a component will establish the processing functionality for all of the objects within that component.

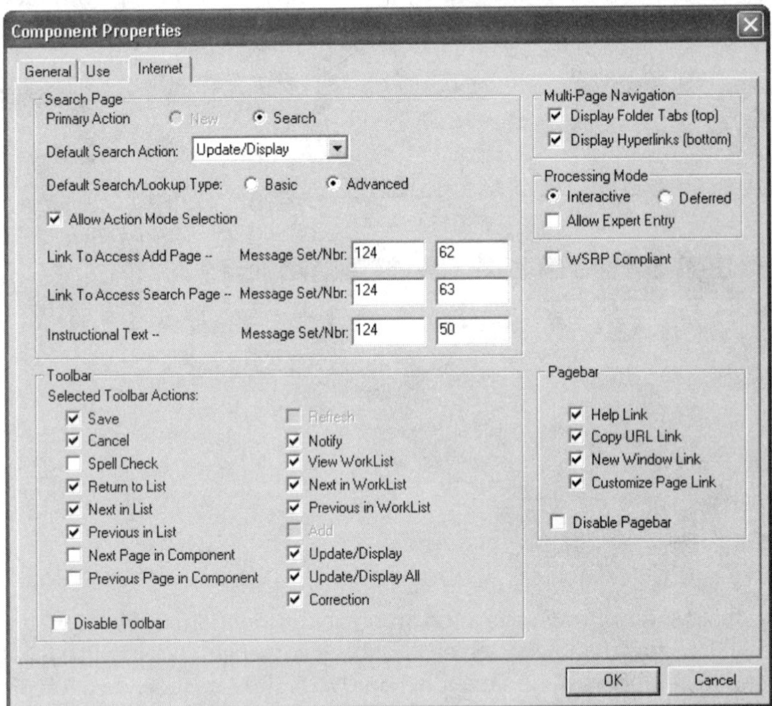

Page Action Options

The page action options are directly related to the actions you can perform on data. The available options are limited to the type of data row that you are trying to retrieve, modify, insert, or update. The rules that are directly linked to effective date are Include History and Correct History actions. It is important to understand that not all tables are effective-dated, and the Include History and Correct History options will only appear in the pages that are effective-dated.

Note that the Update/Display action is easy to implement and directly correlates to the button on the page for Update/Display; however its relation to Include History and Correct History is not as easy to understand. Update/Display All correlates to Include History, and Correction Mode, to Correct History. Update/Display will only retrieve current and add future rows. You can change only future row data—if you are trying to change a current row, this is actually history. Include History will retrieve all rows, and Correct History will allow you to modify and correct current and past data. It is important to understand that each of the corrections and insertions discussed here can only take place if the user has the correct PeopleSoft permission in place that will allow for the data entry or correction.

Update/Display | Include History | Correct History

Page Elements

PeopleSoft pages have three essential types of elements that you can use to design your pages: basic aesthetic elements, for example, lines and pictures; functional elements, which include buttons and links; and data-entry elements, including check boxes and radio buttons. The following are the common elements used in a PeopleSoft page.

- **Frames** Allow you as a Developer to draw a frame around a set of elements and create a group from them. These are display-only boxes that create a grouping of fields on a page.
- **Group boxes** Similar to frames, but they allow for text labels. They group and identify related fields.
- **Horizontal rules** Horizontal lines that are display only.
- **Images** Unchanging graphics on your page; an example would be your Company logo.
- **Text** Static text that is unchanging and can give a set of instructions on a page.
- **Check boxes** These directly correspond to the capturing of data entry for an on/off, yes/no field. A check box has only two options.
- **Radio buttons** Similar to check boxes but allow for a set of options to be chosen in the collection of data entry.
- **Buttons** A button can perform a number of actions, calculate a value, and refresh the fields on the page, open a new page, and help with navigation in the application. Buttons are very dynamic and can be coded to do a variety of actions and navigations.
- **Links** Can redirect the navigation to a new site outside or inside of PeopleSoft.

- **Edit boxes** Allow for data entry. They directly correlate to the field in the database; any limits on type and size are defined by the field. Edit boxes with spell check enabled will display a spell check button.
- **Long edit boxes** Are the same as edit boxes, but they allow for the data entry of longer character strings.
- **Drop-down list boxes** Allow for the selection of a data item for entry from a predefined list.
- **Grids** Grids are spreadsheets on the PeopleSoft page; they allow for the display of one to many relationships on PeopleSoft pages.
- **Scroll areas** These are similar to grids, but the data is displayed in a free-form manner—not in a spreadsheet-type display. Both grids and scroll areas allow for the sharing for key data into each new row that is created. These keys become important in the creation of scroll levels in the component and can cause problems with sharing of data between multiple levels. In Figure 4-10 you can see two of the scroll levels in the JOB_DATA component.

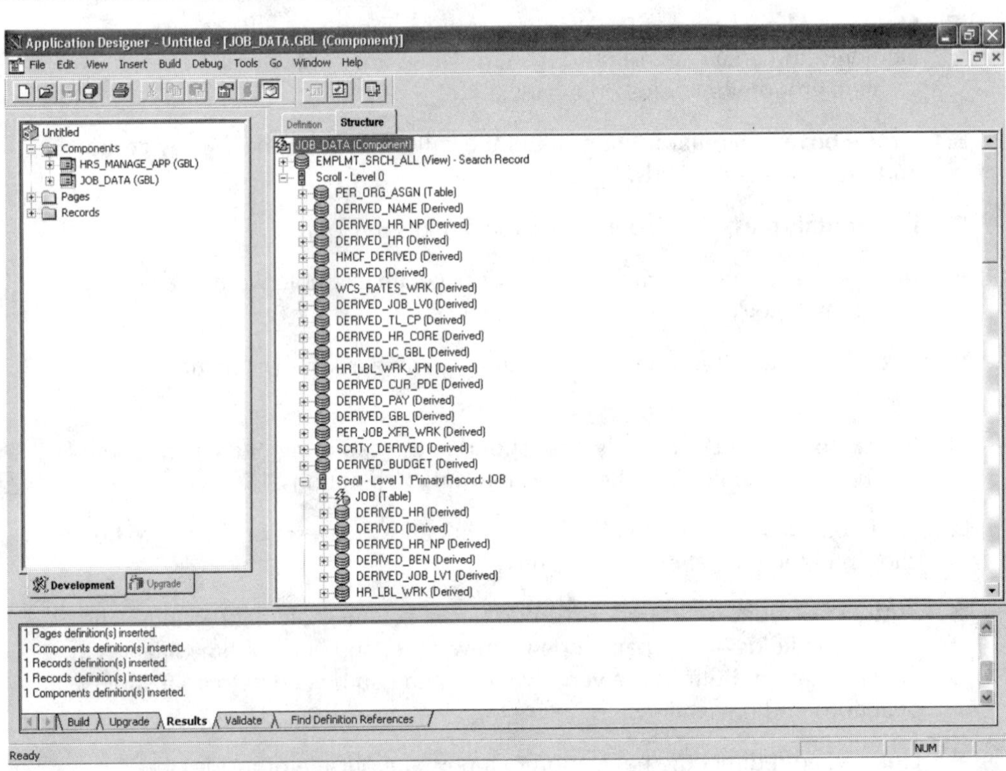

FIGURE 4-10 *Scroll levels in JOB_DATA component*

Components

A *component* is derived from several pages and defines the way that the page will behave in the Internet browser. It is also where you define the pages that display as tabs across the top of the page. Pages and components are closely linked. For example, take a look at the JOB_DATA component in Figure 4-11. Figure 4-12 shows the way the page looks in the application.

The component is based on the page and the properties that define the way that the page will be displayed in the browser. The component interface takes this same approach but exposes the properties to third-party software languages; it consists of the set of properties and methods that follow an object-oriented programming model. You can use the properties or methods specified in the component so that other external applications can gain access to the component. The component interface gives access to external applications with the standard methods in Java, C/C++, COM, and SOA.

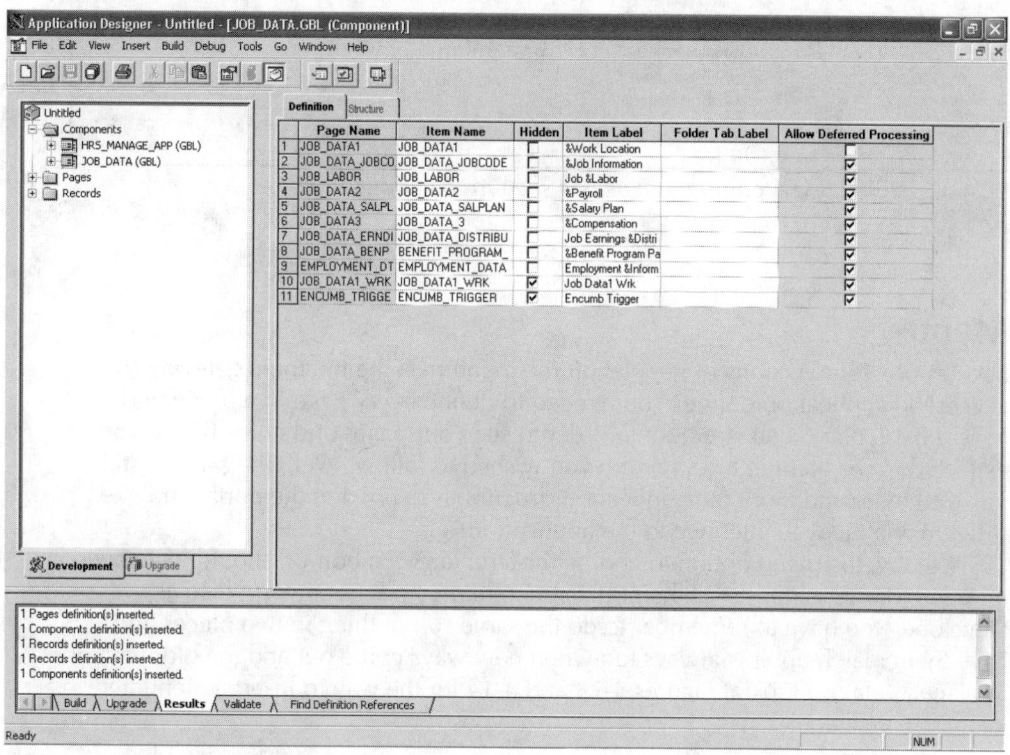

FIGURE 4-11 *JOB_DATA component*

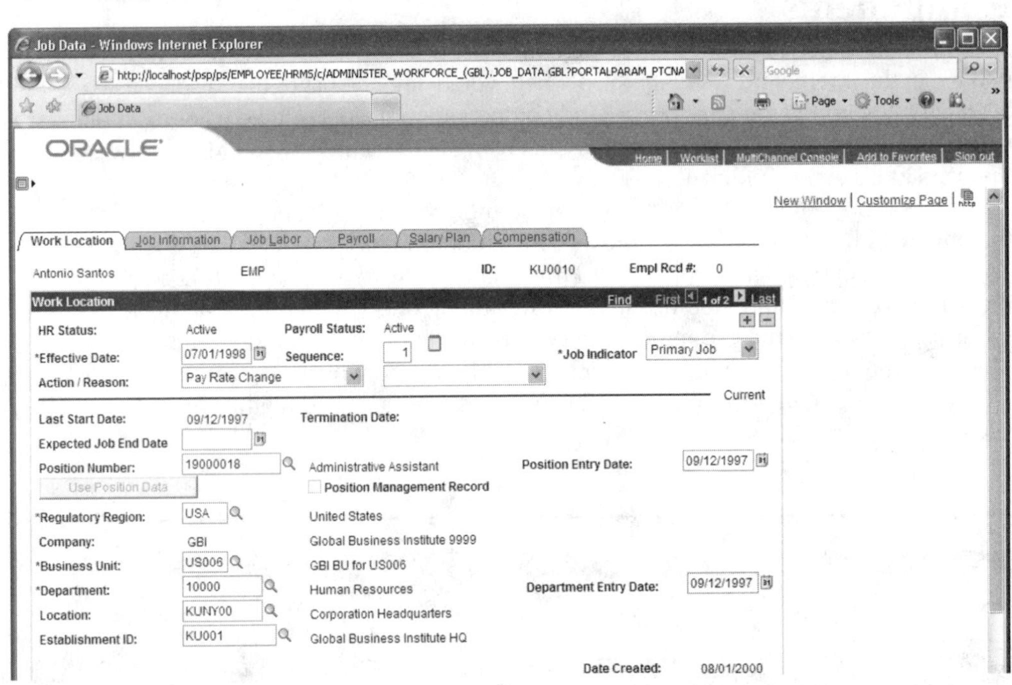

FIGURE 4-12 *JOB_DATA component as it is seen in the application*

Menus

Back in previous versions of PeopleSoft the menu became the main gateway to access the application online. You needed to define every page in a menu and have a particular menu structure in order to see your pages and items where you expected to see them in the structure you wished to follow. Well, the same is still true, but more and more the application structure is defined in the portal and structure via the web interface to the application.

Actually, the menu option to coding the structure of a bolt-on should have been dropped long ago in favor of the portal structure method. But it wasn't, so as a Developer you have to remember to do the same sort of thing in two places and have them match up. It is always fun when new ways come out and the old remains in place. So take a look at Figures 4-13 and 4-14 for the way to insert a menu item,

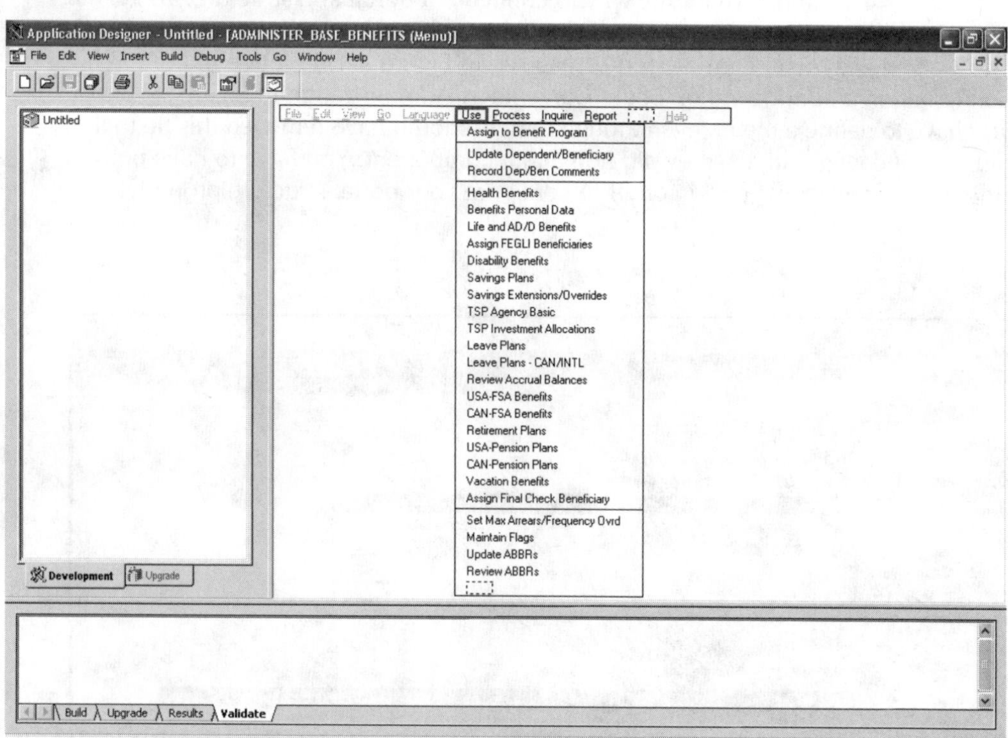

FIGURE 4-13 *Menu structure*

FIGURE 4-14 *Insert a new menu item*

and Figures 4-15 and 4-16 for the way to configure a portal and structure. To get the screen to add a new menu, go to the blank area at the bottom of the menu, right-click, and go to menu item properties you see in Figure 4-14. Notice in the configuration and/or definition of the Content Ref Administration in Figure 4-16 that you have to define a menu (even though Oracle should have removed this tie to the old way of configuration—they did not) and a component. You have to have both "the what" and "the where" in order to configure your portal structure properly.

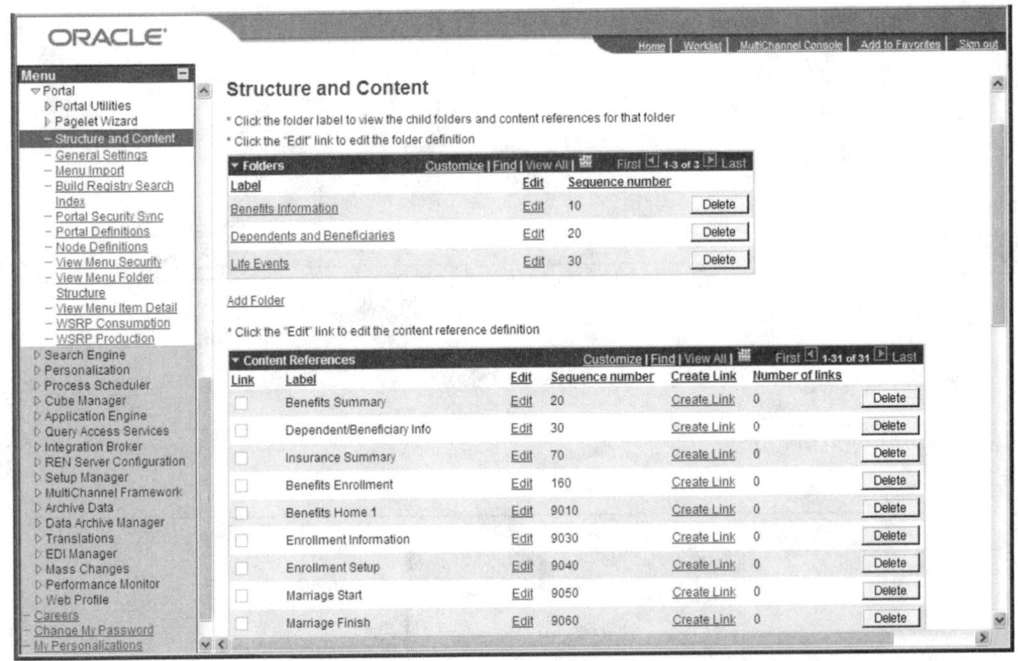

FIGURE 4-15 *Portal structure and content*

FIGURE 4-16 *Content Ref Administration*

Roles and Permission Lists

Permission and security are tied to the page through the component and menu. Notice in Figure 4-17 what is defined in the Permission List object is the menu under the Page tab. A *role* is defined as one or more permission lists, and a permission list is defined as access to one or more pages via the component.

PeopleCode

There are two types of PeopleCode available to you as a Developer: PeopleSoft Component Interface PeopleCode, fired off by an object like a button on an event,

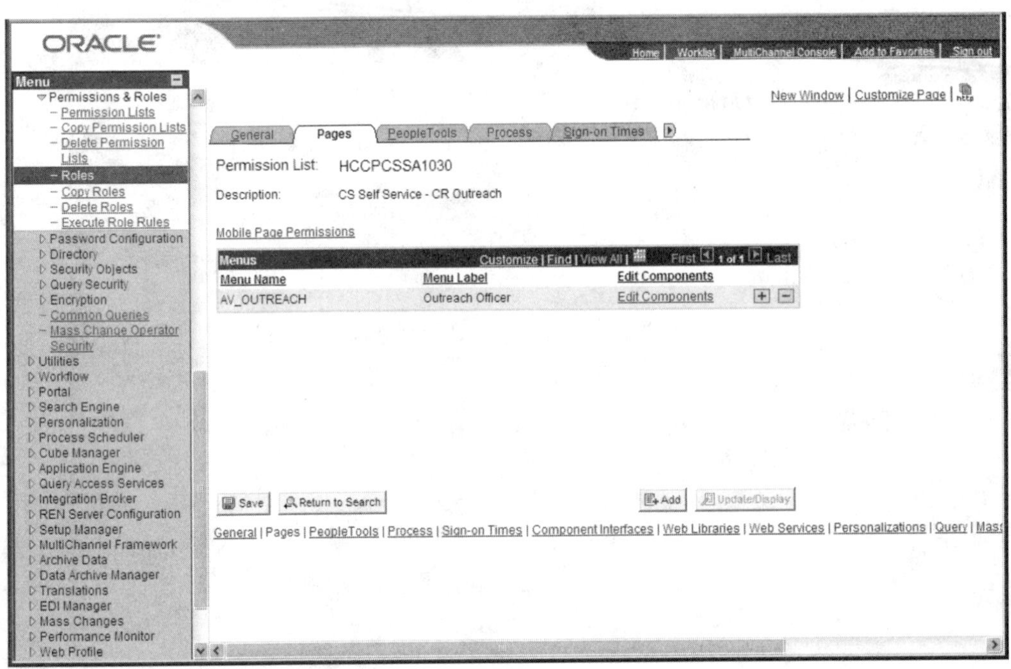

FIGURE 4-17 *Role definition*

and PeopleSoft Application Engine PeopleCode. It is important to understand that PeopleCode is the language that is written via the Application Designer interface. PeopleCode is a PeopleSoft proprietary language that is object-oriented. With its dot notation and methods it is similar in structure to Visual Basic and Java. But it also has features that allow for direct interaction with the database and the ability to embed SQL right into the code.

Chapter 6 will go into detail about the PeopleCode structure, variable declaration, comments, and overall code writing specifics. For now it is important to understand that with Application Designer, with components, or with Application Engine you will be able to write method-driven object-oriented code to create customized bolt-on screens. In Figure 14-18 you can see PeopleCode that was

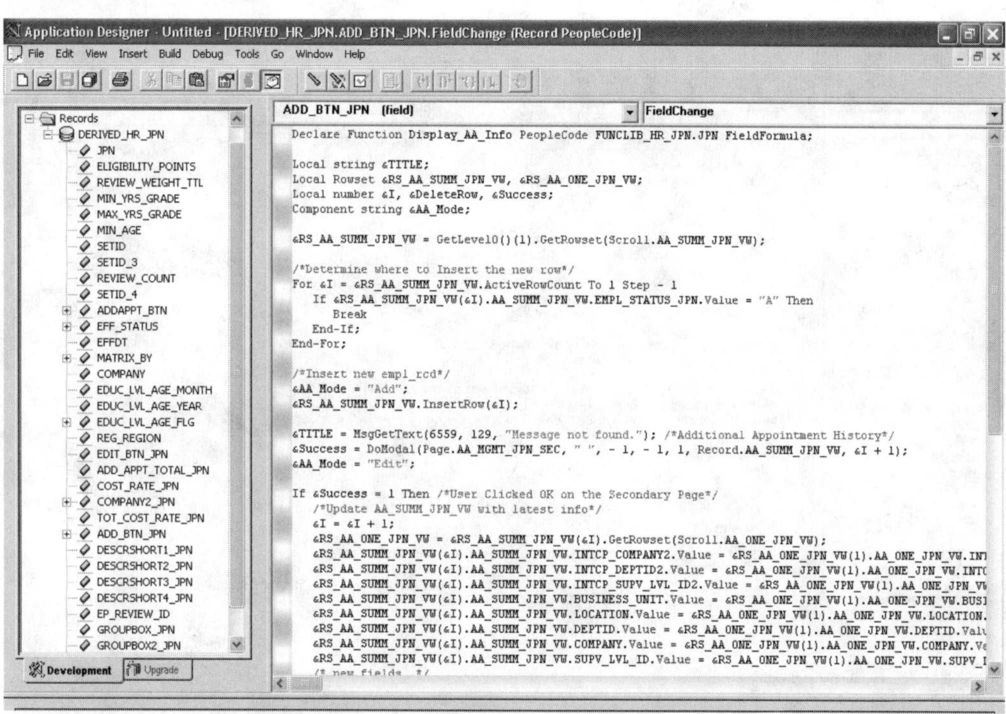

FIGURE 4-18 *Method PeopleCode*

written on a method within a component, and in Figure 14-19 you can see PeopleCode that was written within Application Engine.

HTML

With Derived Records you can display an HTML object on a PeopleSoft page. Why would you want to do that? Well, often you may be asked to make a page more dynamic than straight text. Personally, I was recently asked to do a page that defined the methodologies of a bolt-on—how it worked, where the formulas came from, and so on. The customer wanted it to have embedded hyperlinks to other pages, and a hyperlink to allow for comments to be quickly e-mailed out to the person responsible. They also wanted to use all of the standard web page design elements, like bolding, font sizes, underline, and color. The easiest way to do this

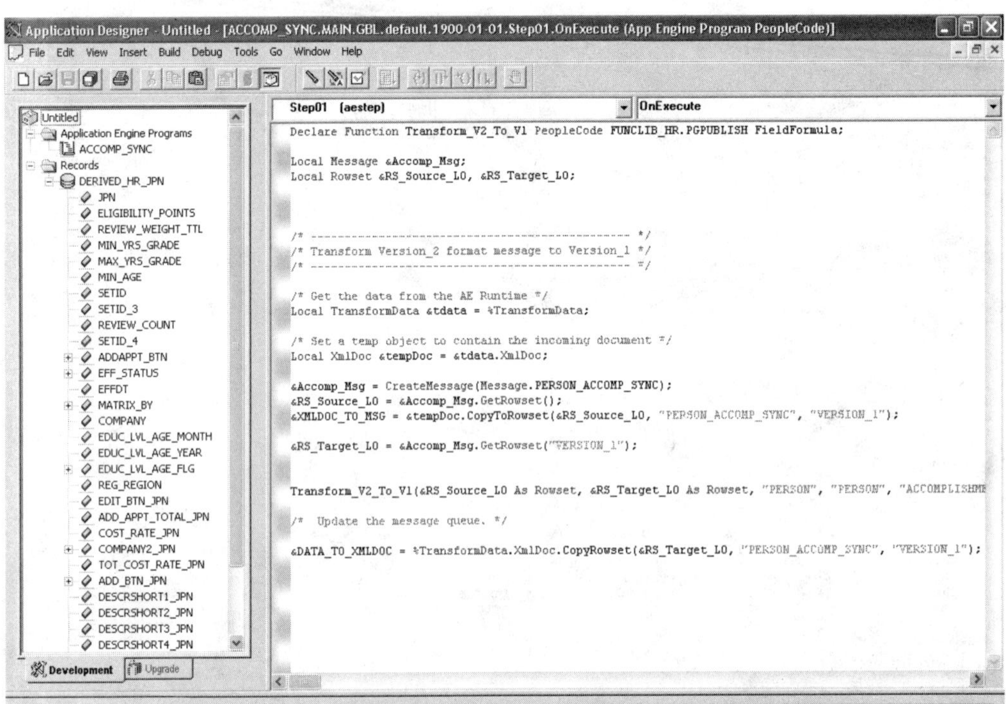

FIGURE 4-19 *Application Engine PeopleCode*

was to embed an HTML object in a page and allow the use in PeopleSoft of standard HTML code. The following are the easy, efficient steps to do this:

1. Create a new HTML object and put your HTML code in the blank object screen.

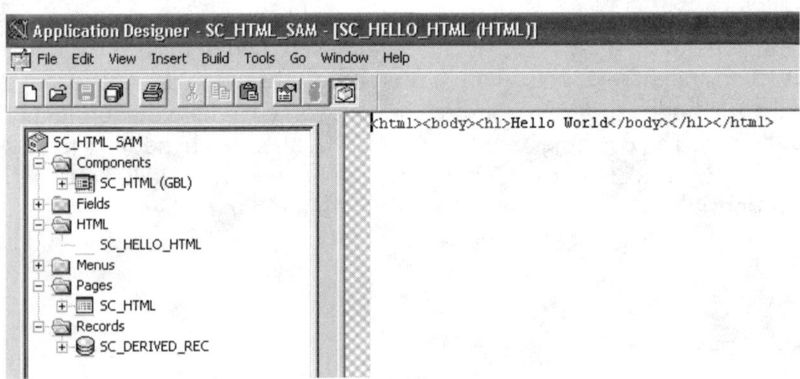

2. Create a Derived Record to store the HTML Field.

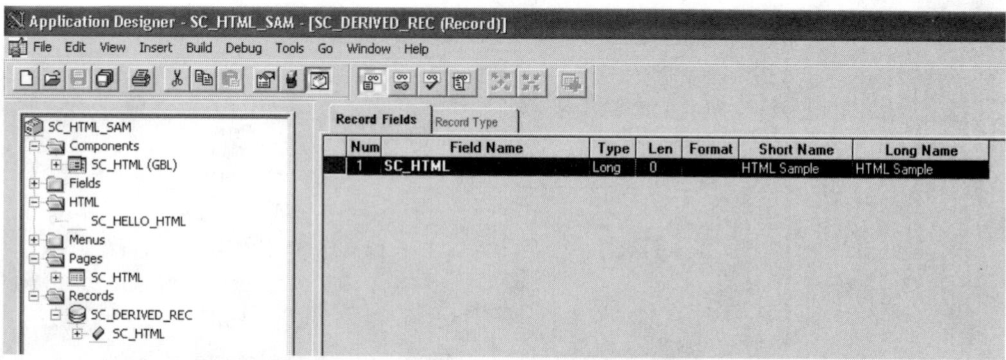

3. Create a Page with an HTML Object area on the page.

4. Set the HTML Object Properties.

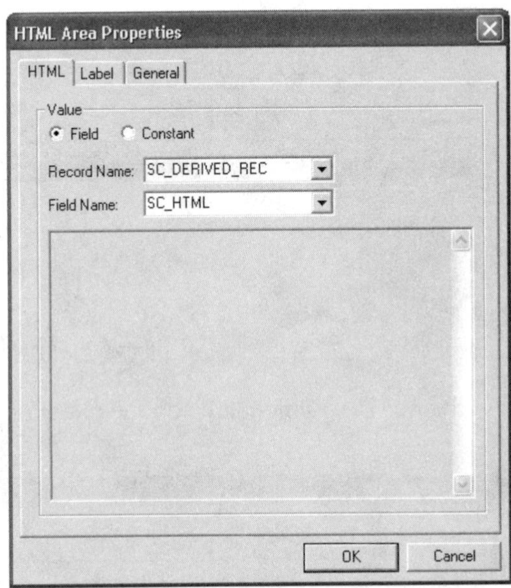

5. Set the Field Formula Property of the HTML Object.

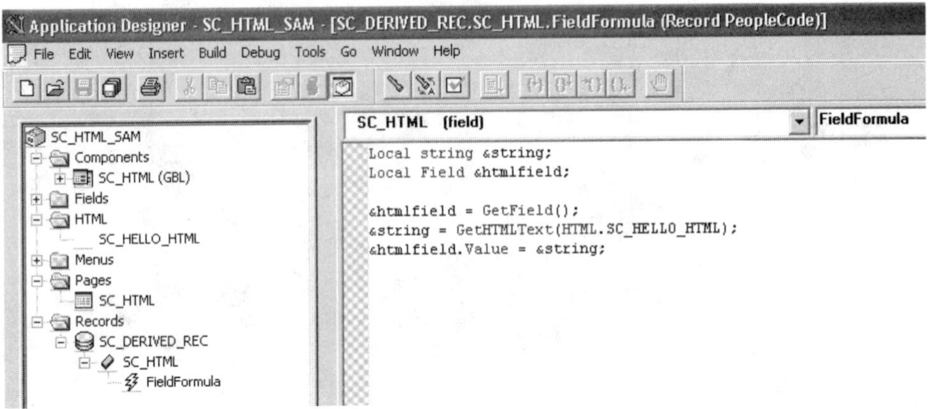

6. Add a page to a component.

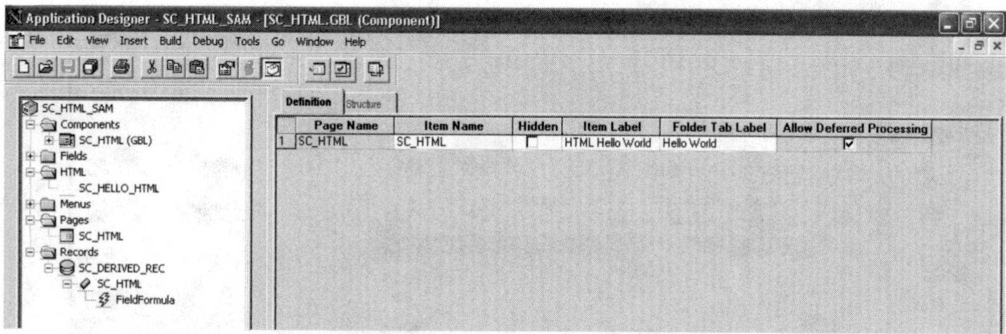

7. Add a component to a menu.

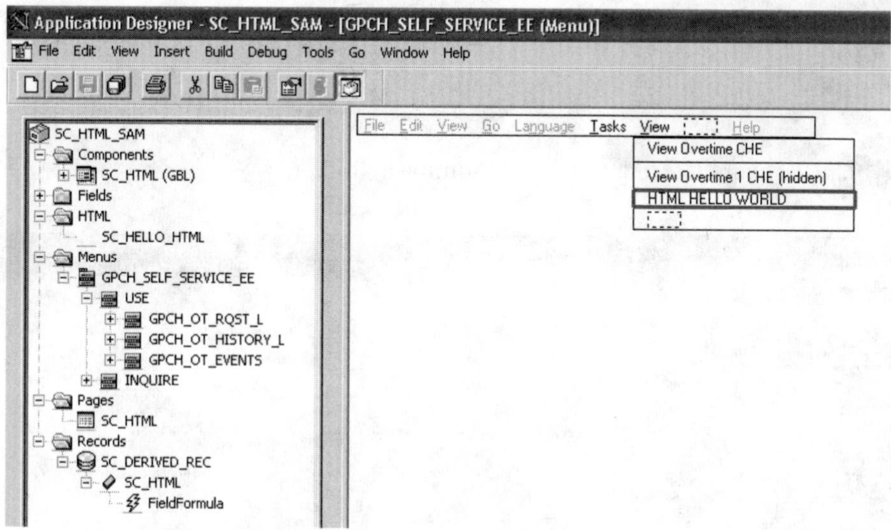

8. Add a component to a portal.

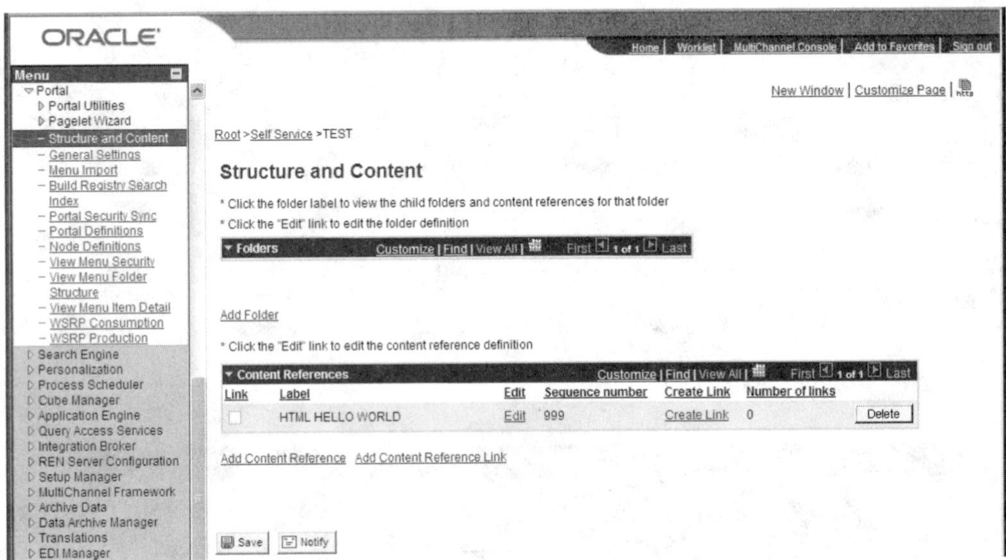

9. Configure Content Reference Administration.

10. Add a component to a permission list.

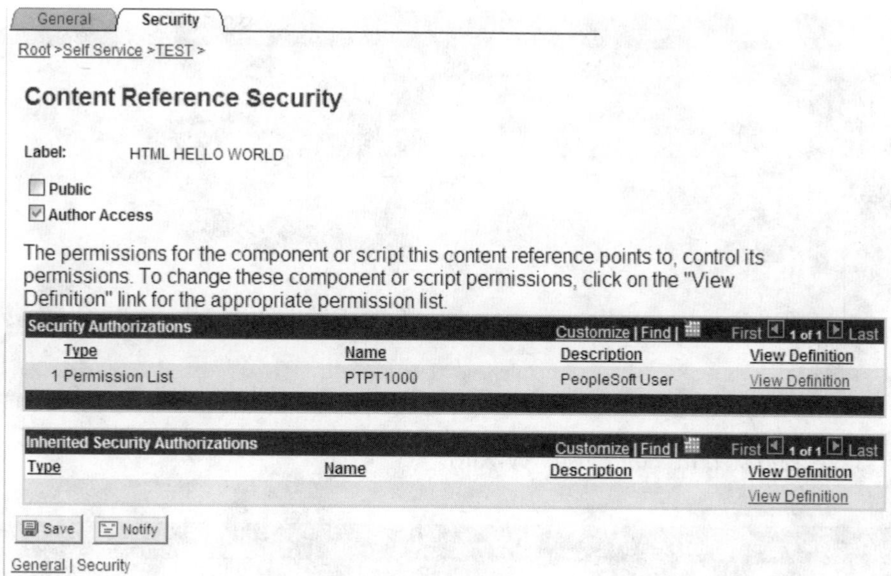

11. Register the Component, Menu, and the Permission List in the Registry Wizard.

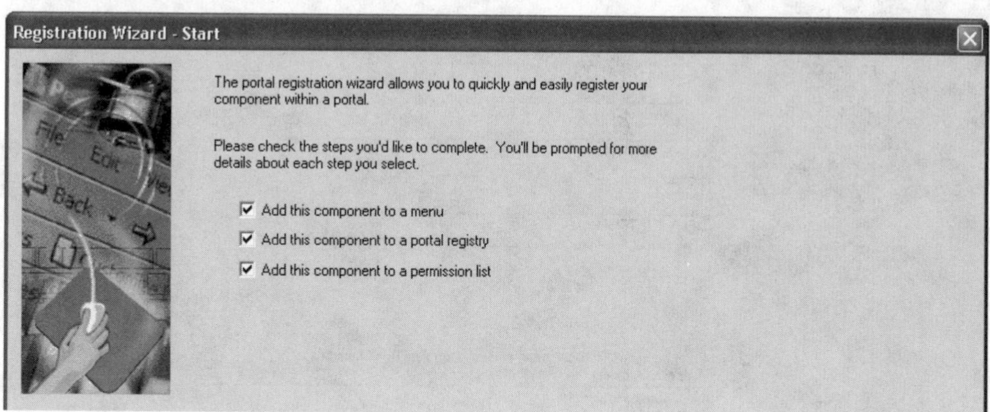

12. First step in the Registry Wizard.

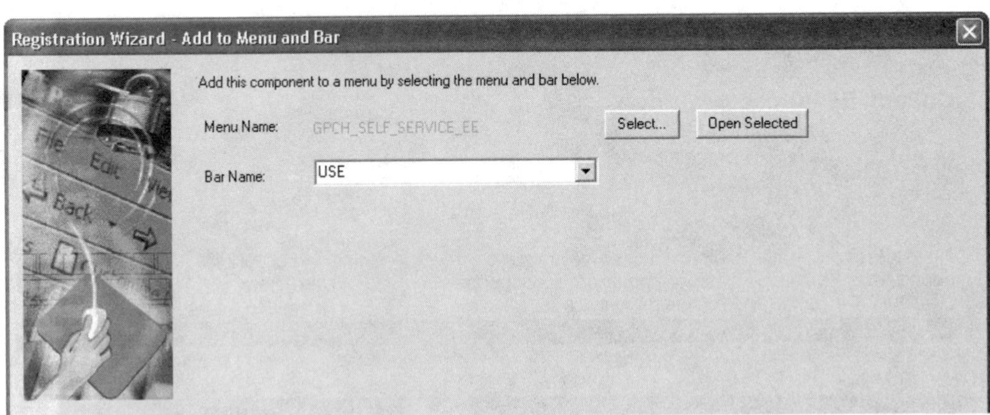

13. Second step in the Registry Wizard.

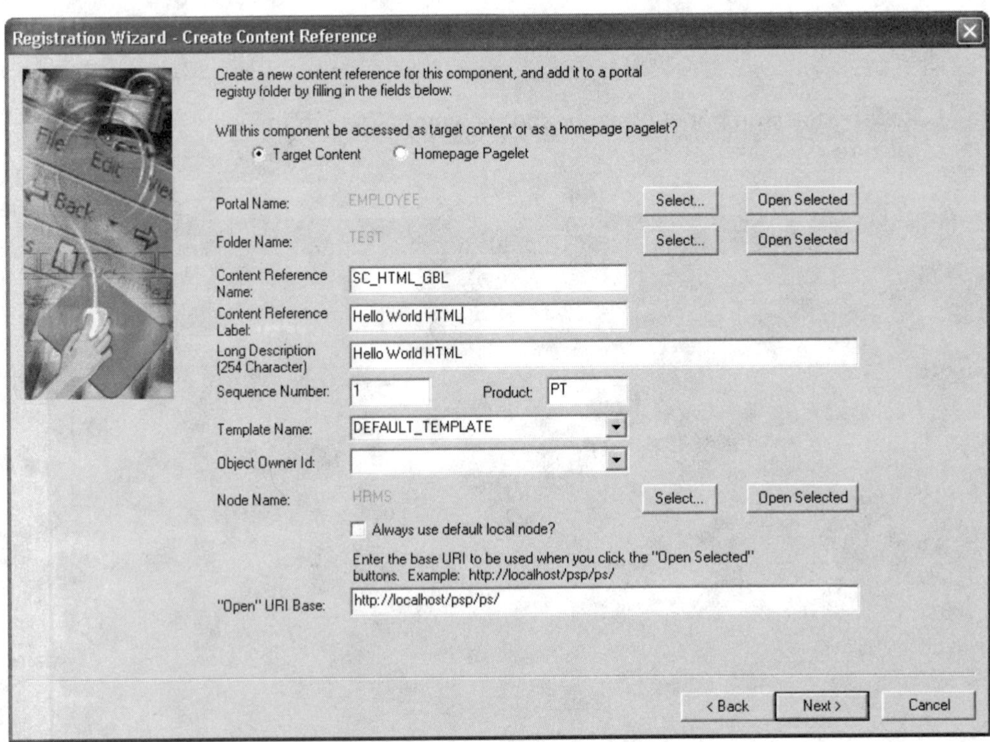

14. Third step in the Registry Wizard.

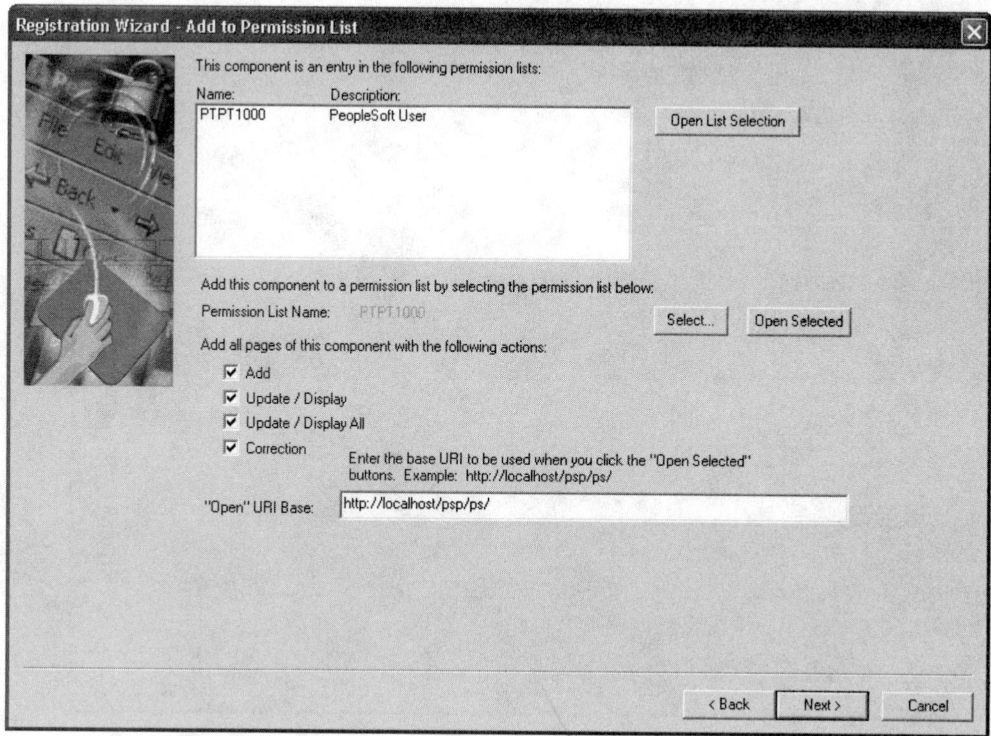

15. Fourth and final step in the Registry Wizard.

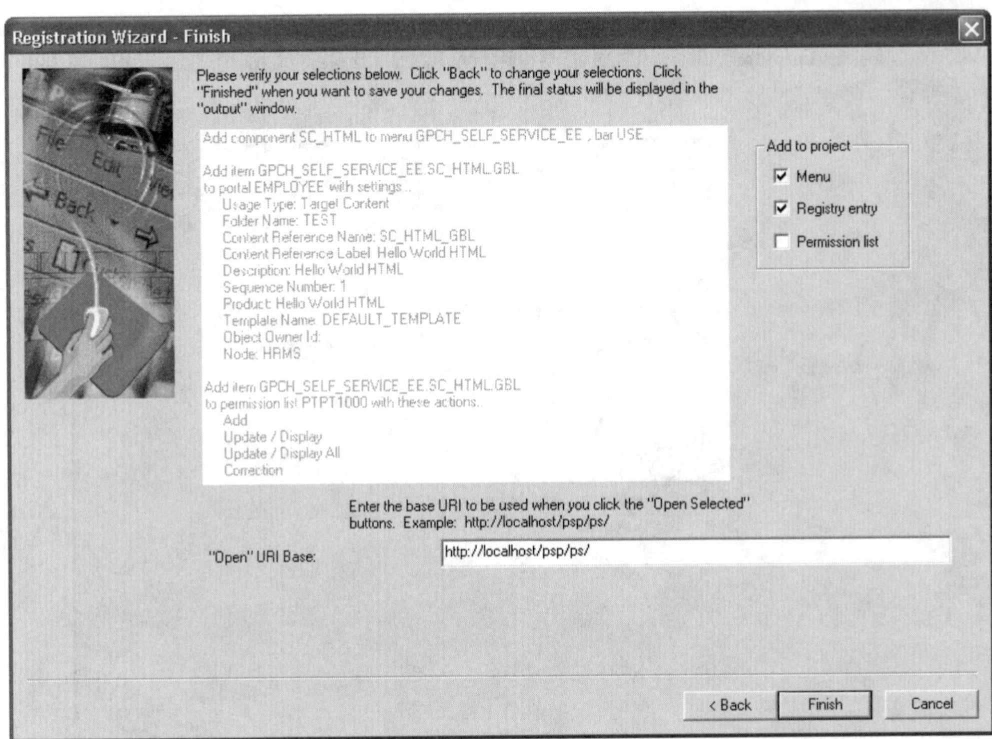

16. View your Hello World Page.

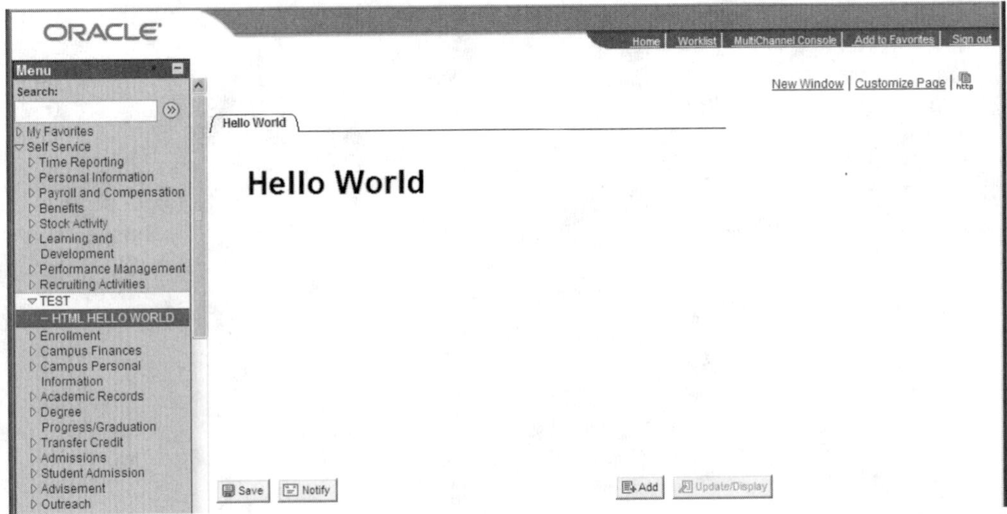

Message Catalogs

You add and maintain system messages using the Message Catalog page. In Figure 4-20 you can see the Message Set 3, which is the General PeopleSoft Messages. You can create your own Message Set and maintain a customized message catalog for your bolt-on. Keep in mind it is just like anything customized that you create in PeopleSoft: it has to be maintained, and you have to make a conscientious effort to make certain your customizations carry over in an upgrade. PeopleSoft reserves all message set numbers up to 20,000. If you create customized message sets or edit a delivered message set with a number less than 20,000, it will be overwritten in future upgrades.

PeopleSoft error messages are maintained by set number and are all stored in the Message Catalog. The sets are organized by category, and the categories range from PeopleTools Message Bar Items and PeopleCode Runtime Messages to PeopleSoft Payroll and PeopleSoft General Ledger application messages. PeopleTools will use some of the messages, but the majority are used by the application and get called by the Error, Warning, Message Box, MsgGet, and MsgGetText built-in PeopleCode functions.

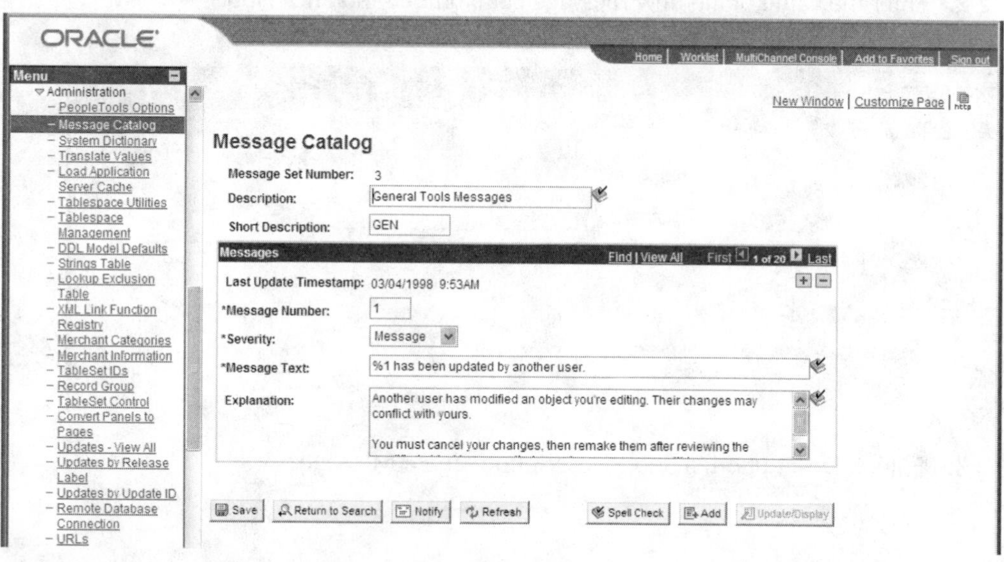

FIGURE 4-20 *Message Catalog—Message Set 3c*

To add a message set:

1. Go to PeopleTools | Utilities | Administration | Message Catalog, and on the search page click Add New Value.

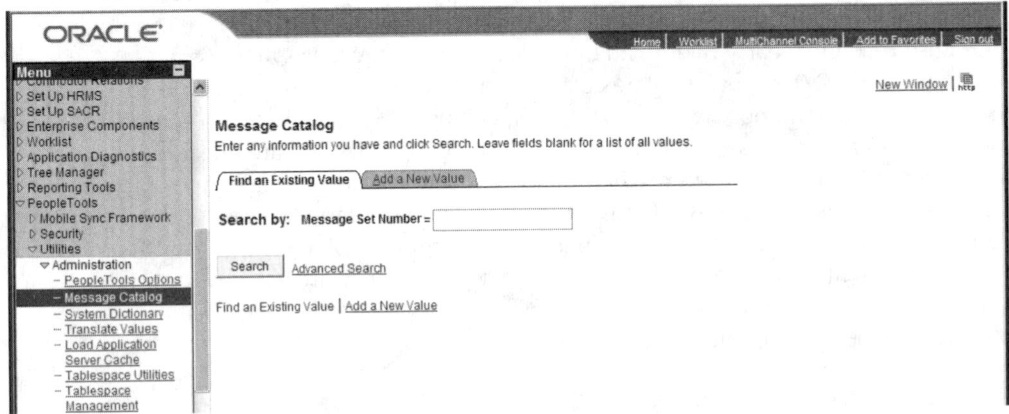

2. Enter the value of the new Message Set Number and click Add.

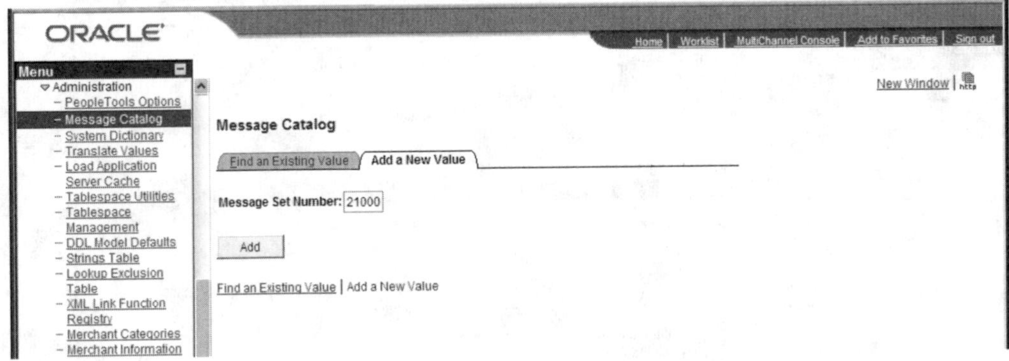

3. Enter a Description, a Short Description, and a Message.

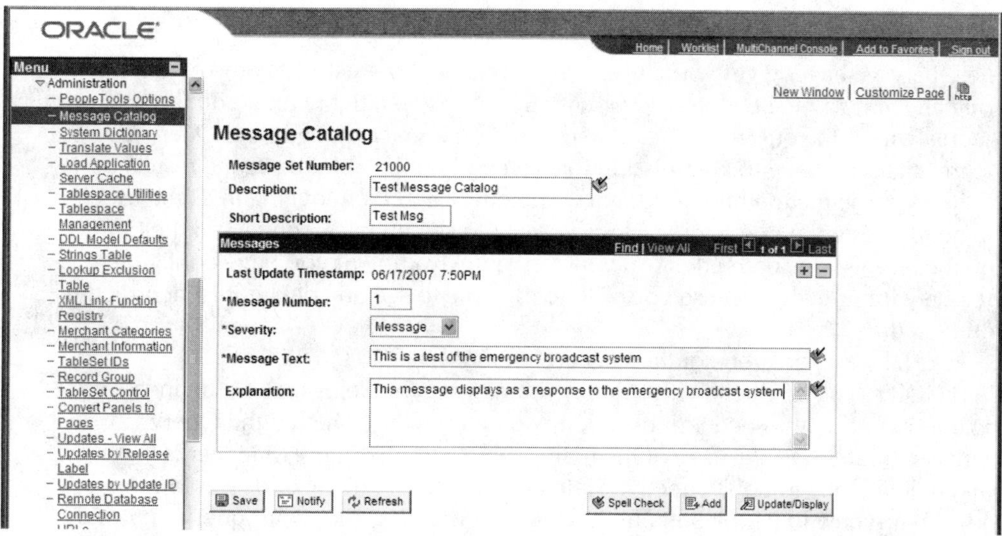

4. Save.

To add a message to a Message Set:

1. Open the Message Set.
2. Click the plus sign button to add a new row.

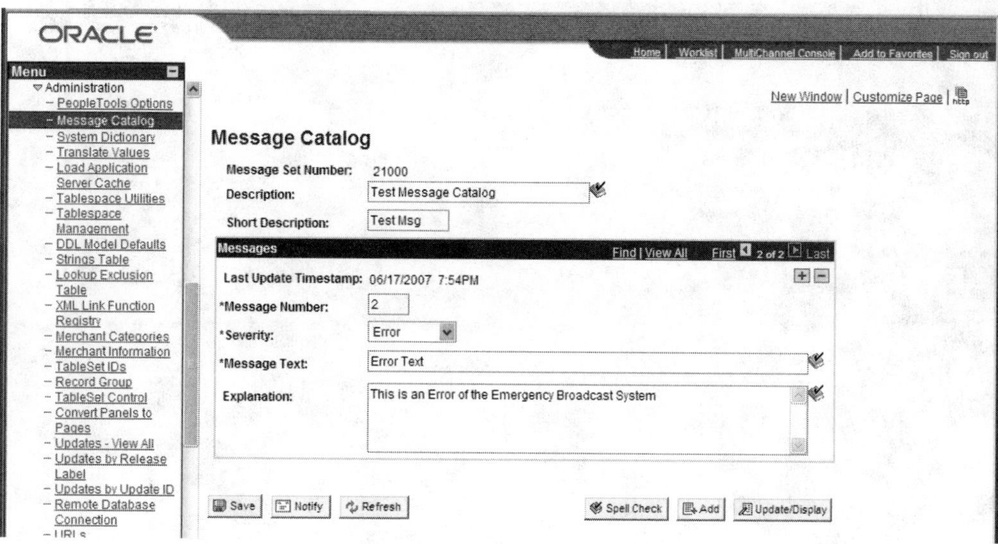

Query Manager

The Query Manager gives you a useful GUI interface to create customized queries. You can create a nice end-user layer with trees to keep a tight handle on the security within the queries. Unless the record you are accessing in the Query is in the tree that you have the permission for, you will not be able to see the results of the query. I use the method of designing the query and then logging in as the user I intend to design the query for in Development to see if I have configured the tree and the permissions correctly. You will very quickly know if you have configured the query incorrectly because you will not be able to see any data if it is incorrectly configured.

Let's take a look at one of the delivered queries, AD703___RECRUIT_CATEGORY_TBL. In the first illustration you can see the fields that are defined in the query. And in the second illustration you can see the SQL that the Query Manager creates for you. One of the main features of the Query Manager is that it will automatically join the Effective Date and Effective Sequence for you properly, so if you are new to PeopleSoft and having a hard time getting your queries properly written, use the Query Manager to help create the queries you need.

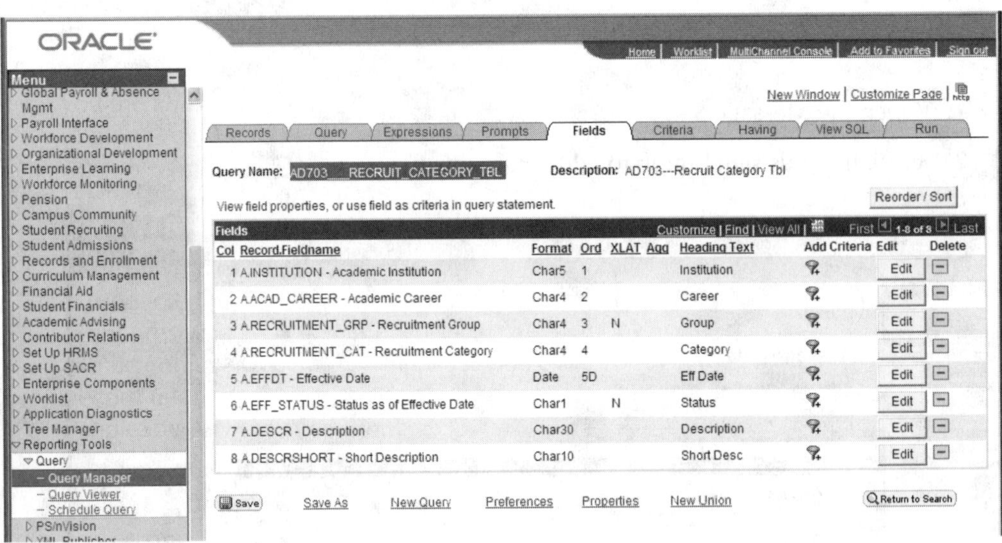

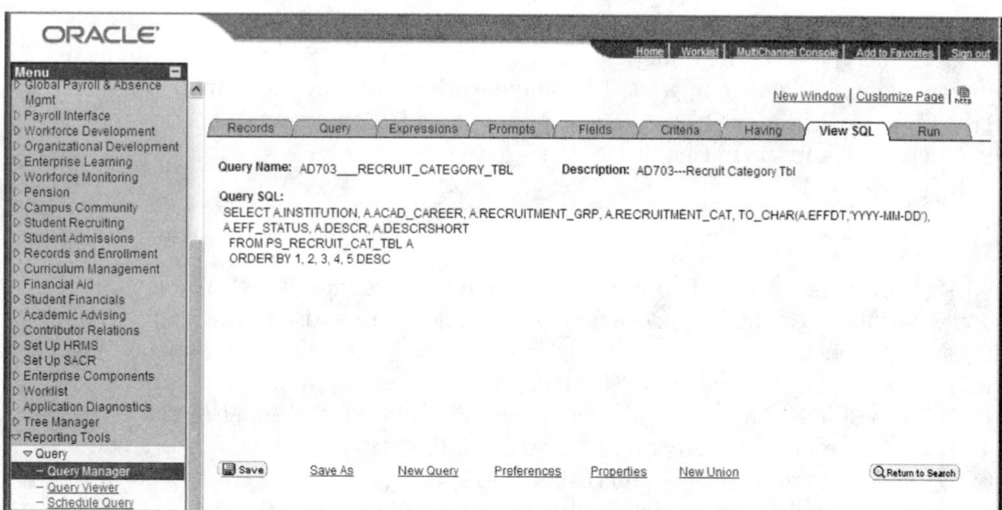

You also get the added advantage in your queries of running them and dropping the results into Excel. This is a nice feature: you can convert your ad hoc queries into queries in the Query Manager, give your customers access, and allow them to run them on demand and put the results into Excel. The next illustration shows the AD703_RECRUIT_CATEGORY_TBL Query results in Excel.

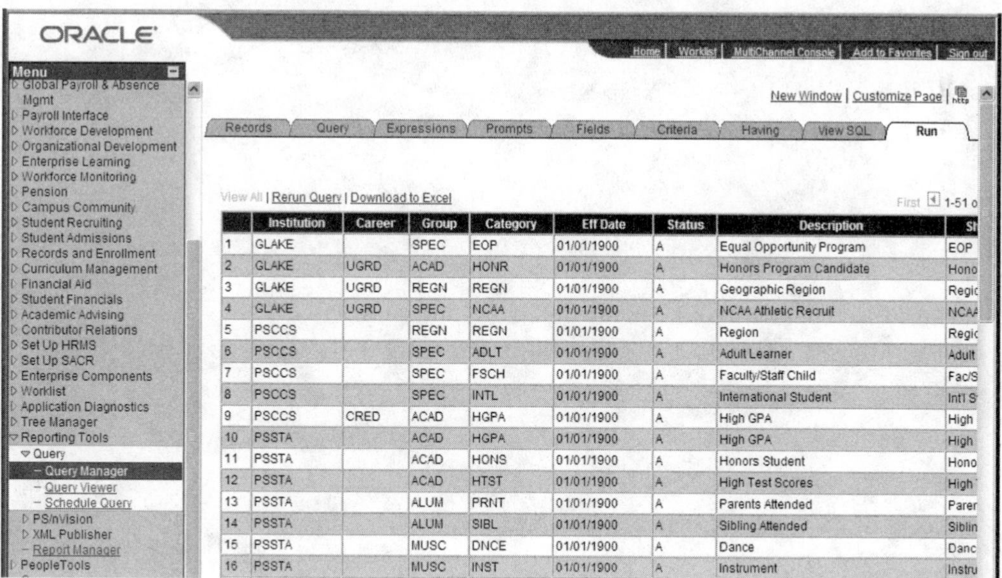

	Institution	Career	Group	Category	Eff Date	Status	Description	Sh
1	GLAKE		SPEC	EOP	01/01/1900	A	Equal Opportunity Program	EOP
2	GLAKE	UGRD	ACAD	HONR	01/01/1900	A	Honors Program Candidate	Hono
3	GLAKE	UGRD	REGN	REGN	01/01/1900	A	Geographic Region	Regic
4	GLAKE	UGRD	SPEC	NCAA	01/01/1900	A	NCAA Athletic Recruit	NCAA
5	PSCCS		REGN	REGN	01/01/1900	A	Region	Regic
6	PSCCS		SPEC	ADLT	01/01/1900	A	Adult Learner	Adult
7	PSCCS		SPEC	FSCH	01/01/1900	A	Faculty/Staff Child	Fac/S
8	PSCCS		SPEC	INTL	01/01/1900	A	International Student	Intl S
9	PSCCS	CRED	ACAD	HGPA	01/01/1900	A	High GPA	High
10	PSSTA		ACAD	HGPA	01/01/1900	A	High GPA	High
11	PSSTA		ACAD	HONS	01/01/1900	A	Honors Student	Hono
12	PSSTA		ACAD	HTST	01/01/1900	A	High Test Scores	High
13	PSSTA		ALUM	PRNT	01/01/1900	A	Parents Attended	Parer
14	PSSTA		ALUM	SIBL	01/01/1900	A	Sibling Attended	Siblin
15	PSSTA		MUSC	DNCE	01/01/1900	A	Dance	Danc
16	PSSTA		MUSC	INST	01/01/1900	A	Instrument	Instru

Users can have the permission (depending on what the security administrator has given them) to save their queries, modify existing queries and save them under a different name, and delete queries. The difference is if they have security permission to the Query Manager or Query Viewer. A more detailed treatment of queries and the Query Tool appears in Chapter 9.

Summary

In this chapter the basics of PeopleSoft development were introduced. You learned about navigation, Application Designer, projects, fields, records, translate values, pages, components, menus, PeopleCode, HTML, message catalogs, and queries. As the book progresses, we will go into detailed coding methods and tips and tricks that you can utilize as a PeopleSoft Developer. It is important to understand the basics before we move quickly on to the advanced topics. The chapter showed you how to create a translate value, an HTML Hello World page, and a basic query with the Query Manager. For more details about Queries, see Chapter 9.

CHAPTER 5

PeopleSoft Pages

his chapter will give you a through understanding of PeopleSoft Pages, how to modify delivered PeopleSoft pages, and how to create them from scratch. We will look at each of the elements that can be placed on a page from aesthetic controls such as static text to data entry controls, and demonstrate how to create your own customized page to accept data into a record. The PeopleSoft page is the main functionality in the PeopleSoft developer's coding bag of tricks. Once you have an understanding of pages you can build on your skills in later chapters to become a proficient PeopleSoft developer.

The Page

This chapter introduces the basic element in the development in PeopleSoft, the page. Earlier versions of PeopleSoft, prior to the introduction of PeopleSoft on the Internet, referred to the page as a *panel.* In Version 8 the "panel" became the "page" because it is a web page.

The most common request that a PeopleSoft developer will get is to make a slight change, such as adding or moving a field or changing a header, to a delivered PeopleSoft page. Any customized bolt-ons that your company may develop would be PeopleSoft pages developed from scratch. Since the page is the main element in PeopleSoft development it is important to understand how to do customizations to a page.

Page Controls

There are three types of controls that are available to use on a page:

- Aesthetic controls
- Data entry controls
- Function and data processing controls

You decide which type of control you want to use based on what type of data you want to display, how you want it displayed, and what you would like the page to look like. In Figure 5-1 you can see the page controls available from the toolbar.

In Figure 5-2 you can see the page controls in order of control. This menu can be seen under Insert on the main menu.

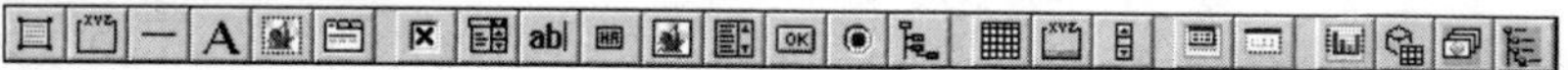

FIGURE 5-1 *Toolbar page controls*

Aesthetic Controls

Aesthetic controls are just what they sound like—controls that allow you to make the page look the way you want, organize it the way you would like, and give messages out to the user of the page with text. Aesthetic controls are not associated with data in the database; they are only used on a one-time basis on a page to give the look and feel you would like. They do not relate back to a record nor do they change the property for reuse on other pages. Aesthetic controls are described in the following sections.

Frame	F
Group Box	B
Horizontal Rule	N
Static Text	X
Static Image	M
Tab Separator	A
Check Box	C
Drop-Down List Box	D
Edit Box	E
HTML Area	H
Image	I
Long Edit Box	L
Push Button/Hyperlink	P
Radio Button	R
Tree	T
Grid	G
Scroll Area	S
Scroll Bar	O
Secondary Page	Y
Subpage	U
Chart	Q
Analytic Grid	Y
ActiveX Controls...	
Current Definition into Project	F7
Definitions into Project...	Ctrl+F7

FIGURE 5-2 *List of page controls on the Insert menu*

Chart

In the following illustration, you can see the drawing of a chart frame, which is a placeholder on the page drawn as a box during design and during runtime using PeopleCode. The chart will be populated with the GetChart field type.

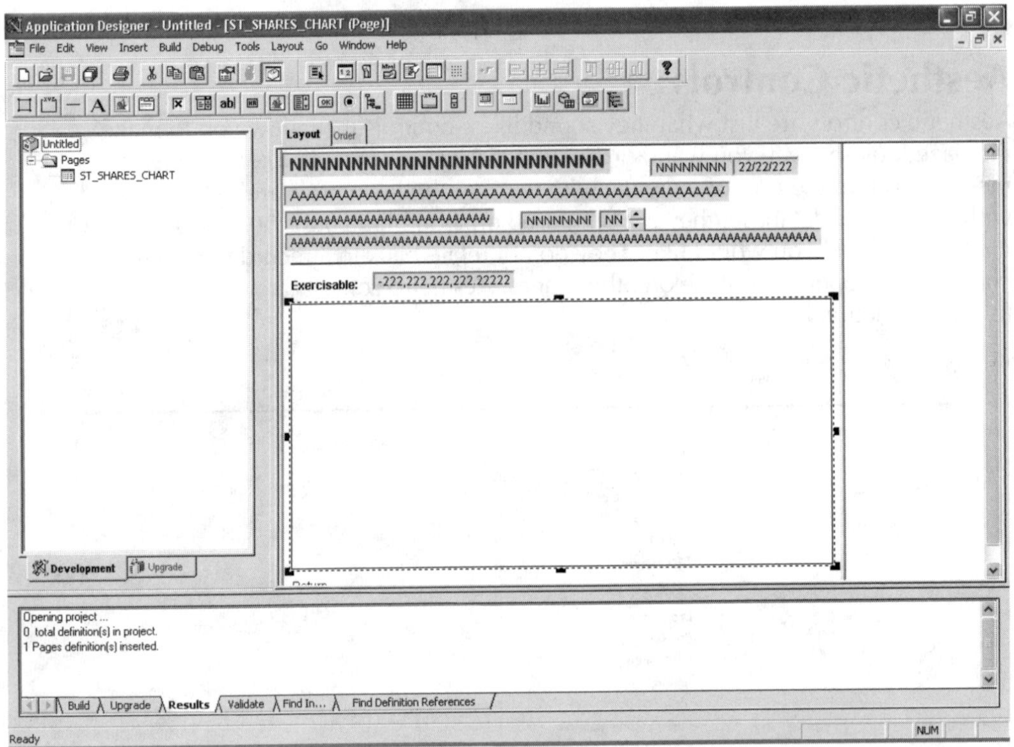

Next, you can see what the chart looks like during runtime, even though the user has not executed any options.

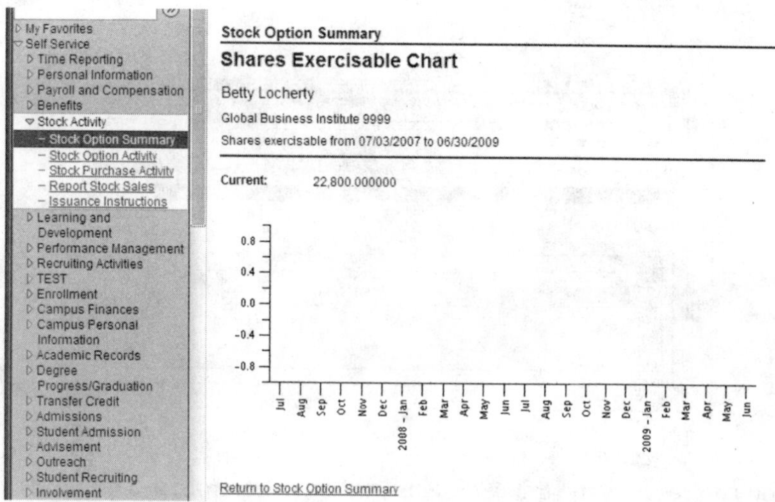

And, finally, you can see the PeopleCode behind the creation of the chart; the difference is you are a regular employee going through Self Service or a Manager. You can clearly see the creation of the X and Y axes for the chart.

```
ST_SHARES_CHART (page)                    Activate

Global CO_NAVIGATN:Stack &MyNavStack;
Global string &CurrCRefName;

Local Chart &StockChart;
Component Rowset &RSChart;
Component number &CurrentChartValue;

/* create return link */
&MyNavStack.initPage( False, 0, 0, True, &CurrCRefName, True);

/* instantiate the chart */
&StockChart = GetChart(CO_CHART_WRK.CHARTFIELD);

/* set data record for the chart */
&StockChart.SetData(&RSChart);

/* set x and y axis data for the specific component */
If %Component = Component.ST_GRANT_SUMM_MGR Then
   &StockChart.SetDataYAxis(CO_CHART_WRK.SHARES_AVAILABLE);
   &StockChart.SetDataXAxis(CO_CHART_WRK.YEAR);
   CO_CHART_WRK.SHARES_EXERCISABLE.Visible = False;
Else
   &StockChart.SetDataYAxis(CO_CHART_WRK.SHARES_AVAILABLE);
   &StockChart.SetDataXAxis(CO_CHART_WRK.MONTH_NAME);
   &StockChart.XAxisLabelOrient = %ChartText_Vertical;
   CO_CHART_WRK.SHARES_EXERCISABLE.Label = MsgGetText(1120, 346, "Message Not Found");
   CO_CHART_WRK.SHARES_EXERCISABLE.Value = &CurrentChartValue;
   CO_CHART_WRK.SHARES_EXERCISABLE.Visible = True;
End-If;
```

Frame

This control draws a frame around a group of controls. Here is the frame in Design mode in Application Designer.

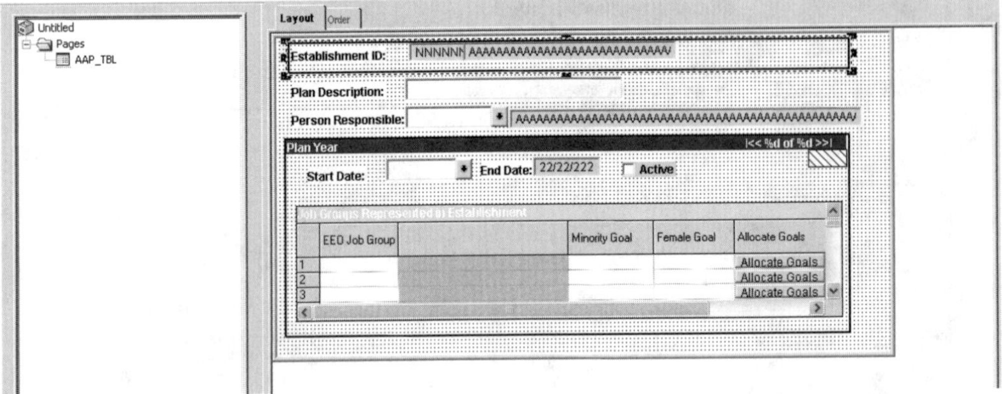

Next, you can see how the frame designates a set of controls as a group. This illustration shows the frame in the PeopleSoft application.

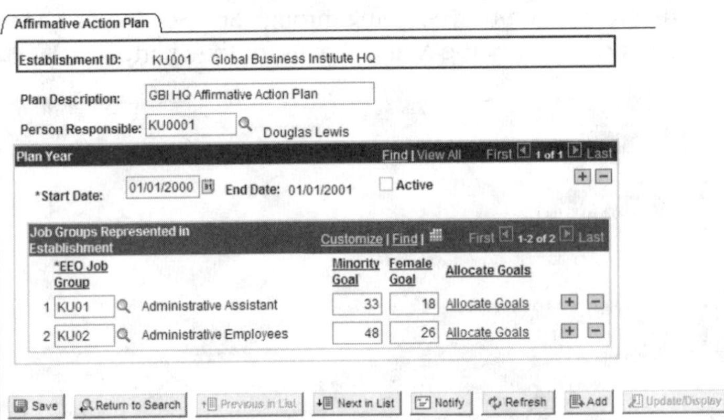

A frame will also help you isolate controls, which will become clearer when you learn how the processing occurs on pages and components. An example is an HTML area; you can draw a frame around it to group it, and then hide the frame. When a frame with HTML is displayed on the Web, it will create an HTML table.

Group Box

A *group box* is a box that you draw around a group of items and give a text label to. For example, here a few group boxes are created in Application Designer on a page, which is denoted as "Group Box Header 1" and represents the property of the header, as shown next.

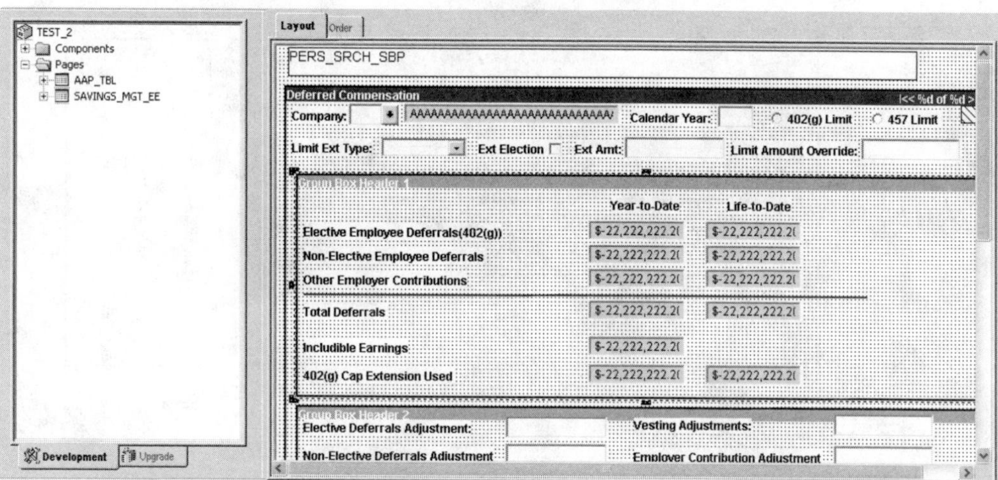

In another example of what a group box looks like in a Web browser, you can see the "Header—457Adjustments" that was added in Application Designer.

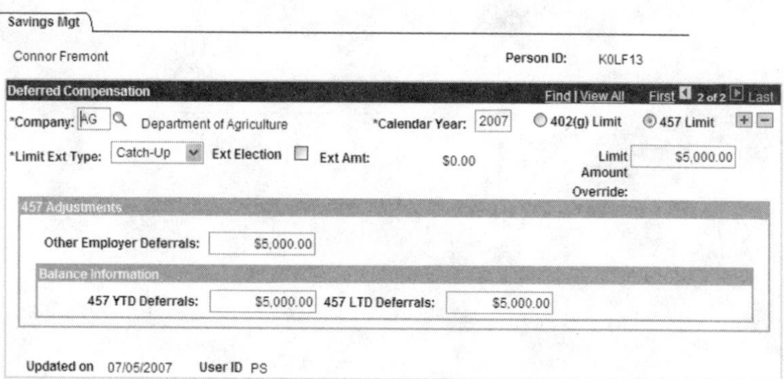

Horizontal Rule

A horizontal rule is a horizontal line that can be drawn on a page to separate items on a page; horizontal lines are not for functionality, but for creating a visual separation on the page. The following illustrations show the horizontal rule in Application Designer, and in the PeopleSoft application.

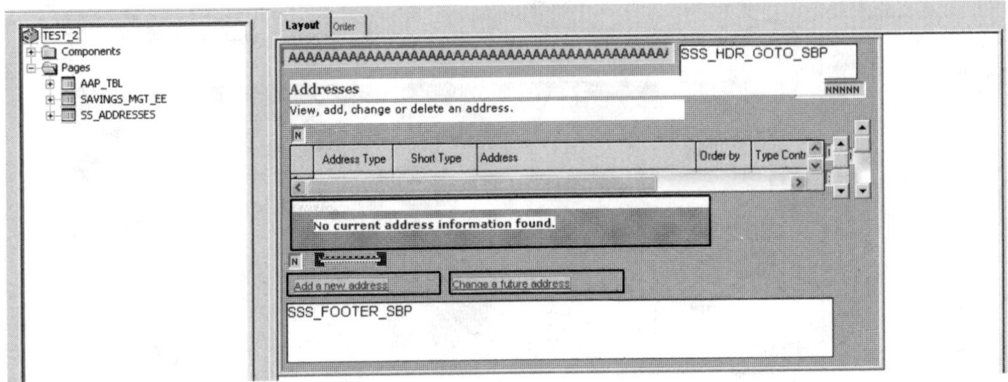

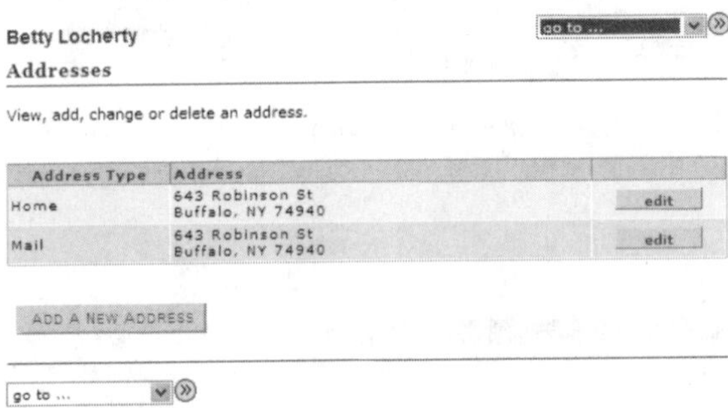

Image

An image allows you to create a frame that can be associated with one of two types of images—a standard Image type field or an ImageReference. An ImageReference can change dynamically during runtime and while the page is displayed. You can use a dynamically changing image to convey information to the user during runtime. Here is an example of an image in Application Designer.

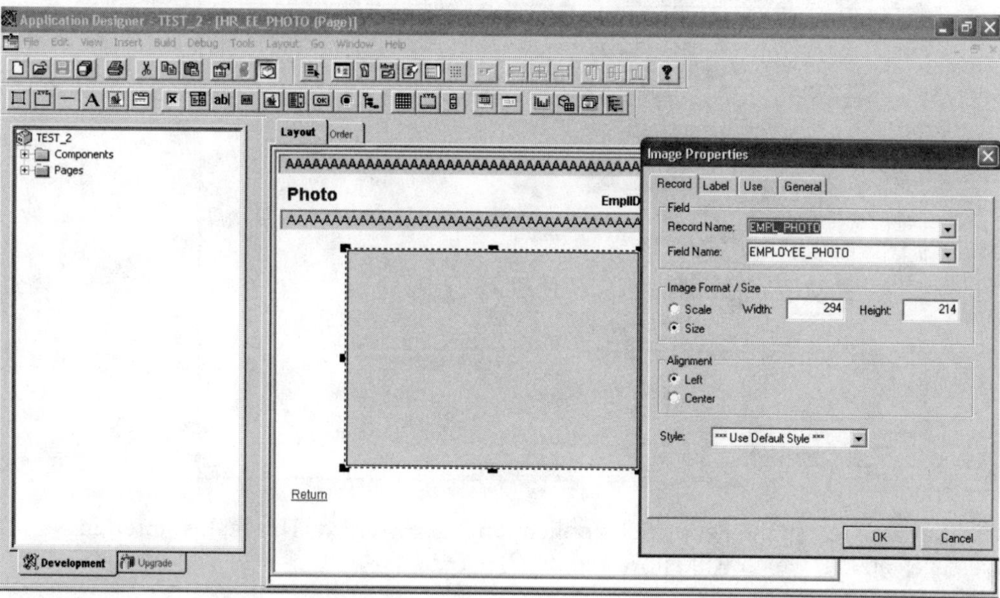

Static Image

A static image is a frame that is associated with a non-changing image. A static image is just what the name implies and it does not change during runtime. It is not associated with a record field but an image definition. An example would be your company logo at the top of the page.

Static Text

Static text can be used to give users instructions on the page. Static text can be any text that does not change on the page. If your text will change, it is best to store it in a message catalog or in HTML rather than in static text. Here's what static text looks like in Application Designer.

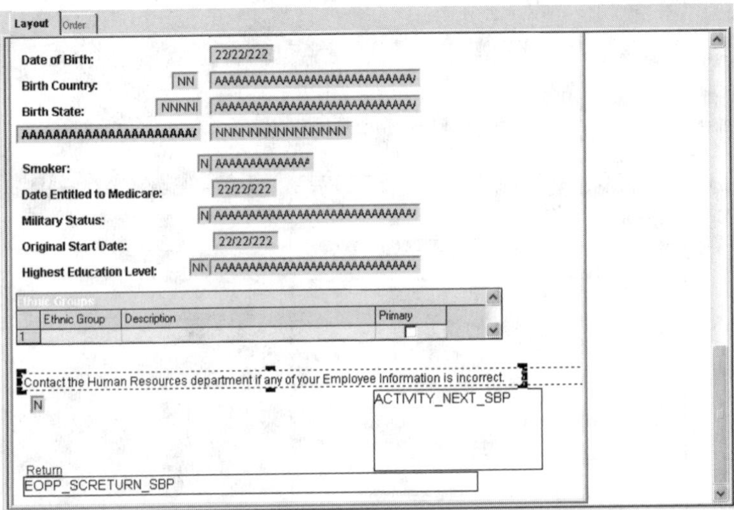

The same text in the PeopleSoft application is shown next. This text is stored in a message catalog, which will allow it to be changed.

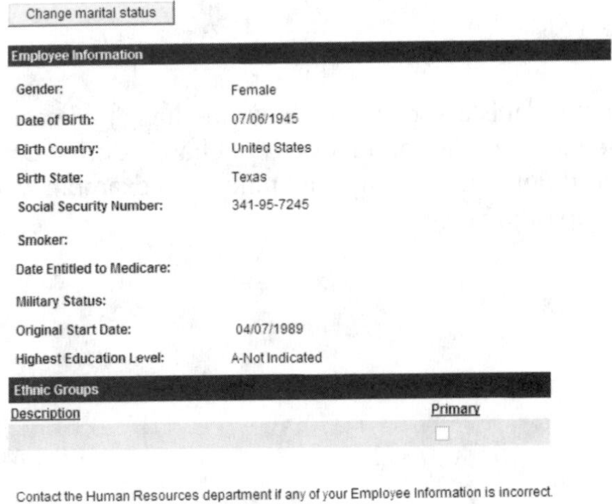

Data Entry Controls

On the page you can have a number of data entry controls including: check boxes, drop-down list boxes, edit boxes, radio buttons, and subpages. The entry controls allow you to choose the way that the data will be entered, manipulated, and/or controlled on the page. If you want to limit the choices for a specific field, you can do that with a drop-down list box with only the list of items to choose from. Radio buttons allow for yes and no choices to be made, check boxes allow for the toggling on and off of preferences, and subpages allow for you to display a second set of data with key relationships.

Check Box

A check box is a toggle switch and represents in code an on or off, or Boolean, function. It is for representing a yes/no, on/off, or 1/0 type of coding. It allows for quick and easy data entry, and saves a yes or no value for the state of the check box—yes if checked and no if unchecked—and upon saving of the form, these values are written to the database. The design of a check box in Application Designer is shown here:

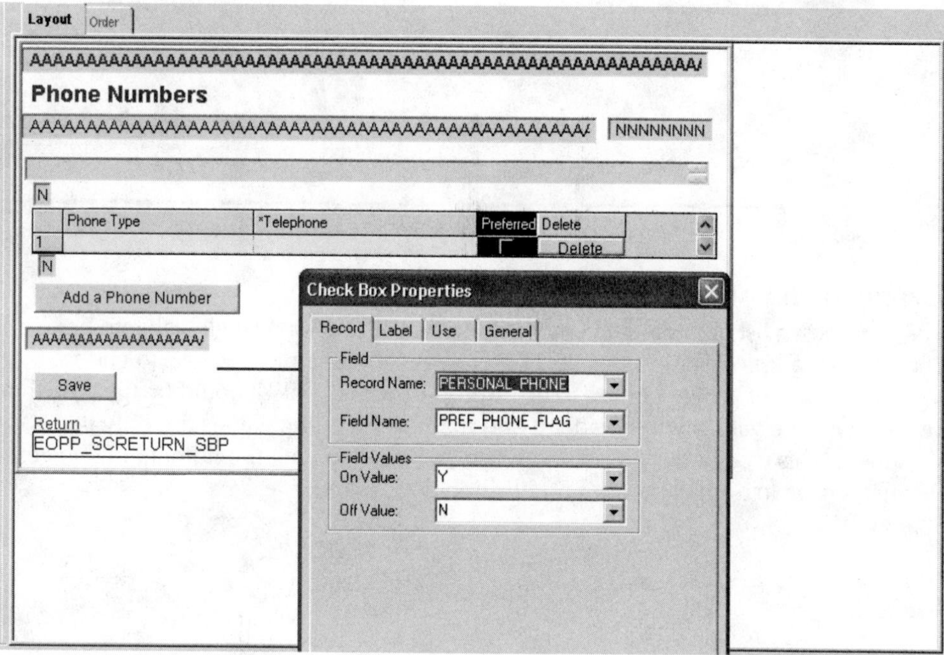

The next illustration shows the check box in the PeopleSoft application.

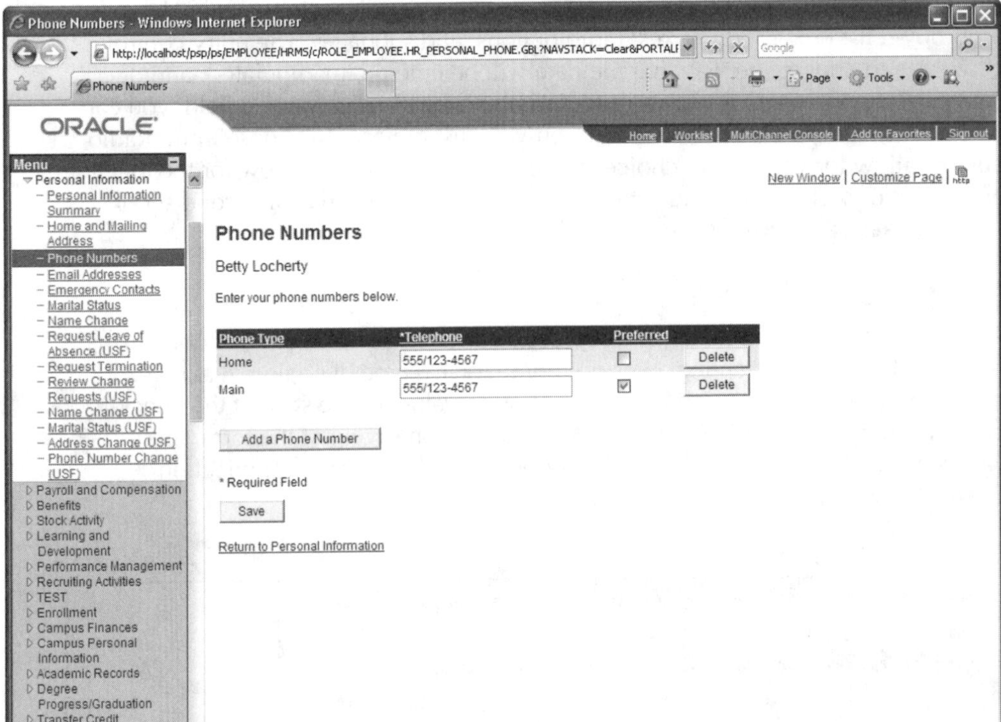

Drop-Down List Box

The drop-down list box is a data entry feature that allows for a single value to be chosen from a list of valid values. It is best to have three or more values to choose from; otherwise, it is over-coding to use a drop-down list box. It could be the case that you know more values will be added and that three starting values are only the beginning. This type of design is good when you want to limit the number of choices that users have to a small number of selections.

The following illustrations show the design of the drop-down list box in Application Designer and in the PeopleSoft application. The words that appear in the drop-down list can be the short XLat, long XLat, or a lookup of a field on a prompt table.

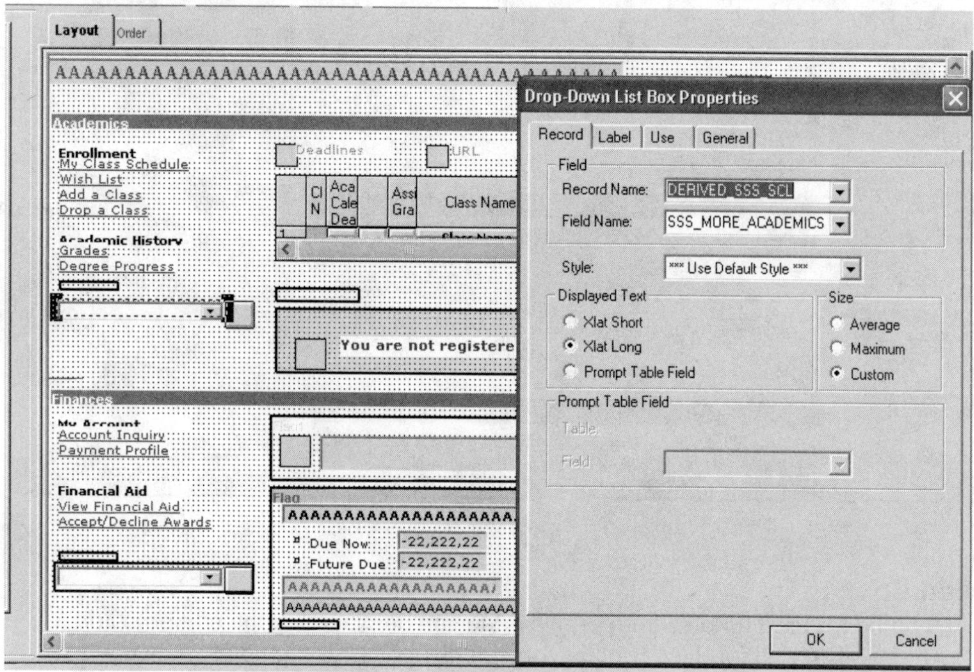

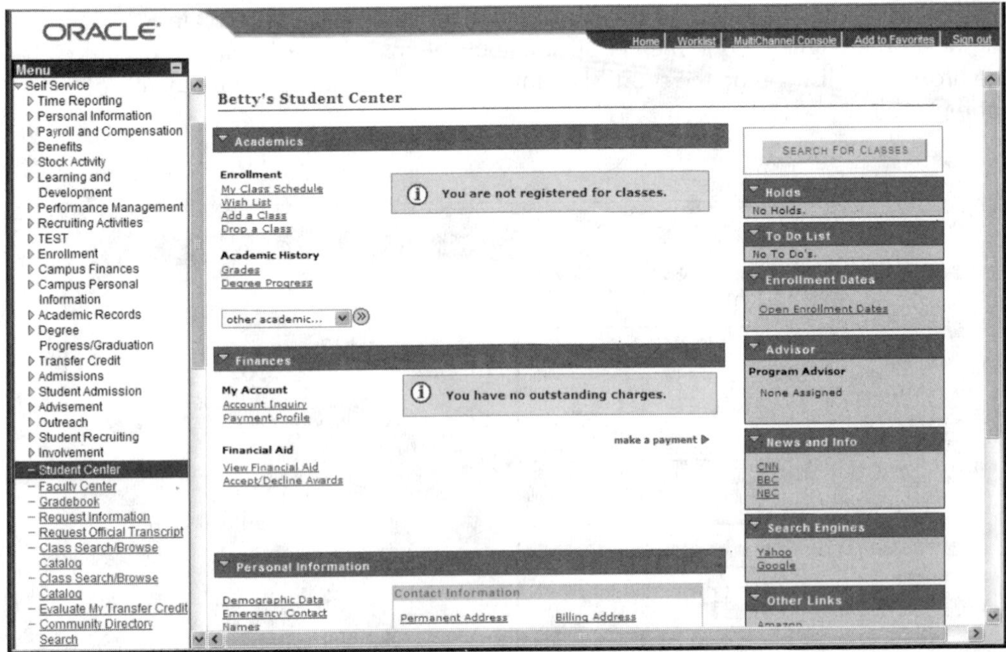

Edit Box

An edit box is used for data entry—any value can be placed in the edit box. Edit boxes are also used for data display; you can display values in fields, derive work records, and/or translate text fields and then make the edit box read-only. The data type for an edit box is text so you want to use an edit box to allow for data entry into a record that has a field that is a character, number, signed number, or date. You can see the edit box design in Application Designer and in the PeopleSoft application, shown next:

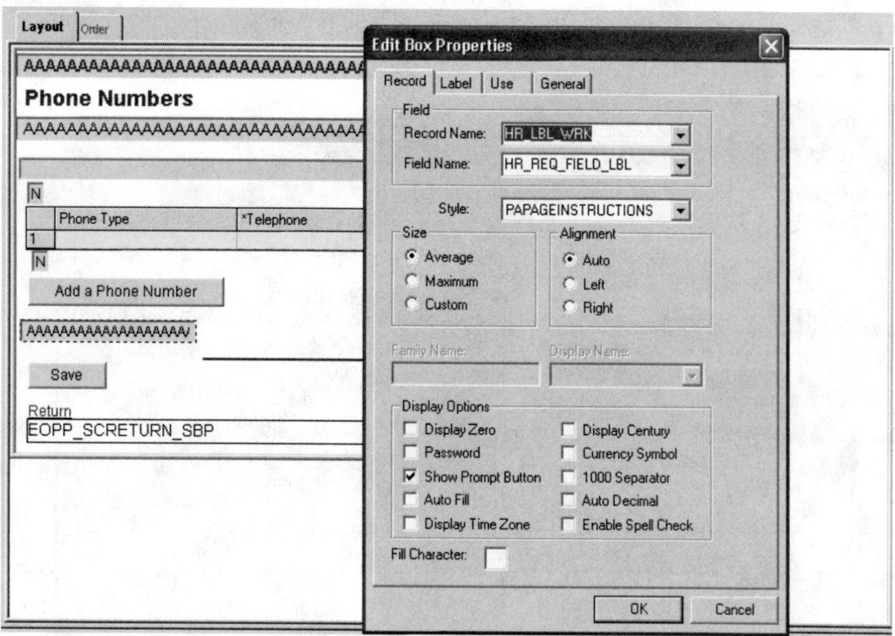

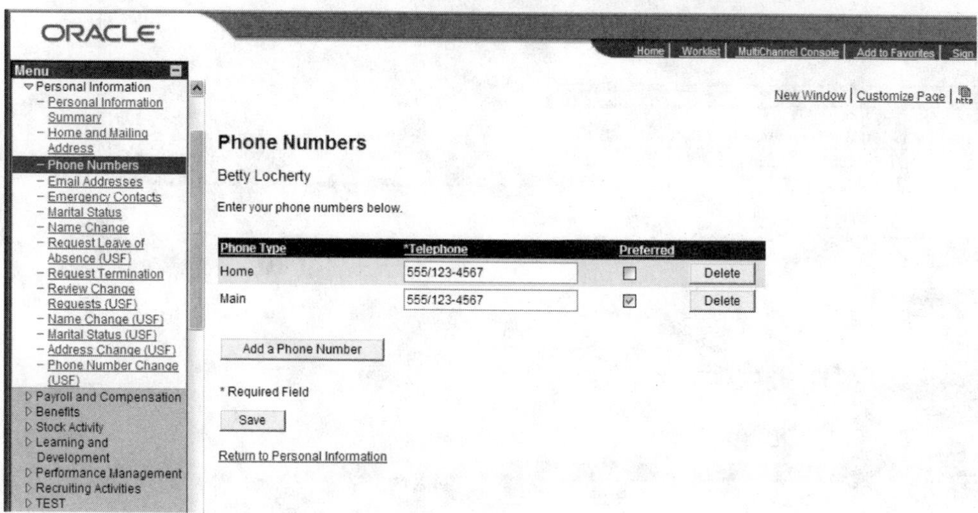

Long Edit Box

A long edit box is almost the same as an edit box; the difference is in size. If your field is a long value a scroll area is added to the edit box, allowing for scrolling through the text. The length is controlled by the contents rather than the size of the field. Common uses are for comments and descriptions. Long edit boxes are good for memo type entries and generally correspond to the "long character" type fields in the database. The long edit box in Application Designer and in the PeopleSoft application are shown here:

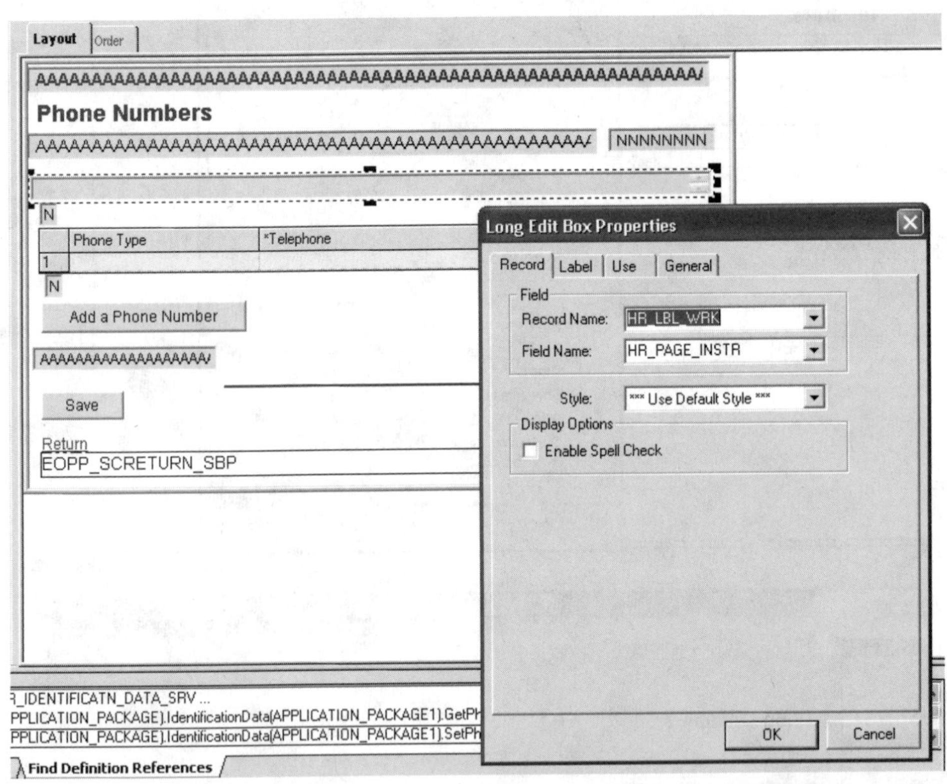

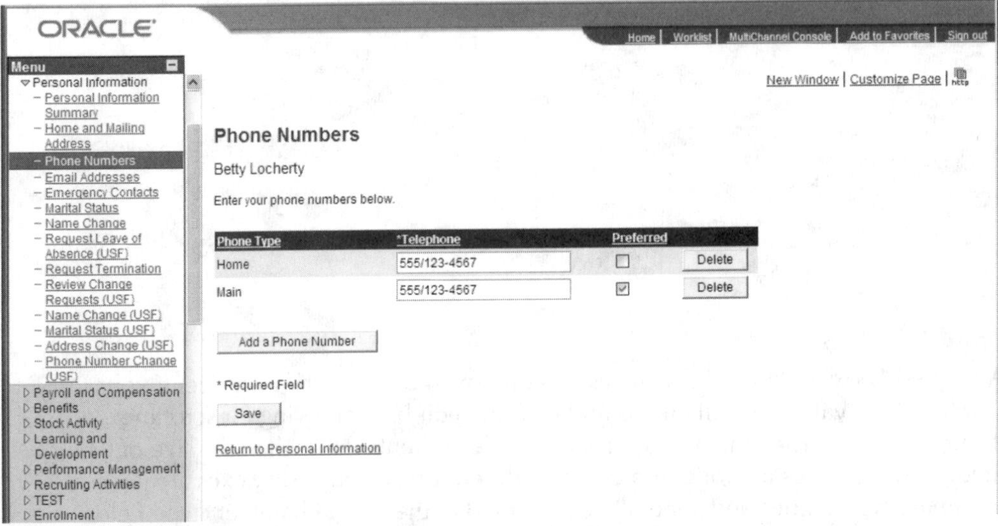

Radio Button

Radio buttons are small round buttons representing a single value that has multiple options. You add radio buttons in groups to show the multiple options that a single value has. PeopleSoft recommends using radio buttons in cases with very few options; for more than a few options, they recommend the use of a drop-down list box. The reason is that drop-down lists will grow dynamically as more choices are introduced, whereas when adding radio buttons the page would need to be modified. In the following illustrations, you can see the design of the radio button in Application Designer and in the PeopleSoft application.

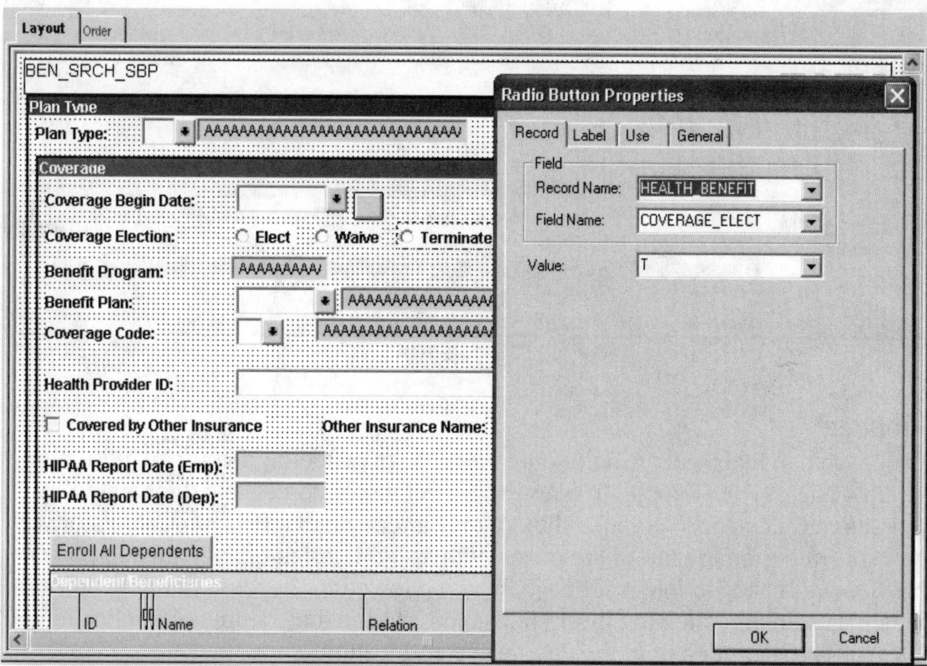

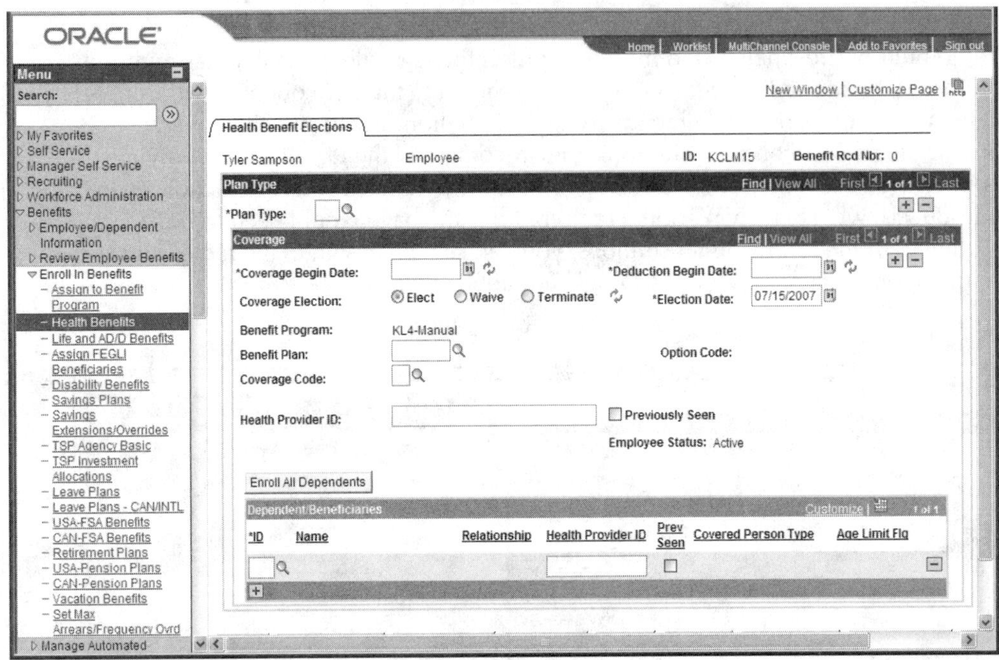

Subpage

A subpage can represent a single source for a page header and you can reuse it on multiple pages. For example, in a recent project the customer asked for a new Retirement Calculation screen, although they already had a Pension Calculator with the main values on the top of the page. With a slight design change the top part of the form was changed into a subpage, which allowed for its reuse multiple times in other pages. In the following illustrations, you can see an example of a subpage in Application Designer and in the PeopleSoft Application.

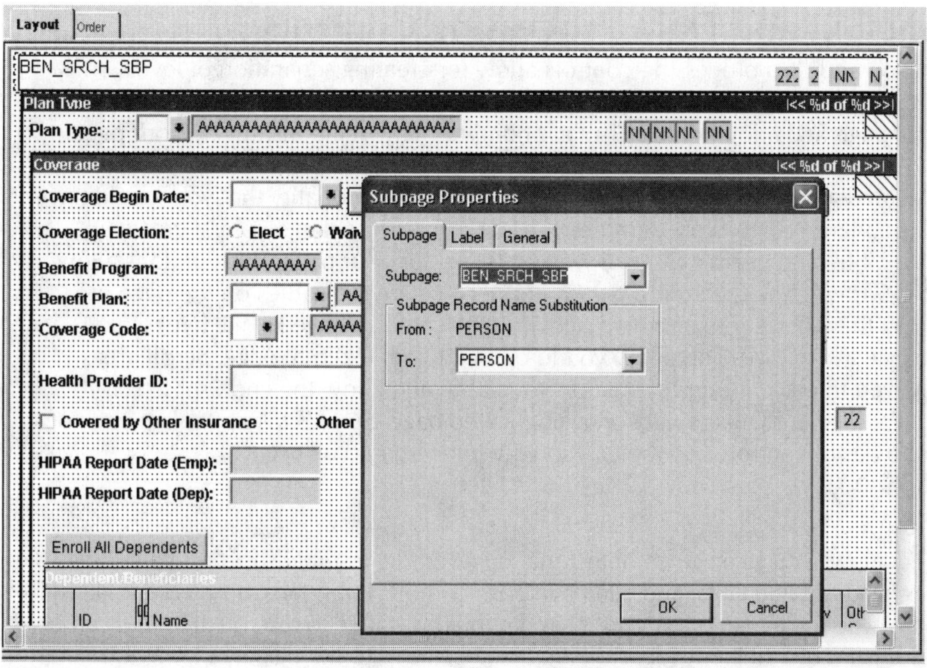
Layout
Order
BEN_SRCH_SBP
Plan Type
Plan Type:
Coverage
Coverage Begin Date:
Coverage Election:
Elect
Benefit Program:
Benefit Plan:
Coverage Code:
Health Provider ID:
Covered by Other Insurance
Other
HIPAA Report Date (Emp):
HIPAA Report Date (Dep):
Enroll All Dependents
Dependent/Beneficiaries
ID
Name
Subpage Properties
Subpage
Label
General
Subpage:
BEN_SRCH_SBP
Subpage Record Name Substitution
From : PERSON
To: PERSON
OK
Cancel

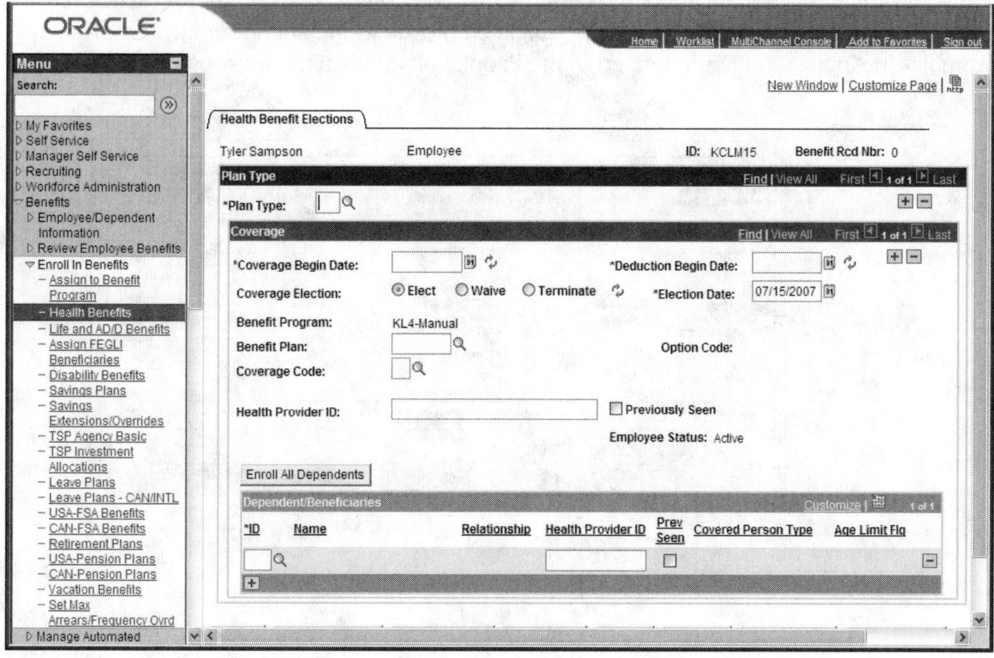
ORACLE
Home
Worklist
MultiChannel Console
Add to Favorites
Sign out
Menu
Search:
My Favorites
Self Service
Manager Self Service
Recruiting
Workforce Administration
Benefits
Employee/Dependent Information
Review Employee Benefits
Enroll In Benefits
Assign to Benefit Program
Health Benefits
Life and AD/D Benefits
Assign FEGLI Beneficiaries
Disability Benefits
Savings Plans
Savings Extensions/Overrides
TSP Agency Basic
TSP Investment Allocations
Leave Plans
Leave Plans - CAN/INTL
USA-FSA Benefits
CAN-FSA Benefits
Retirement Plans
USA-Pension Plans
CAN-Pension Plans
Vacation Benefits
Set Max Arrears/Frequency Ovrd
Manage Automated
New Window
Customize Page
Health Benefit Elections
Tyler Sampson
Employee
ID: KCLM15
Benefit Rcd Nbr: 0
Plan Type
Find | View All
First 1 of 1 Last
*Plan Type:
Coverage
*Coverage Begin Date:
*Deduction Begin Date:
Coverage Election:
Elect
Waive
Terminate
*Election Date:
07/15/2007
Benefit Program:
KL4-Manual
Benefit Plan:
Option Code:
Coverage Code:
Health Provider ID:
Previously Seen
Employee Status: Active
Enroll All Dependents
Dependent/Beneficiaries
Customize
1 of 1
*ID
Name
Relationship
Health Provider ID
Prev Seen
Covered Person Type
Age Limit Flg

Function and Data Processing Controls

Function and data processing controls allow for creating separation of levels on your page. For example, a grid will allow you to embed a spreadsheet type control on the page and allow for the display of one-to-many relationships on your page. An HTML area will allow you to have the functionality of displaying information in HTML and give you as a web developer all of the functionality that you would have with standard HTML—for example, you can bold text, change colors, create an HTML table, and overall create a web page feel for your page. Push buttons allow you to write PeopleCode on a button and recalculate the values on the page or redirect the web user to another page. Buttons can also have HTML hyperlinks associated with them and allow you to open another external page. Scroll areas allow you to place groups of data on your page and allow the end user to scroll through large amounts of data on a single web page. So let's take a look at each of these types of controls and the way in which they could be used.

Grid

A grid allows you to place an object that behaves like a spreadsheet on your page. It has headings and cells, and can have push buttons, links, tabs, and more to allow for any type of navigation. A grid is similar in appearance to a scroll area and can be used instead of a single-level scroll area. Grids allow for the display of one-to-many relationships. So say, for example, you have one employee with multiple dependents and you want all of the data about the dependents. You could use a grid to represent the dependents and the page would have the single employee as the anchor or key. Grid examples in Application Designer and in the PeopleSoft application are shown here:

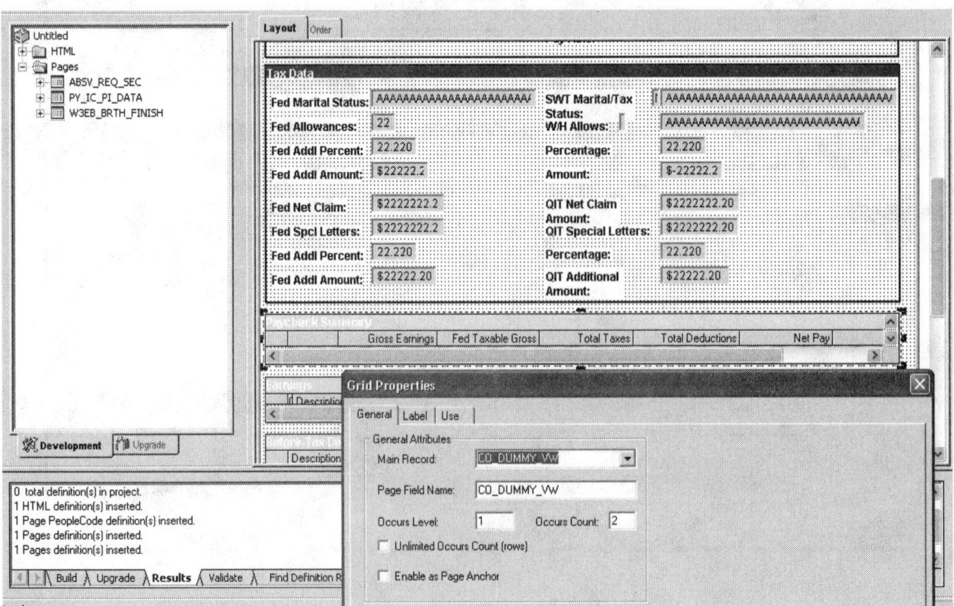

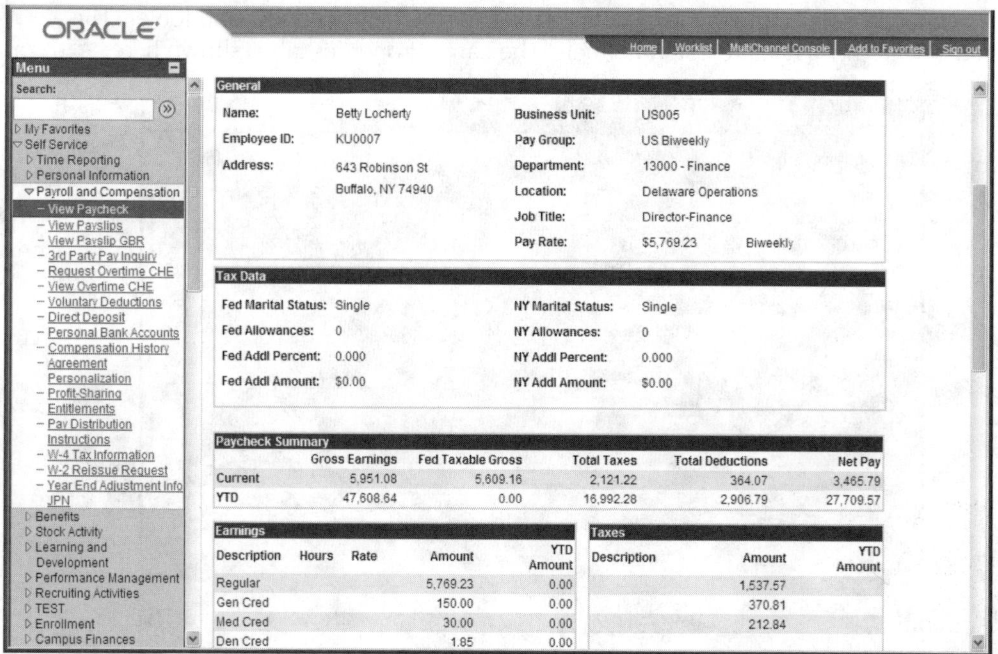

Grid Properties

In a grid you have General properties, Label properties, and Use properties. The General properties define the record and the page field name, which can be the same. The General properties also define the level on which the grid occurs. In this example, you can see the definition of the level and occurrence. The General properties also define the grid as a page anchor and allow unlimited rows.

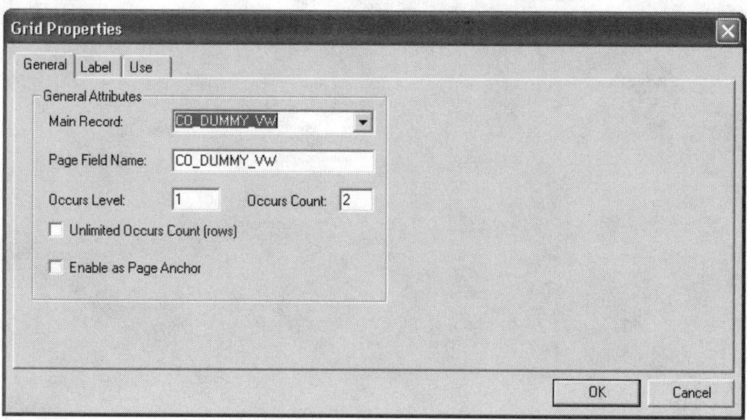

Label properties allow you to define labels for the header, body, and footer. This is also where you declare column labels. The Label Properties tab is shown here:

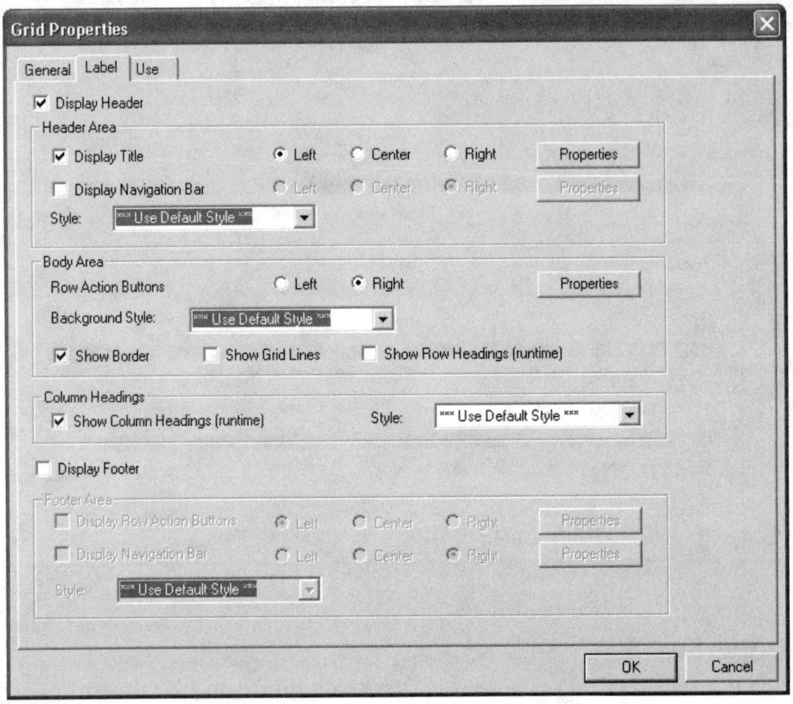

In the Use Properties tab, shown next, you define data options, row selector indicators, pop-up menus, row style, and display options.

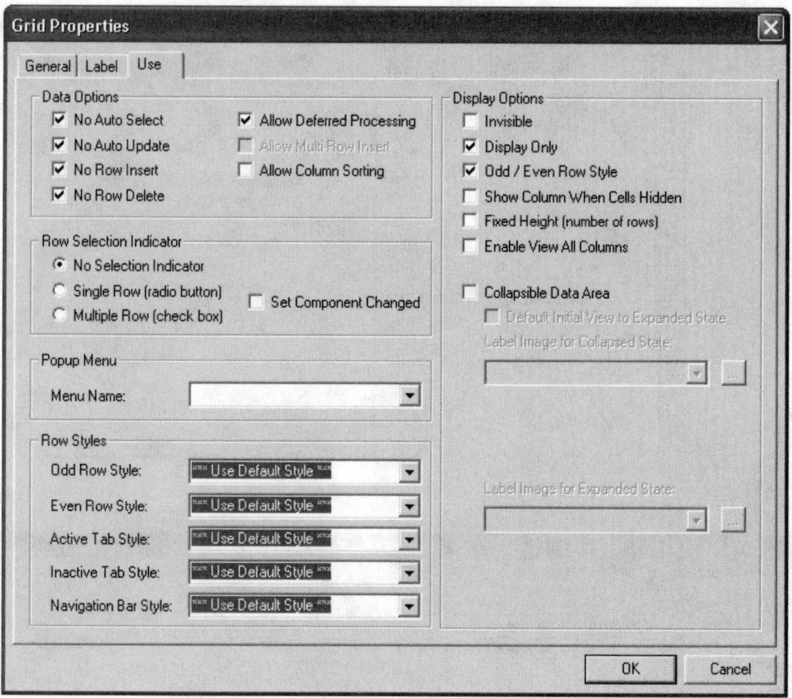

HTML Area

The HTML area gives you as a web designer an HTML object to insert onto a PeopleSoft page. This will provide you with all of the functionality of HTML inside of your PeopleSoft page. All standard HTML code can be written and called to in this object. Take a look at these illustrations. One shows the design of the HTML area; in the second, you can see how to call HTML object in PeopleCode.

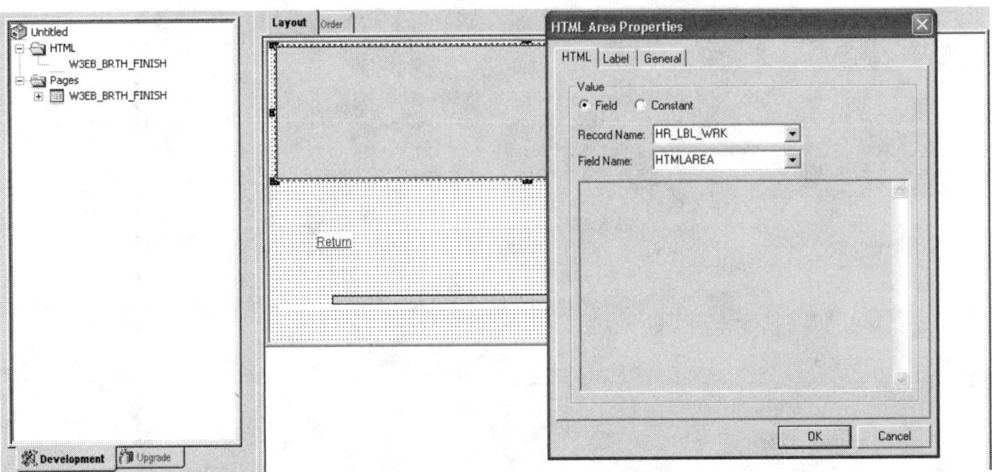

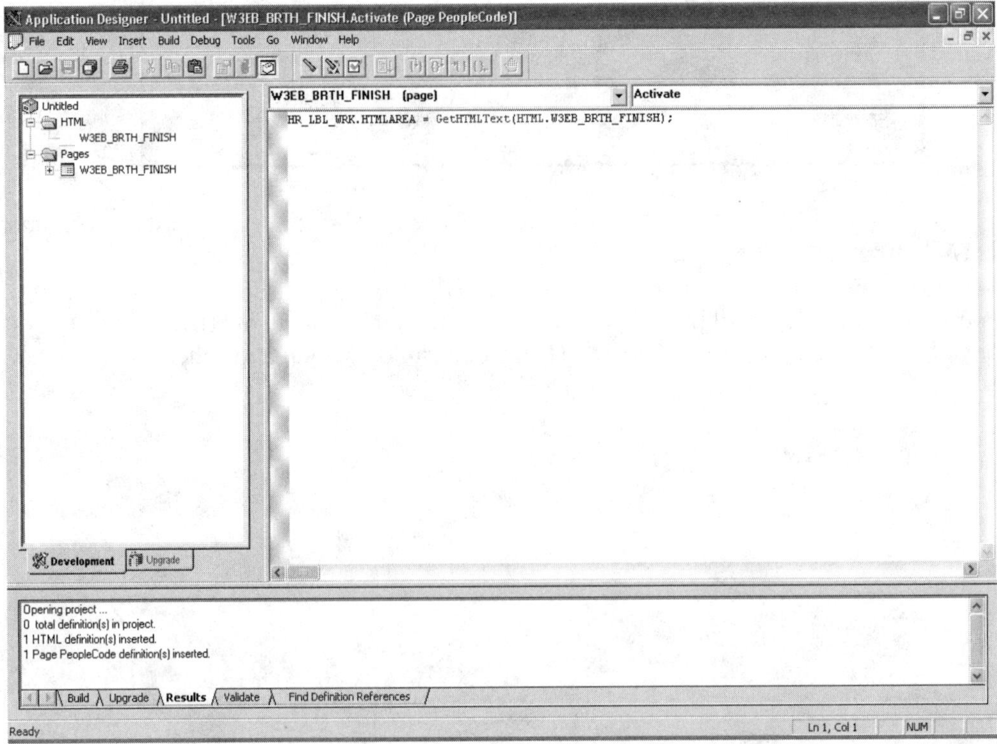

In the next two illustrations, you can see HTML code in Application Designer and HTML code in the PeopleSoft application.

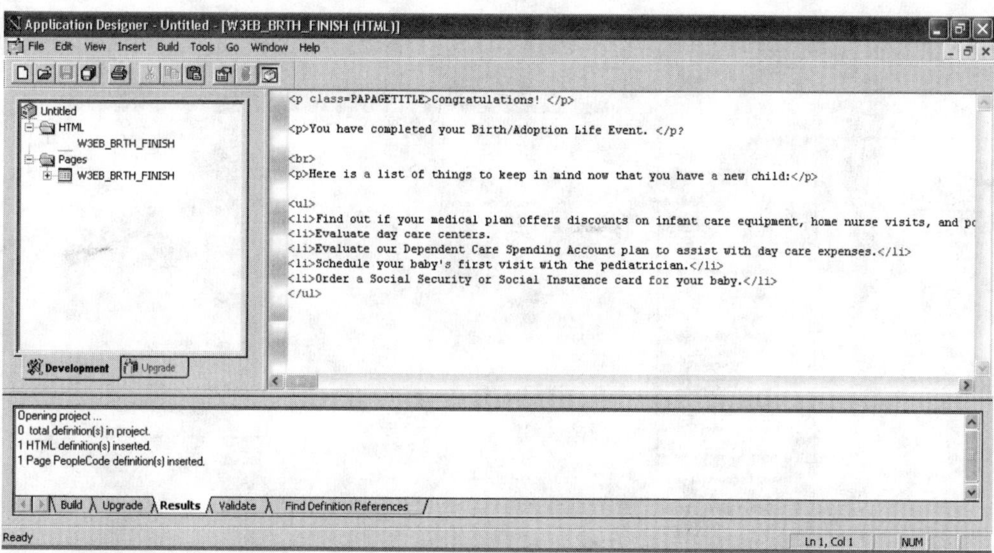

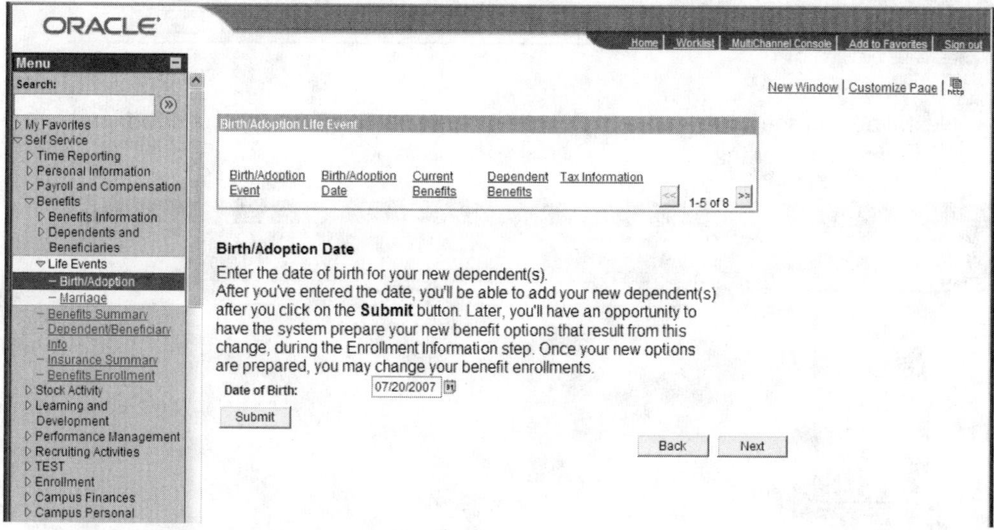

Push Button/Hyperlink

The push button is the basic element on any page design. You can have the push button fire off PeopleCode or go to a hyperlink. It is one of the simplest objects, but can contain some of the most complex code. Here is a basic push button defined in Application Designer.

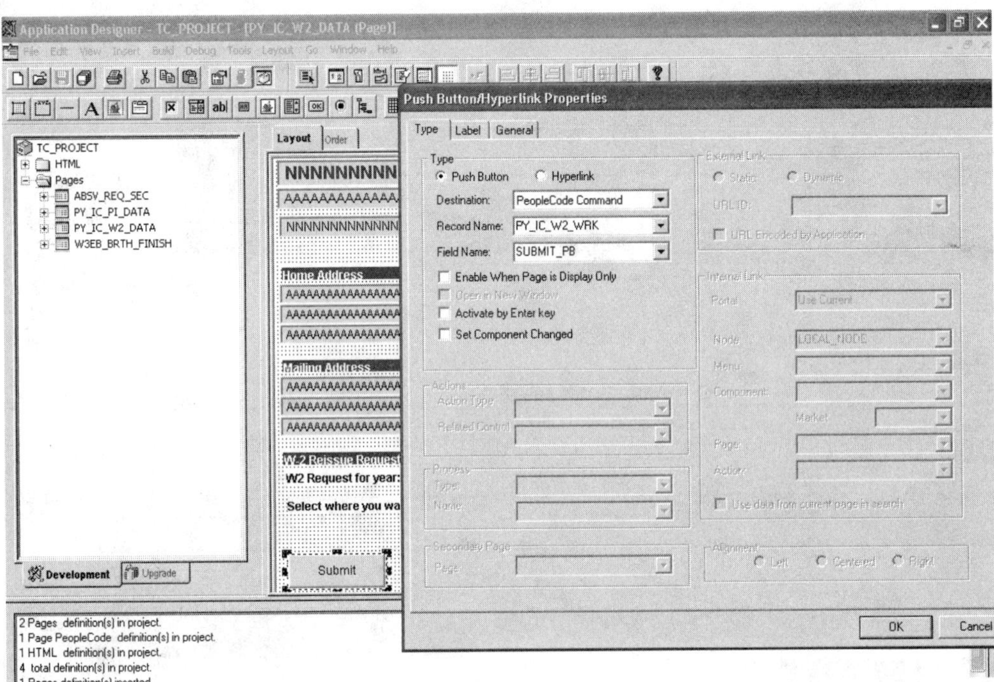

Next, you can see an example of PeopleCode on an event of a push button, and an example of a hyperlink.

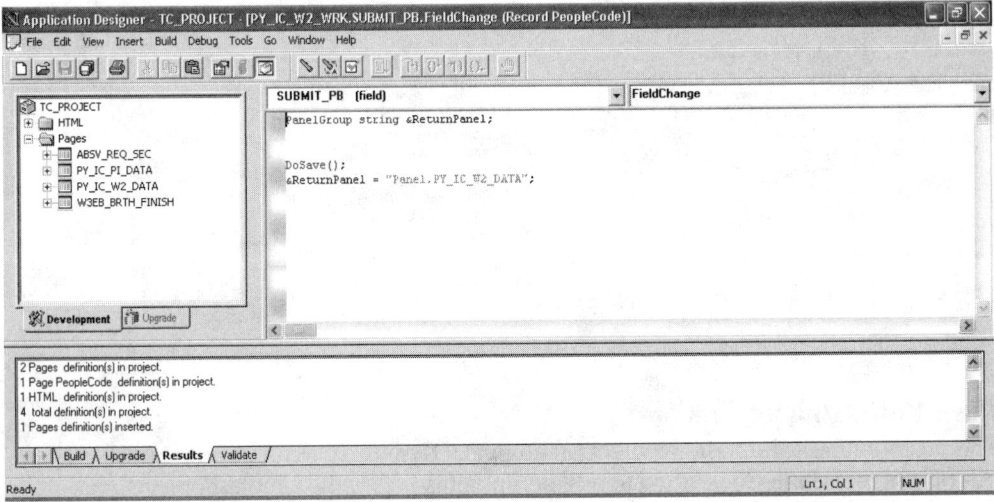

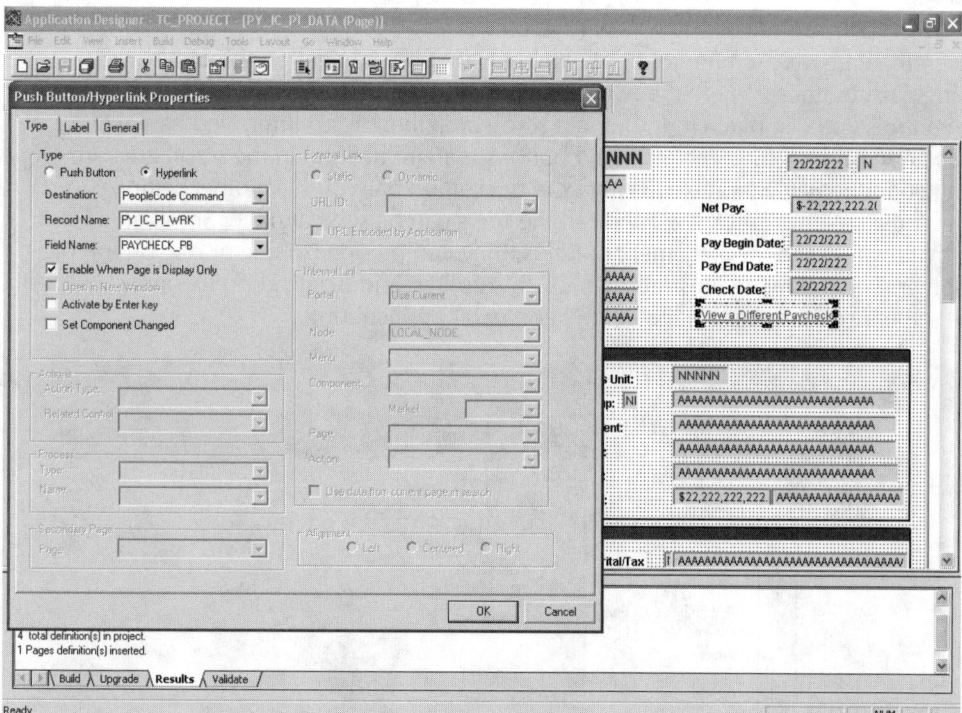

Finally, you see a push button in the PeopleSoft application.

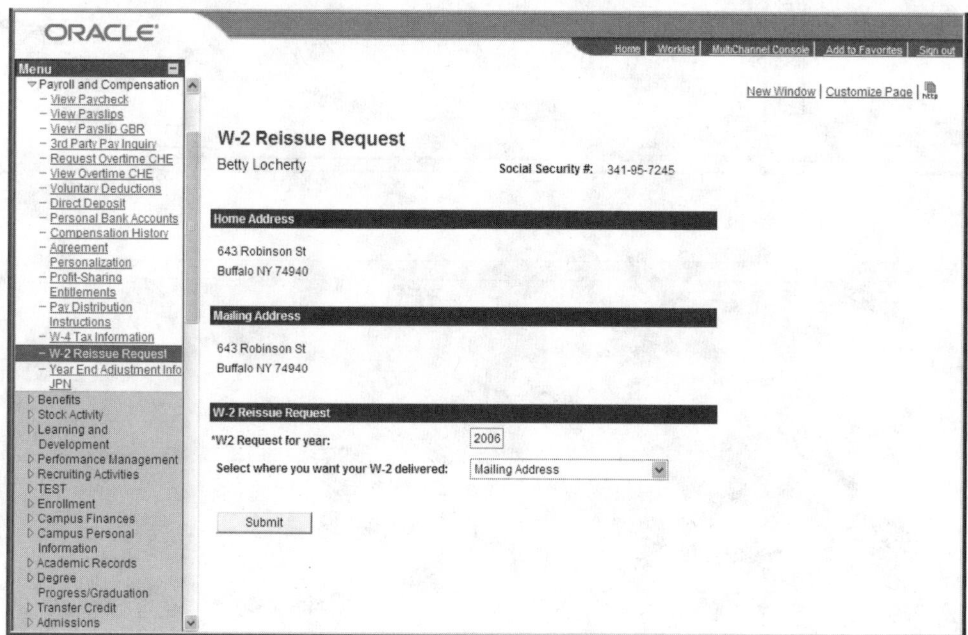

Scroll Area

A scroll area is very similar to a grid. It allows for easy navigation through rows using push buttons. Where the two differ is that in a grid you are limited to the types of controls you can place in it, but in a scroll area there is no limit. You can even place a scroll in a grid. The links and buttons that are defined in the scroll area are defined in the navigation bar. Within the navigation bar you have other settings: Find for searching, and View All so all the rows can be seen at once. Scroll areas also allow for random placement of fields; they can be side by side or one on top of another. The following illustrations show a scroll area in Application Designer and the same scroll area on a page in the PeopleSoft application.

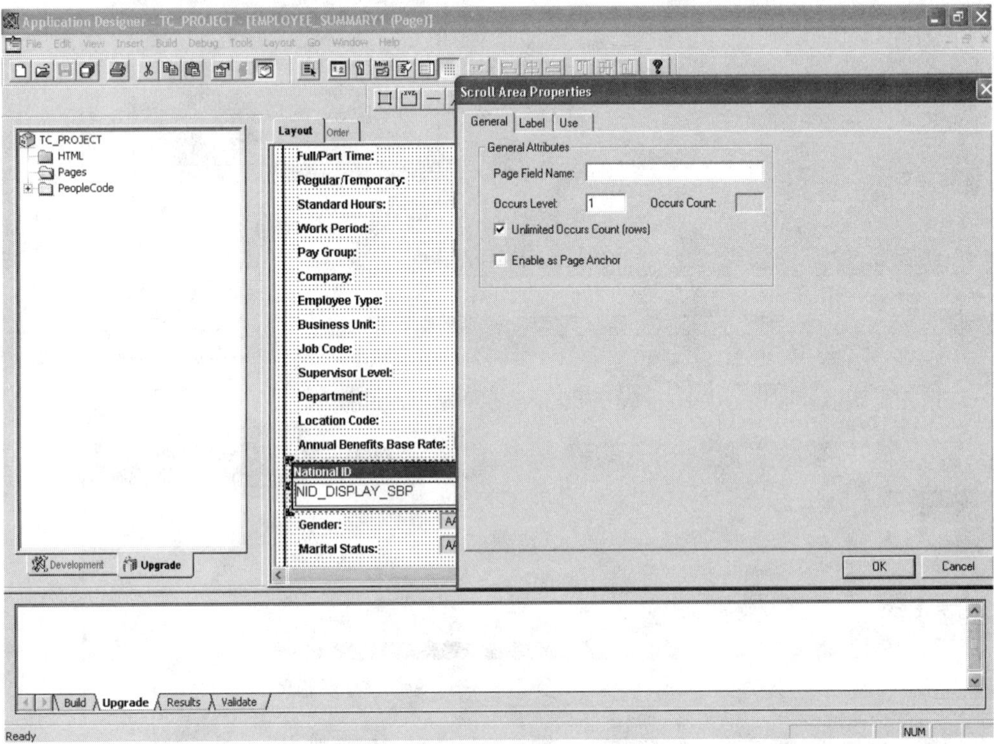

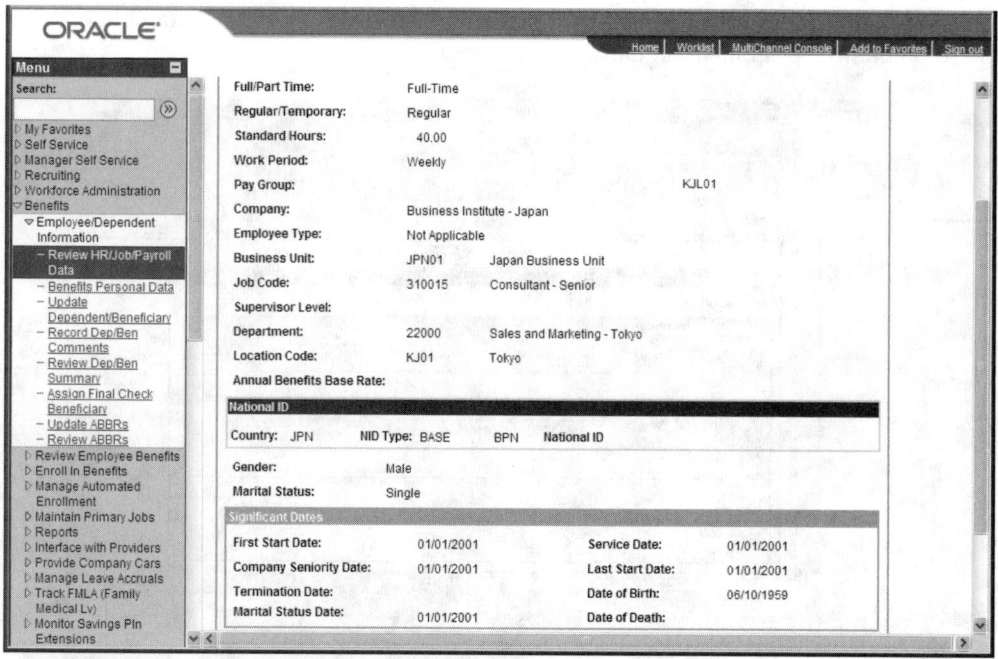

Scroll Bar

Scroll bars contain buttons and links for navigation, but instead of forming an area of data, the scroll bar creates a customized navigation bar. The developer must customize all navigation items and place them on the bar. The bar itself will not appear during runtime; the items that are placed on it display. Here's an example of the scroll bar in the Application Designer and how it is created.

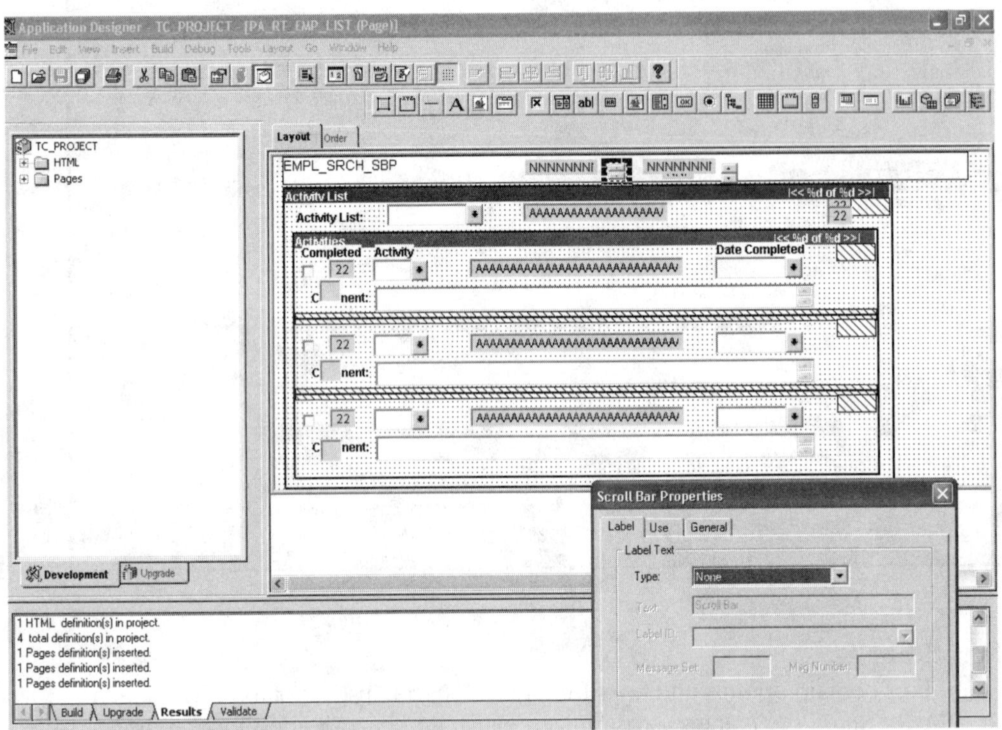

Here's what the comment area with the scroll bar looks like in the PeopleSoft application.

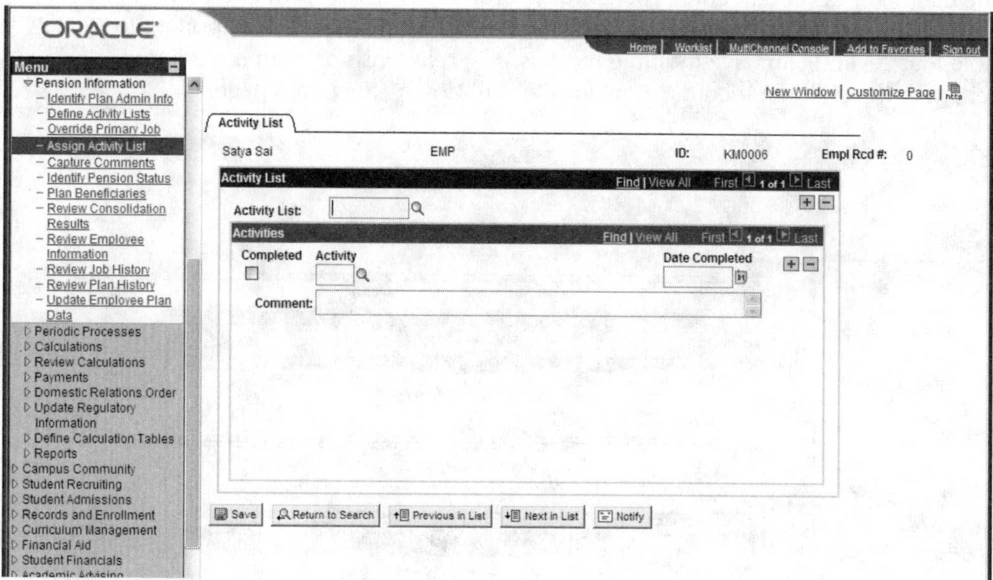

Primary Scroll Record

The primary scroll record directly relates to the SQL table and/or view that is connected to the page via the scroll levels. Each page can have only one primary scroll record, and it cannot be repeated in more than one scroll area on the same level.

The parent/child relationship between the primary or parent scroll record will determine the structure of the other scroll areas on the page. Level 1 is the child to the parent, or Level 0, record. The child record, or Level 1 record, encloses what is on level 0, and Level 2 encloses what is on Level 1, and so on. It is important to note that Level 0 can have multiple records. The relationships from the primary record to the children records allow for the drill-down effect on a page.

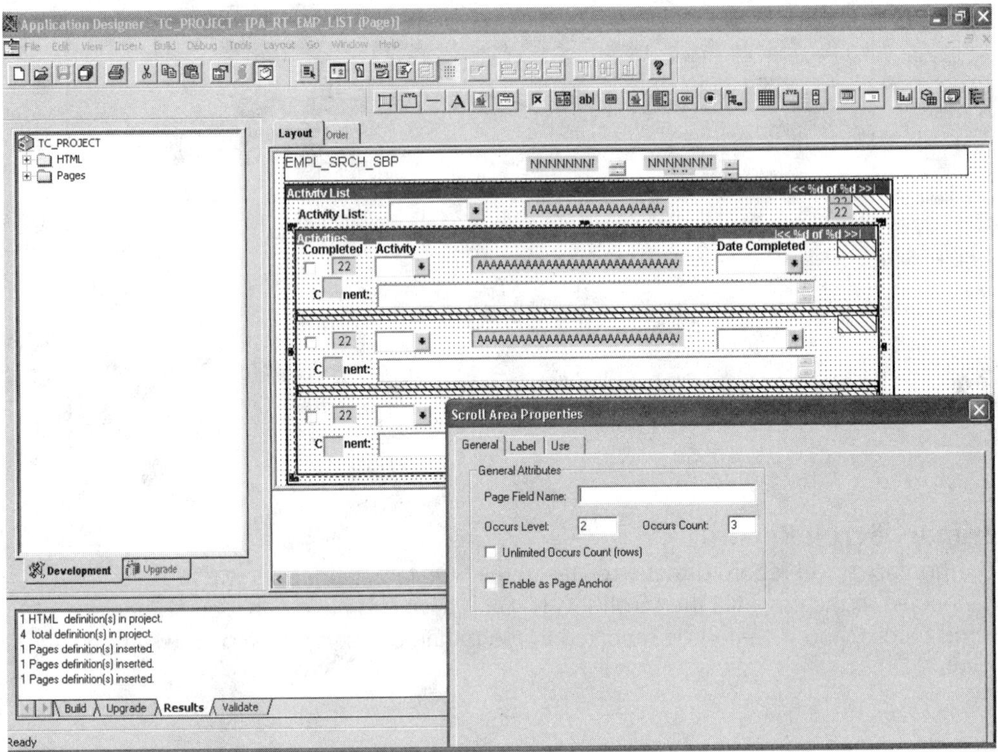

Understanding Component Buffer Structure and Contents

It is important to have a basic understanding of the component buffer structure and its contents if you want to work with levels, and more importantly RowSets. When you are using PeopleCode frequently as a developer you have to refer to data that is stored in the component buffer, which is simply an area in memory that allows you to place data that is active in the component, or in simpler terms, the current record.

There are two ways to refer to data that is in the component buffer: using a scroll path or using PeopleCode with RowSet. At this point in the book we are going to concentrate on the scroll path option. You will learn RowSet manipulation in Chapters 6 and 7.

The fields that display data for the page controls and the rows of data associated with them are stored in the component buffer. One of the fields that contain data would be the primary scroll record. You can access the primary scroll record and direct movement through the available data with PeopleCode.

Secondary Page

A *secondary page* is a control that is invisible at runtime. It allows you to associate a secondary page with the primary or parent page. You then use a command push button or link to redirect the control to the secondary page as a pop-up page. The secondary page is used to gather data and/or display data that is not used as often as the main parent page. You use the DoModal PeopleCode function to display the secondary page. The secondary page is shown in the next two illustrations—the first shows the page displayed in Application Designer, and in the second, you see the PeopleCode.

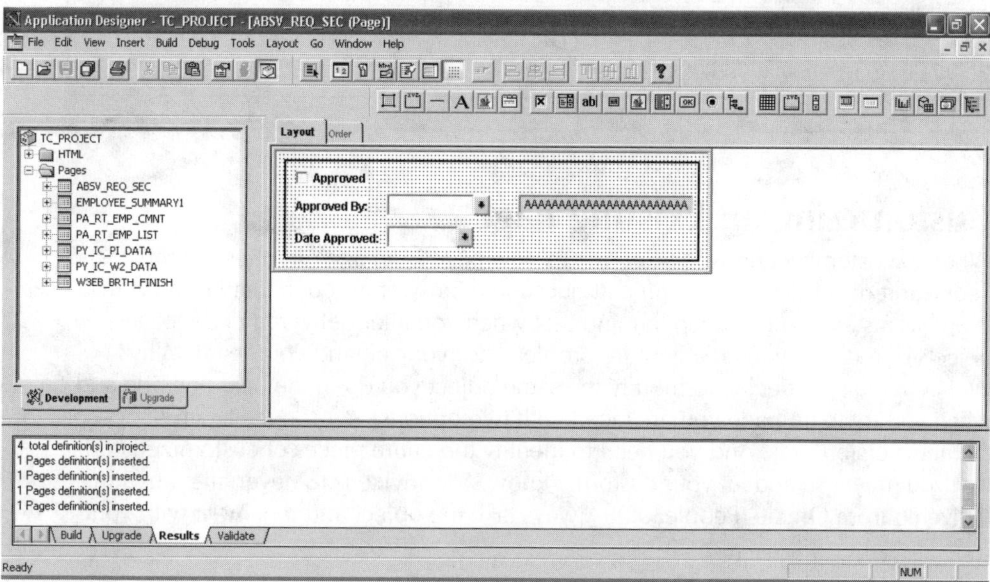

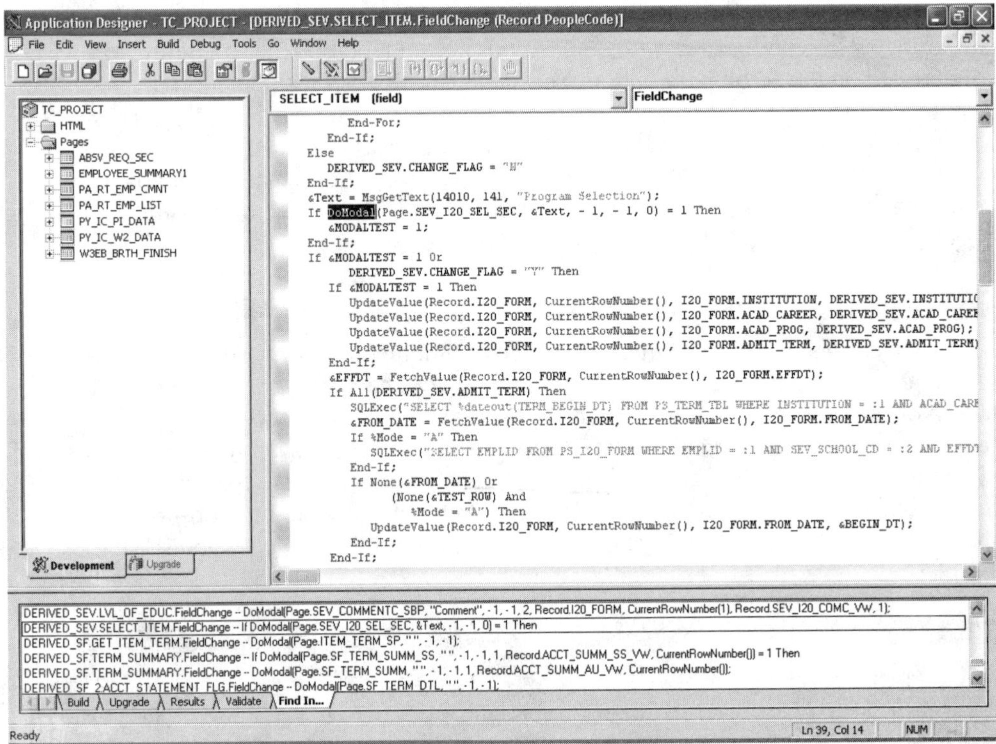

Customizing an Existing Page

When to customize and when to create a new page is an age-old question for PeopleSoft developers. It is a difficult question to answer and one that I hope your shop has a standard for. Keep in mind that when you alter delivered code, pages, objects or records, you create future problems for yourself and your team. Why? Well, Oracle may decide to modify the same object you do in the next upgrade and when you try to upgrade you are faced with two options—customize again or accept the new version as is. And you need to identify the entire pieces of customized code that you may lose and let your customer know. My advice is to never alter anything delivered from Oracle (PeopleSoft). Always take the object and rename it with your company's two-letter naming convention in front of the object. This way you preserve the original and make a copy that you make the customizations in. When upgrading, this will allow you to keep the modified version and not worry about the upgrade scripts overwriting any of your customizations. This then gives you the ability to determine which page you will keep—your old one, a new modified one, or the newly delivered Vanilla.

Let's take a look at customizing an existing page—PA_PLAN_ADMIN. This page is the Pension Plan Administration, Identify Plan Admin Info page. Your employer wants to add a frozen date or end date to the plan. This way you can have existing employees in a pension plan, but not allow new employees to receive it as a benefit. In the first of the following two illustrations, you can see the existing page and the way it looks in the PeopleSoft application. In the second illustration, you can see the current page in the Application Designer.

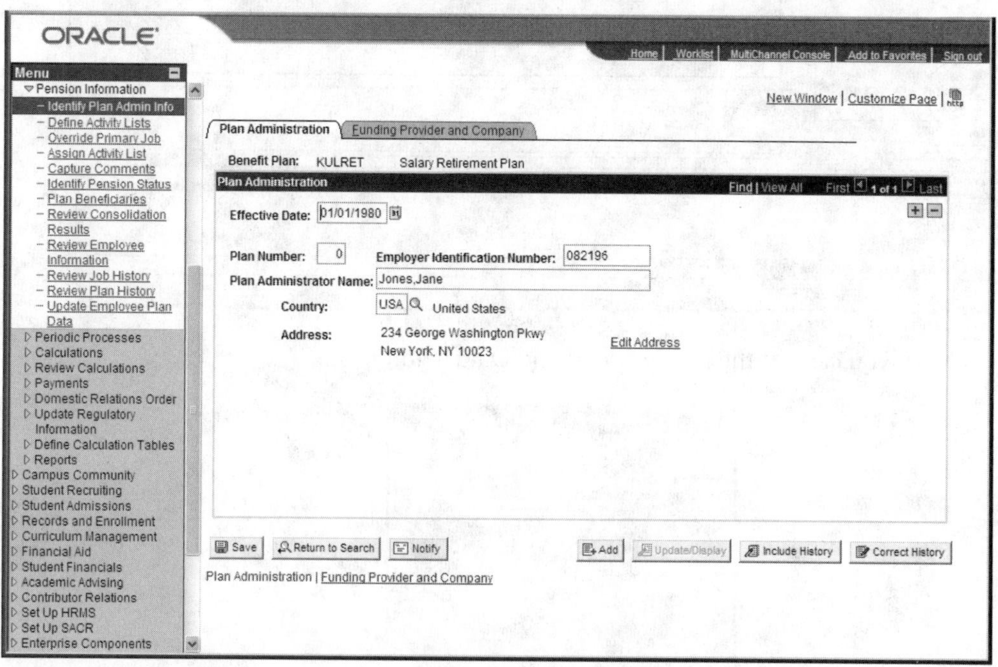

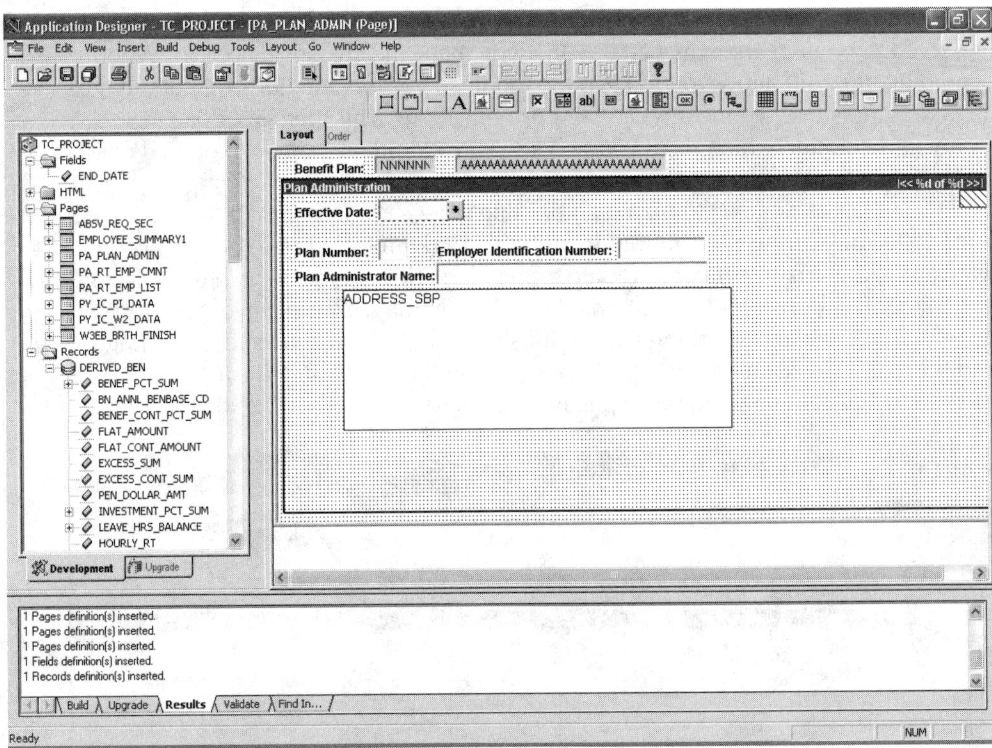

Next, you can see the newly added End Date field.

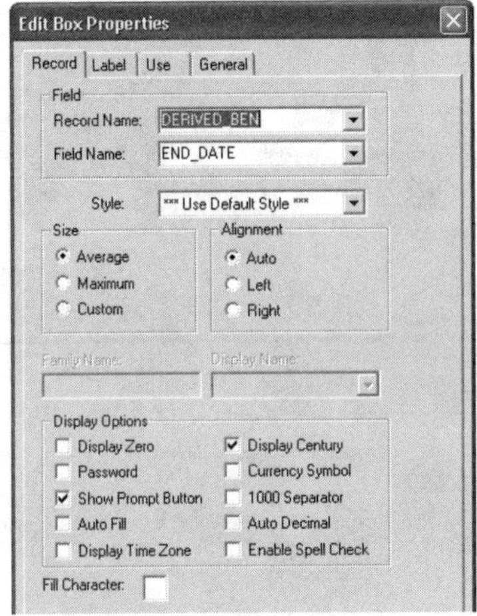

Here's the newly updated page displayed in the PeopleSoft application.

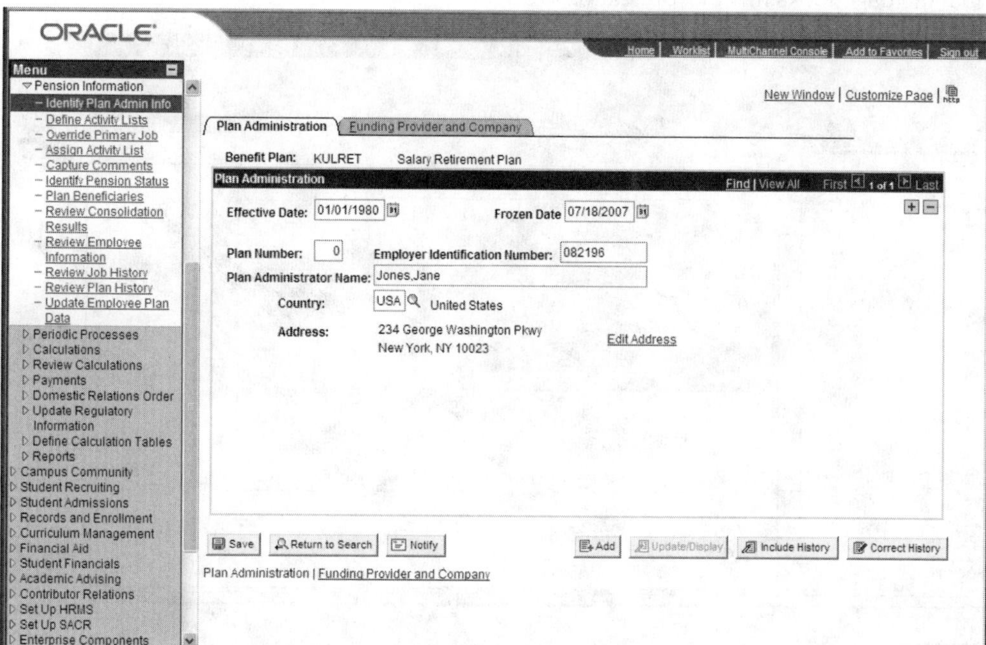

Creating a New Page

Sometimes there is a need to create customized bolt-on applications in PeopleSoft. Maybe your company wants to add a feature that is not currently available in the application. You can create customized-from-scratch pages, menus, records, and the list goes on and on. Keep in mind that with each new upgrade you will need to make certain your customizations carry over into the newly delivered application. You also need to make certain that you update your objects if PeopleSoft modifies a record. With all of this being considered, have fun making customized bolt-ons. Taking a look at the next illustration, you will see the customized page we created in an earlier chapter to show HTML code for the "Hello World" application. Here's what the page looks like in Application Designer.

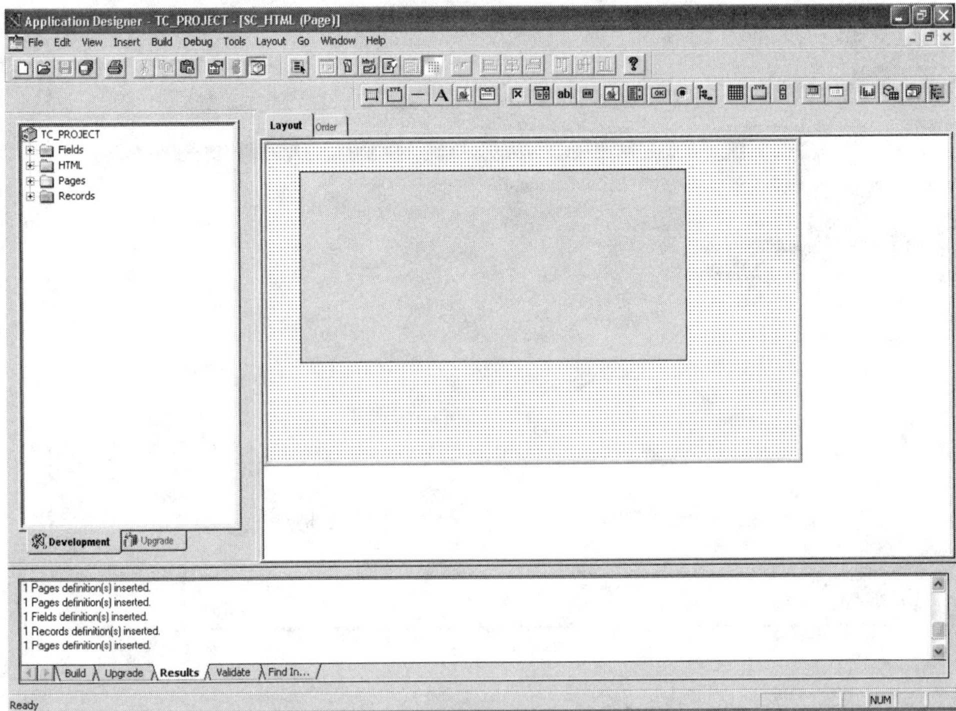

Here is what the page looks like in the PIA.

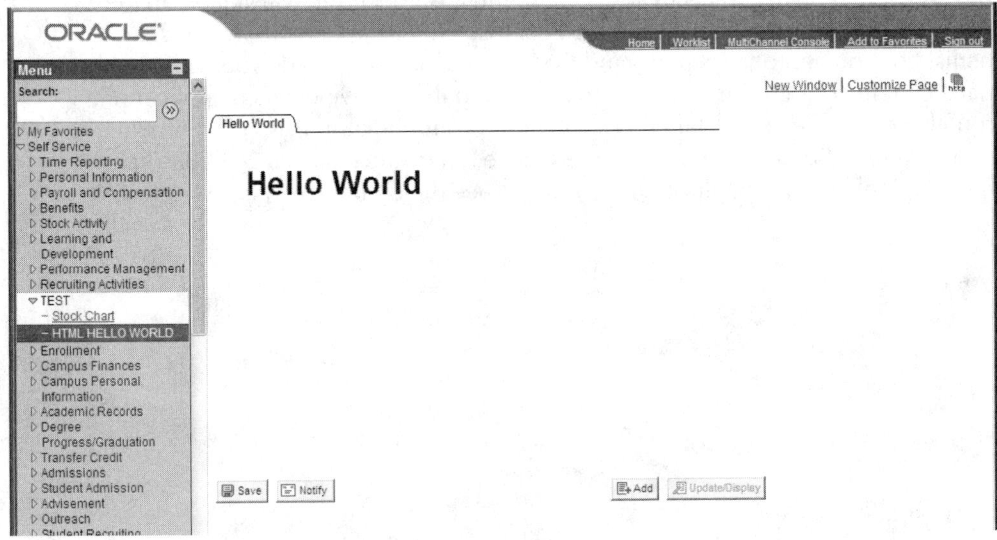

Remember that everything in PeopleSoft is built around a component, so you must have a component to register with the page in the portal. The following is an example of the SC_HTML component that was created to do just this.

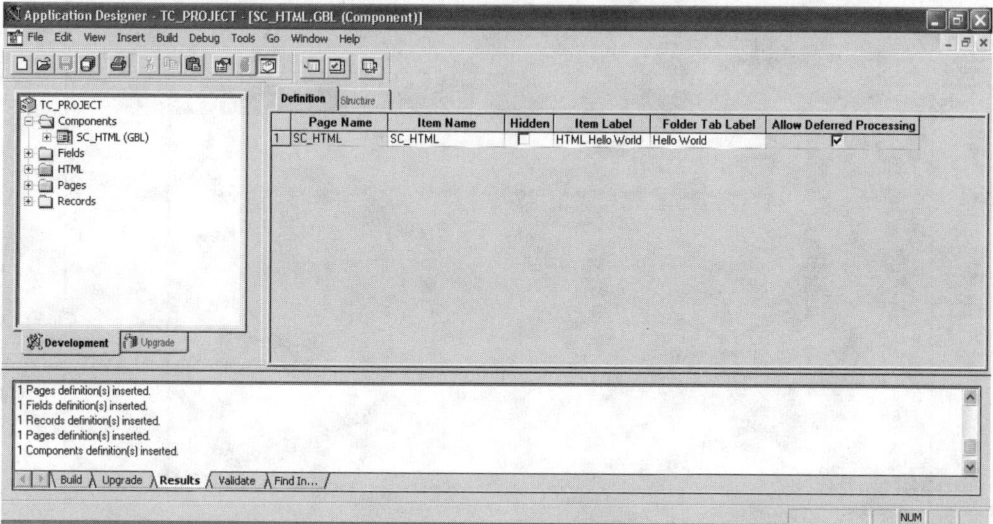

Additional Steps

It is not enough just to create a new page; you have to determine where you will be launching it from in order to determine which menu and which portal to use. The following sections discuss the pieces that are important to have in order to launch your newly created page.

Menus and Portal Registration

When you create a customized page it is important that you associate the page with a menu. Through the menu you will create a portal and structure definition and this will allow you to display your customized page. To register a newly created page, use the Portal Wizard. You can even register the component in more than one portal. In the following illustration, you see the first step in the registration of a component in a portal and on a menu. When you click on the button at the very end of the toolbar with the red cross, the first of the wizard screens opens. You will want all three checks in the first page of the wizard because you want to add this component to a menu, portal register, and a permission list.

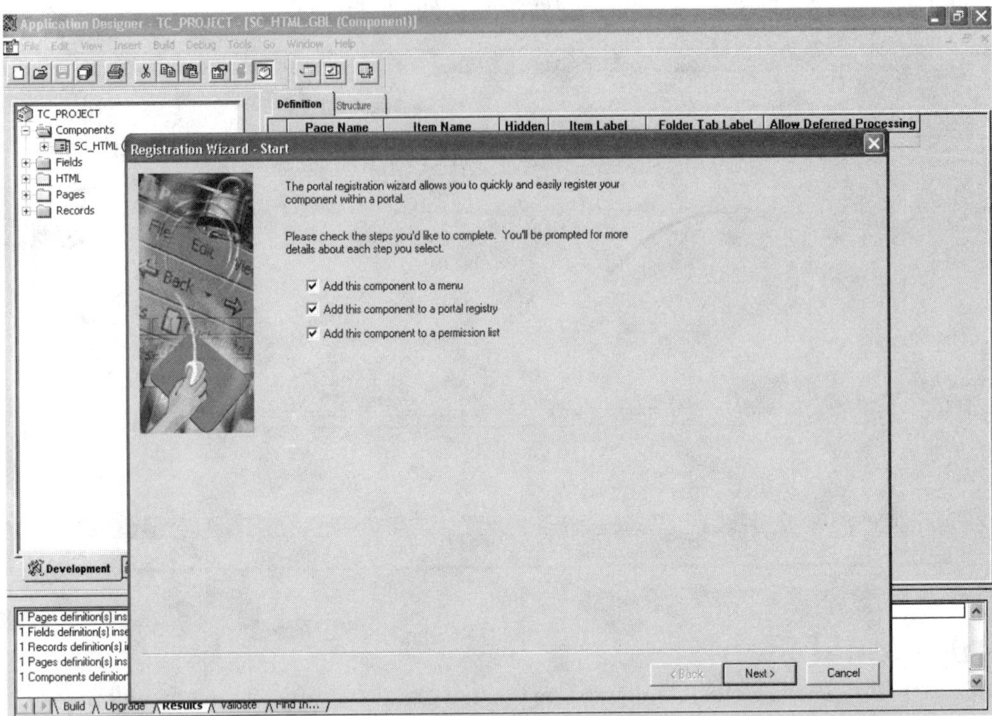

The second page of the Portal Wizard is where you select the menu and bar on which you want to define your component.

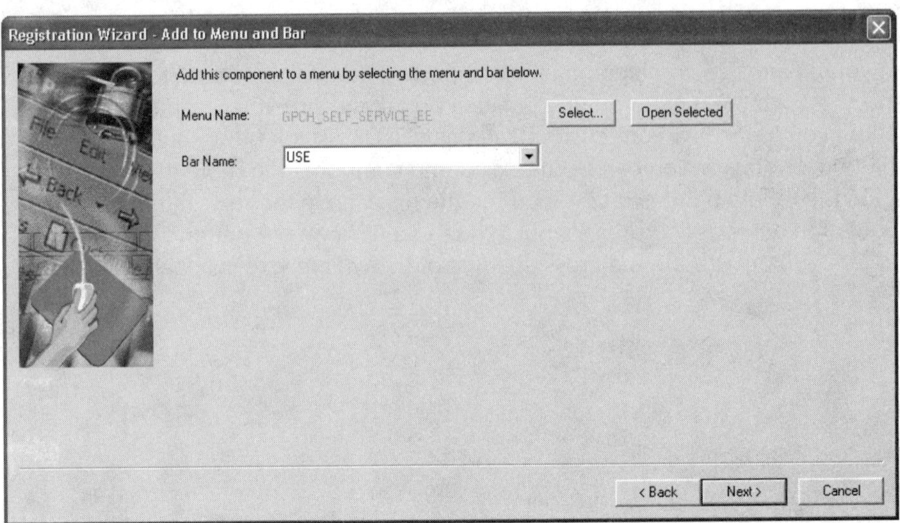

The third page of the wizard is where you define the portal on which your page will reside.

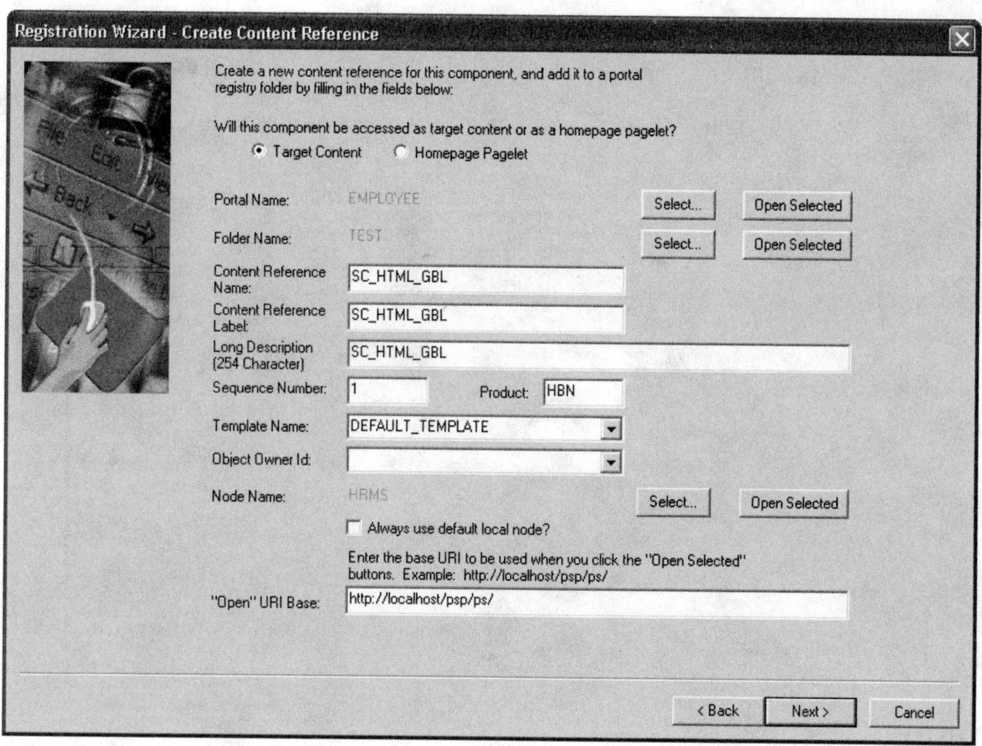

On the final page of the Portal Registery Wizard, you set the permission list you want associated with your component (which is where your page resides).

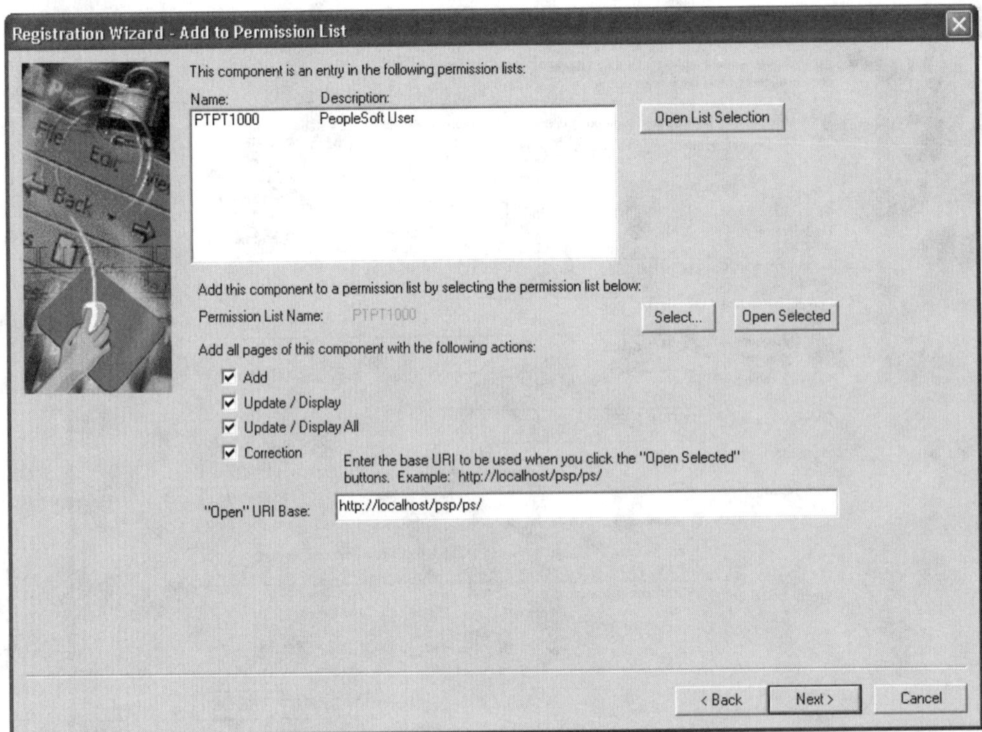

So, as you can see, it is all tied together—you have to have a component, page, menu, permission list, and a place on the portal in order to display your new page. Here's what the end result will look like.

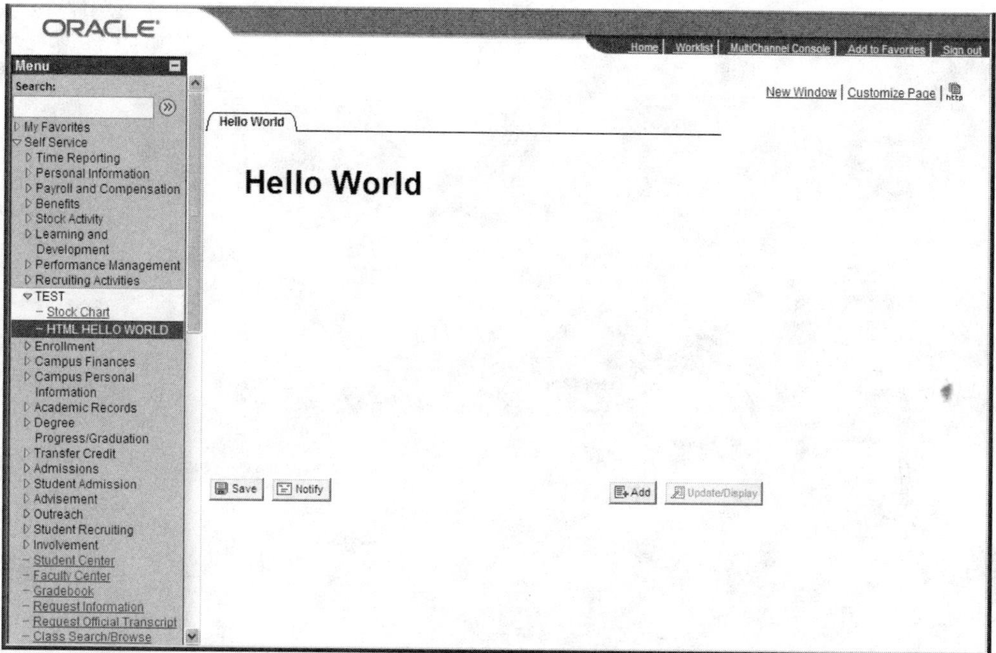

Summary

In this chapter you gained an understanding of PeopleSoft pages, the mainstay of the PeopleSoft development environment. You learned how to create pages from scratch and how to alter delivered pages. You also learned how to associate a page to a component, and register the menu to the portal. All of the elements of the page, including aesthetic controls and data entry controls, as well as ways to drill down on a page, were discussed. Mastery of the page is the first step in becoming a skilled PeopleSoft developer.

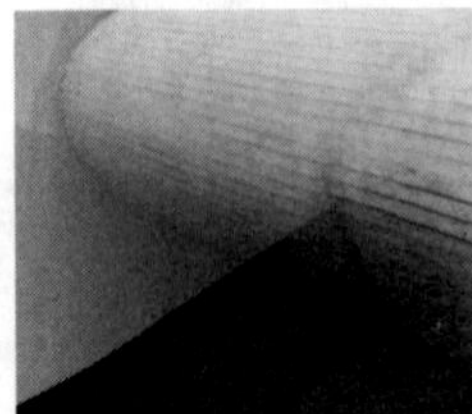

CHAPTER 6

PeopleCode

elcome to the chapter about the meat of PeopleSoft—how to write code. Writing code can be exciting and fun—it is a creative process and it allows you to design and create a working application. It is always gratifying to see your end product being used in business; it truly allows the coder to contribute a work of art to the business world. More than likely this is not the first language you will have written in, and you will see many commonalities between PeopleCode and other languages you have studied, such as COBOL, C, C++, Visual Basic, and Java. As long as you can type code, you only need to follow the structure laid out by the code creators and the syntax for the commands. PeopleSoft makes coding as simple as possible by providing wizards to assist with the structure and syntax.

It is important to follow programming design theory, a topic that will not be covered in this book. If this concept is new to you, then it would be a good idea to get some books, take a class or two, and learn the framework behind programming. If you try to program without understanding the basics of breaking a project into parts and making each component function as a whole, it would be like creating a house without a blueprint or the basic knowledge behind architectural design. Don't get the wrong impression—programming can be self-taught just like any skill, but as with anything worth the time, mastering the fundamentals is key. This chapter will provide you with the fundamentals of the syntax and structure as well as give you the knowledge of where PeopleCode is stored, which event to use, and where to place your code.

Basic Language Syntax and Structure

Code is written in events on objects within PeopleSoft and the Application Designer is used to edit these objects. The key issue is where to place the code and which event fires when. The list of events that fire in PeopleSoft is relatively small, but it can be confusing deciding whether to place the code on the page or on the field (record field). You need to remember that a record comes from the metadata in PeopleSoft and when used in code does not always update the physical data side of the database table. PeopleSoft records can be handled as automatically created arrays, but the division between the metadata and the database tends to confuse.

PeopleCode Editor

You are already familiar with the Application Designer, so now let's take a look at the PeopleCode window and get comfortable with the options. Take a look at the PeopleCode window in Figure 6-1.

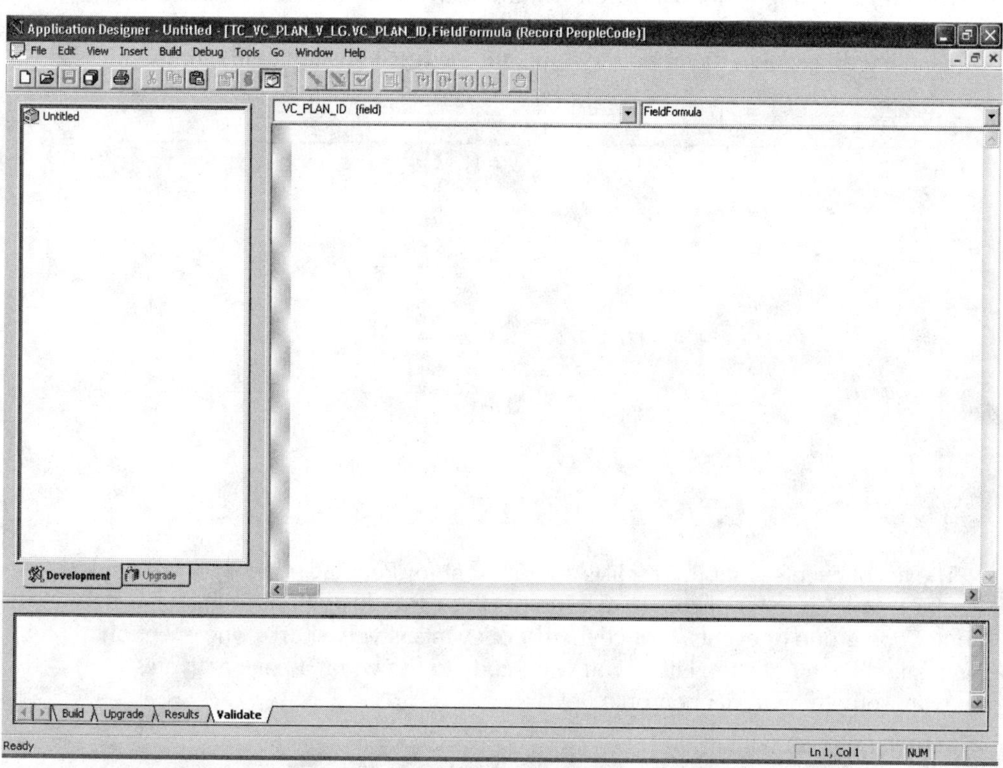

FIGURE 6-1 *PeopleCode window*

NOTE

In Figure 6-1 you may notice the field name that is being used as an example, TC_VC_PLAN_V_LG, makes very little sense. In this chapter it is important to concentrate on learning the code, structure, and syntax, not naming conventions. It is not this book's goal to teach naming conventions; PeopleBooks and external web sites like the one from the University of Utah (http://www.acs.utah.edu/acs/psoft/pol5-1.html) do an excellent job teaching naming conventions.

The programming window is just a white screen that does not look particularly interesting. This is where you enter your code. Notice that there are a number of events in the drop-down menu on the right, and on the left is the field name.

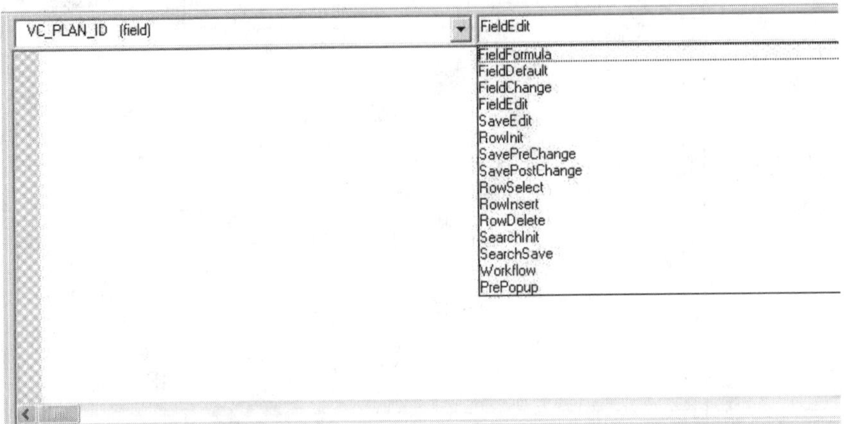

The list of events is short. The lists are different for PeopleCode for record fields than for PeopleCode for pages. Take a look at this next illustration for the page PeopleCode group of events. Notice the list of events is very short—one event on a page, called Page Activate. Either you want code to fire when a page activates or you want something to happen on a field.

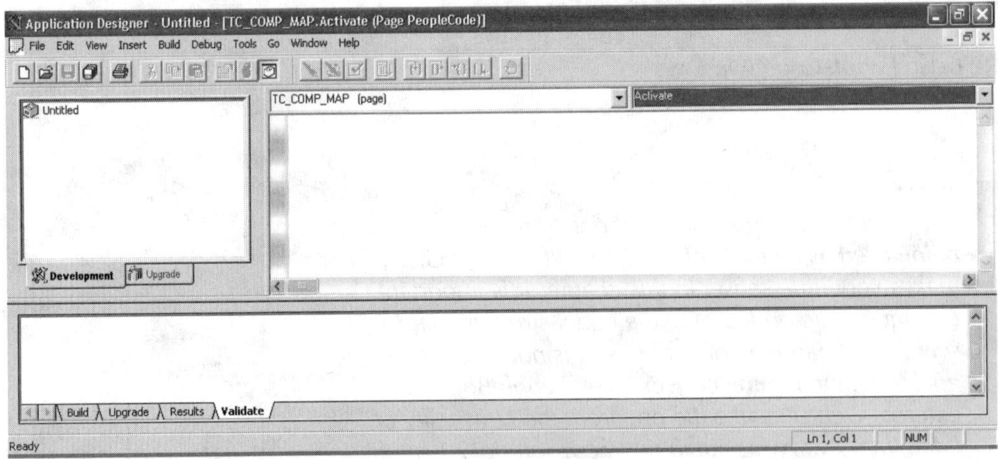

Why do the PeopleSoft metadata and the RDMS data tend to confuse new PeopleSoft programmers so much? Well, it is because you have to wipe out from your mind anything you have learned to this point about databases and developing on the top of databases. Maybe your experience has been with Microsoft Access and you have created forms and reports that are directly related to the table and/or the column in the database. This theory holds true for all types of applications written on databases except in the realm of enterprise-level applications, which are a different concept in development and oftentimes a big step up in the understanding of theory. Remember in previous chapters we talked about the metadata, and that PeopleSoft has a record in the metadata that directly correlates to a table in the database. PeopleSoft also has a field that directly correlates to a column in the database. PeopleSoft can also have a derived work record that does not exist anywhere except in the metadata and is used as a virtual table or array to work with the manipulation of data that does not change the physical table data. These are difficult concepts to grasp, so don't be surprised if it takes some time coding in PeopleSoft before the "light goes on." Entering data and displaying data—or in PeopleSoft-ease, Add, Update/Display, Update/Display All, Correction, and Data Entry—all take place on a PeopleSoft page utilizing PeopleSoft records that have PeopleSoft fields.

Events and Code Placement

This brings us to the important topic of what to write and where. Take a look at the following description:

> "SearchInit PeopleCode performs before the search dialog box displays. SearchSave PeopleCode performs after the operator clicks OK in the search record dialog box. RowSelect PeopleCode is used to filter out rows of data. PreBuild is often used to hide and unhide the pages. FieldDefault attempts to set defaults for fields without a value. FieldFormula performs after FieldDefault completes successfully. RowInit is used to initialize the rows. PostBuild PeopleCode performs after all the component build events have performed. Activate Event is fired every time the page is activated."

I have a copy of this permanently taped up in my cube and it never fails that I have to review it when code is not firing when I expect it to. A couple of points that are missing from the GeekInterview response are FieldEdit and FieldChange, which fire after a user changes, deletes, modifies, or adds a field value. RowInit fires after a new row is inserted, and RowDelete after a row is deleted. It is important to understand all of the available field events: FieldFormula, FieldDefault, FieldChange, FieldEdit, SaveEdit, RowInit, SavePreChange, SavePostChange, RowSelect, RowInsert, RowDelete, SearchInit, SearchSave, WorkFlow, and PrePopup. The response to GeekInterview was written at a time when PeopleSoft had panels and now these events are on the component.

When you are coding in PeopleCode you are not only dealing with a page and a record field, but you will also be coding components, component records, and component record fields. Component PeopleCode, component record PeopleCode, and component record field PeopleCode are all PeopleCode on a component written in different areas or attached in different areas, and each piece of code fires at a different point within the system when it is processing a component. Figure 6-2 shows a component PeopleCode window, and Figure 6-3 shows a component

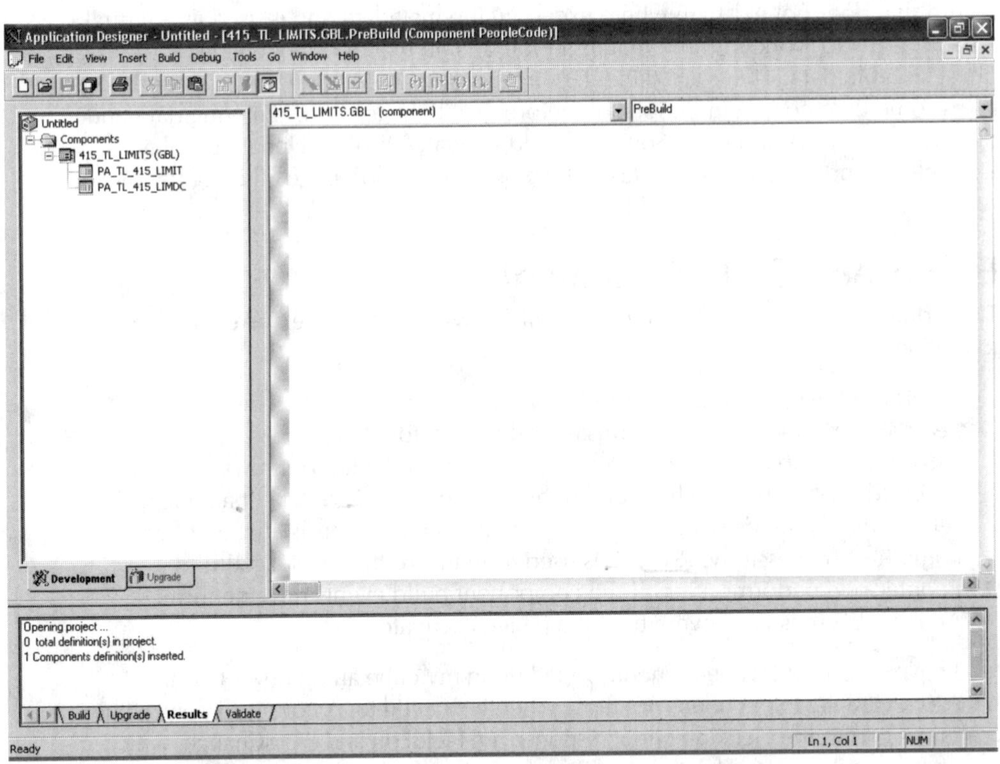

FIGURE 6-2 *Component PeopleCode window*

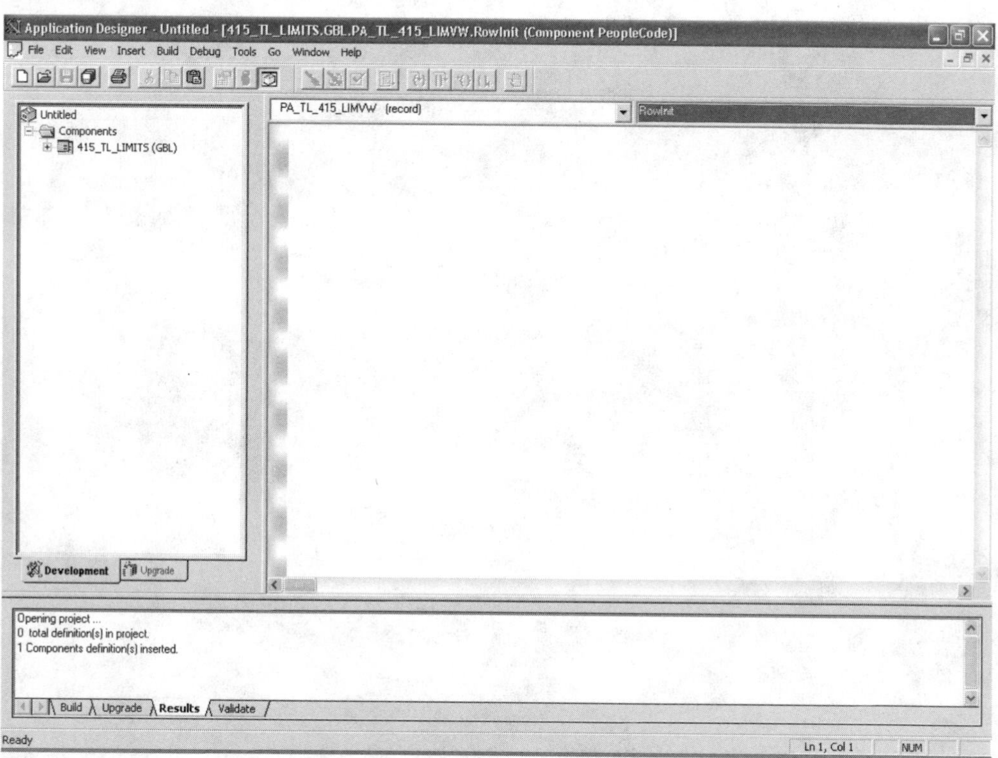

FIGURE 6-3 *Component record PeopleCode window*

record PeopleCode window. In Figure 6-4 you can see a component record field PeopleCode window.

In the component the events are PreBuild, PostBuild, SavePreChange, and SavePostChange. Component record events are RowInit, RowInsert, RowDelete, RowSelect, SaveEdit, SavePostChange, and SavePreChange. Component record field events are FieldDefault, FieldEdit, FieldChange, and PrePopup. (See Table 6-1 for a more detailed description of these events and their usage.) It is important to know that component code fires before component record field, which fires before component record field code.

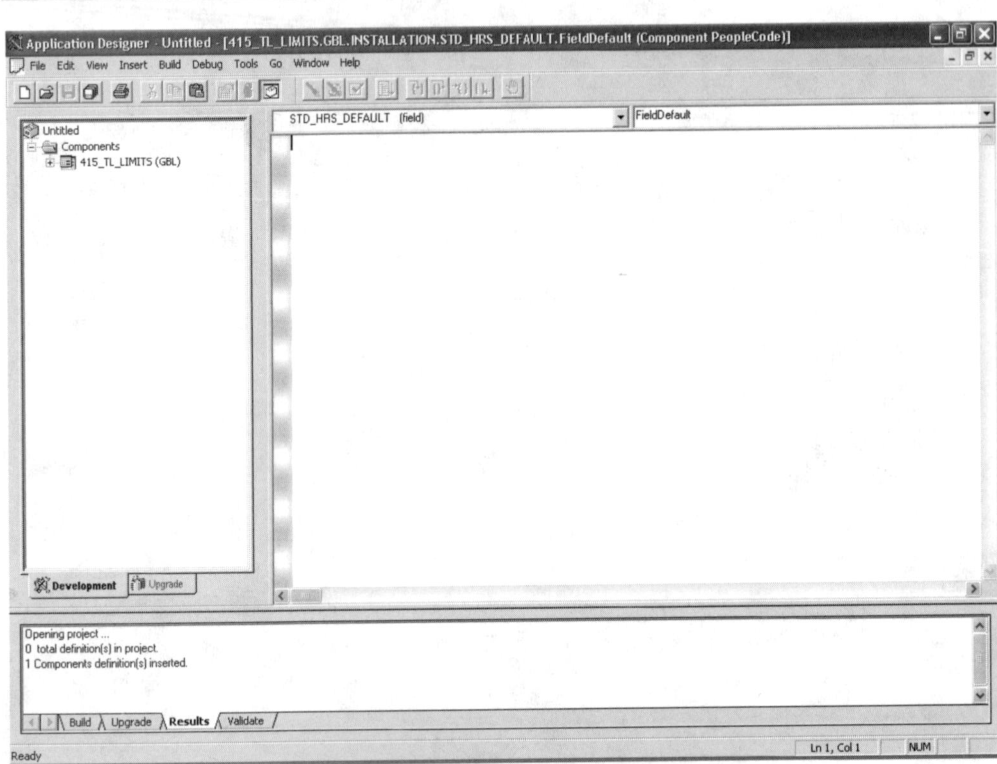

FIGURE 6-4 *Component record field PeopleCode window*

The easiest way to access the PeopleCode Editor on a component is to open the component and select View | View PeopleCode. The PeopleCode Editor window will appear. Click on the left drop-down list box to see a list of objects: the component, the records used by the component, and the fields on those records. The ones in bold already have PeopleCode. Click on the appropriate line to view,

Event	Usage	Types of Use	Comments
PreBuild	Medium	It is fired before the rest of the component build events. The main use is to hide the current page.	This event is associated with page manipulation. PeopleSoft recommends that if you want to hide the current page you use the PreBuild event.
PostBuild	Medium	It is fired after all the other component build events have been initiated. It is often used to hide or unhide pages. It's also used to set component variables.	Can only be associated with components.
SavePreChange	Medium	The Component Processor initiates the SavePreChange event, which fires any SavePreChange events on a record field, a component record, or a component.	It allows you to process data after validation and before the database update.
SavePostChange	Medium	The component processor initiates the SavePostChange PeopleCode event, which fires SavePostChange written on a record field, a component record, or a component.	Use it for processing that needs to occur after the database update; an example is updates to other database tables not in the component buffer.
RowInit	Often	This event is initiated the first time that the component processor encounters a row of data.	RowInit is not field-specific; it fires on all fields and on all rows in the component buffer. Do not use error or warning statements in RowInit; it will cause a runtime error.
RowInsert	Medium	When a user adds a row of data, it generates a RowInsert event. Use RowInsert PeopleCode to processes around the insertion of new rows. Do not write PeopleCode in RowInsert that already exists in RowInit, because a RowInit event initiates after the RowInsert, which causes your code to be fired twice.	RowInsert is written on any field that inserts a row of data. Do not use a warning or error in RowInsert.

TABLE 6-1 *Component Record and Component Record Field Events*

Event	Usage	Types of Use	Comments
RowDelete	Medium	Fires whenever a user tries to delete a row of data from a page scroll area. You use RowDelete PeopleCode to prevent the deletion of a row —with an error or warning statement. You can also perform other processing before row deletion.	RowDelete can be written on any field on the row of data that is being flagged as deleted. RowDelete can be written on record fields and component records.
RowSelect	Medium	RowSelect is fired after the beginning of the component build process (Update, Update/Display All, and Correction). RowSelect can be used to filter data as it is read into the component buffer. This event also occurs after a ScrollSelect.	RowSelect can be written on record fields and component records.
SaveEdit	Medium	SaveEdit fires whenever a user attempts a save on the component. Use this event to validate data on the component fields.	SaveEdit can be written on record fields and components.
SavePostChange	Medium	After updates to the database are made by the component processor, SavePostChange event is fired. You can use SavePostChange to update tables not in your component using SQLExec.	SavePostChange can be written on record fields, components, and component records. Errors or warnings written in this cause a runtime error.
SavePreChange	Medium	After the SaveEdit completes, then the SavePreChange fires. It is the final chance to manipulate the data before the system updates the database.	SavePreChange PeopleCode is not field-specific; it fires on all fields and on all rows within the component buffer.
FieldDefault	Medium	After the FieldChange fires, the component processor runs default processing and redisplays the page.	When the user changes the field to blank or if SetDefault is executed, the FieldDefault fires and sets a default value.

TABLE 6-1 *Component Record and Component Record Field Events* (continued)

Event	Usage	Types of Use	Comments
FieldEdit	Medium	When the field passes through the system edits, the component processor fires the FieldEdit, which triggers any FieldEdits on the record field or the component record field.	You want to place error or warning statements in FieldEdit not the FieldChange event.
FieldChange	Often	Used to automatically change another field when the field that the code is written on changes. One common use is to have code pop up a message when this field changes.	It is similar in functionality to FieldEdit, but this code fires while the cursor is still in the field. In the case of the FieldEdit, firing doesn't happen until after the cursor leaves the field.
PrePopup	Rare	Right before the display of a pop-up menu, this event is fired. You use PrePopup to fire code to change the appearance of the pop-up menu.	Is associated with record fields and component record fields.

TABLE 6-1 *Component Record and Component Record Field Events* (continued)

add, or change code. These lines represent three distinct types of objects: component PeopleCode, component record PeopleCode, and component record field PeopleCode. See an example of this in Figure 6-5.

PeopleCode Event Summary

An event is the way that the PeopleSoft Application Designer associates a program with a definition. Each event is a predefined point in the component processor flow, commonly referred to as the *program flow*. When an event is encountered in the program flow, it fires on a component, which triggers the PeopleCode program associated with it to process. Each definition can be a single definition or it can be one of an event set, a group of PeopleCode events that fire in a program flow. A definition can fall outside of the component processor. External processes include: Application Engine programs, component interfaces, and application packages. There is also the standard sign-on event, which allows for the creation of a session with the PeopleSoft application and resides external to any and all events.

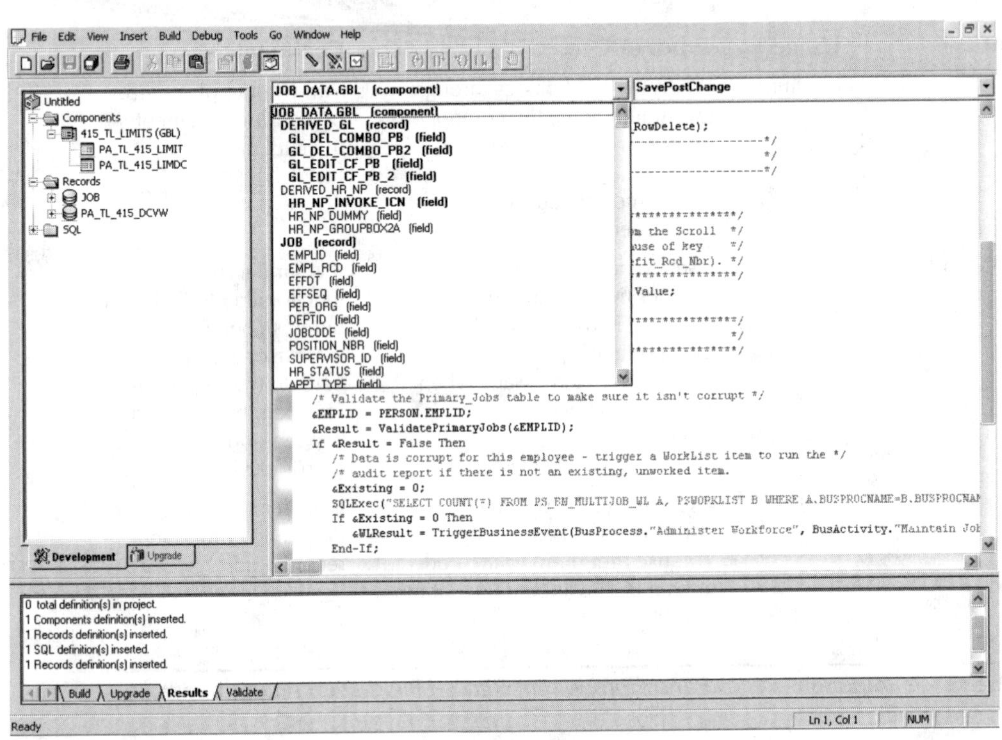

FIGURE 6-5 *Component PeopleCode Editor drop-down menus*

PeopleTools Menus

You have available to you as a developer inside of PeopleSoft two types of menus: standard menus and pop-up menus. Each type of menu is defined separately as a standalone definition within your project. The following illustration shows a menu defined in a project.

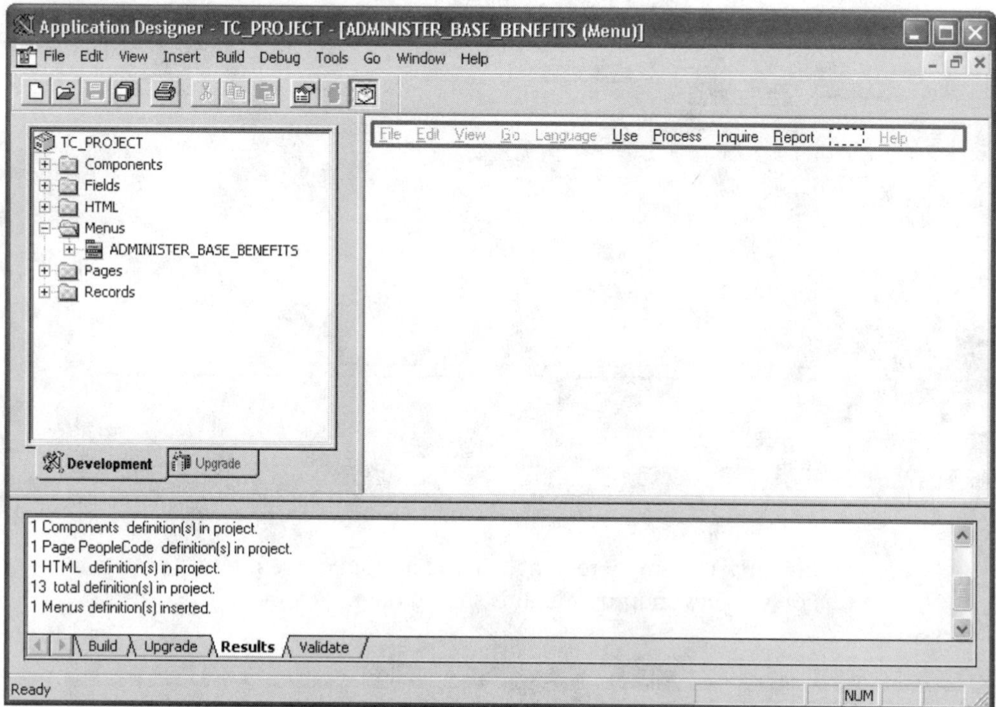

PeopleCode can be used only on pop-up menus, not in standard menus. There is only one event on a pop-up menu to write PeopleCode in—ItemSelected. This event fires whenever a menu item is selected from a pop-up menu. Be careful not to confuse PeopleCode functions such as CheckMenuItem, which changes a menu's appearance, with the ability to fire PeopleCode on a menu.

Defining PeopleCode Pop-Up Menu Items

To define a PeopleCode pop-up menu item, follow these steps:

1. Create a pop-up menu.

   a. In the menu definition, double-click an existing pop-up menu.

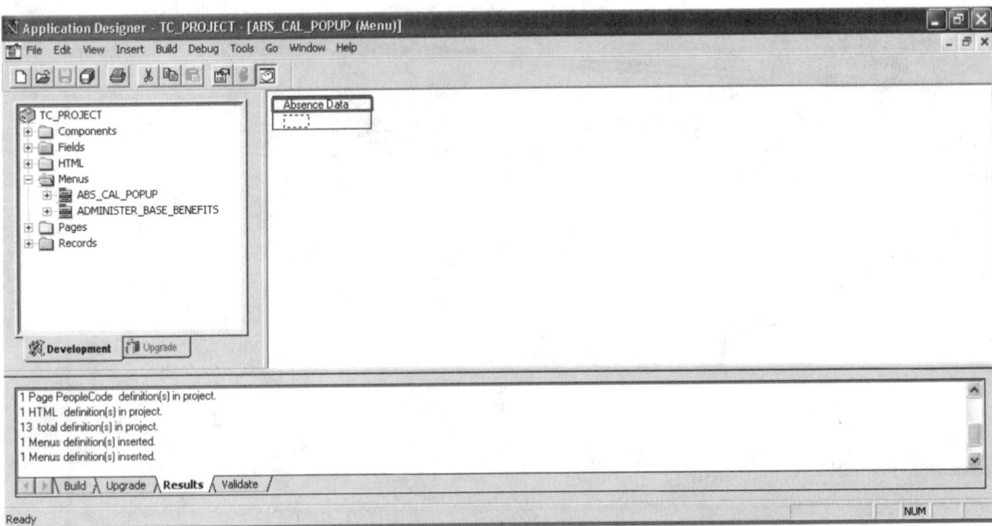

b. Double-click the empty rectangle at the bottom of the menu. The creation of a new pop-up menu is shown here.

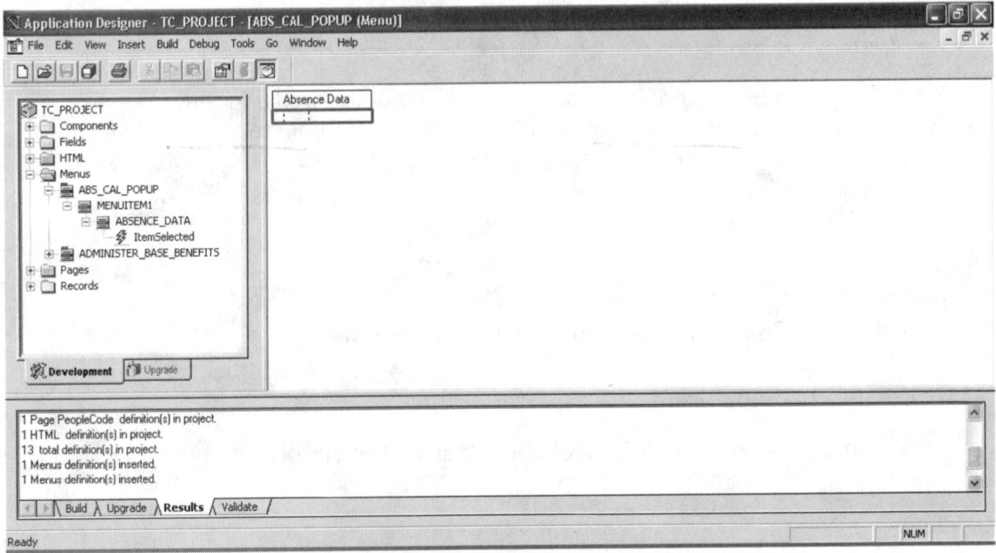

2. Enter a name and a label for the item.

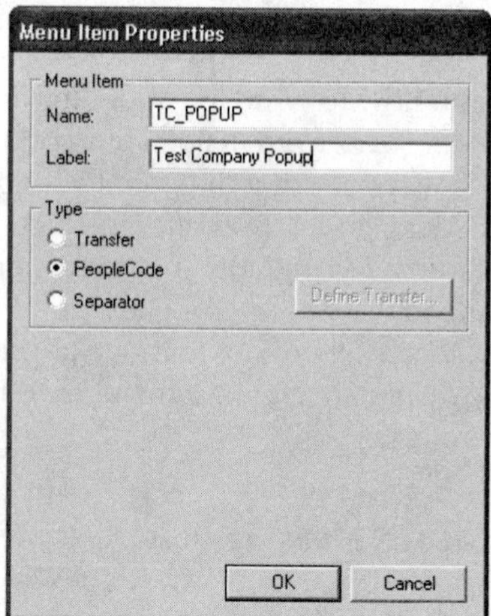

3. Select PeopleCode from the Type group to enter the PeopleCode. Here, you can see the pop-up menu PeopleCode.

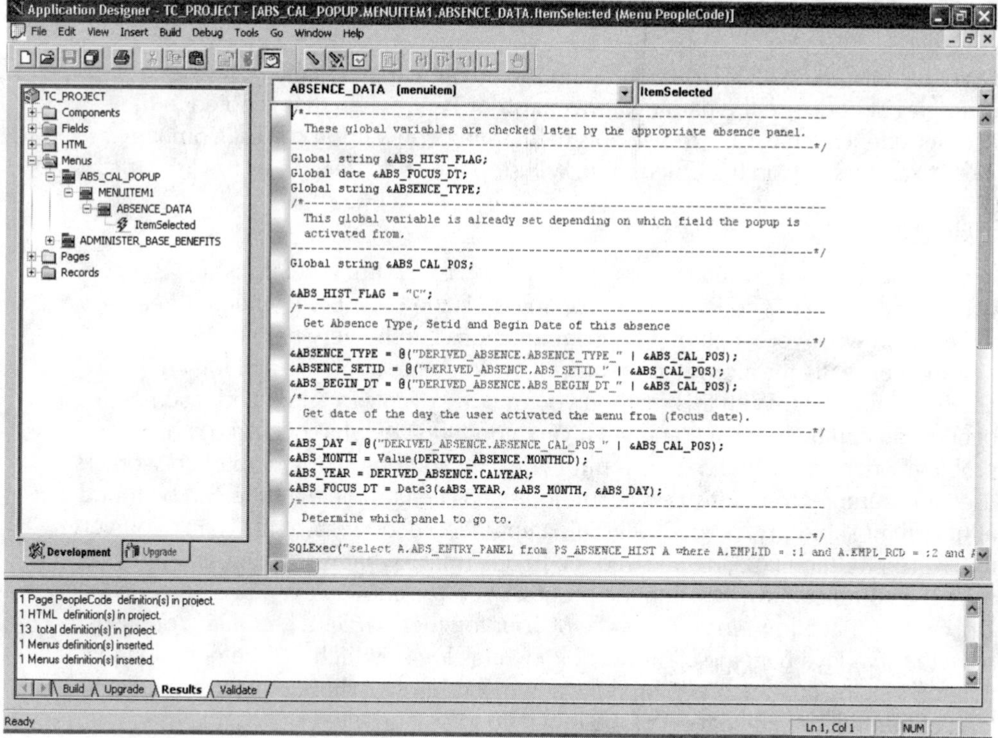

4. Click OK to close and then save your project.

Debugging and Message Functions

Before we get too heavily into how to write the code, it is important for you to understand how to receive messages from inside your code for debugging purposes. The following are some nice ways of using different techniques for debugging. My favorite is the MessageBox. MessageBox fires after the fact. For example, a transfer to a new component will cause a MessageBox not to trigger. MessageBox is one of the most powerful debugging tools in your tool chest as a PeopleSoft developer. The problem is that you have to remark them out to move to production; otherwise, these puppies will just keep firing. So always remember to remove or remark them out when you move your project.

```
MessageBox(0, "", 0, 0, "%1 ",
&rs_Degree(CurrentRowNumber()).HRS_APP_DEG_VW.STATE_OTHER.Visible);

MessageBox(0, "", 0, 0, " %1 * %2 * %3 and %4 and %5 and %6 ",
&TC_RIP_AVG_EARN_36,
&TC_Futr_Svc_Amt, &TC_Ret_Age_Factor, "USD", %Date,
RoundCurrency(&TC_RIP_AVG_EARN_36 * &TC_Futr_Svc_Amt *
&TC_Ret_Age_Factor, "USD",
%Date));
```

Note that the %1, %2, %3, %4, %5, and %6 are all variables; the previous examples of code use the naming convention of TC_ , when that is noted in the PeopleCode examples; TC_ represents the naming convention of Test Company.

A WinMessage, on the other hand, will stop the code dead in its tracks.

```
WinMessage("Test" | &AppName);
```

MessageBox is the preferred method by PeopleSoft. But a WinMessage is a good way to make sure the code you are working on is the code being called. It really depends on what you are trying to. Both functions can be very helpful.

Another really terrific way of debugging is to create a log file and log off anything important. With this method you trap the events in a log, and if something occurs you can trace it back and get a very good idea of what occurred. I had a problem where my search page wouldn't display and one of my helpful co-workers used an example from Jim's PeopleSoft Journal. (The complete article can be found at http://jjmpsj.blogspot.com/2006/09/logging-peoplecode_15.html. Thank you very much, Terry Graff.) Logging allowed me to determine what was being set, and to trace the complete flow through the process. You have to have a place on your Unix server that allows for the storage of your log files *\\PSDV1\LOGS*. You also have to use a Java Logging Framework known as log4j, which can be downloaded at http://logging.apache.org/log4j/docs/download.html. I will not attempt to do any kind of training or explanation of the log4j; you can find a ton of information about it on the web. Just know that it is via this application that the logging to the Unix directory is taking place. Jim, or Jim's PeopleSoft Journal, uses the Java Logging Framework completely as he states, "PeopleCode supports Java objects and

PeopleSoft delivers the log4j lib in the PS_HOME/class directory." The following methods can be invoked within the log4j: debug(), info(), warn(), error(), fatal(), and log(). These methods generate log requests during application execution so your code can be riddled with them and they will log off and never disturb your customers.

Using this logging method can take the place of a WinMessage or a MessageBox. It gives you some very powerful debugging capabilities. You can monitor certain events, log the event, and move the logging capability event into production, whereas with WinMessage and MessageBox you need to remove them prior to moving your project. Otherwise, they will fire and give a message out to the entire world. This is probably not what you want as the thing that makes you famous in your organization as a PeopleSoft developer. Dave Ricker, another one of my really smart co-workers (or should I say legacy co-worker—I followed him and he is a very skilled and talented programmer), always puts If logic in his code to turn logging on and off. I love this because at the top of code right after the variable declarations I have &Diagnostics = 'N' and when I want to debug I set it to &Diagnostics = 'Y'. Very slick, Dave!

```
/*Create a Diagnostics Variable and then use it accordingly */
IF &Diagnostics = 'Y' then
/* call logging
logger.debug("Logger created");
logger.info("Process completed successfully");
Else
/* no logging
End-if;

/* Declare the object variable */
Local JavaObject &logEvent;
/* Instantiate the variable  */
&logEvent = GetJavaClass("org.apache.log4j.Logger").getLogger("Put your
log identifying string message here I.e. page name… Component record
field name….
com.mycompany.mydepartment.PS.Component.Record.Field.Event");
/* Log a message */
&logEvent.debug("In the Test Company tool component... " | &outputVar…
put something meaningful here to log);
```

Message Catalog

Message catalogs represent the messages you want to go out to your customers in the production environment. They are the messages that you want displayed when a wrong value is typed or a button is used incorrectly. PeopleSoft delivers thousands of these in its applications and you can create thousands of your own. With PeopleSoft 8.5 the location of the message catalog is stored in a new record named PSMSGCATDEFN. The old record was PS_MESSAGE_CATALOG.

First, let's take a look at where these message catalogs are stored and you will get a good idea of what they are used for (you can see the main window via the PIA in Figure 6-6). It is important to note that these are used to give information to your application users when they click wrong, enter a wrong value, try to save when they shouldn't, etc. In Figure 6-7 you can see the creation of a new message catalog. In the Type drop-down list, your choices are Cancel, Message, Error, and Warning.

The following snips of code show you ways of determining where your messages are. In an upgrade it is very important to get the message catalogs that were custom created moved over. And with a new table as the location, you want to find all of your messages and move them.

In 8.3 the following SQL will work:

```
SELECT * FROM PS_MESSAGE_CATALOG
```

In 8.9 the following SQL will work:

```
SELECT * FROM PSMSGCATDEFN WHERE MESSAGE_SET_NBR = '20302'
```

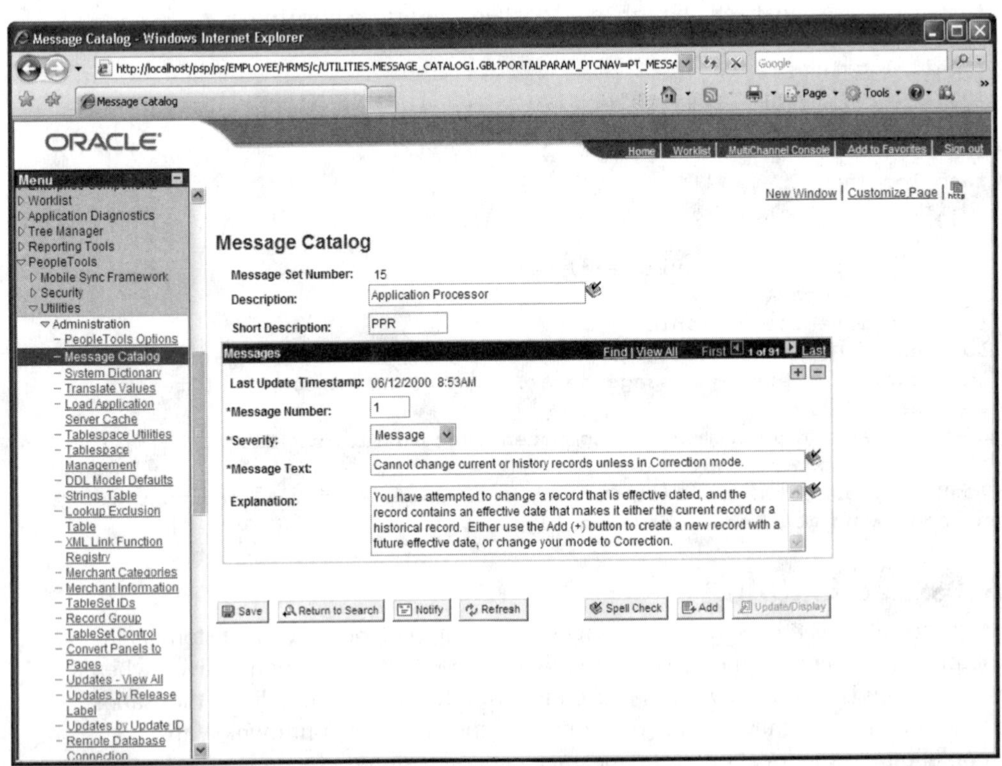

FIGURE 6-6 *Message Catalog definition in the PIA*

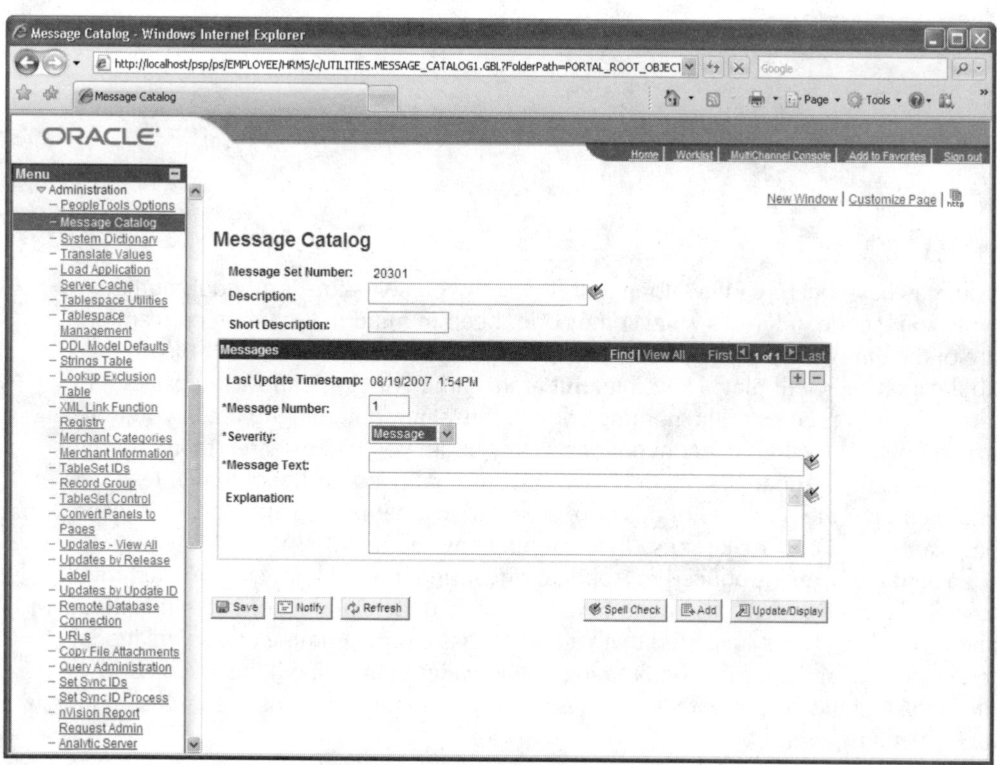

FIGURE 6-7 *Creation of a new message catalog in the PIA*

The following SQL will help you determine what message catalogs have been changed in 8.9 or added:

```
--all
SELECT *
FROM PSMSGCATDEFN
WHERE TO_DATE(SUBSTR(LAST_UPDATE_DTTM,1 ,10)) '01-Apr-06'

-- for ones in your message catalog range for eRecruit in our organization -- we
used 20301 to 20310
SELECT * FROM PSMSGCATDEFN  WHERE TO_DATE(SUBSTR(LAST_UPDATE_DTTM,1 ,10)) '01-Apr-
06'
AND (MESSAGE_SET_NBR > 20300 AND MESSAGE_SET_NBR < 20304)

---metadata record for project Items Item OBJECTTYPE = 25 is for message
--catalogs
--if you know your project name and know the amount above the values
SELECT * FROM PSPROJECTITEM WHERE PROJECTNAME = 'TC714BEN' AND OBJECTTYPE = 25
```

```
---- The 2 sql values should match if I created 6 Message catalogs there
-- should be 6 in your project
SELECT COUNT(*) FROM PSMSGCATDEFN  WHERE TO_DATE(SUBSTR(LAST_UPDATE_DTTM,1 ,10)) >
'01-Apr-06'
AND (MESSAGE_SET_NBR > 20300 AND MESSAGE_SET_NBR < 20304)

SELECT COUNT(*) FROM PSPROJECTITEM WHERE PROJECTNAME = 'SCR714BEN' AND OBJECTTYPE =
25
```

Syntax

You may have been reading along and saying to yourself—this is all cool, but let's write some code. OK, let's write some code. Keep in mind that naming conventions are of the utmost importance in an organization and when writing a full-blown application they will play a key role. But at this time you don't know the basics let alone the ins and outs of the naming conventions. I am not going to teach you the ins and outs of the naming conventions in this book; you can research them, follow your company standards, and, believe me, your quality control people will teach you them. For the purposes of this book, we will just name the variables simply and easily to so that they make sense in a teaching environment.

You have been introduced to Application Designer and I know you are itching to write in this tool. You also need to have a basic understanding of code in general, and if you do not, it is suggested that you take a basic programming course, relational theory course, and a basic programming mathematics course. It will be assumed in this book that the fundamental training is already there and it will not be discussed at an elementary level.

Declaring Variables

The very first skill you have to acquire in PeopleCode is learning how to declare variables. The following sections list the types of variables and provide examples of how to declare them. PeopleCode variables (except object variables) are all preceded with "&" and then the data type of the assignment statement.

ANY

This variable is used when the data that is being returned into this type is unknown. The use of the type ANY will allow PeopleTools to determine the best match for the variable. Undeclared local variables by default become ANY variables. The following code uses an ANY type variable called &Example_Any to be a string in some cases, and a date in other cases.

```
/*Any Variable Declaration */
Local Any &Example_Any;
Local String &Test;
Local String &Test2;
```

```
/* &Example_Any set to a STRING */
&Example_any = "TEST";
REM Concatenation of two strings and &Example_Any is a String
&Example_Any = &Test | ' ' | &Test2;
REM ANY set to a Date--%Date is today's date
&Example_any = %Date;
/*Working with dates when you perform math on a date what do you get in
return?  A
number--look at the following example:*/
&Example_Any = %Date - &birthdate;
/* A number that represents the number of days between
the two is the result */
```

BOOLEAN

This variable is a single bit type that can be TRUE(1) or FALSE(0).

```
REM BOOLEAN Example Declaration
LOCAL BOOLEAN &B_test;
&B_test = False;
```

DATE

This variable is a standard date that in PeopleCode is in the format YYYY-MM-DD and in the Oracle database is in the format DD-MM-YYY. It is important when working with dates to know the base format that your database is using—your DBA could have changed it, and each platform is different.

DATETIME

This variable is exactly what it says—the date with the time—and is in the following format: YYYY-MM-DD-HH.MI.SS.SSSSSS.

TIME

This variable is expressed as HHMISS. When you use a function that uses TIME, it returns a numeric value.

NUMBER

A NUMBER variable is a decimal value or integers; it can be any number that has decimal points. NUMBER and STRING are the most used variable types in PeopleCode.

```
/* Declaration examples of number */
&Number_example1 = 456;
&Number_example2 = 456.78;
&Number_example3 = 0.45678;
&Number_example4 = -456.78;
```

FLOAT

This variable represents a floating decimal point number. You should only use FLOAT when there is a performance gain and when you compare it to using NUMBER and the results of your math are the same—and no effects on the result are found. The FLOAT variable is a number using a machine floating binary point—or double precision. When is it necessary to use this? In exact calculations using decimal fractions or, for the lay person, calculations involving money. Let's take a look at an example: Because one-tenth (1/10 or .1) cannot be exactly represented as a floating binary point, a floating binary point sum of .10 + .10 is not equal to .20. And by default the NUMBER data type in PeopleCode is a floating decimal point representation—this helps a great deal with this problem.

INTEGER

This variable is a whole number with no decimal points. You should only use INTEGER when a performance increase is gained, and as with FLOAT, you should do the entire math in your programming and verify that deviation does not exist. Division &X/&Y is never performed using integer arithmetic in PeopleCode. What is used is floating decimal point arithmetic, even if you declare your variable as an INTEGER type. The INTEGER type is a number represented as a 32-bit signed number with a range of –2,147,483,648 to 2,147,483,647. Just the kind of thing you are going to go right out and memorize—and thanks to a Microsoft Certification exam I had to memorize just such a statistic—but truly remember that the following examples are integers:

```
/* INTEGER declaration */
Local INTEGER &Sample1, &Sample2, &Sample3;
&Sample1 = 44;
&Sample2 = 11000;
&Sample3 = -2200;
```

TIP

Some advice on when to use NUMBER, INTEGER, or FLOAT variables: Use NUMBER when you are unsure, and it will be the primary default way to declare numbers. Use INTEGER when you are counting items; a good example is when you count rows in a rowset. Use FLOAT only when you are performance tuning and the application is already working—and you know what the result should be.

STRING

This variable can be a combination of letters, special characters, and numbers. It is initialized by enclosing the declared string in quotes. You can use either single or double quotes. When you need to enclose a string within a string, one type of quote is enclosed by another type. The "best practice" is to enclose strings in double quotes and embedded strings in single quotes.

```
/*string declaration examples */
&sample_string = "Now is the time for all good men to come to the aid
of their country";

&sample_string2 = "Now is the time for all good men to come to the aid
of their country 'string within a string' declaration";

&sample_string3 = "Now is the time for all good men to come to the aid
of their country "double quoted string within a string" declaration";
```

OBJECT

OBJECT variables have their own data types:

- **PeopleCode Data Buffer Access Types** Field, Record, Row, and Rowset.

```
/* Section for HTML and Totals might be able to move the Totals GSDBEN1 */
/* Drilldown in the Rowset to get year */
&RS0 = GetLevel0();
/* level 1 both Previous and Current year. */
&RS1 = &RS0.GetRow(1).GetRowset(Scroll.ZY_TC_EE_AMT_VW);
&RS2 = &RS0.GetRow(1).GetRowset(Scroll.ZY_TC_EE_CUR_VW);
```

- **PeopleCode Display Data Types** AnalyticGrid, Chart, Grid, GridColumn, and Page.
- **PeopleCode Internet Script Data Types** Cookie, Request, and Response.
- **PeopleCode Miscellaneous Data Types** AESection, AnalyticInstance, Array, Crypt, Exception, File, Interlink, BIDocs, JavaObject (can only be declared as type Local), Message, MCFIMInfo, OptEngine, PostReport, ProcessRequest, RowsetCache, SoapDoc, SQL, SyncServer, TransformData (can only be declared as type Local), XmlDoc, and XmlNode (objects can only be declared as type Local).
- **Global ApiObject Data Type Objects** Session, PSMessages collection, PSMessages, all tree classes (trees, tree structures, nodes, levels, and etc.), and query classes.
- **Local ApiObject Data Type Objects** Meta SQL, Meta HTML, System Variables, and RowSet.

In the Chapter 7 you will see the use of most of these OBJECT types and it will be clearer how, when, and how frequently they are used. For more detailed information on each of the OBJECT types it is highly recommended that you read PeopleBooks for the most detailed and up to date information. You can download a copy of the Oracle PeopleBooks documentation at: http://www.oracle.com/technology/documentation/psftent.html.

Scope

There are three basic variable scopes in PeopleCode: Local, Component, and Global. The following are some examples of declaration statements. There are two types of Local variables: an ordinary Local program variable and a Local function variable. The duration that the variable is "alive" varies depending on the type. A Local program variable is declared and available during the duration of that program, and a Local function variable is available while the function is called and activated.

```
Local String &Last_name;
Local Number &bonus;
Global Number &401k_amt;
Component string &Hello_world;
```

The following is an example of duration from PeopleBooks:

```
Program A (Rec.Field.FieldChange):
local number &temp;
declare function B1 PeopleCode Rec.Field FieldFormula;
/* Uncomment this declaration and comment above to compile this the
first time.
function B1
end-function;
*/
function A1
WinMessage("A1: &temp is " | &temp);
&temp = &temp + 1;
A2();
B1();
A2();
end-function;
function A2
WinMessage("A2: &temp is " | &temp);
&temp = &temp + 1;
end-function;
A1();
Program B (Rec.Field.FieldFormula):
local number &temp;
declare function A2 PeopleCode Rec.Field FieldChange;
```

```
function B1
WinMessage("B1: &temp is " | &temp);
&temp = &temp + 1;
A2();
end-function;
When this is compiled and run, it produces the following output:
A1: &temp is 0
A2: &temp is 1
B1: &temp is 0
A2: &temp is 0
A2: &temp is 2
```

When you look at considering which type of variable to declare—Local, Global, or Component—it is important to understand their differences. The main difference is regarding their life spans:

- **Global** A Global variable is valid during the entire session and can be reset during the session. It is important to understand that its life span is associated with the session and you need to remember to clear and reassign depending on when you plan to use the variable. It is used less often because not that many items need to be valid during the entire session.
- **Component** A Component variable is only valid when the object or page that it was created on is valid. This type of variable is used in component interface coding.
- **Local** A Local variable is valid during the PeopleCode program or function where the variable was defined. It is the most common variable declaration.

Logic Statements

Considering the different types of logic statements that can be used in PeopleCode, let's first look at the simplest—the assignment statement. The assignment statement is the most basic type of code statement in PeopleCode, it consists of a variable "assigned" by an equal sign to a value. The variable is on the left and the value or expression on the right.

```
&sample_string = "Now is the time for all good men to come to the aid
of their
country";
```

If-Then-Else

One of the most common and easiest to use PeopleCode logic statements is the if-then-else statement. It allows you to control the flow of your program, it allows for branching, and it allows processing dependent upon a set of terms. Take a look at the following example. It returns a description when one is present in the table, and if one does not exist in the table, it will return an error explaining that the expected description was not in the table:

```
Local SQL &SQLX;
&SQLX = GetSQL(SQL.ZY_TC_XLAT_SQL, &Field_name, &Field_value);
   If &SQLX.Status = 0 Then
      If &SQLX.Fetch(&Field_Desc) Then
         rem Return &Field_Desc;
         &SQLX.Close();
      End-If;
   Else
      /* use PS error for SQL */
      &TITLE = MsgGet(10640, 24, "SQL Error");
      MessageBox(64, &TITLE, 10640, 23, "SQL Object Not Found in SQL",
SQL.ZY_TC_XLAT_SQL);
   End-If;
&SQLX.Close();
End-Function;
```

Evaluate

Another form of branching in PeopleCode is done using the Evaluate statement. It is used when you have multiple conditions that exist and you need to evaluate each of them. The following is the basic syntax, and then a more complex example follows:

```
Evaluate Expression
     When Comparison 1
          [Statements]
     When Comparison 2          [Statements]
When-Other [optional catch everything else]
End-Evaluate;
```

The When statement with an Evaluate statement will compare the expression using relation operators in the series of When clauses. Think about it the same way you do with If-Then-Else—when the statement evaluates to true, the When is fired off. Once it finishes with the first When it will then evaluate each of the subsequent statements. The following uses an example of Evaluate and When and then shows the same as an If-Then-Else set of statements.

```
Evaluate &Grade
     When >=90
          &Grade_Letter = "A";      When >=80 and <=90
          &Grade_Letter = "B";
     When >=70 and <=80
          &Grade_Letter = "C";
     When >=60 and <=70
```

```
        &Grade_Letter = "D";
    When-Other
        &Grade_Letter = "F";
End-Evaluate;
```

Here's the same code written as an If-Then-Else statement:

```
If &Grade >=90 then
    &Grade_Letter = "A";
Else
    If &Grade >=80 and <=90
       &Grade_Letter = "B";
    Else
        If &Grade >=70 and <=80
            &Grade_Letter = "C";
        Else
        If &Grade >=60 and <=70
             &Grade_Letter = "D";
        Else
             &Grade_Letter = "F";
End-if;      End-if;
        End-if;
            End-if;
```

For

For statements can be very useful tools. They are excellent when you need to execute statements multiple times, and you need to loop or iterate through them. The basic syntax of a For loop is as follows:

```
For &i = 1 to &j
    [Step 1]
    [Code Statement]
End-for;
```

The following code is to get each year's worth of contributions in a 401k and display it out in a particular row. It allows you to loop through and get previous years, and or build years into the future to allow for projection of 401k balances.

```
/* Section for HTML and Totals might be able to move the Totals GSDBEN1 */
/* Drilldown in the Rowset to get year */
&RS0 = GetLevel0();
/* level 1 both Previous and Current year. */
&RS1 = &RS0.GetRow(1).GetRowset(Scroll.ZY_TC_EE_AMT_VW);
&RS2 = &RS0.GetRow(1).GetRowset(Scroll.ZY_TC_EE_CUR_VW);
/* Previous Year */
For &J = 1 To &RS1.ActiveRowCount
/* gether Total for previous */
&PrevAmount = &PrevAmount + &RS1(&J).ZY_TC_EE_AMT_VW.ZY_AMOUNT_PAST.Value;
End-For;
```

While

The While statement is another way to loop and allow for repeated statements in PeopleCode. The loop will process until the expression is false. In a lot of aspects the For loop and the While loop are very similar. Any break within a loop returns control to the next highest level, and processing will continue with the next statement after the loop ends. While loops do have a danger of being written as a runaway loop, with For loops you do have more control. You will know the exact extent and scope of the loop in the first line of the declaration. The While loop on the other hand will loop until false is reached, and if false is never reached it will continue to process—and upset your System Administrator and DBA. The basic format is as follows:

```
While [Logical Expression]
      [Statement]
End-While;
```

The following is an example from "PeopleCode Developer's Guide—PeopleBooks":

```
Local SQL &SQL1, &SQL2, &SQL3;
&rBusExp = CreateRecord(Record.PERSONAL_DATA);
&rBusExpPer = CreateRecord(Record.BUS_EXPENSE_PER);
&rBusExpDtl = CreateRecord(Record.BUS_EXPENSE_DTL);
&rsBusExp = CreateRowset(Record.PERSONAL_DATA,
CreateRowset(Record.BUS_EXPENSE_PER,
CreateRowset(Record.BUS_EXPENSE_DTL)));
&rsBusExpPer = &rsBusExp.GetRow(1).GetRowset(1);
&MYFILE = GetFile("c:\temp\BUS_EXP.out", "W", %FilePath_Absolute);
&MYFILE.SetFileLayout(FileLayout.BUS_EXP_OUT);
&EMPLID = "8001";
&SQL1 = CreateSQL("%selectall(:1) where EMPLID = :2", &rBusExp, &EMPLID);
&SQL2 = CreateSQL("%selectall(:1) where EMPLID = :2", &rBusExpPer, &EMPLID);
While &SQL1.Fetch(&rBusExp)
&rBusExp.CopyFieldsTo(&rsBusExp.GetRow(1).PERSONAL_DATA);
&I = 1;
While &SQL2.Fetch(&rBusExpPer)
&rBusExpPer.CopyFieldsTo(&rsBusExpPer(&I).BUS_EXPENSE_PER);
&J = 1;
&SQL3 = CreateSQL("%selectall(:1) where EMPLID = :2
and EXPENSE_PERIOD_DT = :3", &rBusExpDtl, &EMPLID,
&rsBusExpPer(&I).BUS_EXPENSE_PER.EXPENSE_PERIOD_DT.Value);
&rsBusExpDtl = &rsBusExpPer.GetRow(&I).GetRowset(1);
While &SQL3.Fetch(&rBusExpDtl)
&rBusExpDtl.CopyFieldsTo(&rsBusExpDtl(&J).BUS_EXPENSE_DTL);
&rsBusExpDtl.InsertRow(&J);
&J = &J + 1;
```

```
End-While;
&rsBusExpPer.InsertRow(&I);
&I = &I + 1;
End-While;
&MYFILE.WriteRowset(&rsBusExp);
End-While;
&MYFILE.Close();
```

XLAT

An XLAT item returns true in a component interface if the value is being retrieved from an XLAT table. The following is an example of getting XLAT field values from an XLAT table:

```
/* Get Xlats from XLAT table */
Function Get_XLAT_LONGS(&Field_name, &Field_value, &Field_Desc);
Local SQL &SQLX;
&SQLX = GetSQL(SQL.ZY_TC_XLAT_SQL, &Field_name, &Field_value);
     If &SQLX.Status = 0 Then
          If &SQLX.Fetch(&Field_Desc) Then
               rem Return &Field_Desc;
               &SQLX.Close();
          End-If;
      Else
            /* use PS error for SQL */
            &TITLE = MsgGet(10640, 24, "SQL Error");
            MessageBox(64, &TITLE, 10640, 23, "SQL Object Not Found in SQL",
SQL.ZY_TC_XLAT_SQL);
     End-If;
     &SQLX.Close();
End-Function;
```

Documentation with Comments

Comments are an important element for any programmer. They provide you with a way to internally document your code. The first several lines of each code block should contain information about the what, where, why, and who created, changed, or added to the code. You should try to use language in your comments that makes it easy for anyone to follow along behind your code. This is always a difficult balance to reach; something that is straightforward to you now may not be as clear a year from now—so for your own sanity, over-comment and over-explain. It is very important to comment when you modify delivered PeopleCode so that when your organization upgrades it will be easy to determine what was delivered, what was modified by you, and what was modified in the upgrade.

The following are the different ways you can insert comments into PeopleCode:

- **/* */** Use /* at the beginning of the comment and */ at the end. This is usually used when a block of code is commented out. REM will remark out a single line of code. Put a ; at the end of the REM statement to terminate and note the end of the comment.
- **<* *>** Use <* at the beginning of the comment and *> at the end. This form of commenting is used to comment within another comment.

You will also see /+ +/ used in comments in application classes; they are generated by the compiler. Do not use this syntax to make comments—if you try to, they will be removed by the system the next time you compile or save your PeopleCode.

Note that text in a comment cannot exceed a maximum of 16,383 characters, as shown in the following example:

```
REM This line is commented out and serves as a reference point;
/* ----- Future Earnings Gathered Here ----- */
<*
/* Comment out the PeopleSoft Delivered version of calculating the Rate of the raise
and insert the new Sample Company way of calculating */
Raise_rate(EFFDT, EFFSEQ, COMP_FREQUENCY, COMPRATE, CHANGE_AMT, CHANGE_PCT);
raise_next_rate(EFFDT, EFFSEQ, 0);
*>
```

Summary

In this chapter we covered the basic syntax, structure, and screens used to write PeopleCode. We also looked at how to declare variables, the scope, the lifecycle, and the different ways to use conditional logic. You learned the importance of commenting and the best way to do that in your code, how to debug, how to pull data from the XLAT tables, and the meat of PeopleCode. You will be able to take the knowledge here and move forward into the next chapter and learn some really cool advanced PeopleCode techniques.

CHAPTER 7

Advanced PeopleCode

n this chapter we look a little deeper into PeopleTools, PeopleCode, PeopleSoft's versions of Java and JavaScript, and the component buffer. PeopleCode can be written to offer Web Standard Code compliance, and it is recommended that, when you work with HTML or Java that is embedded in your PeopleCode application, you use these standards. PeopleCode does not have a plug-in that will review whether your code is Web Standard compliant, but Eclipse does have a plug-in for Java. Truly the only time you will run into problems is with your embedded HTML and Java code. This chapter will provide the advanced PeopleCode skills that will make you a more valuable PeopleSoft developer. PeopleSoft is an easy language platform to work in as long as you observe the basics of where code is fired, how to write it efficiently, and the best tool to use to get the desired result.

There are different categories of functions and methods available in PeopleCode; the first category of functions is the PeopleSoft built-in functions, which include string functions and message catalogs. The next type of function is a customized function, which could be an internal PeopleSoft function or an external C or Java function. Also available in PeopleCode is the ability to write methods that call the component buffer. By using functions and methods to call to delivered objects, you can avoid re-inventing the wheel. It is also important to understand what you can do by utilizing functionality and/or writing custom functions to more efficiently manage the processes that are in place in a unique business setting. The concepts introduced in this chapter will require practice; take the time to flex your muscles with the code and learn to create customized functionality. It is time to take the basic skills learned so far and start creating customizations in the PeopleSoft Application.

What Will Be Covered	**Some Common Situations Where Used**
Object and classes	Name and instantiate the objects and classes used in the PeopleSoft component.
Understand the component buffer	Provide the memory buffer for the component.
Functions	Understand that any code could be interpreted as a Function—and deciding how to create and call more traditional Functions.
Application packages	Contain packages or application classes.
Charts	Create charts in PeopleCode.
WSDL bindings for component interface	The necessary infrastructure to process incoming SOAP messages.
Component interface-based web services	Take steps to create a simple component interface-based web services.

What Will Be Covered	Some Common Situations Where Used
Working with the Pagelet Wizard	Take steps to use the Pagelet Wizard.
Automating SaveAs functionality	Create code to automate SaveAs.

Objects and Classes

The PeopleSoft application provides you with a set of delivered classes that can be manipulated with PeopleCode. You can also modify the delivered classes and extend the functionality into classes that you create. Not all of the delivered classes use the GUI, and some of the data structures only occur at runtime. One of the cool things about PeopleCode is that you can manipulate data in the data buffer easily. With classes, you can write code that is more readable and easier to maintain.

Classes

In object-oriented programming a *class* is a language construct used to group related fields and methods; in PeopleCode it is the declaration of an object that can be used as a template to create an instance of that object at runtime. It defines the properties of the object, the methods used for behavior. So it is easier to think of a class as a person, place, or thing; we could, for instance, think of a class dog, with different types of dogs identified as objects. PeopleSoft includes classes such as Array, Field, File, and SQL. As a programmer, you can create your own classes, using the Application class; we will not go into Application classes in any detail in this book, but if you wish to learn about them, you can read: *Enterprise PeopleTools 8.49 PeopleBook: PeopleCode API Reference,* "Application Classes."

Objects

An *object* is a unique instance of the data structure that is defined by the template in the class. So think of the class as a type of dog and one particular Dalmatian dog "Taos" as a specific instance of a dog with unique characteristics that identify him as the one and only spotted demon "Taos." An object has its own values for the defined variables that belong to the class and is put into action with its methods.

For example, the class Dog can have an object Taos, which can have a method of Run. This behavior holds true for classes created by you as the programmer of classes delivered by PeopleSoft. An object is created, or in programmer terms, it is instantiated, from the class; it is at this point you can change its properties. So if we use the same example of the class of Dog and object of Taos, then a *property* would be his orange reflective collar. A property is an attribute of an object. Properties define characteristics such as name and/or value and they also determine the state of the object: if it is visible or not, or deleted or changed.

Properties are of two types: read-only properties, such as the Name and the Author which cannot be set, and non-read-only properties, such as the value or label, which can be set. Objects are very different from other data structures because they include code written in the form of methods—remember Dog.Taos.Run. After Dog. Taos.Run is conceived as a class, an object, and a property, it still shows up in the component buffer (see next paragraph) only when it is *instantiated*. It is fundamentally important to understand that the component buffer must contain exactly the correct number of rows, and that inversely, nothing can be seen in the component buffer (be it object, class, or property) unless it has been instantiated.

Object Instantiation

A class is the blueprint for something, like a bicycle, a car, or a data structure. An object is the actual thing that's built using that class (or blueprint). From the blueprint for a bicycle, you can build a specific mountain bike with 23 gears and a tight suspension. From the blueprint of a data structure class, you build a specific instance of that class. *Instantiation* is the term for building that copy, or instance, of a class.

Understand the Component Buffer

In the simplest terms the *component buffer* is the memory area for everything that is stored for the current or active component. The component buffer is broken down into areas that hold field data and record data. The fields are stored in buffer rows or memory rows that hold a particular piece of data. The records are directly related to page controls, which include the primary scroll records, display records, derived/ work records, and/or translate table records. With PeopleCode you can reference the fields in the buffer, page controls in the buffer, and relate buffer fields from the primary scroll record and related display records. Think of the component buffer as the memory area for the main objects on a page. It gives you a way to manipulate, change, update, and refresh what is currently on the page and only look at or program the active record. A good one-line example taken from an article on SparkPath's TechTalk forum, www.sparkpath.com/techtalk-20061220.php, shows an easy way to see the information in the buffer.

```
&F = GetLevel0()(1).EMPL_CHECKLIST(1).EMPL_CHKLST_ITM(1).EMPL_CHKLST_
ITM.BRIEFING_STATUS;
     Rowset    Row    Rowset    Row    Rowset    Row    Record      Field
```

Understand the Component Processor

The *component processor* is the PeopleTools runtime engine that determines firing order for execution of the application from the time the user requests functionality until the time the database is updated. Why is this important? One of the most difficult things you will encounter when you are programming is determining where

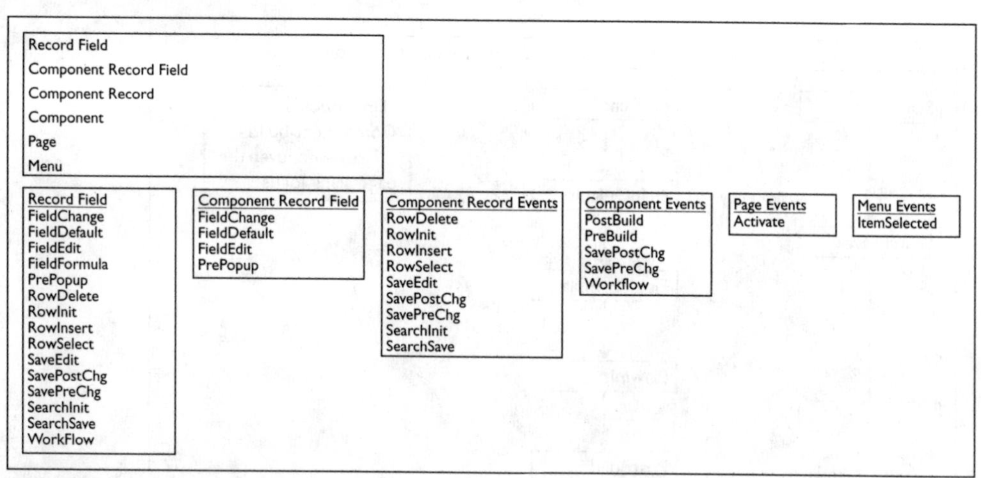

FIGURE 7-1 *Events List*

to place your code. If you think about it, you have several decisions to make; for example, will you place the code on the component, page, record, or field? Well, you can only answer this if you understand what the firing sequence is. What is the order of precedence of the objects, and then what event fires before another? One of the most important things I have tacked up by my desk is a flowchart from my PeopleCode training that defines what and when a piece of code will fire. Figure 7-1 is an Events List, and Figure 7-2 is a recreation of this flowchart to provide nice wall art

Waiting for Action from Customer

Row Insert

1. Add a Row
2. RowInsert
   a. Field Specific? No
   b. Errors or Warnings? No
3. Component Record
   a. PreBuild
   b. Field Default
   c. Field Formula
   d. If 1st time row displayed RowInit Fires Else PostBuild
   e. Activate—fires when Page Gains Focus

Row Delete

1. Delete a Row
2. RowDelete
   a. Field Specific? No
   b. Errors or Warnings? Yes
3. Component Record

Field Changed or Button

1. FieldEdit
   a. Field Specific? Yes
   b. Errors or Warnings? Yes
2. FieldChange
   a. Field Specific? Yes
   b. Errors or Warnings? No
3. Component Record Field

Save

1. SaveEdit
2. SavePreChange
3. WorkFlow
4. --SQL DML
5. SavePostChange
6. --SQL Commit
7. Display Page; wait for action

Pop-up Menu

1. PrePopup
   a. Field Specific? Yes
   b. Errors or Warnings? No
2. ItemSelected
3. Display Page; wait for action

FIGURE 7-2 *Non–Action Event Flowchart*

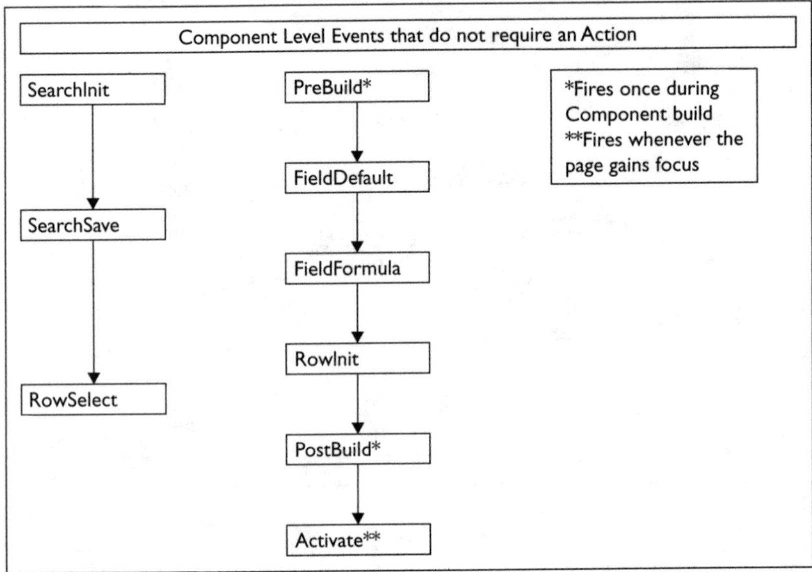

FIGURE 7-3 *Events Waiting for Action Flowchart*

for PeopleSoft developers everywhere. Figure 7-3 shows the events that require an action in a nice flowchart. Table 7-1 shows the list of events and behaviors.

Here are the events that fire errors and/or warnings:

- SearchSave
- FieldEdit
- RowDelete
- RowSelect
- SaveEdit

The following events can be used for calculation:

- RowInit
- FieldChange
- RowDelete
- SavePreChange

Event	Record Field	Component Record Field	Component Record	Component	Function	Field Specific?	Errors or Warnings
SearchInit	X		X		Initialize the search dialog—search record only	Search or ALT key	No
SearchSave	X		X		Validate the search dialog—search record only	Search or ALT key	Yes
PreBuild				X	Hide or unhide page	N/A	N/A
FieldDefault	X	X			Default blank fields	Yes	No
FieldFormula	X				Store FuncLibs, not usually part of the event flow	N/A	N/A
RowInit	X		X		Initialize values, calculate values, and set display	No	No
PostBuild				X	Hide or unhide pages and set component variables	N/A	N/A
Activate	Page				Set characteristics of the page	N/A	N/A
FieldEdit	X	X			Validate one updatable field	Yes	Yes
FieldChange	X	X			Calculate values and set display	Yes	No
RowInsert	X		X		Override effdt and effseq	No	No
RowDelete	X		X		Recalculate totals, gives warning	No	Yes
SaveEdit	X		X		Cross-validate across data in buffer	No	Yes
SavePreChange	X	X		X	This is your last chance to modify data before it is written to the table	No	No
Workflow	X	X		X	Apply business rules	No	No
SavePostChange	X		X	X	SQLExec can alter tables not in buffer; you can also publish messages on this event	No	No
PrePopup	X	X			Alter menu item appearance	Yes	No
ItemSelected	Menu Component				Menu PeopleCode	N/A	No

TABLE 7-1 *List of Events and Behaviors*

The following sections describe the objects, their firing order, and the events that are utilized in the component processor.

How Application Engine Fires off PeopleCode

It is important to understand how Application Engine fires off PeopleCode. If you think about the way Application Engine processes information and what it is utilized for, it is important to understand that Application Engine's functionality is to be a macro for a batch processing flow execution–type program. So in this context you can see that no event fires off the PeopleCode; it is only set with the action, and the only action you get in the PeopleCode window of Application Engine is OnExecute. Thus it is not really an event but just an execution of a step and action within the batch process. Once the programmer understands this and starts to use this understanding to his or her advantage, that programmer has graduated from elementary school to junior high. Then the programmer can start exploring different ways of doing things effectively and really developing killer apps that are user friendly. In this way, PeopleCode has the ability to really accelerate us into a more evolved world of Web 2, whose central theme is making the web more people oriented.

Methods

When you consider what your primary function is when coding in PeopleCode and PeopleSoft—which is to update, insert, and delete data in the database—the methods that are available are mostly for this functionality. Everything about the coding that you will do in PeopleSoft is to manipulate the database; it involves a different mindset than if you learned to code in C, for example. In C you might write data to a database, but it is not a requirement. In PeopleSoft the entire application, the code, the metadata, everything is about the Enterprise database that resides on the back end of the application. If you think of it this way, it will allow you to see the picture when you are working in PeopleCode. So keeping that in mind, let's take a look at some of the most frequently used Record Class database methods:

- Delete
- Insert
- Save
- Update

You may notice that these correlate to the DML (Data Manipulation Language) statements in SQL (Insert, Update, Delete, Merge [with Oracle 9*i*]) and the DQL (Data Query Language)—SELECT. Isn't it interesting that this is so similar to a language that was written to maintain a database? When you are inserting data using

PeopleCode, you can do it in one of three ways. You can use a standard SQLExec statement, but remember, we mentioned earlier that this is not the most efficient way to do it. The recommended way is to use either an Insert method with a Record object or an Insert with a SQL object. You may ask, when do you use one over the other; if you need to loop and run the Insert statement more than one time, it is advisable to use an SQL object; if you only need to do it once, you can use a Record object. The following provides examples of both:

```
/*Record Insert method*/
&TC_REC = CreateRecord(Record.TEST);
&TC_REC.DESCR.Value = "TC" | &TC_I;
&TC_REC.EMPLID.Value = &TC_I;
&TC_REC.Insert();
/*SQL object to insert row */
&TC_SQL = CreateSQL("%INSERT(:1)");
&TC_REC = CreateRecord(Record.TEST);
&TC_SQL.BulkMode = True;
For &TC_I = 1 to 10
&TC_REC.DESCR.Value = "TC" | &TC_I;
&TC_REC.EMPLID.Value = &TC_I;
&TC_SQL.Execute(&TC_REC);
End-For;
```

SQL Objects

An SQL object can be used in any PeopleCode section, for example, in a message subscription, an Application Engine, or a record field. If your SQL changes the database, then limit the placement to the following events:

- SavePreChange
- WorkFlow
- SavePostChange
- Message subscription
- FieldChange
- Application Engine PeopleCode action

The Application Designer SQL Editor can be used to create SQL objects; you populate them with data much as you do when using a cursor. The commands are FetchSQL, Open, or GetSQL.

Declaring an SQL Object in Application Engine

Within Application Engine SQL objects are declared as type SQL.

For example:

```
Local SQL &TC_SQL;

Global SQL &TC_SQL = CreateSQL(SQL.TC_SQL);
```

Binding and Executing SQL Statements

In the binding process the variables are replaced with input values. The placement is determined by the places indicated by the binding placeholders.

The following list shows Meta-SQL functions that are used to replace fieldnames and values in the SQL statement. Using these binding functions allows SQL and PeopleCode to manipulate records without the exact field name within the record.

- %DTTM
- %InsertValues
- %KeyEqual
- %KeyEqualNoEffDt
- %List
- %OldKeyEqual
- %Table
- %UpdatePairs

Array of Any to Place Results

The *Array of Any* is typically used when the number of values needed to run the code is not known. The following is an example of inserting into the TC or Test Company's TEST record.

```
INSERT INTO TC_TESTC (TC_Field1, TC_Field2, TC_Field3, TC_Field4)
VALUES (:1, :2, %DateTimeIn(:3), %TextIn(:4));
```

The values to be placed in the Array of Any that follows, which is named &TC_Any_Array, could be used as the insert.

```
&TC_Any_Array = CreateArrayAny("TC", 1, %DateTime, "judi");
```

The new SQL statement would be as follows:

```
&TC_Any_Array = CreateArrayAny("TC", 1, %DateTime, "judi");
&SQL = GetSQL(SQL.INSERT_TEST);
While /* have logic and processing here */
   &SQL.Execute(&TC_Any_Array);
End-While;
&SQL.Close();
```

SQL Style

Of course everything in code is a matter of style, and that is true of SQL statements as well. The most straightforward way is to write an Open and a Fetch; it is a direct way of processing one row at a time in a contiguous fashion. The following is a sample of that type of SQL code:

```
&SQL.Open("Select x from TC_Test", bind);
While &SQL.Fetch(results)
   /* Processing */
End-While;
```

Another way to process this same type of statement is to base it on something that you change, Update, Insert, or Delete within the SQL.

The following code is an example:

```
&SQL.Open("Update TC_Test set x = y
WHERE a = b");
While /*Processing */
&SQL.Execute(bind);
End-While;
```

Records

PeopleSoft delivers a function for creating records, CreateRecord, which creates a standalone record definition and its fields. You must define this record in advance; however, if you are calling the record from a page, the record is not required to be part of the page definition. This is an important point because records are directly associated with pages. So when you are in Application Engine, you can call records, but the primary way to work with a set of data in an array format is with the State Record. If you want more information about this, please refer to Chapter 11.

When you define a record in PeopleCode with this function, the record life cycle is only within PeopleCode. So what does that mean? Well, if you create a record in code, it is only available through code, not as an object through your project. You already know how to do this and how to build the object within the database as a table; and this type of record is a permanent object within the database. The PeopleCode record is an array within memory to be used in code to cycle through groups of data. Because the record and its field objects are part of code or memory, they are automatically deleted or cleaned up, so to speak, when there are no more references to them in any of the variables. Fields in records are initialized to null values, and no default processing is performed. You need to use the SelectByKey record class method to fill the record, or you can use the SQLExec function and use SQL against a database record.

Keep in mind that PeopleSoft and Oracle have been threatening to get rid of the SQLExec function for years. I do not believe it will happen just as I do not believe they will ever retire PL/SQL; in fact, Oracle released a very powerful web product called Application Express, or AppExp, that is based in PL/SQL. So choices are always an important part of coding decisions. It is also not the most effective way to retrieve data from your tables with SQL (the best way is with MetaSQL). You will see in the Application Engine area of the project that you are asked to rewrite SQLExec Code into SQL sections in Application Engine—this is a good practice, but I live by the philosophy that if it isn't broken, don't fix it, so, if you have a bunch of SQLExec statements that work, do not feel that you will need to rewrite them all; only use this in terms of new code that you plan to write.

```
/*Add to your declaration section */
Local Record &Rec_Curr_Earns, &Rec_Futr_Earns;
Local Rowset &Current_Earnings, &Future_Earnings;
Local SQL &SQL1;

/* BUILD IN CURRENT EARNINGS TO FUTURE TABLE. */
&Current_Earnings = GetRowset(Record.TC_CALC_EARNING);
&Future_Earnings = GetRowset(Record.TC_CALC_FUR_ERN);
&Future_Earnings.Flush();
&SQL1 = CreateSQL("%selectall(:1) Where emplid = :2 and tc_calc_seq_nbr = :3 and
run_cntl_id = :4", &Rec_Curr_Earns, &emplid, &tc_calc_seq_nbr, "TEST");

For &i = 1 To &Current_Earnings.ActiveRowCount
   If &SQL1.Fetch(&Rec_Curr_Earns) Then
      &Future_Earnings.InsertRow(&i);
      &Rec_Curr_Earns.CopyFieldsTo(&Future_Earnings(&i).TC_CALC_FUR_ERN);
      UpdateValue(Record.TC_CALC_FUR_ERN, &i, TC_CALC_FUR_ERN.BEST36_NOTE, "");
      UpdateValue(Record.TC_CALC_FUR_ERN, &i, TC_CALC_FUR_ERN.BEST36_AVG, 0);
      UpdateValue(Record.TC_CALC_FUR_ERN, &i, TC_CALC_FUR_ERN.BEST60_AVG, 0);
      UpdateValue(Record.TC_CALC_FUR_ERN, &i, TC_CALC_FUR_ERN.BEST60_NOTE, "");
   End-If;
End-For;
```

Standalone RowSets

Standalone rowsets are just what their name implies; they stand alone and are not directly associated with a component or page. The primary use of a standalone rowset is to work with data within code that you are not retrieving from the page buffer.

In prior versions of PeopleSoft programmers used to do this with a Derived Work Record—which you can still use, but the fill method will require you to build work pages to load the data. Because standalone rowsets are not related to or connected to the component processor, there is no direct connection to the database, so remember that deletes and inserts with these types of rowsets do not directly change data in the physical table. The standalone rowset can have standard PeopleSoft scopes when declared Local, Global, or Component. The following are some examples:

```
Local Rowset &TC_RS;
&TC_RS = CreateRowset(RECORD.TC_TEST);
```

This creates a rowset with TC_TEST as the level-zero record. The rowset in this example is unpopulated. The behavior of this standalone rowset is the same as an array.

Using the Fill Method

As you may have noted, the rowset is unpopulated—well, that does you no good. So let's take a look at the fill method. The fill method will read records from the database and fill the rowset. The first thing the fill method does is flush out all the contents of the rowset. Remember to include a WHERE condition so that you are only retrieving the relevant rows.

```
Local Rowset &TC_RS;
Local String &TC_EMPLID;
&TC_RS = CreateRowset(RECORD.TC_TEST);
&TC_EMPLID = '117553';
&TC_RS.Fill("where EMPLID = :1", &TC_EMPLID);
```

Using the CopyTo Method

The CopyTo method takes like-named fields from one rowset (the source) and copies them to the new rowset (the destination). In order to do this copy, the fields must match in name unless you specifically define the field with the different names. The method will work for any type of rowset except the Application Engine state record type.

```
Local Rowset &TC_RS1, &TC_RS2;
Local String &TC_EMPLID;
&TC_RS1 = CreateRowset(RECORD.TC_TEST1);
&TC_RS2 = CreateRowset(RECORD.TC_TEST2);
&TC_EMPLID = '117553';
&TC_RS1.Fill("where EMPLID = :1", &TC_EMPLID);
&TC_RS1.CopyTo(&TC_RS2);
```

In the preceding example, &TC_RS1 and &TC_RS2 contain the same data and the fields are named the same. But say you want to use the CopyTo method where you do not have like-named records; in this case, you specify the source and destination explicitly. Take a look at the following example of code:

```
Local Rowset &TC_RS1, &TC_S2;
Local String &TC_EMPLID;
&TC_RS1 = CreateRowset(RECORD.TC_TEST1);
&TC_RS2 = CreateRowset(RECORD.TC_TEST2);
&TC_EMPLID = '117558';
&TC_RS1.Fill("where EMPLID = :1", &TC_EMPLID);
&TC_RS1.CopyTo(&TC_RS2, RECORD.TC_TEST1, RECORD.TC_TEST2);
```

Adding Child Rowsets

Because the first parameter of the CreateRowset method sets the top-level structure, if you pass the name of a record as the first parameter, then the rowset will be based on that record. So say you want to base the structure on a different rowset rather than a record. Take a look at the following example, in which &TC_RS2 will inherit the structure of &TC_RS1:

```
Local Rowset &TC_RS1, &TC_RS2;
&TC_RS1 = CreateRowset(RECORD.TC_TEST1);
&TC_RS2 = CreateRowset(&TC_RS1);
```

To add a child rowset, suppose the following records describe a relationship. The structure is made up of three records:

- TC_PERSONAL_DATA
- TC_BUS_EXPENSE_PER
- TC_BUS_EXPENSE_DTL

To build rowsets with child rowsets, use code like the following:

```
Local Rowset &TC_PER_DTA, &TC_BUS_EXP_PER, &TC_BUS_EXP_DTL;
&TC_BUS_EXP_DTL = CreateRowset(Record.TC_BUS_EXPENSE_DTL);
&TC_BUS_EXP_PER = CreateRowset(Record.TC_BUS_EXPENSE_PER, &TC_BUS_EXP_DTL);
&TC_PER_DTA = CreateRowset(Record.TC_PERSONAL_DATA, &TC_BUS_EXP_PER);
```

Here's a single-line solution:

```
&TC_BUS_EXP = CreateRowset(Record.TC_PERSONAL_DATA,
CreateRowset(Record.TC_BUS_EXPENSE_PER,
CreateRowset(Record.TC_BUS_EXPENSE_DTL)));
```

Functions

Typically when we were taught programming, we were taught that procedures do not return values, but that functions do. Well, in PeopleCode, a function can return a value or not. And any PeopleCode could be determined to be a function. The data types of the values returned by functions can be of any supported data type. When PeopleCode calls a function that is in the same PeopleCode program, a new program evaluation is not started, but if it calls a PeopleCode program that is in another PeopleCode program, then the current program is suspended and the component processor starts loading the program where the function resides. This is important to note because maybe you have variables in Program A, which is the local program that calls the function in Program B. Well, the variables in Program A will no longer be available in the Scope of B. So to complicate matters further, let's speculate that you have variables in A with the same names as variables in B. The variables in A are no longer available and what you will be returning is the values from B, which may or may not be what you expect. Take a look at this example:

```
PeopleCode A1 (RecA.FieldA.FieldChange):
local number &tempA;
declare function B1 PeopleCode Rec.Field FieldFormula;

function B1
end-function;
function A1
WinMessage("A1: &tempA is " | &tempA);
&tempA = &tempA + 1;
A2();
B1();
A2();
end-function;
function A2
WinMessage("A2: &tempA is " | &tempA);
&tempA = &tempA + 1;
end-function;
A1();
PeopleCode B1 (Rec.FieldB.FieldFormula):
local number &tempB;
declare function A2 PeopleCode Rec.FieldB FieldChange;
function B1
WinMessage("B1: &tempB is " | &tempB);
&tempB = &tempB + 1;
A2();
end-function;
When this is compiled and run, it produces the following output:
A1: &tempA is 0
A2: &tempA is 1
B1: &tempA is 0
A2: &tempB is 0
A2: &tempB is 2
```

Recursive Functions

Recursive functions—functions that can call themselves—are supported by PeopleCode. When you do this, the most important thing to remember is what you are passing when you pass variables.

```
Function Func(&j as Number)
&j = 6;
End-Function;
local &y = 2;
Func(&y);
```

So what is the value of &y after the Func(&y) call? It is 6, not 3; if you call Func(Value(&y)), then it will be 2.

One of the categories of built-in functions is ThinkTime functions. Delivered functions in this set suspend processing until one of two things has happened: 1. The user clicks a button (so it waits for a user response). 2. A process reaches completion. Because of the nature of this type of function and how it will wait before processing, it is best not to use this type of function in the following events:

- SavePreChange and SavePostChange
- Workflow
- RowSelect
- Code that fires as a result of a Select, SelectNew, ScrollSelect, ScrollSelectNew, or RowScrollSelectNew function call.

These are the ThinkTime Functions:

- External DLL
- DoCancel
- DoModal
- DoModalComponent
- Exec—only when used synchronously
- Any file attachment function
- InsertImage

- Object functions—only ThinkTime when a user action is required:
  - CreateObject
  - ObjectDoMethod
  - ObjectSetProperty
  - ObjectGetProperty
- Prompt
- RemoteCall
- RevalidatePassword
- WinExec—only when used synchronously
- DoSave
- GetPage
- WinMessage—dependent on which style parameter is used
- MessageBox—dependent on which style parameter is used

Two of the most important functions that you will use are the WinMessage and MessageBox functions. It is important to note that WinMessage is supported only for sake of previous versions of PeopleSoft and is not the recommended way of writing in the new releases. The following is the syntax:

```
MessageBox(style, title, message_set, message_num, default_txt [,
paramlist]);
WinMessage(message [, style] [, title]);
```

Let's take a closer look on the important items that you can set in MessageBox and WinMessage. Notice the style parameter; you need to know what to put there and what it will default to if you leave it blank. It is important to note that the style parameter is ignored unless the message is of type message. As a default in WinMessage if it is omitted, the style will be two buttons: OK and Cancel. Table 7-4 lists the different parameters that you can use for style in both MessageBox and WinMessage.

Of course you can also write your own functions. The following is a function that determines a person's age in months; this is a simple function that is used to

Type	Value	Display
Button	0	One button—OK
Button	1	Two buttons—OK and Cancel
Button	2	Three buttons—Abort, Retry, and Ignore
Button	3	Three buttons—Yes, No, and Cancel
Button	4	Two buttons—Yes and No
Button	5	Two buttons—Retry and Cancel
The following are only available in a Windows Client:		
Default Button	0	First button the default
Default Button	256	Second button the default
Default Button	512	Third button the default
Icon	0	None
Icon	16	Stop sign
Icon	32	Question mark
Icon	48	Exclamation point
Icon	64	Lowercase letter "I" in a circle

TABLE 7-2 *Style Parameters for WinMessage and MessageBox*

know how many months old a person is at retirement. This determines in whole months the eligibility of an employee. This is a useful function. You can change it slightly and determine a person's age in days or years, depending on what you may need to know.

```
InYears PeopleCode FUNCLIB_HR.AGE FieldFormula;
Declare Function AgeInMonth PeopleCode FUNCLIB_HR.AGE FieldFormula;
```

In the first image following, you can see the function AgeInYears, and in the second, you can see the Function AgeInMonth, both declared under the field of Age.

```
&age_in_tot_mos = calcAgeInTotalMonths(&birthdate, SL_DERIVED_USER
.SL_CALC_DT);
AllowEmplIdChg(True);
```

```
AGE (field)                                        FieldFormula
 Function   : AgeInYears
 Purpose    : To Calculate the age in years
 Version    : 16.3.99
 Parameters : &BIRTHDATE, &DEATHDATE
 Returns    : &EMP_AGE as number
*****************************************************/
Function AgeInYears(&BIRTHDATE As date, &DEATHDATE As date) Returns number;
   If None(&BIRTHDATE) Then
      Return 0;
   Else
      If None(&DEATHDATE) Then
         If &BIRTHDATE >= %Date Then
            Return 0;
         End-If
      Else
         If &BIRTHDATE >= &DEATHDATE Then
            Return 0;
         End-If
      End-If;
   End-If;
   &EMP_AGE = 0;
   &BIRTH_YEAR = Year(&BIRTHDATE);
   &BIRTH_MONTH = Month(&BIRTHDATE);
   &BIRTH_DAY = Day(&BIRTHDATE);
   If None(&DEATHDATE) Then
      &CURRENT_YEAR = Year(%Date);
      &CURRENT_MONTH = Month(%Date);
      &CURRENT_DAY = Day(%Date);
   Else
      &CURRENT_YEAR = Year(&DEATHDATE);
      &CURRENT_MONTH = Month(&DEATHDATE);
      &CURRENT_DAY = Day(&DEATHDATE);
   End-If;
   If Not (&BIRTH_YEAR = - 1 Or
```

```
AGE (field)                                        FieldFormula
/*****************************************************
 Function   : AgeInMonths
 Purpose    : To Calculate the residual age in months
 Version    : 16.3.99
 Parameters : &BIRTHDATE, &DEATHDATE
 Returns    : &EMP_MONTH as number
*****************************************************/

/*Residual age in months */
Function AgeInMonth(&BIRTHDATE As date, &DEATHDATE As date) Returns number;
   If None(&BIRTHDATE) Then
      Return 0;
   Else
      If None(&DEATHDATE) Then
         If &BIRTHDATE >= %Date Then
            Return 0;
         End-If
      Else
         If &BIRTHDATE >= &DEATHDATE Then
            Return 0;
         End-If
      End-If;
   End-If;
   &EMP_MONTH = 0;
   &BIRTH_YEAR = Year(&BIRTHDATE);
   &BIRTH_MONTH = Month(&BIRTHDATE);
   &BIRTH_DAY = Day(&BIRTHDATE);
   If None(&DEATHDATE) Then
      &CURRENT_YEAR = Year(%Date);
      &CURRENT_MONTH = Month(%Date);
      &CURRENT_DAY = Day(%Date);
   Else
      &CURRENT_YEAR = Year(&DEATHDATE);
      &CURRENT_MONTH = Month(&DEATHDATE);
```

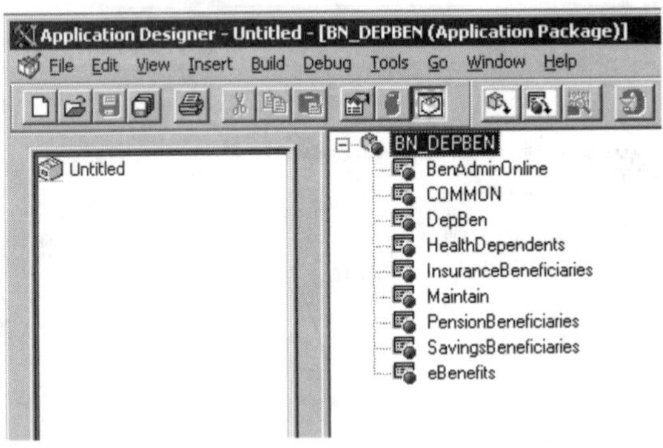

FIGURE 7-4 *Primary Package*

Application Packages

Now the fun begins. Let's take a look at Application Package, which contains packages or application classes. A subpackage is a package within a primary or parent package—this is pretty self-explanatory. Primary packages are noted by a blue database symbol, and subpackages by a yellow database symbol. Figure 7-4 shows the primary package, and Figure 7-5 shows the subpackage. Note the blue versus the yellow. In the example in Figure 7-5 HCR_JOB_PROFILE_EXCEPTIONS is the primary package; JobProfileExceptions and JobProfileExceptions_v1_0 are the subpackages.

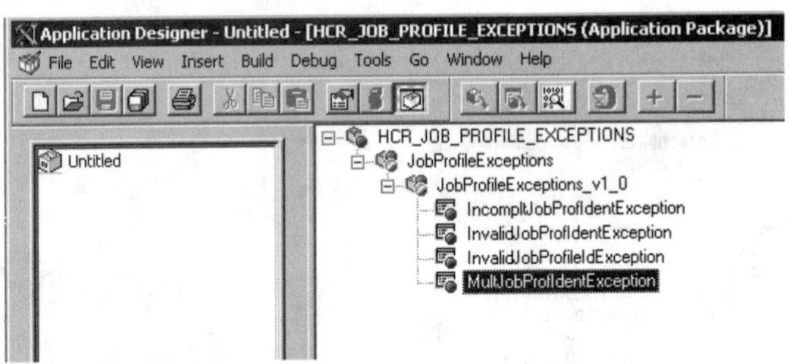

FIGURE 7-5 *Subpackage*

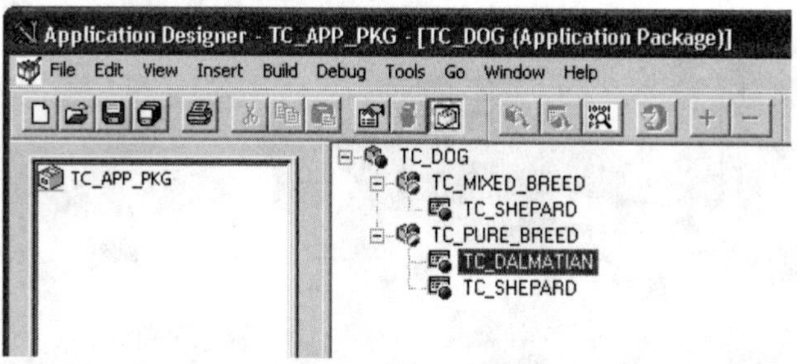

FIGURE 7-6 *Application package naming conventions*

Creating new application packages requires that you understand the naming conventions that you should use. Always remember that naming conventions and such are always suggestions, but that they are for your own good. I don't know how many times I have come back to code I wrote several years before, and if I followed nice, documented standards I was much happier than if I was trying to be a rogue that day—when this happens I usually utter "what was I thinking," so be your own best example.

Take a look at Figure 7-6; it shows you the creation of an application package named TC_DOG. Within that package are two subpackages: one TC_MIXED_BREED and one TC_PURE_BREED. Within these subpackages there are application classes. In the TC_MIXED_BREED you have an application class of TC_SHEPARD, and you also have the same application class in TC_PURE_BREED. Even though TC_SHEPARD in each subpackage shares the same name, it is distinct because of the subpackage definition. The TC_MIXED_BREED subpackage application class TC_SHEPARD is different from the TC_PURE_BREED subpackage application class TC_SHEPARD, just as in the real world a mixed Shepherd is different than a pure breed Shepherd.

How to Create Application Packages

Now for the section I am sure you just skipped right to: how to create your own application packages in Application Designer. First you will need to do everything you have done in the past when working with PeopleSoft: open Application

Designer (see the accompanying illustration) and save your project. The project we will be working on will be named TC_APP_PKG.

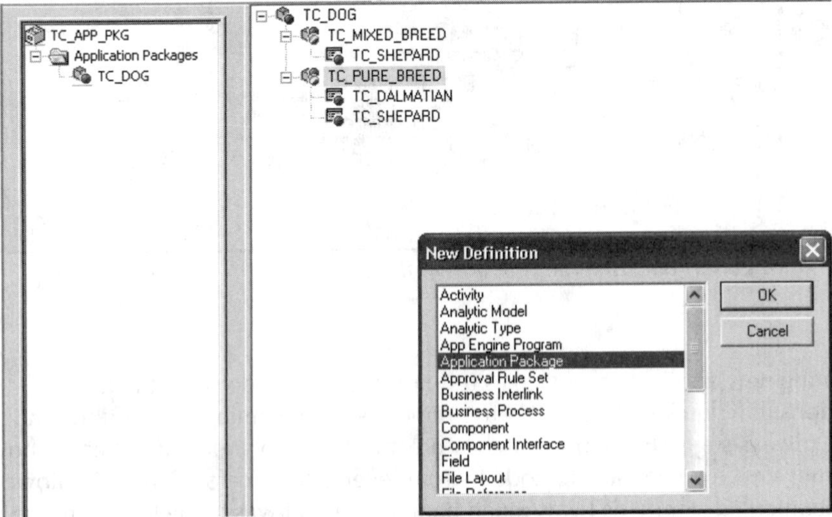

The next step is to create a new Application Package: go to File | New and under New Definition choose Application Package.

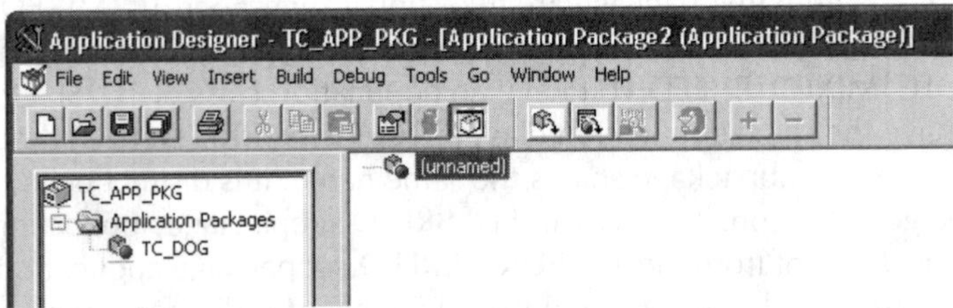

Then choose File | Save As and give it a name. We will be using **TC_TEST**. See the accompanying example.

Make sure you press F7 to include it in your project. See the example of the application package added to the project shown here.

Application Package Editor

The next step in creating an application package is to understand the Application Editor. The illustration shows the menu you get when you right-click in the Application Editor. In Table 7-3 you see the description of each of the menu items and what each helps you do.

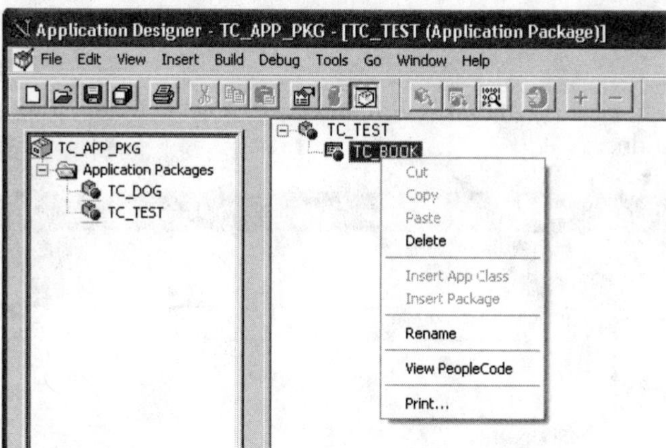

Application Package Classes

The first thing you need to know is that the code you will be writing in the Application Package classes is PeopleCode; you will see that the editor for PeopleCode is Application Designer; you can see the code in the Application Package class

Menu Item	Description
Copy, Cut, and Paste	Not available in the Application Editor. To work around this issue, you can use the clipboard as your copy, cut, and paste area.
Delete	Delete class or package.
Insert App Class	Classes cannot have children or subclasses, so you insert them into an existing package.
Insert Package	Insert an application package.
Rename	Rename a class or subpackage.
View PeopleCode	Will show you the PeopleCode in an Application class.
Print	Will print the Application Package definition and all the PeopleCode.

TABLE 7-3 *Description of Menu Items*

is PeopleCode just like it is when it is written on an Object. Take a look at the following illustration.

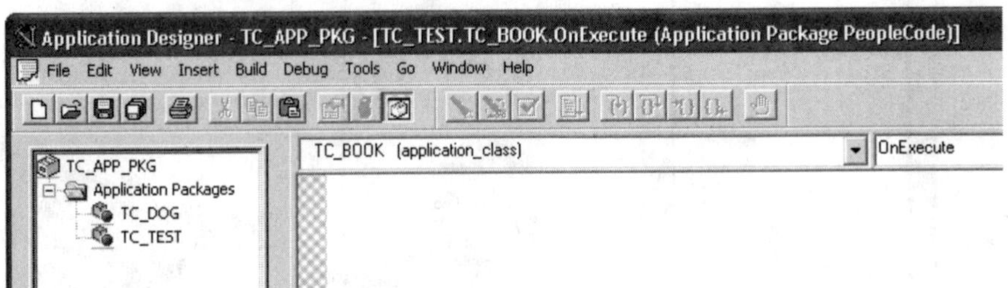

Notice the only event you have available is on Execute of the Application class. This is where your code would be written. In the next illustration you see the PeopleSoft-delivered Application Package BN_DEPBEN and the code that is delivered for Dependent Beneficiary evaluation. I am certain you can think of all kinds of ways in which PeopleSoft has to evaluate this relationship, and this Application Package contains all of the methods.

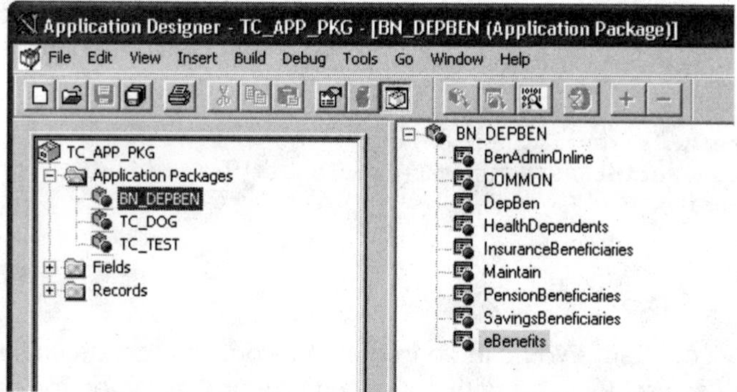

To edit the Application class, right-click the Application class you wish to edit and click View PeopleCode. Edit the Application class just as you would any piece of PeopleCode.

Creating Pagelets and iScript

The iScript is a set of custom-delivered PeopleCode functions that allow you to generate dynamic web content. An iScript has access to requests and responses very similar to ASP; and the responses only render text—just like ASP—so there are limitations. I have read about people wanting to use the write method to store images, but since the write method in iScript can only store text, it seems to be an impossible request. But since I have seen the impossible done many times in many languages, I will not go so far as to say it can't be done—as soon as I do that, someone at a conference is going to show me why I'm wrong. I look forward to being proved wrong, but since the write method only returns text, images might be a bit difficult. iScripts follow the same creation principles as FUNCLIBS; an iScript is a PeopleCode function stored in a record; which sounds simple enough. The basic naming would be ISCRIPT1 event FieldFormula. Remember your function name must start with "IScript_" and unlike the functions we learned about in college this one cannot take any parameters or return a value.

Calling the iScript depends on how it will be used. For example, if it is a pagelet create a CREF in the portal registry by navigating to Portal Objects | Pagelets. Calling the iScript from JavaScript, use a URL; to generate the IScript as a URL, use the built-in function GenerateScriptContentURL.

GetJavaScriptURL

HTML definitions can contain JavaScript programs in addition to HTML. If you have an HTML definition that contains JavaScript, use the GetJavaScriptURL Response method to access and execute the script. This example assumes the existence in the database of a HTML definition called HelloWorld_JS that contains some JavaScript:

```
Function IScript_TestJavaScript()
%Response.WriteLine("<script src= " |
%Response.GetJavaScriptURL(HTML.HelloWorld_JS) | "></script>");
End-Function;
```

Charts

One of the really cool things you can do for your customers is create charts in PeopleCode; you can set them up with a chart control on a page, or you can do it at runtime using an iScript. The pieces that have access to titles and labels are X and Y Axis and the Overlay.

The major components or pieces of a chart are:

- Data
- Legend
- Overlay
- Title
- X and Y Axis

Important Terms

Table 7-4 shows the terms and definitions used for charts.

Available Chart Styles in PeopleSoft are:

- 2D Bar
- 2D Histogram
- 2D Horizontal Bar
- 2DHorizontal Percent Bar
- 2DHorizontal Stacked Bar
- 2D Line
- 2D Percent Bar

- 2D Pie
- 2D Scatter
- 2D Stacked Bar
- 3D Bar
- 3D Percent Bar
- 3D Pie
- 3D Stacked Bar
- Gantt

Term	Definition
Data	Data is pretty self explanatory—it is the information that is populating the chart.
Label	The tag used to name the information on the axis.
Legend	The diagram or map outlining information on the chart.
Legend Overlay	Title for the lines of the superimposed chart.
Overlay	You can have an Overlay Series, an Overlay X Axis, and an Overlay Y Axis. You can also choose the Overlay color field. An Overlay is a line superimposed over the original chart. Or a series or group of lines creating a superimposed chart.
Series	The ability to group or relate data in series. This feature allows you to show Sales information as a chart series and Marketing information as a second series in the same chart.
Title	You can title your X Axis, Y Axis, and Main Chart. The title helps the customer identify what data is represented in the chart.
X Axis	In most charts this is the Horizontal Axis or the thing that is measuring against the data.
Y Axis	Typically the Vertical Axis, except in a bar chart where this is the Horizontal Axis. It is the representative of the data.

TABLE 7-4 *Chart Terms*

Example Code (1):

```
/* ----------------------------------------------------------------
/* Code Example provided by Bryan Norris
/*----------------------------------------------------------------*/
/* chart Section GSDBEN1 Begin*/
/* The Chart object is on a level zero for this page*/
/* Draw CHART */
&oChart = GetChart(ZY_TC_TTL_WRK.CHARTFLDS_NEW);

/* set to Current Rowset */
&oChart.SetData(&RS2);
/* Each Amount and Type */
&oChart.SetDataYAxis(ZY_TC_EE_CUR_VW.ZY_AMOUNT_CUR);
/* Total Amount ZY_TC_EE_CUR_VW.ZY_AMOUNT_CUR */
&oChart.SetDataXAxis(ZY_TC_TTL_WRK.ZY_TOTAL_PERCENT);
/* Types ZY_TC_EE_CUR_VW.ZY_TYPE */
/* All total Base */
&oChart.SetDataSeries(ZY_TC_EE_CUR_VW.TOTAL_SALARIES);
/* all Totals Rewards ZY_TC_EE_CUR_VW.TOTAL_SALARIES*/

/* set Chart type */
&oChart.Type = %ChartType_2DPie;
/* Set Chart Hints */
&oChart.SetDataHints(ZY_TC_TTL_WRK.DESCR);
/* Set Title */
&GraphTitle = &RS2(1).ZY_TC_EE_CUR_VW.YEAR.Value | " Total Rewards";
&oChart.MainTitle = &GraphTitle;
&oChart.YAxisTitle = "Total Rewards";

/* Legend */
&oChart.HasLegend = True;
&oChart.LegendPosition = %ChartLegend_Right;
&myArray = CreateArray(&csh, &benf, &savr, &equ, &per);
&oChart.SetLegend(&myArray);

/* Resets Colors */
&NumArray = CreateArray(4, 15, 12, 8, 5);
&oChart.SetColorArray(&NumArray);

/* PeopleCode trigger */
&oChart.IsDrillable = True;

/* New Chart Class*/
&oChart.YAxisTitleOrient = %ChartText_Horizontal;
/* did not see a change on the Chart */
```

```
&oChart.SetDataColor(ZY_TC_EE_AMT_VW.ZY_AMOUNT_PAST);
/* did not see a change on the Chart */
&oChart.LineType = %ChartLine_Dot;
/* did not see a change on the Chart */
&oChart.GridLines = %ChartGrid_Both;
/* did not see a change on the Chart */
/* chart Section GSDBEN1 End */
/* -------------------------------------------------------------- */
```

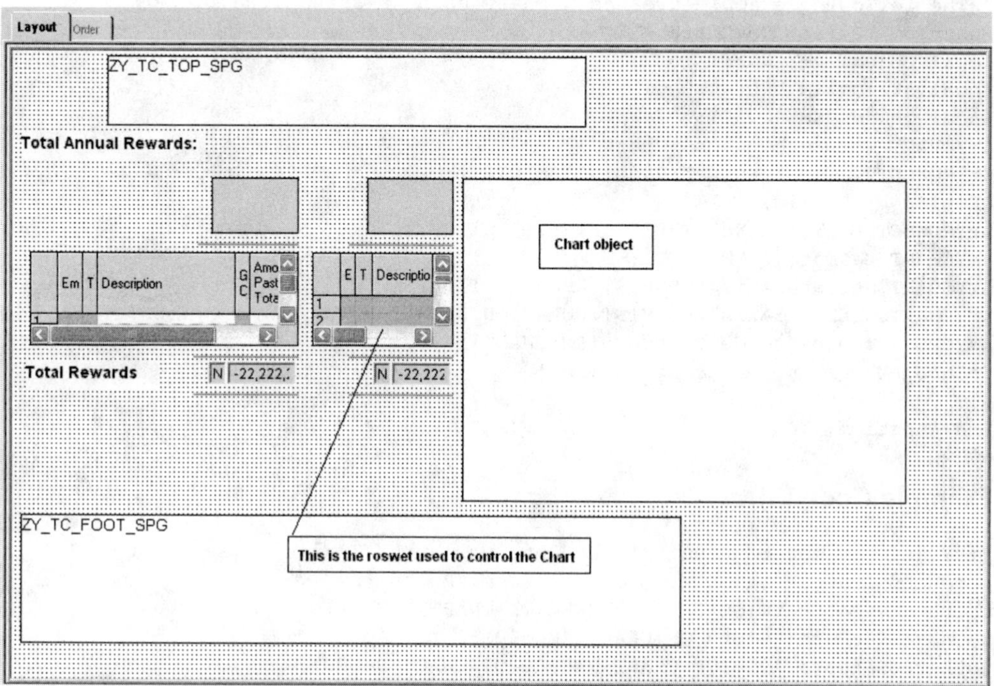

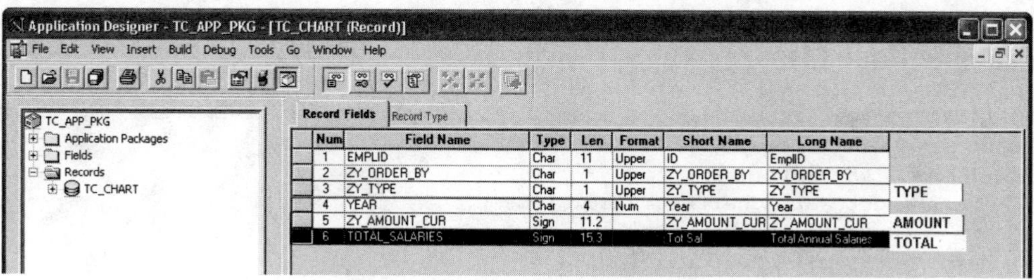

Num	Field Name	Type	Len	Format	Short Name	Long Name
1	EMPLID	Char	11	Upper	ID	EmplID
2	ZY_ORDER_BY	Char	1	Upper	ZY_ORDER_BY	ZY_ORDER_BY
3	ZY_TYPE	Char	1	Upper	ZY_TYPE	ZY_TYPE
4	YEAR	Char	4	Num	Year	Year
5	ZY_AMOUNT_CUR	Sign	11.2		ZY_AMOUNT_CUR	ZY_AMOUNT_CUR
6	TOTAL_SALARIES	Sign	15.3		Tot Sal	Total Annual Salaries

Example Code (2)

```
/*Minimum Code needed for a PeopleSoft Chart Example taken from Oracle
PeopleBooks */
Local Chart &MyChart;
&MyChart = GetChart(ABS_HIST.CHART);
&MyChart.SetData(ABS_HIST);
&MyChart.SetDataYAxis(ABS_HIST.Reason);
&MyChart.SetDataXAxis(ABS_HIST.Duration);
/*The following example creates a chart using a standalone rowset.*/
Function IScript_GetChartURL()
local object &MYCHART;
local string &MYURL;
local rowset &MYROWSET;
&MYCHART = CreateObject("Chart");
&MYROWSET = CreateRowset(Record.ABS_HIST);
&EmplID = %Emplid;
&MYROWSET.Fill("Where EMPLID :=1", &EmplID);
&MYCHART.SetData(&MYROWSET);
&MYCHART.SetDataXAxis(ABS_HIST.ABSENCE_TYPE);
&MYCHART.SetDataYAxis(ABS_HIST.DURATION_DAYS);
&MYURL = %Response.GetChartURL(&MYCHART);
/* use &MYURL in your application */
...
End-Function;
```

Example Code (3)

```
/* Y axis is set to a numeric amount, while the X axis is set to the
products Example taken from Oracle PeopleBooks */
&oChart = GetChart(QE_CHART_DUMREC.QE_CHART_FIELD);
&oChart.SetData(Record.QE_CHART_RECORD);
&oChart.SetDataYAxis(QE_CHART_RECORD.QE_CHART_SALES);
&oChart.SetDataXAxis(QE_CHART_RECORD.QE_CHART_PRODUCT);
&oChart.SetDataSeries(QE_CHART_RECORD.QE_CHART_REGION);
```

Example Code (4)

```
/* Limiting your result set to a smaller manageable subset Example
taken from Oracle PeopleBooks */
Local Chart &MyChart;
&MyChart = GetChart(ChartRec.DisplayField);
&Start = &MyChart.DataStartRow;
/* display the next 20 rows of data */
&MyChart.DataStartRow = &Start + 20;
&MyChart.DataWidth = 20;
```

iScripts and Charts

There are two types of charts supported by PeopleSoft: one is a chart as we have already discussed that is created by using a chart control on a page; the other is generated at runtime with an iScript. To create a chart at runtime, use the CreateObject function, not the GetChart function; this way you can use the GetChartURL Response Class Method to call the URL in your application. The following example creates a chart in an iScript using the CreateObject function to generate a reference to a chart object.

```
/* Example taken from Oracle PeopleBooks */
Function IScript_GetChartURL()
Local Chart &oChart;
Local Rowset &oRowset;
Local string &sMap;
Local string &sURL;
&oChart = CreateObject("Chart");
&oRowset = CreateRowset(Record.QE_CHART_RECORD);
&oRowset.Fill("where QE_CHART_REGION= :1", "MIDWEST");
&oChart.SetData(&oRowset);
&oChart.Width = 400;
&oChart.Height = 300;
&oChart.SetDataYAxis(QE_CHART_RECORD.QE_CHART_SALES);
&oChart.SetDataXAxis(QE_CHART_RECORD.QE_CHART_PRODUCT);
&oChart.SetDataSeries(QE_CHART_RECORD.QE_CHART_REGION);
&oChart.HasLegend = True;
&oChart.LegendPosition = %ChartLegend_Right;
&sURL = %Response.GetChartURL(&oChart);
&sMap = &oChart.ImageMap;
%Response.Write("<HTML><IMG SRC=");
%Response.Write(&sURL);
%Response.Write(" USEMAP=#THEMAP></IMG><MAP NAME=THEMAP>");
%Response.Write(&sMap);
%Response.Write("</MAP></HTML>");
End-Function;
```

IsDrillable

One of the important features of a chart is to allow the user of the application to click a piece of the chart and fire off PeopleCode on the FieldChange event that will drill down into the data. When chart data comes from a record, you can write code on the FieldChange event for Y Axis data; it will generate a Boolean value, true if clicked, false if not. It is important to note that if you have set the IsPlainImage property to true, you will not be able to drill down; when using an iScript, you must use the Set DataURL method of the field that is populated by the URL.

```
&TC_CHART.SetTableXScrollbar(0.20);
&TC_CHART.SetChartArea(TC_CHART_PRJ.TC_CHART_AREA);
&TC_CHART.width = TC_CHART_PRJ.TC_WIDTH;
```

```
&TC_CHART.height = TC_CHART_PRJ.TC_HEIGHT;
&TC_CHART.DataStartRow = TC_CHART_PRJ.TC_FIRST_ROW;
&TC_CHART.DataWidth = TC_CHART_PRJ.TC_SIZE;
&TC_CHART.IsDrillable = TC_CHART_PRJ.TC_DRILLABLE;
```

iScript Security

It is important to note when discussing iScript that in previous versions of PeopleSoft there have been some security issues. If you want to read in depth about this issue you can make a Google search and go to the original documents and read about it from the people who discovered the problem. It is only mentioned here as a caution that it is important to keep up with your PeopleSoft patches to reduce any vulnerability your organization may face. Information taken from the IBM web site notes that the problem "exists in PeopleSoft PeopleTools versions 8.43 and earlier[, which] are vulnerable to cross-site scripting, this is caused by [a] vulnerability in the IScript application. Essentially a remote attacker could embed malicious script within a URL in an HTTP request to the IScript. The script could then be executed in the victim's Web browser within the security context of the hosting site. This allows the attacker to steal the victim's cookie-based authentication credentials and possibly obtain other sensitive information."

To turn on Dynamic Tracing for Debugging:

```
Function IScript_PCTraceOff()
   SetTracePC(0);
End-Function;

Function IScript_PCTraceAll()
   SetTracePC(3596);
End-Function;
```

Turning this tracing on will allow you to leverage iScript's capabilities and not trace an entire session; it would only trace the section of code that would help you debug. A wonderful reference was presented by Chris Heller and David Bain at Grey Sparling at Oracle OpenWorld; see www.erpassociates.com/peoplesoft-corner-weblog/peopletools/browse-the-app-server-filesystem-via-iscript.html.

WSDL Bindings for Component Interface

Within PeopleSoft you have the necessary infrastructure to process incoming SOAP messages; the data maps to the component interfaces. You do this with the WSDL Utility, which produces Web Services Description Language documents in XML format for component interfaces based on the users' permissions. The function is to help development using frameworks that can generate SOAP messages. The following illustrations demonstrate where they are located in the PIA. To find further reading and step-by-step directions on using WSDL Binding, go to PeopleBooks, PeopleSoft Component Interfaces, and WSDL Binding for Component Interfaces.

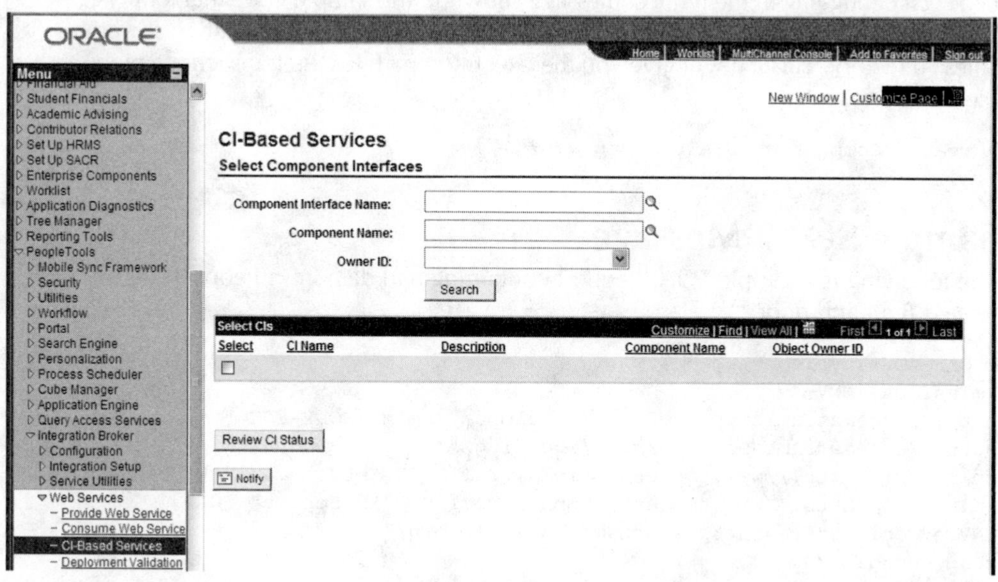

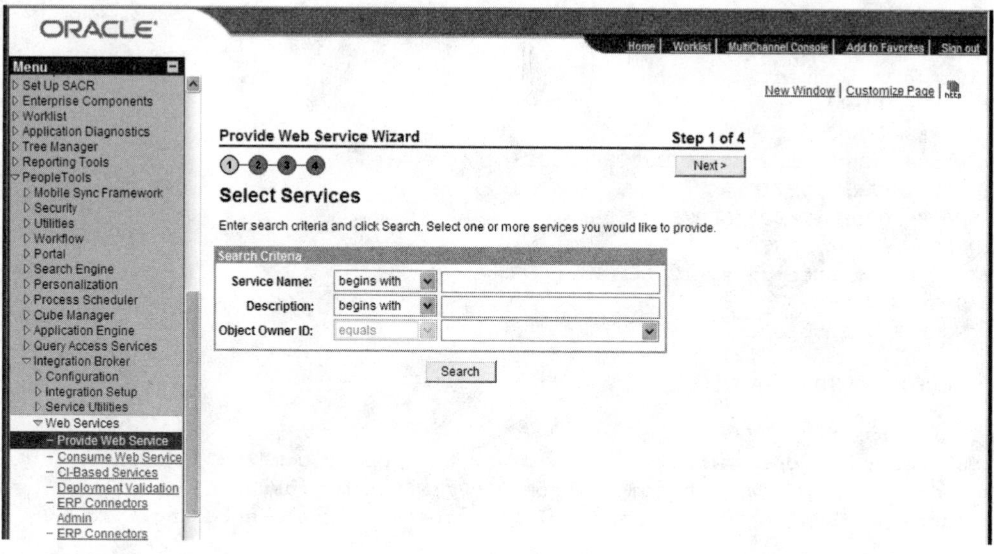

When you first start to work with WSDL and the Component Interface in three-tier mode, which means through an Application Server (Application Designer is using the Application Server to communicate with the database), you should run tests to make certain this three-tier functionality is set up properly at your business. You can set a debug flag in the request message shown in the sample code that follows. What this will do for you is generate a SOAPTOCIxxx log in the application server's "files" directory. This log will give you the execution path for the transactions in the request message.

```
<Create__CompIntfc__STATE debug = "Y">
```

Sample SOAP Message

The following is a sample SOAP request containing bad data from PeopleTools release 8.44 and prior:

```
<SOAP-ENV:Envelope
xmlns:SOAP-ENV="
http://schemas.xmlsoap.org/soap/envelope/" xmlns:SOAP-ENC="
http://schemas.xmlsoap.org/soap/encoding/"
xmlns:xsi="http://www.tc_test_company.com/2007/XMLSchema-instance"
xmlns:xsd="http://www.tc_test_company.com/2007/XMLSchema" SOAP-
ENV:encodingStyle="http://schemas.xmlsoap.org/
soap/encoding/">
<SOAP-ENV:Header>
<Security_Request>
<Username>deanpet</Username>
<Password>tiger</Password>
</Security_Request>
</SOAP-ENV:Header>
<SOAP-ENV:Body>
<Create__testcompany__TC_LEDGER_CODE>
<SETID>SHARE</SETID>
<LEDGER_CODE >TEST</LEDGER_CODE>
<DESCR>testa</DESCR>
</Create__testcompany__TC_LEDGER_CODE>
</SOAP-ENV:Body>
</SOAP-ENV:Envelope>
```

Response from error:

```
<?xml version="1.0"?>
<SOAP-ENV:Envelope xmlns:xsd="http://www.tc_company.com/2007/XMLSchema"
xmlns:xsi="http://www.tc_company.com/2007/XMLSchema-instance"
xmlns:SOAP-ENC=" http://schemas.xml_tc_company.com/soap/encoding/"
```

```
xmlns:SOAP-ENV=" http://schemas.xml_tc_company.com/soap/envelope/"
SOAP-ENV:encodingStyle="http://schemas.xml_tc_company.com/ soap/
encoding/"><SOAP-ENV:Header/><SOAP-ENV:Body><faultcode xmlns="http://
tc_test_ company_temp.com">200</faultcode><faultstring>Component In-
terface API.</faultstring><runcode>0</runcode><detail><keyinformati
on><SETID>SHARE</SETID><LEDGER_CODE>TEST</LEDGER_CODE></keyinformat
ion><messages><type>Message</type><messagesetnumber>15</messagesetn
umber><messagenumber>54</messagenumber><messagetext>The highlighted
field  is required.  You must enter a value for it before proceeding.
{CDW_LEDGER_CODE.DESCRSHORT} (15,54)</messagetext><explaintext>The
specified field is required but does not have a value.</explaintext></
messages><messages><type>Error</type><messagesetnumber>91</messagesetnu
mber><messagenumber>37</messagenumber><messagetext>Error saving Compo-
nent Interface. {CDW_LEDGER_CODE} (91,37)</messagetext><explaintext>
```

An error occurred while saving:

```
</explaintext></messages><messages><type>Error</
type><messagesetnumber>91</messagesetnumber><messagenumber>37</
messagenumber><messagetext>
```

Component interface save error:

```
{CDW_LEDGER_CODE}</messagetext></messages></detail></SOAP-ENV:Body></
SOAP-ENV:Envelope>
```

Response from Success on PT 8.42*x* – 8.43*x*

```
<?xml version="1.0"?>
<SOAP-ENV:Envelope xmlns:xsd="http://www.tc_test_company.com/2007/
XMLSchema" xmlns:xsi="http://www.tc_test_company.com/2007/XMLSchema-
instance" xmlns:SOAP-ENC=" http://schemas.xmlsoap.org/soap/encoding/"
xmlns:SOAP-ENV=" http://schemas.xmlsoap.org/soap/envelope/" SOAP-
ENV:encodingStyle="http://schemas.xmlsoap.org/ soap/encoding/"><SOAP-
ENV:Header/><SOAP-ENV:Body><Create__CompIntfc__CDW_LEDGER_CODEResponse
xmlns="http://psfttemp.org"><notification>1</notification><detail/></
Create__CompIntfc__CDW_LEDGER_CODEResponse></SOAP-ENV:Body></SOAP-
ENV:Envelope>
```

Response from Success on PT 8.44*x*

```
<SOAP-ENV:Envelope xmlns:SOAP-ENV="http://schemas.xmlsoap.org/soap/
envelope/" xmlns:SOAP-ENC="http://schemas.xmlsoap.org/soap/encoding/"
xmlns:xsi="http://www.tc_test_company.com/2007/XMLSchema-instance"
xmlns:xsd="http://www.tc_test_company.com/2007/XMLSchema" SOAP-
ENV:encodingStyle="http://schemas.xmlsoap.org/soap/encoding/">
<SOAP-ENV:Header>
<Security_Request>
```

```
<Username>VP1</Username>
<Password>VP1</Password>
</Security_Request>
</SOAP-ENV:Header>
<SOAP-ENV:Body>
    <Create__CompIntfc__STATE debug = "Y">
<COUNTRY>USA</COUNTRY>
<STATE>MZ1</STATE>
<DESCR>TEST 1</DESCR>
  </Create__CompIntfc__STATE>
  <Create__CompIntfc__STATE debug = "Y">
<COUNTRY>USA</COUNTRY>
<STATE>MZ2</STATE>
<DESCR>TEST 2</DESCR>
  </Create__CompIntfc__STATE>
  <Create__CompIntfc__STATE debug = "Y">
<COUNTRY>USA</COUNTRY>
<STATE>MZ3</STATE>
<DESCR>TEST 3</DESCR>
  </Create__CompIntfc__STATE>
  </SOAP-ENV:Body>
</SOAP-ENV:Envelope>
```

Response:

```
<?xml version="1.0"?>
<SOAP-ENV:Envelope SOAP-ENV:encodingStyle="http://schemas.xmlsoap
.org/soap/encoding/" xmlns:SOAP-ENC="http://schemas.xmlsoap.org/
soap/encoding/" xmlns:SOAP-ENV="http://schemas.xmlsoap.org/soap/
envelope/" xmlns:xsd="http://www.tc_test_company.com/2007/XMLSchema"
xmlns:xsi="http://www.tc_test_company.com/2007/XMLSchema-instance">
    <SOAP-ENV:Header/>
    <SOAP-ENV:Body>
        <Create__CompIntfc__STATE debug="Y">
            <COUNTRY>USA</COUNTRY>
            <STATE>MZ2</STATE>
            <DESCR>TEST 2</DESCR>
        </Create__CompIntfc__STATE>
        <Create__CompIntfc__STATE debug="Y">
            <COUNTRY>USA</COUNTRY>
            <STATE>MZ3</STATE>
            <DESCR>TEST 3</DESCR>
        </Create__CompIntfc__STATE>
        <faultcode xmlns="http://psfttemp.org">200</faultcode>
        <faultstring>Component Interface API.</faultstring>
        <notification>1</notification>
```

```
        <detail>
            <transaction/>
            <transaction/>
            <transaction/>
        </detail>
    </SOAP-ENV:Body>
</SOAP-ENV:Envelope>
```

Message with Errors on PT 8.44*x*:

```
<SOAP-ENV:Envelope xmlns:SOAP-ENV="http://schemas.xmlsoap.org/soap/en-
velope/" xmlns:SOAP-ENC="http://schemas.xmlsoap.org/soap/encoding/"
xmlns:xsi="http://www.tc_test_company.com/2007/XMLSchema-instance"
xmlns:xsd="http://www.tc_test_company.com/2007/XMLSchema" SOAP-
ENV:encodingStyle="http://schemas.xmlsoap.org/soap/encoding/">
<SOAP-ENV:Header>
<Security_Request>
<Username>VP1</Username>
<Password>VP1</Password>
</Security_Request>
</SOAP-ENV:Header>
<SOAP-ENV:Body>
    <Create__CompIntfc__STATE debug = "Y">
<COUNTRY>USA</COUNTRY>
<STATE>MZZZZZZZZZ1</STATE>
<DESCR>TEST 1</DESCR>
  </Create__CompIntfc__STATE>
  <Create__CompIntfc__STATE debug = "Y">
  <COUNTRY>USA</COUNTRY>
  <STATE>MZ2</STATE>
  <DESCR>TEST 2</DESCR>
  </Create__CompIntfc__STATE>
  <Create__CompIntfc__STATE debug = "Y">
  <COUNTRY>USA</COUNTRY>
  <STATE>MZ3</STATE>
  <DESCR>TEST 3</DESCR>
  <NUMERIC_CD>0345</NUMERIC_CD>
  </Create__CompIntfc__STATE>
  </SOAP-ENV:Body>
</SOAP-ENV:Envelope>
```

Response:

```
<?xml version="1.0"?>
<SOAP-ENV:Envelope SOAP-ENV:encodingStyle="http://schemas.xmlsoap.org/
soap/encoding/" xmlns:SOAP-ENC="http://schemas.xmlsoap.org/soap/encod-
ing/" xmlns:SOAP-
```

```
ENV="http://schemas.xmlsoap.org/soap/envelope/" xmlns:xsd="http://www
.tc_test_company.com/2007/XMLSchema" xmlns:xsi="http://www.tc_test_com-
pany.com/2007/XMLSchema-instance">
    <SOAP-ENV:Header/>
    <SOAP-ENV:Body>
        <Create__CompIntfc__STATE debug="Y">
            <COUNTRY>USA</COUNTRY>
            <STATE>MZ2</STATE>
            <DESCR>TEST 2</DESCR>
        </Create__CompIntfc__STATE>
        <Create__CompIntfc__STATE debug="Y">
            <COUNTRY>USA</COUNTRY>
            <STATE>MZ3</STATE>
            <DESCR>TEST 3</DESCR>
            <NUMERIC_CD>0345</NUMERIC_CD>
        </Create__CompIntfc__STATE>
        <faultcode xmlns="http://psfttemp.org">200</faultcode>
        <faultstring>Component Interface API.</faultstring>
        <runcode>0</runcode>
        <detail>
            <transaction>
                <keyinformation>
<COUNTRY>USA</COUNTRY>
                    <STATE>TEST12345678</STATE>
                </keyinformation>
                <messages>
                    <type>Error</type>
                    <messagesetnumber>91</messagesetnumber>
                    <messagenumber>68</messagenumber>
                    <messagetext>TEST12345678 is too long for the field
TC_STATE.STATE (91,68)
```

The value that the field is being set to is too long:

```
</messagetext>
                    <explaintext>
</explaintext>
                </messages>
                <messages>
                    <type>Error</type>
                    <messagesetnumber>91</messagesetnumber>
                    <messagenumber>61</messagenumber>
                    <messagetext>Failed to create the Component Inter-
face</messagetext>
                </messages>
            </transaction>
            <transaction/>
            <transaction>
                <keyinformation>
```

```
                    <COUNTRY>USA</COUNTRY>
                    <STATE>MZ3</STATE>
                </keyinformation>
                <messages>
                    <type>Error</type>
                    <messagesetnumber>91</messagesetnumber>
                    <messagenumber>68</messagenumber>
                    <messagetext>The value 0345 is too long for the
field TC_STATE.NUMERIC_CD (91,68)</messagetext>
                    <explaintext>
```

Component Interface–Based Web Services

Let's take a look at the steps to create a simple component interface–based web service.

1. First go to PeopleTools | Security | Permission and Roles | Permission List and open the permission list.

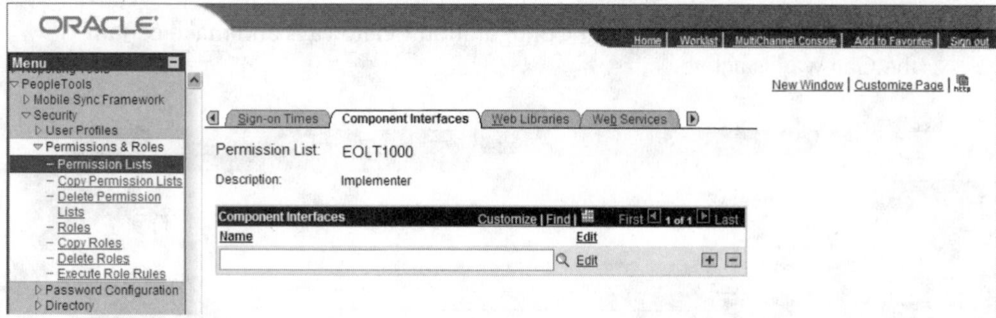

2. Then go to the Component Interface tab and enter your Component Interface name.

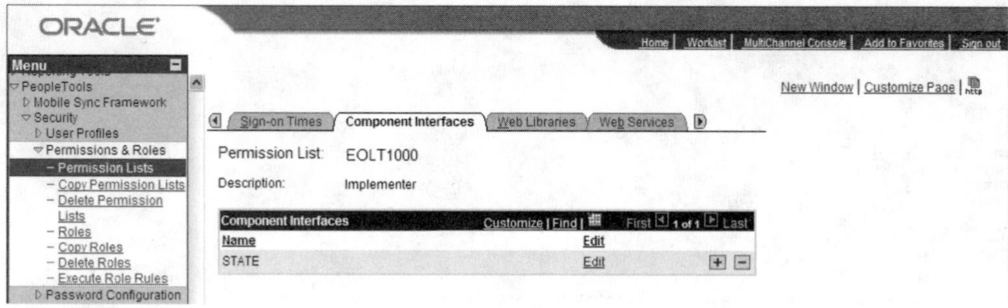

3. Then click the Edit link and grant full access. Save the page.

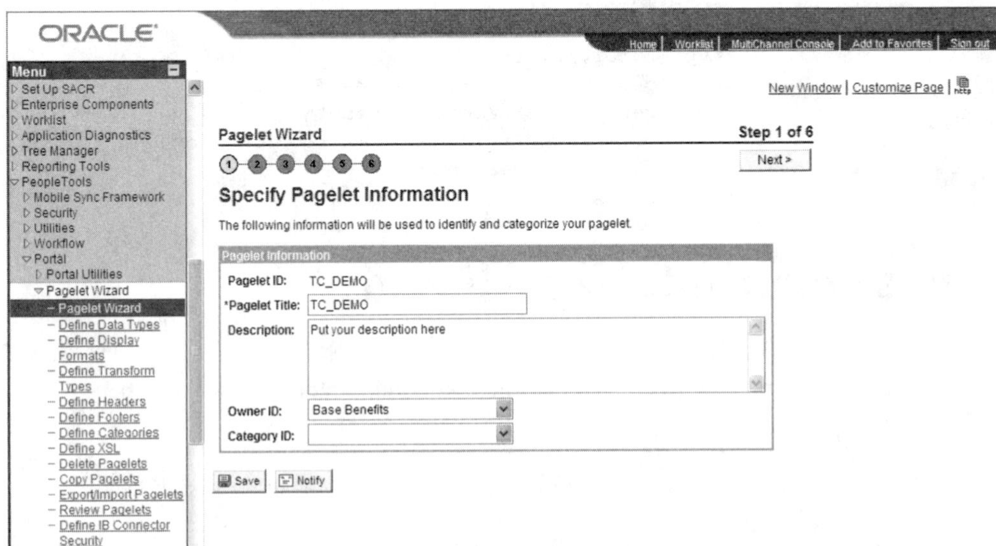

4. Then go to Integration Broker | Configuration | Gateways and make certain the Gateway is active.

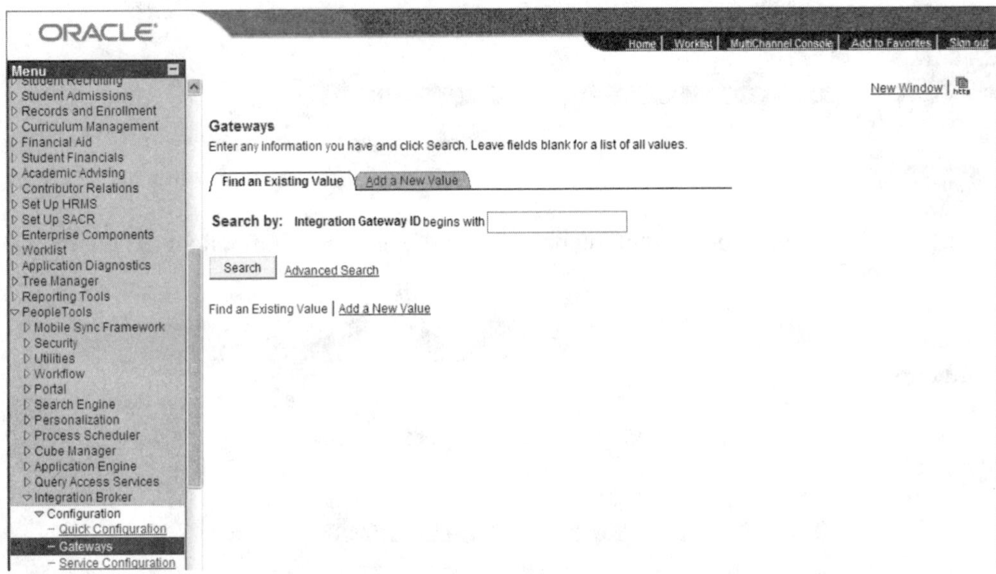

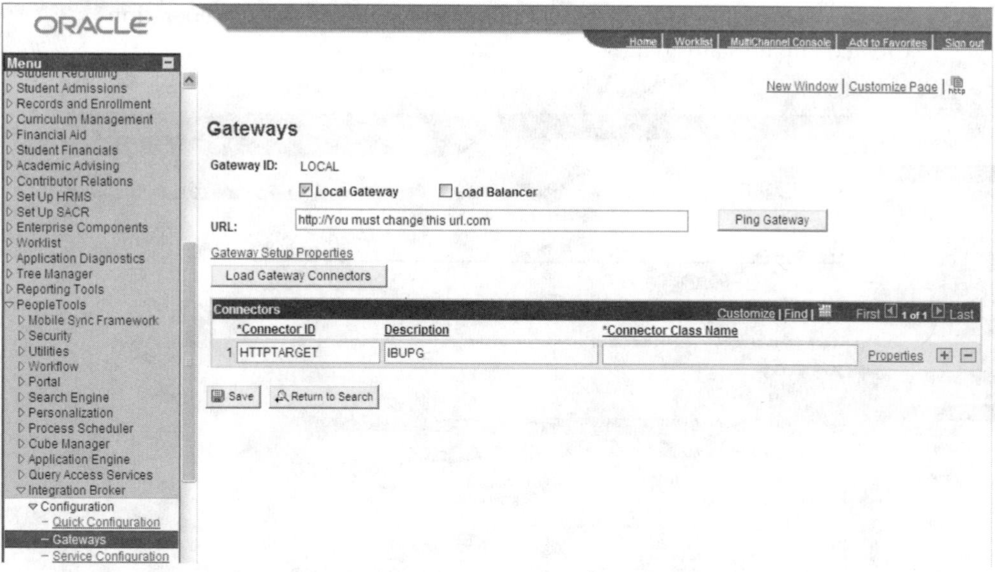

5. Next go to PeopleTools | Integration Broker | Configuration | Service Configurations to make sure all the settings are correct; make certain you set your Target Location.

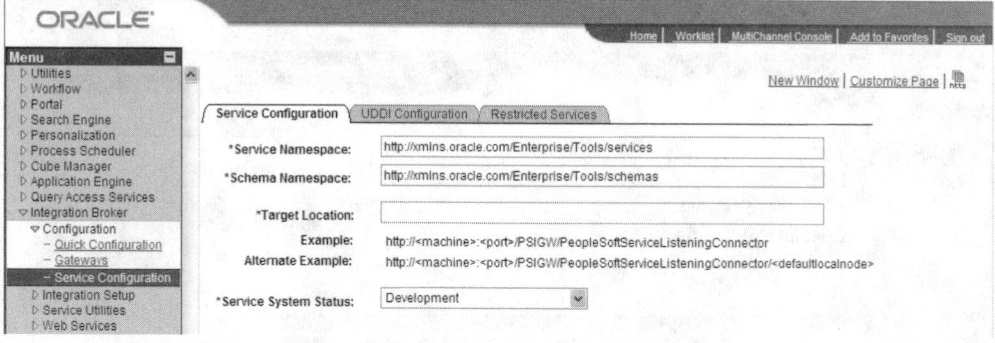

6. Next go to Integration Broker | Web Services | CI-Based Services to open the Component Interface. Make certain you put a check in the check box of the component interface and click Review CI Status. Select the method you wish to expose to the web service and click Display Selected Actions. Then click

Perform Selected Actions. You will then receive the message "Operation Created" in the status bar.

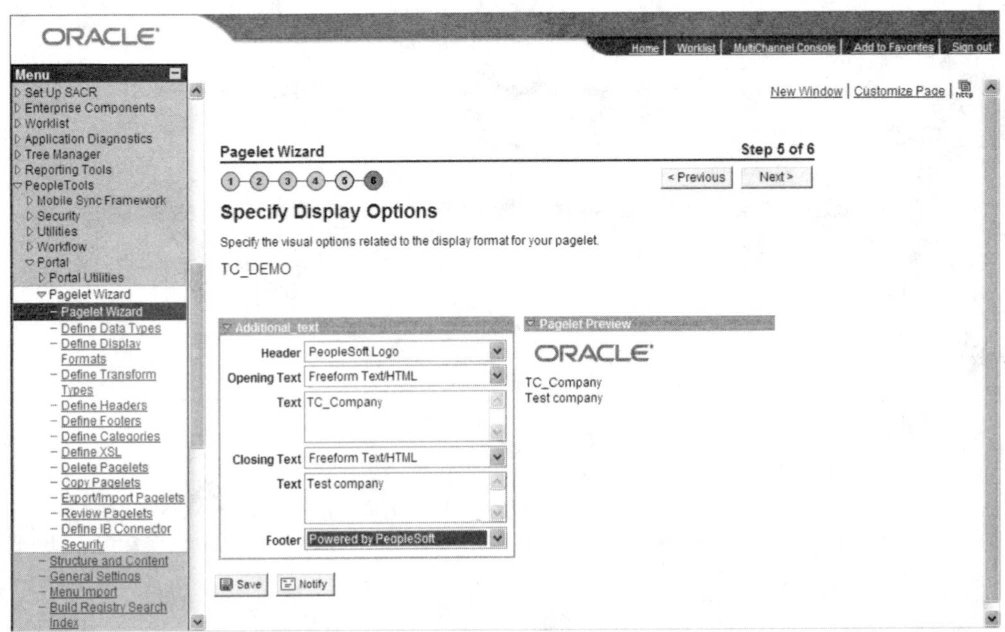

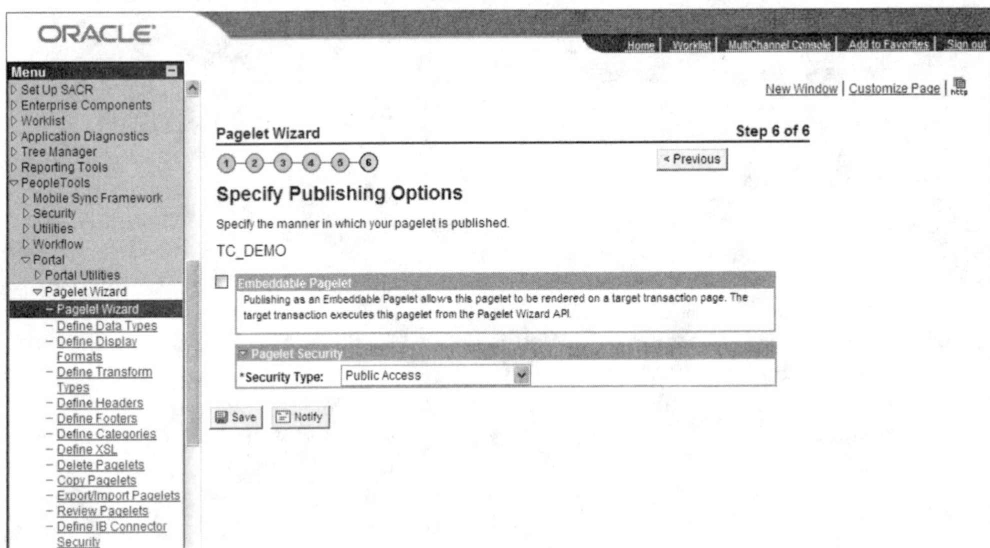

Working with the Pagelet Wizard

Pagelet Wizard allows you to take HTML data sources like Google and add those cool things to your PeopleSoft Portal. Have you ever seen a group add the weather to the main landing page or homepage of an organization in PeopleSoft? They do this by added HTML via a Pagelet Wizard. The following steps teach you how to use the PeopleSoft Pagelet Wizard.

1. First navigate to PeopleTools | Portal | Portal Utilities | Navigation Collections and add your collection.

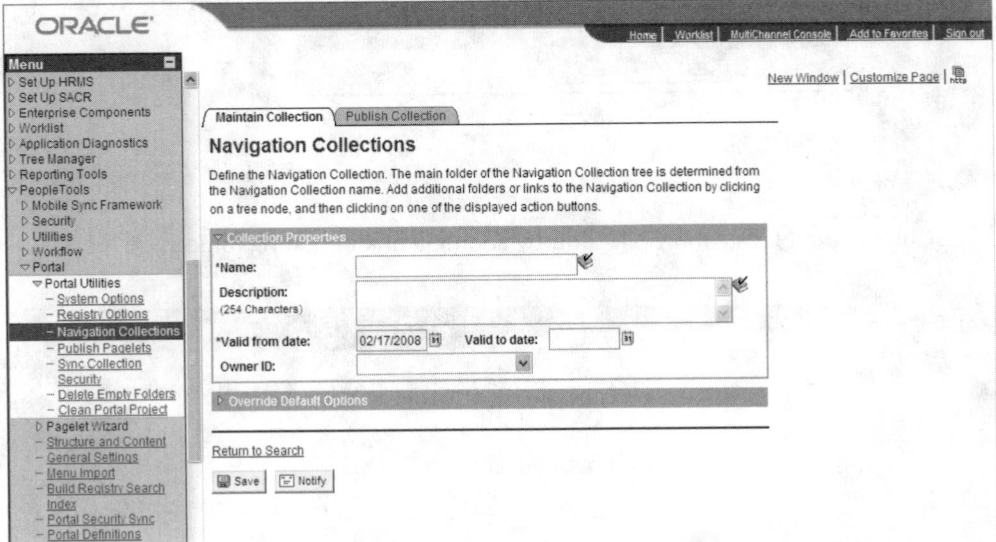

2. Name your collection, provide a description (optional), specify valid dates, and identify the owner.

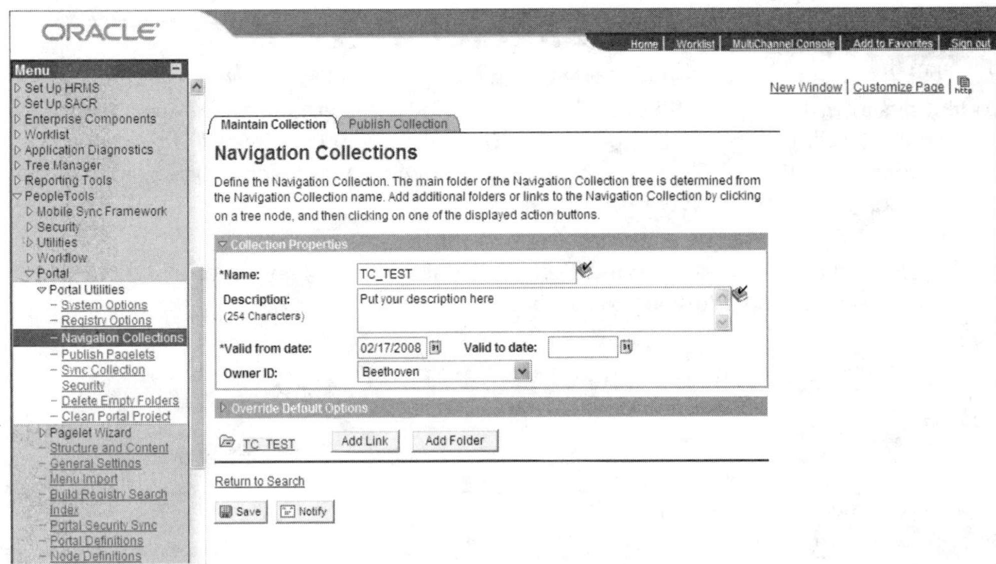

3. Build your Navigation Collection by adding a link or adding folders.

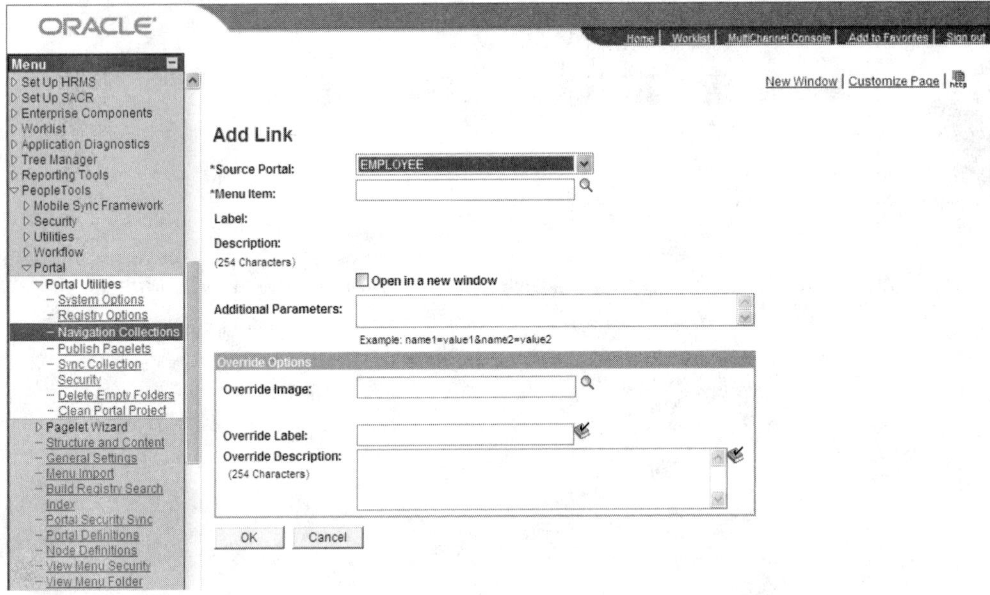

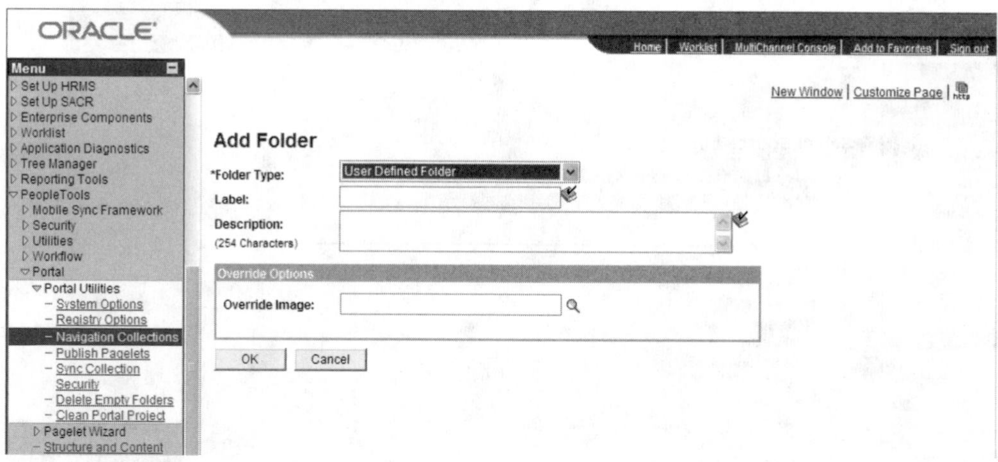

4. When you add a link, make certain you fill in your Source Portal and Source Link.

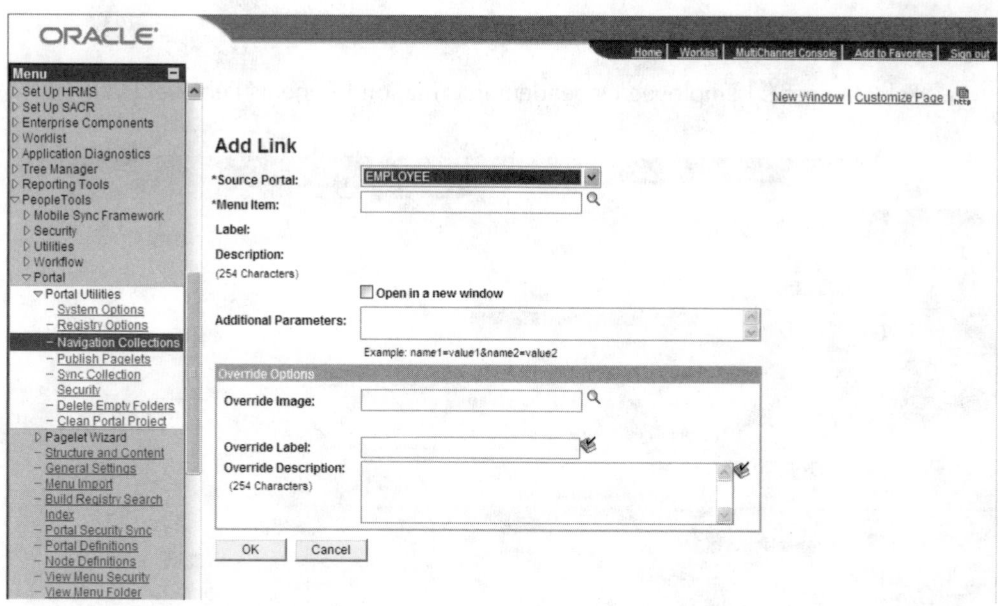

5. You can navigate the menu structure to find the content reference and/or folders you want in your collection.

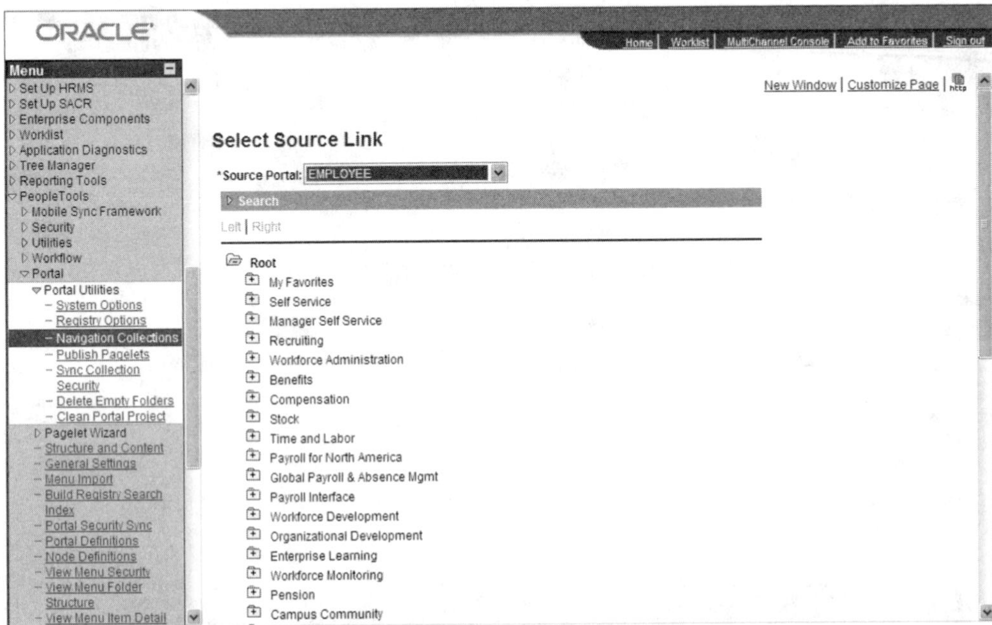

6. Select Benefits | Employee/Dependent Information | Benefits Personal Data.

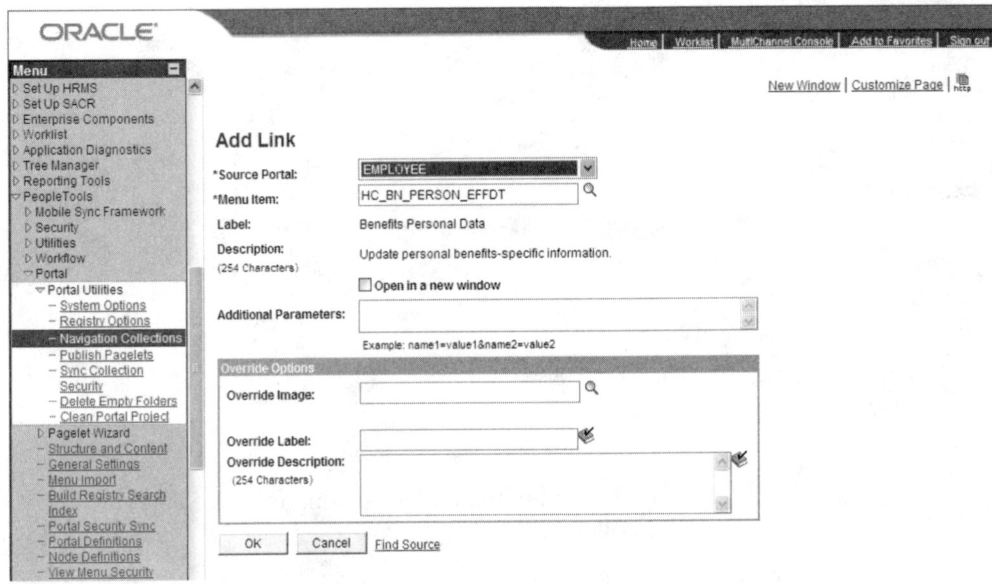

7. Navigate to PeopleTools | Portal | Pagelet Wizard.

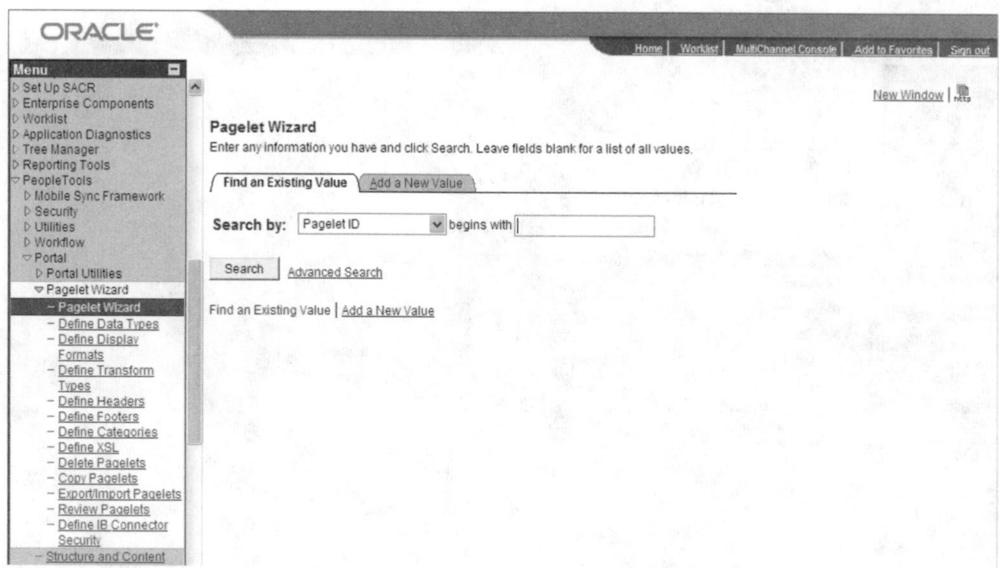

8. Add a New Value and type a Pagelet ID.

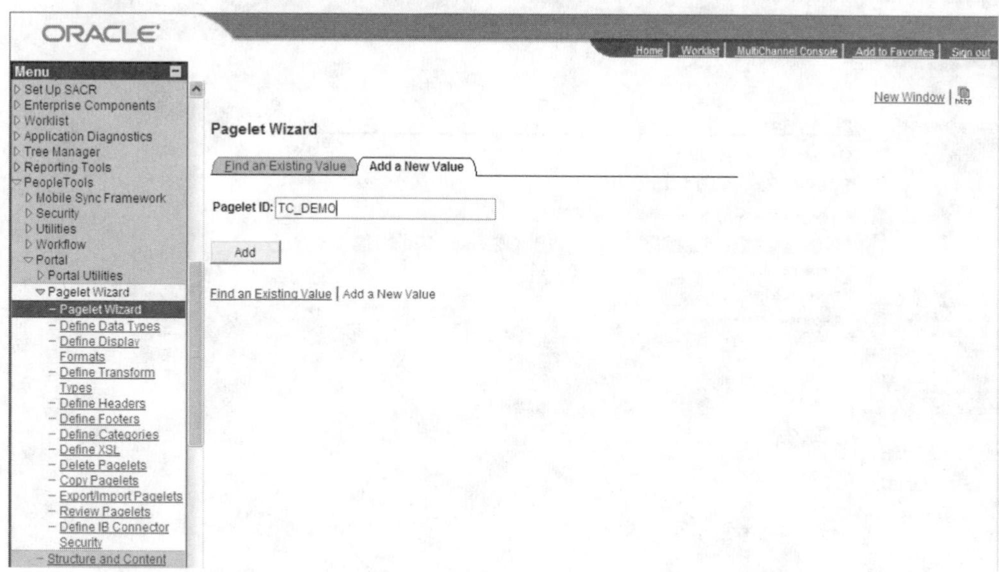

9. Provide a title for the Pagelet, Give Descr, and OwnerId.

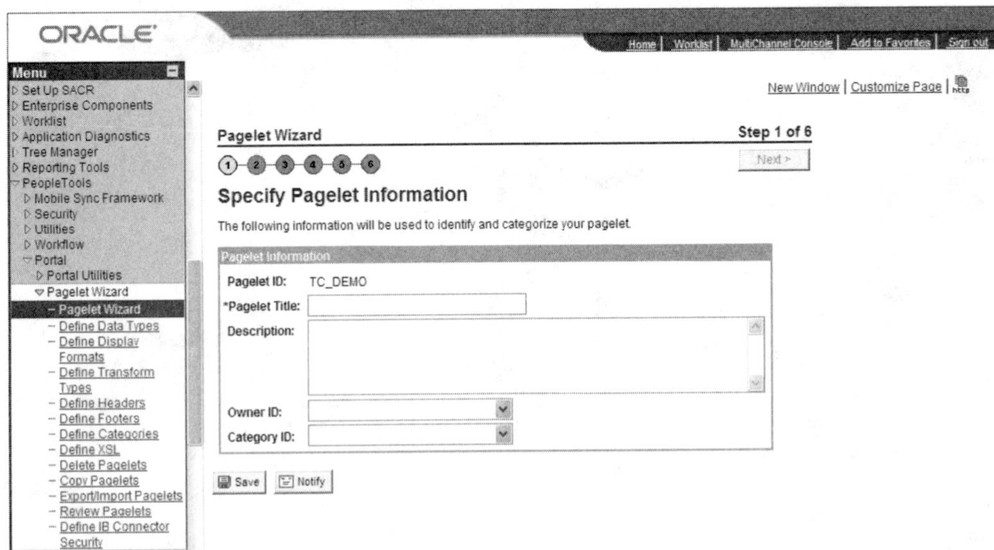

10. Fill in the Title, Description, Owner ID, and Category ID.

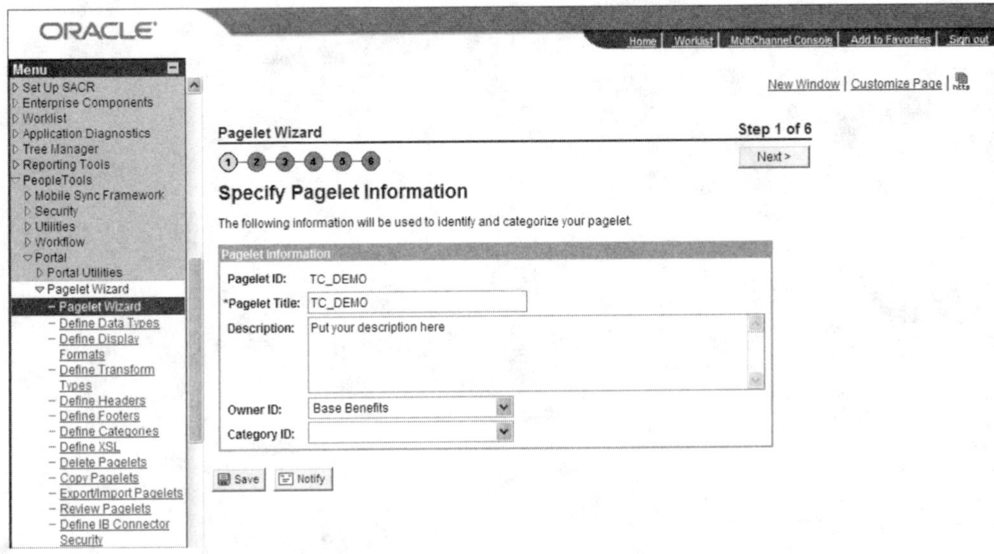

11. Select the Data Source, choose the Data Type, and insert the URL; click Save.

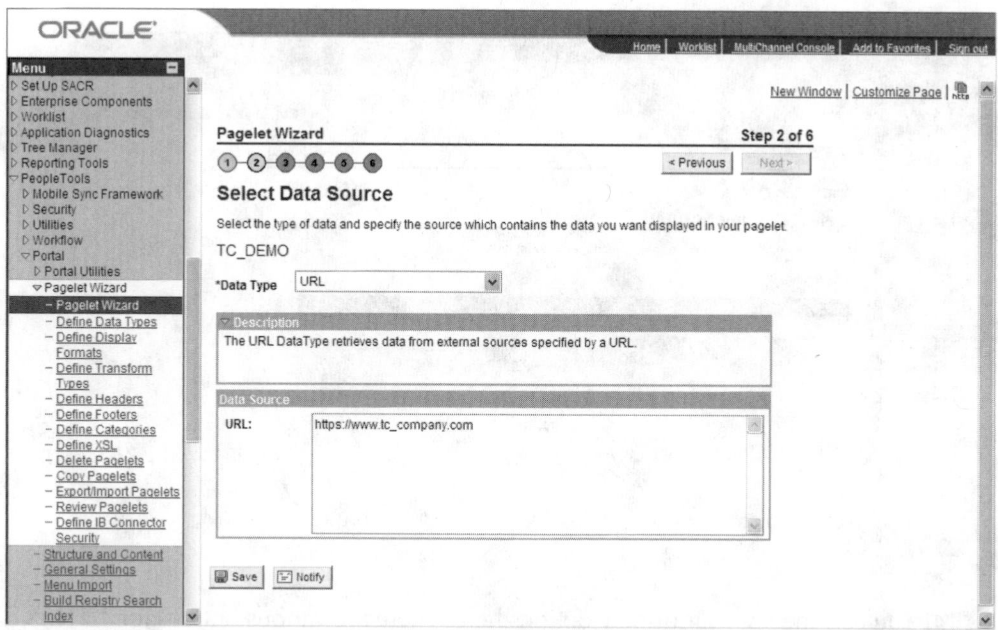

12. Specify the Data Source Parameters, choose the Field Name, Description, Usage Type, Required flag, and an optional Default Value.

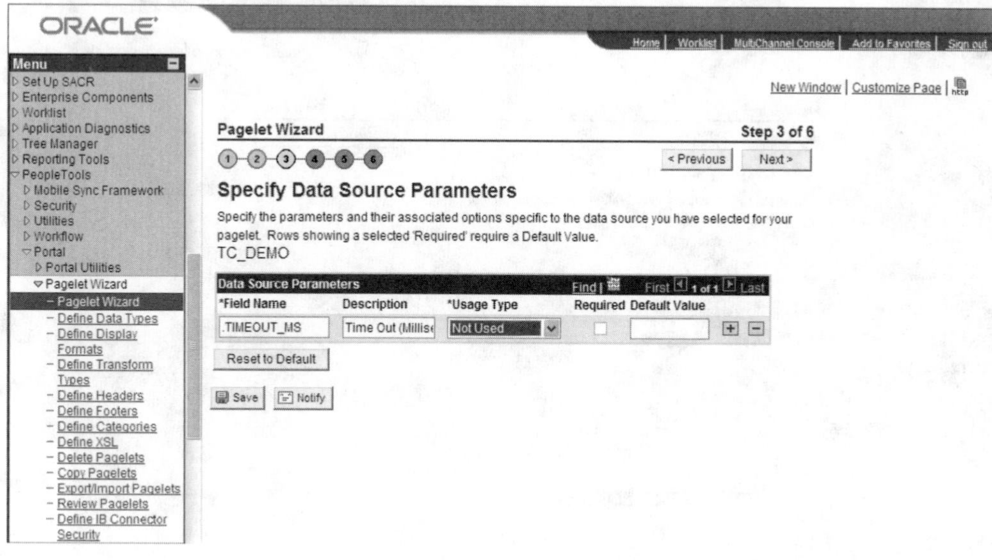

13. Select Display Format, choose between Passthru, which displays your pagelet data as a data source, or specify a custom XSL template for the display.

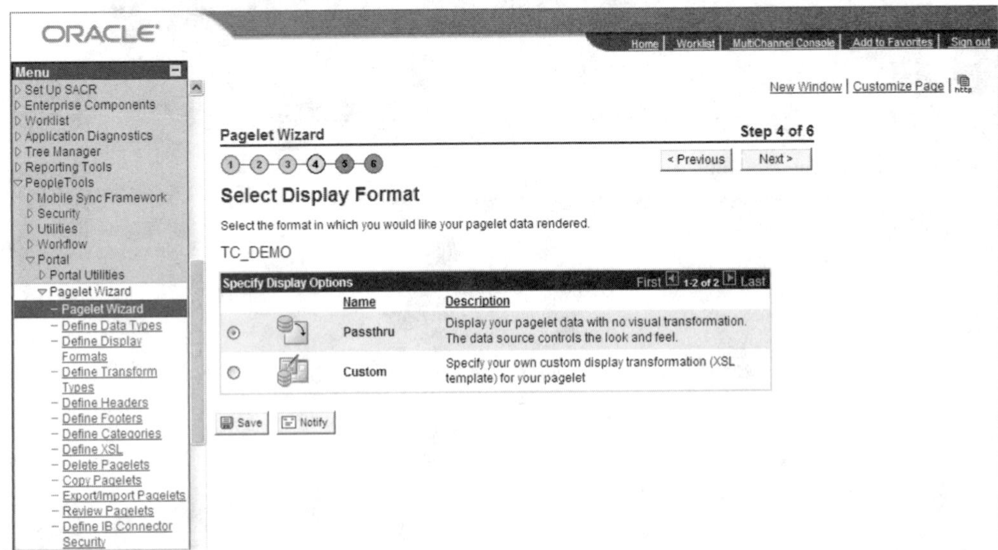

14. You can specify your display options here. There are various options for your navigation collection, including the sizes of images, headers/footers, and PeopleSoft logos.

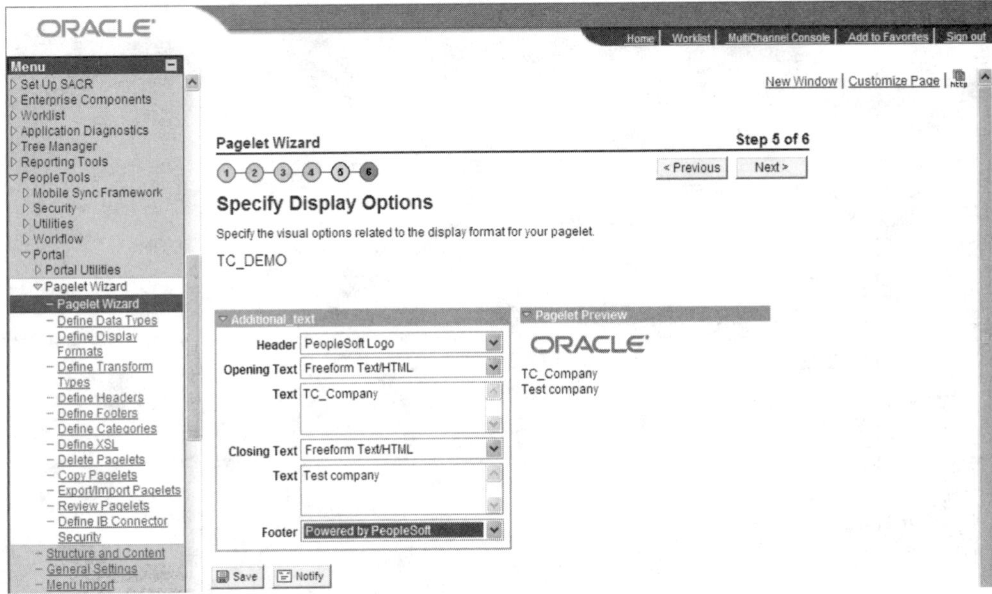

15. You can specify your publishing next. Here we selected Homepage Pagelet and placed it under the PeopleSoft Applications folder.

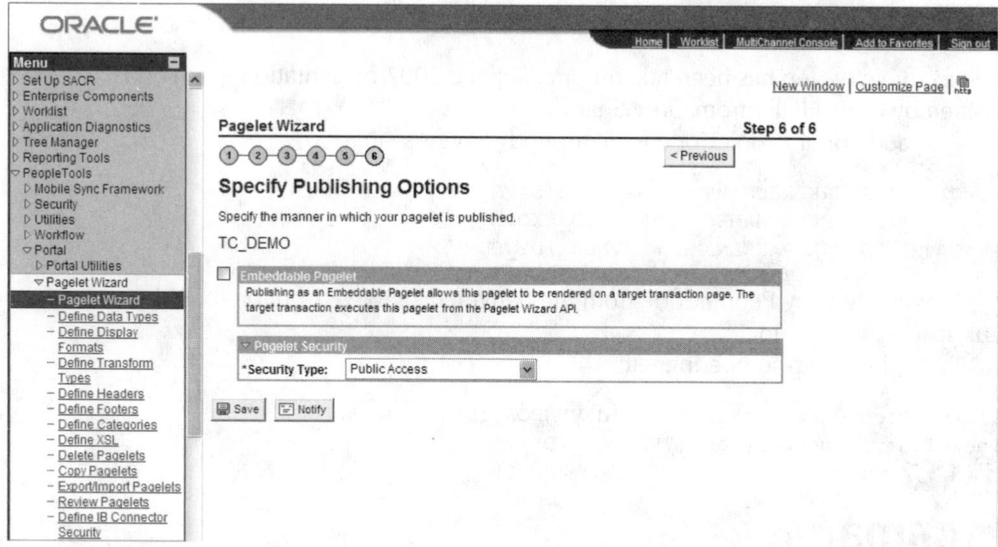

16. Click Save. Test your pagelet by navigating to Home | Personalize Content.

You will see your Navigation Collection in the folder you specified earlier (the Homepage Pagelet folder).

Automating SaveAs Functionality

The following are the steps to automate the SaveAs Functionality:

1. Create a Project with the following "Save As" code.
2. Identify and create a component interface for the component.
3. Set your security.
4. Copy the level 0 record.
5. Delete all fields except for keys.
6. Change the Record type to Work Record.
7. Create a page with the fields from the new record.

8. Add a "Save As" subpage.
9. Add the page to component.
10. Grant security.

The example of step has been taken from Alliance 2007 presentation given and written by Chris Heller from Grey Sparling.

Add additional PeopleCode logic around "Save As" logic:

```
GS_CI_UTILS_WRK.RECNAME = "GS_VNDR_SAVE_AS";
GS_CI_UTILS_WRK.BCNAME = "VNDR_ID_EXCEL";
GS_CI_UTILS_WRK.PANELNAME = "VNDR_ID1_SUM";
```

Optionally copy PeopleCode from the delivered "Save As" button to add application-specific logic.

Example : Auto-numbering, etc.

```
&level0RecordNew.GetField(Field.VENDOR_ID).Value =
&newCI.GetPropertyByName("VENDOR_ID");
```

Summary

This chapter took a deeper look into the more advanced things that can be done in PeopleCode and PeopleTools, using Java and the component interface. It looked at the component buffer, embedding HTML, and Java within the application. The advanced skills needed were outlined to give a developer a toolkit that can take the basics to a more advanced level. These advanced skills will allow for customizations that are sometimes crucial in allowing your business processes to be represented in the PeopleSoft application.

As much as everyone in the industry would like PeopleSoft vanilla to meet all the needs all the time, it is very evident that this is not the case. The skills to know where code is fired, how to write it efficiently, and what is the best tool to use to get the desired result were covered in this chapter. We looked at objects and classes and how to name and instantiate these objects and classes in the PeopleSoft component, the component buffer and how it provides the memory buffer for the component, functions both delivered and custom, application packages (how to write them, call them, and use them in PeopleSoft), how to create custom charts, the WSDL bindings for the component interface, the component interface web services, working with the Pagelet Wizard, and automating the SaveAs Functionality. Many more advanced skills are available in PeopleSoft and PeopleCode, but this chapter has provided a basic toolset for the reader to add to and become an advanced PeopleSoft developer.

PART III

Other Application Development Tools

Part III will introduce you to the new tools available in PeopleSoft, including XML Publisher. This part of the book will also introduce you to a host of tricks taken from several experts and collected into one location. As we move to the Fusion Application, it is more important than ever to learn the new object-oriented skills, while still keeping up the legacy application. This section will provide you with a reference point for the old technology and introduce you to some new Fusion Application technology.

PeopleSoft has a host of other available tools that can be used in PeopleSoft, including BI Publisher, Query Tool, SQR, Application Engine, and (as described in two separate appendixes) COBOL and PL/SQL. You can also utilize Java and place any Java code in an Application Package; refer to Chapter 7, Advanced PeopleCode, to see some examples. Oracle has done many presentations on the available products for reporting. Figure 8-1 shows the available reporting resources taken from the Quest Collaborate 2008 session 34190 "XML Publisher for Project Reporting" by BTRG.

Newer Tools

Newer tools are available in the PeopleSoft development arena, with the biggest advances taking place in the middleware area. At the writing of this book, advances in all areas of development are taking place at Oracle. With the release of the new database platform 11*g* and the data vault, Oracle is taking security, auditing, and reporting to the next level. As developers, we have been asked for years to catch up with the ISO 9000 and Sarbanes-Oxley standards, but without the software tools in areas like the database it was increasingly difficult to meet these demands. Oracle has provided the tools to give application developers a total solution, with the database 11*g*, middleware, and the application front end.

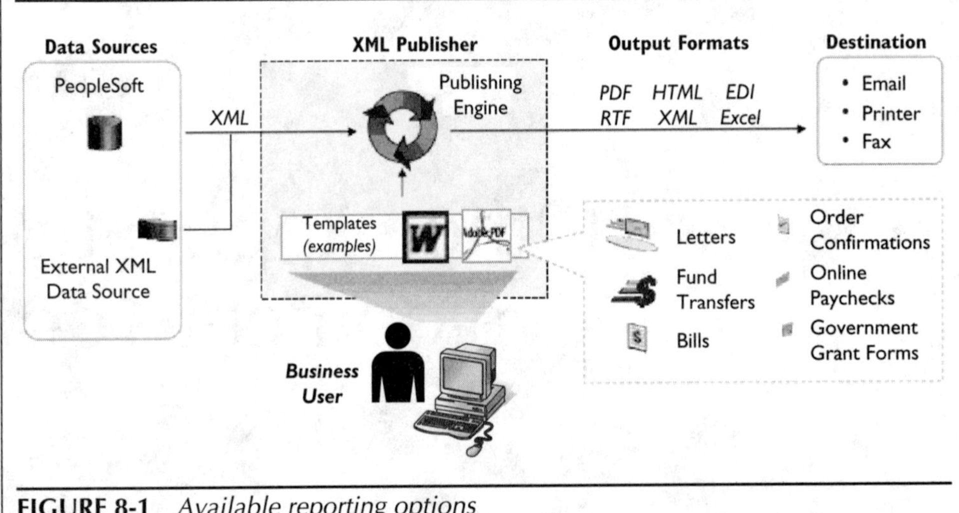

FIGURE 8-1 *Available reporting options*

Fusion Middleware Tools

Oracle Fusion Middleware is a comprehensive middleware family composed of SOA and middleware products, including Oracle Application Server, related Oracle Application Server products and options such as Oracle Identity Management, Oracle Business Intelligence, Oracle BPEL Process Manager, Oracle Web Services Manager, Oracle Business Activity Monitoring, Oracle COREid Products, Oracle Portal and Oracle Integration, Oracle Data Hubs, Oracle Content Services, Oracle Real Time Collaboration, and Oracle Unified Messaging. When used in conjunction with Oracle Fusion Middleware Enterprise Portal, PeopleTools is designed to serve as a point of access for all enterprise applications. In addition, Web services created from PeopleTools' Service Designer and Integration Broker can be automated and orchestrated via Oracle's Fusion Middleware BPEL Process Manager.

Among other new tools included in the launch is PeopleSoft Change Impact Analyzer, designed to allow customers to study the effect of prospective changes to their applications. Also, BI Publisher is now integrated into PeopleTools (called XML Publisher in PeopleTools), increasing the number of options for customized reports. BPEL provides a standard, process-centric way to integrate disparate systems. Oracle's BPEL Process Manager, a key tool in Oracle Fusion Middleware for delivering service-oriented architecture (SOA), supports the industry-standard BPEL specification backed by Microsoft, IBM, SAP, and BEA and is widely recognized as an enterprise blueprint for reducing the cost, complexity, and inflexibility of integration projects.

XML Publisher

XML Publisher (known as BI Publisher in Oracle Development Tools) handles the data formatting and output; it has recently been integrated with PS/Query and PeopleCode, which makes it accessible from Application Engine. It's not a big stretch to see how Application Engine could be enhanced to use BI Publisher natively as an output tool and effectively get rid of the need to use SQR at all.

As of the writing of this book Oracle acquired Hyperion. Version 11 of Hyperion SQR Production Reporting now contains a significant new feature; a new SQR engine for writing rowsets from SQR to XML Publisher.

Query Tool

With PeopleSoft Query, you can create customized reporting in a graphical user interface without having much knowledge of SQL. The most complex part of using the Query Tool is to accurately set up the trees to avoid any problems with security.

Then you just go to the Query Manager and create a query by using a series of check boxes; you can then write very complex queries against the PeopleSoft Records. These queries can then be scheduled in Process Scheduler, linked in Crystal Reports or nVision, and downloaded into Excel. This is a perfect way to create an end-user layer and create a set of data warehouse reports for your customers. Your can spend the time training a superuser in each of your departments and remove yourself from the business of creating ad hoc reports. In this section you will learn about queries: their creation, scheduling, and downloading.

SQR

Structured Query Report Writer is a PeopleSoft-delivered reporting tool. In industry it is used all too often in the place of better and more advanced tools; and with XML on the rise a lot of SQR reports are going to be benched and replaced by XML reports. But there are so many reports in place written in this reporting tool that this book covers SQR. SQR has a robust report-writing environment with complex procedural logic built in. It is also an easy language to learn and come up to speed quickly with. You can combine database retrieval and row processing. You can even embed PL/SQL in your reports and do complex database manipulation.

Application Engine

Application Engine is a batch processing tool provided via Application Designer in PeopleTools. It resembles a macro shell window that allows for calls to SQL, PeopleCode, and or another section. It allows you to do file extraction, carry out database manipulation, e-mail out results to your staff, and embed PL/SQL within PeopleCode.

Application Engine is different than regular batch programs in that it isn't procedural. It focuses on set-based SQL logic and goes to a much deeper level of the underlying application definitions. Describing set-based logic is beyond the scope of this introduction, but suffice it to say that set-based logic is more in line with how SQL is supposed to work, but it's not as familiar to developers who have only worked with procedural logic.

To make an already long story short, Application Engine slowly won converts within PeopleSoft, and by the time that PeopleSoft 8 was being developed, Application Engine was adopted by the PeopleTools team. The front end was converted to being a regular PeopleTool as part of Application Designer, and the back end was rewritten in C++ and given the ability to run PeopleCode as well as SQL logic.

Why would Application Engine show up as part of Oracle Fusion? There are a couple of reasons. One is that Oracle really doesn't have a good tool for batch development. If you look at existing Oracle applications, you'll notice that batch processing is done by writing raw PL/SQL or Pro*C code: not the most straightforward thing for a typical application developer to do. The other thing about Application Engine that fits well within Oracle is that it is a set-based tool. Most of the processing is pushed to the database, and that plays well to Oracle's strengths. Oracle developers themselves list using Application Engine for batch as number 4 in their top ten things for PeopleSoft Enterprise customers to do today to get ready for Fusion.

Does it make sense to train people in SQR or Application Engine for current PeopleSoft customers? The answer is that both have pros and cons. For starters, there aren't many PeopleSoft applications that don't use both SQR and AppEngine, so you need to have some level of skills in both. I think that CRM is the exception here; I know that CRM has no COBOL, and I think that is true for SQR as well.

SQR also has the advantage of being a little bit more independent of the applications. For example, when you want to write an SQR, all you need is a text editor instead of a proprietary tool like Application Designer. You can also run SQRs in any database, not just a PeopleSoft database. Of course, doing so requires that you license SQR independently of the license that you receive with your PeopleSoft applications, but you could actually do it.

Of course, those pros are also part of the cons of SQR. SQR has *zero* understanding of the underlying applications that it's working with. Trees, effective dating, setids, row-level security, related language records, etc., all have to be coded by hand when you're writing SQR code. Not impossible to do, but it's certainly more costly and error prone to build and maintain it by hand.

Chris Heller also talks about the cons that the Application Engine comes with, especially when looking at it from a reporting perspective. Aside from being a very PeopleSoft-specific tool, App Engine lacks any kind of built-in output capability. This was the target of the (never finished) PeopleCode Print project, but there's nothing there today.

Meta-SQL

Meta-SQL expands to platform-specific SQL substrings; it then causes another function to be called, or substitutes a value. Meta-SQL constructs are used in functions that pass SQL strings, such as the following:

- SQLExec
- Scroll buffer functions (ScrollSelect and its relatives)
- PeopleSoft Application Designer dynamic and SQL views
- Some Rowset class methods (Select, SelectNew, Fill, and so on)
- The SQL class

- PeopleSoft Application Engine programs
- Some Record class methods (Insert, Update, and so on)
- COBOL functions

Not all Meta-SQL can be used by all programs. Some Meta-SQL can be used only in Application Engine programs. Other Meta-SQL can only be used as part of an SQL statement in an SQL or dynamic view. If a Meta-SQL construct, function, or metavariable is supported in PeopleCode, it is supported in all types of PeopleCode programs; that is, in Application Engine PeopleCode programs (actions), component interface PeopleCode programs, and so on. Even if a Meta-SQL element is used in PeopleCode, you cannot use Meta-SQL like a built-in function. You can use Meta-SQL in the SQLExec function, the Select method, the Fill method, and so on. Note that Meta-SQL is not available in SQR. There are pros and cons to using Meta-SQL; for example, fewer lines of code are required and you can reuse your code, but SQL is easier to read, so as a developer, you will have to decide what is best for you to pull out of your bag of tricks.

Customization Tricks

One of my favorite tricks, which you will find in Part III, is a method to create a graph on the PeopleSoft page. One of my customers is a group of accountants, and there is just no way to excite an accountant more than to provide him or her with numbers and a graph. You will see how to do that in Part III.

Smarter Ways to Work

In Chapter 12 you will find the best way to do a lot of debugging, problem solving, and graph making, and just a host of ideas on ways that have been learned to solve problems. Also included is a way to turn on and off debugging messages by surrounding them with conditional logic. I hope you enjoy the chapter as much as I did collecting the tips from over the years from many skilled colleagues.

CHAPTER 8

XML Publisher

n this chapter you will get to look at one of the new features of Oracle's Fusion Application. With the release of PeopleTools 8.48, Oracle incorporated Fusion Middleware. This provides you with an easy stepping stone into the new Middleware architecture, which is built on SOA (service-oriented architecture) and is capable of processing 64-bit technology. If you think about it, this is some really monumental stuff, to come this far on the PeopleSoft platform.

So what is XML? Well, XML (the term stands for Extensible Markup Language) is a syntax that describes the structure of data. XML is not a markup language in the pure sense of the word; it is a set of defined rules for creating markup languages. The most popular markup language that you should be familiar with is HTML, or Hypertext Markup Language, which is used to publish to the Internet; we have discussed creating it for pages in PeopleSoft. Two things are required to create and interpret XML: software that can interpret, and the language itself. XML documents reside in files that can be created in simple editors like Microsoft Notepad or Microsoft Word—which makes it very easy to use and create, but then how to incorporate and use it inside of PeopleSoft becomes key. First let's take a look at the XML basics.

Basics of XML

Taking a look at a basic file—12345, John Smith, 0987—the basic three pieces are EMPLID, NAME, and DEPTID. Each piece of information in the flat file is separated by a comma. So here is the XML to pull out these pieces of information.

```
<Employees>
      <Employees>
            <EMPLID>12345</EMPLID>
            <NAME>John Smith</NAME>
            <DEPTID>0987</DEPTID>
      </Employees>
</Employees>
```

The pieces of data that are inside of the brackets (<>) are the markup elements. The information outside of the brackets is data. Each of the pieces of data has a starting and ending tag; the end tag is noted with a /. There is no limit to the tags you can use, create, or rename; so, for example, if you wanted to rename NAME to ENAME, there are no rules in XML that would prevent this.

```
<Employees>
      <Employees>
            <EMPLID>12345</EMPLID>
            <ENAME>John Smith</ENAME>
            <DEPTID>0987</DEPTID>
      </Employees>
</Employees>
```

XML does not qualify as a programming language, and when you are trying to decide within the context of PeopleSoft which is the best solution, it is important to understand the limitations of PeopleSoft. XML is usually stored in a simple text file, and then separate software is required to process and interpret the XML. It is the software that would make any modifications or changes to the application, not XML. XML is only going to provide syntax to add structure to the data and relies completely on the software to carry that out. Let's take a look at the major components of XML:

- **XML declaration** The general characteristics of the document
- **DTD document type declaration** The structure of the document; internal declarations local to the XML document
- **DTD internal subset** DTD contains references to other DTD
- **XML information set** Document content
- **Root element** Encloses all the information
- **Start tag** XML elements have start and end tags
- **End tag** XML elements have start and end tags
- **XML element** The combination of start and end tags collectively makes up an XML element
- **Data** Information between start and end tags

SOAP

SOAP (the Simple Object Access Protocol) is the vocabulary and syntax that allow computers to exchange information based on a structured model. With SOAP, applications can be developed in separate, unrelated systems but enabled to exchange information. One company that I worked for had to exchange information from the KRONOS timekeeping system with the PeopleSoft application; with SOAP and XML it was relatively easy to pass information between the two platforms. For all of the standards involved in using SOAP go to www.w3.org/TR/soap/. Keep in mind that SOAP is just one way to do this; the W3C (World Wide Web Consortium) has an XML Protocol Working Group in place to address some of the standards problems. It is important to understand that you can use WSDL with SOAP; it is a standard middleware protocol supported by PeopleSoft.

So let's take a look at a simple example of WSDL working with SOAP. First, let's set up an imaginary company to sell widgets on the Internet. We will call it www.widgets.com, and we need to set up a site that will allow people to query our database for assembly documents for any widgets that they buy. Of course we have all lost the assembly documentation for our widgets at some point in time. Anyway, a customer can send a request to retrieve the assembly documents from the server using a SOAP request as shown in the following code example:

```
Host: www.widget.com
Content-Type: text/xml: charset="utf-8"
Content-Length: 560
SOAPAction: "http://www.widgets.com/assemblysearch"
<SOAP-ENV:Envelope
      xmlns:SOAP-ENV="http://schemas.xmlsoap.org/soap/envelop/"
      <SOAP-ENV:Body>
            <m:GetAssembly xmlns:m="http://test.widgets.com">
                  <assembly_docs>K2</assembly_docs>
                  <model_number>widget_2</model_number>
            </m:GetAssembly>
</SOAP-ENV:Body>
</SOAP-ENV:Envelope>
```

The SOAP response:

```
<SOAP-ENV:Envelope
      Xmlns:SOAP-ENV="http://schemas.xmlsoap.org/soap/envelope/"
      SOAP-ENV:encodingStyle="http://schemas.xmlsoap.org/soap/encoding/">
      <SOAP-ENV:Body>
            <m:GetAssemblyResponse xmlns :m="http://test.widgets.com">
            <AssemblyApprove>John Smith</AssemblyApprove>
      <m:GetAssemblyResponse>
      </SOAP>-ENV Body>
</SOAP-ENV:Envelope>
```

Let's take a look at the different elements:

- **<definitions>** What is enclosed in the <definitions> element is a set of related services.
- **<types>** What is enclosed in the <types> element allows the specification of low-level data typing for the message or procedure.
- **<message>** Is the individual pieces of the communication and the format of that data.
- **<PortType>** The <PortType> element is the grouping element of the message—it groups it into a single operation.
- **<binding>** The <binding> element is what provides the link between the physical and logical models.

- **<soap:operation>** SOAP can be transmitted by other methods, for example, SMTP; the <soap:operation> element maps the message to the port type.
- **<service>** Is the physical location definition for the end point of communication.

See Chapter 7 for an example of creating a WSDL connection in the Component Interface.

XMLP for PeopleSoft Overview

Oracle has developed a standalone Java-based reporting platform called XML Publisher, or XMLP; it allows you to create reports and forms. The main feature of XML Publisher is the separation of the data extraction from the reporting tool. You can design and create a report layout template with easy-to-use applications like Microsoft Word or Adobe Acrobat; these tools render XML-based data in your template. One template can create many reports in many formats, including HTML, Excel, PDF, and RTF.

The Oracle technology in PeopleSoft makes it available via PeopleSoft Query—which is really cool, because you can create a query and then extract the information via XML into a PDF document. Think about how difficult this is with SQR, for example: you have to create a program and then add beginning procedures and ending procedures, SQCs for layout and opening files, procedures to extract data with SQL, and complicated code for defining the layout of the report. In the new world with XML, you can create a PeopleSoft Query and publish the data in PDF via your XML template. This is much easier, and considering that your end users can create queries, you could put the power of the XML templates in their hands and allow them to create their own reports.

XML Publisher Security

Essentially there are three parts to PeopleSoft XML security:

- Report definitions
- Report running
- Report viewing

When you are working with query-defined reports, the security is easier because the underlying query security governs the XML report security. Because XML does not provide an additional level of security, it is important to note that the running of your reports is governed by one or all of the following: query security, application security, and/or process scheduler security. The same is true with viewing the report definitions: you have to have access to the report definition via the application security. So, for example, for queries, query security is the deciding factor, for data extraction component security determines access, and for processes process security is the key. A query-based report will be run according to the row-level security of the data source. Query-based reports viewed online are controlled by query access groups, and non-query-based reports are controlled by the application.

Setting Up XML Publisher in PeopleSoft

The settings are defined in the xdo.cfg file. Let's take a look at an example:

```
<config version="1.0.0" xmlns="http://xmlns.oracle.com/oxp/config/">
    <properties>
        <!-- System level properties -->
        <property name="xslt-xdoparser">true</property>
        <property name="xslt-scalable">true</property>
        <property name="system-temp-dir">CACHE</property>
        <property name="system-cachepage-size">50</property>

        <!-- PDF compression -->
        <property name="pdf-compression">true</property>

        <!-- PDF Security -->
        <!-- <property name="pdf-security">true</property> -->
        <!-- <property name="pdf-open-password">user</property> -->
        <!-- <property name="pdf-permissions-password">owner</property> -->
    </properties>
</config>
```

The <property name="system-temp-dir">CACHE</property> setting is the cache of the application server, so, for example, on my machine that is set up for writing this book, it is set up in a very simple location of \\PS\CACHE; in most cases, the setting will be more complex; an example would be [PS_HOME]/appserv/[DOMAIN_NAME]/CACHE. You can also specify the application server or process scheduler domain in the xdo.cfg file. You need only update the JavaVM to the option of the xco.cfg in the psappsrv.cfg file. The following code is an example:

Here is psappsrv.cfg before the change:

```
;To pass java options to the jvm loaded via JNI, uncomment JavaVM Options=
;and set it equal to the list of parameters you would like to use.
;The options need to be a blank space separated list of valid java options.
;Consult your JRE vendor for valid java options.
;For example, JavaVM Options=-Xmx256m -Xms128m
JavaVM Options=-Xrs -Dxdo.ConfigFile=../xdo.cfg
```

The new setting:

```
JavaVM Options=-Xrs -Dxdo.ConfigFile=xdo.cfg
```

Keep in mind that any changes that you make to these configuration files will not take effect until you restart the application server. This can be difficult if people are using the system 24/7, so choose the best time, cross your fingers, and restart the machine.

Pages Used

Two pages are used in the setup of XML Publisher in PeopleSoft:

PSXPSETUPRPTCAT: the Report Category Page

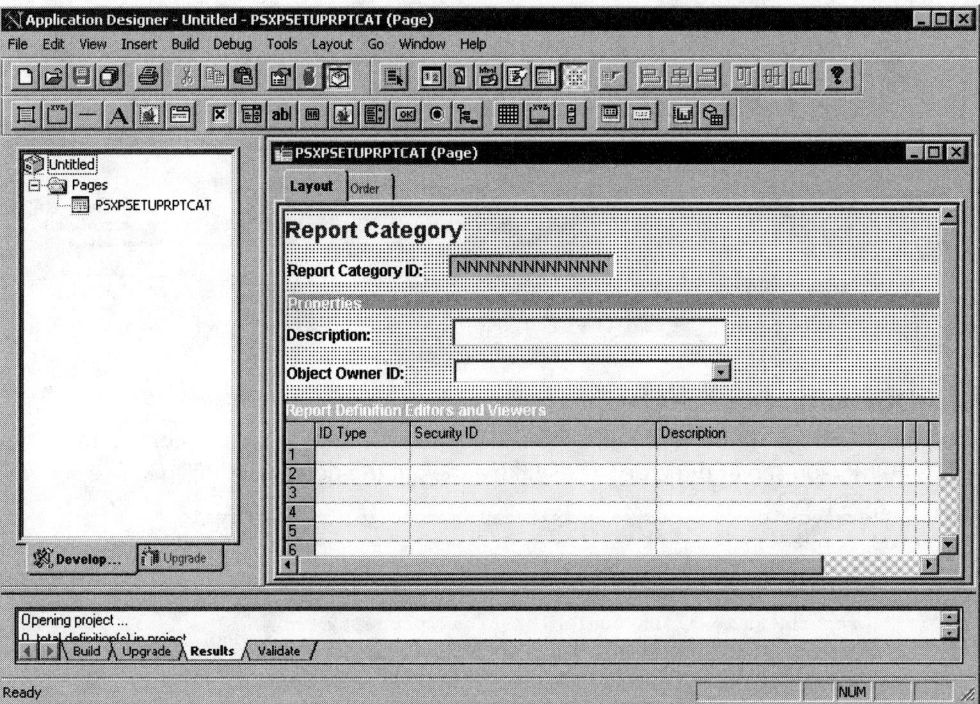

and

PSXPSETUPDWNLD: the Design Helper Page

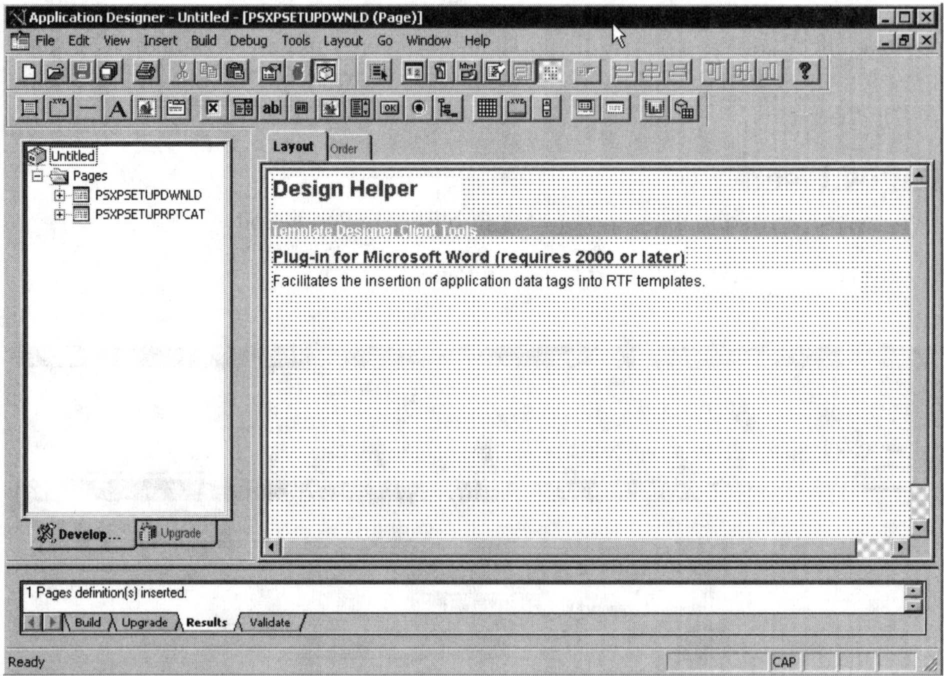

Global Engine Settings

The global settings are defined in the XDO.CFG file; the default location of this file is $PSHOME/app server directory. Let's take a look at the default settings:

```
<config version="1.0.0" xmlns="http://xmlns.oracle.com/oxp/config/">
    <properties>
        <!-- System level properties -->
        <property name="xslt-xdoparser">true</property>
        <property name="xslt-scalable">true</property>
        <property name="system-temp-dir">CACHE</property>
        <property name="system-cachepage-size">50</property>

        <!-- PDF compression -->
        <property name="pdf-compression">true</property>

        <!-- PDF Security -->
        <!-- <property name="pdf-security">true</property> -->
        <!-- <property name="pdf-open-password">user</property> -->
        <!-- <property name="pdf-permissions-password">owner</property> -->
    </properties>
</config>
```

Report Categories

This is a required attribute of any and all report definitions; it is stored in the Content Library with the subtemplates. This allows you to set row-level security to the data of the components. Let's take a look at the XML folder in PeoplesSoft:

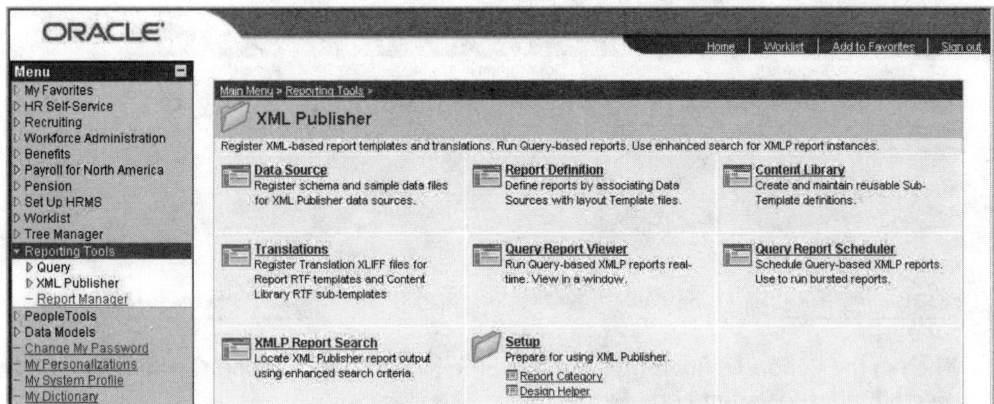

Next you can see the Setup folder, which contains the Report Category and the Design Helpers.

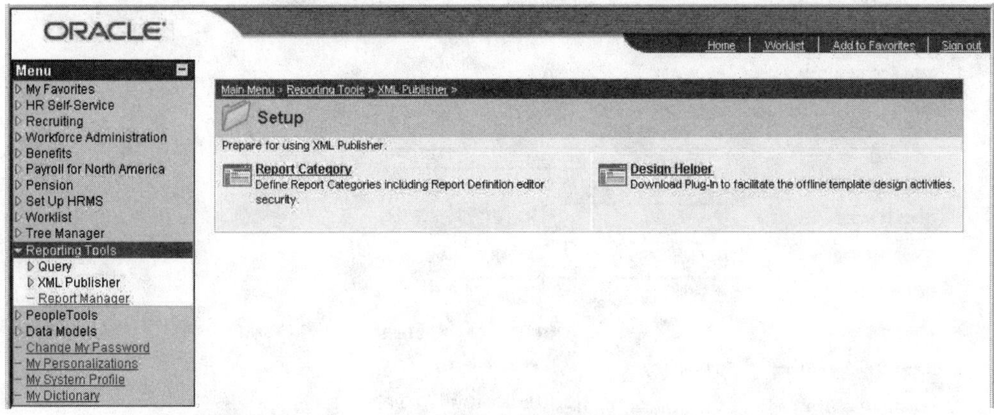

Then you can see the Report Category search record; you can see the setup of the Report Category in Payroll with two PeopleSoft-defined roles.

Report Category

Report Category ID: TC_TEST

Properties

Description: XML Test

***Object Owner ID:** Payroll

Report Definition Editors and Viewers				
***ID Type**	***Security ID**	**Description**	**Read Only**	
Role	Resource Manager	[System] Resource Manager	☐	+ −
Role	Benefits Administrator	[WF] Benefits Administrator	☑	+ −

View All First 1-2 of 2 Last

Save Notify Add Update/Display

Then in the Report Definition you can see the PYW2C07S_EE report, which is the w2c Employee SS form 2007 for payroll.

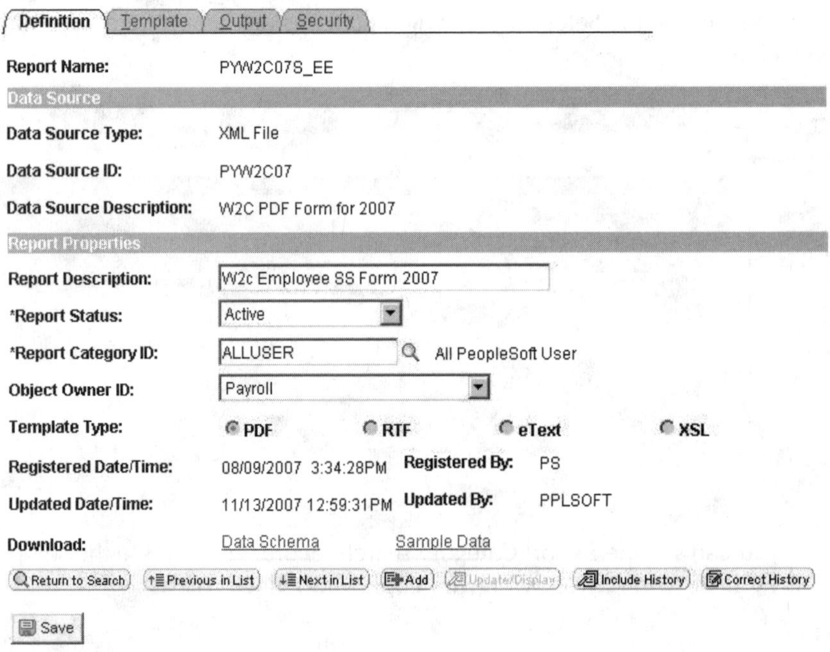

Let's take a look at the key information in creating a Report Category (see the preceding illustration):

- **Report Category ID** Created when you add new data from the Search Record, this defines a group that allows access and the ability to edit the report definitions and the Content Library subtemplates
- **Description (under Properties)** Basic description information of the definition
- **Object Owner ID** The main application that owns the Report Category
- **ID Type** Either Role or User ID
- **Security ID** The name of the Role or User
- **Description (under Report Definition Editors and Viewers)** Description of the Role or User
- **Read Only** This is optional; if you check this box, you set the ID to view the report only in read-only mode, overriding other security on the query or component

Template Design Helpers

When you create templates, you can use the design helper to quickly insert application data tag placeholders right into your templates. Next you can see the page that displays the link to the plug-in for Microsoft Word and the folder it downloads. If your PeopleSoft Application is not enabled to go to this link, you will have to work with your system administrator to get access to this download to get the tool. Read more about creating PDF templates in the section Report Templates later in this chapter.

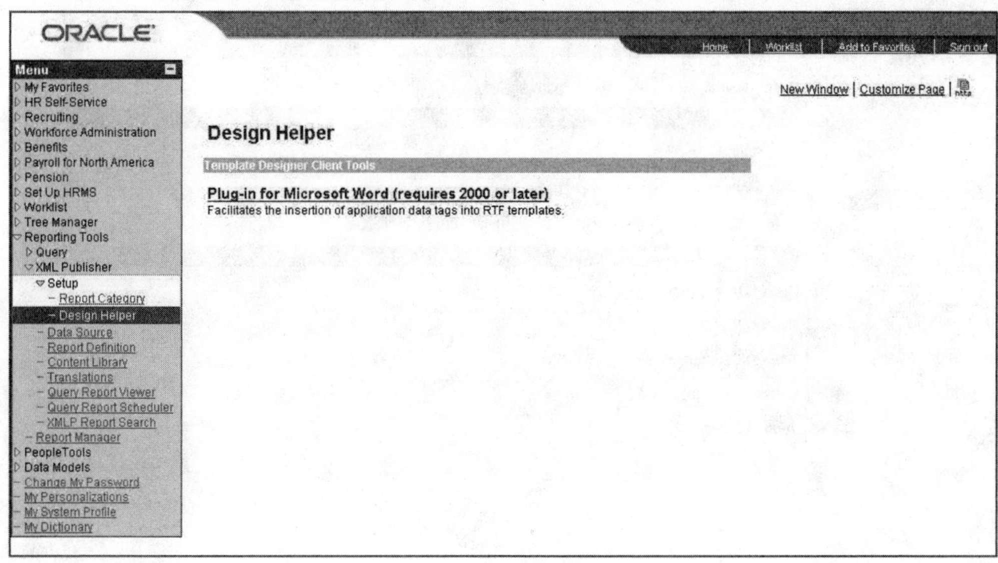

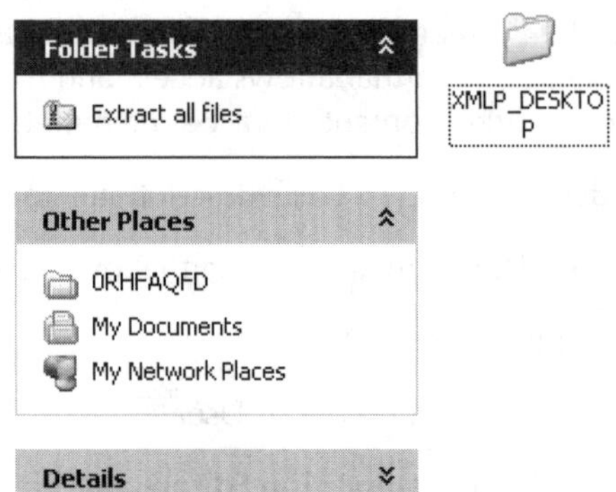

XML Report Publisher

First let's take a look at using the XML Report Publisher and the available tabs on the setup page. Keep in mind that at this point we are only looking at the page so that you can become familiar with it. This is not the first step in creating an XML report; the first step is to define your data, i.e., create your query, and then you must have your template defined, and then you can define your report and set up your options. Take a look at the PeopleSoft-delivered XML report PYW2C07S_EE, which is the Employee's W2c report for 2007.

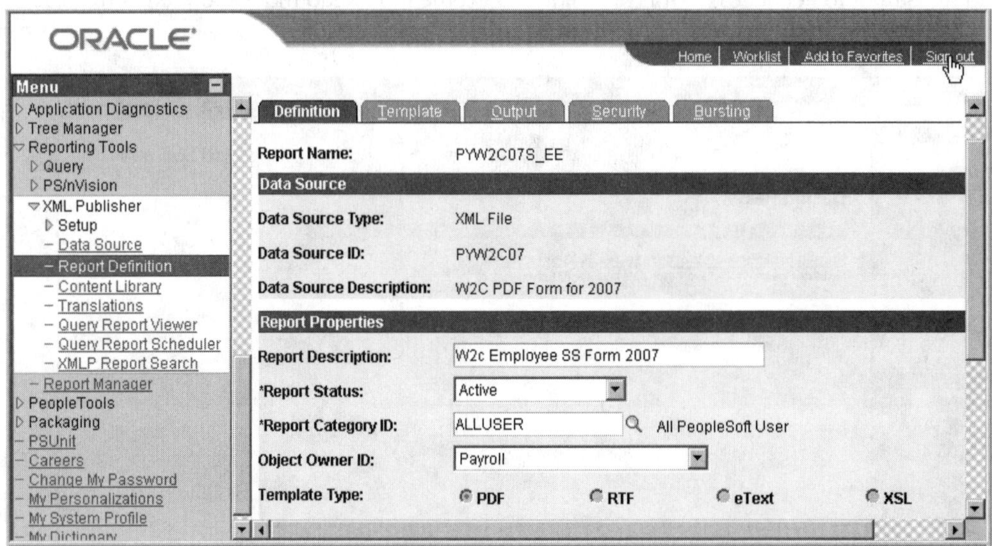

The Definition tab contains the main information about the report, such as the report name, data source type, data source ID, data source description, report description, report status, report category ID, object owner ID, template type, days before purge, registered date and time, updated date and time, and where to download the data.

- Report Name: the unique report name
- Data Source Type: the options are PS Query, Rowset, XML Document, or XML File
- Data Source ID: You choose the Data Source ID according to registered data sources; queries do not have to be registered data sources.
- Data Source Description
- Report Description
- Report Status
- Report Category ID
- Object Owner ID
- Template Type
- Days Before Purge
- Registered Date/Time
- Updated Date/Time
- Registered By
- Updated By
- Download

Here is the Template Definition Page.

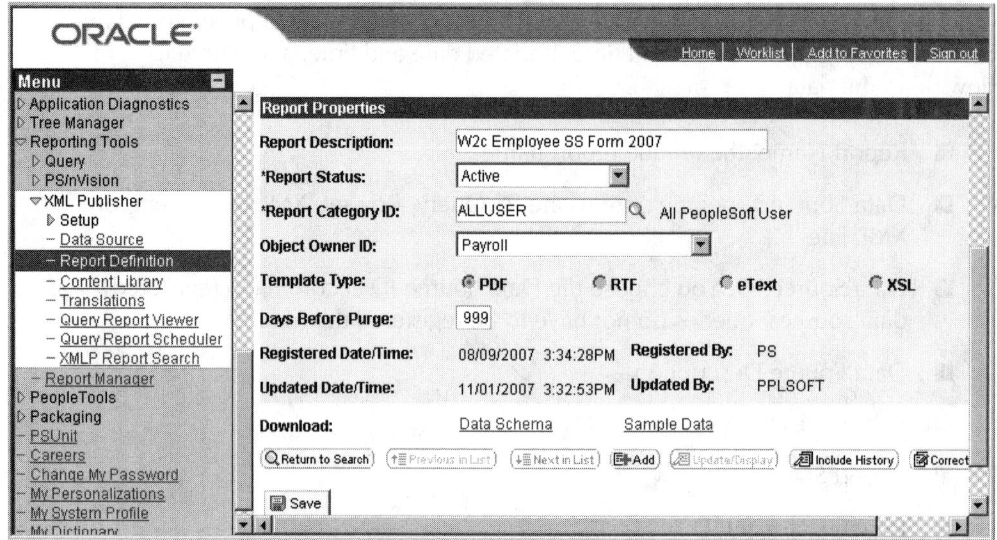

The flow of the process to work with an XML report is outlined in Figure 8-2.

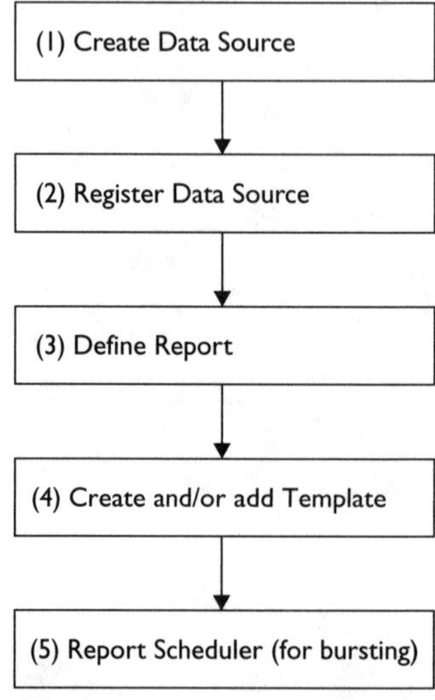

FIGURE 8-2 *Process flow for XML reports*

Create Data Source

It is important to remember that there are two main pieces to XML reports; unlike SQRs, XML is composed of a data piece (the Data Source) and the template piece. Usually you will see the PeopleSoft developer designing the data piece and the functional business team member performing the template piece. But just like anything in the real business world, it could also be one person wearing two hats. You can have a few different types of data sources, including PeopleSoft Queries, rowsets, XML document objects, XML files, and XSD files. Let's take a look at each type. With XML files and XSD files, you will first create an Application Engine that will generate either the file or the data in the case of the XML file or else will establish the schema layout in the case of the XSD file.

It is important when working with XML Publisher in PeopleSoft to have an understanding of the XML Application Packages, which include the XML Publisher Classes. This way you can manipulate the XML information programmatically. These classes are not built-in classes, so unlike when working with rowsets, fields, or records, you must import them into your program rather than call to them directly. Let's take a look at the classes that are in the Application Package complete with Import statements:

```
import PSXP_RPTDEFNMANAGER:*;
import PSXP_REPORTMGR:*;
import PSXP_XMLGEN:*;
import PSXP_ENGINE:*;
```

The asterisks after the package name on the import statement will make all the named packages be available—this does not include subpackages within the named packages. Now let's take a look at how to use some of this code to set up a rowset as a data source. The following code was taken from the PeopleSoft tipster web site, http://peoplesofttipster.com/2007/05/24/xml-publisher-within-peoplesoft/:

```
/*Populating the RowSet */
import PSXP_XMLGEN:*;

/*create rowsets */
&rs_compensation CreateRowSet(Record.COMPENSATION);
&rs_job CreateRowSet(Record.JOB);

/*Fill Parent */
&rs_job.Fill("where EMPLID like 'K0G00%'");

/*Fill Child */
For &I = 1 to &rs_Job.ActiveRowCount
      &row =  &rs_Job.GetRow(&i);
      &rs = &row.GetRowSet(Scroll.COMPENSATION);
      &rs.Fill("WHERE EMPLID = :1", &row.JOB.EMPLID.Value;
```

```
End-For;
/*Output Files */
/*Create XSD */
&rds = create psxp_xmlgen:RowSetDS();
&myschema = &rds.GetXSDSchema(&rs_Job);
&f1 = GetFile("C:\temp\rpt01.xsd", "W", %FilePath_Absolute;
&f1.WriteLine(&myschema);
&f1.Close();
/*Create Sample XML File */
&myXMLFile = &rds.GetXMLData(&rs_Job, "c:\temp\rpt01.xsd");
&f2 = GetFile("c:\temp\rpt01.xml", "W", %FilePath_Absolute);
&f2.WriteLine(&myXMLFile);
&f2.Close();
/*Code taken from a presentation by Duncan Davies */
```

Register Data Source

Now that we have looked at how to populate XML with a RowSet, let's take a look at using a PeopleSoft Query. If you do not know how to make a PeopleSoft Query, then refer to Chapter 9 for a step-by-step direction for query creation; here we will only be looking at populating a data source from a query. The first step is to create your query. Then you register the data source by going to the data source page located under Reporting Tools | XML Publisher | Setup | Data Source, where you will see the page shown next. The first setting is the Data Source Type, which can be PSQuery, Rowset, XML Doc, or XML File; next is the Data Source ID.

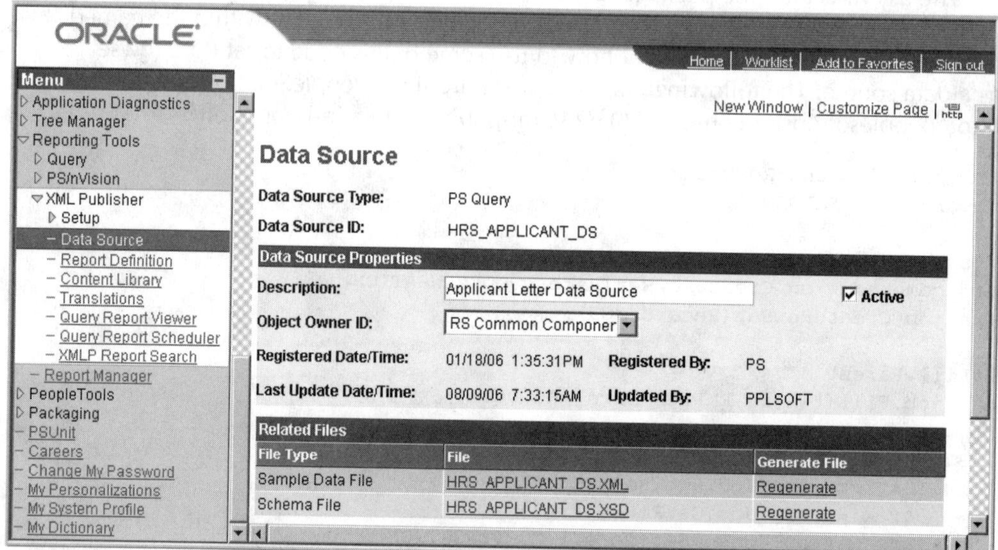

When you are working with PSQuery as the data source, PeopleSoft pulls the data source ID from the Query Manager—which is why it is important to create your query before you register the data source. Next in the settings is the Description, which is pretty self-explanatory. The Object Owner ID is optional and is the product, feature, or application that owns the data source. Registered Date/Time is the read-only field maintained by the system noting the date and time created. Last Update Date/Time is a read-only system-maintained field as well that stores the date and time of the last update. Active sets a data source to be actively chosen when you are creating a report definition; if the Data Source is inactive, you will not see it when you try to create a report. Registered By is the UserID of the person who first registered the data source. Updated By is a read-only field that is maintained by the system to show the last person who updated the field.

Next you create a report definition with the query. In the first illustration following you can see the Report Definition page. Your report has a description, a status, a report category ID, an Object Owner ID, a Template Type, and a place to download the data. Next, if you click the Data Schema link, you will see a pop-up window asking if you want to save the XSD file; click Save to create the XML Schema. The next step in the process is to click the Sample Data link to generate the XML data file from PeopleSoft. Then, again, you will see a dialog box asking if you want to Save or Open. Click Open. Let's take a look at the code example right after the illustrations.

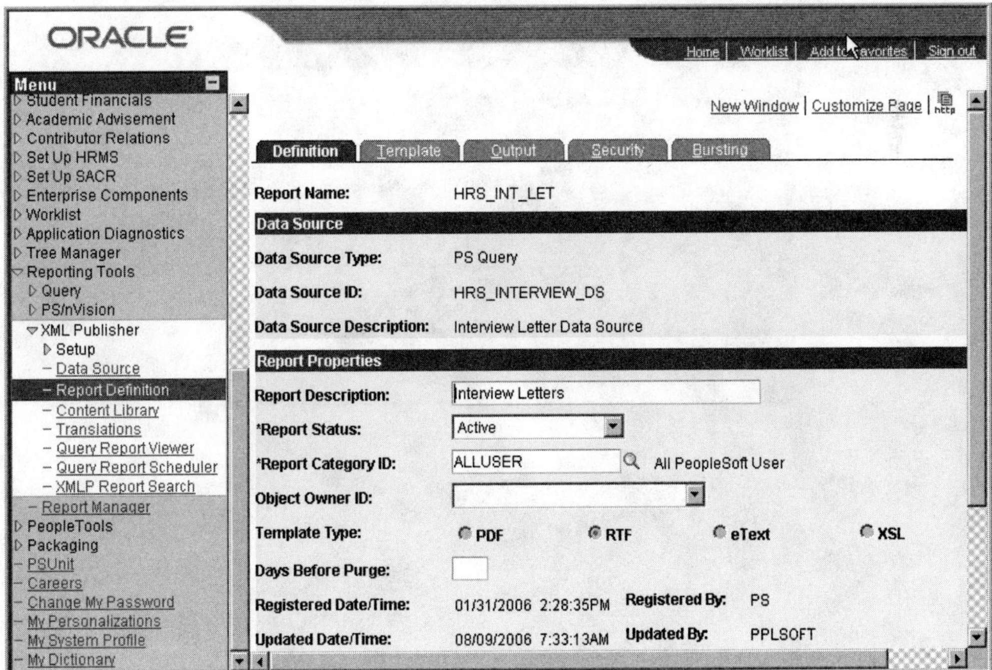

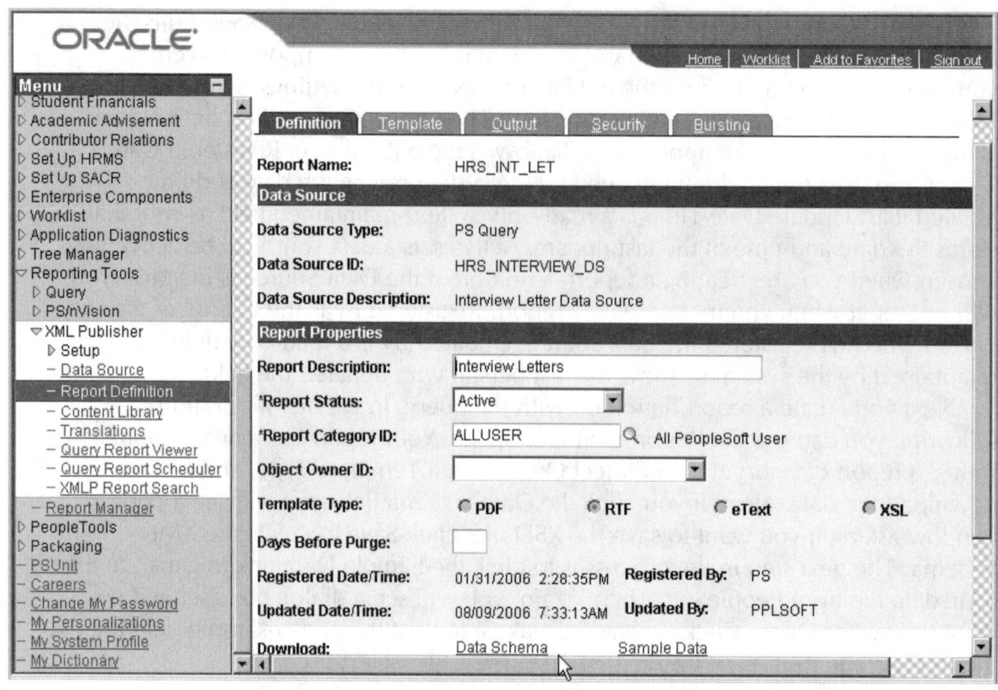
ORACLE
Home | Worklist | Add to Favorites | Sign out
Menu
Student Financials
Academic Advisement
Contributor Relations
Set Up HRMS
Set Up SACR
Enterprise Components
Worklist
Application Diagnostics
Tree Manager
Reporting Tools
Query
PS/nVision
XML Publisher
Setup
Data Source
Report Definition
Content Library
Translations
Query Report Viewer
Query Report Scheduler
XMLP Report Search
Report Manager
PeopleTools
Packaging
PSUnit
Careers
Change My Password
My Personalizations
My System Profile
My Dictionary
Definition
Template
Output
Security
Bursting
Report Name: HRS_INT_LET
Data Source
Data Source Type: PS Query
Data Source ID: HRS_INTERVIEW_DS
Data Source Description: Interview Letter Data Source
Report Properties
Report Description: Interview Letters
*Report Status: Active
*Report Category ID: ALLUSER All PeopleSoft User
Object Owner ID:
Template Type: PDF RTF eText XSL
Days Before Purge:
Registered Date/Time: 01/31/2006 2:28:35PM Registered By: PS
Updated Date/Time: 08/09/2006 7:33:13AM Updated By: PPLSOFT
Download: Data Schema Sample Data

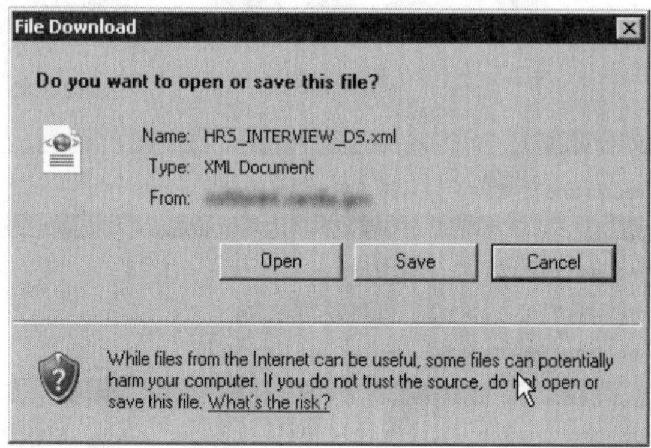
File Download
Do you want to open or save this file?
Name: HRS_INTERVIEW_DS.xml
Type: XML Document
From:
Open
Save
Cancel
While files from the Internet can be useful, some files can potentially harm your computer. If you do not trust the source, do not open or save this file. What's the risk?

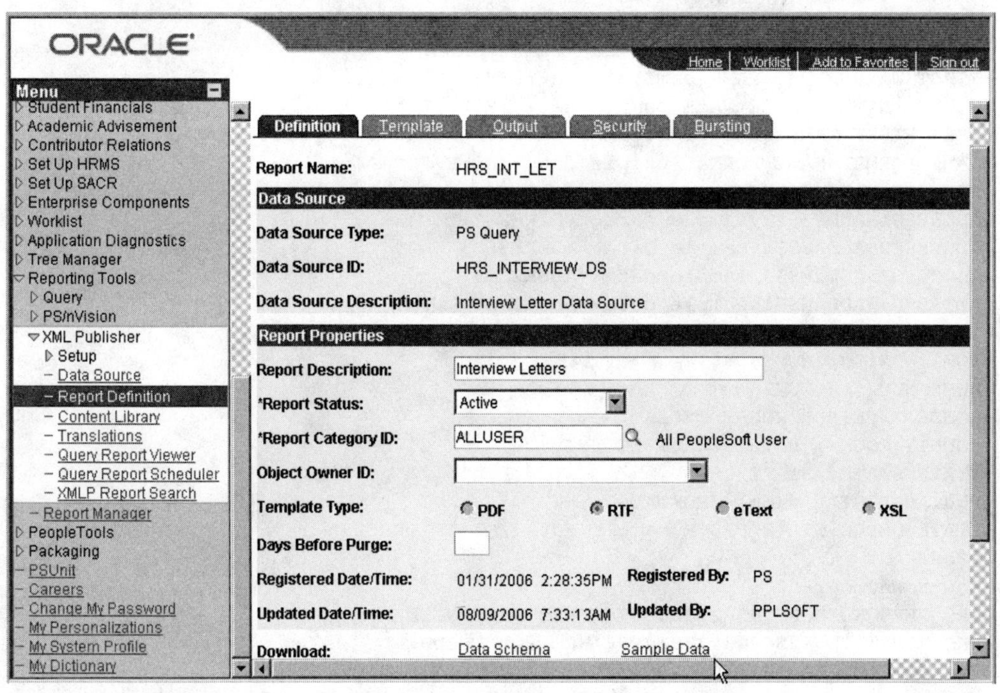


```
<?xml version="1.0" ?>
<query numrows="2" queryname="HRS_INTERVIEW_DS"
xmlns:xsi="http://www.w3.org/2001/XMLSchema-instance"
xsi:noNamespaceSchemaLocation="">
<row rownumber="1">
<HRS_PERSON_ID>681507202028096</HRS_PERSON_ID>
<HRS_RCMNT_ID>347494994791389</HRS_RCMNT_ID>
<HRS_RCM_INT_ID>471162448426785</HRS_RCM_INT_ID>
<HRS_INT_ID>809015552653811</HRS_INT_ID>
<HRS_INTERVIEWER_ID>HRS_INTERVI</HRS_INTERVIEWER_ID>
<HRS_INT_DT>2008-04-06</HRS_INT_DT>
<HRS_START_TM>16:14:11</HRS_START_TM>
<HRS_END_TM>16:14:11</HRS_END_TM>
<HRS_INTVW_LEVEL>H</HRS_INTVW_LEVEL>
<INTVW_LOCATION>INTVW_LOCATION sample data</INTVW_LOCATION>
<RECRUITER_COMMENTS>RECRUITER_COMMENTS sample data</RECRUITER_COMMENTS>
<NAME_DISPLAY>NAME_DISPLAY sample data</NAME_DISPLAY>
<NAME>NAME sample data</NAME>
<NAME_INITIALS>NAME_I</NAME_INITIALS>
<NAME_PREFIX>NAME</NAME_PREFIX>
<NAME_SUFFIX>NAME_SUFFIX sam</NAME_SUFFIX>
```

```
<NAME_TITLE>NAME_TITLE sample data</NAME_TITLE>
<LAST_NAME>LAST_NAME sample data</LAST_NAME>
<FIRST_NAME>FIRST_NAME sample data</FIRST_NAME>
<MIDDLE_NAME>MIDDLE_NAME sample data</MIDDLE_NAME>
<PREF_FIRST_NAME>PREF_FIRST_NAME sample data</PREF_FIRST_NAME>
<NAME_FORMAL>NAME_FORMAL sample data</NAME_FORMAL>
<COUNTRY>COU</COUNTRY>
<ADDRESS1>ADDRESS1 sample data</ADDRESS1>
<ADDRESS2>ADDRESS2 sample data</ADDRESS2>
<ADDRESS3>ADDRESS3 sample data</ADDRESS3>
<ADDRESS4>ADDRESS4 sample data</ADDRESS4>
<CITY>CITY sample data</CITY>
<NUM1>NUM1 s</NUM1>
<NUM2>NUM2 s</NUM2>
<HOUSE_TYPE>HO</HOUSE_TYPE>
<COUNTY>COUNTY sample data</COUNTY>
<STATE>STATE</STATE>
<POSTAL>POSTAL sampl</POSTAL>
<STATE_DESCR>STATE_DESCR sample data</STATE_DESCR>
</row>
<row rownumber="2">
<HRS_PERSON_ID>670056298963378</HRS_PERSON_ID>
<HRS_RCMNT_ID>625694342884420</HRS_RCMNT_ID>
<HRS_RCM_INT_ID>907536472057687</HRS_RCM_INT_ID>
<HRS_INT_ID>204207983807229</HRS_INT_ID>
<HRS_INTERVIEWER_ID>HRS_INTERVI</HRS_INTERVIEWER_ID>
<HRS_INT_DT>2008-04-06</HRS_INT_DT>
<HRS_START_TM>16:14:11</HRS_START_TM>
<HRS_END_TM>16:14:11</HRS_END_TM>
<HRS_INTVW_LEVEL>H</HRS_INTVW_LEVEL>
<INTVW_LOCATION>INTVW_LOCATION sample data</INTVW_LOCATION>
<RECRUITER_COMMENTS>RECRUITER_COMMENTS sample data</RECRUITER_COMMENTS>
<NAME_DISPLAY>NAME_DISPLAY sample data</NAME_DISPLAY>
<NAME>NAME sample data</NAME>
<NAME_INITIALS>NAME_I</NAME_INITIALS>
<NAME_PREFIX>NAME</NAME_PREFIX>
<NAME_SUFFIX>NAME_SUFFIX sam</NAME_SUFFIX>
<NAME_TITLE>NAME_TITLE sample data</NAME_TITLE>
<LAST_NAME>LAST_NAME sample data</LAST_NAME>
<FIRST_NAME>FIRST_NAME sample data</FIRST_NAME>
<MIDDLE_NAME>MIDDLE_NAME sample data</MIDDLE_NAME>
<PREF_FIRST_NAME>PREF_FIRST_NAME sample data</PREF_FIRST_NAME>
<NAME_FORMAL>NAME_FORMAL sample data</NAME_FORMAL>
<COUNTRY>COU</COUNTRY>
<ADDRESS1>ADDRESS1 sample data</ADDRESS1>
<ADDRESS2>ADDRESS2 sample data</ADDRESS2>
```

```
<ADDRESS3>ADDRESS3 sample data</ADDRESS3>
<ADDRESS4>ADDRESS4 sample data</ADDRESS4>
<CITY>CITY sample data</CITY>
<NUM1>NUM1 s</NUM1>
<NUM2>NUM2 s</NUM2>
<HOUSE_TYPE>HO</HOUSE_TYPE>
<COUNTY>COUNTY sample data</COUNTY>
<STATE>STATE</STATE>
<POSTAL>POSTAL sampl</POSTAL>
<STATE_DESCR>STATE_DESCR sample data</STATE_DESCR>
</row>
</query>
```

The next type of data source we will take a look at is the XML Document Object, or what is known as the XMLDoc. XMLDoc is PeopleSoft's XML parser; it enables you to have access to data in an XML file just as you would a database. It is based on W3C standards and uses XPath, which provides the directory structure. The Zutshi Group has an excellent example of how to work with XMLDoc and how to handle a SOAP message; see www.zutshigroup.com/site/tech/peoplesoft_soap_example.

The first thing to understand is the premise behind the example. Zutshi is trying to take a message from a third-party system and determine if the user exists and that the Social Security number that the third-party system has is valid. They do this with a SOAP message because opening a gateway to transmit protected data such as a Social Security number is not a good idea. Step 1 is the SOAP message.

Two parameters are passed, 1. OPRID, and 2. SSN. In the following message, the system is trying to verify if "bob_smith" has the SSN of "999999999."

```
<?xml version="1.0"?>
<SOAP-ENV:Envelope xmlns:SOAP-
ENC="http://schemas.xmlsoap.org/soap/encoding/"
xmlns:SOAP-ENV="http://schemas.xmlsoap.org/soap/envelope/">
  <SOAP-ENV:Body>
    <ValidateSSN>
      <OPRID>bob_smith</OPRID>
      <SSN>999999999</SSN>
    </ValidateSSN>
  </SOAP-ENV:Body>
</SOAP-ENV:Envelope>
```

Step 2, the response or return message, will be from "OnRequest" PeopleCode and the XML response will be parsed as

```
tbd
```

In step 3, the implementation, you create a message definition and name it NX_VALIDATE_SSN; then you assign it to a Message Channel that is active. On the Message click View PeopleCode and insert the following code in the OnRequest PeopleCode:

```
/*******************************************/
/* CUST399 - 02/25/2005 - Ayush Zutshi       */
/* Provide SSN Validation to 3rd party via   */
/* SOAP Web Service                          */
/*******************************************/
Local XmlDoc &request, &response;
Local string &ssn, &result, &req_oprid, &req_ssn;
Local boolean &error;
Local SOAPDoc &soapReq, &soapRes;

/* Process the request() */
&request = GetMessageXmlDoc();
&soapReq = CreateSOAPDoc();
&soapReq.XmlDoc = &request;
&OK = &soapReq.ValidateSOAPDoc();
&req_oprid = &soapReq.GetParmValue(1);
&req_ssn = &soapReq.GetParmValue(2);

/* Validate the SSN */
SQLExec("select S.NATIONAL_ID from PSOPRDEFN O, PS_PERS_NID S
where O.OPRID = :1 and O.EMPLID = S.EMPLID
and S.NATIONAL_ID_TYPE= 'PR'", &req_oprid, &ssn);
If &ssn = &req_ssn Then
   &result = "True";
Else
   &result = "False"
End-If;

/* Assemble the Response */
&soapRes = CreateSOAPDoc();
&soapRes.AddMethod("ValidateSSN", 0);
&soapRes.AddParm("Result", &result);
&OK = &soapRes.ValidateSOAPDoc();

/* Return the Response */
&response = &soapRes.XmlDoc;
ReturnToServer(&response);
```

To create schemas from messages and to test message schemas you need to work with the Integration Broker. If you take a look at the next illustration, you can see the Integration Broker menu; here you can create a SOAP template, use the

Message Schema Builder, or work with the Schema Tester to test Message Schemas against XML. This menu is also where you can work with Service Administration and WSDL. The next step in the process is to work with your template.

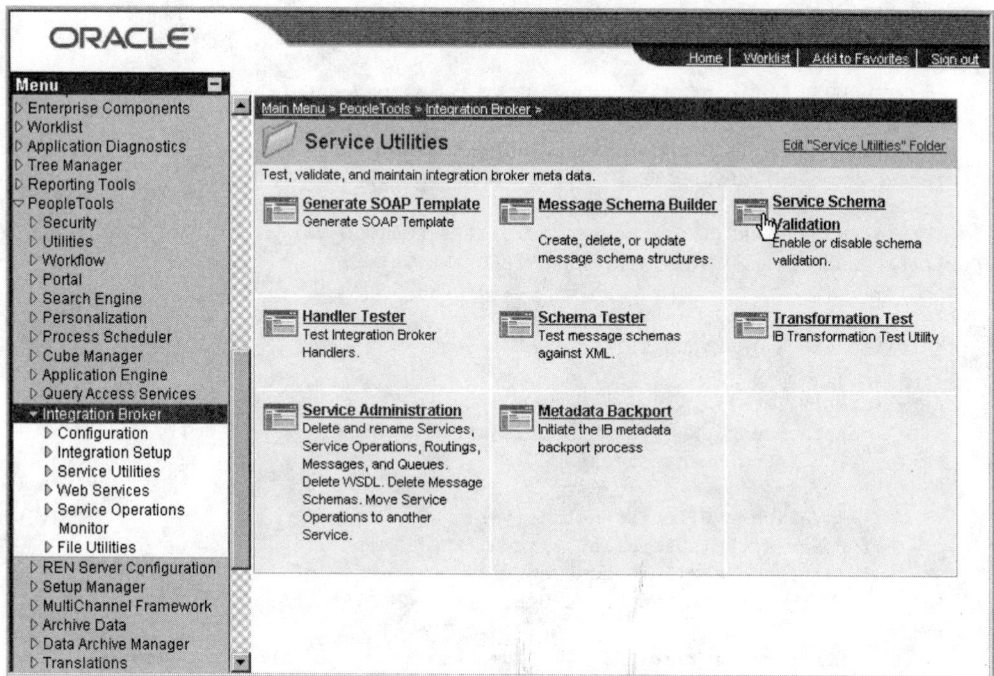

Another way of working with XML is a file that is provided to you from an outside source. Of course none of us works in an environment where we have anything except PeopleSoft, but just in case you are in one of the places that gets files of an XML type from another application, here is the way to code retrieval of that data:

```
/* mdu ICE 1568175000 */
import PSXP_XMLGEN:QueryDS;
import PSXP_RPTDEFNMANAGER:DataSourceDefn;
Declare Function DeleteLocalDirectory PeopleCode PSXPFUNCLIB.FUNCLIB
FieldFormula;
Component PSXP_RPTDEFNMANAGER:DataSourceDefn &coDataSrcDefn;
Local Rowset &RS;
Local string &strFile, &FieldName, &UserFile, &strFileName;
Local string &strSessionID;
Local array of string &FnamesAry;
```

```
Local File &hFile;
Local number &Ret;
Local JavaObject &joXsdParser;

&strSessionID = UuidGen();
&RS = GetLevel0();
try
   /*** The User defined XML file needs to be uploaded by the user ***/
   /*** Determine which row has been clicked ***/
   &FieldName = &RS(1).GetRowset(Scroll.PSXPDATFLD_VW)
(CurrentRowNumber()).PSXPDATFLD_VW.FIELDNAME.Value;
   If None(&FieldName) Then
      &FieldName = &RS(1).GetRowset(Scroll.PSXPDATFLD_VW)
(CurrentRowNumber()).PSXPDATASRC_WK2.FIELDNAME.Value;
   End-If;

   If &FieldName = "SAMPLEDATFILE" Then

      /*** XML File ***/
      If AddAttachment(URL.FILEDB_XMLP, &strSessionID | "/", ".xml",
&UserFile, 0) = %Attachment_Success Then

         /*** Validate File Extension ***/
         If Upper(Right(&UserFile, 3)) <> "XML" Then
            /*** Remove File Attachment ***/
            &Ret = DeleteAttachment(URL.FILEDB_XMLP, &strSessionID | "/" |
&UserFile);
            Error MsgGetText(235, 4, "The file to upload must be of type
%1", "XML");
         End-If;

         /* Set the Sample File property on the Data SOurce object */
         /* 1-- First detach sample file to App Server */
         CreateDirectory(GetEnv("PS_SERVDIR") | "/files/XMLP/" |
&strSessionID, %FilePath_Absolute);
         &strFileName = GetEnv("PS_SERVDIR") | "/files/XMLP/" |
&strSessionID | "/" | &UserFile;
         If GetAttachment(URL.FILEDB_XMLP, &strSessionID | "/" | &UserFile,
&strFileName) <> %Attachment_Success Then
            /* we've got a pb */
            &Ret = DeleteAttachment(URL.FILEDB_XMLP, &strSessionID | "/" |
&UserFile);
            Error MsgGet(235, 5, "Error downloading file from database");
         End-If;

         /* 4-- Delete temporary database file */
```

```
         &Ret = DeleteAttachment(URL.FILEDB_XMLP, &strSessionID | "/" |
&UserFile);

         /* Convert file path to platform specific */
         &FnamesAry = FindFiles(&strFileName, %FilePath_Absolute);
         If &FnamesAry.Len <> 1 Then
            DeleteLocalDirectory(GetEnv("PS_SERVDIR") | "/files/XMLP/" |
&strSessionID, %FilePath_Absolute + %Remove_Subtree);
            Error MsgGet(235, 67, "Error reading generated file from app
server");
         End-If;
         &strFileName = &FnamesAry [1];

         /* 2.2-- Set File Name */
         &coDataSrcDefn.AddSampleDataFile(&strFileName);

         /*** Update Data Source Field names ***/
         PSXPDATASRC_WRK.SAMPLEDATFILE.Value = &UserFile;
         PSXPDATASRC_WK2.PSXP_DWNLOAD_FILE.Label = &UserFile;
         PSXPDATASRC_WK2.PSXP_DWNLOAD_FILE.Enabled = True;
         /* PSXPDATASRC_WRK.LASTUPDDTTM.Value = %Datetime; */

         /* 3-- Delete disk-based file */
         DeleteLocalDirectory(GetEnv("PS_SERVDIR") | "/files/XMLP/" |
&strSessionID, %FilePath_Absolute + %Remove_Subtree);
         PSXPDATASRC_WK2.PSXP_FLACTION_HLNK.Label =
PSXPDATASRC_WK2.PSXP_FLACTION_HLNK.GetShortLabel("REGENERATE");
      End-If;
   End-If;
catch Exception &Err
   Local string &sSub1, &sSub2, &sSub3, &sSub4, &sSub5;
   Evaluate &Err.SubstitutionCount
   When > 4
      &sSub5 = &Err.GetSubstitution(5);
   When > 3
      &sSub4 = &Err.GetSubstitution(4);
   When > 2
      &sSub3 = &Err.GetSubstitution(3);
   When > 1
      &sSub2 = &Err.GetSubstitution(2);
   When > 0
      &sSub1 = &Err.GetSubstitution(1);
   End-Evaluate;
   Error MsgGet(&Err.MessageSetNumber, &Err.MessageNumber, &Err.ToString(),
&sSub1, &sSub2, &sSub3, &sSub4, &sSub5);
end-try;
```

Create Templates

One of the first pieces you need to have besides a data source is a template and/or a subtemplate. There are a few software platforms you can use in XML to create templates. The first platform we will look at is RTF style in Microsoft Word; we will also look at PDF using Adobe Acrobat. It is important to note that if you are using Adobe Acrobat, the version supported by PeopleSoft is version 5.0, PDF version 1.4. If you use a later version, you will have to use the File | Reduce File Size option to save your file as an Adobe 5.0–compatible file. It is important to mention Excel templates. The functionality of using Excel is pretty clumsy and information released from Oracle states that we can expect an Excel template soon; however, we may not see good functionality until the next release of PeopleTools.

Let's take a look at some instructions provided by Oracle at www.oracle.com/technology/obe/obe_bi/xmlp_ps/index.html#t4. Download the template file named Personal_Data_Pay.rtf and place it in your c:\temp directory. Here you see Personal_Data_Pay.rtf opened in Microsoft Word.

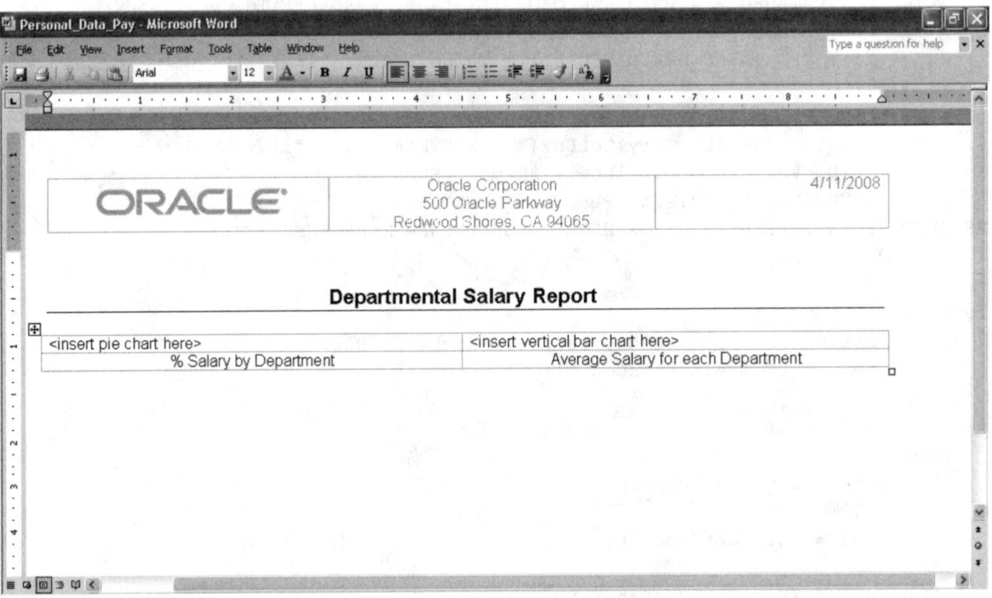

Within each template layout you can retrieve one or more versions, with the most recent being identified by the effective date. The following are the important settings from this page:

- Effective Date
- Status
- Template File
- Upload
- Download
- Preview

Subtemplates

Subtemplates are all about reuse; it never fails that you have text, logic, or images you want to use on multiple reports; well, why create a new report every time you need to use this data? Just use a subtemplate. A good example is the company information. Maybe you have multiple locations, but of course you only have one headquarters. Well, store the headquarters information in a subtemplate and call to it from your reports; this way, you only have to create this setup once.

The way you call the subtemplate files is with XSL commands from the main template file. You can only use subtemplates in RTF and XSL type templates. Of course, if you call to a nonexistent subtemplate, you will receive an error, so it is a good idea to verify the subtemplate when you are creating the main report template. You will receive the error through Process Scheduler, so it will be very obvious what happened and you can either call a different subtemplate or remove it. All the subtemplate files are stored independently and are not registered with a data source. Because of this if the subtemplate calls to any fields, they had better be in the data source of your main template or you will receive an error. So remember that the data source of the main report is also the data source of the subtemplate.

You register subtemplates in the component provided for this, which is the Content Library. The metadata that is stored about the subtemplate file includes name, description, language, Owner ID, category, effective date, and status. Security is applied through the report category. Subtemplate names are not available to the end users; both the template and the subtemplate are put together with the XML Publisher engine, and connection and creation of the two as one report is seamless to the end user. Because of this, previewing the report via the web application is the only way to see the end product. The name of the PeopleSoft page that is used to maintain subtemplates is PSXPSUBTMPLDEFN. Let's take a look at the Content Library. In the first illustration, you see the menu navigation, and in the second, you see the Content Library page for a subtemplate.

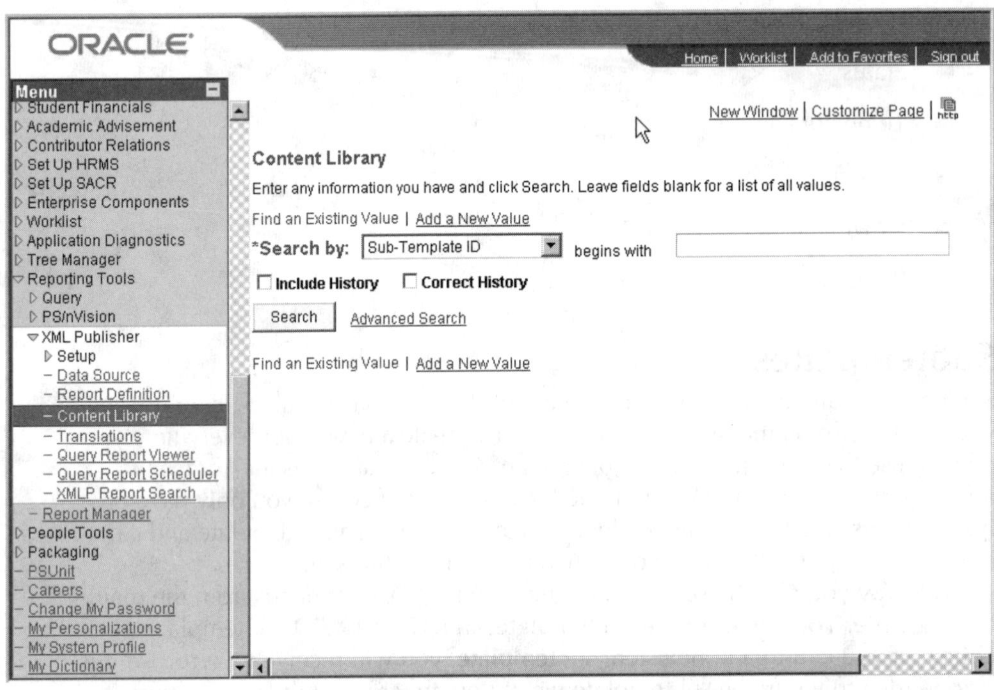
ORACLE
Home | Worklist | Add to Favorites | Sign out
Menu
Student Financials
Academic Advisement
Contributor Relations
Set Up HRMS
Set Up SACR
Enterprise Components
Worklist
Application Diagnostics
Tree Manager
Reporting Tools
Query
PS/nVision
XML Publisher
Setup
Data Source
Report Definition
Content Library
Translations
Query Report Viewer
Query Report Scheduler
XMLP Report Search
Report Manager
PeopleTools
Packaging
PSUnit
Careers
Change My Password
My Personalizations
My System Profile
My Dictionary
New Window | Customize Page
Content Library
Enter any information you have and click Search. Leave fields blank for a list of all values.
Find an Existing Value | Add a New Value
*Search by: Sub-Template ID begins with
Include History Correct History
Search Advanced Search
Find an Existing Value | Add a New Value

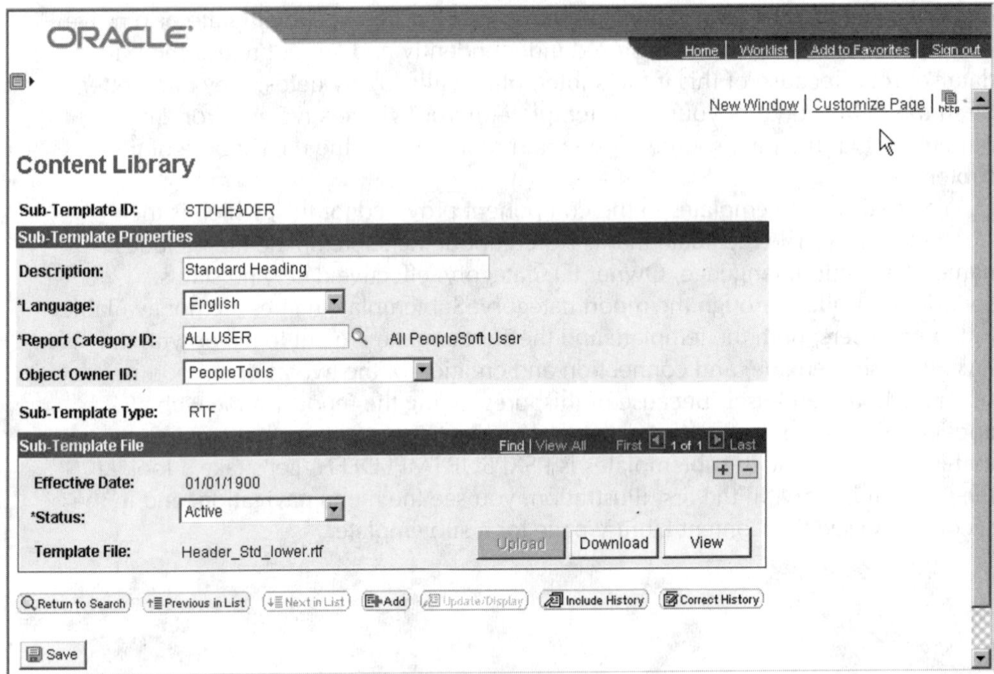
ORACLE
Home | Worklist | Add to Favorites | Sign out
New Window | Customize Page
Content Library
Sub-Template ID: STDHEADER
Sub-Template Properties
Description: Standard Heading
*Language: English
*Report Category ID: ALLUSER All PeopleSoft User
Object Owner ID: PeopleTools
Sub-Template Type: RTF
Sub-Template File
Find | View All First 1 of 1 Last
Effective Date: 01/01/1900
*Status: Active
Template File: Header_Std_lower.rtf
Upload Download View
Return to Search Previous in List Next in List Add Update/Display Include History Correct History
Save

Template Translations

You can create template translations only for file types of RTF; the processing is based on the standard Localization Interchange File Format (XLIFF) .xlf processing. Both subtemplates and templates can have related XLIFF files. The XLIFF files include the translation for each content element, which includes all the fixed values on a template, or anything that is not supplied by the data source. When the translation is complete, the XLIFF file is uploaded and integrated into the XML Publisher. The first illustration here shows the translation of a subtemplate and the second shows the translation of a template. From this screen you can Download the RTF file, Preview the report, or Generate a Translatable File.

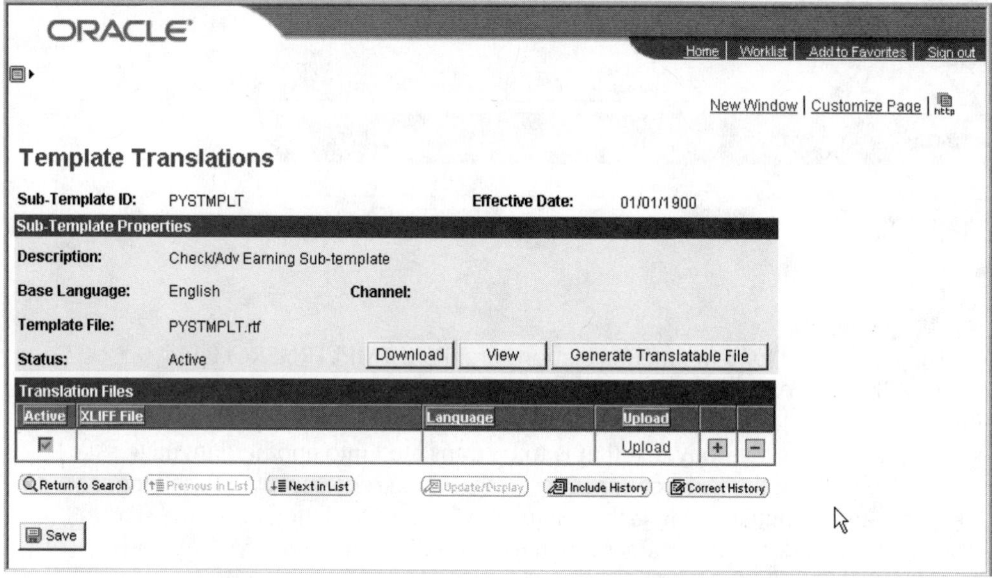

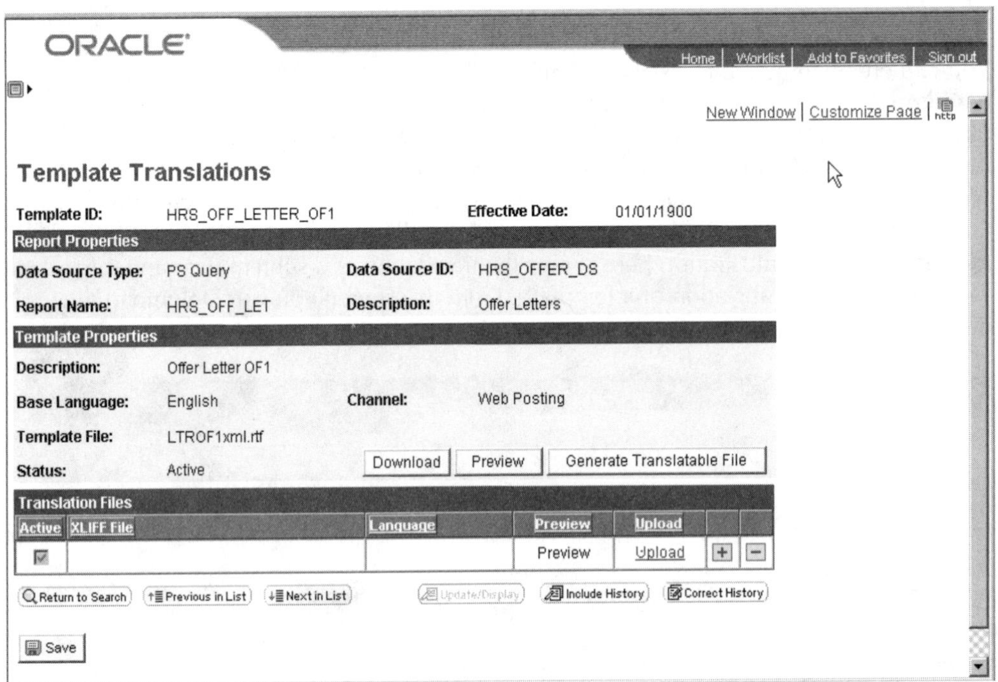

The pages used for template translations are: PSXPTMPLTRNSRCH and PSXPTMPLTRNS. Another important aspect of template translations is the translation file, or the XLIFF file. The file is generated, and it includes the template's static headings as well as the body text that is to be translated into another language. At the top you will see the <source-language> tag, which represents the base language. And the <target-language> tag is the language you are translating to. At the start the <source-language> and the <target-language> are the same. Once you upload the translated file into the database, the <target-language> tag must be changed to the translated language code. The value needs to be one of the two-character ISO language codes: fr equals French, jp equals Japanese, and the file type will be of extension .xlf. If you forget to change the <source-language> and it equals the <target-language>, you will get an error.

The following is an example of an XLIFF file:

```
<?xml version="1.0" encoding="utf-8" ?>
- <xliff version="1.0">
- <file source-language="en-US" target-language="fr-FR" datatype="XDO"
original="orphen.rtf" product-version="orphen.xlf" product name="">
<header />
- <body>
- <trans-unit maxbytes="4000" maxwidth="15"
size-unit="char" translate="yes">
```

```
<source>Total</source>
<target>Totale</target>
<note>Text located: body/table</note>
</trans-unit>
- <trans-unit maxbytes="4000" maxwidth="22"
size-unit="char" translate="yes">
<source>Seq Name/</source>
<target>Nom de Seq/</target>
<note>Text located: body/table/table header</note>
</trans-unit>
```

Report Templates

I'm sure as you can figure out by the naming that a template is the design or layout of your XML report. What you are planning on displaying plays a major role in the template you choose to use; so what type of data do you have and where do you wish to display it? Keep in mind that IE (Internet Explorer) does not natively support svg graphics, and you need an SVGView viewer in order to see charts, which can be downloaded from Adobe at http://www.adobe.com/svg/viewer/install. The following is a list of template types, and we will take a look at each one to help you decide what would be best in your situation. First and most popular is PDF template, then for your Word format the RTF template, then the eText template, and XSL templates.

The most popular report template is PDF, which is a prerendered report that is filled with data at runtime. All you do is map your XML data source to the PDF form fields and presto bingo! You have your PDF form. PDF has faster report generation than RTF. It is best to use PDF templates when you have a predefined form, for example, a government form—a good example is a W2 form—or a simple form-based report that you wish to generate quickly and that does not require complex things like charting or complex formatting.

The next type of report template is RTF. The RTF engine is the core of XMLP and is based on W3C XSL-FO standards. It is the most scalable of the report templates. You use this type of report when you want a fully rendered report; that is, the PDF output is generated at runtime with the XSLFO. This type of report gives you as the designer complete control over the formatting, and you can include charts, dynamic tables, and conditional formatting. This type of report is generally slower than PDF because it is far more complex.

The eText templates are RTF-type templates that generate flat text outputs that can be transmitted to a bank or other vendor for EFT Electronic Funds Transfer or EDI Electronic Date Interchange. Because this type is used to transmit data as an electronic communication, placement and format are very specific and you must follow all of the standards.

XSL templates are the most complex and difficult type of template from PeopleSoft. You can manage them from the Oracle XML Publisher and JDeveloper much easily. For further information, go to Oracle's guide titled "Oracle XML Publisher Core Components Guide, XSL, SQL, and SXL-FO Support."

PDF Templates

PDF templates are the easiest templates to work with and create; they do not require a plug-in, and the mapping feature for XML data elements is enabled automatically when the PDF template file is uploaded into the XML Publisher, the Reporting Definition, or the Template page. This functionality allows you to quickly match form fields to a PDF template data schema field tag or tags. If you are lucky and have a third-party PDF template, you don't have to worry about mapping data tags if you create a PDF template with field names that match the XML data tags, but make certain the names are the same. Oracle provides us with the following guidelines when working with PDF templates:

- **The PDF document must allow editing** To determine this, check the security settings in File | Document Properties | Summary Page.
- **It must be Adobe Acrobat 5.0 compatible** If you are using a later version, go to File | Reduce File Size and select Make Compatible With Acrobat 5.0 And Later.
- **Files must have form fields for placement of application data; each tag must be unique** If you do not have a form field use Adobe Professional version to add field tags. If you have duplicates or non-unique tags use Adobe Profession to update the tags
- **No embedded JavaScript** XML Publisher removes it during the Map Enablement function when you generate the report.

Processing PDF Oracle provides us with the following rules regarding Oracle's XML Publisher Core Engine:

- The XML hierarchy is ignored.
- A search for the tag that matches the field name starts at the end of the XML file.
- The first match of the tag is used for the field value.
- If a tag is not found, it will look at the map file, if it has one.

Creating PDF Templates So you have a PDF template that was provided to you by an outside vendor. You can take the template, and instead of changing the names, you use XML Publisher to map the fields to your concurrent XML elements. You then register the PDF template in the Template Manager. When you have a PDF template that doesn't contain the field, you must have the full Adobe Acrobat

Professional product to add the fields. You have two options to create fields in Adobe:

- Create the field with your own name. If you choose this option, you have to map the fields to the XML elements in your XML file.
- Create the fields with the same names as the XML elements in the output XML file. When you use the same names, mapping is not required.

Once you have aligned the fields to the XML elements, then you can upload the template into the Report Definition by clicking the Upload button on the Reporting Tools | XML Publisher | Report Definition | Template page.

Mapping Data Tags The PDF templates that you will get from your third-party vendors will have form fields that already exist in the form template. Your XML data element requires a mapping to know where it should print the data on a form. When you take a PDF form with editable form fields and map those fields to the XML schema fields that are created by PeopleSoft query, the template becomes ready for use by XML Publisher, which allows for easy mapping of data tags.

Prior to performing this mapping, you need to preprocess the file. The preprocessing requires an OPEN schema for the report's data source. You will need Adobe Acrobat Standard or above and version 6 or above for template mapping. If your PDF form does not have form fields, you can insert them with the Professional version of Adobe.

Here are steps to create a PDF template by mapping using Adobe Acrobat:

1. Upload the PDF template file by clicking the template file Upload button on the Reporting Tools | XML Publisher | Report Definition | Template page.
2. Generate the file by clicking the map file Generate button. This will create a map-enabled PDF with the letter *m* added at the end of the file, so if your original is named sample.pdf, the new name will be samplem.pdf.
3. Map your data tags to the form field tags.
4. Save the file with a new name.
5. Upload the mapped PDF Reporting Tools | XML Publisher | Report Definition | Template page by clicking the Map Upload button.

RTF Templates

You will be using Microsoft Word to create RTF templates. The first thing you want to do is download the delivered XML Publisher Template Builder plug-in. To do this go to the Reporting Tools | XML Publisher | Setup | Design Helper page; the plug-in will help with the insertion of application data tags into your RTF template. The Template Builder is not required to create templates in Microsoft Word, but it will help with the creation by automating functions.

A Word Template Builder Tutorial File is available after you install the plug-in; it is located in the \\Word Template Builder\doc directory of the folder where you installed the Oracle XML Publisher Desktop, XML Publisher Template Builder plug-in. Sample reports are also available in <Your Installation Directory>\ xmlp_desktop. The next step is to download the XML schema and sample data files by clicking the Data Schema and Sample Data links at Reporting Tools | XML Publisher | Report Definition page for your query. Then you load the schema and sample data into the document from inside the Word Template Builder toolbar menu by clicking Data | Load Schema or Load XML Data. You are then ready to design your template in the RTF document; you can either use the downloaded schema or create your own. You then upload the completed template into the report definition—click the Upload button from Reporting Tools | XML Publisher | Report Definition | Template page.

Subtemplates

When you are creating your template, you can include one or more subtemplates. And within your subtemplate you can have multiple subtemplate components; they are noted by the start and end template indicators.

```
<?template:component_name?>
<?end template?>
```

Syntax for two components:

```
<?template:peoplesoft?>
Redwood Shores
500 Redwood Shores Drive
Redwood City, CA 97865
<?end template?>
<?template:oraclelogo.7?>
Logo_Oracle
<?end template?>
```

The start of template 1 is template:peoplesoft; the start of template 2 is template:oraclelogo. Each template ends with the end template tag.

When you are importing a subtemplate that is stored in the Content Library, you must place the following syntax at the top of the primary template file:

```
<?import.psxmlp://sub-template_NAME?>
```

where you have the sub-template_name as a registered subtemplate ID in the Content Library and the example is <?import:psxmlp://STDHEADER?>. The syntax must be in Normal text.

The next important piece of syntax is how to call the subtemplate. You must place the following syntax in the primary template file in the location of the desired text or XSL instructions from the subtemplate file—where peoplesoft is the component name:

```
<?call-template:peoplesoft?>
```

It is best to test your template and subtemplate using Template Builder before you upload it to PeopleTools. This is to ensure your subtemplate is accessible to your template in the file system. The following syntax is how you import—note the triple slashes:

```
<?import:file:c:///template_directory/subtemplate.rtf?>
```

Defining Reports

By following the steps at the preceding template section, you can insert your data into your RTF template in Microsoft Word, add graphs, or create a table. Let's look at the important steps you would need to take to define the report in PeopleSoft.

Report Name: PYW206N_GVT

Data Source

Data Source Type: XML File

Data Source ID: PYW206

Data Source Description: W2 PDF Form for 2006

Report Properties

Report Description: W2 Government Print Form 2006

***Report Status:** Active

***Report Category ID:** ALLUSER All PeopleSoft User

Object Owner ID: Payroll

Template Type: PDF RTF eText XSL

Days Before Purge: 999

Registered Date/Time: 09/05/2007 1:21:08PM **Registered By:** bsando

Updated Date/Time: 12/03/2007 6:39:36PM **Updated By:** bsando

Download: Data Schema Sample Data

Return to Search | Previous in List | Next in List | Add | Update/Display | Include History | Correct History

It is important to remember the four steps for creating a report. Defining your report is the second step. To understand the four steps refer to Figure 8-3 below, taken from Quest Collaborate 2008 session 34190 "XML Publisher for Project Reporting" by BTRG.

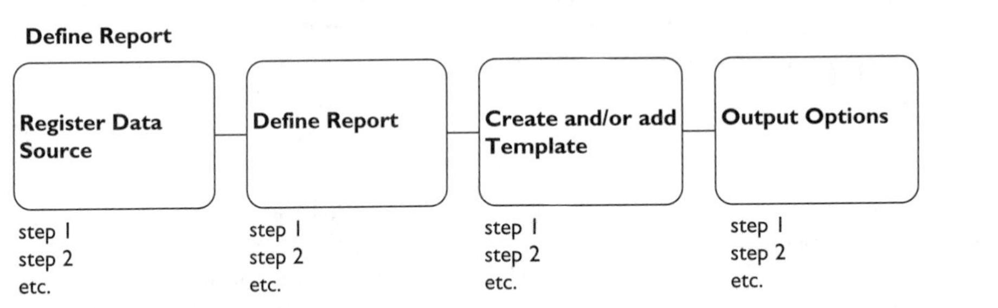

FIGURE 8-3 *The four steps to report creation*

Output Options

Let's take a look at the Output page shown next. Depending on the type of format type you have, you will see any number of types HTML, PDF, RTF, and XLS; the example shown is of a PDF format type. You want to enable all of the format types that you would like to see the report in, as well as choose a Default format type. The Output Location is Any, File, Printer, or Web. Any allows the user to select any of the types File, Printer, or Web. The other types then limit the choice that the user will see.

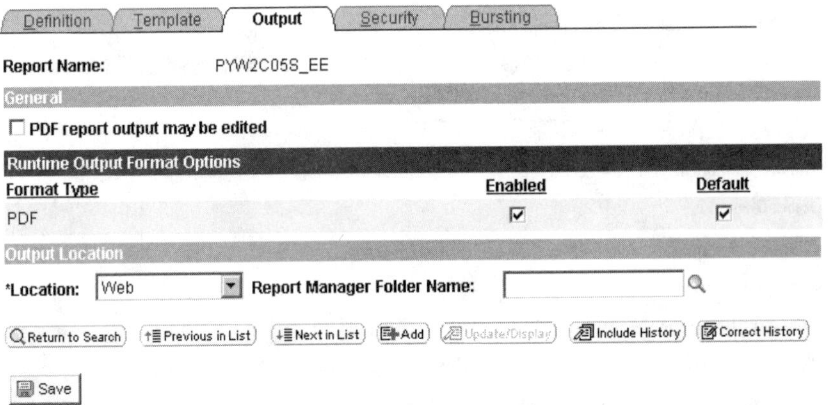

Report Scheduler with Bursting Options

Bursting is an advanced feature that is available only when you run your reports through Process Scheduler. Bursting is just what the name implies. It is used to generate a template multiple times with different data sets. While you are bursting, you can generate individual report files from the different data sets, resulting in secure separate output. An example would be if you wanted to generate a report for a vendor, then one for the customer, and then one for the employee.

You need to have a good understanding of the data and the schema when you set up bursting; if you make incorrect entries you will get an error at runtime. You can define bursting only if the report's data source has an associated schema file. Because this is an advanced feature, you will need security to be a report developer and implement bursting. The PeopleSoft-delivered permission list is PTPT2600. Let's take a look at the bursting page: the first illustration shows the bursting and template settings, and the second shows the security settings and search keys.

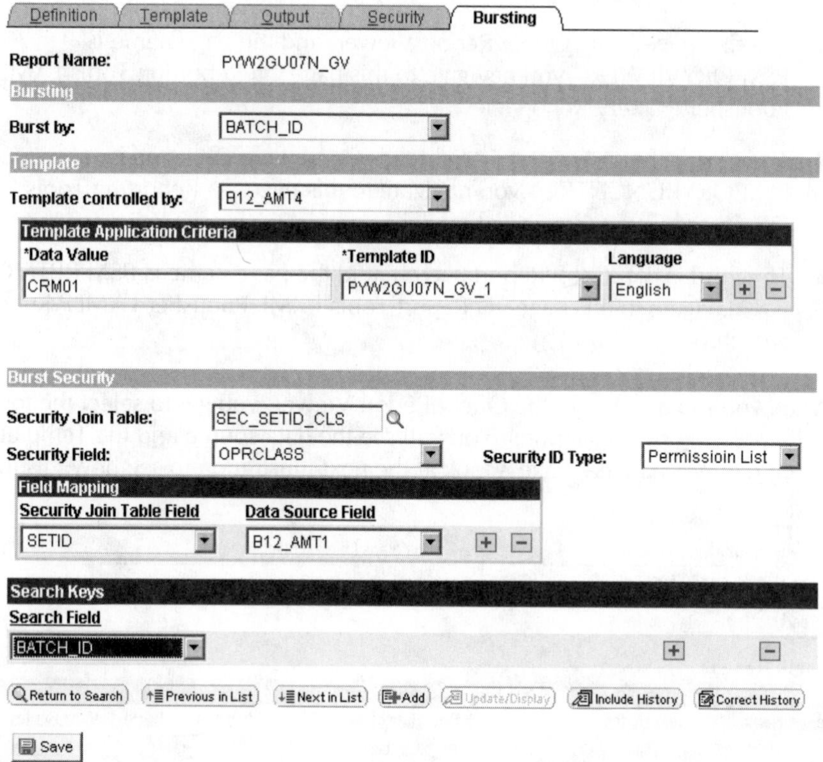

You set a Burst By field to enable report bursting; once it is selected, the report generates multiple files at runtime, with a separate report instance each time a unique value is seen in the Burst By field. So in the example in the first illustration, each time there is a new Batch_ID a new report is generated. Assigning a template in your bursting is optional. What this feature does is dynamically drive a template assignment at runtime based on the data. So if you want a different template for your customer and vendor, you can do that. Security for Bursting is also an optional setting. It enables you as the developer to determine how the reports are posted in Report Manager. Say one user on the team needs permission to see Customer reports and another should see Vendor reports; you can implement this type of report-level security with the Bursting Security settings. The Search Key setting is also optional; it provides you with a way to locate your desired report from the Report Manager repository.

Running XML Reports

Three pages are used by PeopleSoft to run XML Publisher Reports:

- The first page is the Query Report Viewer, and the page name is PSXPQRYVIEWER—you navigate to this page via Reporting Tools | XML Publisher | Query Report Viewer.
- The next is the Query Report Scheduler, and the page name is PSXPQRYRUNCNTRL—you navigate to this page via Reporting Tools | XML Publisher | Query Report Scheduler.
- The third is the XMLP Report Search, and the page name is PSXPRPTMGR—you navigate to this page via Report Tools | XML Publisher | XMLP Report Search.

When you run a report in the Query Report Viewer, you get to select the format for online viewing of your reports. You will see the data source and the Template ID, which can be changed. Take a look at the next illustration to see how this looks.

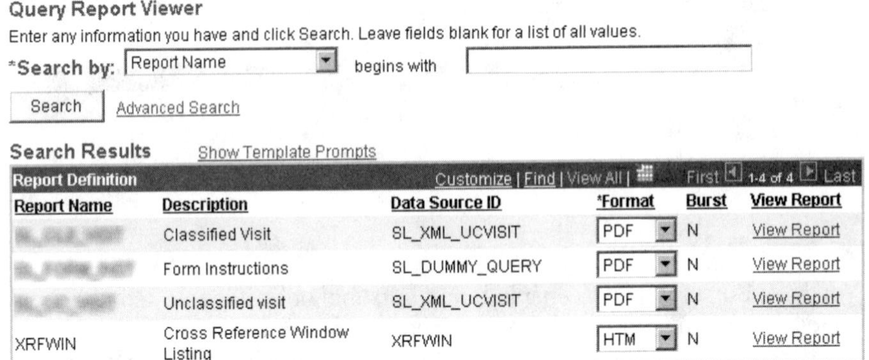

You can schedule XML Reports in the Query Report Scheduler. This allows you to select runtime parameters for query-based reports, monitor the report process request, and post and secure the results to either the Report Manager, a printer, or the Process Scheduler file directory. You can see this page here for the Query Report Scheduler.

Query Report Scheduler

Run Control ID: jhotsin Report Manager Process Monitor Run

Language: English

Report Definition

Report Name: XRFWIN Cross Reference Window Listing

Template ID: XRFWIN_1

Template As Of Date: 05/05/2008 **Channel:**

Go to XMLP Report Search

Save Notify Add Update/Display

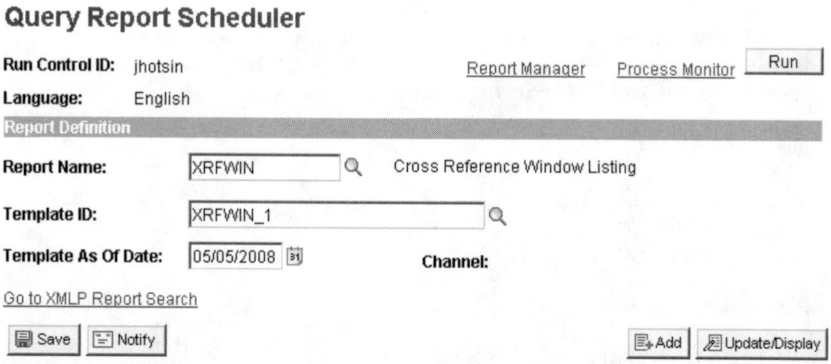

Take a look at the next illustration to see the XML Publisher Report Search page. This page allows you to search for a report that is delivered or created previously by you or your co-workers.

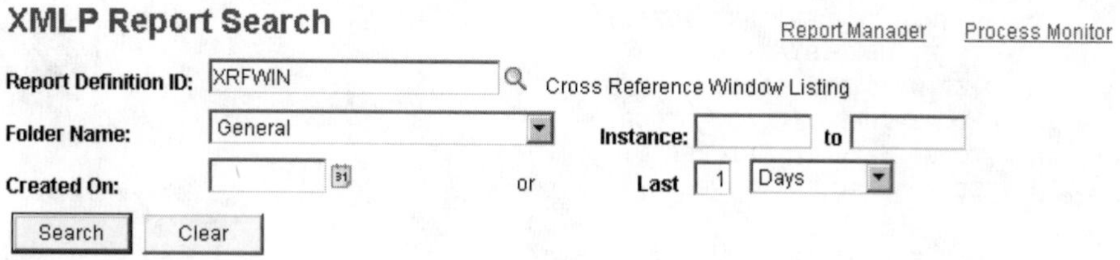

XMLP Report Search Report Manager Process Monitor

Report Definition ID: XRFWIN Cross Reference Window Listing

Folder Name: General **Instance:** to

Created On: or **Last** 1 Days

Search Clear

Using XML and Email

A really handy piece of code is being able to run your Query, populate it into your PDF report via XML and email it out to a set of employees. The following code does this from a fieldchange event on a button.

```
/*  On the click of the button, Create the PDF form for the manager to print
out and send to the organization office */

import PSXP_RPTDEFNMANAGER:*;
import PSXP_REPORTMGR:*;

Declare Function GetDirSeparator PeopleCode PSXPFUNCLIB.FUNCLIB FieldFormula;
Declare Function GetFileExtension PeopleCode PSXPFUNCLIB.FUNCLIB FieldFormula;
Declare Function DeleteLocalFile PeopleCode PSXPFUNCLIB.FUNCLIB FieldFormula;
```

```
Local string &sRptDefn, &sTmpltId, &sLangCd, &sOutFormat;
Local string &emplid, &org, &errorflag, &location, &purpose, &org_flg;
Local date &AsOfDate, &startdt, &enddt, &relstart, &relend, &effdt;
Local Record &rcdQryPrompts;
Local string &sOutPutFormat, &sTemplateId, &sFileext, &sOutputfile;
Local string &sDirSep, &sOutputDir, &sDataDir, &RptOutputDir;
Local PSXP_RPTDEFNMANAGER:ReportDefn &oRptDefn;

Component string &MAIL_START;

Local string &MAIL_TO, &MAIL_CC, &MAIL_BCC, &MAIL_SUBJECT, &MAIL_TEXT,
&MAIL_FILES, &MAIL_TITLES, &MAIL_SENDER;
Local number &MAIL_FLAGS;

Local string &MAIL_CONTENT_TYPE;

&MAIL_START = MsgGetExplainText(20301, 215, "");
&desc = " ";

/* Set initial values */
&errorflag = "N";
&emplid = PERSON.EMPLID.Value;
&org = TC_EP_WRK0.TC_DEPTNAME_ABBRV;
&startdt = TC_EP_WRK0.START_DATE;
&enddt = TC_EP_WRK0.END_DATE;
&location = TC_EP_WRK0.TC_LOC_DESCR;
&purpose = TC_EP_WRK0.TC_DESCR50_1;
&org_flg = TC_EP_WRK0.TC_ORG_FLAG;

/*  Set report definition and template */
&AsOfDate = %Date;

If &org_flg = "Y" Then
   &sRptDefn = "TC_ORG_VISIT";
   &sTemplateId = "TC_ORG_VISIT_1";
   &MAIL_TITLES = "Org_Visit_Form.PDF";
Else
   &sRptDefn = "TC_STD_VISIT";
   &sTemplateId = "TC_STD_VISIT_1";
   &MAIL_TITLES = "STD_Visit_Form.PDF";
End-If;

/* Validate that values exist or send error message */
If RTrim(&org) = "" Then
   MessageBox(0, " ", 0, 0, "Visiting Org has not been selected");
   &errorflag = "Y";
Else
   If RTrim(String(&startdt)) = "" Then
      MessageBox(0, " ", 0, 0, "Visit Start Date must be entered");
      &errorflag = "Y";
   Else
```

```
      If RTrim(String(&enddt)) = "" Then
         MessageBox(0, " ", 0, 0, "Visit End Date must be entered");
         &errorflag = "Y";
      Else
         If RTrim(String(&location)) = "" Then
            MessageBox(0, " ", 0, 0, "Location of Visit must be entered");
            &errorflag = "Y";
         Else
            If RTrim(String(&purpose)) = "" Then
               MessageBox(0, " ", 0, 0, "Purpose of Visit must be entered");
               &errorflag = "Y";
            End-If;
         End-If;
      End-If;
   End-If;
End-If;

If &errorflag = "N" Then
SQLExec("Select %dateout(TC_begin_dt), %dateout(TC_expected_end_dt),
%dateout(TC_effdt) from TC_EP_JOB1_VW where TC_EMPLID = (:1) and TC_deptname_
abbrv = (:2) and TC_rel_status = 'A'", &emplid, &org, &relstart, &relend,
&effdt);

   If IsDate(&relstart) Then
      /*   date good */
   Else
      &relstart = &effdt;
   End-If;

   If &startdt < &relstart Or
         &startdt > &relend Then
      MessageBox(0, " ", 0, 0, "Visit Start Date: " | &startdt | " is not in
relationship range --  start date: " | &relstart | "  end date: " | &relend);
      &errorflag = "Y";
   Else

      If &enddt > &relend Or
            &enddt < &relstart Then
         MessageBox(0, " ", 0, 0, "Visit End Date: " | &enddt | " is not in
relationship range --  start date: " | &relstart | "  end date: " | &relend);
         &errorflag = "Y";
     End-If;
   End-If;

   /* Set the value of the descrlong  to the concatenated string  that is set
in previous peoplecode */


   &MAIL_FLAGS = 0;
   &MAIL_TO = "test@test.com";
   &MAIL_CC = "";
```

```
   &MAIL_CC = "test2@test.com";
   &MAIL_SUBJECT = "TC - STD - Visit Forms ";
   &MAIL_TEXT = &MAIL_TITLES;

/* Set the content type this is in position #11 of the send mail function */
   &MAIL_CONTENT_TYPE = "Content-type: text/html; charset=utf8";
     If &errorflag = "N" Then
        try
           /* detect system directory separator */
         &sDirSep = GetDirSeparator();

         /* create process directory */
         CreateDirectory("XMLP", %FilePath_Relative);

         /* get report definition object */
         &oRptDefn = create PSXP_RPTDEFNMANAGER:ReportDefn(&sRptDefn);
         &oRptDefn.Get();

         /* output directory */
   &RptOutputDir = GetEnv("PS_SERVDIR") | &sDirSep | "files" |  &sDirSep |
"XMLP" | &sDirSep | UuidGen();
         &sOutputDir = &RptOutputDir | &sDirSep | "RptInst";
         &sDataDir = &RptOutputDir | &sDirSep | "Data";
         CreateDirectory(&sOutputDir, %FilePath_Absolute);
         CreateDirectory(&sDataDir, %FilePath_Absolute);

         &oRptDefn.OutDestination = &RptOutputDir;
         /* MessageBox(0, "", 0, 0, " report output dir " | &RptOutputDir);*/
         /* Output format */
         &sOutPutFormat = "PDF";

         /*fill query runtime prompt record */
         &rcdQryPrompts = &oRptDefn.GetPSQueryPromptRecord();
         &rcdQryPrompts.GetField(Field.TC_EMPLID).Value = &emplid;
         &rcdQryPrompts.GetField(Field.DESCRSHORT).Value = &org;
         &rcdQryPrompts.GetField(Field.START_DATE).Value = &startdt;
         &rcdQryPrompts.GetField(Field.END_DATE).Value = &enddt;
         &rcdQryPrompts.GetField(Field.TC_LOC_DESCR).Value = &location;
         &rcdQryPrompts.GetField(Field.TC_DESCR50_1).Value = &purpose;
         &oRptDefn.SetPSQueryPromptRecord(&rcdQryPrompts);

         /*generate report*/
         &oRptDefn.ProcessReport(&sTemplateId, %Language_User, &AsOfDate,
&sOutPutFormat);
         &sFileext = GetFileExtension(&sOutPutFormat);

         /*publish report */
        CommitWork();
         &sRptDir = &RptOutputDir;
         &sReportFile = &sRptDefn | "." | &sOutPutFormat;
```

```
         &sRptFilePath = &sRptDir | &sDirSep | "RptInst" | &sDirSep |
&sReportFile;

         rem MessageBox(0, "", 0, 0, " report file path " | &sRptFilePath);

         &ret = SendMail(0, &MAIL_TO, &MAIL_CC, "", &MAIL_SUBJECT, &MAIL_
TEXT, &sRptFilePath, &MAIL_TITLES, "", "", &MAIL_CONTENT_TYPE, "", "");

         If &ret <> 0 Then
            MessageBox(0, "", 0, 0, " Error with email return code " | &ret);
         Else
            MessageBox(0, "", 0, 0, " Email has been sent to:  " | &MAIL_TO |
"  " | &sOutputfile);
         End-If;


         /* display the output */
         /*  &oRptDefn.DisplayOutput();*/
         /* cleanup */
         DeleteLocalFile(&sOutputfile, %FilePath_Absolute);
         catch Exception &err
         Local string &sSub1, &sSub2, &sSub3, &sSub4, &sSub5;
         Evaluate &err.SubstitutionCount
         When > 4
            &sSub5 = &err.GetSubstitution(5);
         When > 3
            &sSub4 = &err.GetSubstitution(4);
         When > 2
            &sSub3 = &err.GetSubstitution(3);
         When > 1
            &sSub2 = &err.GetSubstitution(2);
         When > 0
            &sSub1 = &err.GetSubstitution(1);
         End-Evaluate;
         Error MsgGet(&err.MessageSetNumber, &err.MessageNumber,
&err.ToString(), &sSub1, &sSub2, &sSub3, &sSub4, &sSub5);
      end-try;

   End-If;
End-If;
```

Integration Broker

The Integration Broker is your mechanism for communicating via XML files with third-party systems. The way this works is that the third-party application can accept and process XML messages that are posted by PeopleSoft using connectors or by adding in custom-built connectors using the Integration Gateway. The main way to do this is with asynchronous messages from PeopleSoft to the third-party application using the File Output connector. To be able to do this, you must configure some internal structures and processes. The following are the pieces that you need to understand how to set this up.

- **Message** This is a container for the data that goes into the XML. It has basic information such as records and fields. You must have your message in Active status to send the XML file.
- **Message Channel** This is the mechanism for placing your records into logical groups. Each Message belongs to only one Message Channel, and it must have an Active or Run status for the Message to be delivered.
- **Message Node** This specifies which Gateway will receive the message.
- **Integration Gateway** This is the program that runs on the PeopleSoft Web Server; it is the physical hub between PeopleSoft and the third party.
- **Target Connector/Handler** These are Java programs that run from the Integration Gateway and determine the destination of the XML file. PeopleSoft is delivered with connectors HTTP, FTP, SMTP, JMS, POP3, and Simple File.
- **PeopleCode** This is your language or programming tool that you use via Peopletools to create more complex functionality. You can only initiate a message using PeopleCode. You trigger this code with an event; an example would be creating a new database row via your page.

Let's take a look at configuring Integration Broker to send an asynchronous outbound message to the File Output connector:

Step 1 is to bring up the Integration Broker menu, which is located at PeopleTools | Integration Broker and can be seen here.

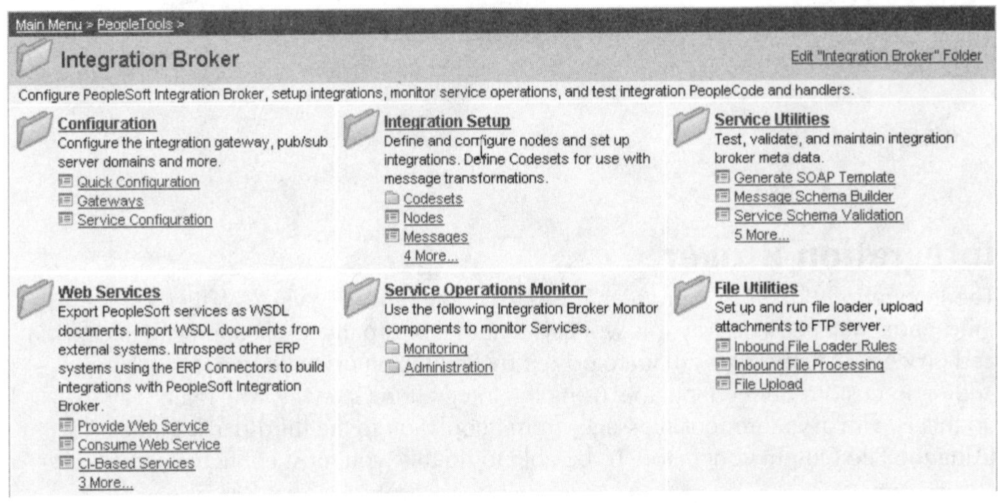

Make certain the message is active and routed to the Message Channel.

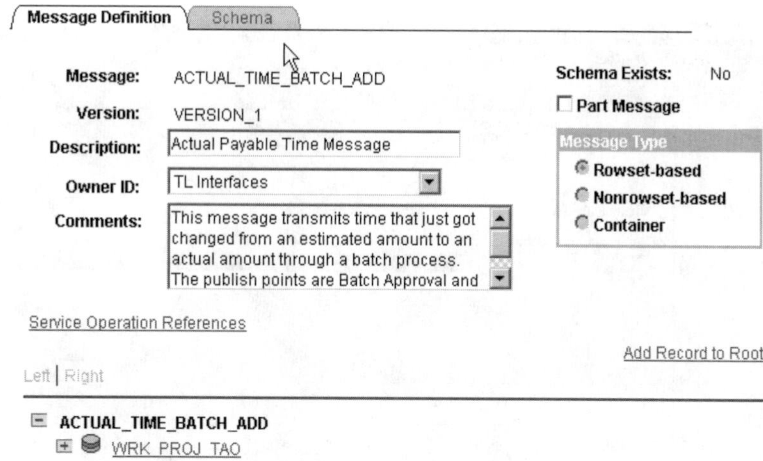

Configure the Message Channel using the steps that follow:

1. Open Application Designer.
2. Create a sample Project named **EXAMPLE1**.

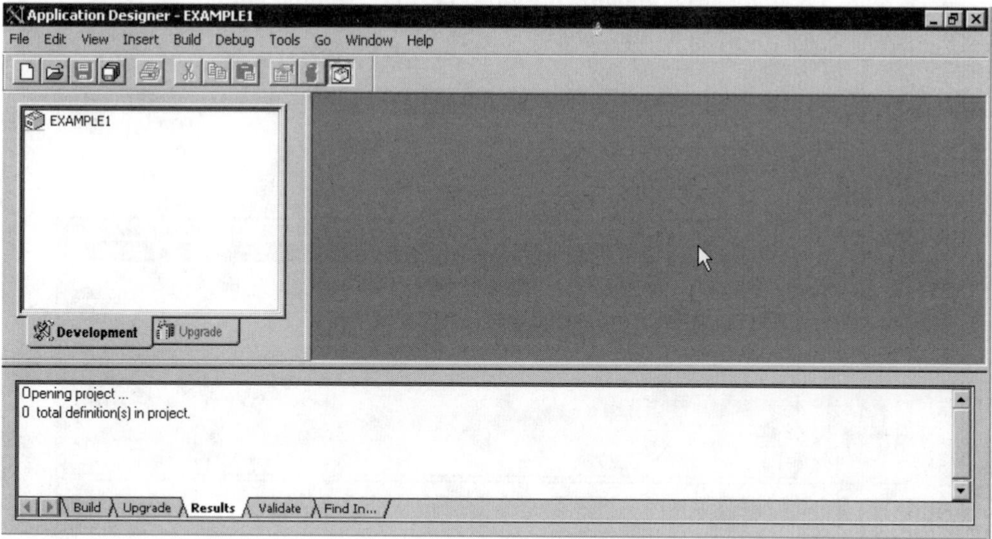

3. Create a field and name it **EXAMPLE_CHAR**.

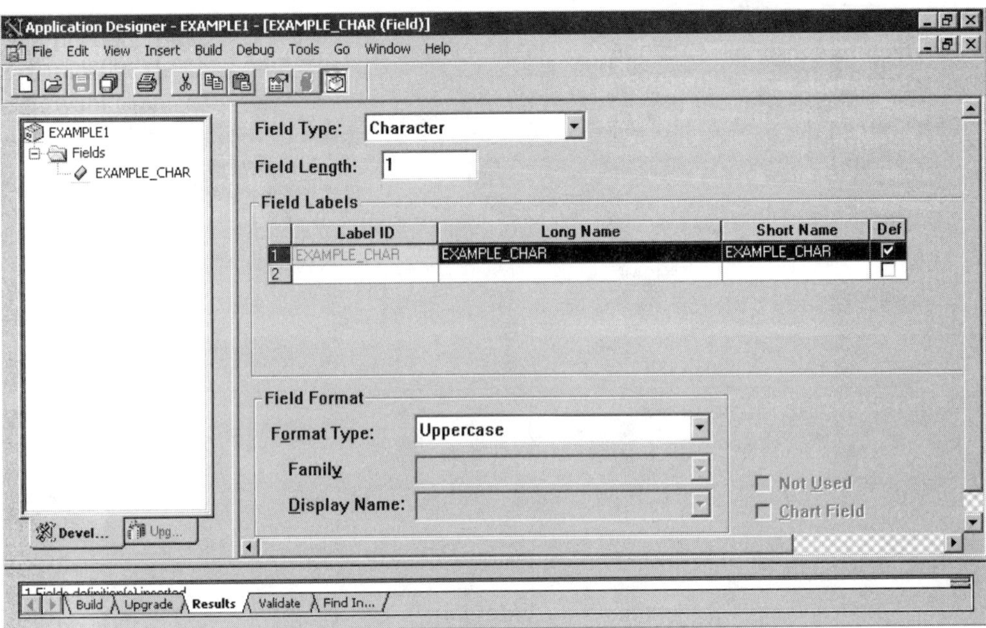

4. Create a new record and name it **EXAMPLE_REC**, add the field EXAMPLE_CHAR to it, and build the physical table.

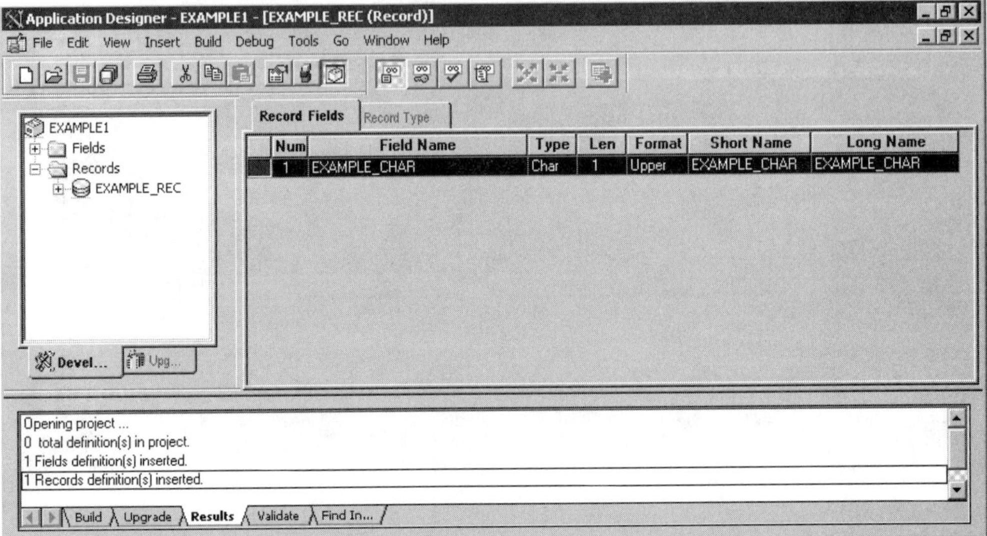

5. Create a new Message Channel and call it **EXAMPLE_CHANNEL**. On the properties dialog box, set the status to Run. Configure the security for the message monitor so that the channel can be displayed.

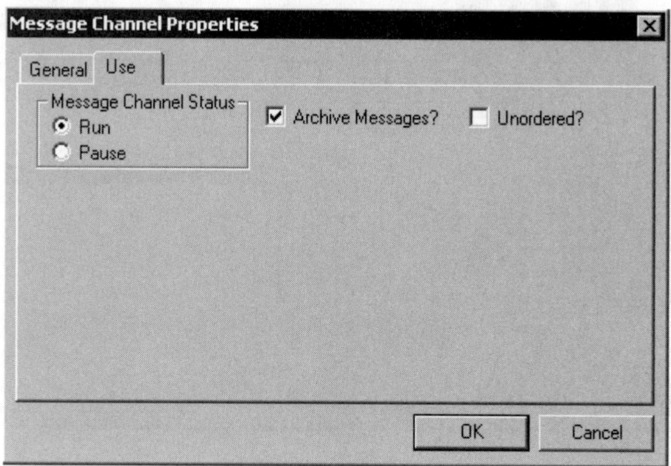

6. Create a new message through the PIA:

   a. Add the EXAMPLE_REC record to VERSION_1 of this message.

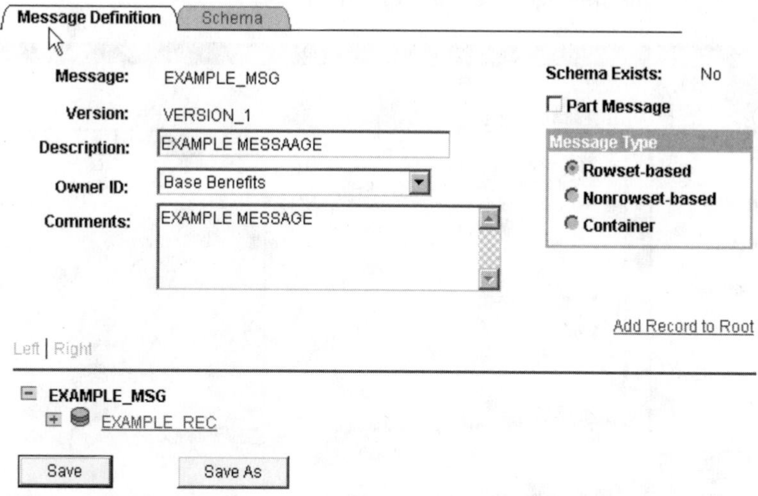

b. Set the Message Channel to **EXAMPLE_CHANNEL**.

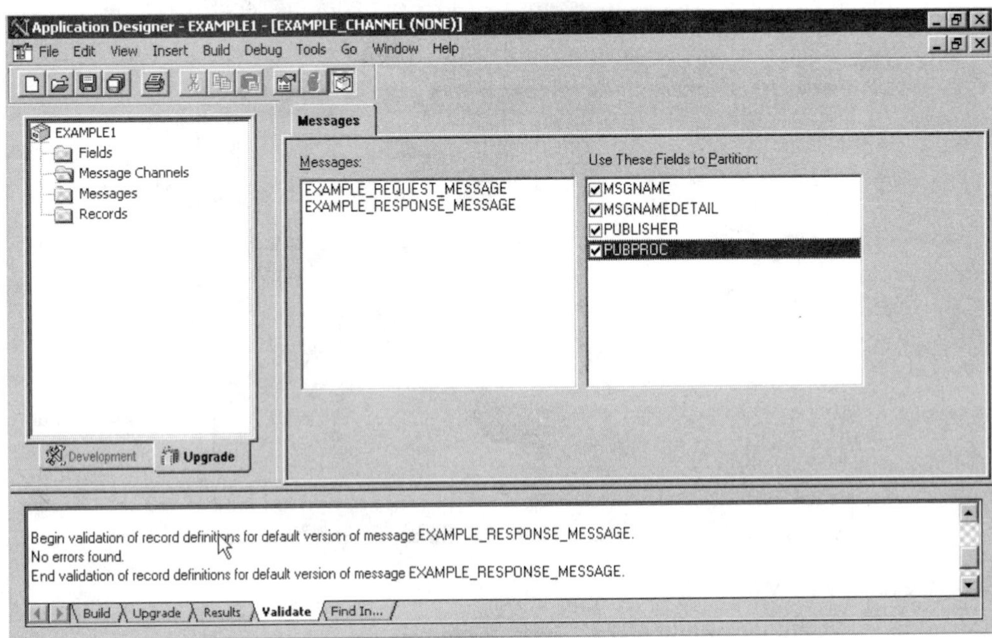

c. Save the message as EXAMPLE_MSG.

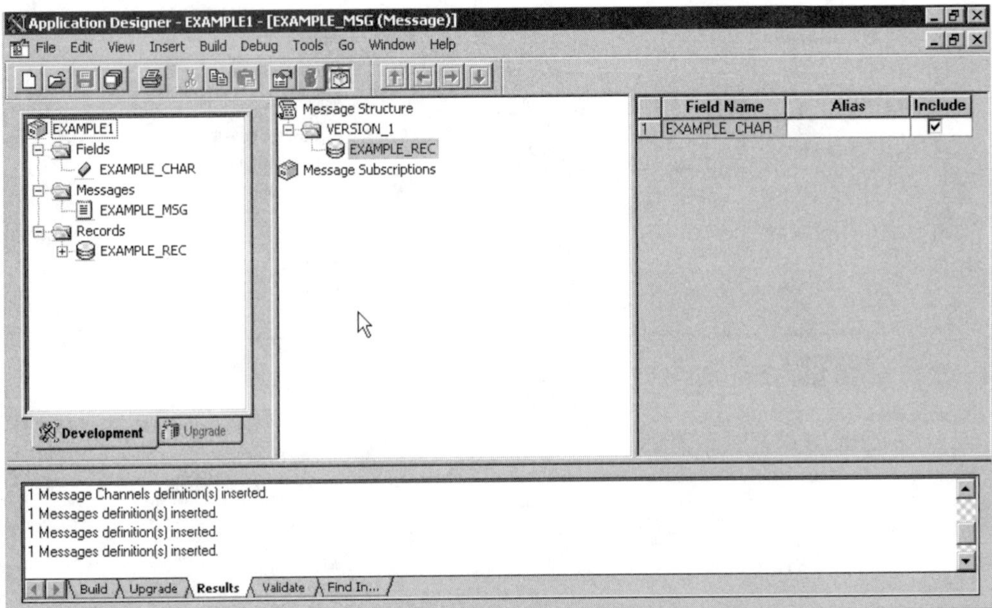

7. Add the subscription LocationSync to your project and add the code that is shown next.

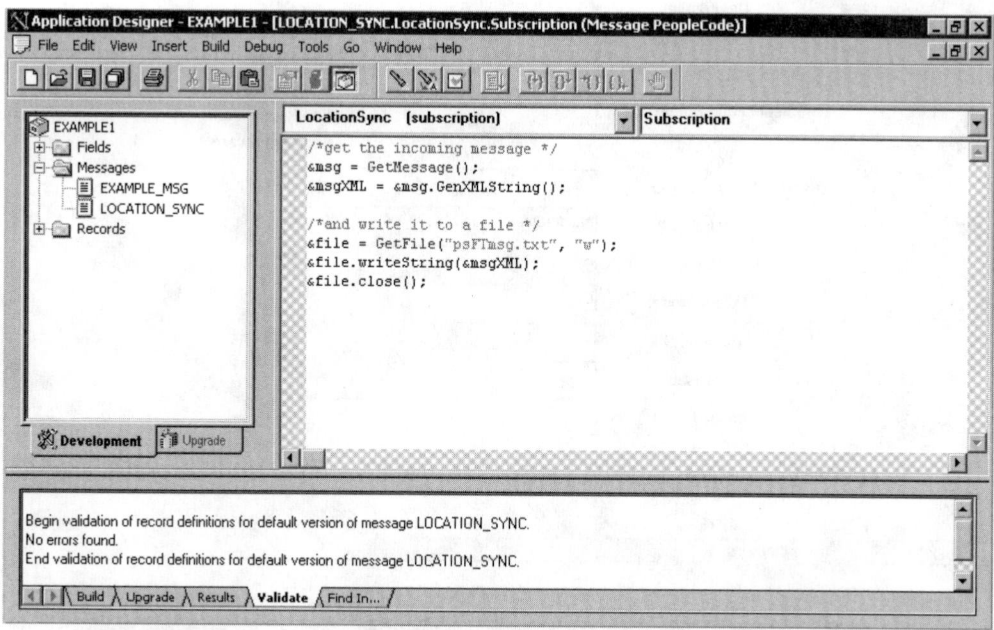

8. Create a new node, calling it **Example**, and add the location **http://<serverName:port>/PSIGW/PS89listeningConnector**.

Node Definitions | Connectors | Portal | WS Security | Routings

Node Name: EXAMPLE

***Description:**

***Node Type:** PIA

Default Local Node

Local Node

Active Node (checked)

***Authentication Option:** None

Non-Repudiation

Segment Aware

***Default User ID:**

Hub Node:

Master Node:

Company ID:

IB Throttle Threshold:

Image Name:

Code Set Group Name:

Contact/Notes   Properties

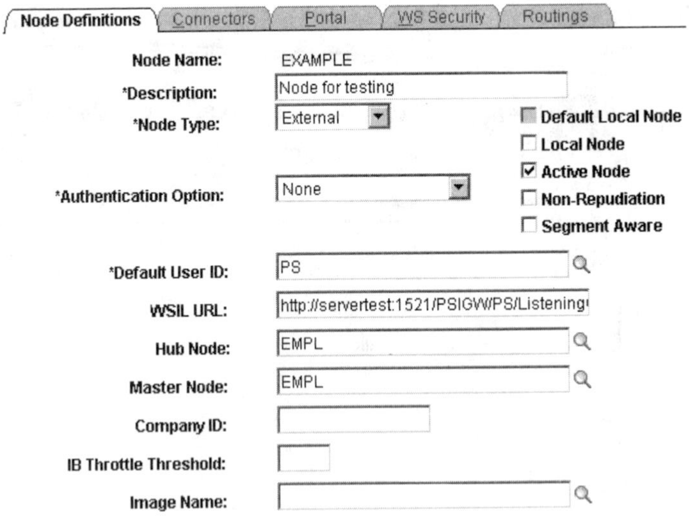

9. Select the Connectors tab and set the Gateway ID and the Connector ID.

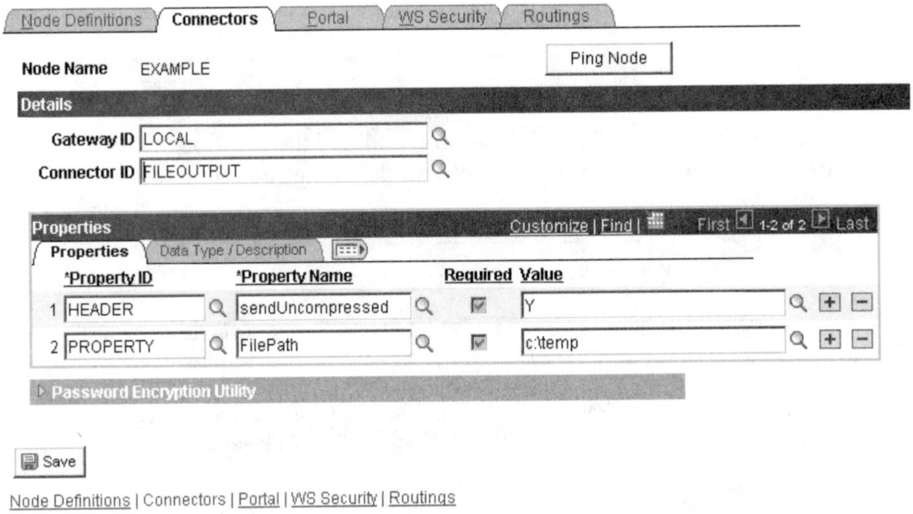

10. Add a Routing Definition.

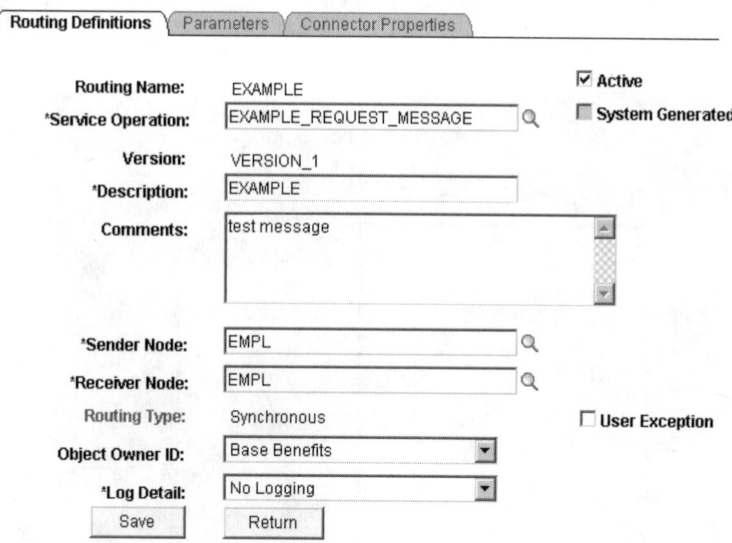

11. Add your newly created Node from the PIA into your project.

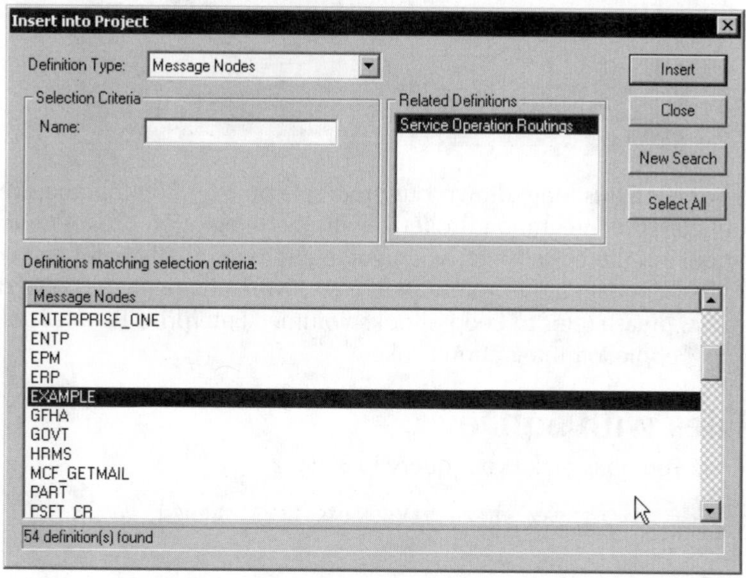

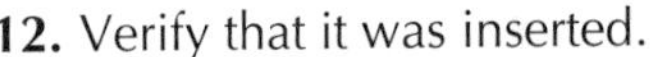

12. Verify that it was inserted.

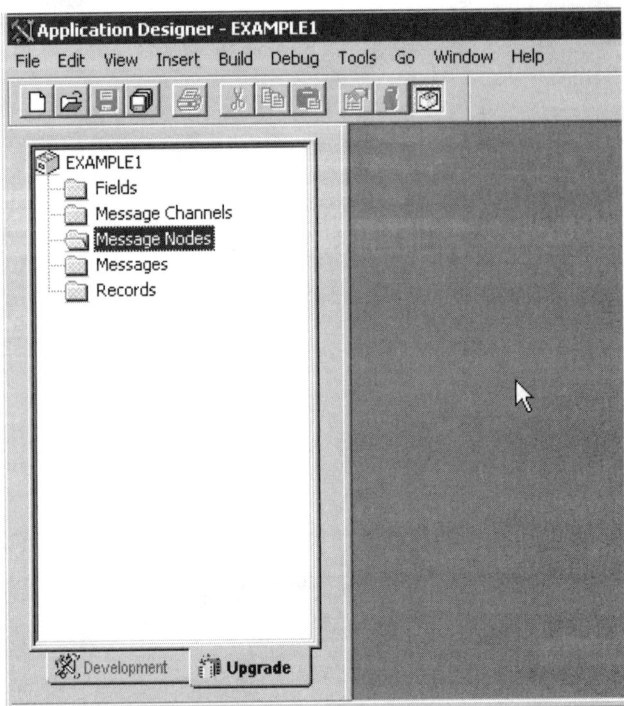

After reviewing this long, drawn-out process, you may find that the simplest way to configure the Integration Broker is with the Integration Broker Quick Configuration, but there are times when you need to manually enter each of these pieces to accommodate a third-party-delivered XML document. To delve deeply into this topic, please refer to PeopleBooks volume "Enterprise PeopleTools 8.49 PeopleBook: PeopleSoft Integration Broker."

XML Files with SqlDev

The first thing you do is make your query in SQL.

```
select * from PSXLATITEM where FIELDNAME like 'ABSENT_AF%'
```

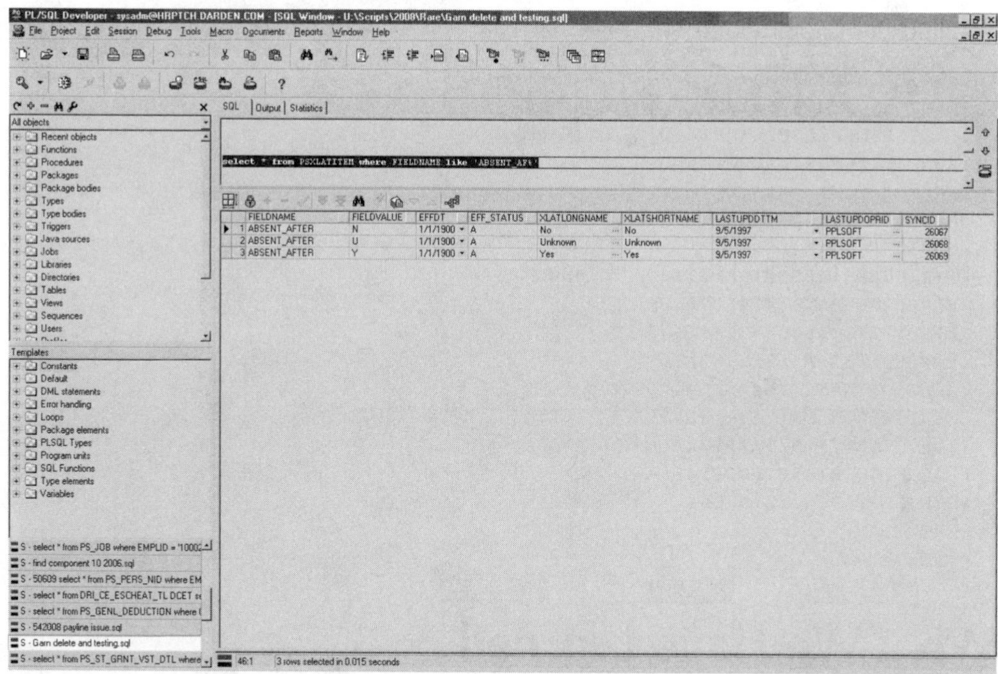

Then highlight the rows you want, right-click Export Results, and choose XML File from the list of four. This will create a file like the one shown next, which is the result from the preceding SQL statement.

```
  <?xml version="1.0" ?>
- <ROWDATA>
- <ROW>
  <C0>1</C0>
  <FIELDNAME>ABSENT_AFTER</FIELDNAME>
  <FIELDVALUE>N</FIELDVALUE>
  <EFFDT>1/1/1900</EFFDT>
  <EFF_STATUS>A</EFF_STATUS>
  <XLATLONGNAME>No</XLATLONGNAME>
  <XLATSHORTNAME>No</XLATSHORTNAME>
  <LASTUPDDTTM>9/5/1997</LASTUPDDTTM>
  <LASTUPDOPRID>PPLSOFT</LASTUPDOPRID>
  <SYNCID>26067</SYNCID>
  </ROW>
- <ROW>
  <C0>2</C0>
  <FIELDNAME>ABSENT_AFTER</FIELDNAME>
  <FIELDVALUE>U</FIELDVALUE>
  <EFFDT>1/1/1900</EFFDT>
```

```
<EFF_STATUS>A</EFF_STATUS>
<XLATLONGNAME>Unknown</XLATLONGNAME>
<XLATSHORTNAME>Unknown</XLATSHORTNAME>
<LASTUPDDTTM>9/5/1997</LASTUPDDTTM>
<LASTUPDOPRID>PPLSOFT</LASTUPDOPRID>
<SYNCID>26068</SYNCID>
</ROW>
- <ROW>
<C0>3</C0>
<FIELDNAME>ABSENT_AFTER</FIELDNAME>
<FIELDVALUE>Y</FIELDVALUE>
<EFFDT>1/1/1900</EFFDT>
<EFF_STATUS>A</EFF_STATUS>
<XLATLONGNAME>Yes</XLATLONGNAME>
<XLATSHORTNAME>Yes</XLATSHORTNAME>
<LASTUPDDTTM>9/5/1997</LASTUPDDTTM>
<LASTUPDOPRID>PPLSOFT</LASTUPDOPRID>
<SYNCID>26069</SYNCID>
</ROW>
</ROWDATA>
```


What We Have Learned

Always keep in mind the four major steps for creating a XML; these steps are outlined in Figure 8-4 from Quest Collaborate 2008 session 34190 "XML Publisher for Project Reporting" by BTRG. Note the inclusion of the step to create the data

FIGURE 8-4 *Four steps for creating an XML report*

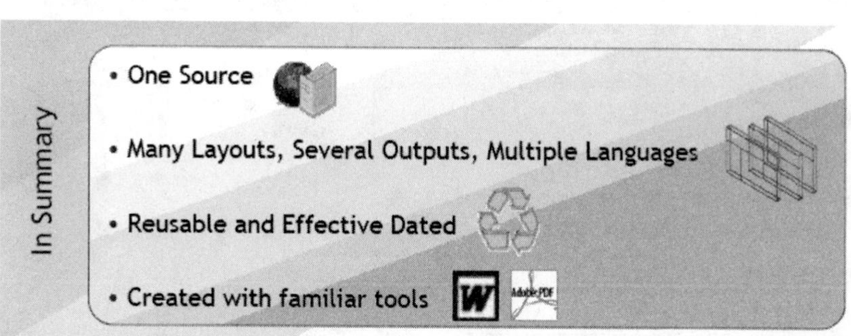

FIGURE 8-5 *Summary of steps*

source as the first step. This is crucial to the success of your XML report. Figure 8-5 is the summary of the steps, also taken from Quest Collaborate 2008 session 34190 "XML Publisher for Project Reporting" by BTRG.

1. Create your data source.

Records | Query | Expressions | Prompts | **Fields** | Criteria | Having | View SQL | Run

Query Name: FPA_ADR **Description:** Address

View field properties, or use field as criteria in query statement. Reorder / Sort

Fields Customize | Find | View All | First 1-5 of 5 Last

Col	Record.Fieldname	Format	Ord	XLAT	Agg	Heading Text	Add Criteria	Edit	Delete
1	A.EMPLID - EmplID	Char11				ID		Edit	
2	A.NAME_PREFIX - Name Prefix	Char4				Prefix		Edit	
3	A.NAME - Name	Char50				Name		Edit	
4	B.BIRTHDATE - Date of Birth	Date				Birthdate		Edit	
5	B.BIRTHPLACE - Birth Location	Char30				Birthplace		Edit	

Save | Save As | New Query | Preferences | Properties | New Union | Return to Search

2. Create your Report Definition.

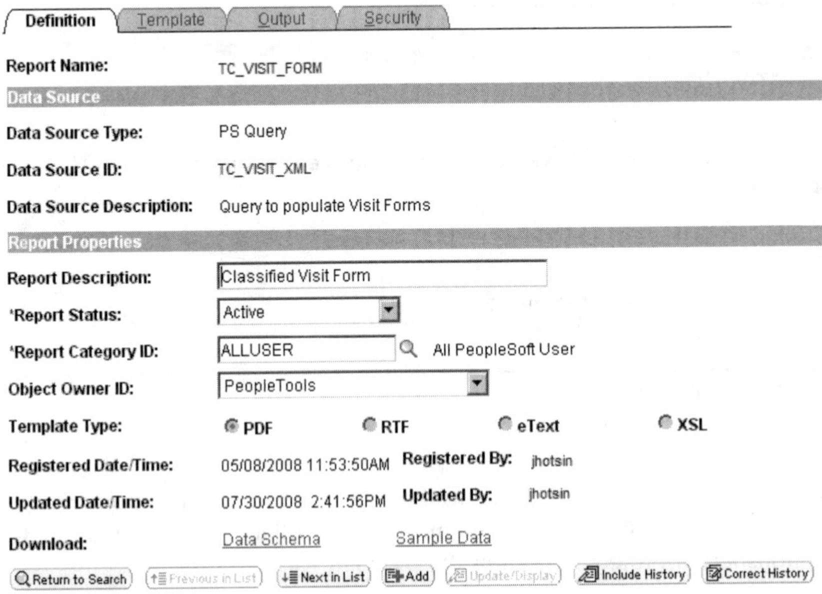

3. Define your Template.

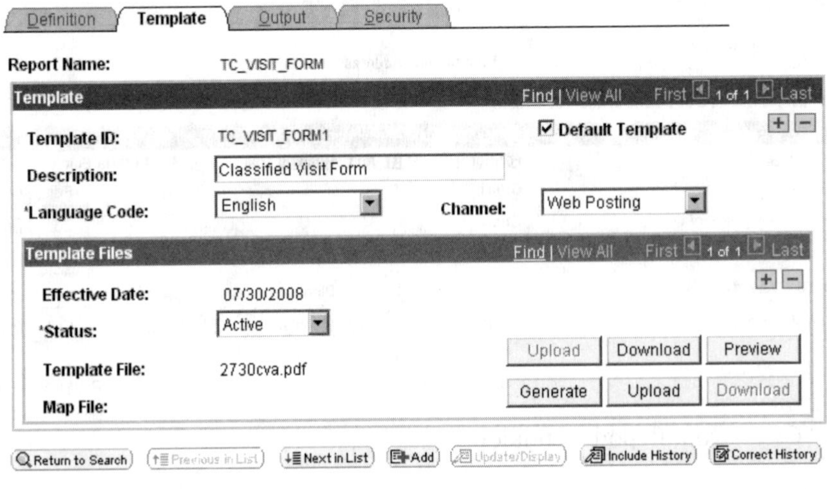

4. Define your Output.

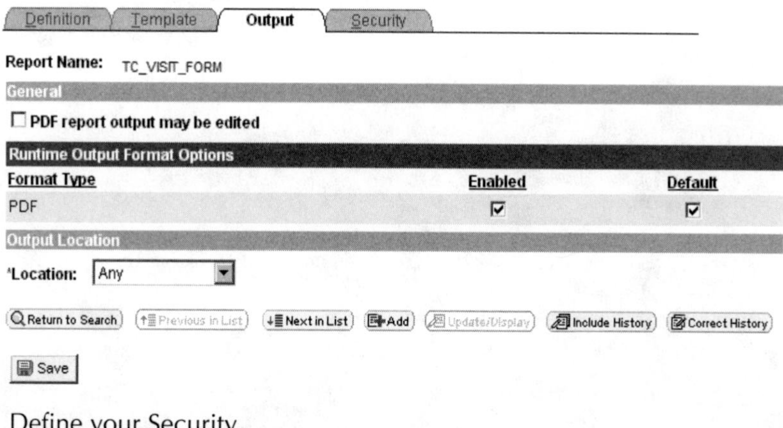

5. Define your Security.

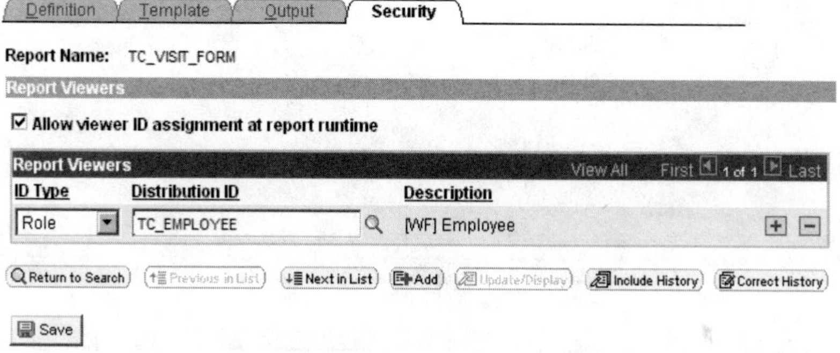

6. PeopleCode to Generate Report:

```
/* detect system directory separator */
&sDirSep = GetDirSeparator();

/* create process directory */
CreateDirectory("XMLP", %FilePath_Relative);

/* get report definition object */
&oRptDefn = create PSXP_RPTDEFNMANAGER:ReportDefn(&sRptDefn);
&oRptDefn.Get();

/* output directory */
&RptOutputDir = GetEnv("PS_SERVDIR") | &sDirSep | "files" | &sDirSep | "XMLP" | &sDirSep | UuidGen();
&sOutputDir = &RptOutputDir | &sDirSep | "RptInst";
&sDataDir = &RptOutputDir | &sDirSep | "Data";
CreateDirectory(&sOutputDir, %FilePath_Absolute);
CreateDirectory(&sDataDir, %FilePath_Absolute);

&oRptDefn.OutDestination = &RptOutputDir;
/* MessageBox(0, "", 0, 0, " report output dir " | &RptOutputDir);*/
/* Output format */
&sOutPutFormat = "PDF";

/*fill query runtime prompt record */
&rcdQryPrompts = &oRptDefn.GetPSQueryPromptRecord();
&rcdQryPrompts.GetField(Field.EMPLID).Value = &emplid;
```

```
/*generate report*/
&oRptDefn.ProcessReport(&sTemplateId, %Language_User, &AsOfDate, &sOutPutFormat);
&sFileext = GetFileExtension(&sOutPutFormat);


/*publish report */

CommitWork();

&sRptDir = &RptOutputDir;

&sReportFile = &sRptDefn | "." | &sOutPutFormat;
&sRptFilePath = &sRptDir | &sDirSep | "RptInst" | &sDirSep | &sReportFile;



/*&ret = SendMail(0, "jhotsin@test.com", "jhotsin@test.com", "jhotsin@test.com", "TEST", "TEST", &sRptFilePath, "TEST", "", "",
"TEST", "", "");*/

/* cleanup */
DeleteLocalFile(&sOutputfile, %FilePath_Absolute);
```

7. Define PDF Fields.

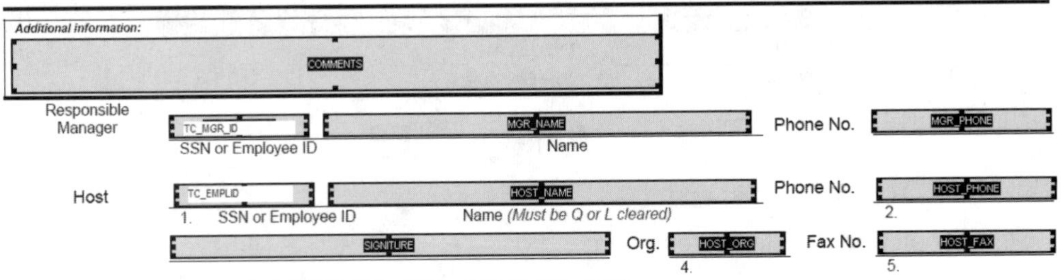

Summary

In this chapter you learned the basics of XML in PeopleSoft. XML is a very complex topic, but it can be simplified in PeopleSoft. The easiest way is to create a query as your data source, register your query as a data source, define your report, add your .PDF template, and schedule the report to run with Report Scheduler. You can also work with XML through the Integration Broker, or SQLDev.

XML is the new accepted standard for reporting, but the question that seems to come up most often is, will XML replace SQR, COBOL, or Application Engine? The answer to this question is no. XML Publisher in PeopleSoft is great for reporting when data is clearly aligned with a query and can be reported out in a .PDF form. A good example is a W2 tax form. But this in no way will replace the depth of programming that you get with SQR or COBOL, and the extensive batch processing that you get with Application Engine. It is a good skill to add to your tool chest, but it will be an addition to the existing tools you are using in PeopleSoft.

CHAPTER 9

PeopleSoft Query

eopleSoft delivers a reporting tool called Query. It is a user-friendly tool for non-technical individuals to retrieve data without knowing how to use SQL (Structured Query Language). This tool can be set up two ways. Some users can have access to create Query reports, while others can only run the queries. Determining how to set up the tool will depend on your environment.

The individual creating the query will have to have basic knowledge about the table structures. This will enable them to pull the correct data for their query. The tool will guide them through joining two or more tables and formatting the data to their specifications. The tool also helps users avoid creating bad queries or Cartesian joins, but queries can bog down the system if not created efficiently.

Data can be viewed on a grid and pushed out to Excel or HTML. Queries can be set up to run on a schedule. There is a lot of flexibility with queries that will enable your end user to be more productive.

The following chapter describes the steps needed to create simple queries. It starts from the creation of the query tree, moves on to the permission list, and ends up creating a simple query that uses the information that was set up. These basic concepts can be used to create very complicated queries.

Query Security

The first step to creating queries is setting up the security. This requires creating a query tree and setting up a permission list that allows access to the query trees. Within the tree all tables that the end user is allowed to view must be included. If a table is not in the query tree, then the query will not be available for the end user to run.

Creating Access Group Trees

Query Access Manager is the administration tool for creating and maintaining your query trees. Navigate to People Tools | Security | Query Security | Query Access Manager.

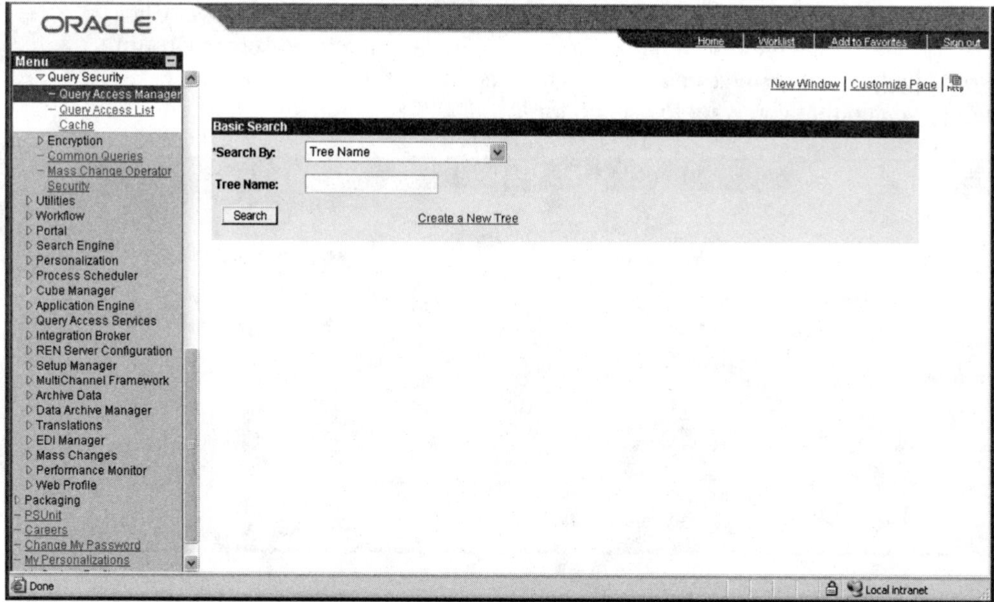

Creating

This page gives the option to retrieve an existing tree for modification or create a new tree. Click Create A New Tree. This will take you to the Definition And Properties page, shown in the following illustration.

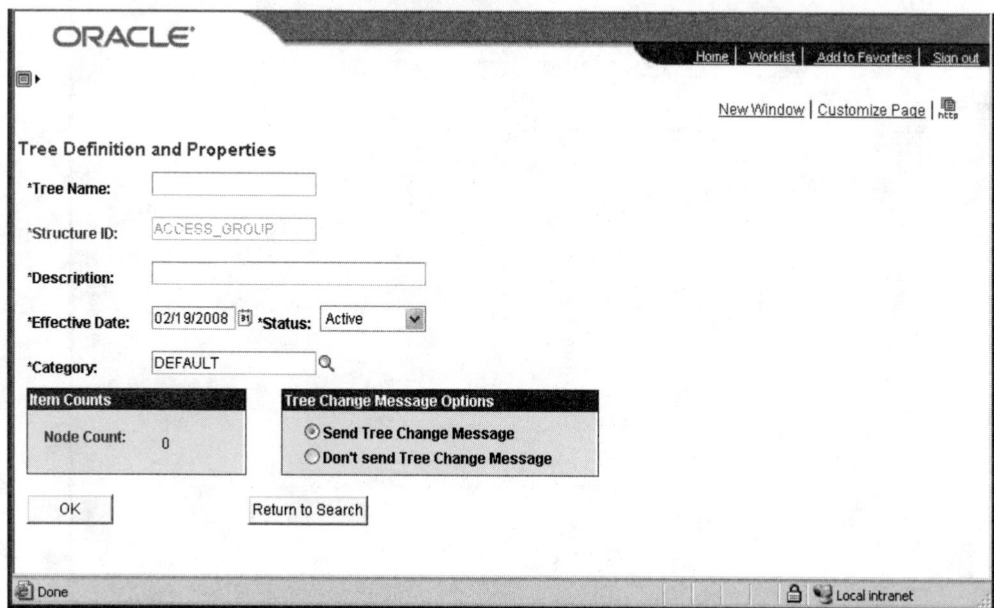

Enter a tree name and a description, and verify that the status is active. Click OK. The next page requests a name for the root node of the tree (Access Group). Normally this will be the same name as the tree, but if there is already an access group created that you want to use, go for it.

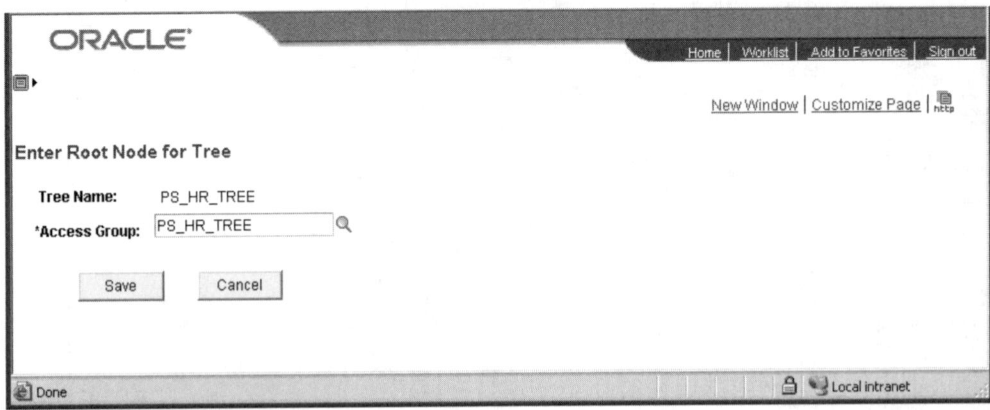

Save the page after you have entered an access group. If this is a new access group, the following page requests a description and definition for the access group. Click OK when finished.

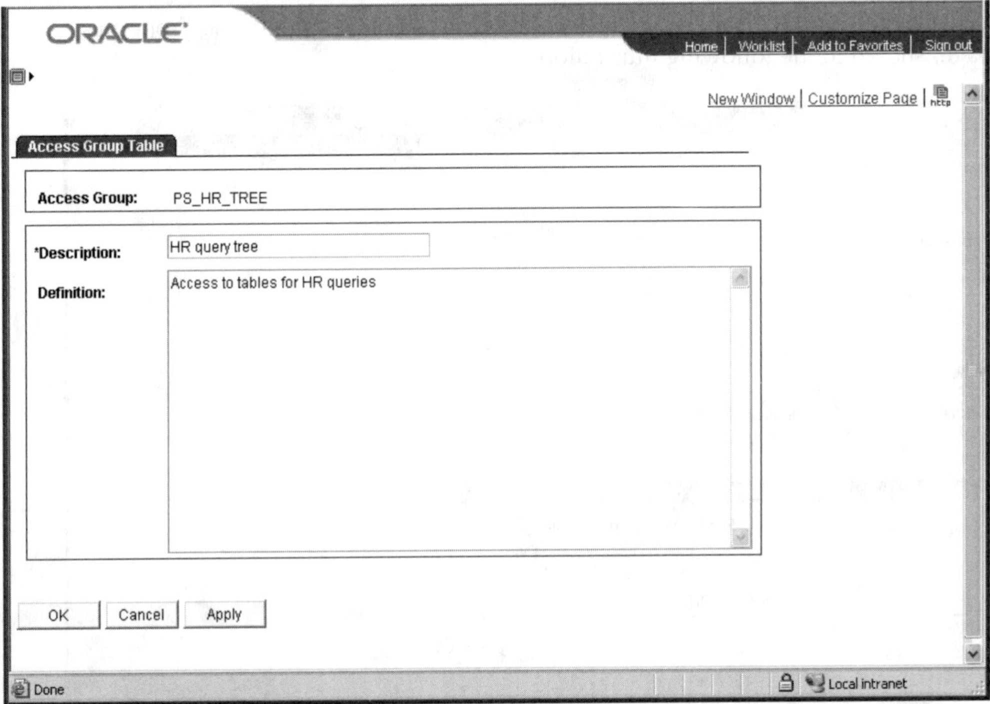

Now you have created a tree with an access group, as you can see in the following illustration. These access groups allow you to set up security for different end users.

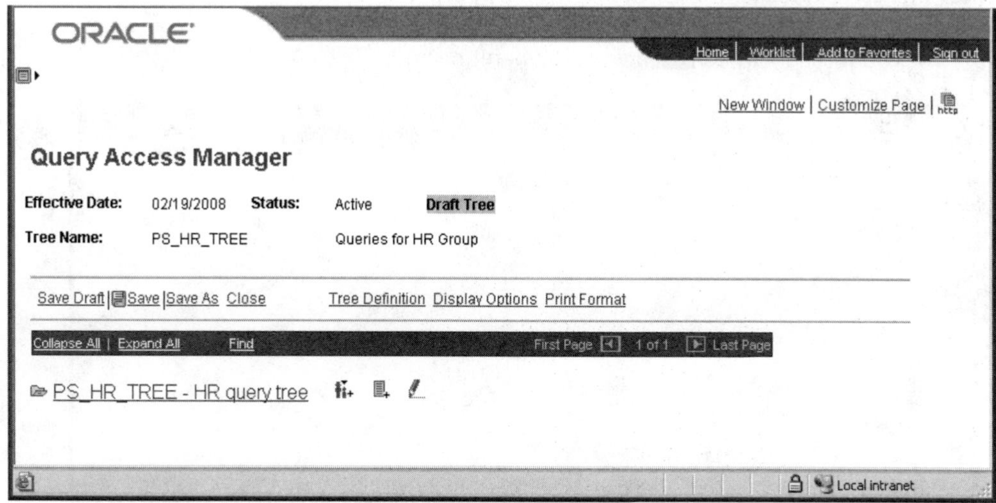

Adding Records

The next step is to add the tables to your node. To the right of your main node are icons. These icons enable you to add nodes and information to your tree. Different icons will be available, depending on which node is being utilized. Table 9-1 describes each of the icons.

Icon	Name	Description
	Add Sibling	Add a sibling folder
	Add Child	Add a child folder
	Add Record	Add a record to the folder
	Delete Node	Delete the folder or record
	Cut	Cut the folder or record and then it can be pasted to another node
	Edit Data	Edit information for the access group folder or record description

TABLE 9-1. *Query Security Icons*

To keep your trees easy to read, it is recommended that you group your tables in common folders. Click the Add Child icon. This will prompt you to name your folder, which will be a new access group. Make sure you have focus on your new folder and select the Add Record icon. This will bring up the following page for you to enter or look up a record (table) name. Do not include the PS prefix; if you want PS_JOB, you just specify JOB. Click Add when finished.

ORACLE

Home | Worklist | Add to Favorites | Sign out

New Window | Customize Page

Insert Child Record

*Record (Table) Name: job

Add Cancel

Local intranet

You can repeat this process to enter as many tables you want included in that access group (folder). The following illustration shows how records have been added to the access group folder JOB-RECORDS.

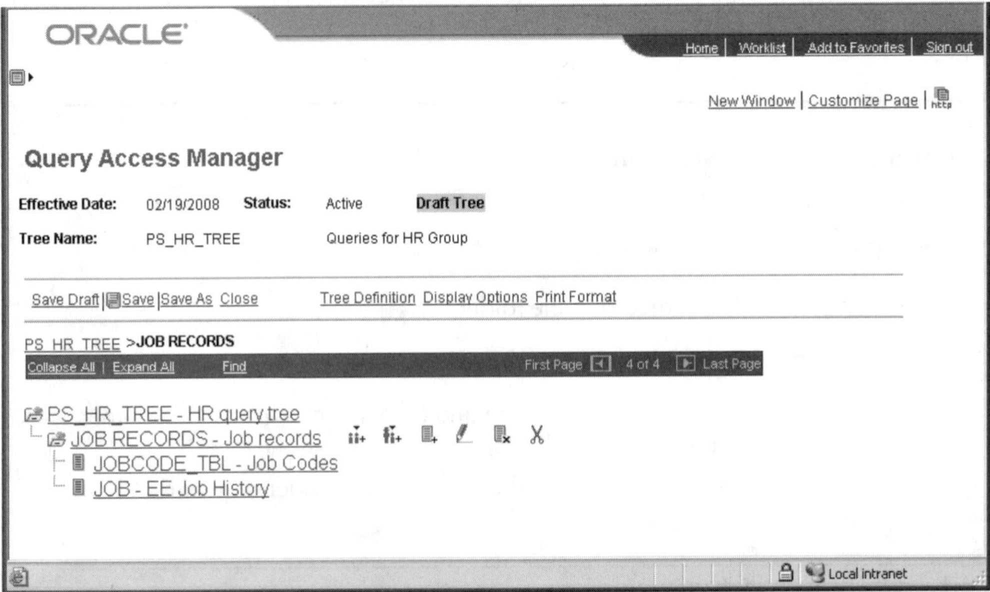

To add another folder, click an existing folder so that it has the focus. Then click the Add Sibling icon. This will create a new folder. Follow the same process to add records to this folder. The following illustration shows an example of how a query tree with multiple folders and records may look.

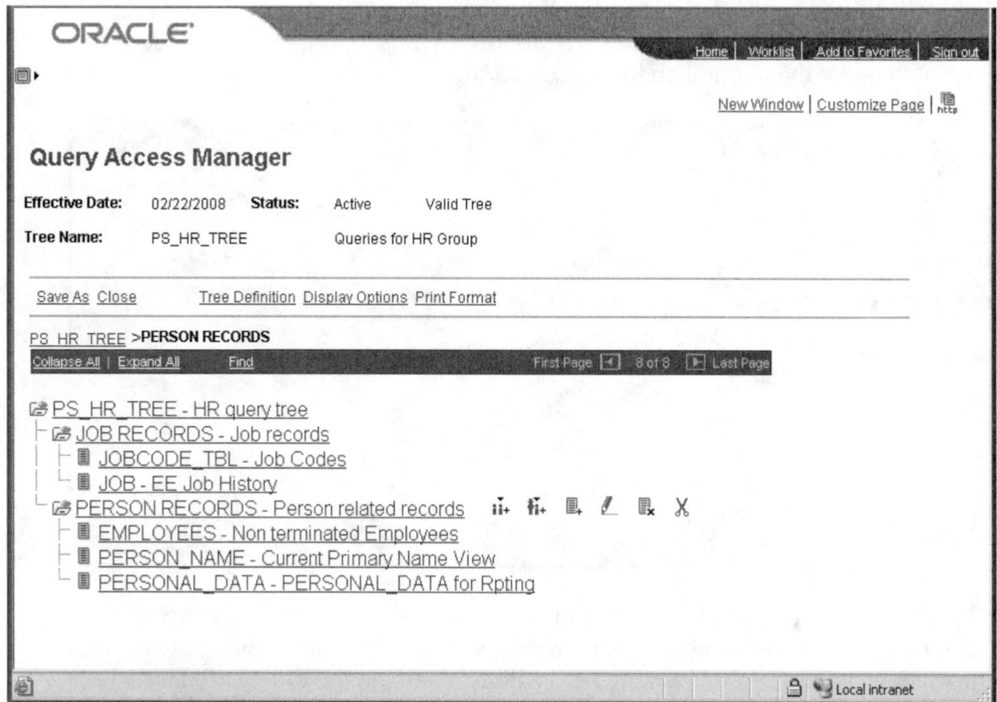

Remember to save your query tree when you are done. It is also a good idea to save intermittently to ensure none of your work gets lost.

You need to develop a strategy on how you will manage your Query Security. A hierarchy might be by module and permissions, such as AP MANAGER, AP CLERK, PAYROLL MANAGER, PAYROLL CLERK, etc. Another element of strategy is whether to add custom tables to delivered query security views, or to create custom-query security views. Also, there are important PeopleTools tables that are not associated with modules but are often queried for metadata, such as PSTREENODE, which are usually for developers and kept in something like the TOOLS query security node.

PeopleSoft delivers query security trees already created that include the delivered tables, so it is possible to start using PS Query "out of the box" and simply add the custom tables and views that are user defined. All records have to be defined as PeopleTools records; it is not enough that it is defined to the database, but the underlying database is of course the actual record or view, usually with the PS prefix.

Permissions

For your end users to be able to have access to run queries and utilize the records in your tree, a permission list should be created. This permission list should be added to one of their roles. Navigate to PeopleTools | Security | Permission And Roles | Permission List to create the permission list.

Select the Add A New Value tab. The following illustration shows the Add page. Enter a name for the permission list and click Add.

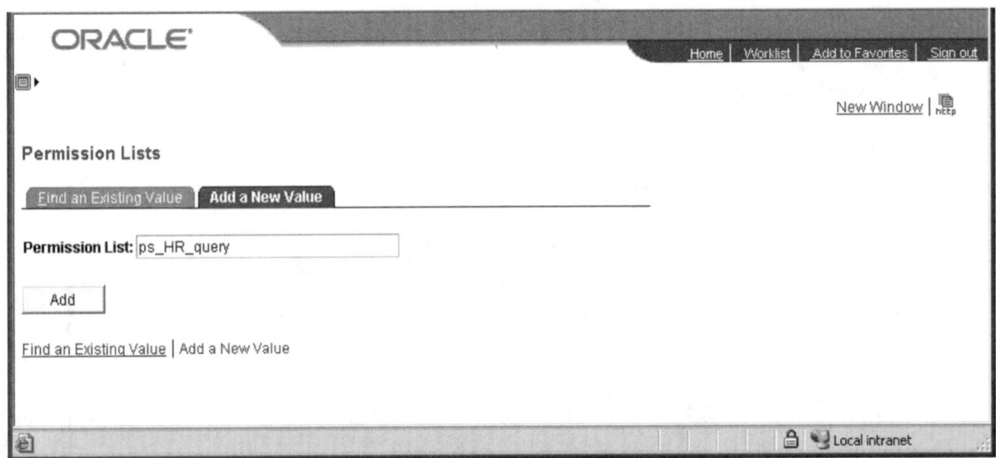

On the General tab add a description for your permission list. Then click the Pages tab. Add the menu name **Query Manager**. Click the Edit Components link. The following illustration shows all the pages available on the Query Manager menu.

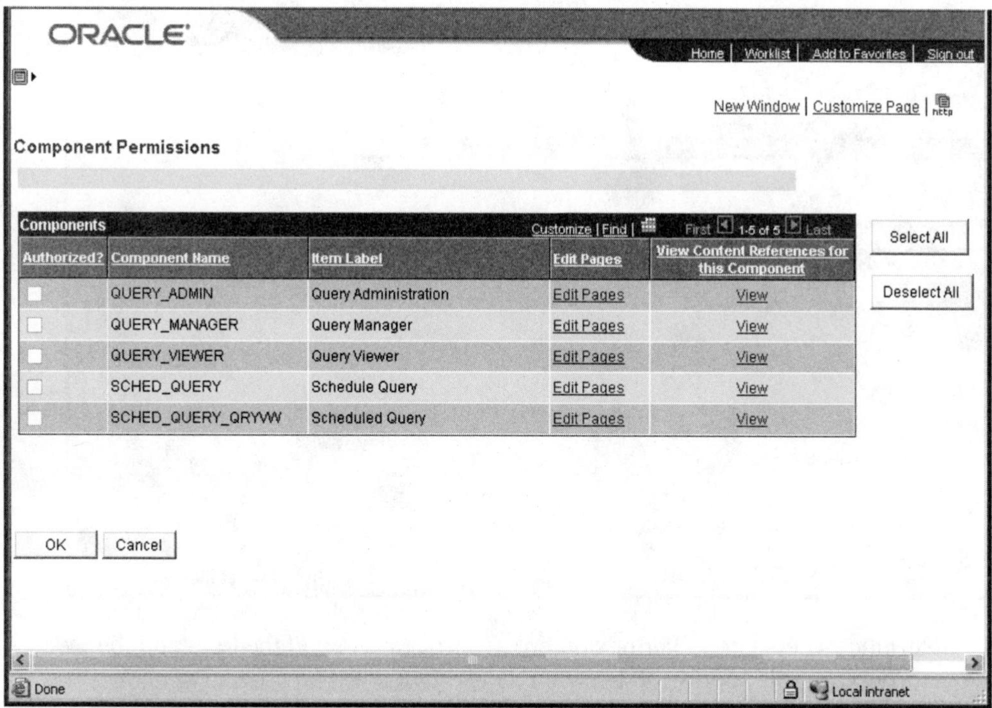

This page allows you to give certain access to your end user. The following describes what each of these pages can do.

- **Query_Admin** This page allows for viewing of all queries. The ability to kill a query is done from this page.
- **Query_Manager** This page allows the creation and running of queries. Give access to this page only if you want your end user to create and change queries.
- **Query_Viewer** This page will only allow the end user to run queries they have access to.
- **Sched_Query** This page allows for the scheduling of queries.
- **Sched_Query_Qryvw** This page will allow the end user to view only the scheduled queries that they have access to.

Edit each of the pages to give the desired permission to your end users and then click Add. Next select the Query tab. You have two types of permissions to set up, as shown in the next illustration.

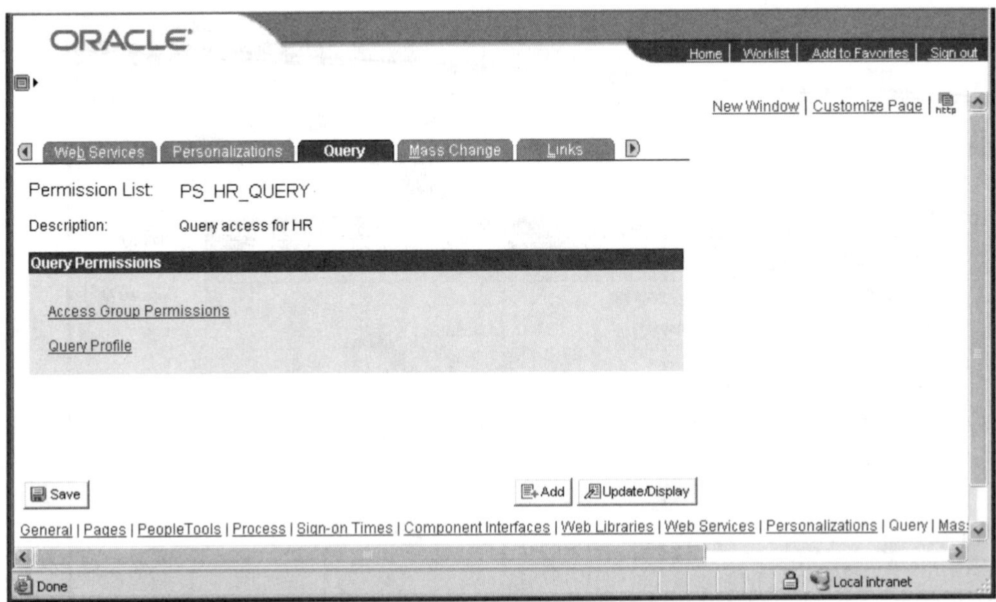

Select the Access Group Permission link. This page is to add the trees and the access group that this permission list will include. One tree can contain many access groups. Each access group can be selected in the permission list. Since it is set up in a hierarchical structure, permissions given to the higher access groups will include the lower access groups. As you can see in the following illustration, the trees and access group created earlier are added to this page. When all trees and access groups are added, click OK.

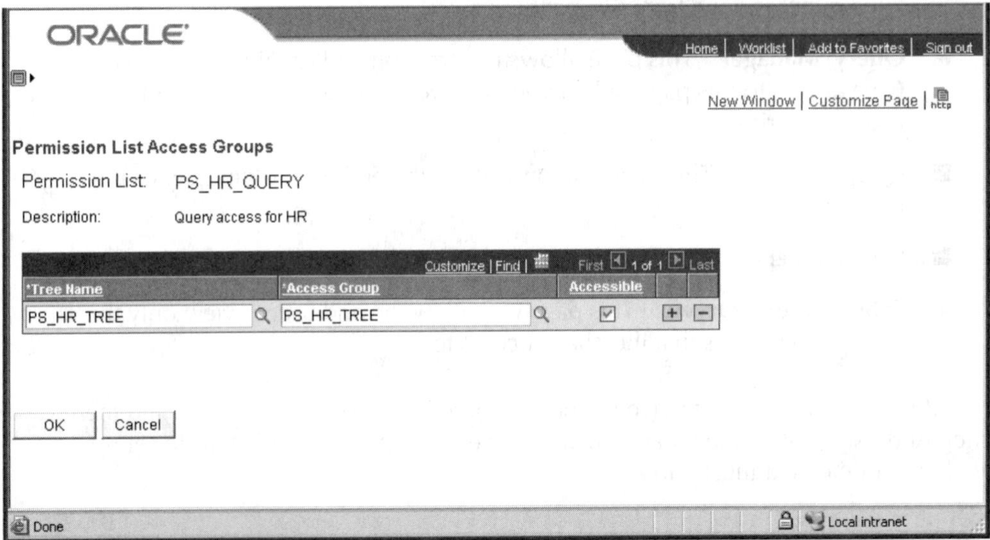

Next select the Query Profile. The following illustration shows the page. On this page you can force certain attributes on the queries that the end users can run. You can set parameters on how the query can be used and how it is outputted. For end users that will be able to create queries, advanced SQL options can be set. These SQL options are provided to prevent runaway queries. Unfortunately these don't completely prevent runaway queries, so additional measures are needed. Two such additional measures are

- Turning on the Query Monitor option.
- Doing additional work at the database level. Since PeopleSoft is "database agnostic," each database has its own ways of preventing runaway SQL.

For more information, refer to the following web site:

```
http://books.oaks.ohio.gov/PSOL/fin88/eng/psbooks/tpsq/
chapter.htm?File=tpsq/htm/tpsq09.htm
```

To save your permission list, click OK. Attach it to a role that the end user currently uses or create a new role.

ORACLE
Home | Worklist | Add to Favorites | Sign out
New Window | Customize Page
Permission List PS_HR_QUERY
Description: Query access for HR
PeopleSoft Query Use
Only Allowed to run Queries
Allow creation of Public Queries
Allow creation of Role, Process and Archive Queries
Maximum Rows Fetched: (0 = Unlimited)
Maximum Run Time in Minutes: (0 = Unlimited)
PeopleSoft Query Output
Run
Run to Excel
Advanced SQL Options
Allow use of Distinct
Allow use of 'Any Join'
Allow use of Subquery/Exists
Allow use of Union
Allow use of Expressions
Maximum Joins Allowed: (9 = Unlimited)
Maximum 'In Tree' Criteria: (9 = Unlimited)
OK Cancel
Done
Local intranet

Query Process Overview

Now that you have a tree and permissions set up, you can create your first query. First you need to determine what kind of query your end user is requesting, how it will be used, and what information you require to produce the query.

Query Types

PeopleSoft has delivered six different types of queries. These types are available depending on the permissions given to the end user.

- **User query** Uses the Query Manager to retrieve data from the database.
- **Reporting query** Basically the same as a user query, except it is designed to be used with other reporting tools, such as Crystal Reports, PS/nVision, Cube Manager, and XML Publisher.
- **Process query** A batch query used with Application Engine and the Query API.
- **Role query** Used with workflow, to determine who should receive e-mails or work list entry. This query returns a list of roles.
- **Archive query** Used by PS Archive Manager for archiving.
- **PS/nVision query** Creates a specific data source for PS/nVision reports and matrix layouts.

Query Steps

There are seven major parts to creating a query. Only a few of these steps are required, but they may be needed depending on the query requirements.

1. **Select Records** Data is stored in records (tables). Depending on the request, you will need to select the records that store the correct data.
2. **Select Fields** Identify the fields from the records that are needed in the query.
3. **Using expression (optional)** Expressions are new fields that can be the following: fields that are not on your records, fields combined into one field, or fields using aggregate functions (for example, sums, counts).
4. **Using prompts (optional)** Requesting input from the end user (for example, Date range).

5. **Selection criteria (optional)** Applying criteria to the data that is being selected to reduce the data returned from the database (for example, only rows that were created in the current year).
6. **Having criteria (optional)** Another type of selection criteria, used when the field you are checking is an aggregate value (for example, only pull departments with more than five employees).
7. **Run query** View the results of the query.

Links and Icons Within Query Manager

While working within Query Manager, you will see common links and icons that can be clicked to get to another page or provide a service. Table 9-2 will help you when you are creating your queries.

Link/Icon	Name	Description
Add record	Add record	This link will return you to the query tab where fields can be added.
Show fields	Show Fields	This link will show the fields included in the record.
Col	Column Number	This will show the current column number for each field.
	Expanded Folder	This shows that the record is expanded. Click it to collapse.
	Collapsed Folder	This shows that the record is collapsed. Click it to expand.
	Criteria	Add criteria for the field you are on.
	Lookup	Look up a table or a field.
31	Calendar	Brings up a calendar to select a date.
	Delete	Deletes the object.

TABLE 9-2. *Links and Icons*

Creating New Queries

Query Manager is the tool PeopleSoft delivers to create queries. End users do not need to know how to create SQL, but they do need a basic understanding of the table structures that they will be pulling data from. You can find Query Manager by navigating to Reporting Tools | Queries | Query Manager. You will see the following page. You can search for an available query or create a new one.

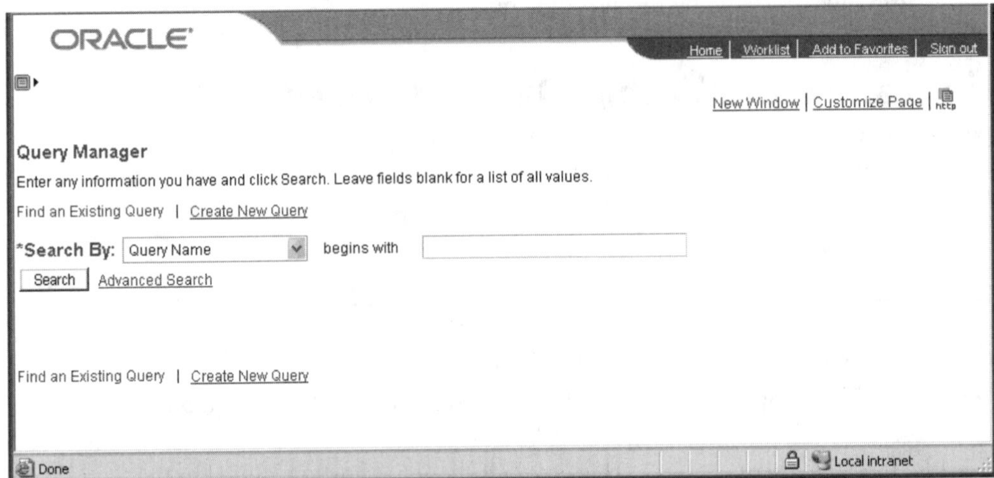

Selecting Records

Select Create New Query to bring up the first page of the Query Manager, which is the Records tab. You are now ready to select the first record needed for your query. All records are displayed with their record name, not including the "PS_". Enter the name of your record or the beginning of it. The next illustration shows how the page will look with the records that you have access to and begin with your search criteria.

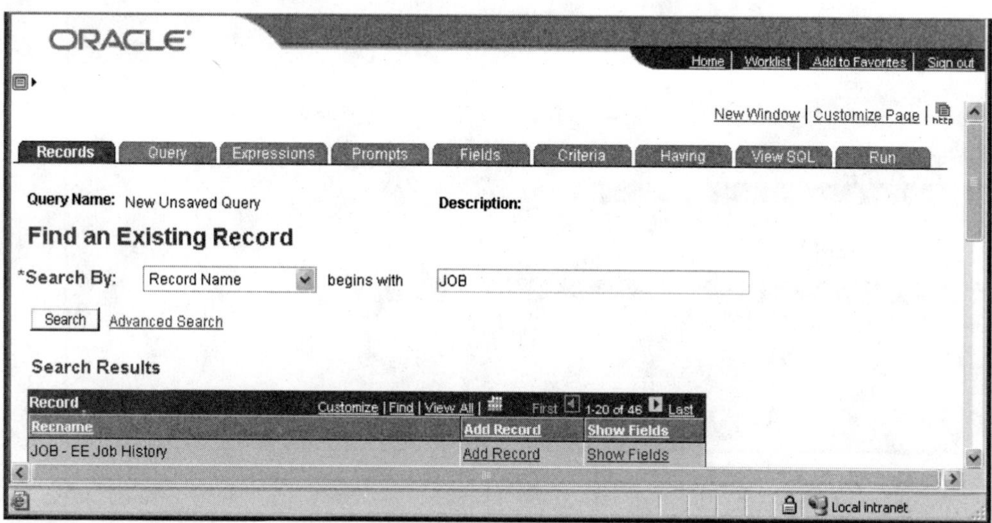

If you want to see what fields are available, you can click the Show Fields link. If this record does not include the field you want, you can search for other records. Click the Add Record link to add the record to your query. If this is an effective-dated record, the following pop-up message will be shown. It will automatically insert criteria to get the most current row into the Criteria tab and take you to the Query tab for fields to be selected.

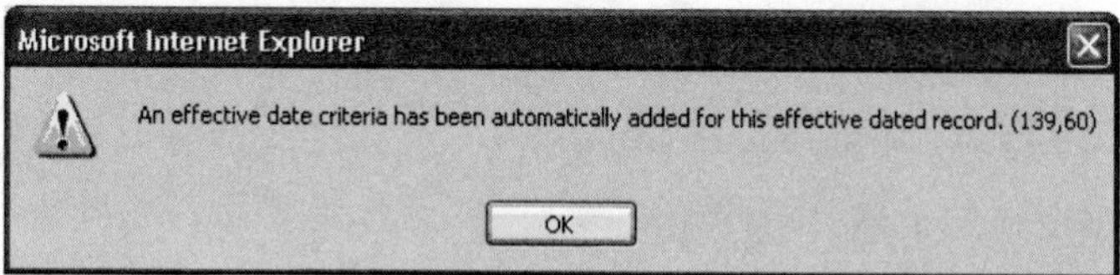

To add fields from other records, go back to the Records tab and search for the next record you want to add. When adding more than one record to your query, the Query Manager will try to help in joining the records. The first question it will ask is how the two records should be joined. The standard join will match any fields that are the same name. The left outer join will take all rows from the left record even though it may not find a match with the right record. It will also ask what record it should join to, since you may have multiple records in your query.

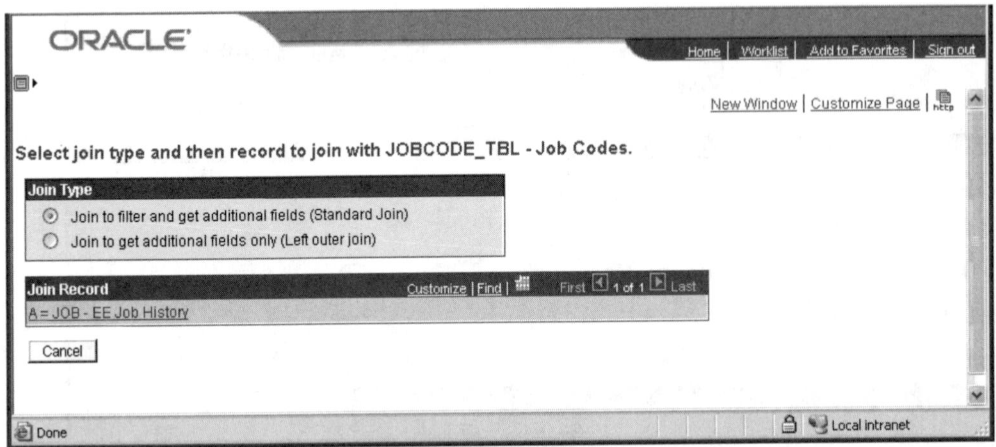

If common fields are found it will suggest how the records should be joined. You have the option at this time to deselect any matches it has found. Depending on your data, you may not want to match on all fields. When the join is the way you want it, click Add Criteria. This will add the join to the Criteria tab.

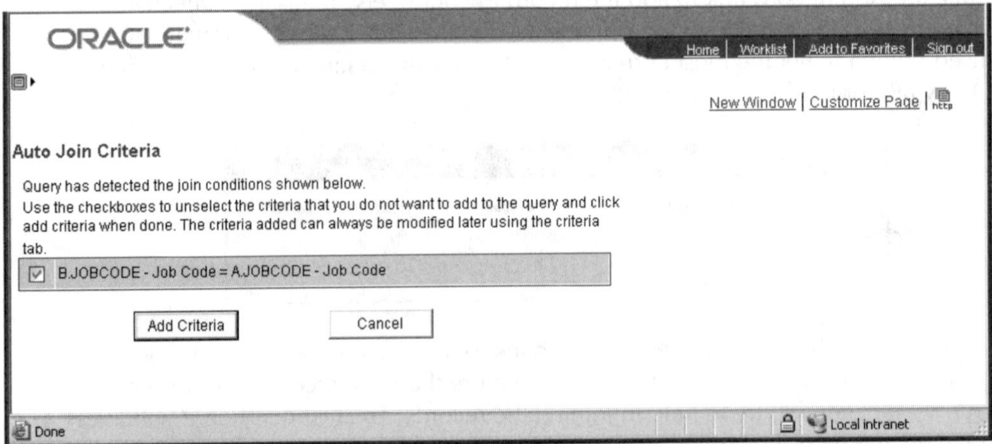

Sometimes Query Manager cannot make a match. If this occurs, you need to join the records yourself using the Criteria tab, which will be shown later in this chapter.

Fields

Once you have added the record, you can select the fields you want to include in your query. Click in the check box to add the field to your query. You also have the option at this time to add criteria by clicking the Criteria icon. Here you can see how a field has been checked.

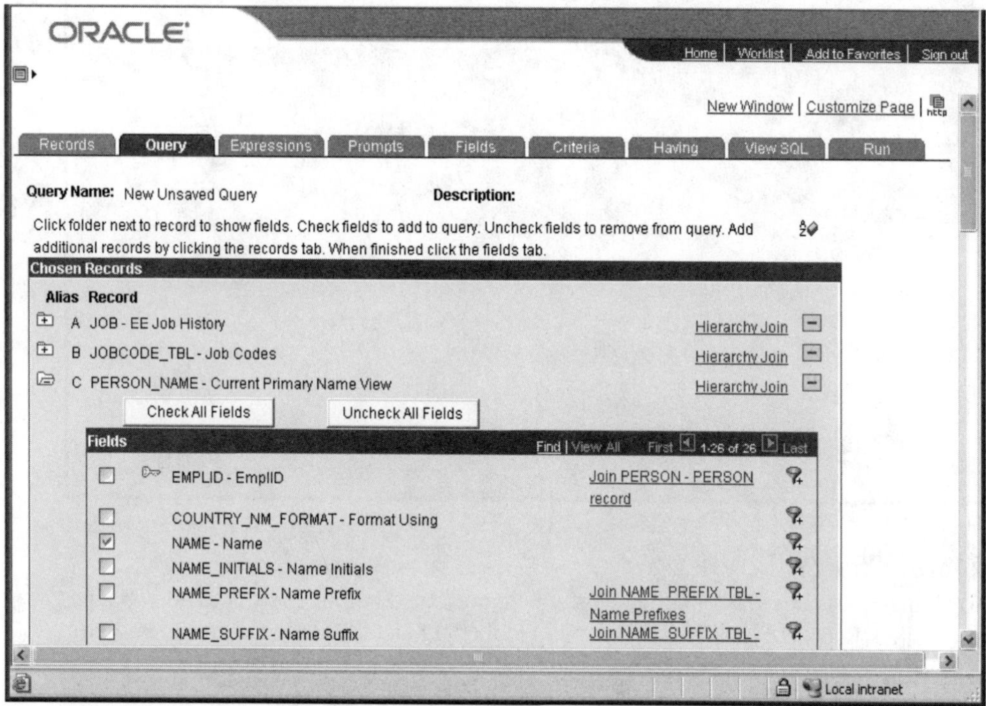

At any time you can go back to the Query tab and add or remove fields, depending on the requirements for your query. When you have selected all the records and fields needed for your query, click the Fields tab. This tab will show all fields that have been selected from the records. It gives the format and the heading for each of the fields. You cannot add new fields from this page, but you can delete them by clicking the Delete icon on the line that contains the field name.

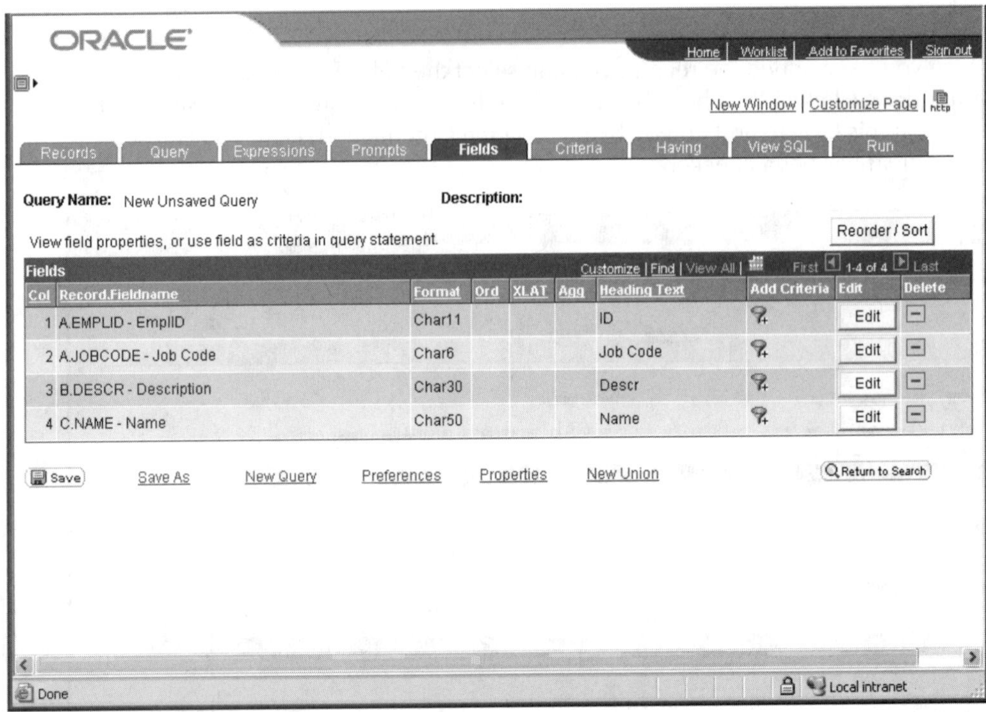

Reorder/Sort

To change the order in which the fields will be presented in the report or to add/change a sort, click Reorder/Sort. This will take you to the Edit Field Ordering page shown here.

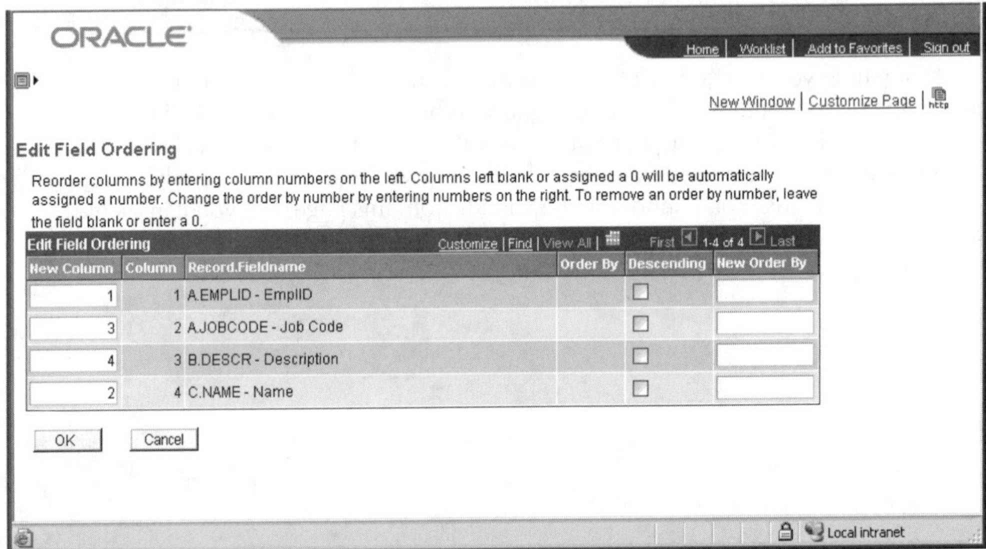

Use the New Column field to place the fields in the correct columns. This is done by entering a column number from 1 to the number of fields in your query. Use New Order By to sort your fields when the query is run. Check the box in the descending column if that is a requirement; otherwise, the default will be ascending. When you are done, click OK to return to the fields page. The fields will be shown in the new order.

Edit Field Properties

To edit the heading or field name or to create an aggregate from this field, click the Edit button in the same row. The Edit Field Properties page will be shown.

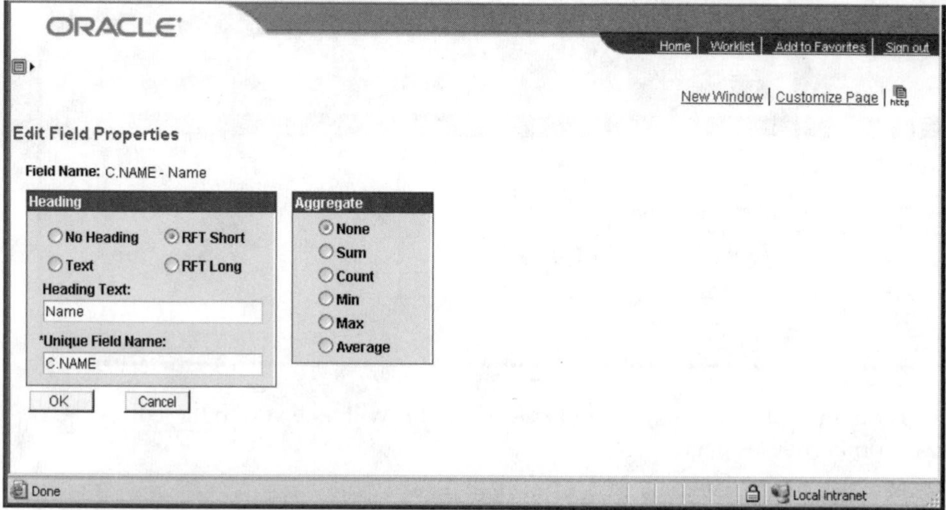

This page will allow you to change the heading. You get the option to have no heading, create your own text, or use the short or long defaults that were created with this field. The query will default to the short name created with the field. You can also change the field name; this is only recommended when you are creating an expression. If this field was selected from a record, it is best to leave it alone, so that you retrieve the correct data. There are different aggregate functions that can be used on the field.

- **None** Default.
- **Sum** This is used with numeric fields to add up the value of a field for all the rows that are returned.
- **Count** This will count the number of records that are returned.
- **Min** This will return the record with the lowest value.
- **Max** This will return the record with the highest value.
- **Average** This is used with numeric fields. It will calculate an average amount for all the rows returned.

When you have made all your changes to this page, click OK and you will be returned to the Fields page.

Expressions

Sometimes the field you require is not in the database or you want to create a field with a combination of one or more fields. In the Query Manager these types of fields are called expressions. Click the Expressions tab and you can create fields to be added to your query.

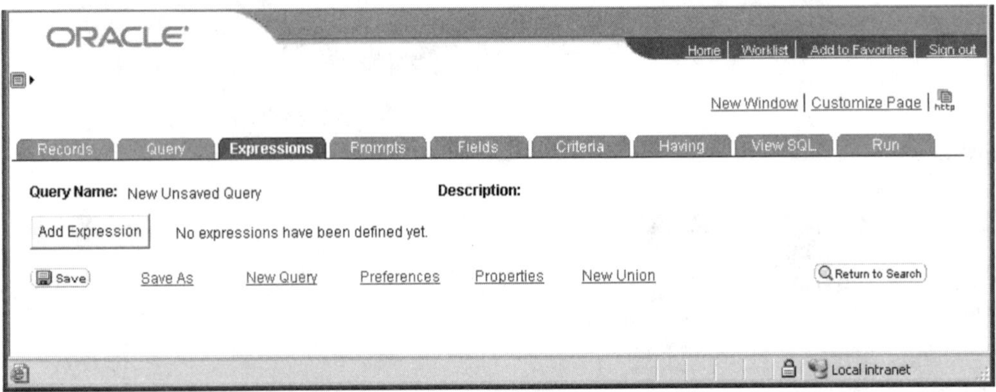

To add an expression, click Add Expression; this will take you to the Edit Expression Properties page.

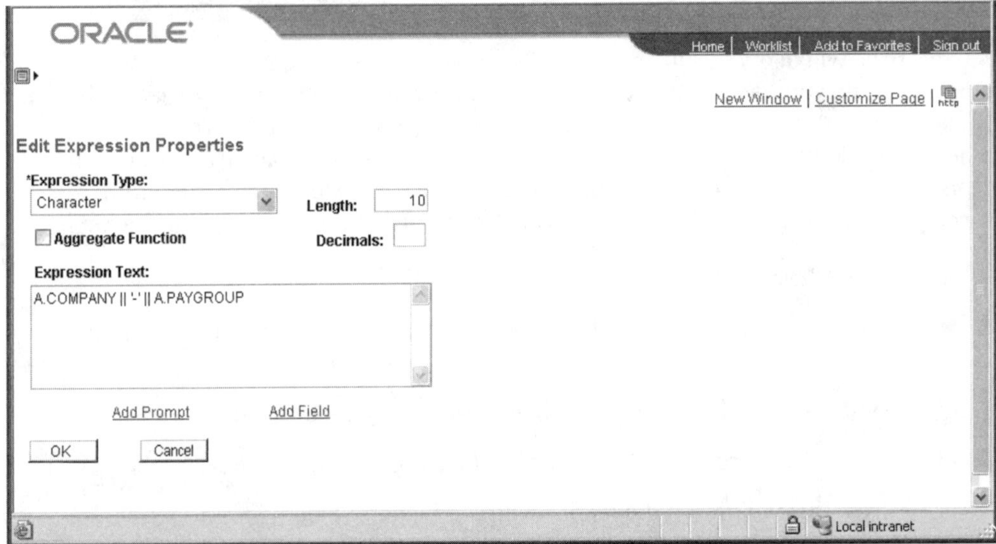

On this page you can determine the Expression Type, Length, and Decimals setting, as well as if it is an aggregate function. You can add a prompt value to your expression or a field from the records that are included in your query.

The following values are valid expression types:

- Character
- Date
- DateTime
- LongCharacter
- Number
- Signed Number
- Time

Enter in your expression in the Expression Text box. You can set up equations, create new fields, and combine fields. The following are examples:

```
A.Company || '-' || A.Paygroup
Round(A.Annual_rate + B.Bonus,2)
```

When you have completed creating your expression, click OK to return to the Expressions page. You can now see the expression you created. This expression can be added to the field's page by clicking the Use As Field link. It will show up at the end of your fields list. If you decide not to include this expression, you can delete it by clicking the Delete icon. You can go back and edit this expression at any time by clicking Edit. There is also an option to add criteria using this expression by clicking the Criteria icon.

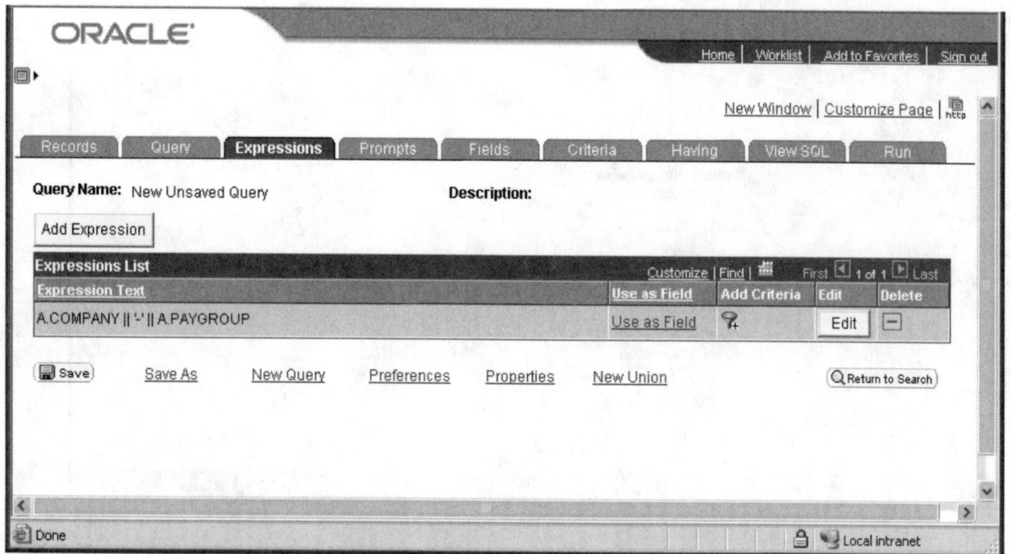

Prompts

To make your query more dynamic, you may want to request information from the end user. This is done by clicking the Prompts tab. Prompts can be set up on this page or from the Criteria setup.

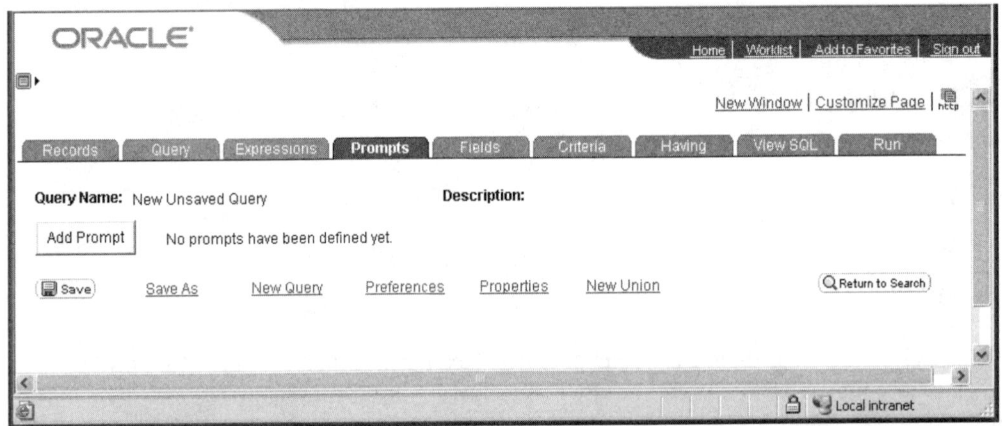

This page will list the prompts that you currently have set up or will allow you to add new ones by clicking Add Prompts. This will take you to the Edit Prompt Properties page.

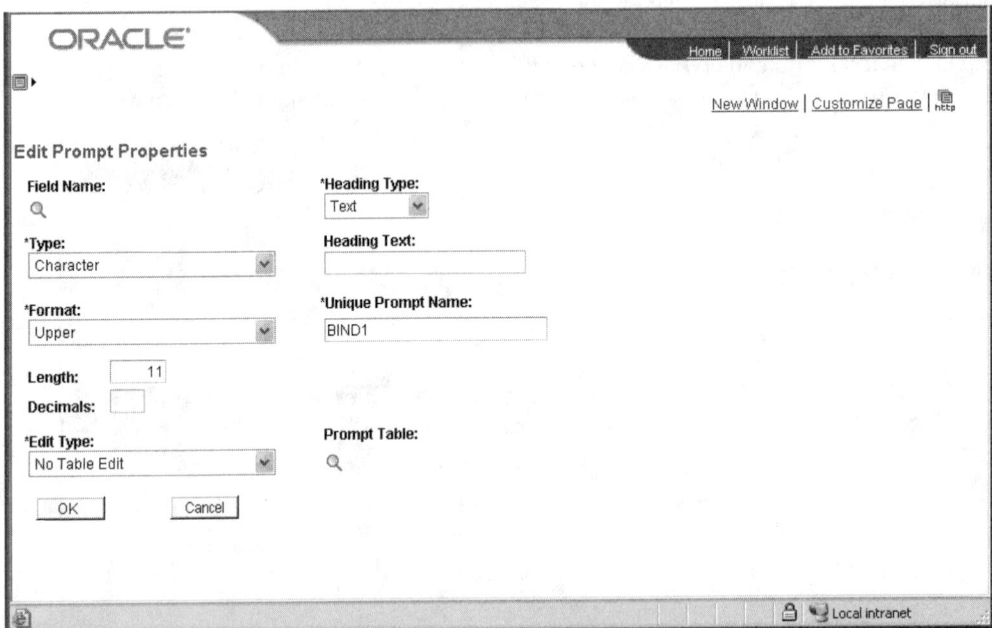

Select a field name by using the Lookup icon. This will list all stored field names. You can refine your search by adding criteria in the Search By field. Double-click the field you want to use as a prompt field.

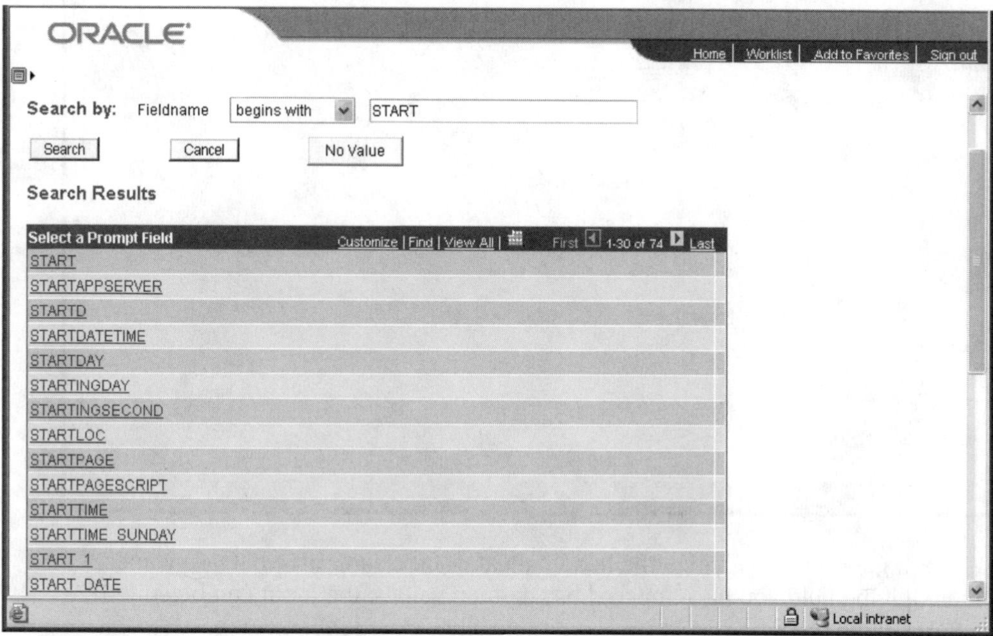

You will then be returned to Edit Prompt Properties. As you can see next, the attributes that are stored with the field are used. These attributes were set up when the field was originally created within PeopleTools.

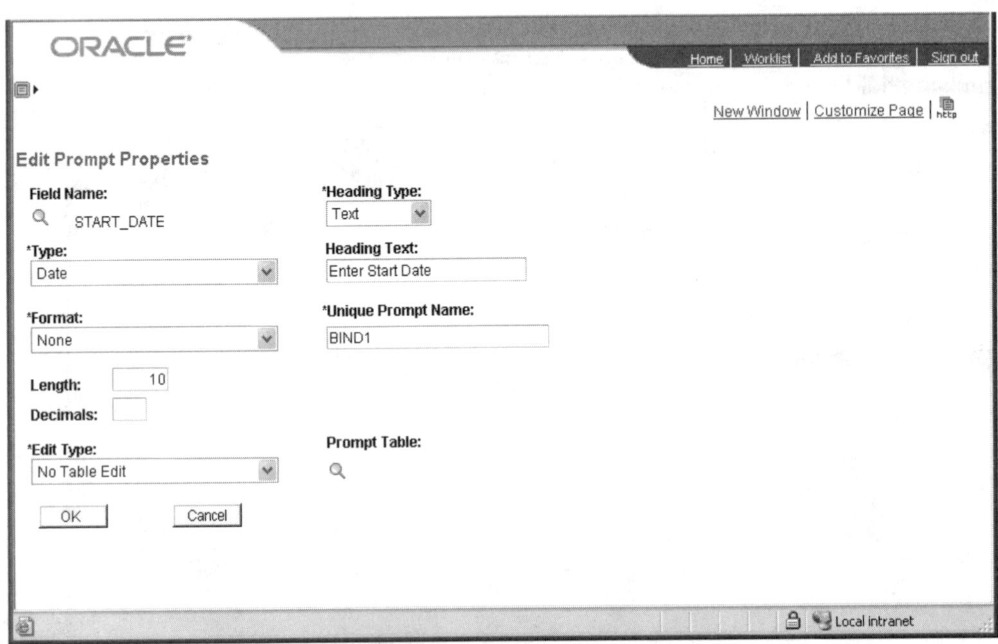

It is a good idea to change the heading text to be clearer on what you want entered. If the field you have entered has defined values, the input can be edited against a table or xlatvalues (limited defined values stored in the database for this field). There are three types of Edit Types:

- **No Table Edit** Data entered will not be validated.
- **Prompt Table** You add a prompt table that the input would be validated against.
- **Translate Table** Validates against the translate table attached to this field.

When you are done with the prompt properties, click OK. This will return you to the Prompt page. Your new prompt will now be listed. To edit the prompt, click

Edit; this will return you to the Edit Prompt Properties page. To delete the prompt, click the Delete icon. Continue to add whatever prompts you may need.

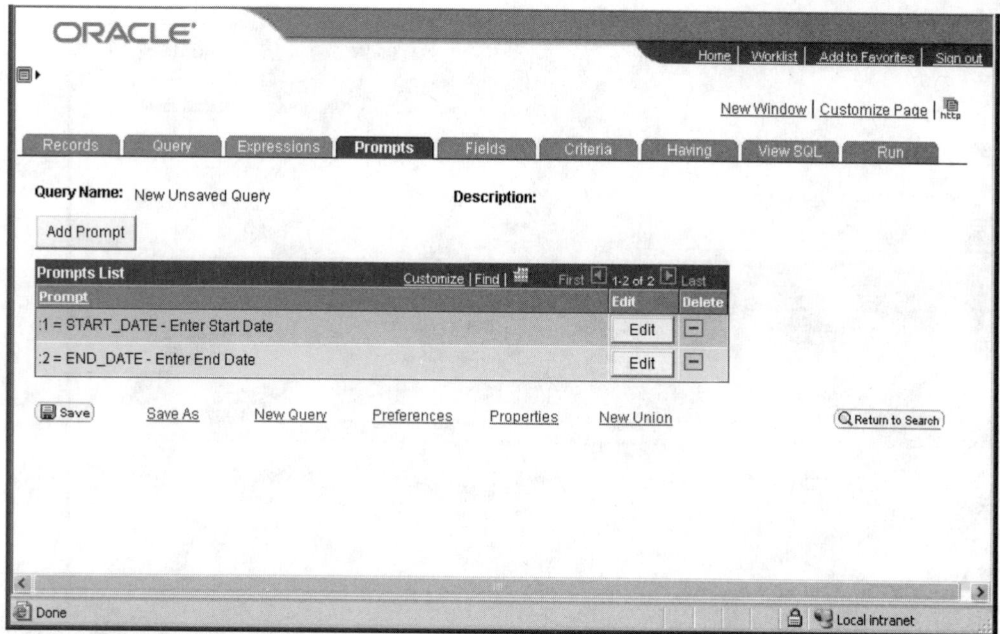

Criteria

After you have selected what fields you want to show in your query, you may want to reduce the amount of data to be returned. If you are creating this query for a manager, they may only want to see their employees or a subset of their organization. You may want to use prompt fields against the data to reduce the records returned. Criteria are equivalent to the where clause in an SQL statement. To subset your data, click the Criteria tab.

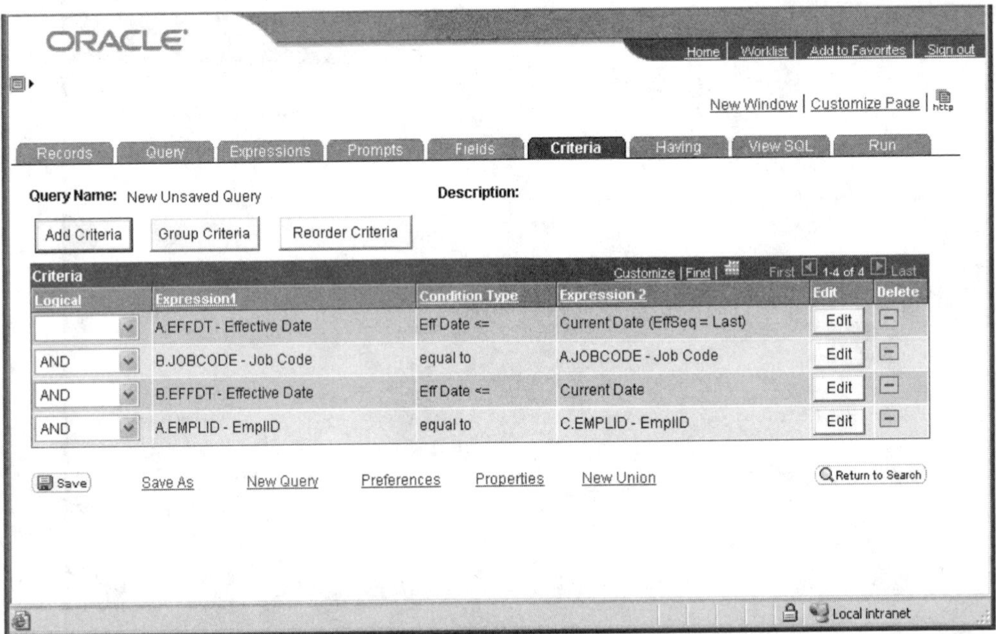

This page will list all the criteria that have been created. As you can see, there are already rows entered. These were created when you added the records. Since one of the records we added had an effective-dated row, criteria were added to only select the max effective date as of current date. This is done using a function Current Date(EffSeq = Last). Criteria were added to join Record A with Record B and Record A with Record C. Each of these criteria uses a Logical operator between each of the criteria statements. The operators "and" and "or" are available for selection. To edit the information of each criterion, click Edit; it will take you to the Edit Criteria Properties. To delete a criterion, click the Delete icon.

Edit Criteria Properties

To add new criteria, click the Add Criteria button. This will take you to the Edit Criteria Properties page.

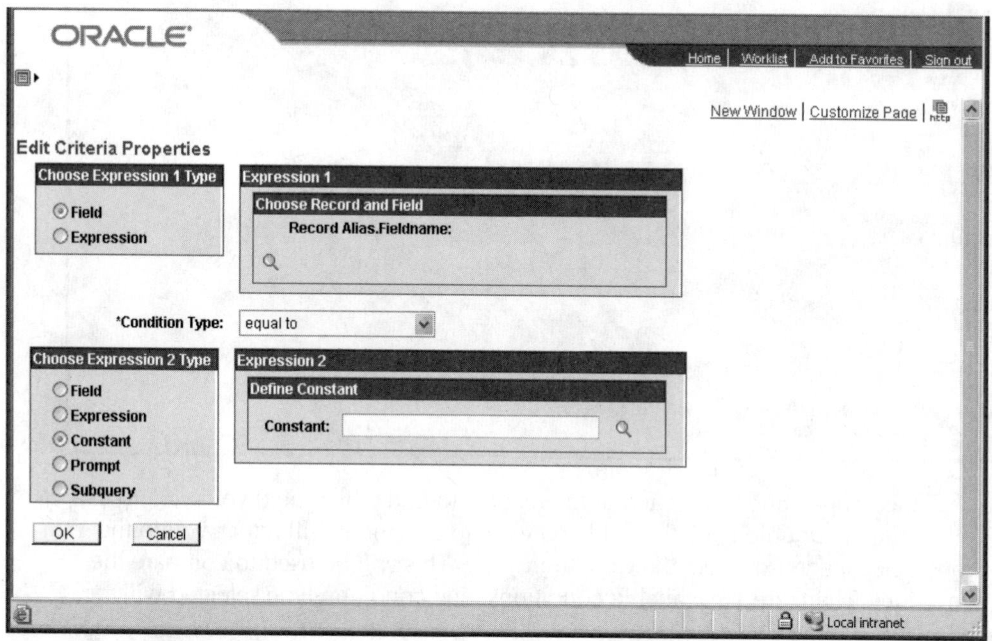

On this page you can use a field or an expression to compare to another field or expression or to a constant or a prompt, or else you can use a subquery. Select the Expression 1 Type. If a field is selected, use the Lookup icon in the Expression 1 box to get a list of fields available for selection. If an expression is selected, click the Expression link to select an expression that you have created.

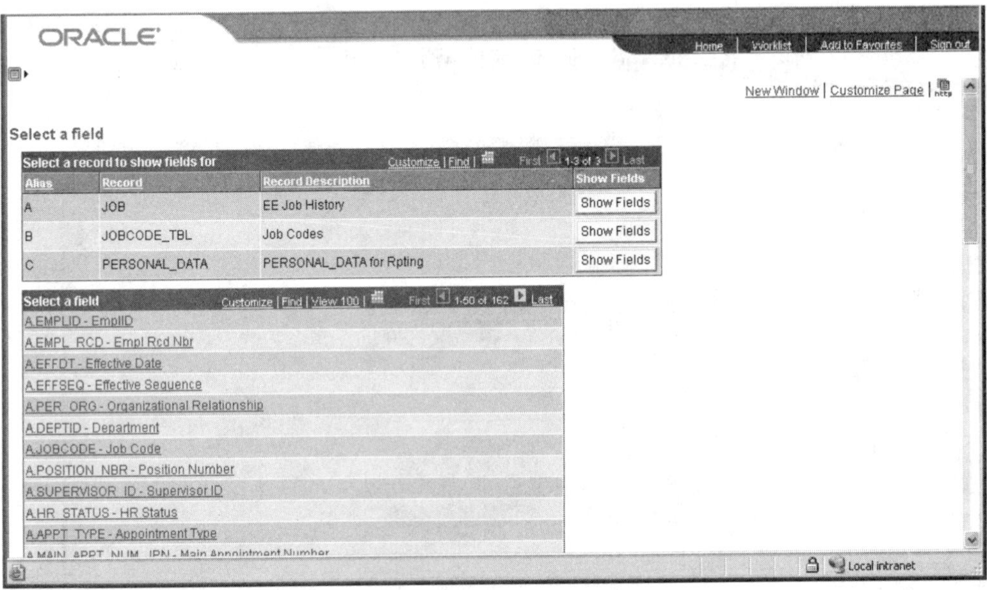

You can open and close each of the records to find which field you want to use in the criteria. Double-click the field you want to use and it will return you to the Properties page. Next select the Condition Type. This will be used to compare the two values. There are 16 available conditions. The condition type selected will determine what information is needed for the Expression 2 box.

- **Between** This will check if the value of Expression 1 is between two other values. In the Expression 2 box you will have to give these two values. This works well with fields, expressions, and prompts.
- **Does not exist** This will check if Expression 1 exists in the Expression 2 value. This is good to use with subqueries.
- **Equal** This will check if Expression 1 equals Expression 2. This works well with all Expression 2 types.
- **Exists** This will check if Expression 1 exists in the Expression 2 value. This is good to use with subqueries.
- **Greater than** This will check if Expression 1 is greater than Expression 2. This works well with all Expression 2 types.
- **In list** This will check if Expression 1 equals one of the values in the list for Expression 2. This works well with all Expression 2 types. If a constant is given, it will allow you to build a list.
- **In tree** Compares the value to a selected set of tree nodes, uses the Select Tree Node List page to create the list.

- **Is not null** This will check if Expression 1 is not null. Expression 2 is not available. Normally used with dates.
- **Is null** This will check if Expression 1 is null. Expression 2 is not available. Normally used with dates.
- **Less than** This will check if Expression 1 is less than Expression 2. This works well with all Expression 2 types.
- **Like** This will check if Expression 1 is like Expression 2. You use the wildcard '%' to add on to partial constants.
- **Not between** This will check if the value of Expression 1 is not between two other values. In the Expression 2 box you will have to give these two values. Works well with fields, expressions, and prompts.
- **Not equal to** This will check if Expression 1 does not equal Expression 2. This works well with all Expression 2 types.
- **Not greater than** This will check if Expression 1 is not greater than Expression 2. Same as less than or equal to. This works well with all Expression 2 types.
- **Not in list** This will check if Expression 1 does not equal one of the values in the list for Expression 2. This works well with all Expression 2 types. If a constant is given, it will allow you to build a list.
- **Not in tree** Compares to a selected set of tree nodes; uses the Select Tree Node List page to create the list that it should not be in.
- **Effective Seq** Used with effective-dated records.

After the condition type has been created, select from the Expression 2 Type. You have more choices here.

- **Field** This is a field within one of the records you have included in the query.
- **Expression** This is an expression you created in the Expression tab.
- **Constant** This is any value you key.
- **Prompt** This is a prompt that you can create at this time, using the lookup icon or selecting one that you have already created from the prompt page. A list of prompts will be provided if you select the prompt number.
- **Subquery** This allows you to create another query to use as validation within your current query. It will be shown in the Advanced Query topics.

Once you are done setting up your criteria properties, click OK to return to the Criteria page. You page will now look something like the following.

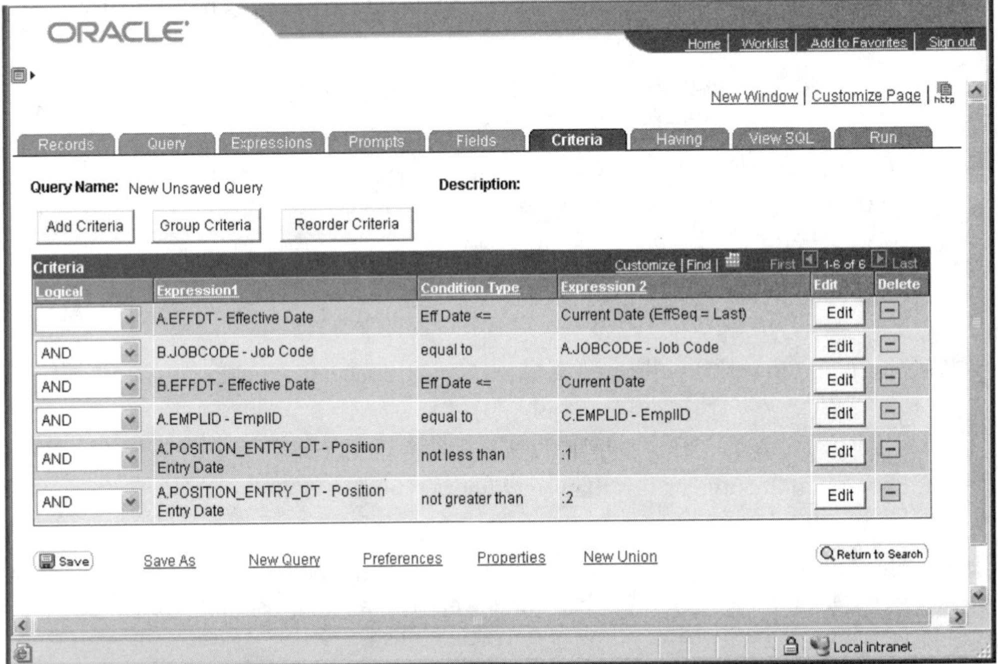

Group Criteria

After you have entered your criteria, you may need to group them, so that you pull the correct data. This can be done by clicking Group Criteria. On this page you can enter parentheses around the criteria that you need grouped together. This is normally useful when you have "or" conditions. Click OK to return to the Criteria page.

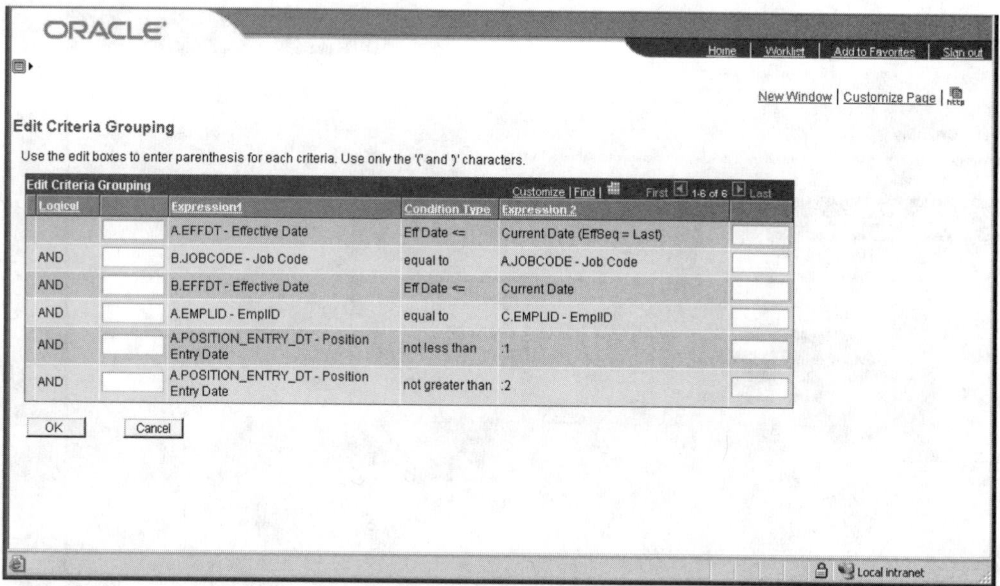

Reorder Criteria

Since criteria can be added from multiple pages of the Query Manager, they may not be in the order needed for your grouping. Click Reorder Criteria to change the order of the criteria. It works the same as reordering your fields. Enter a number from 1 to the number of criteria you have in the list. When you click OK, you can see the new order on the Criteria page.

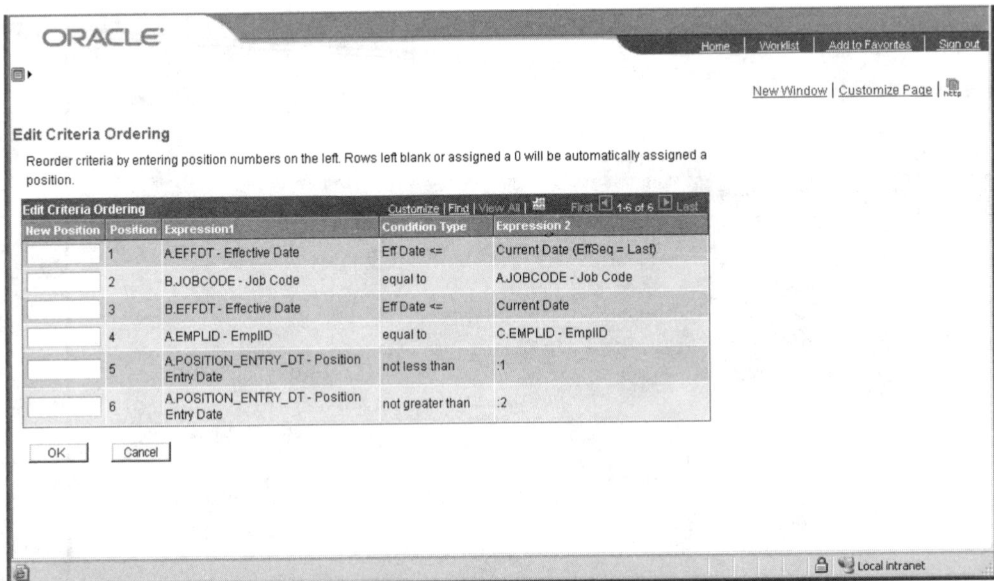

Saving

Before we test our query, we should save it, in case we have done something incorrectly that locks up the computer. We do not want to lose all the work we have done. At the bottom of the screen, there are buttons and links. Click Save.

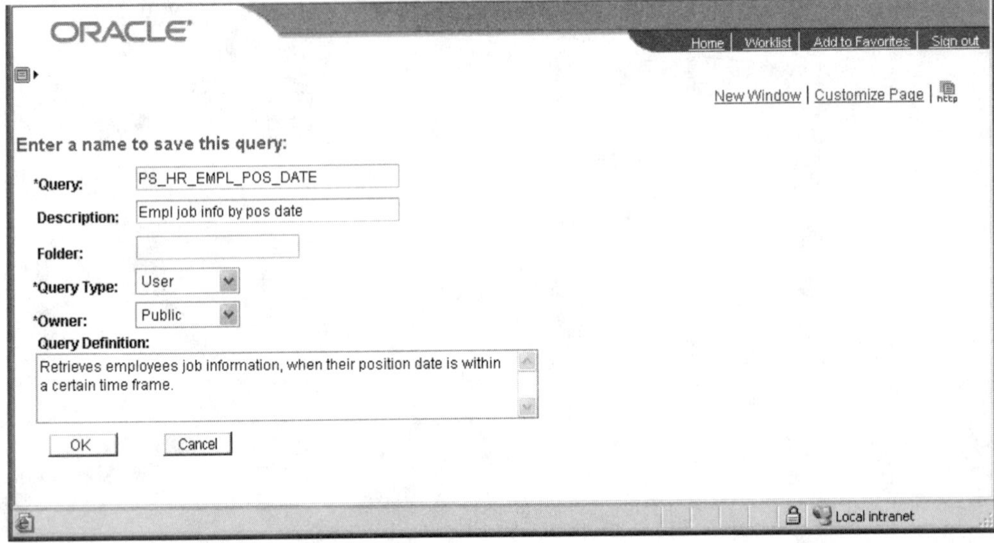

Enter a name for your query. Try to structure your names so that they are meaningful and easy for the customers to find. Enter a description for the query. If want to keep separate folders, enter a folder name. Folders can also be assigned later if you do not have the structure created yet. Set the query type and owner of the query to public or private. Private will let only the creator run and view the query. Public will allow anybody with access to the records to run the query. The Query definition is to document the query and track change control that is needed for audits. Click OK when you are done.

Previewing

Now it is time to test your query. Throughout this chapter we have been building a query, so let's look at the results. Click the Run tab to start your query. If you have any prompts set up, they will be displayed, as shown here.

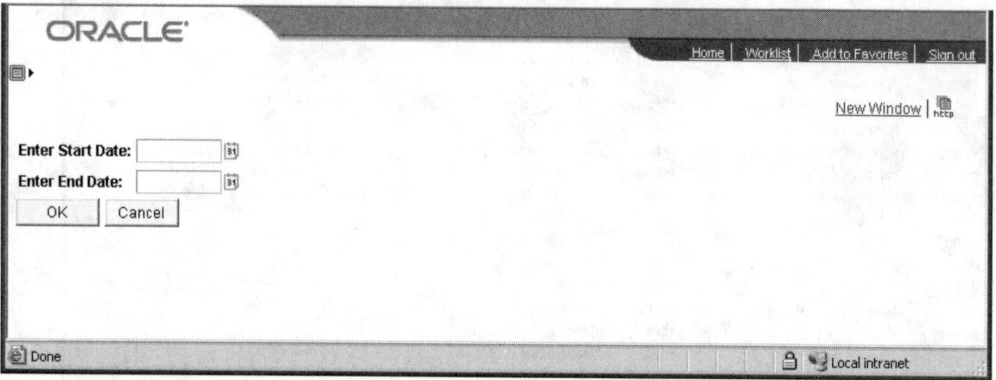

This page is asking for start and end dates. Since these are date fields, Query Manager provides a Calendar icon to help the end user select a valid date. After valid dates have been entered and the OK button has been selected the query will continue. The results will be displayed as a grid. The following page is a sample of the results created by the query.

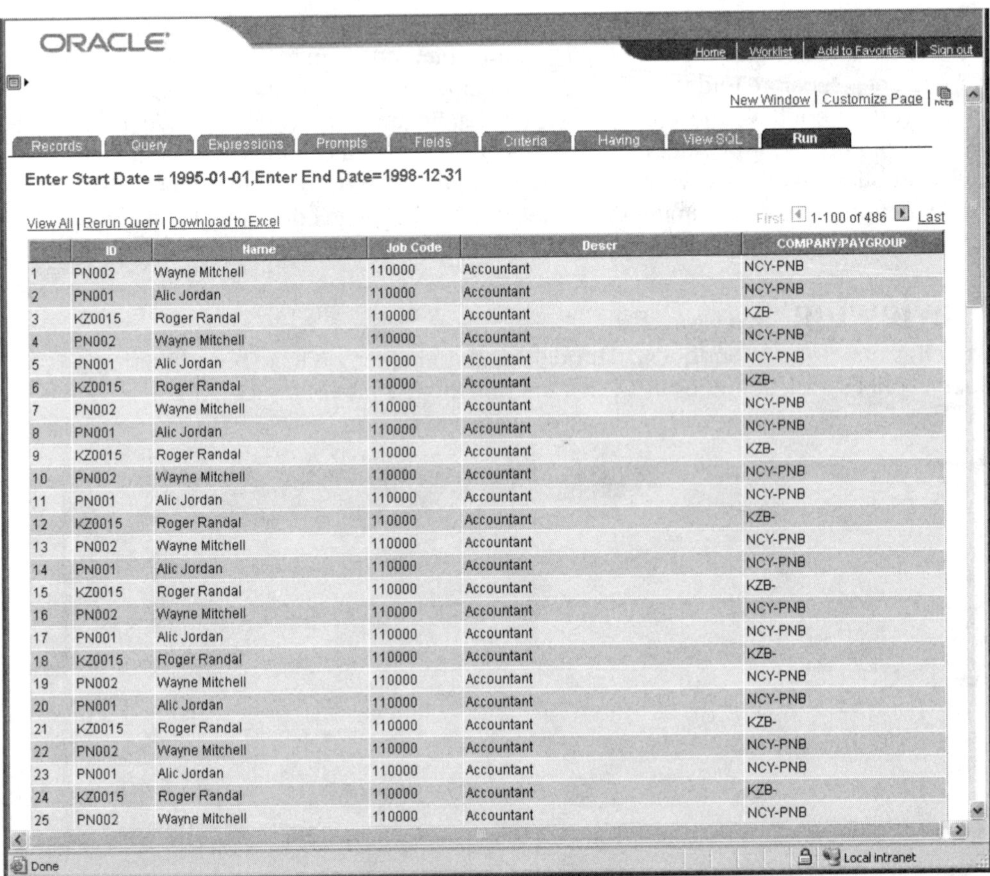

	ID	Name	Job Code	Descr	COMPANY/PAYGROUP
1	PN002	Wayne Mitchell	110000	Accountant	NCY-PNB
2	PN001	Alic Jordan	110000	Accountant	NCY-PNB
3	KZ0015	Roger Randal	110000	Accountant	KZB-
4	PN002	Wayne Mitchell	110000	Accountant	NCY-PNB
5	PN001	Alic Jordan	110000	Accountant	NCY-PNB
6	KZ0015	Roger Randal	110000	Accountant	KZB-
7	PN002	Wayne Mitchell	110000	Accountant	NCY-PNB
8	PN001	Alic Jordan	110000	Accountant	NCY-PNB
9	KZ0015	Roger Randal	110000	Accountant	KZB-
10	PN002	Wayne Mitchell	110000	Accountant	NCY-PNB
11	PN001	Alic Jordan	110000	Accountant	NCY-PNB
12	KZ0015	Roger Randal	110000	Accountant	KZB-
13	PN002	Wayne Mitchell	110000	Accountant	NCY-PNB
14	PN001	Alic Jordan	110000	Accountant	NCY-PNB
15	KZ0015	Roger Randal	110000	Accountant	KZB-
16	PN002	Wayne Mitchell	110000	Accountant	NCY-PNB
17	PN001	Alic Jordan	110000	Accountant	NCY-PNB
18	KZ0015	Roger Randal	110000	Accountant	KZB-
19	PN002	Wayne Mitchell	110000	Accountant	NCY-PNB
20	PN001	Alic Jordan	110000	Accountant	NCY-PNB
21	KZ0015	Roger Randal	110000	Accountant	KZB-
22	PN002	Wayne Mitchell	110000	Accountant	NCY-PNB
23	PN001	Alic Jordan	110000	Accountant	NCY-PNB
24	KZ0015	Roger Randal	110000	Accountant	KZB-
25	PN002	Wayne Mitchell	110000	Accountant	NCY-PNB

While you are on this screen, you have the following options:

- **View All** View all the results.
- **Rerun Query** Rerun the query with different input values.
- **Download to Excel** Query results will open up in Excel so that they can be saved or manipulated within Excel.

When you are done viewing the results, click any of the tabs to return to the Query Manager pages. At this point, you can make changes to your query, create a new query, or save your query.

Advanced

So far you have learned how to create basic queries by selecting fields, creating prompts, and setting up criteria. This is how you will create the majority of the queries required by your end users. Query Manager does provide some other pages to help with advanced types of requests.

View SQL

Query Manager is building the SQL required to pull the data from the database. On the View SQL tab, you can see how the information you have entered into Query Manager has been converted into SQL. This SQL is useful if you are having problems pulling the correct data. If you have other tools (like SQL Plus, Toad), you can copy the SQL and play with it in these tools. It is also helpful to view the SQL and see if you have grouped your criteria correctly. The following screen shows a sample of how your SQL may look.

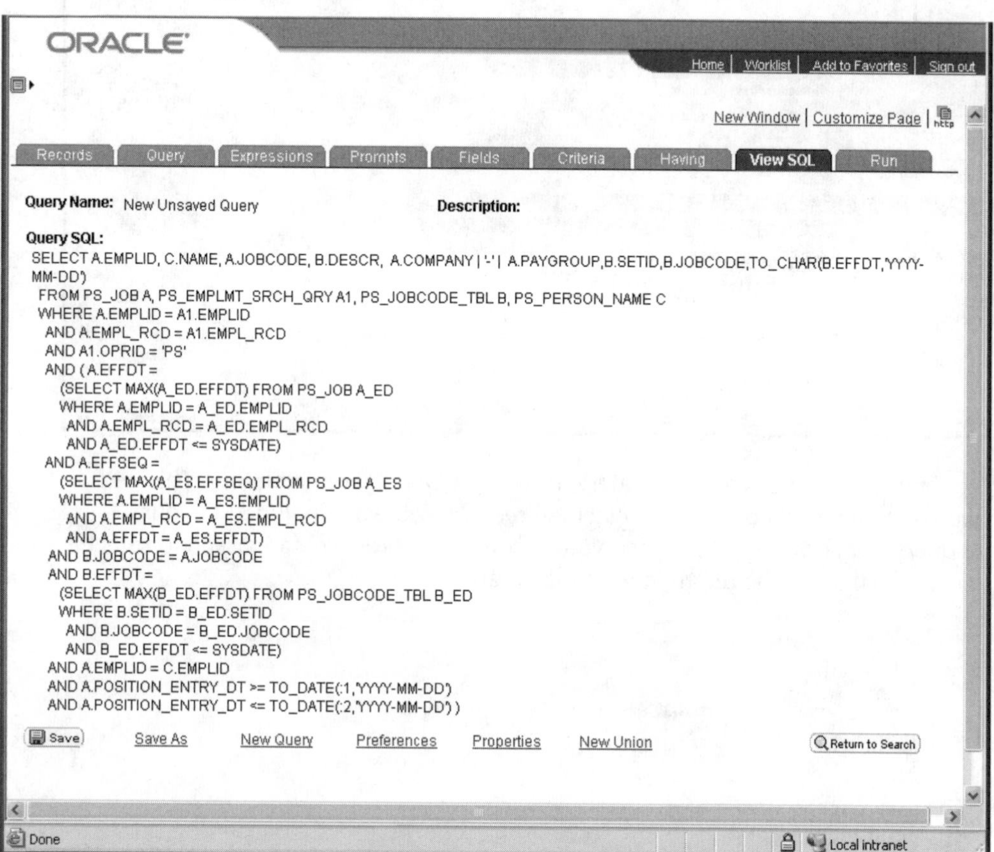

Subquery

Subqueries can be used within the criteria properties. Use subqueries when you need to compare a field against the results of another query. The results of the query must be the same field type that is being compared. An example could be if you want to select only IDs of employees who have not taken the safety course. Another may be you do not want to select the latest effective row from the job record. You may want to pick the latest row, for instance, according to a date given by the end user. Using the query we have created so far, we are going to change the effective-dated record to use a subquery to get the latest row based on the end date given by the end user. The following page shows how to set up the Edit Criteria Properties page.

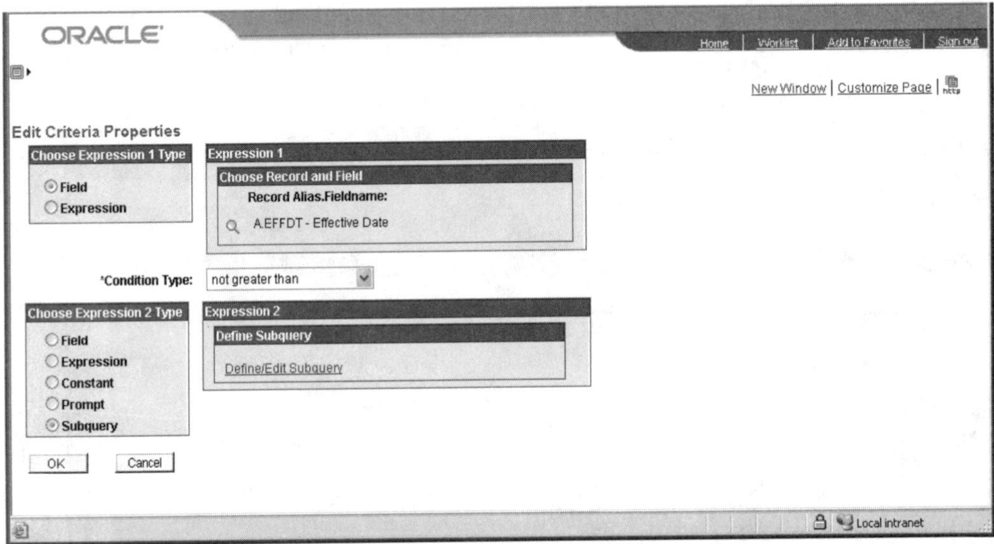

The Expression 2 type is Subquery; now click Define/Edit Subquery. This will take you to the Records page to select the records you want included in your subquery. Once you have selected your record or records, you are asked to select a single field that will be returned from this query.

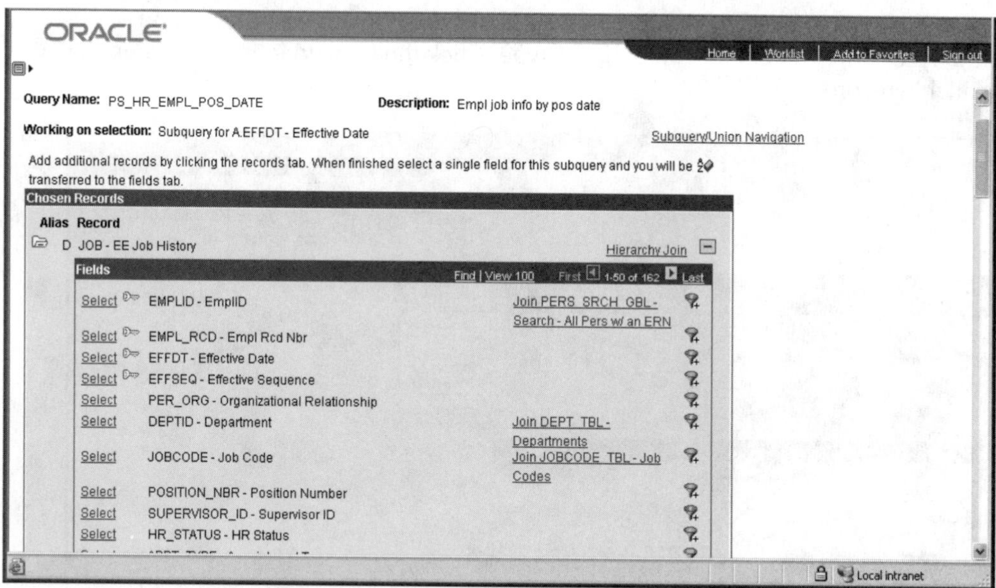

This field will be added to your field's page. For this example we want to get the max value of a field, so we are not going to select a record; we are going to create an expression.

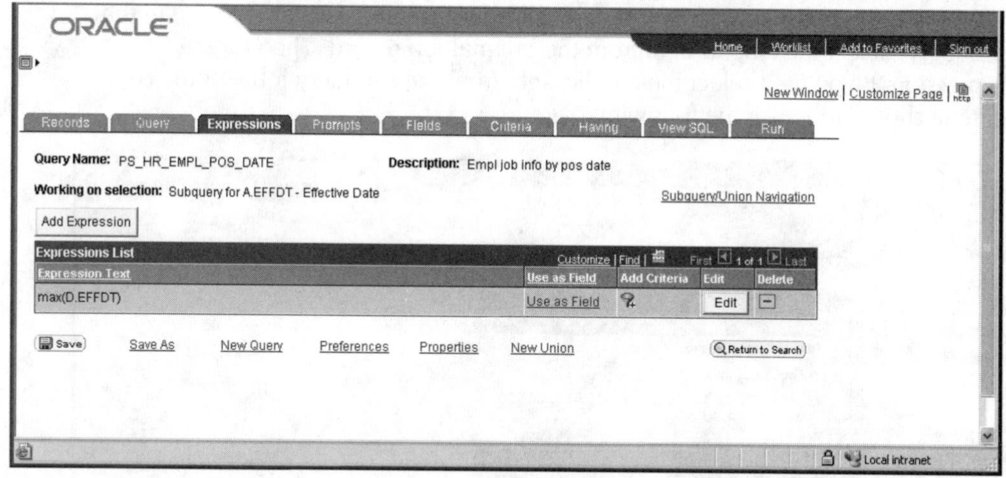

In this expression we are using the aggregate function of "max" to return the latest effective date from the query. This is the field that will be returned in the query, so click the Use As Field link so that it will be added to the Fields page. Now we have to add criteria for the subquery. First we need to join our Job record from our original query to the job record in our subquery, so that it will get the correct employee. Select a field for Expression 1 type. Click the Lookup icon to bring up the available records.

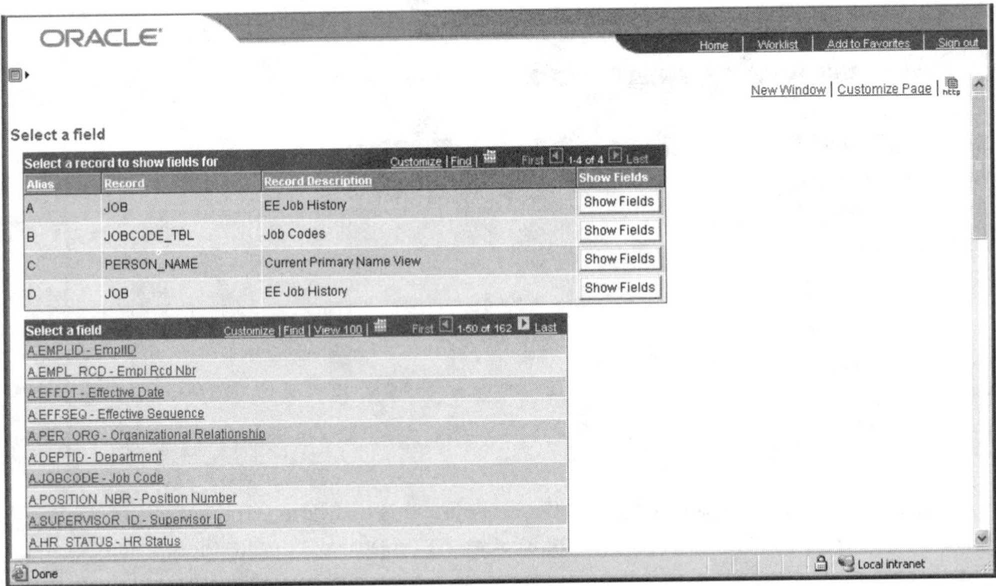

As you see, the records from the original query are also available to use in the subquery. Select the emplid field from the original job record. Then for the Expression 2 type field select the emplid field from the subquery job record. Your criteria should look like the following page:

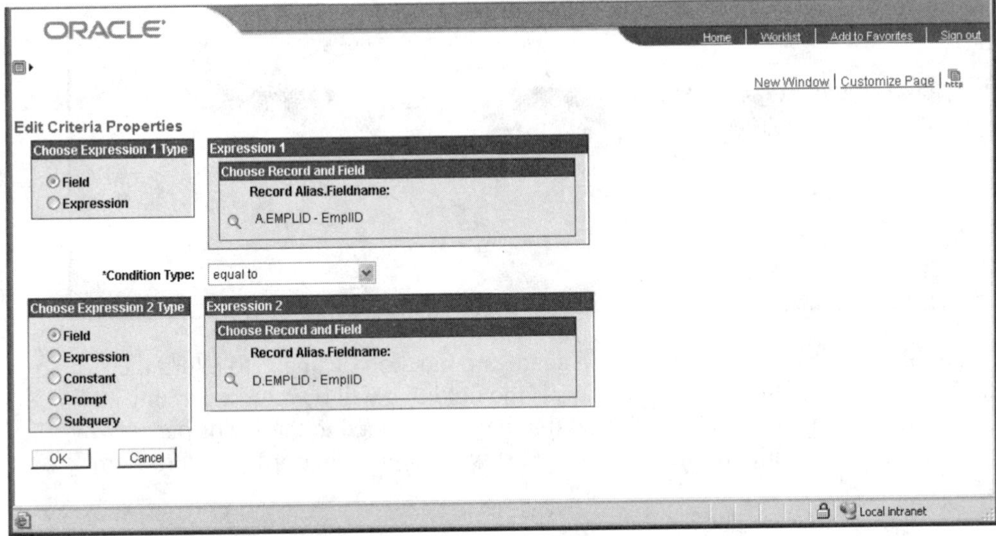

Now we need to have the effdt from the subquery job record to use the prompt field created in the original query. All prompts created in the original query and in the subquery are available for selection. Your criteria should look like the following page:

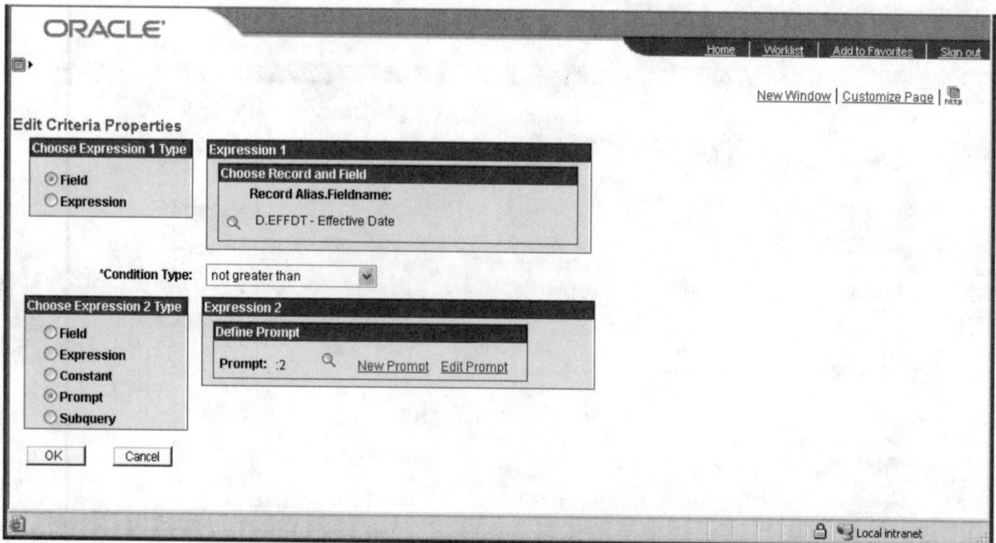

Since you are using a subquery, a navigation link has been provided to go to each query. Click the Subquery/Union Navigation link to go to the following page:

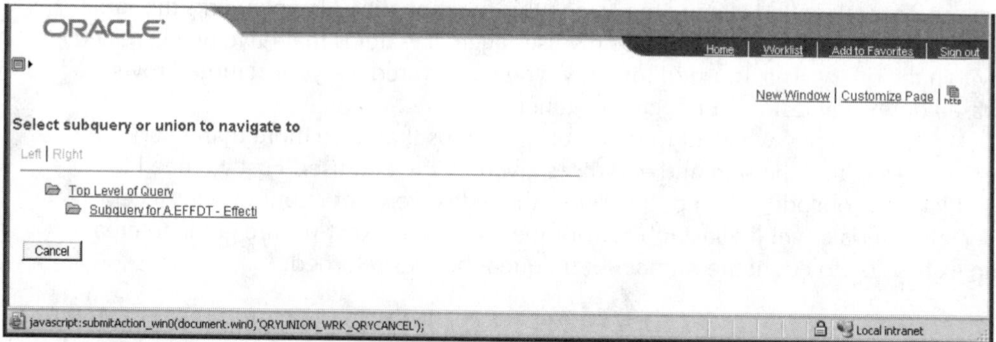

This page will allow you to move from the main query to any queries or unions that have been created. Click the link for the Top Level Of Query to return to the main query. Now we are ready to run our modified query. It still requires us to enter the start and end dates. The following is a sample of the query results.

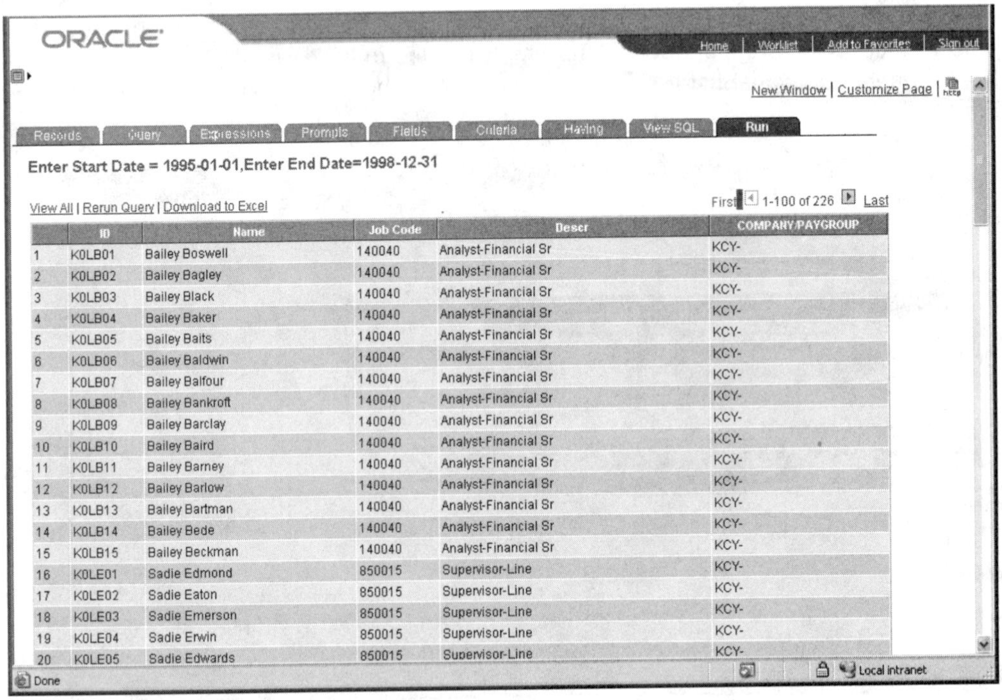

ORACLE

Home | Worklist | Add to Favorites | Sign out

New Window | Customize Page | http

Records | Query | Expressions | Prompts | Fields | Criteria | Having | View SQL | Run

Enter Start Date = 1995-01-01,Enter End Date=1998-12-31

View All | Rerun Query | Download to Excel

First 1-100 of 226 Last

	ID	Name	Job Code	Descr	COMPANY/PAYGROUP
1	KOLB01	Bailey Boswell	140040	Analyst-Financial Sr	KCY-
2	KOLB02	Bailey Bagley	140040	Analyst-Financial Sr	KCY-
3	KOLB03	Bailey Black	140040	Analyst-Financial Sr	KCY-
4	KOLB04	Bailey Baker	140040	Analyst-Financial Sr	KCY-
5	KOLB05	Bailey Baits	140040	Analyst-Financial Sr	KCY-
6	KOLB06	Bailey Baldwin	140040	Analyst-Financial Sr	KCY-
7	KOLB07	Bailey Balfour	140040	Analyst-Financial Sr	KCY-
8	KOLB08	Bailey Bankroft	140040	Analyst-Financial Sr	KCY-
9	KOLB09	Bailey Barclay	140040	Analyst-Financial Sr	KCY-
10	KOLB10	Bailey Baird	140040	Analyst-Financial Sr	KCY-
11	KOLB11	Bailey Barney	140040	Analyst-Financial Sr	KCY-
12	KOLB12	Bailey Barlow	140040	Analyst-Financial Sr	KCY-
13	KOLB13	Bailey Bartman	140040	Analyst-Financial Sr	KCY-
14	KOLB14	Bailey Bede	140040	Analyst-Financial Sr	KCY-
15	KOLB15	Bailey Beckman	140040	Analyst-Financial Sr	KCY-
16	KOLE01	Sadie Edmond	850015	Supervisor-Line	KCY-
17	KOLE02	Sadie Eaton	850015	Supervisor-Line	KCY-
18	KOLE03	Sadie Emerson	850015	Supervisor-Line	KCY-
19	KOLE04	Sadie Erwin	850015	Supervisor-Line	KCY-
20	KOLE05	Sadie Edwards	850015	Supervisor-Line	KCY-

Done | Local intranet

Having

Since you cannot use an aggregate field in the selection criteria, the Query Manager has another tab called Having to provide this functionality. Having works the same way as the Criteria page, except it only uses aggregate fields that have been created within the query. This is useful for when you want to reduce your returned rows based on the values of your aggregate function.

In this example, we want to return only the jobs that have more than five employees within the start and end dates given by the end user. First we need to add Job and Jobcode_tbl, and then select the fields we want in our query. Accept default criteria to get the last job row for the employee. Next we are going to create an expression to count the number of unique jobcodes returned.

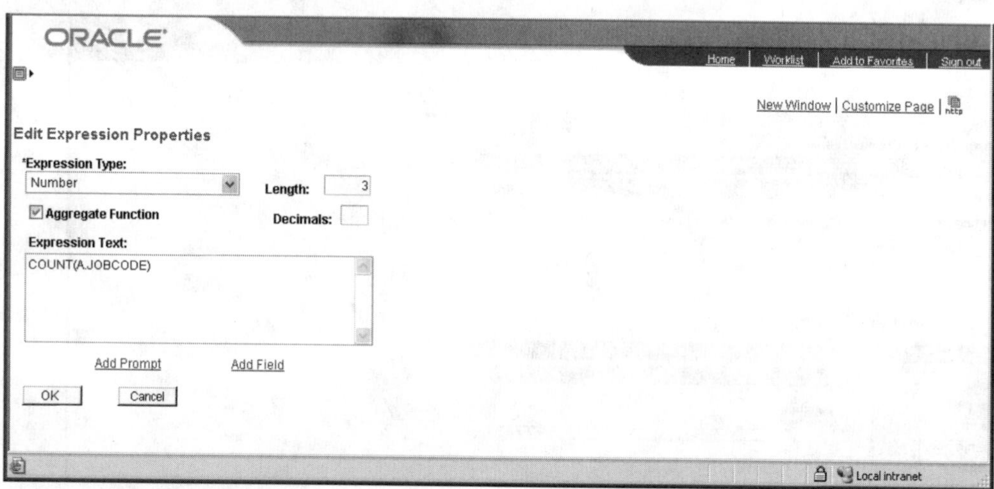

Use this expression as a field in your query. Now click the Having tab. It will take you to the following page. If any automatic having criteria had been created, they would show up on this page.

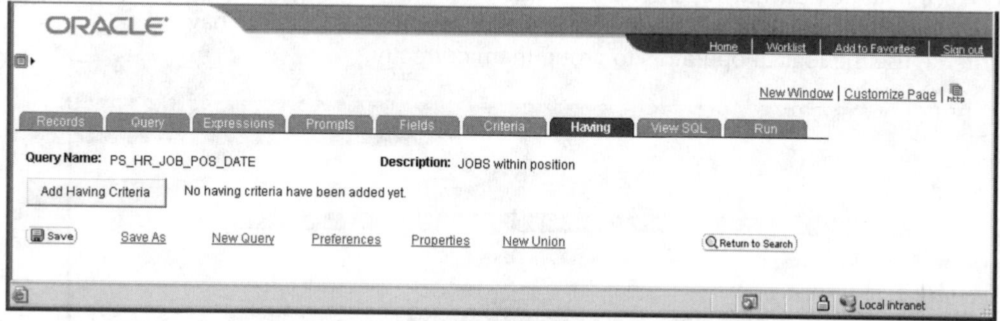

Next click Add Having Criteria to go to the Having Criteria Properties page. It works the same as the Selection Criteria Properties page except that your Expression 1 should be an aggregate function value. In this example we only want to show jobcodes that have more than five employees attached to them.

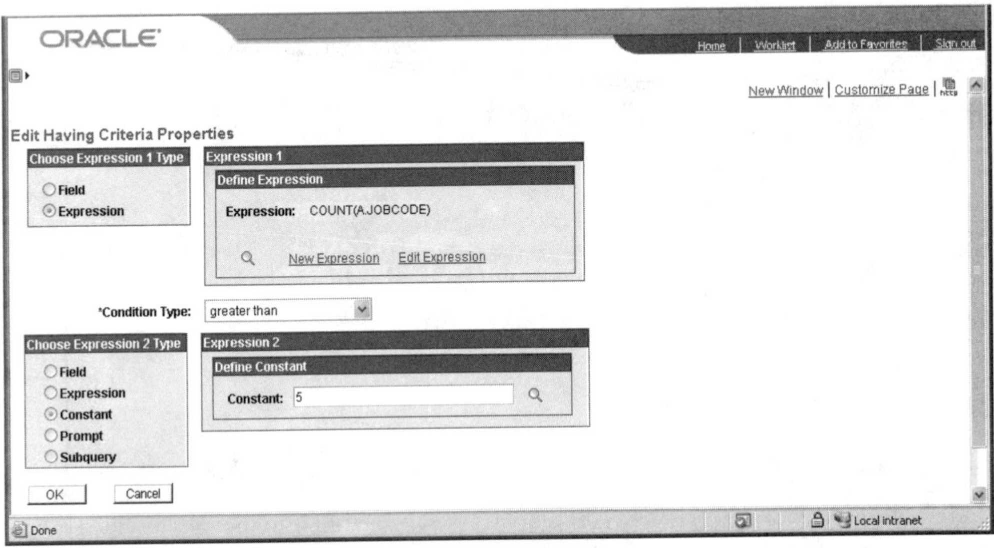

When you are done with the page, click OK to return to the Having page. You can see that the new having criteria have been added. To change the criteria, click Edit. To delete the criteria, click the Delete icon. If you have multiple having criteria, use the logical operators to group them correctly.

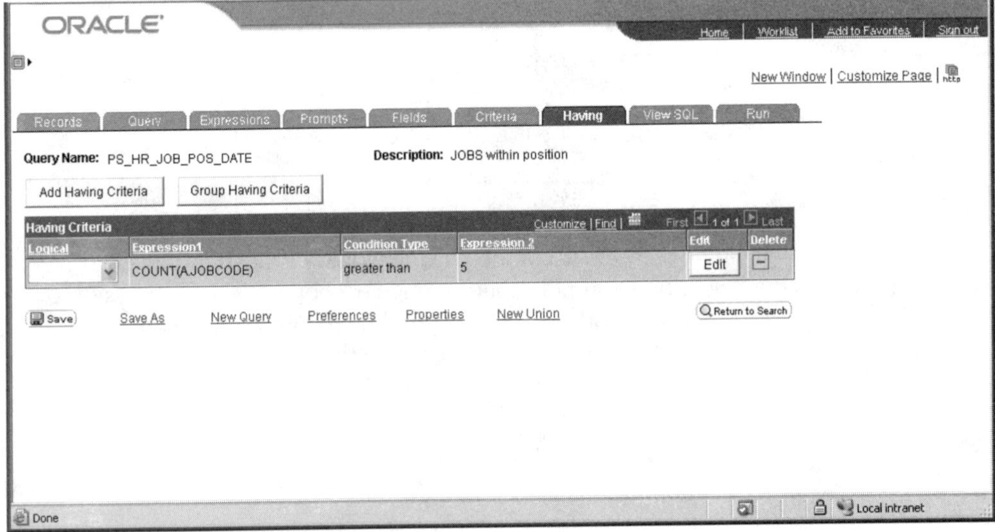

Now that we have set up our query, let us run it and view the results. The following is a sample of the report using the start and end dates given.

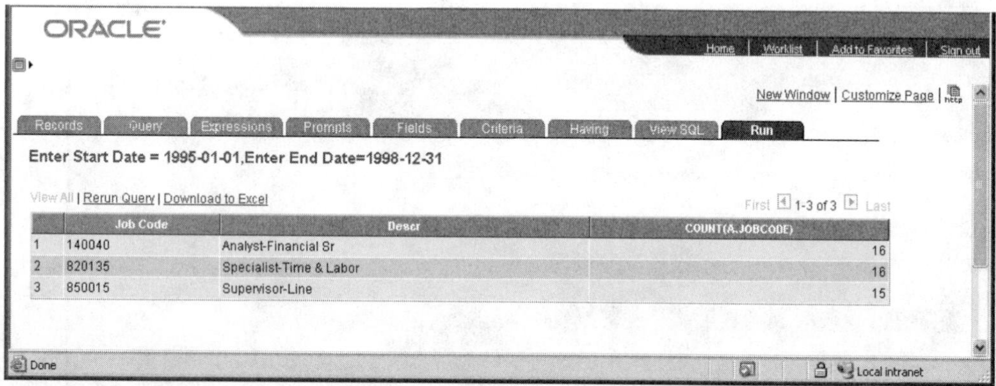

New Union

Query Manager allows for unions between two queries. This will return data from more than one query at the same time. The NewUnion link is at the bottom of the page. After you have created your first query, you can click this link to create other queries. There are a few requirements to use the Union function.

- Selected fields must be the same.
- Fields must have the same data type.
- Column must have the same display order.

Navigation between the unions is the same as when you have a subquery. You can click the Subquery/Union Navigation link to view the hierarchical list of queries.

Scheduling

Queries can be scheduled through the Process Scheduler. This is another way you can get information to your end users, without giving them access to Query Manager. End users can view output using the Report Manager. Go to Reporting Tools | Query | Schedule Query to get to the Schedule query page.

Select or create a Run Control ID for this request. Select the query name that you want to schedule. There is a Search button to look up the available queries. Enter in a description of the query. If any prompts are needed, use the Update

Parameters link to provide the values. Click Save to save the changes you have made to this page.

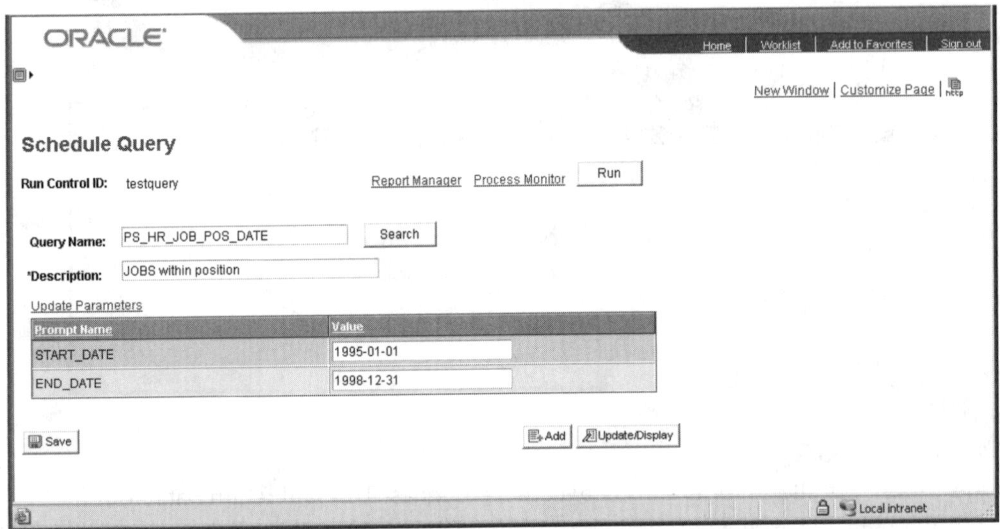

To submit the request, click Run. On this page you can set up the following:

- **Server Name** Name of server that the job should run on.
- **Recurrence** Set up when this job should run if it should recur.
- **Time Zone** Defaults to system time zone.
- **Run Date** Set to the first date you want this to start running.
- **Run Time** Set to the time you want this to start running.
- **Format** Select the output format.
- **Distribution** Click the link to define detail distribution criteria.

Click OK to set the request up to run. Your job will run when the criteria you have set up have been met. You can view the status by using the Process Monitor. The query results can be viewed by using the Report Manager.

Query Viewer

Query Viewer is provided for end users who need to view and print only queries that have been provided for them. These end users do not have access to the Query Manager. You can find the Query Viewer by navigating to Reporting Tools | Queries | Query Viewer.

End users can search for queries that they have the permissions to view. They can run the query, but they must select how they want the output to be displayed. They can select HTML or Excel. Here is a sample of what an end user may see while in Query Viewer.

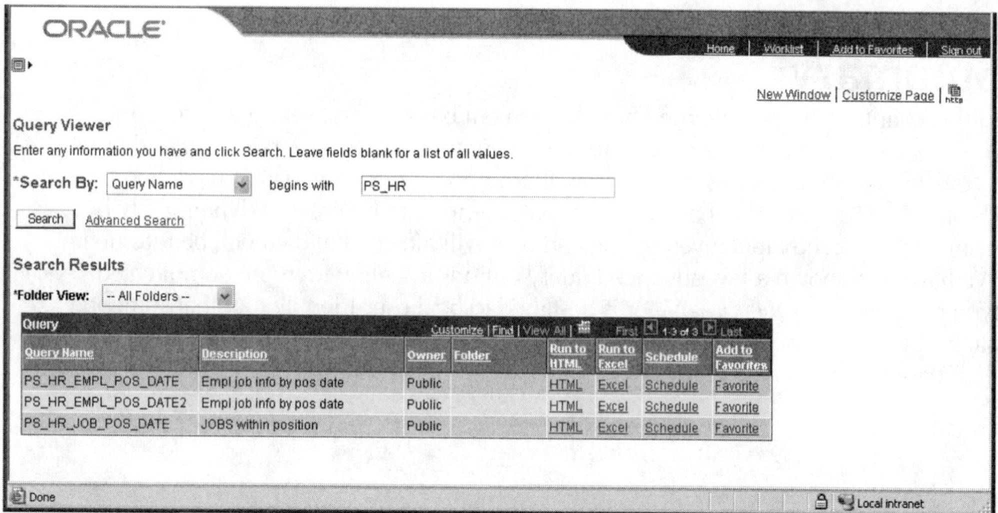

Query Tables

The objects that are created within the Query Manager are stored in tables. For example, PSQRYFIELD stores the names of all the fields used in a query. This has a Field SELNUM, which is also included on PSQRYSELECT, which stores details of select requirements. Then PSQRYCRITERIA holds details of criteria, and so on. The SQL that you see on the SQL tab is generated on the basis of all these tables rather than being stored on a particular table. The full list of tables involved in Query is as follows:

- **PSQRYFIELD** Stores all fields used in all aspects of query operation.
- **PSQRYDEFN** Stores high-level query definitions with version numbers. Non-English definitions are stored in PSQRYDEFNLANG and PSQRYHEADLANG.
- **PSQRYRECORD** Stores all records used in all aspects of query creation.
- **PSQRYSELECT** Stores all SELECT requirements by select type, including union, subselect, join.
- **PSQRYCRITERIA** Stores all criteria expressions in code format.

- **PSQRYBIND** Stores runtime prompt data.
- **PSQRYEXPR** Stores the text associated with each criteria expression.
- **PSQRYLINK** Stores the relationships to child queries.

Summary

In this chapter you have learned how to create a basic query, set up the tree, and provide access to the tables needed for the query to run. You can train your end users to create their own queries or just show them how to run queries that have been created for their use. You have learned that queries can be created dynamically by using prompts. The input given by the end user will affect what data will be returned. We have also shown a few advanced query options to help with more complicated type requests. The Query Manager is designed to be a user-friendly tool that someone can use without any programming background, but users do need to understand how their data is stored in the database.

CHAPTER 10

Structured Query Reporting

his chapter introduces the Structured Query Reporting (SQR) programming language used for extracting data from the database, reporting, and writing files. We will look at how SQR uses Structured Query Language (SQL) to communicate with relational databases. The SQR tool has its own language and structure; when used with SQL, it can produce reports and files. You will learn SQR procedures, commands, and functions that will enable you to produce informative files and reports. PeopleSoft recommends that SQR be used only for reporting because application edits are not applied when data is changed using the SQL commands.

Prior to PeopleTools release 8.46, SQR was the main reporting tool delivered with the PeopleSoft suite. PeopleSoft bought the SQR code a few versions ago before Brio was bought by Hyperion. Since then there have been many enhancements to SQR, but PeopleSoft ships with an old version. The latest version is now part of a suite with pixel-perfect reports such as W2 statements and can be had from Oracle (which bought Hyperion) with additional licensing costs. The name "SQR" has been largely retired from the Hyperion version; it is now simply a part of the Production Reporting component of Hyperion System 9. If you want to leverage your staff's SQR expertise, SQR Integrator is a third-party add-on for ETL and uses SQR to do the data warehouse. It has a GUI drag-and-drop business process mapping layer, which becomes the SQR program.

SQR Basics

SQRs can be run through the process scheduler, an editor tool, and most scheduling software. It is a powerful tool that can be used to update, change, and delete data. The following section will discuss different editing tools and how SQR programs are processed.

Editors

A variety of tools can be used to create your SQR program. Any basic text editor will work (for example, Notepad or WordPad). There are free shareware products, such as Programmer's File Editor, that allow the processing of SQR outside of

PeopleSoft. There are also products that can be purchased that were created to run SQRs (SQR Runner). These products can edit and validate the SQR written before it is added to the application. Using any of these products requires access to the database. The following illustrations show how the code would look in each of these tools.

Using Notepad is the easiest method, but there are no editing functions to help with structure or formatting. To run an SQR, you must use a bat file or the application, as shown here.

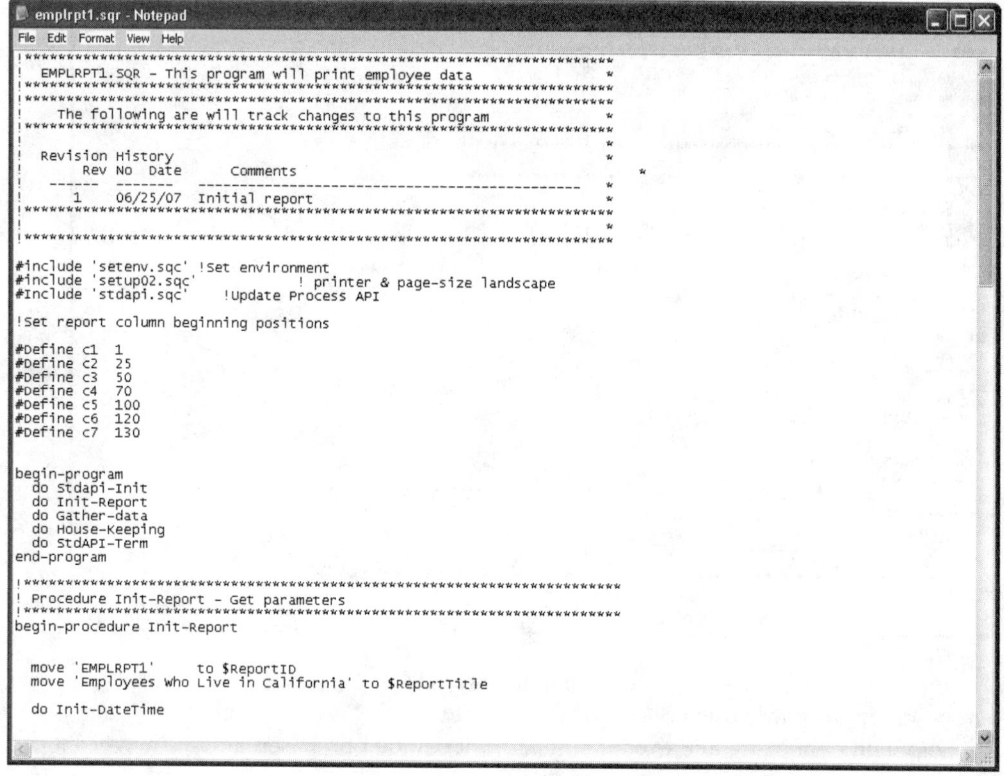

```
emplrpt1.sqr - Notepad
File Edit Format View Help
!****************************************************************************
!  EMPLRPT1.SQR - This program will print employee data                    *
!****************************************************************************
!****************************************************************************
!    The following are will track changes to this program                  *
!****************************************************************************
!                                                                          *
!  Revision History                                                        *
!       Rev No  Date      Comments                                         *
!    ------  -------  --------------------------------------------         *
!      1    06/25/07  Initial report                                       *
!****************************************************************************
!                                                                          *
!****************************************************************************

#include 'setenv.sqc' !Set environment
#include 'setup02.sqc'            ! printer & page-size landscape
#Include 'stdapi.sqc'    !Update Process API

!Set report column beginning positions

#Define c1  1
#Define c2  25
#Define c3  50
#Define c4  70
#Define c5  100
#Define c6  120
#Define c7  130


begin-program
  do Stdapi-Init
  do Init-Report
  do Gather-data
  do House-Keeping
  do StdAPI-Term
end-program

!****************************************************************************
! Procedure Init-Report - Get parameters
!****************************************************************************
begin-procedure Init-Report


  move 'EMPLRPT1'      to $ReportID
  move 'Employees Who Live in California' to $ReportTitle

  do Init-DateTime
```

Programmer's File Editor is a freeware tool that you can download at http://www.download.com/3640-2352-904159.html. This tool is like Notepad in that it will not help with formatting but can be set up to run your SQR from a DOS prompt. It is a great tool to have when working with any text data.

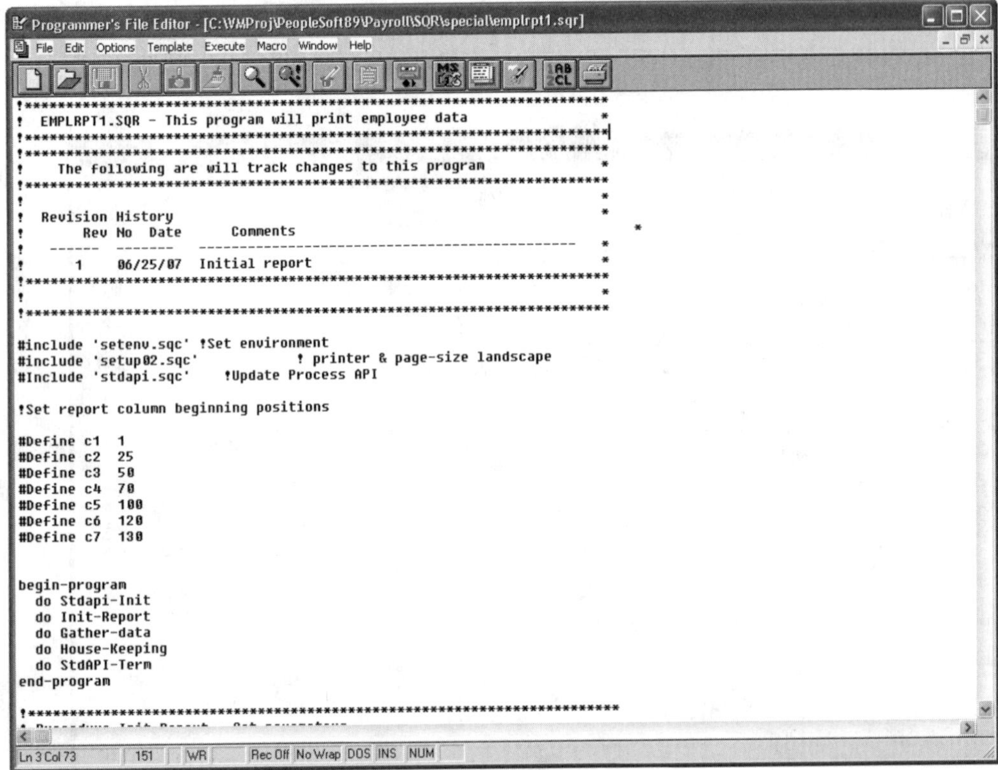

SQR Runner was specifically designed to create SQR programs. It must be purchased. It has formatting editors to ensure that the SQR is created correctly. It can help with debugging and execute the SQR. It can be purchased at http://www.sqr-runner.de/subd/index.php?categoryid=10.

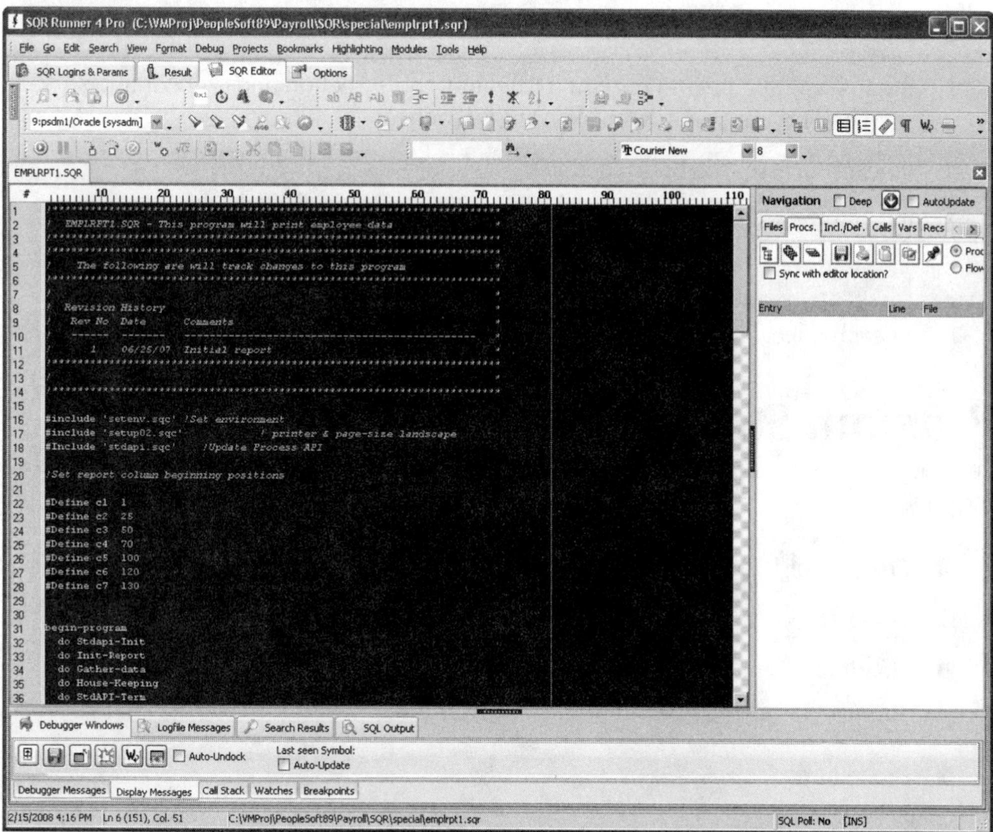

Whatever tool you decide to use, you will need to understand the basic structure and language of an SQR.

Processing

Two passes are made through the SQR when it is being run. The compile pass does the following:

- Inserts all #include files (SQC) into the source program
- Interprets and validates the SQR code and SQL statements
- Preprocesses #Commands (#Define, #Include, #IfAnd, #IFDef)
- Allocates work buffers
- Processes the Begin-Setup section

The execution pass will process the SQR in the following order.

1. It starts with the Begin-Program (or Begin-Report) section and will continue until an End-Program (or End-Report) is reached.
2. It next processes the body sections.
3. It then processes the Begin-Heading section. This will set up the heading for the report and will print at the top of each page.
4. Finally, it processes the Begin-Footing section. This will print at the bottom of each page.

Program Structure

There is a basic structure to all SQR programs. It consists of the following five sections:

- Program or Report
- Setup
- Heading
- Footing
- Procedures

Program or Report

This section controls the flow of the SQR program, by calling procedures, utilizing modular programming techniques.

```
Begin-Program
  (Commands)
End-Program
```

Within this section all SQR programs must include the delivered setenv.SQC to identify the platform-specific environment. This tells the SQR what environment it needs to run on. More SQCs that can be included will be discussed later in this chapter.

```
#include 'setenv.sqc'
```

Setup

This section will describe the report characteristics (i.e., page size, columns, form feeds, charts). Declare commands reside in this section.

```
Begin-Setup
(Commands)
End-Setup
```

Heading

This section will contain commands that will print a heading at the top of each report page. "#" represents the total number of lines reserved for the heading. PeopleSoft delivers standard headings (SQC files) that can be added using the #include at the beginning or end of the SQR program.

```
Begin-Heading #
(Commands)
End-Heading
```

Footing

This section will contain commands to print the footer on each report page. PeopleSoft delivers standard footers (SQC files) that can be added using the #include.

```
Begin-Footing #
(Commands)
End-Footing
```

Procedures

A procedure is how you organize the program to produce the desired report. It will process SQR commands and paragraphs (SQL, Document, and Select), but each procedure must have a unique name.

```
Begin-Procedure procedure_name
(Paragraphs)
(Commands)
End-Procedure procedure_name
```

Variables and Commands

Variable names can be any length and are not case sensitive. The following are valid runtime variables. Text and Date fields begin with "$". Numbers begin with "#". Database records and fields begin with "&". Runtime variables do not have to be explicitly declared. Text and Date variables are initialized with null and zero for numeric variables, by default all numeric variables are created as a data type of float. SQR delivers many reserved variables, which are maintained within SQR.

Examples of String and Date Variables

```
$Name
$CurrDate
```

Examples of Numbers

```
#Amount
#Age
```

Examples of Database Fields

```
&JobCode
&Emplid
```

Data Types

SQR support many data types for variables. These can be explicitly defined within the Declare-Variable command. If variables are not explicitly defined they will use the default for that data type.

- **Decimal** Decimal lets you define the precision after the decimal point. The precision can be 1 to 38, with the default at 16.

  ```
  Decimal Variable_Name [(precision)]
  Decimal   #Salary(2)
  Decimal #Age(1)
  ```

- **Float** This is the default if a #variable is used and not declared. The values after the decimal point can be any number; this is dependent on the machine that it is being executed on.

  ```
  Float Variable_Name
  Float #AnnSal
  ```

- **Integer** This is a numeric value with no values after the decimal point.

  ```
  Integer Variable_Name
  Integer #Year
  ```

- **Date** This variable identifies that these are Date fields and will be formatted accordingly. This will also allow date functions to be used on these fields.

  ```
  Date Variable_Name
  Date $Curr_Date
  ```

- **Text/Char** This identifies that the values are string variables.

```
Text Variable_Name
Text $Empl_Name
```

- **List** List variables contain a list of other variables. Assign the list to a variable name that starts with '%'.

```
LIST (number_variable1|string_variable1,
number_variable2|string_variable2,...)
Let %ListAddress = List($address1, $address2,
$city,$state,$zip);
```

Output File Type

SQR reports are stored on your file server. When running through the process scheduler, you can determine how you want your output to look without doing any coding. The following are a list of output file types that are available:

- **PDF** Adobe Acrobat Reader is the default type for SQR output when it is executed through process scheduler unless it changed. This outputs the report to a nice readable format. Most users are comfortable with this format.
- **SPF** This is the printer-independent format, so that the format can be created for a specific printer.
- **CSV** This is a text comma-delimited file. This format is good when the data need to be imported into Excel or Access.
- **HTM** This creates the report in HTML format, so that the report can be pushed to the web.
- **LIS** This is the default output for SQR. When the file is executed locally this file type will show up in the C:\temp library. It is not very pretty but is good for testing.
- **LOG** This is where errors will be displayed. Also, any shows or displays within the program will be outputted to the log.
- **OUT** This will only show up when the SQR is executed through a process scheduler. It will show all the paths that were used.

Reserved Variables

Reserved variables are variables that SQR has predefined. You can use these variables in your program, instead of having to create a function or code to retrieve the values. SQR has system variables that can be used with any database and there are also variables created that only work with PeopleSoft.

PeopleSoft Variables

The following is a list of variables that were created to work with PeopleSoft applications. They get values that are specific to PeopleSoft functionality.

- **$prcs_oprid** This will return the Operator Id of the person executing the SQR.
- **$prcs_run_cntl_id** This will return the Run Control Id that is being used to execute the SQR. This is helpful if parameters are being passed through a run control record.
- **$AsofToday** This will return the system Date in the native format.
- **$Asofnow** This will return the system Time in the native format.
- **$SysDateTime** This will return the system Date and Time in the native format.
- **ReportDate** This will return the Date from the report, in the date format used in the report.
- **ReportTime** This will return the Time from the report, in the time format used in the report.
- **SQL_Statement** This will output text when there is an SQL error.

System Variables

System variables can be used with any applications. Since SQRs are system independent, the programs that are produced can run against any database that you may have access to. This list is a sample of system variables provided with the SQR language.

- **#current-column** Holds the current column on the report page.
- **#current-date** Will return the current date and time for the local machine that is being used.
- **#current-line** Holds the physical line number on the report page.
- **#end-file** When reading a file, it will determine if the file is at the end. False is stored as 0 and True is stored as 1.

```
If #end-file then
  break
End-if
```

- **#page_count** Stores the current page number. This is used by different SQCs to print the page number on reports.
- **#return-status** This value comes from the operating system. If the SQR fails, this value can be outputted for debugging.
- **#sql-count** Counts the rows that are affected in an SQL statement.
- **#sql-error** Stores the last text message when there is an error. This value can be displayed in the log to help with debugging.
- **#sql-status** Status of each SQL query.
- **#sqr-hostname** The name of the machine that the SQR is being executed on.
- **#sqr-max-columns** Gives the maximum columns in the report.
- **#sqr-max-lines** Gives the maximum lines in the report.
- **$sqr-database** Stores the database that the SQR is being executed against. Valid databases are ORACLE, DB2, ODBC, SYBASE, and INFORMIX.
- **#sqr-pid** Stores the process id for the current execution of the SQR.
- **$sqr-program** Stores the name of the SQR program. This is also used by delivered SQC headers to print on the report.
- **$sqr-report** Stores the name of the SQR report, to be printed on reports.
- **$sqr-ver** The version of SQR that is being used.

Declare-Variable

This variable is used to explicitly define variables. If it is within the setup section, these variables will be global. When used in a local procedure it will be known only to that procedure.

```
Declare-variable

  [DEFAULT-NUMER= {Decimal [(precision)]} | Float | Integer}
  [Decimal Variable_Name [(precision)]]
  [FLOAT Variable_Name]
  [INTEGER Variable_Name]
```

```
  [DATE Variable_Name]
  [TEXT Variable_Name]
End-Declare
declare-variable
    decimal  #Age(1)
    integer  #year
    date     $curr_date
    text  $Empl_name
end-declare
```

Substitution Variables

Substitution variables are declared at the beginning of your program with a #define statement. This is where columns for the print statement would be stored. These variables can be referenced within brackets anywhere in the program.

```
Example
#Define C1  5
#Define C2  20
...
Print Name (+1, {C1})
Print Phone (0, {C2})
```

Move and Let Commands

There are two commands that can be used for assigning values to variables. The first is the MOVE command. This will copy data from one storage location to another. The source data can be a literal or a variable. The target variable must be a user-defined field; an edit mask can be used to format the data.

```
MOVE source data to target_variable [edit_mask]
MOVE $Id to $SSN   xxx-xx-xxxx
```

The second command is the LET statement. This is used to assign values or expressions to user-defined variable. Expressions can use a combination of operand, operators, and functions.

```
LET target-variable = expression
LET #total = #total + #salary
```

Display and Show Commands

The following commands are used for debugging. They will write the statements into the log file. The DISPLAY statements will write only one variable on each line. This variable can contain an edit mask. To stop a carriage control at the end of the line, use a noline option.

```
DISPLAY {variable | literal} [edit_mask] [noline]
Display  'Total Salary = '  noline
Display  #total
```

Using a SHOW command will allow multiple literals or variables to be written on the same line. Edit mask is also allowed to format variables.

```
SHOW {variable | literal} [edit_mask] [{variable | literal} [edit_mask]...]
Show 'Total Salary =  ' #total  '  Total Employees = '  #totemp
```

SQR Program Commands

The following SQR commands used in conjugations with SQL commands will enable a program to be written that can modify, manipulate, and format the data requirements.

Comments

To include comments in your program, use the exclamation mark (!). Comments are used to document your program.

DO Command

This command is used to call a procedure. The procedure must exist within the SQR or an included SQC file. When the procedure has completed, it will return to the following statement. A parameter list can be passed to the procedure. Each variable is separated by a comma.

```
DO procedure_name [(parm_list)]
Do Get-Name
```

IF Command

This command is used for conditional testing of variables. All IF commands end with an END-IF. ELSE commands are executed if the condition is false. SQR uses the logical operators of =, <, <=, >=, >, <> and the Boolean operators "and", "or", and "not".

```
If condition
      {When condition is true}
[Else
      {When condition is false}]
End-If
```

```
If    #total > 50,000
      Let $overflag = 'Y'
Else
      Let $overflag = 'N'
End-if
```

EVALUATE Command

The EVALUATE command is another way to do conditional testing when there are multiple processes to be done depending on the value. Each EVALUATE command must end with an END-EVALUATE. Each variable is evaluated against the when variable or literal. Condition statements can include logical operators (=, <, <=, >=, >, <>), but Boolean operators are not allowed. An OR command can be simulated by having multiple WHEN commands without any other SQR commands between them. A WHEN-OTHER condition will catch all other values. Add a BREAK command to exit out of the EVALUATE statement.

```
EVALUATE {literal | variable}
      WHEN condition_1
            {When condition_1 true}
            [Break]
      WHEN condition_2
            {When condition_2 true}
            [Break]
      WHEN-OTHER
           {When none of the other conditions are true}
END-EVALUATE
Evaluate  &Status
      When 'A'
            Let #activecount = #activecount + 1
      When 'L'
            Let #leavecount = #leavecount + 1
      When-Other
            Let #termcount = #termcount + 1
End-Evaluate
```

WHILE LOOP Command

This command will continue to process statements when the condition is true. A WHILE LOOP is ended by an END-WHILE. A BREAK command can be added to exit the WHILE LOOP for other conditions, besides the WHILE condition.

```
WHILE condition
      {Statements when condition is true}
END-WHILE
While &emplid = $prevemplid
      Do Get-Salary-Data
      Do Get-Tax-Data
End-While
```

BREAK Command

The BREAK command can be used to exit EVALUATE and WHILE statements.

```
BREAK
Evaluate  &Status
     When 'A'
          Let #activecount = #activecount + 1
          Break
     When 'L'
          Let #leavecount = #leavecount + 1
          Break
     When-Other
          Let #termcount = #termcount + 1
End-Evaluate
```

EXIT-SELECT Command

These commands are similar to the BREAK commands, but are used to exit an SQL SELECT statement.

```
EXIT-SELECT
Let #count = 0
Begin-select
Select
Emplid
Name
     If #count =100
       Exit-select
     Else
       Let #count = #count + 1
     End-if
From ps_personal_data
End-Select
```

GOTO Command

This command will branch to a program section.

```
GOTO {Label}
Begin-Procedure GetHighSalary
If #total < 50,000
      GoTo GetHighSalaryExit
End-if
GetHighSalaryExit:
End-Procedure GetHighSalary
```

STOP Command

The STOP command will terminate an SQR command. By adding the option of quiet to your code, it will suppress the Trace file.

```
STOP [Quiet]
If #activecounts < 1
       Show 'No active employees to process'
       Stop
End-if
```

Delivered Formatting Commands and Functions

PeopleSoft delivers many commands and functions to be used for data manipulation. This section will demonstrate a few string manipulations, date conversions, and numeric functions.

STRING Function

The STRING function allows the concatenation of two or more fields or variables by using a common delimiter.

```
STRING {String1 | Variable1} {String2 | Variable2} … {StringN | VariableN}
   BY {Delimiter}
   INTO  Results_String
String &LastName &FirstName by ', ' into $FullName
```

SUBSTR and UNSTRING Functions

There are two main functions that separate out a portion of a string. SUBSTR requires a starting point and the number of characters that are being extracted.

```
Let $NewString = SUBSTR({String|Variable}, {Starting Position}, {Length})
Let $FirstInitial = SUBSTR(&FirstName, 1, 1)
```

UNSTRING will separate string variables into multiple strings depending on the delimiter.

```
UNSTRING {String|Variable}
             BY {Delimiter}
        INTO {Results_String1 … Results_StringN}
Unstring $FullName by ',' Into $FirstName $LastName
```

LENGTH Function

The LENGTH function will return the length of the string or variable, including any spaces.

```
Let Numeric = LENGTH({String|Variable})
Let #LastNameLen = Length(&LastName)
```

EDIT Functions

To format a string, use the EDIT function. This is normally used in the PRINT function, but sometimes it will be necessary to format the string for output.

```
Let String = EDIT({String|Variable}, edit_mask)
Let $SSN = EDIT(&SSN, 'XXX-XX-XXXX')
```

RTRIM and LTRIM Functions

To remove unwanted characters use the RTRIM and LTRIM functions. They will remove characters from the right and left sides of the string.

```
Let NewString = {Rtrim|LTrim} ({String|Variable}, UnwantedCharacter)
Let $JobCode = Rtrim(&Jobcode, ' ')
Let $Sal = Ltrim($Total, '$')
```

RPAD and LPAD Functions

To add characters to a string, use the RPAD and LPAD functions. This allows for all the strings to be the same length.

```
Let Newstring = {Rpad|Lpad} ({String|Variable}, Max_length, Character)
Let $FullName = Rpad(&FullName, #largestName, ' ')
Let $Sal = Lpad($EmpSal, 7, '0')
```

UPPERCASE and LOWERCASE Commands

To insure that your string variables are all the same case, use the Uppercase or Lowercase commands.

```
{UPPERCASE|LOWERCASE}  String
Uppercase $FullName
Lowercase $JobDescr
```

TO_CHAR Function

To change a numeric variable from a number to a string, use the TO_CHAR function.

```
Let String = TO_CHAR(Numeric)
Let $Salary = To_Char(#Totalary)
```

TO_NUMBER Function

To change a string variable to a numeric, use the TO_NUMBER function. This will only work if the string variable contains only numeric characters.

```
Let Numeric = TO_NUMERIC({String|Variable})
Let $AnnualSal = To_Numeric(&Annual_Sal)
```

Basic Arithmetic

There are two ways to do basic arithmetic. SQR uses the standard operators with the LET command ('+', '–', '*', '/').

```
Let Numeric = {Numeric1|Variable1} Operator1 {Numeric2|Variable2}
[Operator2
{NumericN|VariableN}]
Let #Total = #Total + #EmplSal
Let #AvgSal = #Total / #TotCount
```

Arithmetic Functions

SQR also has the following functions: ADD, SUBTRACT, MULTIPLY, and DIVIDE. The new value is stored in the Target field. These functions allow for optional arguments to round and test for errors.

```
Add {Numeric|Variable} TO Target_Numeric[Round = nn]
Subtract {Numeric|Variable} from Target_Numeric [Round = nn]
Multiply {Numeric|Variable} Times Target_Numeric [Round = nn]
Divide {Numeric|Variable} into Target_Numeric [On-Error = {High|Zero}] [Round = nn]
Add #EmplSal to #Total
Subtract 1 from #TotEmp
Multiply #hours times #TotEmp Round=2
Divide #TotCount Into #AvgSal On-Error=Zero Round=2
```

ROUND Function

The ROUND function is used to specify decimal precision. This is used with the LET command calculations. The precision may be for 0 to 38 positions to the right of the decimal point. Any value 5 or above will round up to the next value dependent on the decimal precision.

```
Let Numeric = ROUND({Numeric|Variable}, Precision)
Let #AvgSal = Round(#Total/#TotCount, 4)
```

TRUNC Function

The TRUNC function drops all digits beyond the precision value.

```
Let Numeric = TRUNC({Numeric|Variable}, Precision)
Let #Amount = Trunc(#hours * #rate, 2)
```

ISNULL and ISBLANK Functions

To check for an empty variable, use the ISNULL function. This function can be used on strings or dates. It will return a Booleon value, 1 for true and 0 for false. This is good to use when checking for valid inputs. A string is considered empty if the length is zero. A date is considered empty if it contains null values.

```
ISNULL({String|Date})
If ISNULL($Input_date)
      Show 'No Date Entered'
      Stop
End-if
```

To check for white space use the ISBLANK function. White spaces can be null, tab, carriage control, line feed, and form feed characters.

```
ISBLANK({String|Date})
If ISBLANK($Input_Name)
      Show 'No Name Entered'
      Stop
End-if
```

STRTODATE Function

To convert a string to a date, use the STRTODATE function. This function will return the date representation of the string based on the edit mask. If a date mask is not specified, then the default will use SQR_DB_DATE_FORMAT delivered in the PSSQR.INI file.

```
Let Date = STRTODATE(String [, edit_mask])
Let $YearEndDate = STRTODATE ('12/31/2007', 'MM/DD/YYYY')
```

DATETOSTR Function

To convert a date to a string, use the DATETOSTR function. This uses the same date defaults.

```
Let String = DATETOSTR(DATE [, edit_mask])
Let $Birthdate = DATETOSTR(&Birthdate, 'MM/DD/YYYY')
```

DATENOW Function

To get today's date, use the DATENOW function. It will return the operating system's date.

```
Let String = DATENOW()
Let $Totay = DATENOW()
```

DATEADD Function

To add to a date, use the DATEADD function. This function allows the following date units (year, quarter, month, week, day, hour, minute, or second) to be added or subtracted from a given date.

```
Let String = DATEADD(Date, date units, amount)
Let $AddTenYears = DateAdd($Today, 'year', 10)
```

DATEDIFF Function

To find the difference between two given dates, use the DATEDIFF function. This function will return the value in the following date units (year, quarter, month, week, day, hour, minute, or second).

```
Let Numeric = DATEDIFF(Date1, Date2, date units)
Let #age = DATEDIFF($Today, $Birthdate, 'year')
```

SQR Arrays

To save multiple rows of the same type of data, it is best to work with SQR arrays. Arrays are temporary storage units of data to be used within the SQR program. The following commands are used to work with arrays: CREATE-ARRAY, CLEAR-ARRAY, GET, PUT, ARRAY-ADD, ARRAY-SUBTRACT, ARRAY-MULTIPLY, and ARRAY-DIVIDE. The first step is to create an empty array with the required fields.

```
Create-Array Name={ArrayName}
       Size= {number}
       Field = {name:type[:occurs][=initial_value]}
Clear-Array Name={ArrayName}
```

This example will create an array, load data, and then clear the array.

```
Create-Array Name=Employees_by_Dept
       Size=12
       Field=Month:Char
       Field=DeptCnt:3
Put 'Jan' 4 6 10  Into Employees_by_Dept(0)
       Month DeptCnt(0) DeptCnt(1) DeptCnt(2)
Put 'Feb' 7 2 4  Into Employees_by_Dept(0)
       Month DeptCnt(0) DeptCnt(1) DeptCnt(2)

...
Put 'Dec' 5 4 5  Into Employees_by_Dept(0)
       Month DeptCnt(0) DeptCnt(1) DeptCnt(2)
Clear-Array Employees_by_Dept
```

Printing

The PRINT command can be used to control how the information should be viewed by the end user. These commands can be used within a paragraph (explicit printing) or attached to the SQL (implicit printing). The PRINT command uses three coordinates (line, column, length), which are optional, to determine where to place the information on the report. These coordinates can be fixed or relative to another position, by using a plus or minus sign. EDIT-MASK can be used to format the field being shown.

```
Print {Variable|Literal} ([line][, [column][,[length]]]) format edit-mask
Print 'My Company'       (1,1,10) Center
```

Format Options

There are different format options available. Not all format options are compatible with each other, or with some printers. Here are a few commonly used options.

- **Bold** Causes the value to be in bold type
- **Box** Creates a box around the value
- **Center** Centers the value across the page
- **Fill** Fills the length buffer with the character
- **Shade** Places a shaded box around the data
- **Money** Uses the money edit mask
- **Number** Uses the standard number edit mask
- **Underline** Underlines the value
- **Wrap** Wraps the characters when it is a long text field

ON-BREAK

SQR programs can print data from the SELECT statements. This is done using the ON-BREAK function. The ON-BREAK function has the following options that are used to determine how to print the field.

- **Print=Always** Always prints the value of the field
- **Print=Change** Only prints if the value of the field changes
- **Print=Change/Top-Page** Starts a new page when the value changes

- **Skiplines=nn** Identifies how many lines to skip
- **Procedure=procedure-name** Calls a procedure
- **After=procedure-name** Calls the procedure after a break
- **Before=procedure-name** Calls the procedure before a break
- **Level** Determines level of break

The following is an example of how the On-Break function can be used in an SQR program. Company is used as a page break, so that all employees within a company will be shown on the same page.

```
Begin-Select
Company (,1,4)  On-Break Print=Change/Top-Page
Emplid (,15,10)
Name (, 35,40)
From Ps_Employees
Order by Company, Name
```

EDIT-MASK

EDIT-MASK allows the formatting of the variable being printed. There are specific types of masks depending on the field type.

Text Masking

- X Takes the place of each character of the field
- B Will insert a space instead of the character
- ~ Skips the value of the character in the field
- / Tells the system to use the character(s) following a backslash as a literal
- | Used to concatenate different basks

Numeric Masking

- 9 Will print the number of the field, zero fill to the right decimal, and space fill to the left.
- 8 Will print the number of the field, zero fill to the right of the decimal, trim leading blanks, and left justify the number.
- 0 Will print the number of the field and zero fill to the left.
- . The dot will be added when the field is printed.

- , The comma will be added when the field is printed.
- $ Will print the number and a dollar sign to the right of the number. Using one dollar symbol will print in a fixed position; using more than one dollar symbol will print to the left of the number.
- B Will print the number unless it is a zero, in which case it will convert to a blank space.

Date Masking (Case Sensitive)

- **MM** Two-digit month (01–12)
- **MON** Three-character abbreviation for the month
- **MONTH** Full name of the month
- **Day** Name of the day
- **DD** Two-digit day of the month (01–31)
- **D** Day of the week (1–7)
- **YYYY** Four-digit year
- **YY** Two-digit year (current century is assumed)
- **RR** Two-digit year (century is calculated)
- **Q** Quarter of the year (1–4)
- **WW** Week of the year (1–53)
- **W** Week of the month (1–5)
- **HH** Hour of the day 24-hour clock
- **MI** Minutes (0–59)
- **SS** Seconds (0–59)
- **AM PM** Time indicator
- **B** Will add a blank space

These are just a few of the edit masks available. For a complete list, go to Oracle's PeopleSoft Library People Books, SQR Language Reference, Copyright © 1988–2005 PeopleSoft, Inc. Table 10-1 provides examples of using masks.

Mask	Type	Value	Result
(XXX)BXXX-XXXX	Text	1234567890	(123) 456-7890
AcctNo:~~XXXX	Text	001234	AcctNo:1234
9,999.99	Numeric	100	100.00
099999	Numeric	100	000100
$$,$99.99	Numeric	100	$100.00
$9,999.99	Numeric	100	$100.00
9999.99PF	Numeric	–100	(100.00)
9999	Numeric	–100	–100
MM/DD/YYYY	Date	12-31-2006	12/13/2006
DAY,BDD-MON-YY	Date	12-31-2006	Sunday, 31-Dec-06
MONTH	Date	12-31-2006	December
Q	Date	12-31-2006	4
WW	Date	12-31-2006	52
HH:MI:SS	Date	092015	09:20:15

TABLE 10-1. *Commonly Used Edit Masks*

PeopleSoft delivers a report repository for viewing of all reports and processes through the PeopleSoft applications. There are many options to automatically display your output (Web, CSV, text, PDF). For more extensive capabilities for managing SQR output, go to http://blog.greysparling.com/2005/08/report-distribution-with-3rd-party.html.

Graphics

SQR supports different graphical objects that enable the use of charts, graphs, labels, and images. These types of objects enhance reports and forms. Be aware that not all printers will support these features. Controlling the position of a graphic on a page can be tricky, since the SQR will start at the upper-left corner after it has printed the graphic. SQR delivers different commands to help create these graphic objects.

DECLARE-CHART

This command will define all the basic features of the chart. The types of charts available are line graphs, bar charts, histograms, area charts, XY scatter plots, and high-low-close graphs.

```
Begin-Setup
Declare-Chart  {Chart Name}
  Title={'Chart Title'}
  Type = {Line|Pie|Bar|Stacked-Bar|100%-Bar|Overlapped-Bar|
floating|Bar|Histogram|Area|Stacked|100%-Area|XY-Scatter-Plot|        High-Low-
Close}
  Legend = {YES|NO}
  Legend-Placement = {Center-Right|Center-left|Upper-Right|Upper-Left|  Upper-
Center| Lower-Right | Lower-Left | Lower-Center}
  X-Axis-Label= {'Label Name'}
  Y-Axix-Label = {'Label Name'}
End-Declare
End-Setup
```

The following will declare a bar chart.

```
Begin-Setup
Declare-Chart  Employees_By_Department
       Title = 'Count of employees by Department'
       Type = STACKED-BAR
       Legend = YES
       X-Axis-Label  = 'Months'
       Y-Axis-Label = '# of Employees'
End-Declare
End-Setup
```

PRINT-CHART

After a chart has been declared it can be referenced within the PRINT-CHART function. Normally, a data-array is used to populate the chart and with this data a Print-Chart can be created.

```
Print-Chart {ChartName} (X [,Y])
       Data-Array = {ArrayName}
       Data-Array-Row-Count= number
       Data-Array-Column-Count = number
       Data-Array-Column-Labels = {None|ArrayName|Label}
       Sub-title = {Subtitle}
Print-Chart Employees_By_Department (+5 ,10)
       Data-Array = Employees_by_Dept
       Data-Array-Row-Count= 12
       Data-Array-Column-Count = 3
       Data-Array-Column-Labels = (Dept1, Dept2, Dept3)
       Sub-title = 'By Month'
```

DECLARE-IMAGE

Images can personalize your document, such as company logos or images that represent the data on the document. To use an image it must be saved in the SQRDIR directory, or a full path must be specified. This image can be used later within a PRINT-IMAGE command.

```
Declare-Image ImageName
       [Type = {EPS- FILE |HPGL- FILE |GIF- FILE |JPEG- FILE |BMP- FILE }]
       [Image-Size = (width, height)]
       [Source = File_name]
End-Declare
Declare-Image Company_Logo
       Type = JPEG-FILE
       Image-Size = (10, 20)
       Source = 'My_Company_Logo.JPG'
End-Declare
```

PRINT-IMAGE

PRINT-IMAGE will use the information from the DECLARE-IMAGE to print the image on the document. Definitions of type, image size, and source can be overwritten at the PRINT-IMAGE command.

```
Print-Image ImageName (row, column)
      [Type = {EPS- FILE |HPGL- FILE |GIF- FILE |JPEG- FILE |BMP- FILE }]
      [Image-Size = (width, height)]
      [Source = File_name]

Print-Image Company_Logo (+4, 30)
      Image-Size = (15, 30)
```

Structured Query Language

Structured Query Language (SQL) is used within the SQR program to extract data from the database. To use these commands, one needs to know their tables within the database. All the examples in this section will reference the PeopleSoft HRMS database. All SQL commands, including columns, must start left-justified. Any SQR commands included within the SQL command must be indented; otherwise, an error will occur. The main commands are BEGIN-SELECT and BEGIN-SQL.

BEGIN-SELECT

This command is used to extract data from the database. This is where columns are identified for use within the SQR program. Each column, unless specified, will start with an "&" and then the column name. Each column is flush left without a comma following. If more than one field has the same database column name, you must add a synonym starting with "&".

The following example is reading two tables, getting three variables from these tables, and using the SQR command DO to call another paragraph. It will then print the variables retrieved.

```
Begin-Procedure  Get-Empl-Job
Begin-Select
A.EMPLID
A.NAME    &NAME
B.JOBCODE   &JOBCDE
     Do Get-Job-Desc
FROM PS_PERSONAL_DATA A,
       PS_JOB B
WHERE   ......
END-SELECT
Print &A.Emplid   (+1,1)
Print &Name        (+0, 10)
Print &Desc                (+0, 40)
End-procedure Get-Empl-Job
```

BEGIN-SQL

This command is used for all other SQL commands (INSERT, UPDATE, DELETE, etc.). These statements are used to manipulate data in the database. You must have the appropriate access to the database to use these SQL statements.

```
Begin-SQL on-error={procedure_name or STOP|WARN|SKIP}
       {SQL statements}
End-SQL
```

This example is updating the field work_location in the Job table where the work_location currently equals "BuildingA".

```
Begin-Procedure  Update-location
Let $location = 'BLDG1'
Begin-SQL
UPDATE PS_JOB
SET WORK-LOCATION = $location
WHERE WORK_LOCATION = 'BuildingA'
End-SQL
End-procedure Update-location
```

Effective Dated Rows

This PeopleSoft application utilizes effective dated rows throughout the system to keep history. This allows for processing based on certain dates. Future dated rows can be entered in advance and not affect how data is processed on the current date.

History can be retrieved based on certain dates for audit purposes. When retrieving these records for reporting, you will want to select only the most current row for the time frame you are reporting for. The table PS_JOB is used to store job data for employees. The following example will show how to get the current job row.

```
Begin-Select
A.EMPLID
A.NAME    &NAME
B.JOBCODE      &JOBCDE
     Do Get-Job-Desc
FROM PS_PERSONAL_DATA A,
       PS_JOB B
WHERE  A.EMPLID = B.EMPLID
AND B.EFFDT = (SELECT MAX(EFFDT) FROM PS_JOB B1
               WHERE B.EMPLID = B1.EMPLID
                AND B.EMPL_RCD = B1.EMPL_RCD
                AND B1.EFFDT <= $DATEIN)
AND B.EFFSEQ = (SELECT MAX(EFFSEQ) FROM PS_JOB B2
               WHERE B.EMPLID = B2.EMPLID
               AND B.EMPL_RC = B2.EMPL_RCD
               AND B.EFFDT = B2.EFFDT)
END-SELECT
```

Dynamic Query Variables

Dynamic query variables allow parts of the SQL statement to be built prior to using it within the SQL. The statement is stored as a string variable and when used it will be shown with brackets around it [$statement]. These dynamic variables allow you to build SQL statements based on user input. The following will request input on how the data should be selected. This information will be used to build a Where clause.

```
Let $Quote = '"'
Input $choice  "Do you want employee by State (S) or Company (C)'
If $Choice = 'S' then
      Input $State 'Enter the two character State:'
      Let $Where =  'State = ' || $quote || $State || $quote
Else
      Input $Company 'Enter the Company Code:'
      Let $Where =  'Company = ' || $quote || $Company || $quote
End-if;
Begin-Select
Emplid

Name
From PS_EMPLOYEES
Where [$Where]
End-Select
```

Running an SQR

To run an SQR from Windows, you need to have permissions to all the tables needed by your program in the database. If you are using an SQR tool, like SQR runner, follow their setup process to run SQR. You can use delivered executables, which are normally stored on your server. The next illustration shows all the available fields that may need to be filled out depending on your setup.

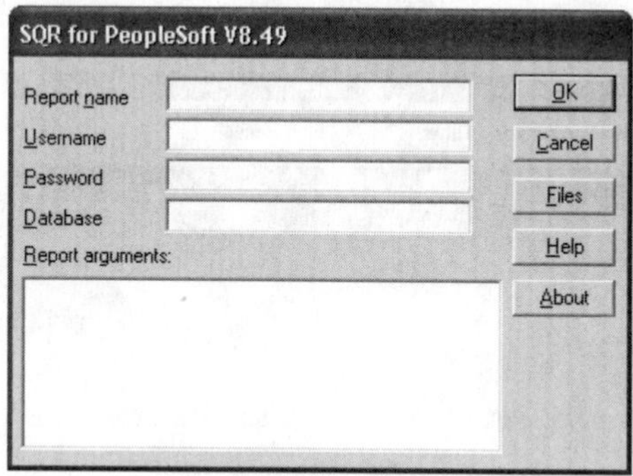

Running SQR from a Bat File

SQRs can also be run by creating a bat file, to be used at a command line or through a script. For further explanation of the options using the bat file, go to http://www.ontko.com/sqr/sqrcard6.html#SQR_COMMAND_LINE.

Running SQR Through the Process Scheduler

To run an SQR through the process scheduler requires that a page and component be set up. Refer to Chapter 5 for information on creating a page and a component, adding them to a menu, and setting up permissions. After an SQR has been created and saved to the correct PeopleSoft libraries, a process definition needs to be created.

To set up the process definition within PeopleSoft, follow these steps:

1. Within PeopleSoft HRMS select PeopleTools | Process Scheduler | Processes. You will add a new process. The system will display the Add Process Definition Box. The Process Type will be SQR Report. The Process Name will be the same as your program name. Be aware that this name must not be longer than eight characters in length. In the following illustrations, you can see that there are three pages that can be set up. Only the Process Definition and Process Definition Options pages are required; the others are optional.

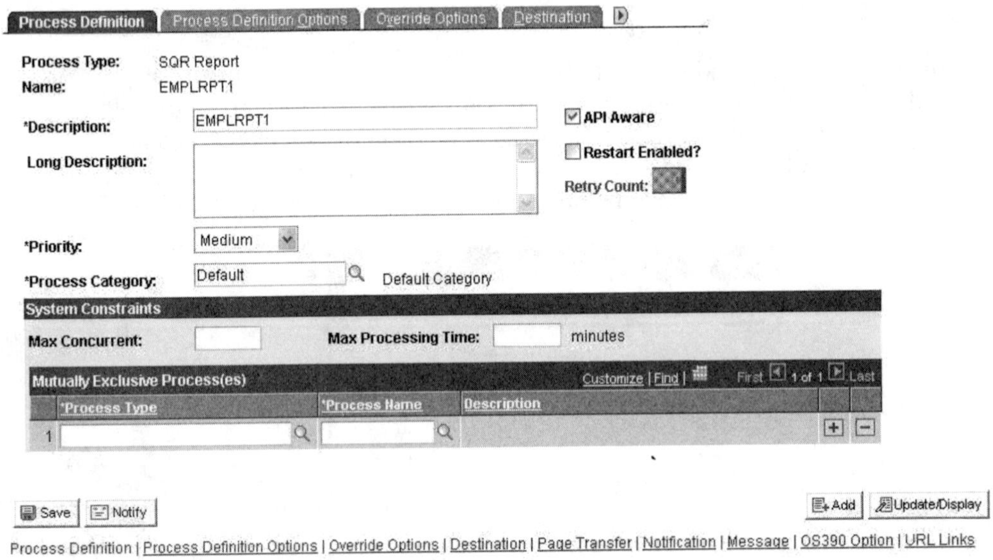

Process Definition | Process Definition Options | Override Options | Destination

Process Type: SQR Report
Name: EMPLRPT1

*Description: EMPLRPT1
API Aware
Long Description:
Restart Enabled?
Retry Count:

*Priority: Medium
*Process Category: Default Default Category

System Constraints

Max Concurrent: Max Processing Time: minutes

Mutually Exclusive Process(es) Customize | Find | First 1 of 1 Last

	*Process Type	*Process Name	Description
1			

Save Notify Add Update/Display

Process Definition | Process Definition Options | Override Options | Destination | Page Transfer | Notification | Message | OS390 Option | URL Links

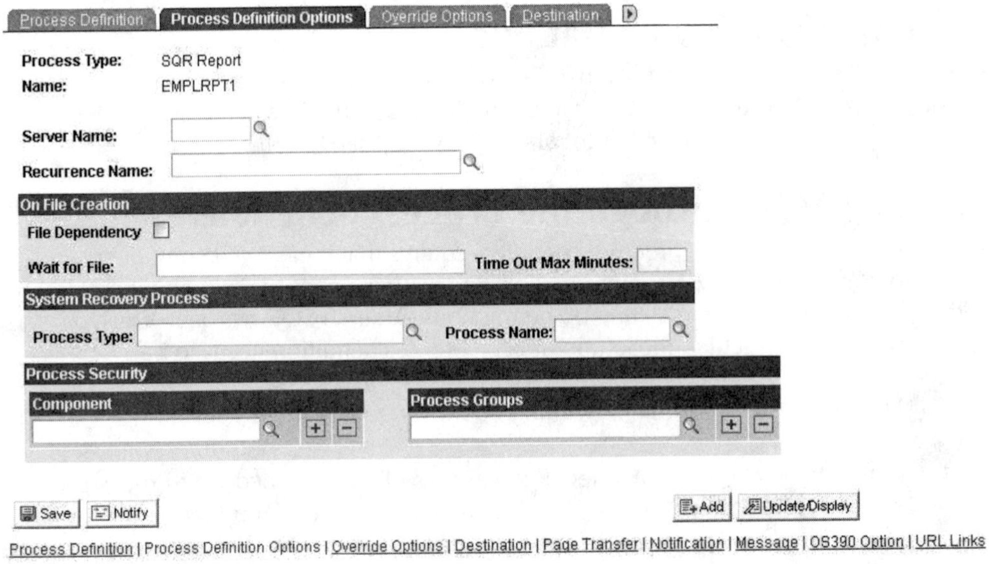

Process Definition | Process Definition Options | Override Options | Destination

Process Type: SQR Report
Name: EMPLRPT1

Server Name:
Recurrence Name:

On File Creation

File Dependency
Wait for File: Time Out Max Minutes:

System Recovery Process

Process Type: Process Name:

Process Security

Component
Process Groups

Save Notify Add Update/Display

Process Definition | Process Definition Options | Override Options | Destination | Page Transfer | Notification | Message | OS390 Option | URL Links

2. Fill out the description and other requirements on the Process Definition page.
3. On the Process Definition Options page, select a server and set up the security by connecting it to a component that contains your run control page.
4. Click Save to save the definition. You are now able to go to your menu and run your SQR program.

Running SQR from PeopleCode

Sometimes it will be necessary to launch an SQR within PeopleCode. This will allow the customer to run a job or have it triggered if certain criteria are met. This can be done by using delivered PeopleSoft functions: CreateProcessRequest() and Schedule(). Two required parameters are needed by the CreateProcessRequest(): Process_Type and Process_Name. For Process_Type use "SQR Report" for a single SQR or "PSJob" for multiple SQRs that have been scheduled as a job. Process_Name is the name of your SQR or job, which has been set up with Process Definition. The following will provide an example of how the PeopleCode should be set up to run a single SQR program.

```
Local ProcessRequest &SQRrequest;
! Create the process Request object
&SQRrequest = CreateProcessRequest("SQR Process", "EMPLRPT1");
&SQRrequest.RunControlID = "MYRUNCNTRL_ID";
&SQRrequest.SetOutputOption("Web", "PDF", "", "EMPLRPRT1");
! With the information stored above. The Schedule method can be used.
&SQRrequest.Schedule();
If &SQRrequest.status <> 0 then
   !  An error has occurred
End-if;
```

Using SQC Files

PeopleSoft delivers many SQC files with their software. These are commonly used procedures and statements that can be used in any SQR program. SQC files are added to your program using the #include operator. The non-PeopleSoft naming standard for Include files is .inc, but PeopleSoft uses SQC as their naming convention. The Include file is often the source of an error when debugging, and the developer will have to open the Include file to read the entire procedure to debug. Like SQR files, Include files have to reside in the correct libraries.

Your program can use any procedures included in these SQC files. People Books delivers a comprehensive list of delivered SQC files. Table 10-2 describes commonly used SQC files (taken from PeopleTools 8.1 SQR training class manual, Appendix E).

File Name	Description
ADDRESS.sqc	Addresses formatting routines
AMASKFTD.sqc	Inputs logic for user-entered dates
AMASKFTD.sqc	Inputs logic for fiscal year end
AMBATCH.sqc	Processes SQR batch messages
AMCURPRI.sqc	Currency precision printing
AMCV1000.sqc	CSV parser
AMCV2000.sqc	Interface loader
AMDCBULD.sqc	Requests array processing
ASKDEPT.sqc	Inputs logic for user-entered department codes
ASKEFFDT.sqc	Inputs logic for effective dates
ASKFISYR.sqc	Inputs logic for fiscal year
BDIMPORT.sqc	Imports mass PeopleSoft data
BENASOF.sqc	Inputs logic for user-entered date
BENDEPS.sqc	Gets dependent records
BENOTR.sqc	Populates tables for ps_benefits_data
BENPERS.sqc	Populates table for ps_benefits_data
BIRADFTC.sqc	Business unit defaults
BIRADFTX.sqc	Tax defaults
BNPRIJOB.sqc	Finds primary job
CHKADVPR.sqc	Check/advice printer and page size
CHRTFLD.sqc	Accounts payable chart fields
CURDTTIM.sqc	Defines date functions for retrieving current dates and times
DATEMATH.sqc	Defines many date functions to compute dates
DATETIME	Contains general routines to format date and time
DBRVND	Gets all vendors
DDDINDEX	Audits index
DDDTABLE	Audits Record/SQL table
DDDIEWS	Audits views

TABLE 10-2. *Commonly Used SQC Files*

File Name	Description
DBGETCW	Gets calendar and view information
DBGETVAL	Masks run control value
DBIWHERE	Constructs Where clause for the SELECT statement
DPRNCTL1	Retrieves run control
FSADATES	Flexible spending account date routines
FSGENRND	Generic rounding
GETACTS	Gets action reason from the action reason table
GETBALID	Gets balance ID for calendar year from the installation table
GENBENNM	Gets benefit name
GETDATCD	Gets year, quarter, and month codes from $asofdate
GETDEDBL	Gets deduction balances
GETDEDNM	Gets deduction name from the deduction table
GETEMPPAD	Gets personal data for an emplid
GETEMPNM	Gets employee and applicant name from Personal_Data and Applicant_Data
GETERNBL	Gets earnings balances
GETERNNM	Gets earnings name from the earnings table
GETEVCLS	Gets the benadmin event class name
GETJOBTL	Gets job title from the job code table
GETPRIMJ	Gets primary job
GETPYMSG	Gets text of pay messages
GETRPTPD	Gets reporting period for benefits reports
GLACCDTA	Gets data from the account table
GLFUNC	GL miscellaneous functions
GLHDG01	Standard heading #1 for GL printed reports
GLHDG07	Standard heading #7 for GL printed reports
GLMASIMP	Imports mass PeopleSoft data
LDADROPT	Loads a lookup table with the paycheck address options

TABLE 10-2. *Commonly Used SQC Files* (continued)

File Name	Description
MASSCHNG	Mass change processing shared procedures
MASSFILE	Mass change file Unload/Load procedures
MASSLAYO	Mass change layout definition
NETINWDS	Converts net pay to words
NIDFORMT	Formats nationalid
NUMBER	Contains general routines to format numbers
NUMTEST	Numeric test
OECHANGE	Audits change and delete fields
OEGETSHR	Shared OE routines
PCNUMFMT	Number formatter
PLCOMMON	Gets field information for all commonly used values
POCEDI	Creates files for purchase order EDI
PTHDG01	Standard heading #1 for printed reports
PTSET01	Printer and page-size initialization (portrait)
PTSET02	Printer and page-size initialization (landscape)
PTSET02a	Printer and page-size initialization (landscape)
READXLAT	Read Translate table for the desired values
RECLIST	Returns a string list separated with a comma with the fields of a given record
RESET.sqc	Contains the standard footing section
ROTNAME10	Converts from "last suffix, first" to "last first mid in"
ROTNAME3	Converts $name from "last,first,prefix" to its three components
RPTSUMMRY	Prints summary information
SETENV.sqc	Defines database, operating system, and printer type variables
SETLYOUT	Sets the layout for the SQR report
SETUP01	Standard setup section (portrait orientation)
SETUP02	Standard setup section (landscape orientation)
SETUP31.sqc	Printer and page-size initialization (portrait)

TABLE 10-2. *Commonly Used SQC Files* (continued)

File Name	Description
SETUP32.sqc	Printer and page-size initialization (landscape)
SFBARCD	Bar code set up and control flags
SQLERR	SQL error-handling procedures
SQLERR1	SQL error-handling procedures
SQRTRANS	Translates SQR strings to given language
STDAPI.sqc	Defines variables for the process scheduler
STDERROR	Standard error processing
STDHDG01.sqc	Defines a standard heading to be printed on the reports
STDDTR20	Reports description and fiscal year
STDINIT	Reports initialization and timing routines
SYSAE	Application engine audits
SYSAUDIT	PS system audits
SYSFIELD	PS DB field definition edit report
SYSMENU	PS menu item edit report
SYSOPSEC	PS operator security audit
SYSPPLCD	PS PeopleCode program manager name report
SYSRECRD	PS record definition edit report
SYSTREE	PS tree structure edit report
TAXRNCTL	Retrieves data from tax reporting run control record
TIMEMATCH	SQR time arithmetic procedures
TXOVRFLW	Tax amounts overflow splitting utility
UTILS	Printing utilities
W2SORT	Controls W2 sort
WFACT	Finds missing activity objects
WFBP	Finds missing business process items
WFHP	Finds missing homepage items
WLGEN	Worklist generator

TABLE 10-2. *Commonly Used SQC Files* (continued)

File Functions

SQR programs are very useful in reading and writing external files. It is a good tool to use to create interfaces to external systems. There are seven commands provided with SQR to help process external files: CLOSE, DELETE, EXISTS, OPEN, READ, RENAME, and WRITE.

CLOSE

This command is optional unless there are more than 256 files being opened, but it is good coding practice to always close the files before you end your program.

```
CLOSE {filenum}
Close 10
Close 20
```

DELETE

This command will delete the file from its location. This is a good idea when you want to insure an input file does not get processed twice. If the delete is successful the file status will be a 0.

```
Delete(filename)
#status = delete($bonus_in)
```

EXISTS

This command will check to make sure the file exists before continuing to process. A return of 0 tells you the file exists.

```
Exists(filename)
#status = exists($bonus_in)
```

OPEN

Before a file can be read or written to, you must open it. Within this command a file name is established and attached to a file number, type of file (read or write), file length, and status of the file. A maximum of 256 files can be opened at one time. The file name needs to be fully qualified, including a complete path. The file can be opened three different ways. For-Reading will only read data and process it sequentially. For-Writing will create a new output file or overwrite an existing file at the same location. For-Append will add data to the end of an existing file or create a new file. Record lengths can be set to fixed or they can vary in size but it should be set to the longest record written out. The status allows for error checking insuring that the file is open. This value must be numeric; zero indicates success and –1 indicates failure.

```
OPEN {filename} As {filenum}
FOR-READING | FOR-WRITING | FOR-APPEND
RECORD = {length} [:FIXED | VARY]
STATUS = {variable}

OPEN 'C:\temp\datain.txt' as 10
FOR-READING
RECORD=80:FIXED
STATUS = #Datein10
If #Datain10 = -1
   STOP QUIET
End-If
```

READ

The READ command will sequentially read each record until the SQR variable #end-file has been reached (set to –1). When reading this command, refer to the file number.

```
READ {filenum} into {variable}:{length}
```

There are two ways that the data can be read in. The first way is to read the file into a single field, then parse it out into separate fields using the SUBSTR function.

```
While 1=1
       Read 10 into $DataIn:80
       If #END-FILE = 1
             Break
       End-if
       Let $Emplid = Substr($DateIn,1,6)
       Let $EmpName = Substr($DateIn, 10,40)
End-While
```

The second way is to read it into each field; you just have to account for the total length of the record. If there are data you do not want to include, they must be assigned a dummy variable.

```
While 1=1
     Read 10 into $Emplid:6
          $Dummy1:4
          $EmpName:40
          $Dummy2:30
     If #END-FILE = 1
          Break
     End-if
End-While
```

RENAME

This command will rename the files. This is another way to insure the file is not processed twice, but the data need to be kept for backup purposes. A return of 0 will let you know that the rename was successful.

```
Rename(filename1, filename2)
#status = Rename($bonus_in, $bonus_in_bkup)
```

WRITE

This command will write out variables or literals to a file set to For-Writing or For-Append. Refer to file using the file number.

```
WRITE {filenum} into {variable}:{length}
WRITE 20 from $EmpName:40
              $EmpAddress:40
```

Compiler Functions

These functions are used during the compile phase. The compile phase will determine if the statements should be compiled. This will speed up processing, when testing the validity of the input values. It also does not have to be removed to be moved to production.

#DEBUG

This function is used with the –Debug flag on the command line. It tests and debugs code without having to take it out when the program is moved to production.

```
#DEBUG SQR command
#DEBUG show 'Total of employees is ' #empcount
```

#DEFINE

This function declares a value for a substitution variable. It sets up static variables for specific values. These variables do not start with a "$" or "#".

```
#Define Variable Value
#Define Column1   5
#Define Male M
```

Compile Directive

This function will only compile the code within if the statement meets the criteria. There are five delivered compile directives:

- **#IF** If the statement is true, then it will compile the next statements. Only simple if statements are allowed. Can be nested up to 10 times.
- **#ELSE** When the #IF statement is false it will compile these statements.
- **#ENDIF** Ends the #IF directive.
- **#IFDEF** When a substitution variable has been declared with a #DEFINE or an ASK command, these statements will be compiled.
- **#IFNDEF** This will compile when a substitution variable has not been declared.

```
#IF {literal|variable} operate {literal|variable}
#IFDEF substitution variable
#IFNDEF substitution variable
begin-setup
  ask mailtype 'Home or Mail or None(H,M,N)'
end-setup
begin-procedure Main
#if {mailtype} = 'H'
  ...code for H here
#else
#if {mailtype} = 'M'
  ...code for M here
#else
#if {type} = 'N'
  ...code for N here
#else
  show 'H, M or N not selected. Report will not run.'
  stop
#endif
#endif
#endif
End-Procedure Main
```

#INCLUDE

This function shows how all SQC and .inc files are available for use within the SQR. #Include files can be at the beginning or end of the program since they are processed during the compiling phase.

```
#INCLUDE '{SQC name | .inc name}'
#INCLUDE 'mysqc.sqc'
```

HTML

SQR delivers commands that will generate and publish HTML files and reports. To provide your company up-to-date technology and utilize the Internet capabilities, this section will get you started on producing these HTML files and reports. If the report you have created is just what you want, but you want to publish it to the Internet or an intranet, add –PRINTER:HT when running the program. This will automatically convert the output into HTML 3.0 format. Within your SQR program, you can enhance your document by adding titles and background colors for the body and navigation bar using the PRINT-DIRECT command.

```
Print-Direct [Nolf]
      [printer= {HTML}
      Text
Print-Direct Printer=html '%%Title Monthly Department Counts'
To specify links use the target option.
Print-Direct Printer=html '%%Href target = "_top" http://www.myweb.com
```

To use more complicated HTML tags and features, include the html.inc file. This will allow the usage of delivered HTML procedures. At the beginning of an SQR program html_on needs to be called.

```
Do html_on
```

In addition, a large page-size needs to be allocated within a DECLARE-LAYOUT command to prevent page breaks. Page breaks within the HTML will cause bad data to be shown. HTML procedures must be used around the print statements to format the document properly. Table 10-3 lists some of the procedures available for formatting. Each procedure requires an end to the procedure.

Example of a Header Record

```
Do html_h2
Print 'Company Status Report' (1,1)
Do html_h2_end
```

Example of Blinking Text

```
Do html_blink
Print 'This text blinks' (1,20)
Do html_blink_end
```

Example of Creating a Link

```
Do html_a ('HREF=myhome.html')
Print 'Go to myhome' (1,1)
Do html_a_end
```

Procedure	Description
Html_table	Creates a table
Html_caption	Creates a caption
Html_tr	Creates rows
Html_th	Creates column heading
Html_td	Creates column
Html_h2	Creates a level 2 heading
Html_blink	Blinks the text
Html_stike	Strikes out the text
Html_sub	Subscript
Html_a('HREF=myhome.html')	Creates links
Html_p	Creates paragraph breaks
Html_br	Creates line breaks

TABLE 10-3. *Commonly Used HTML Procedures*

To publish the finished SQR report or file, work with your webmaster to establish a directory on the server that these documents can be copied to. Then anyone can go to this location and view the report.

```
http://www.mycompanyserver/departmentcountreport.html
```

Sample Programs

This program will retrieve records from Job and Personal data and print the information.

```
!***********************************************************************
!  EMPLRPT1.SQR - This program will print employee data               *
!***********************************************************************
!***********************************************************************
!    The following are will track changes to this program             *
!***********************************************************************
!                                                                      *
!  Revision History                                                    *
!   Rev No    Date    Comments                                  *
!   ------  -------   -------------------------------------------     *
!      1    06/25/07 Initial report                                    *
```

```
!***********************************************************************
!                                                                      *
!***********************************************************************

#include 'setenv.sqc'    !Set environment
#include 'setup02.sqc'    ! printer & page-size landscape
#Include 'stdapi.sqc'    !Update Process API
!Set report column beginning positions

#Define c1 1
#Define c2  25
#Define c3  50
#Define c4  70
#Define c5  100
#Define c6  120
#Define c7  130

begin-program
  do Stdapi-Init
  do Init-Report
  do Gather-data
  do House-Keeping
  do StdAPI-Term
end-program

!***********************************************************************
! Procedure Init-Report - Get parameters
!***********************************************************************
begin-procedure Init-Report


  move 'EMPLRPT1'      to $ReportID
  move 'Employees Who Live in California' to $ReportTitle

  do Init-DateTime
  do Init-Number
  do Get-Current-DateTime

end-procedure Init-Report

!***********************************************************************
! Heading
!***********************************************************************
begin-heading 10
! Include header code as needed, example:
    #include 'stdhdg01.sqc'

    print 'LAST NAME'                                   (+1,{C1})
    print 'FIRST NAME'                                  (00,{C2})
    print 'EMPLID'                                      (00,{C3})
    print 'ADDRESS'                                     (00,{C4})
```

```
    print 'CITY'                                      (00,{C5})
    print 'STATE'                                     (00,{C6})
    print 'ZIPCODE'                                   (00,{C7})

    print '________________'                      (+1,{C1})
    print '________________'                      (00,{C2})
    print '__________'                            (00,{C3})
    print '__________'                            (00,{C4})
    print '__________'                            (00,{C5})
    print '__________'                            (00,{C6})
    print '__________'                            (00,{C7})

   Let #ln_cnt = 10

end-heading

begin-procedure House-Keeping
! This will show in the Log file
  Show '   '
  Show '   '
  Show 'Report completed successfully '
end-procedure House-Keeping

! This will read the personal_data table and get the requested information
! for printing
begin-procedure Gather-Data

BEGIN-SELECT

EMPLID       &EMPLID
LAST_NAME    &LASTNAME
FIRST_NAME   &FIRSTNAME
ADDRESS1     &ADDRESS1
CITY         &CITY
STATE        &STATE
POSTAL       &ZIP

  do Print-report

FROM PS_PERSONAL_DATA
WHERE STATE = 'CA'
ORDER BY LAST_NAME, FIRST_NAME

END-SELECT
end-procedure Gather-Data

!-------------------------------------------------------------------------
!   Print Report
!-------------------------------------------------------------------------
begin-procedure Print-report
```

```
if #ln_cnt > 50
   new-page
end-if

print &LASTNAME                                  (+1,{C1})
Print &FIRSTNAME                                 (00,{C2})
print &EMPLID                                    (00,{C3})
print &ADDRESS1                                  (00,{C4})
print &CITY                                      (00,{C5})
print &STATE                                     (00,{C6})
print &ZIP                                       (00,{C7})

Let #ln_cnt =  #ln_cnt = +1
end-procedure

!*  INCLUDE SQC
#Include 'reset.sqc'      !Reset printer procedure
#Include 'curdttim.sqc'   !Get-Current-DateTime procedure
#Include 'datetime.sqc'   !Routines for date and time formatting
#include 'datemath.sqc'   !Routines for date calculation
#include 'number.sqc'     !Routines to format numbers
```

The following illustration shows the resulting page using this program.

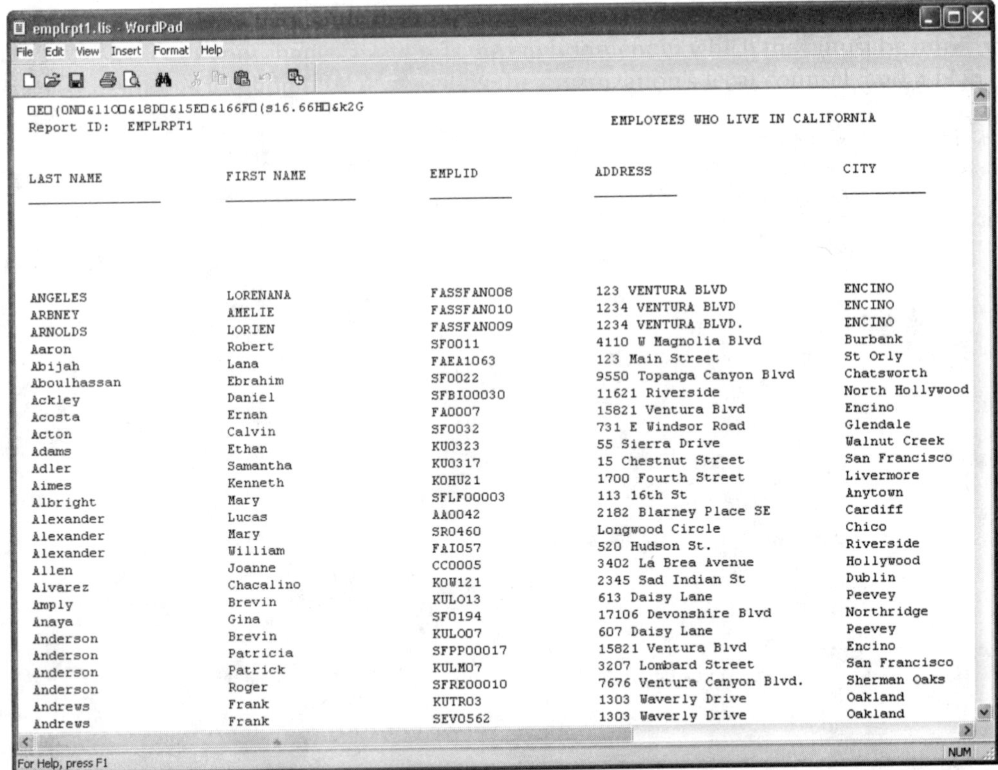

LAST NAME	FIRST NAME	EMPLID	ADDRESS	CITY
ANGELES	LORENANA	FASSFAN008	123 VENTURA BLVD	ENCINO
ARBNEY	AMELIE	FASSFAN010	1234 VENTURA BLVD	ENCINO
ARNOLDS	LORIEN	FASSFAN009	1234 VENTURA BLVD.	ENCINO
Aaron	Robert	SF0011	4110 W Magnolia Blvd	Burbank
Abijah	Lana	FAEA1063	123 Main Street	St Orly
Aboulhassan	Ebrahim	SF0022	9550 Topanga Canyon Blvd	Chatsworth
Ackley	Daniel	SFBI00030	11621 Riverside	North Hollywood
Acosta	Ernan	FA0007	15821 Ventura Blvd	Encino
Acton	Calvin	SF0032	731 E Windsor Road	Glendale
Adams	Ethan	KU0323	55 Sierra Drive	Walnut Creek
Adler	Samantha	KU0317	15 Chestnut Street	San Francisco
Aimes	Kenneth	KOHU21	1700 Fourth Street	Livermore
Albright	Mary	SFLF00003	113 16th St	Anytown
Alexander	Lucas	AA0042	2182 Blarney Place SE	Cardiff
Alexander	Mary	SR0460	Longwood Circle	Chico
Alexander	William	FAI057	520 Hudson St.	Riverside
Allen	Joanne	CC0005	3402 La Brea Avenue	Hollywood
Alvarez	Chacalino	KOW121	2345 Sad Indian St	Dublin
Amply	Brevin	KUL013	613 Daisy Lane	Peevey
Anaya	Gina	SF0194	17106 Devonshire Blvd	Northridge
Anderson	Brevin	KUL007	607 Daisy Lane	Peevey
Anderson	Patricia	SFPP00017	15821 Ventura Blvd	Encino
Anderson	Patrick	KULM07	3207 Lombard Street	San Francisco
Anderson	Roger	SFRE00010	7676 Ventura Canyon Blvd.	Sherman Oaks
Andrews	Frank	KUTR03	1303 Waverly Drive	Oakland
Andrews	Frank	SEV0562	1303 Waverly Drive	Oakland

This program will read in a file, get information from the database, and write out a new file. It also demonstrates simple error handling if the files are not available and the employee cannot be found.

```
!***********************************************************************
!  READWRTE.SQR - This program will print employee data               *
!***********************************************************************
!***********************************************************************
!    The following are will track changes to this program             *
!***********************************************************************
!                                                                     *
!  Revision History                                                   *
!   Rev No     Date     Comments                                        *
!   ------  -------   ---------------------------------------------   *
!      1    06/25/07  Initial report                                  *
!***********************************************************************
!                                                                     *
!***********************************************************************

#include 'setenv.sqc' !Set environment
#Include 'setup32.sqc'  !printer and page-size initialization
#Include 'stdapi.sqc'    !Update Process API

begin-report
  do Stdapi-Init
  do Open-files
  do Read-data
  do House-Keeping
  do StdAPI-Term
end-report
begin-procedure House-Keeping
  ! Close Files
  Close 10
  Close 20
  ! Write out to log how many records written
  Show '   '
  Show '   '
  Show 'Total Records Written to file: ' #totins edit 999
end-procedure House-Keeping
begin-procedure Open-files
!  Open-files for input and output
   Open 'C:\TEMP\SUPPADDS.PRN' As 10
   For-Reading
   Record=19:Fixed
   Status = #Open10
   if #Open10 = -1
      Display 'Could not open file C:\TEMP\SUPPADDS.PRN'
      Stop Quiet
   end-if
   Open 'C:\TEMP\InsertSUPPADDS.TXT' As 20
```

```
      For-Writing
      Record=400:Fixed
      Status = #Open20
      if #Open20 = -1
         Display 'Could not open file C:\TEMP\InsertSUPPadds.TXT'
         Stop Quiet
      end-if
   end-procedure Open-files

   begin-procedure Read-Data
   !  Read Data from input file sequentially

   While 1=1
     Read 10 into $Emplid:10
                  $dummy:1
                  $Amount:8

     If #END-FILE = 1
       Break
     End-if

     Do Get-Empl-Data
   End-While
   end-procedure Read-Data

   !**************************************************************************
   !  PROC Get-Empl-Data
   !      Get employee name and address for output file that will be
   !      used to send a letter with the award information
   !**************************************************************************
   BEGIN-PROCEDURE Get-Empl-Data
   Let $found = 'N'
   BEGIN-SELECT
   Name          &Name
   Address1      &Address1
   Address2      &Address2
   City          &City
   State         &State
   Postal        &Zip
      Let $found = 'Y'
   FROM PS_PERSONAL_DATA
   WHERE EMPLID = $Emplid
   END-SELECT
   If $found = 'Y'
      Do Write-File-out
   else
      ! Write an error message to the log
      Show ' Emplid not found on Database ' $Emplid
   end-if

   END-PROCEDURE Get-Empl-Data
```

```
!**********************************************************************
!  PROC Write-File-out
!    Create an output file in the format needed, then write out
!**********************************************************************
BEGIN-PROCEDURE Write-File-out
!    Create a comma delimited file for output.
Let $output = $emplid || ', '  || &Name || ', ' || &Address1 || ', ' ||
&Address2
|| ', ' || &City || ', ' || &State || ', '|| &Zip || ', ' || $amount

WRITE 20 FROM $output:400
Add 1 to #totins
END-PROCEDURE Write-File-out

#Include 'reset.sqc'      !Reset printer procedure
#Include 'curdttim.sqc'   !Get-Current-DateTime procedure
#Include 'datetime.sqc'   !Routines for date and time formatting
```

In the following illustrations, you can see the new files.

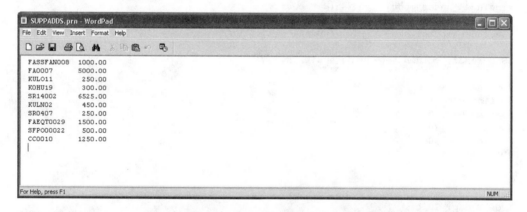

```
FASSFAN008  1000.00
FA0007      5000.00
KULO11       250.00
KOHU19       300.00
SR14002     6525.00
KULN02       450.00
SR0407       250.00
FAEQT0029   1500.00
SFP000022    500.00
CC0010      1250.00
```

InsertSUPPADDS.TXT - Notepad

File Edit Format View Help

```
FASSFAN008, ANGELES,LORENANA, 123 VENTURA BLVD,  , ENCINO, CA, 91436,  1000.00
FA0007, Acosta,Ernan, 15821 Ventura Blvd,  , Encino, CA, 91436,  5000.00
KULO11, Baron,Brevin, 611 Daisy Lane,  , Peevey, CA, 94762,   250.00
KOHU19, Berry,Julie, 4050 Piemonte Drive,  , Pleasanton, CA,  ,   300.00
SR14002, Cabalbag,Ruben, 6200 N. Dunrobin Ave,  , Lakewood, CA, 90713,  6525.00
KULN02, Chandler,Melissa, 101 Peabody Street,  , Walnut Creek, CA, 94596,   450.00
SR0407, Cushman,Kelly, 803 La Jolla Drive,  , Saugus, CA, 67890,  250.00
FAEQT0029, Dariara,Ortegano O, 3 PECAN ALLY,  , ROSEMEAD, CA, 91770,  1500.00
SFP000022, Davidson,Lisa M, 15821 Ventura Blvd, Suite 220, Encino, CA, 91436,   500.00
CC0010, Dominguez,Sarah Jessica, 5099 Maple Drive,  , Dublin, CA, 94275,  1250.00
```

Sometimes it is useful to test an SQR program outside of the PeopleSoft application, but as a developer you want it ready to run through the process scheduler, so that you do not have to recode. This program will show how to run a program that requires input values.

```
!***********************************************************************
!  CANEWHIR.SQR - This program will print California new employee data *
!                 For a specified time frame                           *
!***********************************************************************
!***********************************************************************
!    The following will track changes to this program             *****
!***********************************************************************
!                                                                      *
!  Revision History                                                    *
!   Rev No     Date    Comments                                       *
!   ------  -------   -------------------------------------------     *
!      1    06/25/07  Initial report                                   *
!***********************************************************************
!                                                                      *
!***********************************************************************

#include 'setenv.sqc'        !Set environment
#include 'setup02.sqc'         ! printer & page-size landscape
#Include 'stdapi.sqc'        !Update Process API

!Set report column beginning positions

#Define c1  1
#Define c2  25
#Define c3  50
#Define c4  70
#Define c5  100
#Define c6  120
#Define c7  130

begin-program
  do Stdapi-Init
  do Init-Report
  do Gather-data
  do House-Keeping
  do StdAPI-Term
end-program

!***********************************************************************
! Procedure Init-Report - Get parameters
!***********************************************************************
begin-procedure Init-Report

  move 'CANEWHIR'     to $ReportID
  move 'New Hire Employees Who Live in California' to $ReportTitle

  do Init-DateTime
```

```
  do Init-Number
  do Get-Current-DateTime

  !Determine if you are running from within PS or another method
  !Process Instance will be null if not within PS

  if $Prcs_Process_Instance = ''
     input $START_DT MAXLEN=11 'Please Enter  Beginning Date (mm/dd/yyyy) '
     let $START_DT = strtodate(rtrim($START_DT, ' '), 'mm/dd/yyyy')
     input $END_DT MAXLEN=11 'Please Enter End Date (mm/dd/yyyy) '
     let $END_DT = strtodate(rtrim($END_DT, ' '), 'MM/DD/YYYY')
  else
      do Select-Parameters
  end-if

end-procedure Init-Report

!***********************************************************************
! Heading
!***********************************************************************
begin-heading 10
! Include header code as needed, example:
    #include 'stdhdg01.sqc'

    print 'LAST NAME'                                   (+1,{C1})
    print 'FIRST NAME'                                  (00,{C2})
    print 'EMPLID'                                      (00,{C3})
    print 'ADDRESS'                                     (00,{C4})
    print 'CITY'                                        (00,{C5})
    print 'STATE'                                       (00,{C6})
    print 'ZIPCODE'                                     (00,{C7})

    print '________________'                         (+1,{C1})
    print '________________'                         (00,{C2})
    print '__________'                               (00,{C3})
    print '__________'                               (00,{C4})
    print '__________'                               (00,{C5})
    print '__________'                               (00,{C6})
    print '__________'                               (00,{C7})

   Let #ln_cnt = 10

end-heading

begin-procedure House-Keeping
! This will show in the Log file
  Show '   '
  Show '   '
  Show 'Report completed successfully '
end-procedure House-Keeping
```

```
! This will read the personal_data and employment table and get the
! requested information for printing
begin-procedure Gather-Data
BEGIN-SELECT
P.EMPLID          &EMPLID
LAST_NAME         &LASTNAME
FIRST_NAME        &FIRSTNAME
ADDRESS1          &ADDRESS1
CITY              &CITY
STATE             &STATE
POSTAL            &ZIP
  do Print-report
FROM PS_PERSONAL_DATA P,
     PS_EMPLOYMENT E
WHERE STATE = 'CA'
AND P.EMPLID = E.EMPLID
AND E.HIRE_DT BETWEEN $START_DT AND $END_DT
ORDER BY LAST_NAME, FIRST_NAME
END-SELECT
end-procedure Gather-Data
!-------------------------------------------------------------------
!   Print Report
!-------------------------------------------------------------------
begin-procedure Print-report
if #ln_cnt > 50
   new-page
end-if

print &LASTNAME                                   (+1,{C1})
Print &FIRSTNAME                                  (00,{C2})
print &EMPLID                                     (00,{C3})
print &ADDRESS1                                   (00,{C4})
print &CITY                                       (00,{C5})
print &STATE                                      (00,{C6})
print &ZIP                                        (00,{C7})
Let #ln_cnt =  #ln_cnt = +1
end-procedure

begin-procedure select-parameters
!Get parameters from Run Control Record
Begin-SELECT On-Error = SQL-Error
FROMDATE
THRUDATE
     let $START_DT = &FROMDATE
     let $END_DT = &THRUDATE
from PS_run_cntl_per067
where OPRID        = $prcs_oprid
and RUN_CNTL_ID  = $prcs_run_cntl_id
end-select
end-procedure
```

```
!*  INCLUDE SQC
#Include 'reset.sqc'      !Reset printer procedure
#Include 'curdttim.sqc'   !Get-Current-DateTime procedure
#Include 'datetime.sqc'   !Routines for date and time formatting
#include 'datemath.sqc'   !Routines for date calculation
#include 'number.sqc'     !Routines to format numbers
```

The results of running this program are shown in the following illustrations.

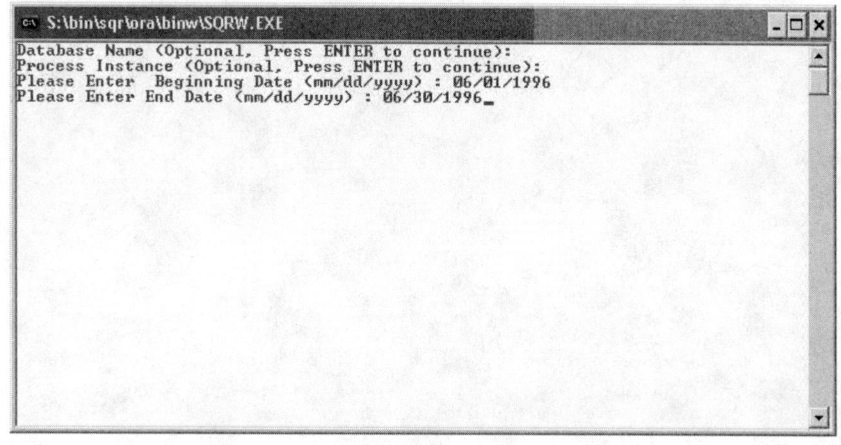

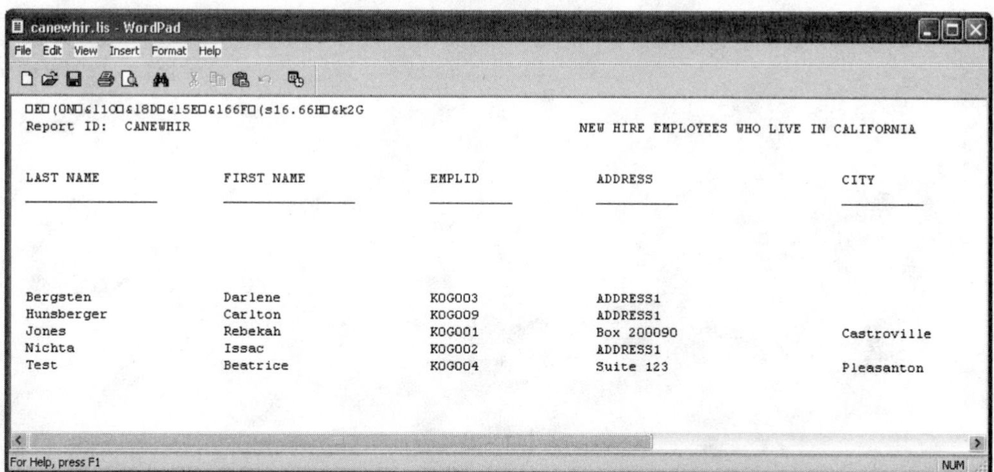

Summary

In this chapter you have learned how to use the SQR language to retrieve, manipulate, and write reports. Integrating it with SQL commands allows the retrieval of fields from the database. You have been introduced to adding charts and images to your document and how to convert your document to HTML. SQR programs are good for providing informative reports and getting data in and out of the database. There are a lot of valuable free tools out there, such as using SQR to create XML spreadsheets. Other useful links regarding SQR can be found at www.sqr-info.com.

CHAPTER 11

Application Engine

his chapter introduces a powerful SQL processing tool called Application Engine (AE). Designed to run small and large batch processes using SQL and PeopleCode, it is an alternative to using COBOL or SQR programs, with benefits. Application Engine programs do not need to be compiled and do not generate SQL. They just execute SQL statements that are provided. Application Engine is integrated into the PeopleTools suite, and the execution component is written in C++. All objects created within the Application Engine are stored within the database. This allows the use of the graphical tool Application Designer for developing the AE program. All fields, records, functions, component interfaces, Meta-SQL, and other objects are available to be used within the Application Engine program. Reusability is one of the greatest benefits available with creating Application Engine programs.

History

The first few releases of PeopleTools did not include Application Engine. The only way to do batch processing was to use COBOL or SQR. A PeopleSoft coder created Application Engine, using PeopleTools for the front end and COBOL for the back end. It was based on SQL logic and worked with PeopleTools definitions, instead of being procedural. When the PeopleTools team decided to incorporate Application Engine, they converted the back end to C++ and added the use of PeopleCode. Application Engine has evolved and continues to be upgraded with new features, while COBOL and SQR have not changed much. The main problem with Application Engine was that it did not have a reporting tool. With the addition of XMLP in the 8.46 tools release, Application Engine can be used to create reports and charts.

Application Engine vs. SQR

There is a great debate among programmers as to what should you use to code customizations—SQR or Application Engine? Many programmers are familiar with SQR, so it is easy to find coders. Application Engine is relatively new, and there is less familiarity with the product. Some programmers just use the PeopleCode part of Application Engine because they do not understand the set-based SQL language. Many of the delivered reports are written in SQR. Application Engine has knowledge of all the objects in the application, whereas SQR is a stand-alone language. Application Engine can utilize any code that is stored in the database, whereas unless it is written as an SQC, SQR has to re-add the code each time.

Looking forward to the Oracle Fusion, Application Engine is going to be included. Currently, Oracle does not have a good batch processing tool. Since Application Engine is a set-based tool, it pushes processing to the database, and this fits well with Oracle products. It does not look as if Oracle is planning to invest in SQR. Even at the conferences the emphasis is to use Application Engine as the primary batch tool. Our recommendation is to do new customizations in Application Engine, so that it will be easier to move forward with Fusion. As time permits, convert SQR to XML Publisher or Application Engine, depending on the function.

Application Engine

All Application Engine programs are designed and maintained within the Application Designer (Chapter 4). To create a new Application Engine program, log on to Application Designer. Use the new function to select Application Engine. It will open a new AE program with a Main section already created. MAIN is the name of the section that is usually called first. The name MAIN is specified in the Application Engine definition. If the programmer decides to call it something else, such as MAIN_SECTION, then MAIN_SECTION should be specified in the definition of the App Engine. Before programming can begin, you must save this program. The following illustration shows a new Application Engine ready for programming.

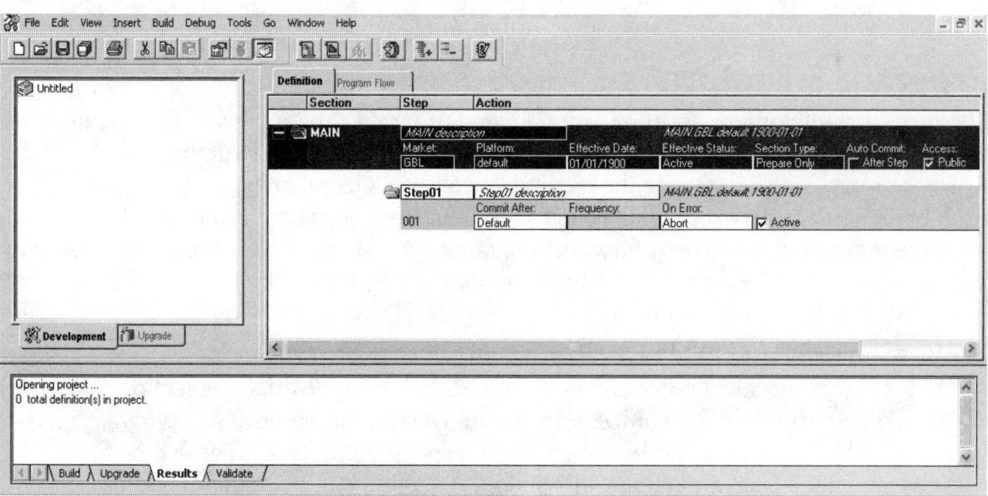

The Application Engine program can also be viewed as a program flow by clicking the tab. The following illustration shows how this would look.

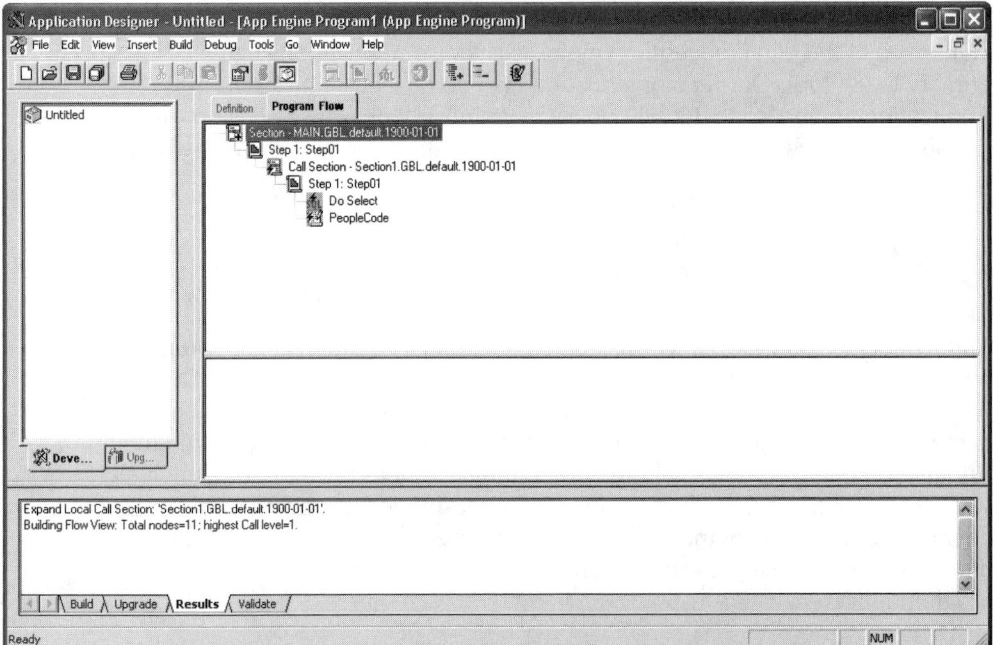

Program Structure

The program structure for an Application Engine program can be viewed graphically in a definition structure or through a program flow. The definition structure uses folders to represent objects; use the expand or compress icons to expand/compress each of the folders. To expand all, select View | Expand All. There is a hierarchical structure that must be followed for your program to run successfully. There are three components in the hierarchical structure: sections, steps, and actions.

Sections

An AE program must always contain one section defined as "MAIN." A section contains one or more steps to process an action. Depending on how you program your AE, multiple sections can be created to run specific processes. These other sections are called from an action Call section. A section can be added by right-clicking a section and selecting Insert Section.

Section Parameters For each section parameters can be set up to help maintain the program. The next illustration shows the default parameters.

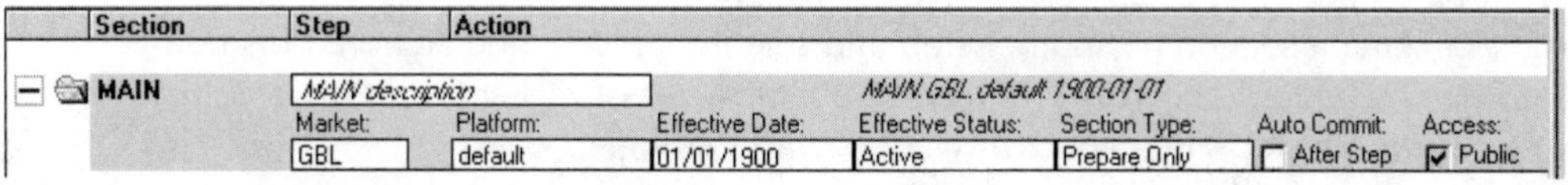

Section	Step	Action					
MAIN	MAIN description			MAIN.GBL.default.1900-01-01			
	Market:	Platform:	Effective Date:	Effective Status:	Section Type:	Auto Commit:	Access:
	GBL	default	01/01/1900	Active	Prepare Only	After Step	Public

The following table describes each parameter. These are all optional and do not need to be changed for your program to work. Using some of these parameters can make your program easier to read and understand.

Parameter	**Description**
Section Name	This is the name of the section. A default name will be given when a section is added. It can be changed, but there is an 8-character limit.
Description	Description of what the section does. There is a 20-character limit.
Market	The default value is GBL for global, but it can be changed if a specific market is required.
Platform	It will default to the current platform but can be set up to run on a certain platform.
Effective Date	This will only allow this section to run if the system date is after the date entered in this parameter. The default is 01/01/1900.
Effective Status	This will activate or inactivate a section. Active is the default.
Section Type	Used for abnormal termination. The default value is "Preparation Only".
Auto Commit	Check the box if you want the commit to be done after each step; otherwise, it will be committed at the end of the program.
Access	If Public is checked, it will allow this section to be called from any other app engine program; otherwise, it can only be used by the current program.
Comments	Documentation. To view, right-click the section and select Show Comments.

Steps

Steps are processed sequentially within the section. There can be one or more steps within a section. Each step can have one or more actions. A step can be added by right-clicking a section or another step and selecting Insert Step/Action. This new step will be added following where your cursor was last. An action is always inserted with a step since you will want to start coding.

Step Parameters For each step there are parameters that can be set up to help maintain the program. These have been described in the following table. The available parameters are shown next.

Parameter	Description
Step Name	This is the name of the step. A default name will be given when a step is added. It can be changed, but there is an 8-character limit.
Description	Description of what the step does. There is a 20-character limit.
Commit After	Tells the AE program when to commit. There are three choices: • **Default** Follow the Auto Commit from section. • **Later** Commit will be done later. • **After Step** When step has completed.
Frequency	Controls how often within a Do While, Do Until, or a Do Select a commit is issued. Default is blank.
On Error	Action to take if there is an error during the step. • **Abort–Default** Messages will be written to log and terminate. • **Ignore** Messages will be written to log and continue. • **Suppress** No messages will be written to log and continue.
Active	This will allow you to activate or deactivate a step. This helps during development, to be able to test different steps. Test one step by deactivating all other steps.
Comment	Add comments to document the step process.

Action

Multiple actions can be processed within a step, but each action type can only be used once within the same step. Once an action type has been created for the step, it is not available to use. Action types available to use are Do When, Do While, Do Select, PeopleCode, SQL, Call Section, Log Message, Do Until, and XSLT. These action types will be defined in detail under Action Types, later in this chapter.

Action Parameters For each step there are parameters that can be set up to help maintain the program. This illustration shows what parameters are available for an SQL action. Each action parameter is described in the following table.

Parameter	Description
Action Name	This is the name of the action. A list of available actions is available in the drop-down.
Description	Description of what the action does. There is a 20-character limit
Reuse Statement	Default is No. This statement allows the SQL to convert any %bind variables from the state records into real bind variables :1, :2, ... These real bind variables can be used in other SQL statements within the AE program.
Do Select Type	Only available when a Do Select Action is being used. Select/Fetch is the default to get one record at a time. Other options available are Re-Select and Restartable.
On Return	Only available when PeopleCode action is used. Abort is the default. Other options are Break and Skip Step.
Message Set, Number, Parameters	Only available when Log Message action is being used. Can send message from the message log table to the jobs log file.
No Rows	Only available when SQL action is being used. Continue is the default to process all rows. Other options are Abort, Section Break, Skip Step.

Properties

With every Application Engine program created, a Properties box is available for documenting the program. Use the properties to keep track of changes, connect tables, and set up properties for the AE program. There are four tabs available in the Properties box: General, State Records, Temp Tables, and Advanced. To open the Properties tab, go to File | Definition Properties or click the Properties icon.

General

The General tab is the place to enter in a description of the AE and any comments that are needed for documentation and change control. An owner can be assigned, and the Last Updated information will be updated when you click OK.

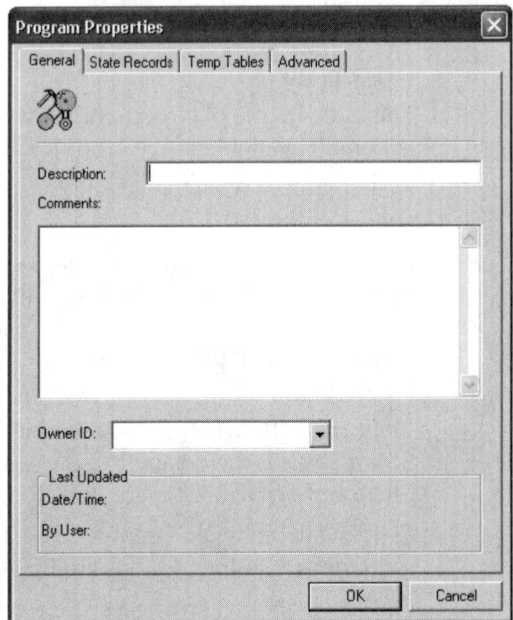

State Records

The State Records tab is the area where you can attach one or more state records to your AE program. A state record allows variables to be passed between the actions. It is like the working storage section in a COBOL program. A state record can be an SQL table or a derived work record. The variables stored in a derived work record will be lost at the end of the AE program execution.

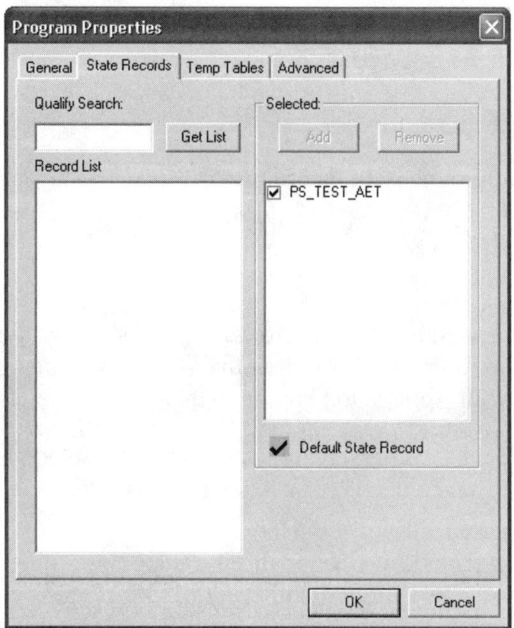

The state record must have certain attributes. The first field in the record must be PROCESS_INSTANCE, and it must be a key field. Any other field within PeopleSoft, custom or delivered, can be added to the state record. A state record must be saved with a name that ends with AET. This will allow it to come up in the list for valid state records. Any PeopleCode attached to this state record will not be executed during an AE program.

The state record PS_TEST_AET has the following fields:

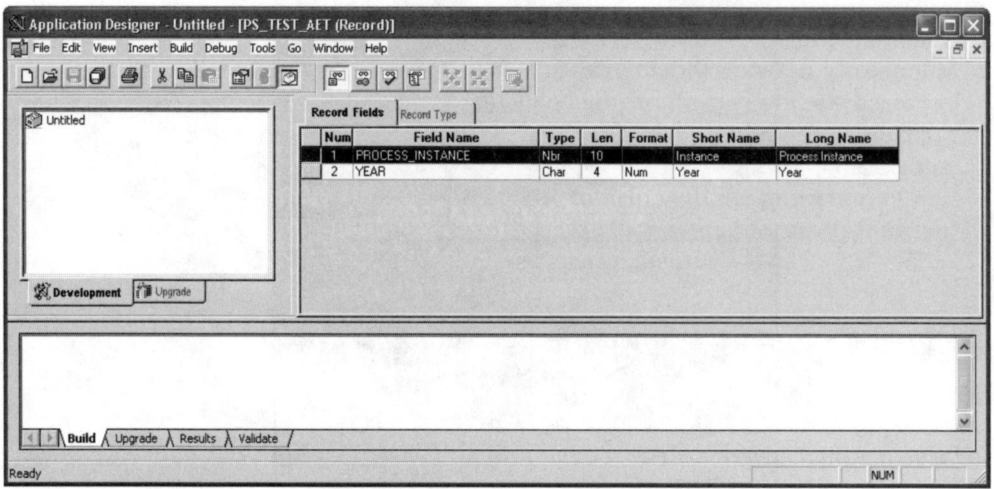

Num	Field Name	Type	Len	Format	Short Name	Long Name
1	PROCESS_INSTANCE	Nbr	10		Instance	Process Instance
2	YEAR	Char	4	Num	Year	Year

To store data in the state record, use %Select.

```
%Select(Year)
Select Year
From PS_TEST_RUN_CONTROL
```

To retrieve data from the state record, use %Bind.

```
Insert %Bind(Year) into PS_TEST_FILE
```

Temp Tables

Temporary tables are used for parallel processing. This allows the Application Engine Program to be run multiple times at the same time. There are six steps you must take to set up your Application Engine to take advantage of parallel processing.

Define Temporary Table When creating a new record, select the type Temporary Table. The Process Instance needs to be a key on the table. Save the record with an ending of TAO.

Set the Temporary Table This will create the number of available instances of the temporary table, depending on the PeopleTools Option screen. Build the temporary table. The number instance will be appended to the table name (for instance, PS_TEMP_TAO1).

Assign to Application Engine Program Within the AE properties, on the Temp Tables tab, add the table to the selected list.

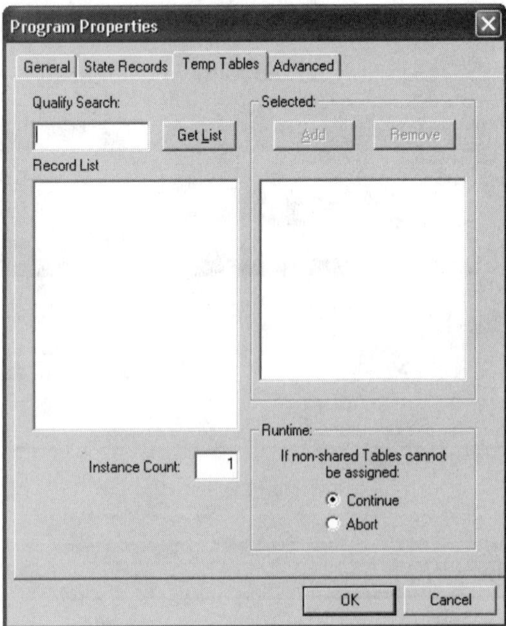

For Batch Processing On the Temp Tables tab set the number of table instance that will be used by the AE program. Also determine how the AE program will proceed if all the instances are taken, Continue or Abort.

Build/Rebuild Temporary Table After changing the instance, you will need to rebuild the temporary table.

Adjust Meta-SQL Use %Table to reference the temporary table. The AE program will keep track of what temporary table instance it is using. All data is deleted from the temporary table before it is used in the AE program.

Advanced Tab

The Advanced tab has optional properties that can be used to control your Application Engine program. When Disable Restart is checked, it will not allow the Application Engine Program to be restarted if it fails. If this AE program was created to hold public callable objects and not run on its own, check the Application Library box. Check the Batch Only box when the AE program should run only in batch mode. To assign a default message set, enter the number. It will be shown whenever a Log Message action is used without a message set number. There are multiple program types available to be used with an AE program. Standard is the default Program Type.

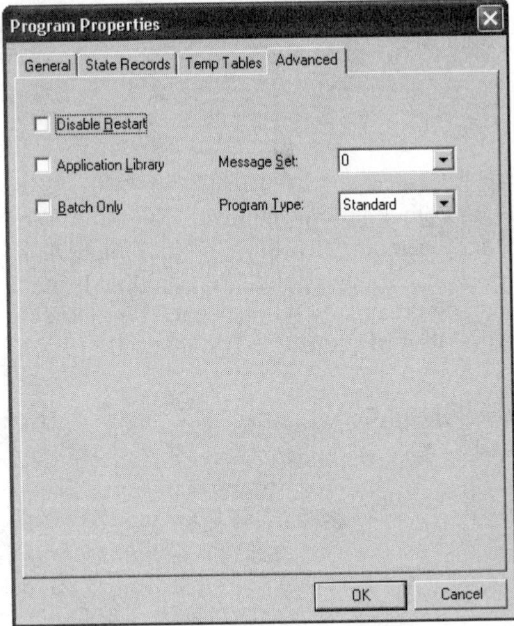

Action Types

Action types are where the actual programming is done. They can be a series of actions used together in a step or a single action. The purpose of your code will determine which action would be best to use.

Do When

Do When is a conditional action that will process other actions that follow when the condition is true. It is comparable to an "If" statement in other languages. When we say the condition is true, we mean that the SQL returns one or more rows. If the SQL in the Do When doesn't return any rows, then the step after won't be executed. If the SQL returns one or more rows, then the next following step will be executed once. The following table is an example of how to use the Do When within your program.

Section	Step	Action Type	Code	Description
Main	Step1	Do Select	`%Select(Year) Select Year from PS_RUN_CONTROL`	Get Year from the Run Control Record.
	Step2	Do When	`Select 'X' from PS_TEST_REC where Year = %Bind(Year)`	Get the record with the correct year.
		SQL	`Update PS_TEST_NEW_REC Set Year = %Bind(Year)`	Update the new test record with the year.

Do While

Do While will loop through other actions while the condition is true. It will continue to execute all actions that follow until the looping SQL is false. This requires code within another action to change the data that is making the looping SQL true; otherwise, you will create an endless loop. The following table shows how a Do While would be used in code.

Section	Step	Action Type	Code	Description
Main	Step1	Do Select	`%Select(TotEmp) Select Count from PS_RUN_CONTROL`	Get total employees for processing from Run Control.
	Step2	Do While	`Select 'X' from PS_TEST_REC where Count <= %bind(TotEmp)`	Get as many records as determined from the run control record.
		SQL	`Update PS_TEST_REC Set Count = Count + 1`	Update the count.

Do Select

Do Select will loop through the records and is normally used to populate the state record. As each record is stored, other actions within the same step will be processed. There are three types of looping rules that can be used with Do Select. The Default is Select/Fetch. This will read one record at a time and then execute other actions within the same step. Reselect will only read the first row of data over and over again. This could cause an endless loop, unless there is code in one of the other actions to stop the selection. Restartable acts the same way as Select/Fetch, but a commit is done within the loop, so that the program can be restarted if there is a problem. The following table shows how to use a Do Select.

Section	Step	Action Type	Code	Description
Main	Step1	Do Select	`%Select(Year) Select Year from PS_RUN_CONTROL`	Get Year from Run Control Record.
	Step2	Do Select	`%Select(Emplid, Name) Select Emplid, Name from PS_TEST_REC where Year = %Bind(Year)`	Get the records with the correct year.
		SQL	`Insert into PS_TEST_NEW_REC Set Emplid = %Bind(Emplid), Name = %Bind(Name)`	Insert into the new test record with employees that match the year.

PeopleCode

PeopleCode is used within the Application Engine when data has to be manipulated, or else when already developed code, component interfaces, or application packages and functions are used. Refer to Chapter 6 for basic PeopleCode programming. To store and receive data from the state record, use the full qualified state record name plus the field name (for example, PS_TEST_AET.YEAR). Variables within the PeopleCode can be defined as Local, Global, and Component. Local variables are only used by the PeopleCode they are in. Global and Component variables can be used throughout the Application Engine program. To use the on-return parameter that was set on the action, use Exit(1). This will cause the program to Abort, Break, or Skip Step, depending on how it was set. The default is Exit(0), which will continue the Application Engine program no matter what is set on the return parameter. This allows for validation to be done within the PeopleCode that can affect processing of the AE program. The following table shows code for the usage of PeopleCode with the AE program.

Section	Step	Action Type	Code	Description
Main	Step1	Do Select	`%Select(Year) Select Year from PS_RUN_CONTROL`	Get Year from the Run Control Record.
	Step2	Do Select	`%Select(Emplid, Name, Salary) Select Emplid, Name, Salary from PS_TEST_REC where Year = %Bind(Year)`	Get the records with the correct year.
		PeopleCode	`Local number &Salary, &Bonus; &Salary = PS_TEST_AET. Salary; If &Salary> 50000 &Bonus = &Salary * .10; Else &Bonus = &Salary * .05; End-if; PS_TEST_AET.Bonus = &Bonus`	Calculate a bonus.
		SQL	`Update PS_TEST_REC Set Bonus = %Bind(Bonus) Where Emplid = %Bind(Emplid) And Year = %Bind(Year)`	Update the bonus field in the record where Emplid and Year match.

SQL

SQL actions are used for insert, update, and delete SQL statements. SQL actions can appear by themselves or be used with any of the conditional actions. This table shows an example of an update SQL statement.

Section	Step	Action Type	Code	Description
Main	Step1	Do Select	`%Select(Year) Select Year from PS_ RUN_CONTROL`	Get Year from the Run Control Record.
	Step2	Do Select	`%Select(Emplid, Bonus) Select Emplid, (Salary * .10) from PS_TEST_ REC where Year = %Bind(Year)`	Get the record with the correct year and calculate a bonus.

Section	Step	Action Type	Code	Description
		SQL	`Update PS_TEST_REC Set Bonus= %Bind(Bonus) Where Emplid = %Bind(Bonus) And Year = %Bind(Year)`	Update the record with the bonus amount where Emplid and Year match.

Call Section

Call Section is used when another section is needed. This allows for actions to be used within new steps. It also helps with the readability of the Application Engine program. The following table shows how to use a Call Section.

Section	Step	Action Type	Code	Description
Main	Step1	Call Section	`SETUP`	Call section Setup.
	Step2	Call Section	`UPDATE`	Call section Update.
SETUP	Step1	Do Select	`%Select(Year) Select Year from PS_RUN_CONTROL`	Get Year from the Run Control Record.
UPDATE	Step1	Do When	`Select 'X' from PS_TEST_REC where Year = %Bind(Year)`	Get the record with the correct year.
		SQL	`Update PS_TEST_NEW_REC Set Year = %Bind(Year)`	Update the new test record with the year.

Log Message

The Log Message action is useful for writing messages to the log file as you run your application engine program. These can help diagnose problems and provide control numbers. Messages stored in the message catalog can be used by providing the message set and number. Parameters can be sent as part of the message. For custom messages, create with a message set greater than 20000. A Log Message is used in the following table.

Section	Step	Action Type	Code	Description
Main	Step1	Do When	`Select 'X' from PS_TEST_REC where Count > %BIND(MAXCOUNT)`	Only process this step if count is above Max Count.
		LOG MESSAGE	`Message Set : 21000 Number: 50 Parameter: %BIND(PS_TEST_AET.MAXCOUNT)`	When count is above Max Count, send a message to the log.

Do Until

Do Until is another conditional action. It will continue to loop, executing all actions within the step while the condition is true. This process also requires code within another action to change the data that is making the looping SQL true; otherwise, you will create an endless loop. The following table shows how to use the Do Until statement.

Section	Step	Action Type	Code	Description
Main	Step1	Do Select	`%Select(TotEmp) Select Year from PS_ RUN_CONTROL`	Get Year from the Run Control Record.
	Step2	Call Section	`InsertEmps`	Call a section to Insert Employees.
		Do Until	`Select 'X' from PS_ TEST_REC where Count > %bind(TotEmp)`	Continue until Tot employees processes.

XSLT

XSLT is for program transformation. This action can only be used if it is specified within the Properties tab that the Application Engine program is a Transformation program. For more information on XSLT, refer to PeopleBooks Information Broker.

Running Application Engine Programs

To run an Application Engine program, you will need a run control, a page, a component, and permissions. Refer to Chapter 5 for creating a page, including a component, adding it to a menu, and setting up permissions. After an AE program has been created, a process definition needs to be created.

Process Definition

This section will show how to set up the process definition within PeopleSoft. Within PeopleSoft HRMS, go to PeopleTools | Process Scheduler | Processes. You will add a new process. The system will display the Add Process Definition box. The Process Type will be Application Engine. The Process Name will be the same as your program name. In the next two illustrations, you can see that there are multiple setup tabs. Only the Process Definition and Process Definition Options tabs are required; the others are optional. Fill out the Description and other requirements on the Process Definition page. On the Process Definition Options page, select a server and set up the security by connecting it to a component that contains your run control page. Click Save to save the definition. You are now able to go to your menu and run your AE program.

Process Definition | Process Definition Options | Override Options | Destination

Process Type: Application Engine
Name: PS_TEST_AE
*Description: PS_TEST_AE
API Aware
Long Description:
Restart Enabled?
Retry Count: 0
*Priority: Medium
*Process Category: Default Default Category

System Constraints

Max Concurrent: Max Processing Time: minutes

Mutually Exclusive Process(es) Customize | Find | First 1 of 1 Last

*Process Type *Process Name Description

1

Save Notify Add Update/Display

Process Definition | Process Definition Options | Override Options | Destination | Page Transfer | Notification | Message | OS390 Option | URL Links

Process Definition | Process Definition Options | Override Options | Destination

Process Type: Application Engine
Name: PS_TEST_AE

Server Name:
Recurrence Name:

On File Creation

File Dependency
Wait for File: Time Out Max Minutes:

System Recovery Process

Process Type: Process Name:

Process Security

Component | Process Groups

Save Notify Add Update/Display

Process Definition | Process Definition Options | Override Options | Destination | Page Transfer | Notification | Message | OS390 Option | URL Links

Using a Batch File

Sometimes you will want to test your AE program before you set it up within the PeopleSoft application, or you may want to set it up to run through external scheduling software. The use of a .bat file allows for this type of process. You will have to know how PeopleSoft is set up on your client machine to create the correct mappings in your .bat file. Here is an example:

```
\\ServerName\bin\client\winx86\PSAE.exe -CD database -CO USERID -CP
PASSWORD -R PS_TEST_RUN_CONTROL -AI PS_TEST_AE
```

The following table describes all the parameters that can be used with the Application Engine command line.

Parameter	Value	Required	Description
-CT	Database Types	Yes	Valid Database types: ORACLE, MICROSFT, DB2, DB2UNIX, SYBASE, INFORMIX
-CS	Server Name	Only required fro Informix and Sybase	Server Name
-CD	Database Name	Yes	Name of Database
-CO	User Id	Yes	The user ID that has access to the database
-CP	User Password	Yes	The password of the user ID
-R	Run Control Id	Yes	The run control table name
-AI	Application Engine Name	Yes	The name of the Application Engine program that needs to run
-I	Process Instance	Yes	The default is 0, unless there is a specific Process Instance number.
-DEBUG	Yes/No	No	The default is No. If Yes, it will launch the program within a debugger.
-DR	Yes/No	No	The default is No. If Yes, it will disable restart.

Parameter	Value	Required	Description
-TRACE	Number	No	1-Step Trace 2-SQL Trace 128-Timing statements 256-PeopleCode 1024-Stores Timing 2048-Database explain 4096-Stores Database
-DBFLAGS	Number	No	The default is 0. To disable the %UpdateStats Meta-SQL, use 1.
-TOOLSTRACESQL	Number	No	1-SQL statements 2-SQL statement variables 4-database-level commands 8-Row Fetch 16-All other API calls 32-Set Select Buffers 64-DB API–specific calls 128-COBOL timing statements 256-Sybase Bind 512-Sybase Fetch 4096-Manager information 8192-Message Agent
-TOOLSTRACEPC	Number	No	1-Instructions 2-List program steps 4-Variable assignments 8-Fetched values 16-Stack usage 64-Start of program 128-External function call 256-Internal function call 512-Parameter value 1024-Function return values 2048-All statements

Meta-SQL and Meta Variables

Since the power in Application Engines lies in the use of SQL commands, PeopleSoft delivers Meta-SQL. Some of these Meta-SQL commands are unique to Application Engine. Meta-variables can be used to get system-defined values. They are like reserved words in other languages. In this section we show how some of the most common delivered Meta-SQL and meta-variables are used. For more delivered Meta-SQL, refer to PeopleTools.

%AsofDate

%AsofDate will return the processing date of the Application Engine program.

```
Local Date &CurrDate;
&CurrDate = %AsofDate;
```

%Bind (Only Used in AE Programs)

%Bind is used to retrieve fields from the state record.

```
%Bind([Record Name.]Fieldname)
Insert into PS_TEST_REC
(Emplid, Bonus)
Values (%Bind(Emplid), %Bind(Bonus))
```

%Concat

%Concat will join two fields together. This is helpful when data needs to be stored into one field.

```
Fieldname1 %Concat Fieldname2
%Select (Emplid, Name)
Select Emplid, first_name %Concat last_name
From PS_PERSON_NAME
```

%CurrentDateIn

%CurrentDateIn will return the current system date used in SQL statements.

```
Select Emplid, Effdt
From PS_JOB
Where effdt < %CurrentDateIn
```

%CurrentDateOut

%CurrentDateOut is used to write out the current system date to a date field.

```
%Select(CurrDate, Emplid)
Select %CurrentDateOut, Emplid
From PS_TEST_REC
```

%Date

%Date will return the current system date.

```
Local Date CurrDate;
CurrDate = %Date;
```

%DateIn

%DateIn will be used when a date variable is being used as input variable. This will format the date correctly to the date format required by the database.

```
%DateIn(Date value)
Select Emplid, Name
From PS_Job
Where effdt > %DateIn('2007-12-01')
```

%DateOut

%DateOut should be used whenever you are selecting a date from the database and using it within your program as a date field.

```
%DateOut(Date  value)
%Select(Emplid, Bonus, Effdt)
Select Emplid, Bonus, %DateOut(Effdt)
From PS_TEST_REC
Where Effdt = %Bind(StartDate)
```

%DateAdd

%DateAdd will add the number of days to the date. If the number is negative, it will subtract the days from the date.

```
%DateAdd(Date value, Number)
Select Emplid, Bonus, %DateAdd(Effdt,30)
From PS_TEST_REC
```

%DateDiff

%DateDiff will return the number of days between two date fields.

```
%DateDiff(Date value, Date value)
Select Emplid, Bonus
From PS_TEST_REC
Where %DateDiff(%DateIn('2007-12-31',effdt) < 30
```

%InsertSelect

%InsertSelect will do an insert based on the Select statement. The fields are based on an Insert record. Fields can be overwritten by adding them to the end of the Meta-SQL. If no override field is added, the fields with the same name will be used.

```
%InsertSelect([Distinct,]Record Name of Insert, Record Name of Select,
[Where Clause])[,Override Field = value]
%InsertSelect(PS_TEST_NEW, PS_TEST_REC, where Year = '2007')
```

%OperatorId

%OperatorID will return the user ID of the person currently logged in and running the Application Engine Program. This will help when trying to retrieve the correct record from a Run Control record.

```
%Select(effdt, erncd, amount)
Select %Dateout(effdt), erncd, amount from PS_Test_Run_Control
Where oprid = %OperatorId
```

%ReturnCode

%ReturnCode is the return code for the last Application Engine step that was performed. If the step is successful, the %ReturnCode is set to 0.

%Round

%Round will round the number to the precision given as the factor. A factor is the number past the decimal point.

```
%Round(Number, Factor)
Select %Round(hour_sal,2)
From Ps_job
Where emplid = %bind(emplid)
Select %Round(Annual_sal,0)
From PS_JOB
Where emplid = %bind(emplid)
```

%RunControl

%RunControl will return the run control ID that is currently being used to run the Application Engine program.

```
%Select(effdt, erncd, amount)
Select %Dateout(effdt), erncd, amount from PS_Test_Run_Control
Where oprid = %OperatorId
And run_cntl_id = %RunControl
```

%Select (Only Used in AE Programs)

%Select is used with the Do Select action. It will store all your fields in the default AET record. Fieldnames must be valid fields in the state record.

```
%Select(Fieldname1, Fieldname2, Fieldname3...)
%Select(Emplid, Name)
Select Emplid, Name
From PS_TEST_REC
```

%SelectAll

%SelectAll will select all the fields from the records. It will default the Date fields to %DateOut. This is good to use with the CreateSQL functions when most of the fields from the record will need to be used.

```
CreateSQL("%SelectAll(:1)",&TestRec);
```

%SelectInit (Only Used in AE Programs)

%SelectInit works the same as the %Select for storing the fields on the State Record. The only difference is that it clears the State Record fields before inserting the new data. This is helpful if the select returns no rows. The data in the state record will be blank or null, depending on the data types.

```
%SelectInit(Fieldname1, Fieldname2, Fieldname3...)
%Select(Emplid, Name)
Select Emplid, Name
From PS_TEST_REC
```

%Substring

%Substring will take portions of a string when you give it the starting position and the length of the new string.

```
%Substring(String, Starting Position, Length)
Select Emplid, %Substring(Org_unit,3,2)
From PS_TEST_REC
```

%Table (Only Used in AE Programs)

%Table will return the full table name. If it is a temp table, it will return the table instance that is being used.

```
%Table(TableName_TAO)
&SQL = "Select from %Table(:1) where " | emplid | " = :2";

SQLExec(&SQL, @("RECORD." | "Temp_TAO"), &emplid);
```

%Truncate

%Truncate works like %Round but will remove all numbers after the factor.

```
%Truncate(Number, Factor)
Select %Truncate(Bonus,0)
From PS_TEST_REC
Where emplid = %bind(emplid)
```

%Upper

%Upper will convert the data in the string to uppercase. This is useful if you want to be consistent in checking for string values.

```
%Upper(String)
Select Emplid, Name
From PS_PERSON_NAME
Where %Upper(Name)  like 'san%'
```

Printing Application Engine Programs

Hard copy documentation is sometimes hard to retrieve from PeopleTools for some objects. That is not the case for Application Engine programs. PeopleTools delivers the option to print your AE program in the program flow layout or in the program definition. It also lets you decide what parts of the AE program you would like to print. The following illustration shows what options are available for printing when you are on the program definition page.

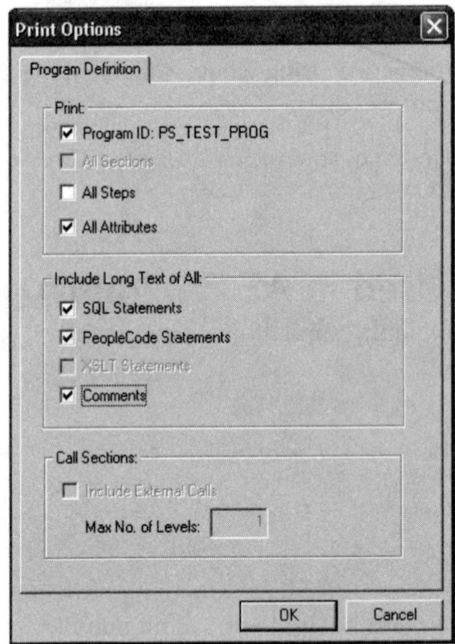

From this screen you can select to print the entire Application Engine program, or just the current section or step that you are in. You can also decide to print any of the long text (SQL, PeopleCode, and Comments). The following is the report if the whole AE program is printed.

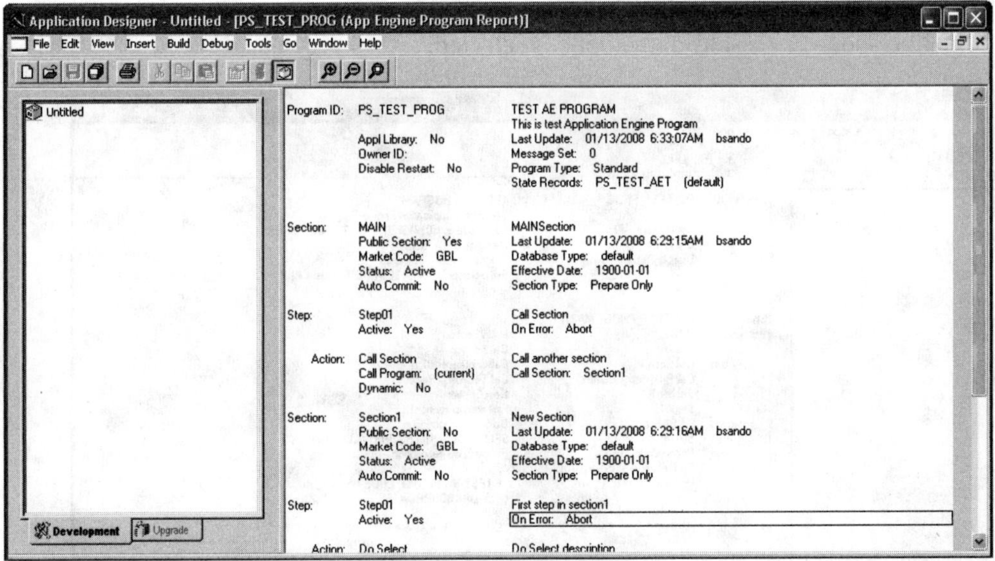

The options are basically the same for printing the Program Flow of the program. The following illustration shows these options. The options that can be selected have the check box available.

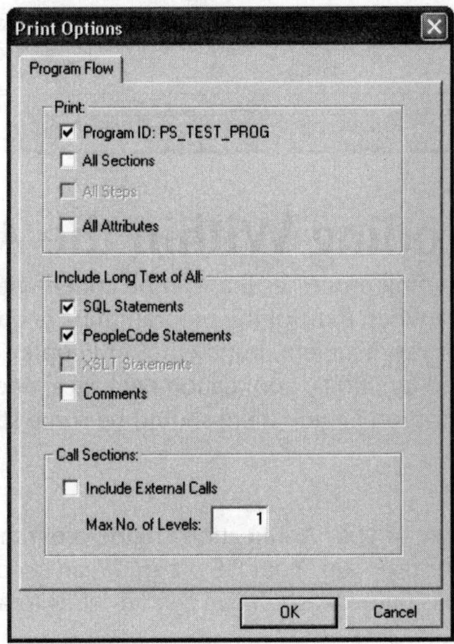

Depending on what options you select, it will produce different results. This illustration shows the results of the options selected.

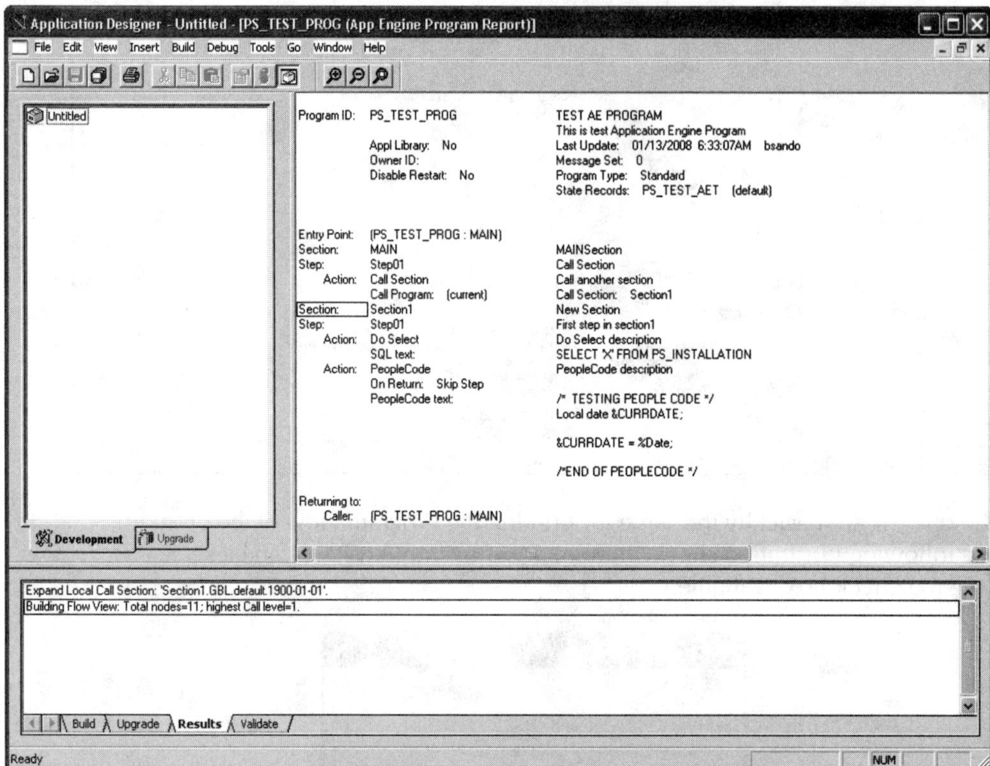

Advanced Coding Within the App Engine

There are many programming processes that can be coded with an Application Engine program. It is best when most of the programming is done with SQL statements. This makes it very efficient, but the use of PeopleCode actions allows the use of many delivered functions, application packages, and component interfaces. For any Application Engine there should be some structure.

Using E-Mail

Depending on the purpose of your Application Engine program, the use of the e-mails can enhance your program. Your AE program can send an e-mail when the process is complete or has failed. Also, it can send e-mails to a group of employees with the same criteria. The e-mail function SendMail is used within the PeopleCode action. Refer to PeopleBooks for all the options available with this function.

```
SendMail(flags, Email_Address, CC, BCC, subject, text)
SendMail(0, &EMAIL, "", "", &SUBJECT, &TEXT);
```

Input and Output Files

Reading input files and creating output files helps with interfacing to other applications. There is still a lot of work done in Excel, Access, and text files. Using input and output files with an AE program can help you use and create data for external applications. Within your PeopleCode action, an external file should be declared a Global variable so that it can be used throughout your AE program. The path and filename need to be explicitly defined. There are delivered functions that help with using files. GetFile will open a file:

```
GetFile(File Name, {R,W,U},[Char Set],[Path Type])
GetFile(&path | &filename, "W", %FilePath_Absolute)
```

To check to see if the file is open, use FileName.Open; to write to the file, use FileName.Writeline; and to read, use FileName.Readline. Use a while loop with the Readline function to process multiple rows of data. Format your data for output with a file layout or create a comma-delimited file. This will make it easy for users to read the data into their applications.

```
Local File &Infile;
Local String &Allfile, &Emplid, &Name;
&InFile = GetFile(&path | &filename, "W", %FilePath_Absolute)
If &Infile.Open then
  While &InFile.Readline
      &Allfile = &Infile;
      &Emplid = Substring(&Allfile,1,6);
      &Name = Substring(&Allfile,10,20);
     ....  Process Data....
   End-While;
&Infile.Close;
End-if;
```

Reading Records

When using PeopleCode, there are many ways to retrieve data from the database. When using pages or components, it is best to use CreateRowSet to retrieve data from the screen. It can also be used in an Application Engine program, but it just requires more programming to keep track of what row you are on. A better solution is to use CreateRecord with a CreateSQL function. This will instantiate a record and use SQL to retrieve the rows.

```
Local record &TestRec;
Local SQL &TestSql;
Local string &Emplid;
Local number &Bonus;
&Bonus = 0;
&TestRec = CreateRecord(PS_TEST_REC);
&TestSql = CreateSql("%SelectAll(:1) where EMPLID = :2",&TestRec, &Emplid);
While &TestSql.Fetch(&TestRec)
     &Bonus = &Bonus + &TestRec.Bonus;
End-While;
```

Sample Programs

The following are two simple Application Engine programs. They will show how an AE program can be structured. For any Application Engine there should be some structure for readability. The following sample programs show the basic recommended structuring of the sections.

- **Main** Required section
- **Setup** All setup work needed for the Application Engine program to work properly
- **Process** Working sections, these sections will process all the work
- **Cleanup** Closing file and finalizing any processing

Inserting Records

This sample program will insert records into a Bonus Table.

The run control record has the following fields:

```
PS_TEST_RUN_Control
Oprid
Run_cntl_id
Effdt
Erncd
Amount
```

The AET record has the following fields:

```
PS_BONUS_AET Table
Process_instance
```

```
Effdt
Erncd
Amount
TotCnt
```

This Application Engine program will get information from the Run control, get the employees that fit the criteria, and insert the information into a Bonus Record. It will also track how many records it has inserted and write it out to the log. This Application Engine Progam PS_Bonus is shown in the following table.

PS_BONUS

Section	Step	Action	Code
Main	Step01	Call Section	`Setup`
	Step02	Call Section	`GetData`
	Step03	Call Section	`CleanUp`

Setup	Step01	Do Select	`%Select(effdt, erncd, amount)`
			`Select %Dateout(effdt), erncd, amount`
			`from PS_Test_Run_Control`
			`Where oprid = %OperatorId`
			`And run_cntl_id = %RunControl`

GetData	Step01	Do Select	`%Select(emplid)`
			`SELECT b.emplid`
			` FROM ps_service_date a`
			` WHERE service_yrs = 5`

	Step02	SQL	`Insert Emplid, effdt, amount into`
			`PS_Bonus_Table values (%bind(Emplid),`
			`%bind(effdt), %bind(amount))`

	Step03	PeopleCode	`Local number &totinsert;`
			
			`&totinserts = PS_TEST_AET.TotCnt + 1;`
			` PS_TEST_AET.TotCnt = &totinserts;`

CleanUp	Step01	PeopleCode	`/* Write to the log Total records`
			`inserted */`
			`Local number &totinsert;`
			`&totinserts = PS_TEST_AET.TotCnt;`
			`MessageBox(0, "" ,0 ,0 , "Number of`
			`records Inserted: " | &totinserts);`

Writing a File

This sample program will retrieve Sick Time Earnings from the database and write out a comma delimited file.

The run control record has the following fields:

```
PS_TEST_RUN_Control
Oprid
Run_cntl_id
Begin_dt
End_date
```

The AET record has the following fields:

```
PS_TEST_AET Table
Process_instance
Begin_dt
End_date
Emplid
Name
Tot_hrs
```

The following Application Engine program will get information from the Run Control Record and store it in an AET record, as shown in the following table. This information will be used to pull the requested data. This data will be written out as a comma-delimited text file.

PS_WRITE_SICK

Section	Step	Action	Code
Main	Step01	Call Section	`Setup`
	Step02	Call Section	`GetData`
	Step03	Call Section	`CleanUp`

Setup	Step01	Do Select	`%Select(begin_dt, end_date)`
			`Select %Dateout(begin-dt),`
			`%Dateout(End_date) from PS_Test_Run_`
			`Control`
			`Where oprid = %OperatorId`
			`And run_cntl_id = %RunControl`

Section	Step	Action	Code
	Step02	PeopleCode	`Global File &Sickfile;` `Local string &StringHdr1,` `&StringHdr2, &Blnkstr, &filename,` `&path;` `Local date &currdate;` `&filename = "SickTime.txt";` `&path = "\\myserver\stage\data\";` `&currdate = %Date;` `&Blnkstr = " ";` `&Sickfile = GetFile(&path |` `&filename, "W", %FilePath_Absolute)` `&StringHdr1 = "Sick Time File -` `daterun= "	&currdate;` `&StringHdr2 = "Emplid, Name, Total` `Sick Hours";` `&Sickfile.WriteLine(&StringHdr1);` `&Sickfile.WriteLine(&Blnkstr);` `&Sickfile.WriteLine(&StringHdr2);`

GetData	Step01	Do Select	`%Select(emplid, name, tot_hrs)`
			`SELECT b.emplid`
			`,b.name`
			`, SUM(a.oth_hrs)`
			`FROM ps_pay_oth_earns a`
			`, ps_pay_check b`
			`WHERE a.company = b.company`
			`AND a.paygroup = b.paygroup`
			`AND a.pay_end_dt = b.pay_end_dt`
			`AND a.off_cycle = b.off_cycle`
			`AND a.page_num = b.page_num`
			`AND a.line_num = b.line_num`
			`AND b.paycheck_status = 'F'`
			`AND a.pay_end_dt >= %Bind(Begin_dt)`
			`AND a.pay_end_dt <= %Bind(end_date)`
			`AND erncd = 'SIC'`
			`GROUP BY b.name , b.emplid ,`
			`HAVING SUM(a.oth_hrs) <> 0`

	Step02	Call Section	`WriteData`

Section	Step	Action	Code
WriteData	Step01	PeopleCode	Global File &Sickfile; Local string &string, &emplid, &name; Local number &tothours; &emplid = PS_TEST_AET.EMPLID; &name = PS_TEST_AET.NAME; &tothours = PS_TEST_AET.TOT_HRS; &string = &emplid | "," | &name | ", " | &tothours; If &Sickfile.IsOpen Then &Sickfile.WriteLine(&string); End-If;
CleanUp	Step01	PeopleCode	/* Close file */ Global File &Sickfile; &Sickfile.Close();

Summary

In this chapter you have learned how to create an Application Engine program. You've learned what the structure looks like and how, when created properly, such a program can be a very powerful programming tool. AE programs should be used for most of your batch processing since they have access to all the PeopleSoft objects. They can read and write files from other applications and take advantage of delivered edits when component interfaces are called from within the AE program. This will keep the data integrity the same as if it were keyed through the application. They also have a good print view that can be used for documenting your AE program in a hard/soft copy format.

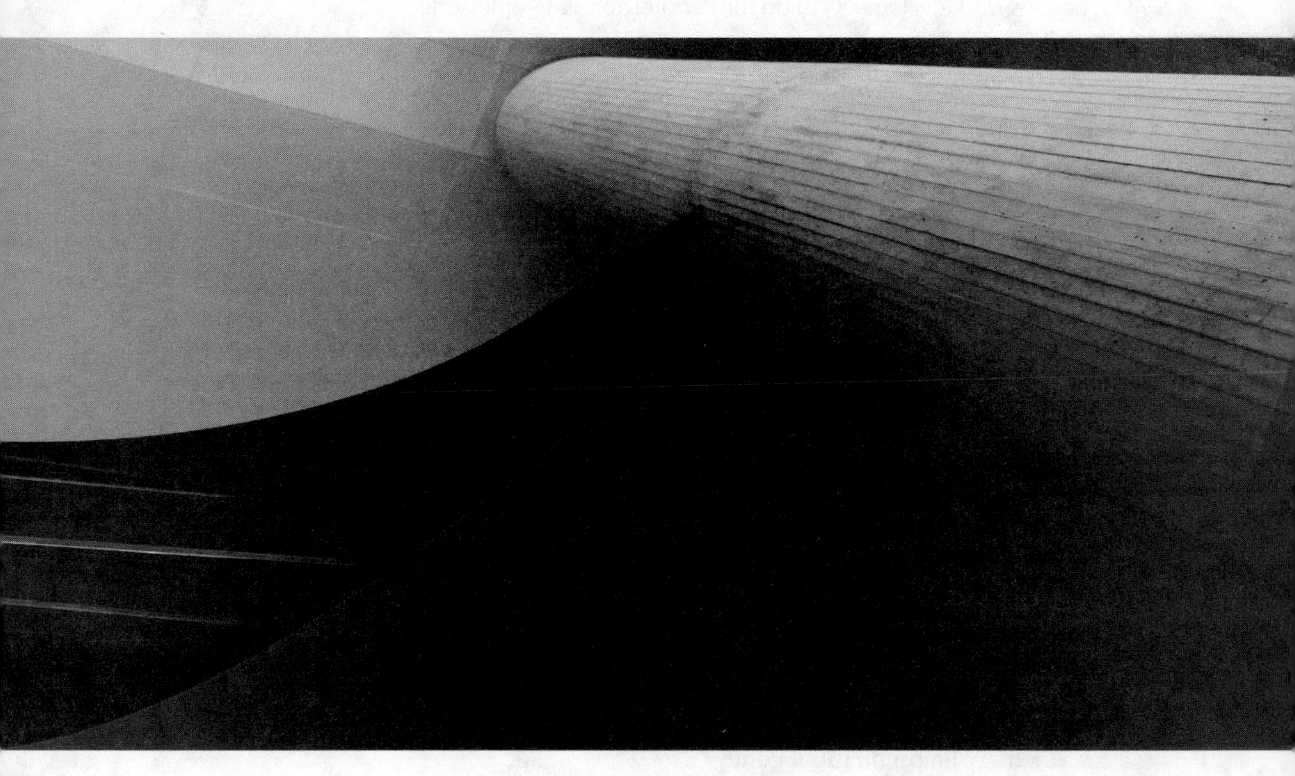

CHAPTER 12

Tips and Tricks

In this chapter we will look at some of the tricks of the trade and learn how to do things more efficiently. You will learn when to use what language and where to place your code. And you will learn the answers to the all-important question, how do I debug this situation? Over the years I have saved in my bag of tricks many ideas found on the Internet or provided by other developers. You will be given a list of handy web sites, suggestions on where to go when you can't find the answer, and a sample of my favorites saved over the years. I hope that you will find each of them as cool and handy as I did.

Quick Answer Web Sites

The best and the quickest source for PeopleSoft Tips and Tricks is the web. Of course you can do the easiest thing and type your problem or error message directly into Google and search, which nine times out of ten will return just what you need. In my group at work, the team has put together a list of web sites that is updated frequently in our SharePoint web site. The following is the list that currently exists:

- https://www.peoplesoft.com/corp/en/login.jsp
- http://jjmpsj.blogspot.com/
- http://blogs.oracle.com/jesper_andersen/
- http://oraclefusion.blogspot.com/
- http://blog.psftdba.com/
- http://peoplesoftexperts.blogspot.com/
- http://psguyblog.blogspot.com/index.html
- http://manalang.wordpress.com/2006/02/01/adding-live-search-to-peoplesoft-enterprise/
- http://blog.greysparling.com/
- http://www.searchpsoft.com/

In the following article Larry Grey goes deeply into how to create queries with parameters. "This is an important way to run an nVision report, and you can use it to create simple prompt queries. One of the ways it has been used for my team is to allow the customer to determine a date range over which they would like data for a specific query and then dump the results into an Excel spreadsheet. Our team does not work on nVision, and although I have experience on a financial team, some of the tips from this web site can be taken in small pieces and applied in numerous ways. Take a look at http://blog.greysparling.com/2006/05/nvision-with-query-prompts.html and see if you can think of several different applications of this unique way of creating queries that prompt the end user."

My favorite and most accurate place to get direction is PeopleBooks. Unfortunately, sometimes PeopleBooks doesn't have the easiest or most straight-to-the-point examples to follow, but that said, it is still the number one place to learn anything related to PeopleCode, PeopleTools, or the PeopleSoft application. Your group should have PeopleBooks installed at an easy-to-locate web site, but if it doesn't, you can download your very own copy and install it locally on your machine. Download your version, or if you want to read about the newest, latest, and greatest version, you can also download that and study to your hearts content:

www.oracle.com/technology/documentation/psftent.html

My next favorite place to get help is my network of friends. But what if you are new to PeopleSoft or the industry and don't have a network of friends? You can get them through the user groups. Quest is where the PeopleSoft user groups primarily ended up after the Oracle acquisition, and IOUG also has a very active PeopleSoft SIG that deals primarily with DBA issues in the PeopleSoft application. You can join Quest for free at www.questdirect.org/questdirect/; you can join IOUG for free at www.ioug.org/networking/peoplesoft.cfm.

The next recommendation is to go to as many training sessions, user group meetings, conferences, and Oracle-sponsored training sessions as you are allowed. The more exposure, the more practice, and the more networking you can do, the quicker your skill level will increase. One of my favorite conferences is COLLABORATE, co-sponsored by IOUG (Independent Oracle Users Group), Quest International, and OAUG (Oracle Application User Group). Consider these groups as you would consider a lobbyist; they have direct connections with Oracle and have the power to make your voice heard. The more you give to these types of groups, the more you will get in return to help your career. Some suggestions for tech groups:

- http://peoplesoft.ittoolbox.com/groups/#
- http://tech.groups.yahoo.com/group/peoplesoft-fans/

Keep in mind too that one of your greatest resources as a PeopleSoft customer is MetaLink. You can use it to query for your specific problem or open a case to have a team of top PeopleSoft gurus look into your problem.

Metadata Tips

One of the most important things in an application upgrade, a tools upgrade, or even a database upgrade is to understand the difference between your physical database and the metadata. In a recent Tools upgrade, PeopleSoft changed the default on their indexes. Instead of defaulting to ASC sort order, PeopleSoft decided to change the default on date data types to DESC. At first thought, you may say, "So what?" Well, if you have a bolt-on written that matches up your year and month in a rowset, the order in which the data loads and retrieves is very important. It will no longer behave the way it had for many years, in this case since 1999. Only after members of my team beat their heads against a brick wall for many days was it discovered that the indexes were different—the code was fine and had been since 1999, but the new way the data came back prevented the data from loading in the way expected. So, as you can see, the metadata can really adversely affect your application and the overall health of your database. The tip for this problem is to have your DBA do a compare between schemas to the index level. See the sample code at the end of this section.

Another really handy tip in the world of metadata concerns how you locate your objects in the metadata. Well, you use SQL and you write queries against the metadata tables. Here are some examples:

```
--use to find component and panel
SELECT *
FROM PSAUTHITEM
WHERE PNLITEMNAME = 'TC_PENSION_CURRENT'
--BARITEMNAME IS Component
--PNLITEMNAME IS Panel
-------------------------------------------------------------------
--how to find metadata record in PeopleSoft to use to make SQL
--for example
OPEN Definition
------Definition: Record
--also
------FOR NAME enter: PS
------FOR Description: Role
------FOR TYPE dropdown: TABLE
-------------------------------------------------------------------
--permission list
SELECT *
FROM PSCLASSDEFN
WHERE CLASSID = 'CPEB1000' OR CLASSID = 'XCBP1010' OR CLASSID = 'TC_DEV'
--Roles for users
SELECT *
FROM PSROLEMEMBER
WHERE ROLEUSER = 'jsmith'
--examples
jsmith  PAPP_USER
jsmith  PeopleSoft USER
jsmith  TC_EMPLOYEE
```

```
jsmith  TC_ER_RECRUITER
jsmith  TC_ER_RECRUITER_ADMIN
jsmith  TC_HR_APP_DATA
jsmith  TC_HR_EDUC_DTA
--meta records for roles
--L0 high level one row
SELECT *
FROM PSROLEDEFN
WHERE  ROLENAME = 'TC_EMPLOYEE'
--L1 Next Level
SELECT *
FROM PSROLECLASS
WHERE ROLENAME = 'TC_EMPLOYEE' AND (CLASSID = 'CPEB1000' OR CLASSID =
'XCBP1010')
SELECT *
FROM PSROLECLASS
WHERE (CLASSID = 'CPEB1000' OR CLASSID = 'XCBP1010' OR CLASSID = 'TC_DEV')
----watch out for redirects Security definitions can be buried very deeply.
```

One of the handiest tables of metadata is PSQRYSTATS, which reports on the usage of PSQuery queries, one of the most sought-after pieces of information because it tells what the business is really interested in seeing.

```
SELECT *
FROM PSQRYSTATS
```

It also tells you if a query is running slow. If you don't turn on Query Statistics, however, it will not gather this information. You turn it on by going to PeopleTools | Utilities | Administration | Query Administration. PSQRYSTATS and PSQuery metadata in general is more effective if your organization has some type of prefix-naming convention for custom queries, such as 0POxxxxxx for Purchasing Queries, 0APxxxxxx for AP queries, etc., because this segregates the queries by subject matter.

The next tip is how to find the page in PeopleSoft (the portal system). The following query, which was created by Bryan Norris, gathers the portal information. The fields are narrowed down to one `PORTAL_URLTEXT`. He uses the component name to retrieve the rows for gathering the address. Take a look at the example:

```
SELECT *
FROM PSPRSMPERM A, PSPRSMDEFN B
WHERE A.PORTAL_NAME = B.PORTAL_NAME
AND A.PORTAL_REFTYPE = B.PORTAL_REFTYPE
AND A.PORTAL_OBJNAME = B.PORTAL_OBJNAME
AND B.PORTAL_URI_SEG2 = 'HR_SSTEXT_LANG'
--Run this SQL too:
SELECT 'https://[server name]/psp/[instance name]/EMPLOYEE/HRMS/' || 'c/' ||
```

```
PORTAL_URI_SEG1 || '.' || PORTAL_URI_SEG2 ||'.'|| PORTAL_URI_SEG3' AS
Address_string
FROM PSPRSMPERM A, PSPRSMDEFN B
WHERE A.PORTAL_NAME = B.PORTAL_NAME
AND A.PORTAL_REFTYPE = B.PORTAL_REFTYPE
AND A.PORTAL_OBJNAME = B.PORTAL_OBJNAME
AND B.PORTAL_URI_SEG2 = 'HR_SSTEXT_LANG'
----You need to find the component that the page uses.
```

This will then return the value of the page address in the browser. Just paste it into the browser, and you will go to the page you are looking for in PeopleSoft. Once you find the page, you're good to go. This process can be refined, but this should get you started on creating your own queries against the metadata to help you locate that needle in a haystack on the page in the PeopleSoft application.

Let's take a look at how Bryan found the metadata Tables in Peoplesoft. The following shows you the result of looking for records that have the description of Portal.

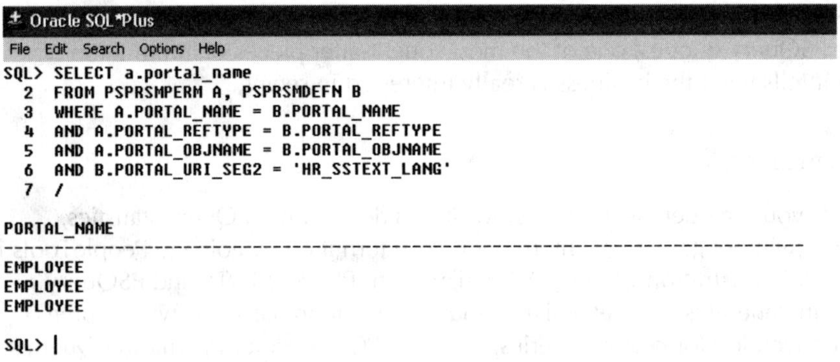

```
Oracle SQL*Plus
File Edit Search Options Help
SQL> SELECT a.portal_name
  2  FROM PSPRSMPERM A, PSPRSMDEFN B
  3  WHERE A.PORTAL_NAME = B.PORTAL_NAME
  4  AND A.PORTAL_REFTYPE = B.PORTAL_REFTYPE
  5  AND A.PORTAL_OBJNAME = B.PORTAL_OBJNAME
  6  AND B.PORTAL_URI_SEG2 = 'HR_SSTEXT_LANG'
  7  /

PORTAL_NAME
------------------------------------------------------------------------------
EMPLOYEE
EMPLOYEE
EMPLOYEE

SQL> |
```

From there how did he find the component to put in the SQL? He found the prompt record, and from there he kept doing a find definition reference from record to page to component to menu (even searching through projects the objects are attached to) to each object, and presto!

```
Page HR_SSTEXT_LANG
Results Fine Definition Reference
Searching for references to page HR_SSTEXT_LANG ...
Found in component: HR_SSTEXT_LANG.GBL
Found in Project: UPGDBCOMP1
Found in Project: UPGDBCOMP2
Search completed and 3 reference(s) found.
```

Another really handy tip on the metadata is to find out if a process has a process scheduler. Why is this important? Well, after one of our senior developers left, we quickly discovered that all of his jobs stopped running. This was because they were scheduled to run under a user that no longer existed. Take a look at the following:

```
--How to find if a process has a process Scheduler
--What page it has attached, and type
--Also who runs the process, even people who are gone
--Who ran what process
--is there a process scheduler for an SQR or process app engine
--also description plus Page
SELECT A.PRCSTYPE,
A.PRCSNAME,
PNLGRPNAME,
DESCRLONG
FROM PS_PRCSDEFN A, PS_PRCSDEFNPNL B
WHERE A.PRCSTYPE = B.PRCSTYPE
AND A.PRCSNAME = B.PRCSNAME
AND B.PRCSNAME = 'SHRS104U'
--what user ran what process
SELECT *
FROM PS_PMN_PRCSLIST
WHERE RUNCNTLID = 'jharmst'
SELECT *
FROM PS_PMN_PRCSLIST
WHERE RUNCNTLID = :RUNCNTLID
--who ran this process
SELECT *
FROM PS_PMN_PRCSLIST
WHERE PRCSNAME = 'SHRS104U'
SELECT *
FROM PS_PMN_PRCSLIST
WHERE PRCSNAME = :PRCSNAME
--To find the who and the process
SELECT *
FROM PS_PMN_PRCSLIST
WHERE RUNCNTLID = :RUNCNTLID
AND PRCSNAME = :PRCSNAME
SELECT *
FROM PS_PMN_PRCSLIST
WHERE RUNCNTLID = :RUNCNTLID
AND PRCSNAME = :PRCSNAME
```

It never hurts to be able to know who, what, and what type when it comes to permissions. Take a look at the following metadata. The first query will retrieve which role and which OPRID, whereas the second will retrieve the operator alias, and the third will show the definition of the operator.

```
SELECT * FROM PS_ROLEXLATOPR
SELECT * FROM PSOPRALIAS
SELECT * FROM PSOPRDEFN
```

On my team we quickly discovered you can have a problem if a particular OPRID is the owner of a scheduled process in Process Scheduler. The following SQL will find if a process has a Process Scheduler, what page it has attached, the type, and who ran the process.

```
--is there a process scheduler for an SQR or process app engine
--also desc plus Page
SELECT A.PRCSTYPE,
A.PRCSNAME,
PNLGRPNAME,
DESCRLONG
FROM PS_PRCSDEFN A, PS_PRCSDEFNPNL B
WHERE A.PRCSTYPE = B.PRCSTYPE
AND A.PRCSNAME = B.PRCSNAME
AND B.PRCSNAME = 'SHRS104U'
--what user ran what process
SELECT * FROM PS_PMN_PRCSLIST WHERE RUNCNTLID = 'jsmith'
SELECT * FROM PS_PMN_PRCSLIST WHERE RUNCNTLID = :RUNCNTLID
--who ran this process
SELECT * FROM PS_PMN_PRCSLIST WHERE PRCSNAME = 'SHRS104U'
SELECT * FROM PS_PMN_PRCSLIST WHERE PRCSNAME = :PRCSNAME
--the who and the process
SELECT * FROM PS_PMN_PRCSLIST
WHERE RUNCNTLID = :RUNCNTLID AND  PRCSNAME = :PRCSNAME
SELECT * FROM PS_PMN_PRCSLIST
WHERE RUNCNTLID = :RUNCNTLID AND  PRCSNAME = :PRCSNAME
```

The following is a handy small SQL to find records with fields. Note that you can use any field name. It is nice because it shows you how many times a field is used and where. It also shows the indexes so that you can determine where it is used as a key.

```
--find records with these keys
SELECT * FROM PSRECDEFN A
WHERE RECTYPE = 0
AND INDEXCOUNT = 1
AND A.Recname =
(SELECT Recname FROM PSRECFIELD B WHERE FIELDNAME = 'APPLID' AND
B.RECNAME = A.RECNAME )
AND A.Recname =
(SELECT Recname FROM PSRECFIELD C WHERE C.FIELDNAME = 'JOB_REQ_NBR' AND
C.RECNAME = A.RECNAME )
AND A.Recname =
(SELECT Recname FROM PSRECFIELD D WHERE D.FIELDNAME = 'APP_DT' AND
D.RECNAME = A.RECNAME )
AND RECNAME NOT LIKE '%GVT%'
AND RECNAME NOT LIKE 'UPG%'
```

```
AND RECNAME NOT LIKE 'APPEXP%'
AND RECNAME NOT LIKE 'HROFFERDAT%'
AND RECNAME NOT LIKE '%TAO%'
AND RECNAME NOT LIKE '%AET%'
AND RECNAME NOT LIKE '%TEO%'
AND RECNAME NOT LIKE 'PS_IV_SCHED_TIMES'
```

Just recently I was helping a teammate on a problem he was having with an Application Engine. The Application Engine was referring to a field that he had put in his view the first time he had created the view, although he had long since deleted it, but much to his dismay the Application Engine was seeing the field in the metadata and not the table in the Production Application, so it was giving a nice error to his customer. The following is what we used to determine that the metadata was different from the desc in the database. Of course in this case we used the Field and Record metadata queries, but I have included the common ones, because you just never know what you might need to find.

```
--Projects
select * from PSPROJECTDEFN
select * from PSPROJECTITEM
--fields
select * from PSDBFIELD
--records
select * from PSRECDEFN
select * from PSRECFIELD
--Pages
select * from PSPNLDEFN
select * from PSPNLFIELD
--components
select * from PSPNLGRPDEFN
select * from PSPNLGROUP
--menus
select * from PSMENUDEFN
select * from PSMENUITEM
--Peoplecode
select * from PSPCMNAME
select * from PSPCMPROG
--user
select * from PSOPRDEFN
select * from PSROLEUSER
Select * from PSOPRALIAS
select * from PS_ROLEXLATOPR
```

Another recent problem our team had was with the upgrade from PeopleTools 8.46 to PeopleTools 8.49. The indexes changed, and instead of defaulting to ASC sort order on the dates, it changed to defaulting to DESC, which caused a problem in our code that was loading into a RowSet. The following is a good script to have the DBA run and give you anytime you want to upgrade your tools to know if anything has changed down to the index level. You can modify this MINUS query to fit your environments or to add additional columns—whatever will help you diagnose your problem.

```
SELECT table_name, index_name, descend
FROM user_ind_columns@PSDV1
MINUS
SELECT table_name, index_name, descend
FROM user_ind_columns@pspr1
```

XLAT Changes in 8.9

The xlat table is now XLATtable; Peoplesoft delivers a view of the example SQL. Note that the naming convention does not have a PS_ in front of the record. The following SQL statements show the new tables:

```
SELECT * FROM PSXLATItem
SELECT * FROM PSXLATdefn
SELECT * FROM XLATtable_VW
```

Security Overview of Primary Table Relations

The following are SQL statements that join the relevant tables to determine who can access what and what can be accessed by whom.

```
/* all User IDs */
SELECT OPRID
FROM PSOPRDEFN
ORDER BY OPRID
/* all role names */
SELECT ROLENAME
FROM PSROLEDEFN
ORDER BY ROLENAME
/* all permission lists (class names) */
SELECT CLASSID
FROM PSCLASSDEFN
ORDER BY CLASSID
/* users --> roles */
SELECT ROLEUSER, ROLENAME
FROM PSROLEUSER
ORDER BY ROLEUSER, ROLENAME
/* users --> permission lists (class names) */
SELECT DISTINCT UR.ROLEUSER, RP.CLASSID
```

```
FROM PSROLEUSER UR, PSROLECLASS RP
WHERE UR.ROLENAME = RP.ROLENAME
ORDER BY UR.ROLEUSER, RP.CLASSID
/* users --> components */
SELECT DISTINCT UR.ROLEUSER
, PC.MENUNAME
, PC.BARNAME
, PC.BARITEMNAME
, PC.PNLITEMNAME
FROM PSROLEUSER UR, PSROLECLASS RP, PSAUTHITEM PC
WHERE UR.ROLENAME = RP.ROLENAME
AND RP.CLASSID = PC.CLASSID
ORDER BY UR.ROLEUSER, PC.MENUNAME, PC.BARNAME, PC.BARITEMNAME,
PC.PNLITEMNAME
/* roles --> permission lists (class names) */
SELECT ROLENAME, CLASSID
FROM PSROLECLASS
ORDER BY ROLENAME, CLASSID
/* roles --> components */
SELECT DISTINCT RP.ROLENAME
, PC.MENUNAME
, PC.BARNAME
, PC.BARITEMNAME
, PC.PNLITEMNAME
FROM PSROLECLASS RP, PSAUTHITEM PC
WHERE RP.CLASSID = PC.CLASSID
```

You would use these pivot tables in Excel to create reports for Technical Auditors, or there is a way in SQL to pivot tables as well if you know the distinct names of the roles.

```
SELECT DISTINCT
,CASE WHEN RP.ROLENAME = 'APCLERK'
           THEN 'Has Privileges'
            ELSE 'No Privileges'
           END AP_CLERK
,CASE WHEN RP.ROLENAME = 'APMANAGER'
           THEN 'Has Privileges'
            ELSE 'No Privileges'
           END AP_MANAGER
, PC.MENUNAME
, PC.BARNAME
, PC.BARITEMNAME
, PC.PNLITEMNAME
FROM PSROLECLASS RP, PSAUTHITEM PC
WHERE RP.CLASSID = PC.CLASSID
```

PIA Tips

When you are working in the application, there are little things that become nice to have features and that your customers may request. Or maybe you just like going the extra mile. The following section of Tips and Tricks will cover some of the things that you may encounter as your career as a PeopleSoft developer continues. You may know some of them, and some of them may be new, but hopefully you will find value in the tips that are offered. The first one covers how you make a button default and have it fire off when the customer presses ENTER. In this illustration the customer would like the Career's page Apply Now Continue Button to be activated with the ENTER key. The illustration shows you the page through the PIA.

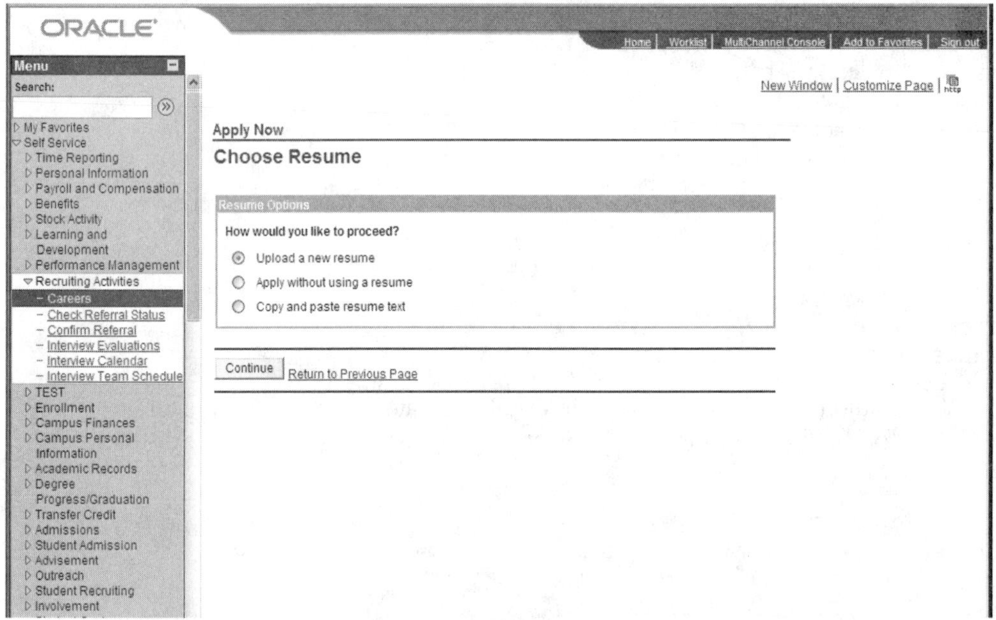

In the next illustration you see the properties of the Push Button/Hyperlink via Application Designer. You can see under the Type tab that there is a check box for Activate By Enter Key. Place a check here and your button or hyperlink will be activated when your customer presses ENTER.

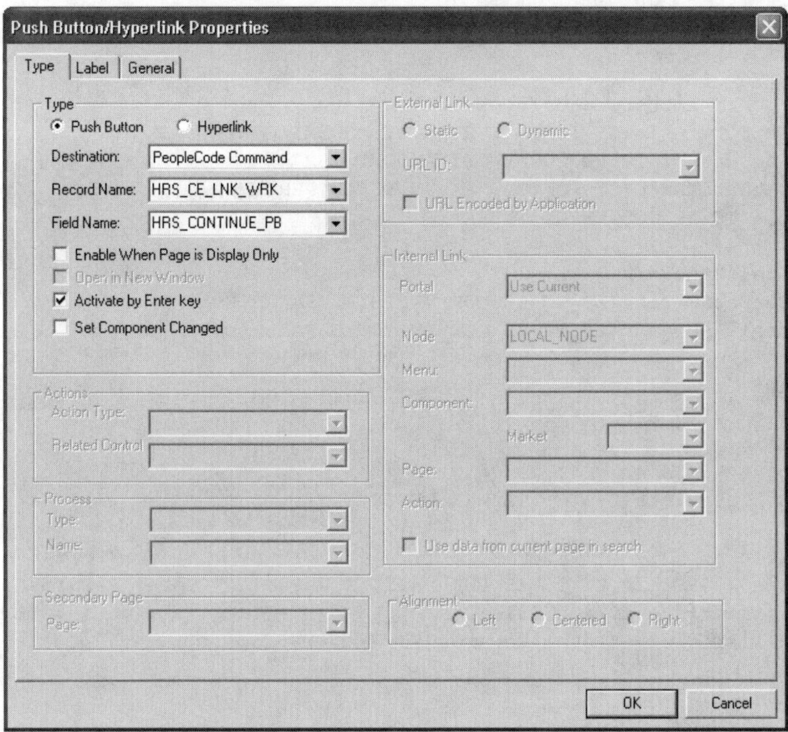

Creating a Graph on a Page

It is always nice to go the extra mile and add in things that you know your customers will like and appreciate. A graph is one of those things; customers of your application always like to see any kind of mathematical or financial data graphically. Or any type of statistics, for example, how many job openings compared to how many applicants. I am certain you can think of a bunch of cool ways to incorporate a graph into your application. The following is the basic code and a simple implementation. The first illustration that follows shows the page design and the layout of the chart, and the next shows the record and the correlation to the variable. Here is the code that would implement a graph:

```
/* chart Section GSDBEN1 Begin*/
/* The Chart object is on a level zero for this page*/
/* Draw CHART */
&oChart = GetChart(ZY_TC_TTL_WRK.CHARTFLDS_NEW);
```

```
/* set to Current Rowset */
&oChart.SetData(&RS2);

/* Each amount Amounts and Types */
&oChart.SetDataYAxis(ZY_TC_EE_CUR_VW.ZY_AMOUNT_CUR);
/* Total Amount ZY_TC_EE_CUR_VW.ZY_AMOUNT_CUR */
&oChart.SetDataXAxis(ZY_TC_TTL_WRK.ZY_TOTAL_PERCENT);
/* Types ZY_TC_EE_CUR_VW.ZY_TYPE */

/* All total Base */
&oChart.SetDataSeries(ZY_TC_EE_CUR_VW.TOTAL_SALARIES);
/* all Totals Rewards ZY_TC_EE_CUR_VW.TOTAL_SALARIES*/

/* set Chart type */
&oChart.Type = %ChartType_2DPie;

/* Set Chart Hints */
&oChart.SetDataHints(ZY_TC_TTL_WRK.DESCR);

/* Set Title */
&GraphTitle = &RS2(1).ZY_TC_EE_CUR_VW.YEAR.Value | " Total Rewards";
&oChart.MainTitle = &GraphTitle;
&oChart.YAxisTitle = "Total Rewards";

/* Legend */
&oChart.HasLegend = True;
&oChart.LegendPosition = %ChartLegend_Right;
&myArray = CreateArray(&csh, &benf, &savr, &equ, &per);
&oChart.SetLegend(&myArray);

/* Resets Colors */
&NumArray = CreateArray(4, 15, 12, 8, 5);
&oChart.SetColorArray(&NumArray);

/* PeopleCode trigger */
&oChart.IsDrillable = True;

/* New Chart Class  */
&oChart.YAxisTitleOrient = %ChartText_Horizontal;
&oChart.SetDataColor(ZY_TC_EE_AMT_VW.ZY_AMOUNT_PAST);
&oChart.LineType = %ChartLine_Dot;
&oChart.GridLines = %ChartGrid_Both;

/* chart Section GSDBEN1 End */
```

When making a customized bolt-on application, consider simply adding charts like these and the queries of the data tables all onto one component consisting of a series of PIA pages. By doing this, in effect you have provided the end user with a full "dashboard" where the results of the bolt-on application, such as the usage, the statistics, trends, KPIs, various pivoted views, etc., are all instantly available at the same time the bolt-on is released. Such a component is very easy to build, simply saving the queries, and then putting each one individually on a grid, or using graphics as just described.

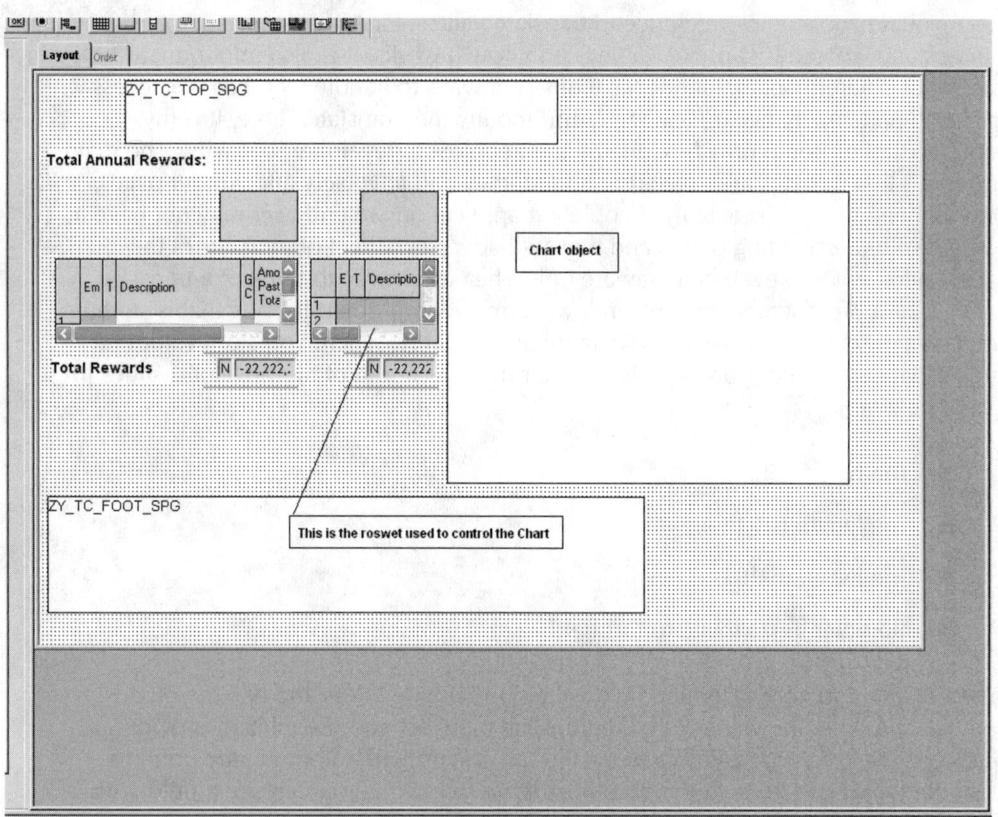

Record Fields | Record Type

Num	Field Name	Type	Len	Format	Short Name	Long Name	
1	EMPLID	Char	11	Upper	ID	EmplID	
2	ZY_ORDER_BY	Char	1	Upper	Order by	Order by	
3	ZY_TYPE	Char	1	Upper	Type	Type	Type
4	YEAR	Char	4	Num	Year	Year	
5	ZY_AMOUNT_CUR	Sign	11		Current Amouts	Current Amouts	amount
6	TOTAL_SALARIES	Sign	15.3		Tot Sal	Total Annual Salaries	Total

Translate Values

I don't know about anyone else, but for some reason translate values always kill me. I can't seem to ever remember where they are located, how to change them, where to set a default, or how to change them based on the page. I guess it is because I do them so infrequently that I always have to look them up; either way I thought it would be good to have this as a section in the Tips and Tricks under the PIA so that you would have a quick reference to translate values. First it is important to understand what the Translate Table is and how it works. It is also important to note here that different organizations have different ways to handle who has the access rights to update, change, delete, add, and modify the Translate Table. It is my opinion that it should only be done by the PeopleSoft developer, but why? The main reason is that if things are deleted or added, they can adversely affect other pages, components, and objects in the PeopleSoft application; an end user may not have a complete understanding of this and thus will adversely affect other users of the application without even being aware of it. The easiest way to think of a translate table is as a prompt table or (in Windows terms) a drop-down list box that is stored in a system table. It is similar to a data dictionary table, where you store values for fields that don't need prompt tables of their own. As a rule of thumb, store values in a translate table if

- The type is Character
- The length is 1 to 4
- The list is small
- No other fields relate to this field

It is important to note that if the field values are of type Y Yes and N No, you do not need to enter the values into the translate table because PeopleSoft provides a delivered field for that—PSYESNO—and the system will automatically point to that field and its values. In the first illustration following you can see a field with translate values; this is where you would make changes or additions. Then you can see that in the record definition it is of type XLat edit, which tells you that it is a field with translate values. Then you go to the field to see the actual values.

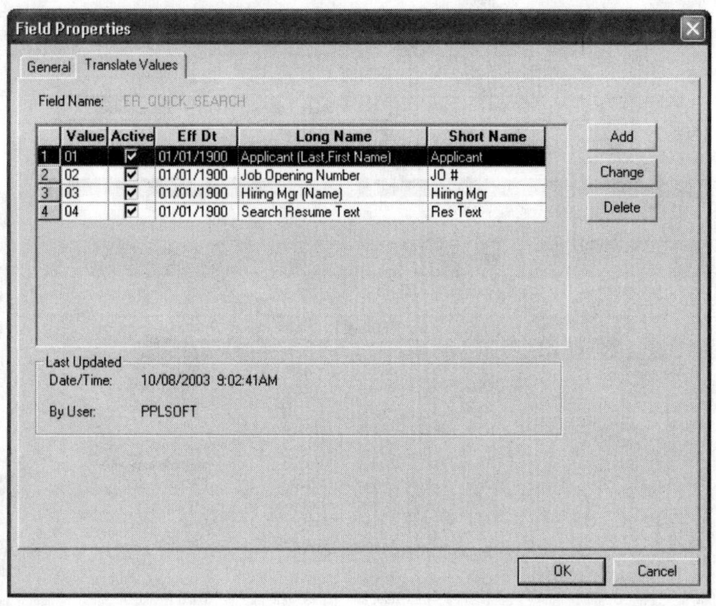

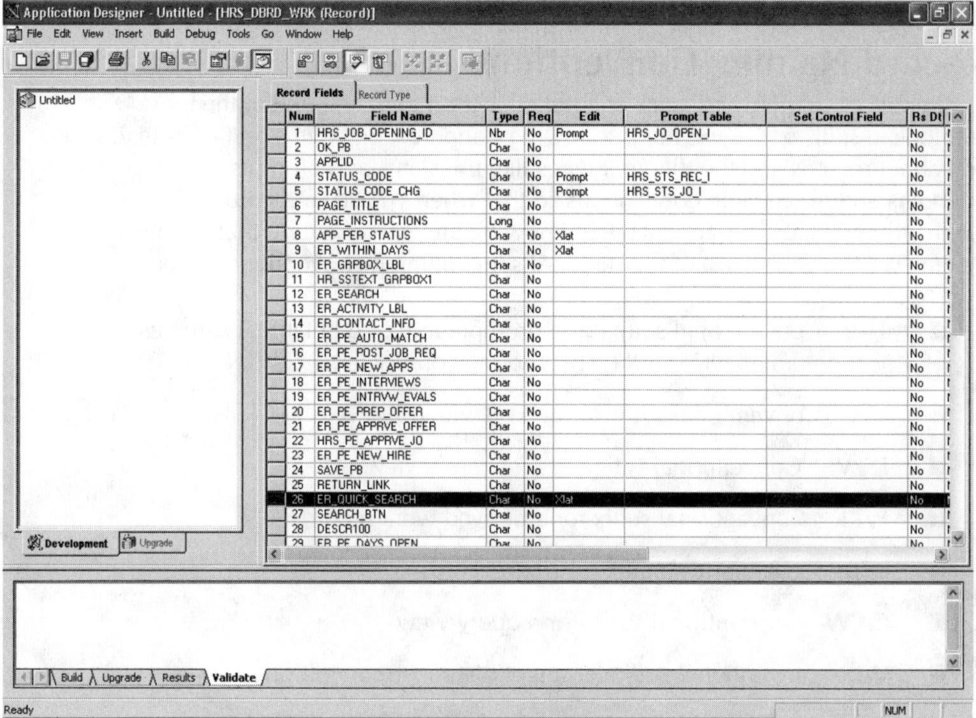

HRS_DBRD_WRK (Record)

Record Fields | Record Type

Num	Field Name	Type	Req	Edit	Prompt Table	Set Control Field
1	HRS_JOB_OPENING_ID	Nbr	No	Prompt	HRS_JO_OPEN_I	
2	OK_PB	Char	No			
3	APPLID	Char	No			
4	STATUS_CODE	Char	No	Prompt	HRS_STS_REC_I	
5	STATUS_CODE_CHG	Char	No	Prompt	HRS_STS_JO_I	
6	PAGE_TITLE	Char	No			
7						
8						
9						
10						
11						
12						
13						
14						
15						

HRS_STS_REC_I (Record)

Record Fields | Record Type

Num	Field Name	Type	Len	Format	Short Name	Long Name
1	STATUS_AREA	Char	1	Upper	Area	Recruitment Area
2	STATUS_CODE	Char	3	Upper	Status	Status Code
3	DESCR	Char	30	Mixed	Descr	Description
4	DESCRSHORT	Char	10	Mixed	Short Desc	Short Description
5	OPEN_STS_IND	Char	1	Upper	Open	Open
6	STATUS_PHASE	Char	1	Upper	Phase	Recruitment Phase
7	MUTUALLY_EXCLUSIVE	Char	1	Upper	Exclusive	Mutually exclusive
8	DEFAULT_STS_IND	Char	1	Upper	Default	Default Status
9	COMPLETE_STS_IND	Char	1	Upper	Complete	Complete
10	HRS_DRFT_STS_IND	Char	1	Upper	Draft	Draft
11	HRS_APRV_STS_IND	Char	1	Upper	Approval Sts	Approval Status
12	HRS_DND_APRV_IND	Char	1	Upper	Denied	Approval Denied
13	HRS_DFLT_APRV_IND	Char	1	Upper	Default	Approval Default
14	DATA_TYPE_CD	Char	1	Upper	Data Type	Data Type CD

Record Naming Conventions

It is important in a Tip and Trick chapter or section to define one of the most overlooked skills or tips, which is following standards. Since this section is teaching you about records and the different types like translates and prompts, it is important to understand the naming conventions so that when you see a record with a given name, you will have the advantage of knowing the type of record that you are dealing with. Here is a list of the standard suffix naming conventions for records:

- **_TBL** Conventional suffix for a prompt table or edit table. Examples: the location table LOCATION_TBL and the country table COUNTRY_TBL
- **_VW** Conventional suffix for an SQL view
- **_DVW** Conventional suffix for a dynamic view
- **_WRK** Conventional suffix for a derived work record
- **_SBR** Conventional suffix for a subrecord
- **_QVW** Conventional suffix for a query view
- **_WL** Conventional suffix for a worklist record definition

The following is a list of standard naming prefix conventions for records:

- **R_** Conventional prefix for Structured Query Report reports
- **AUDIT_** Conventional prefix for records that store audit information
- **WEBLIB_** Conventional prefix for record definitions that store Internet scripts
- **FUNCLIB_** Conventional prefix for record definitions that contain written PeopleCode functions, as opposed to built-in functions
- **DERIVED_** Conventional prefix for shared record–derived work records

COBOL

The main tip to remember with COBOL is the location of the external SQL statements. Unlike a lot of languages that you are used to, PS COBOL does not store the SQL statements in the code or even in an external file; it stores them in a table in PS. In order to change them, you need to change the SQL statement in the table. This can come back and bite you if you change PS-delivered COBOL and then do an upgrade and your SQL goes back to the original, so remember to work closely with your DBA to ensure any changes you make here will not be lost. In the first illustration following, the PS_SQLSTMT_TBL is described and you see the columns that you are working with. Next you see a sample SQL statement from the table.

```
SQL> desc ps_sqlstmt_tbl
 Name                                      Null?    Type
 ----------------------------------------- -------- ----------------------------
 PGM_NAME                                  NOT NULL VARCHAR2(8)
 STMT_TYPE                                 NOT NULL VARCHAR2(1)
 STMT_NAME                                 NOT NULL VARCHAR2(7)
 STMT_TEXT                                 NOT NULL LONG
```

```
SQL> select stmt_text from ps_sqlstmt_tbl where pgm_name = 'SRPCSMLS';

STMT_TEXT
--------------------------------------------------------------------------------
DELETE FROM PS_MLSTN_ATMPT WHERE EMPLID = :1 AND INSTITUTION = :2 AND ACAD_CAREE
DELETE FROM PS_SSR_MLSTATM_NZL WHERE EMPLID = :1 AND INSTITUTION = :2 AND ACAD_C
INSERT INTO PS_STDNT_CAR_MLSTN (EMPLID, INSTITUTION, ACAD_CAREER, ACAD_PROG, EFF
insert into PS_SSR_MLSTATM_NZL (EMPLID, INSTITUTION, ACAD_CAREER, ACAD_PROG, EFF
insert into PS_MLSTN_ATMPT (EMPLID, INSTITUTION, ACAD_CAREER, ACAD_PROG, EFFDT,
INSERT INTO PS_STDNT_MLSTN (EMPLID ,INSTITUTION ,ACAD_CAREER ,ACAD_PROG ,EFFDT)
Select A.MILESTONE, C.MILESTONE_COMPLETE, B.MILESTONE_NBR, B.CRSE_ID, B.ATTEMPT_
SELECT B.SSR_ENRL_CRS_MLSTN FROM PS_ACAD_CAR_TBL A ,PS_SSR_ACD_CAR_NZL B WHERE A
SELECT B.STRM FROM PS_SSR_CRS_MILESTN A, PS_STDNT_ENRL B, PS_CLASS_TBL C WHERE A
SELECT A.MILESTONE ,B.ACAD_PROG ,A.CRSE_ID ,C.START_DT FROM PS_SSR_CRS_MILESTN A
SELECT A.INSTITUTION ,A.ACAD_CAREER ,A.ACAD_PROG ,A.EFFDT ,B.MILESTONE_NBR ,B.MI

STMT_TEXT
--------------------------------------------------------------------------------
UPDATE PS_SSR_MLSTATM_NZL SET CRSE_ID = :1 WHERE EMPLID = :2 AND INSTITUTION = :
```

SQL and PL/SQL

Every good PeopleSoft programmer should be well versed in SQL, and in the case of Oracle you should also be well versed in PL/SQL. In this section we will discuss the basics; if you are already well versed in the subject, most of this will be redundant and boring for you, but if you are new to subject, this is your essential foundation that will serve you well through your programming career. In Appendix A in the book you can find an entire section on using PL/SQL in PeopleSoft.

First it is important to understand the basic commands. In my teaching I always discuss the different categories of SQL commands. Most books and teachers list SQL commands as residing in two different categories, DDL (Data Definition) or DML (Data Manipulation Language). There two types of commands that are left out when you do this: your basic SELECT (which some authors consider the DQL, or Data Query Language—I like this explanation; it doesn't leave me thinking I have left something off) and your Security and Analysis commands, which some authors put in with the DDL commands, although they do not really manipulate any data but simply give access to users and allow DBAs to analyze results. So let's take a look at an easy layout and a memory technique to retain these commands.

DQL—Data Query Language:

- SELECT

DML—Data Manipulation Language:

- INSERT
- UPDATE
- DELETE
- MERGE

DDL—Data Manipulation Language (I always remember these commands with a pneumonic device, Dr. CAT):

- DROP
- RENAME
- CREATE
- ALTER
- TRUNCATE

Last but not least, the Security and Analysis Group:

- GRANT
- REVOKE
- ANALYZE

SELECT

First let's take a look at examples of DQL, or simply the SELECT statement, depending on which camp you are in concerning how SQL commands are grouped. Either way, this will be your most used command in SQL as a PeopleSoft developer. Next is the code for a basic SELECT statement against the PS_BEN_PER_DATA table that contains things like name, address, phone number, and birth date for Personnel that receive Benefits. The illustration shows the results of that query.

```
SELECT emplid, birthdate
from PS_BEN_PER_DATA
/
```

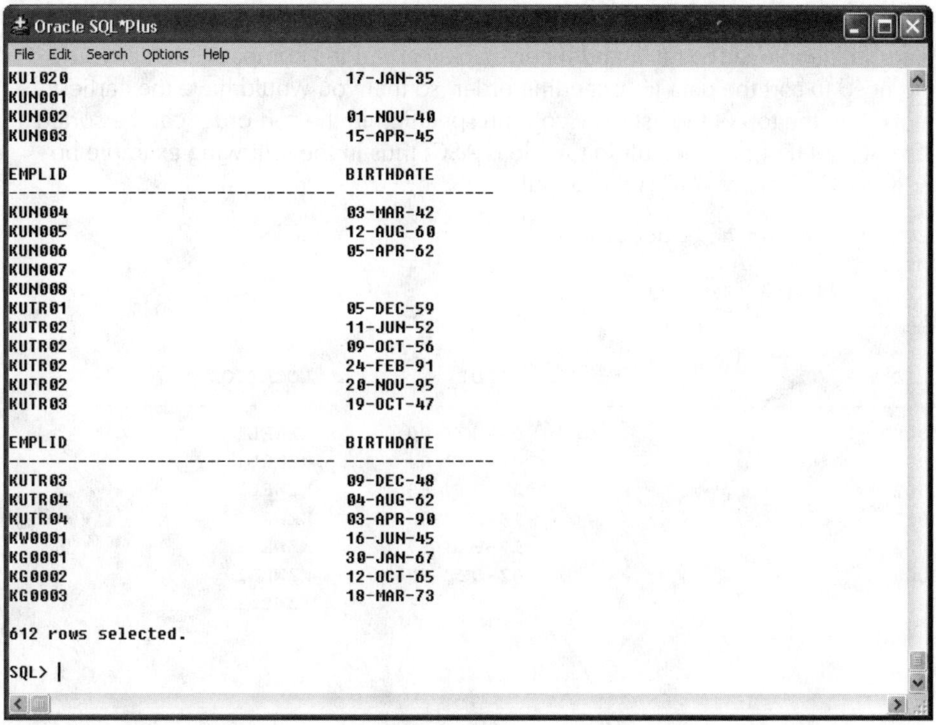

```
Oracle SQL*Plus
File  Edit  Search  Options  Help
KUI020                            17-JAN-35
KUN001
KUN002                            01-NOV-40
KUN003                            15-APR-45

EMPLID                            BIRTHDATE
--------------------------------- ---------------
KUN004                            03-MAR-42
KUN005                            12-AUG-60
KUN006                            05-APR-62
KUN007
KUN008
KUTR01                            05-DEC-59
KUTR02                            11-JUN-52
KUTR02                            09-OCT-56
KUTR02                            24-FEB-91
KUTR02                            20-NOV-95
KUTR03                            19-OCT-47

EMPLID                            BIRTHDATE
--------------------------------- ---------------
KUTR03                            09-DEC-48
KUTR04                            04-AUG-62
KUTR04                            03-APR-90
KW0001                            16-JUN-45
KG0001                            30-JAN-67
KG0002                            12-OCT-65
KG0003                            18-MAR-73

612 rows selected.

SQL> |
```

ORDER Data on Your SELECT

Basic SELECT queries return your data in a random order. Rarely is that of much use, so it is important to learn that you can order your data in Ascending or Descending order. Maybe you need to know when the first employee started his or her job at a location. You would do the following query against the PS_JOB table.

```
SELECT emplid, effdt, location f
FROM ps_job
WHERE location = 'KZWEL1'
/
EMPLID                              EFFDT            LOCATION
--------------------------------- --------------- --------------------
KZ0006                              01-JAN-00        KZWEL1
KZ0007                              01-DEC-97        KZWEL1
KZ0007                              14-NOV-98        KZWEL1
KZ0007                              03-MAY-99        KZWEL1
KZ0007                              06-MAY-01        KZWEL1
KZ0007                              30-JUN-01        KZWEL1
KZ0008                              06-NOV-80        KZWEL1
KZ0008                              07-SEP-99        KZWEL1
KZ0008                              12-DEC-99        KZWEL1
```

Well, this doesn't help you much because in order to know who started first and if they are still employed to track and receive an award at the company picnic, you would need to sort the data in ascending order, so that you would have the earliest employee on the top of the list. Any column specified in the sort order can be sorted either ASC or DESC; the default in Oracle is ASC; thus in the following example no order is given, because ASC is the default.

```
SELECT emplid, effdt, location
FROM ps_job
WHERE location = 'KZWEL1'
ORDER BY effdt
/
EMPLID                              EFFDT            LOCATION
--------------------------------- --------------- ---------------------
KZ0008                              06-NOV-80        KZWEL1
KZ0001                              04-MAR-84        KZWEL1
KZ0002                              23-JUN-85        KZWEL1
KZ0013                              16-SEP-86        KZWEL1
KZ0003                              10-FEB-87        KZWEL1
KZ0006                              02-OCT-87        KZWEL1
KZ0012                              06-FEB-91        KZWEL1
```

Function	SQL Example	Purpose	Result
`Concat(char1, char2)`	`select concat('judi', 'doolittle') from dual;`	Char1 concatenated with char2	judidoolittle
`Initcap(char)`	`select initcap('judi')from dual;`	Returns char with first letter in uppercase	Judi
`Lower(char)`	`select lower('JUDI') from dual;`	Returns char with all letters in lowercase	judi
`Replace(char, search_string, replace_string)`	`select replace('ascout', 'a', 'girl') from dual;`	Replaces the search string with the replacement string	girlscout
`Substr(char, m[,n])`	`select substr('STUVWXYZ', 5, 3) from dual;`	Portion of char, beginning at character *m, n* characters long, where *m* and *n* are integers; if *n* is left off, it returns all characters to the end of char	WXY
`Upper(char)`	`select upper('judi') from dual;`	Char with all letters in uppercase	JUDI

TABLE 12-1 *Common SQL String Functions*

One of the most important tools that Oracle provides us with as developers is functions; they enable the manipulation of the data so that it can be analyzed. The first set of functions to look at is the string functions, which come in two classes: one that returns characters and one that returns numbers. Table 12-1 shows common SQL string functions. The examples in the table will use the internal Oracle table "dual," which is useful in SQL and PL/SQL when you only need to return one row of data. The "dual" table can also be used to return the current system date and time or, in the case of PeopleSoft, the system date of the database server machine.

In Table 12-2 the commonly used numeric functions are listed, with syntax and examples from "dual"; keep in mind this is only a small sample of commonly used numeric functions; there are many more available.

Table 12-3 lists the String to Number functions, and Table 12-4 lists the Date functions.

Date formatting can be done to change the display of the date. You use the TO_CHAR function with the date and the format mask to get the desired results. Table 12-5 offers a sample of the most commonly used format models.

Function	SQL Example	Purpose	Result
`ABS(n)`	`select abs(18.2) from dual;`	Absolute Value of *n*	18.2
`CEIL(n)`	`select ceil(18.2) from dual;`	Smallest integer greater than or equal to *n*	19
`EXP(n)`	`select exp(4) from dual;`	Returns *e* raised to the *n*th power	54.59815
`LN(n)`	`select LN(4) from dual;`	The natural log of *n*	1.38629436
`LOG(m,n)`	`select log(4,2) from dual;`	The logarithm base *m* of *n*	.5
`MOD(m,n)`	`select mod(4,3) from dual;`	The remainder of *m* divided by *n*	1
`POWER(m,n)`	`select power(4,3) from dual;`	Raised to the *n*th power	64
`ROUND(n[,m])`	`select round(54.23, 0) from dual;`	*n* rounded to *m* places right of the decimal; *m* omitted equals 0 places	54
`SIGN(n)`	`select sign(-.2) from dual;`	Returns –1 if *n*<0, 0 if *n*=0, and 1 if *n*>0	–1
`SQRT(n)`	`select sqrt(3.4) from dual;`	Square root	1.84390889
`TRUNC(n[,m])`	`select trunc(4.56, 0) from dual;`	*n* truncated at *m* decimal places	4

TABLE 12-2 *Common Numeric Functions*

Aggregate functions act on an entire row of data, unlike the character or numeric functions that act on a single row at a time. So, for example, an aggregate function will add up a set of rows to give you a total, much as you would do a sum column in Excel. Table 12-6 lists the most commonly used Aggregate functions and offers examples of the results.

Function	SQL Example	Purpose	Result
`ASCII(char)`	`select ascii('a') from dual;`	Decimal representation of the character	97
`INSTR(char1, char2, n, m)`	`SELECT INSTR('This is a test','is',1,2) FROM dual;`	The position of the *m*th char2 in char1 beginning from the *n*th position	6
`LENGTH(char)`	`select length('Bryan') from dual;`	Returns the length of the char	5

TABLE 12-3 *String to Number Functions*

Function	SQL Example	Purpose	Result
`ADD_MONTHS(d,n)`	`select add_months('01-JAN-2007', 6) from dual`	The date *d* plus *n* months	01-JUL-07
`MONTHS_BETWEEN(b1, b2)`	`select months_between('22-OCT-2007', '01-FEB-2008') from dual;`	Months between *b1* and *b2*	-3.3225806
`SYSDATE`	`select sysdate from dual;`	Returns the current date and time of the database server	22-OCT-07

TABLE 12-4 *Date Functions*

Mask	SQL Example	Purpose	Result
Y, YY, YYY, YYYY	`select to_char(sysdate, 'YYYY') from dual;`	Return just the 1-, 2-, 3-, or 4-digit year	2007
MM	`select to_char(sysdate, 'MM') from dual;`	Month 01–12 for each month of the year	10
DD	`select to_char(sysdate, 'DD') from dual;`	Day of the month	22
D	`select to_char(sysdate, 'D') from dual;`	Day of the week 1–7; 1=Sunday—7=Saturday	2

TABLE 12-5 *Format Models*

Function	SQL Example	Purpose	Result
`Count(expr)`	`select count(*) from ps_job;`	A count of the non-null columns by row	2955
`Avg(expr)`			
`Sum(expr)`			
`Min(expr)`			
`Max(expr)`			

TABLE 12-6 *Aggregate Functions*

Joins

Outer joins in Oracle are declared in the WHERE clause through the use of the (+) symbol. An inner join, also known as a simple join, is joined together by the keys. In most databases (except for Application databases) this join would be on the primary and foreign keys, but in applications that are made to run on any platform regardless of the database that is on the back end, they do not have keys in the traditional sense. What they do have is indexes; keys are configured only in the metadata on the record within the PeopleSoft application; in the database they are simply indexes. This can tend to confuse the idea of joining. The inner and outer joins are the Oracle standard way of joining, but there is also the ANSI standard approach to joins, which moved the syntax of the join to the from clause. There are two types that are important to understand in ANSI standard joining: 1) the right outer join, or right join, and 2) the left outer join, or left join.

```
--Simple Join
SELECT A.EMPLID, A.NAME, B.address1
 FROM PS_PERSONAL_DATA A, PS_addresses B
 WHERE A.EMPLID= B.EMPLID
 and a.emplid like 'AD617%'
 and b.Address_type IS NULL
 /
no rows selected
--Outer Join
SELECT A.EMPLID, A.NAME
FROM PS_PERSONAL_DATA A, PS_addresses B
WHERE A.EMPLID= B.EMPLID (+)
and a.emplid like 'AD617%'
and b.Address_type IS NULL
EMPLID   NAME
-----------------------------------------------------------------
AD6170 Thomas Person
AD6171 Kim Pheng
AD6172 Nick Ramirez
AD6173 Raul Guzman
AD6174 Aaron Ramos
AD6175 Dale Ramsey
AD6176 Bill Randle
AD6177 John Ray
AD6178 Gary Redding
AD6179 Ginger Redman
10 rows selected.
```

To create easy-to-follow examples of all of the join types with the data that is provided in the PeopleSoft sample tables would become incredibly complex. So the following SQL creates table examples will give us sample data to work with to create a learning environment to understand the different types of joins. Please feel free to follow along and create the tables and data for practice purposes.

```
--1. create a table with test employees and descriptions
CREATE TABLE tc_empl_test(emplid varchar(6), descr varchar(5));
--2. create a second table to join to with test employees and descriptions
create table tc_empl_test2(emplid varchar(6), descr2 varchar(5));
--3. Insert data into the two tables for the sample queries.
INSERT INTO tc_empl_test VALUES('E1234', 'Empl1');
INSERT INTO tc_empl_test VALUES('E6789', 'Empl2');
INSERT INTO tc_empl_test2 VALUES('E1234', 'Addr1');
INSERT INTO tc_empl_test2 VALUES('E9876', 'Addr2');
--4. Right Outer Join

--5.  Left Outer Join
SELECT emplid, descr, descr2
FROM tc_empl_test a NATURAL LEFT JOIN tc_empl_test2 b;

EMPLID             DESCR           DESCR2
------------------ --------------- ---------------
E1234              Empl1           Addr1
E6789              Empl2
SELECT emplid, descr, descr2
FROM tc_empl_test a RIGHT OUTER JOIN tc_empl_test2 b
USING(emplid);
EMPLID             DESCR           DESCR2
------------------ --------------- ---------------
E1234              Empl1           Addr1
E9876                              Addr2
```

Group By and Having

Earlier in this chapter we discussed the functions that work on sets of rows. You can also group sets of rows to gather types of information into groups. You will see in your career as a PeopleSoft developer that you will write a number of Group By queries. Having is the way to apply criteria to the group; it provides the same filtering as you would receive using a WHERE clause. The difference is that the condition is on the set of rows rather than being a single value returned in a row. The following are simple examples:

```
--Group by Example
SELECT emplid, SUM(total_gross)
FROM ps_pay_check
GROUP BY emplid;
```

```
EMPLID                              SUM(TOTAL_GROSS)
---------------------------------- ----------------
KC0001                                      7416.48
KC0018                                     26068.17
KC0009                                      5032.47
KC0036                                      2076.93
KC0007                                      7065.03
KC0005                                        10044
KU0096                                     12063.25
KUTR03                                     23740.96
KU0062                                     24692.96
L00009                                       2995.2
L00013                                        89536
--HAVING Example
SELECT emplid, SUM(total_gross)
FROM ps_pay_check GROUP BY emplid
HAVING SUM(total_gross) > 82000
EMPLID                              SUM(TOTAL_GROSS)
---------------------------------- ----------------
L00013                                        89536
KU0001                                    110283.78
KU0002                                     82763.53
```

Special Set Operators

A relational database is a mathematical set of data and operates on the same principle as relational algebra or set theory. SQL queries are written and used on sets of data rather than on a single returned row of data. Because of this you can use set operators, the main three of which are UNION, INTERSECT, and MINUS. As the name implies, UNION is where the two are the joined or the same overlapping data, INTERSECT is where they cross, and MINUS is where they are different in sets. The following are examples of UNION and MINUS:

```
SELECT A.ACTION, A.PAYGROUP, COUNT(*)
FROM PS_JOB A, PS_RUN_CNTL_HR B
WHERE A.ACTION_DT BETWEEN B.FROMDATE AND B.THRUDATE
AND A.ACTION IN ( 'HIR','TER','POS', etc. )
AND A.PAYGROUP IN ( 'HOURLY','WEEKLY','MONTHLY')
AND B.OPRID = 'ME'
AND B.RUN_CNTL_ID = 'MySpecialQueryRange'
GROUP BY A.ACTION, A.PAYGROUP
UNION
SELECT B.ACTION, C.PAYGROUP, 0
FROM XLATTABLE B, PS_PAYGROUP_TBL C
WHERE B.FIELDNAME = 'ACTION'
AND B.FIELDVALUE IN ('HIR','TER','POS', etc.)
AND B.EFFDT = (SELECT MAX(B1.EFFDT) FROM XLATTABLE B1 etc.)
```

```
AND C.COMPANY = 'MYCOMPANY'
AND C.PAYGROUP IN ( 'HOURLY','WEEKLY','MONTHLY')
AND C.EFFDT = (SELECT MAX(C1.EFFDT) FROM PS_PAYGROUP_TBL C1)
--MINUS Example
/*put records with too many rows into the exclusion table*/
INSERT INTO psrecxl
SELECT recname
FROM lux_cand
WHERE num_rows > 100
MINUS
SELECT recname
FROM psrecxl
```

System Catalog

Oracle has a number of system catalog tables available with information about the underlying tables that directly correlates to the metadata in PeopleSoft. The most useful of these is USER_TABLES. Keep in mind that the keyword USER implies the owner of the table, and in the PeopleSoft schema this is the SYSADM USER. If you run this under SYSTEM, your USER name, or any other schema, the result will be very different and you may wonder why some tables are missing. The following is the most common query written against the USER_TABLE system catalog:

```
SELECT table_name
FROM user_tables
WHERE table_name LIKE 'PS_PAYROLL%';

TABLE_NAME
----------------------------------------------------------------------
PS_PAYROLL_ACCRUAL
PS_PAYROLL_DATA
PS_PAYROLL_DAT_LNG
```

External Content References

The PIA has a set of menus that allow users to interact with data in the database. The way that it does this is with content references. Sometimes it is beneficial to make external content references, where the term external refers to web pages that are outside of the PeopleSoft application, not necessarily outside of your organization. The menu pagelet consists of a tree of folders and content references. Moving through the branches of the tree (the folders) and navigating to the content references is the primary way of navigating within PeopleSoft applications. So let's learn how to create a new external content reference. The following are the basic settings you will need, as provided by Natasha Garcia:

- **Usage Type** HTML Template
- **Storage Type** Remote by URL
- **Node Name** LOCAL_NODE
- **URL Type** PeopleSoft Script
- **Record Name** WEBLIB_SLEXTLNK
- **Field Name** ISCRIPTLINK
- **PeopleCode Event Name** Field Formula
- **PeopleCode Function Name** IScript_NewWindow
- **Additional Parameters** link="externallink"

The additional parameter name should be the link, and the value should be quoted, for example, link="http://www.ssa.gov/OACT/quickcalc/".

The first of the following illustrations shows you the Structure and Content section of the Portal Menu system, followed by the Pension folder (where you would click Add Content Reference) and then the Content Reference page blank. Remember the settings just listed; this is where you would enter them. You will also need the following code:

```
HTML Code - SL_HTMLNEWWINDOW
<html>
<head>
<script language="javascript">
function newWindow(){
   var newWin = window.open(%BIND(:1));
}
window.onLoad = newWindow;
</script>
</head>
<body onLoad="newWindow()">
The link should open in a new browser window.  If not, please click
<a href=%BIND(:1) target="new">here</a>.
</body>
</html>
PeopleCode FieldDefault for ISCRIPTLINK
Function ISCRIPT_NewWindow()
   &link = %Request.GetParameter("link");
   &link = &link;
   %Response.Write(GetHTMLText(HTML.SL_HTMLNEWWINDOW, &link));
End-Function;
```

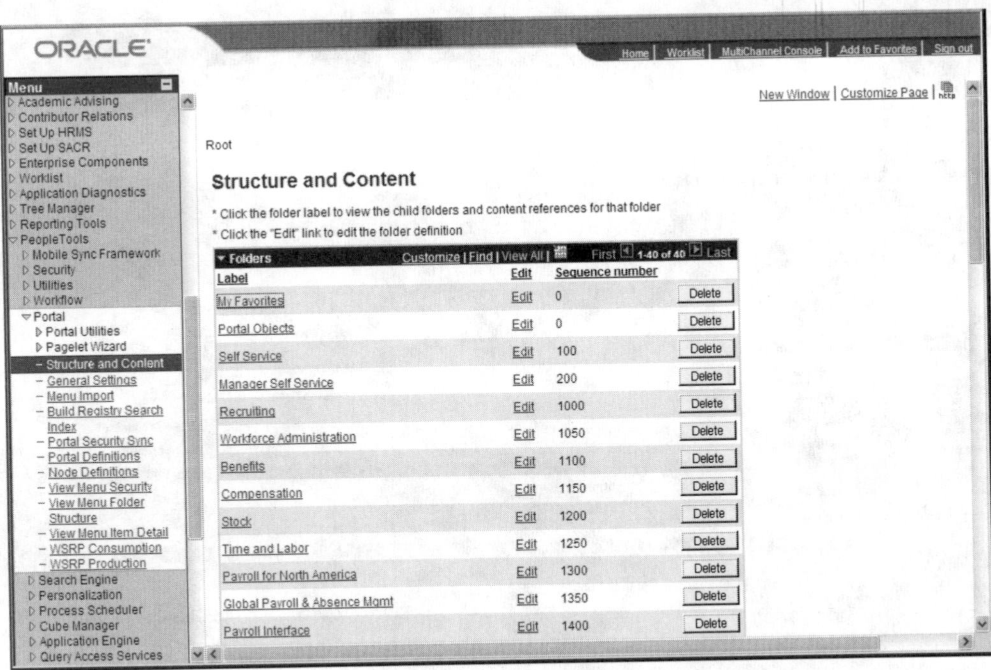
ORACLE
Home | Worklist | MultiChannel Console | Add to Favorites | Sign out
Menu
Academic Advising
Contributor Relations
Set Up HRMS
Set Up SACR
Enterprise Components
Worklist
Application Diagnostics
Tree Manager
Reporting Tools
PeopleTools
Mobile Sync Framework
Security
Utilities
Workflow
Portal
Portal Utilities
Pagelet Wizard
Structure and Content
General Settings
Menu Import
Build Registry Search Index
Portal Security Sync
Portal Definitions
Node Definitions
View Menu Security
View Menu Folder Structure
View Menu Item Detail
WSRP Consumption
WSRP Production
Search Engine
Personalization
Process Scheduler
Cube Manager
Application Engine
Query Access Services
New Window | Customize Page
Root
Structure and Content
* Click the folder label to view the child folders and content references for that folder
* Click the "Edit" link to edit the folder definition
Folders
Customize | Find | View All | First 1-40 of 40 Last
Label
Edit
Sequence number
My Favorites Edit 0 Delete
Portal Objects Edit 0 Delete
Self Service Edit 100 Delete
Manager Self Service Edit 200 Delete
Recruiting Edit 1000 Delete
Workforce Administration Edit 1050 Delete
Benefits Edit 1100 Delete
Compensation Edit 1150 Delete
Stock Edit 1200 Delete
Time and Labor Edit 1250 Delete
Payroll for North America Edit 1300 Delete
Global Payroll & Absence Mgmt Edit 1350 Delete
Payroll Interface Edit 1400 Delete

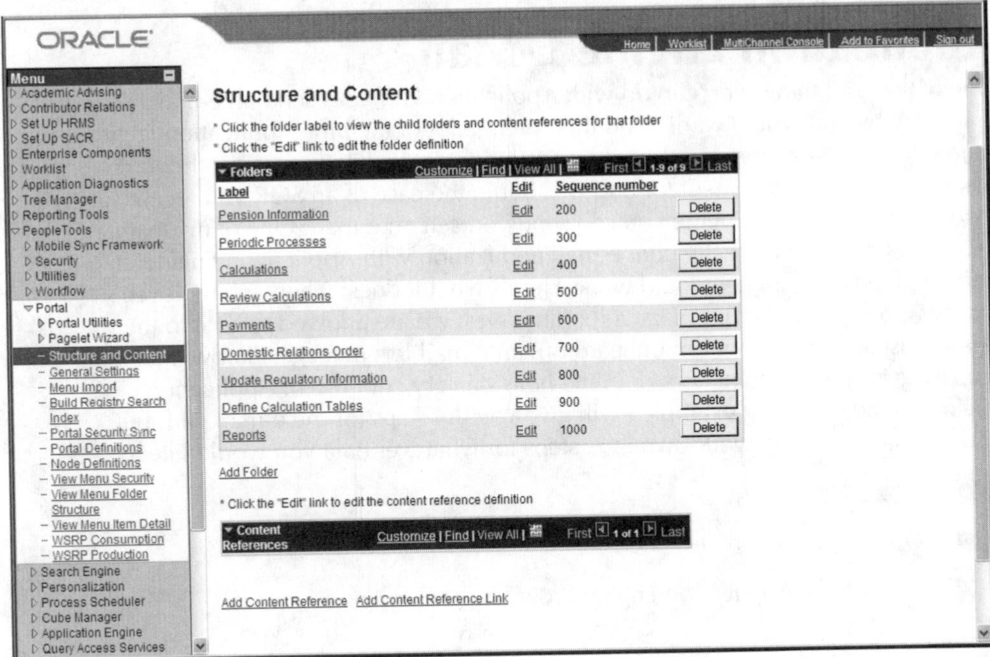
ORACLE
Home | Worklist | MultiChannel Console | Add to Favorites | Sign out
Menu
Academic Advising
Contributor Relations
Set Up HRMS
Set Up SACR
Enterprise Components
Worklist
Application Diagnostics
Tree Manager
Reporting Tools
PeopleTools
Mobile Sync Framework
Security
Utilities
Workflow
Portal
Portal Utilities
Pagelet Wizard
Structure and Content
General Settings
Menu Import
Build Registry Search Index
Portal Security Sync
Portal Definitions
Node Definitions
View Menu Security
View Menu Folder Structure
View Menu Item Detail
WSRP Consumption
WSRP Production
Search Engine
Personalization
Process Scheduler
Cube Manager
Application Engine
Query Access Services
Structure and Content
* Click the folder label to view the child folders and content references for that folder
* Click the "Edit" link to edit the folder definition
Folders
Customize | Find | View All | First 1-9 of 9 Last
Label
Edit
Sequence number
Pension Information Edit 200 Delete
Periodic Processes Edit 300 Delete
Calculations Edit 400 Delete
Review Calculations Edit 500 Delete
Payments Edit 600 Delete
Domestic Relations Order Edit 700 Delete
Update Regulatory Information Edit 800 Delete
Define Calculation Tables Edit 900 Delete
Reports Edit 1000 Delete
Add Folder
* Click the "Edit" link to edit the content reference definition
Content References
Customize | Find | View All | First 1 of 1 Last
Add Content Reference
Add Content Reference Link

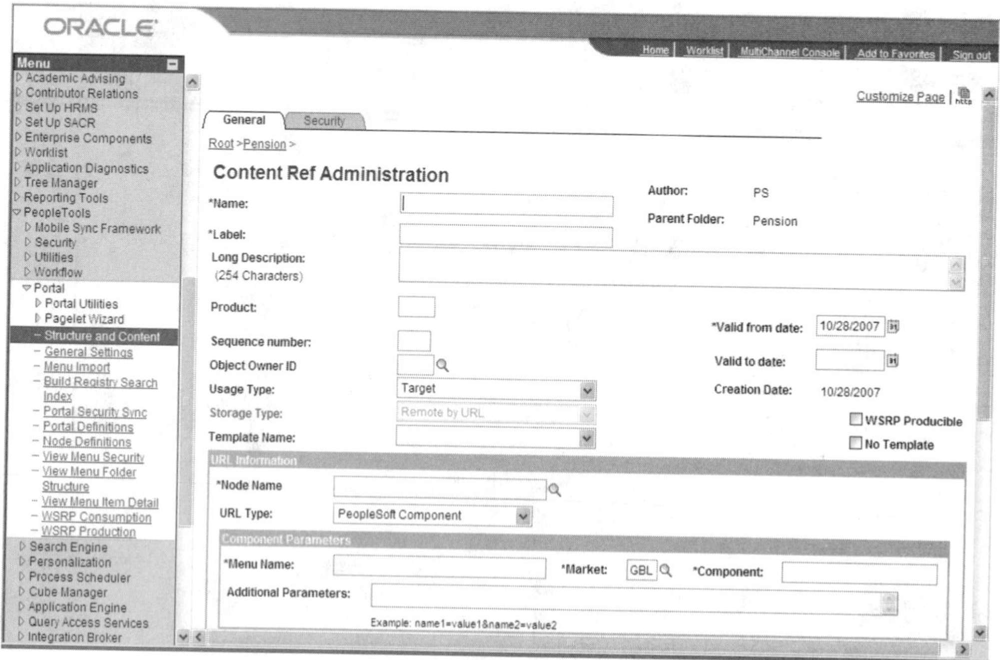

Application Engine E-Mail

One of the cool things you can do with Application Engine is send an e-mail. You may ask why you would want to do this. Well, a lot of the time Application Engine is used to process a large number of inserts, updates, or deletes as a batch job. You could see it as a replacement for an SQR, but in the case of an SQR you receive a report—in Application Engine you can send yourself an e-mail. One of my team, Otis Stewart, created a really cool e-mail application with Application Engine; it works in the way a trigger would work. Here's what it does: when an employee reaches a trigger of overuse of vacation time (yes, we are allowed to go into the red—unusual, I know, but not unheard of), an e-mail lets managers know that employee is close to going too far in the hole—a very cool use of Application Engine. In the following example I will give you the steps for the e-mail part, but you will have to create your own SQL steps for whatever data you would like to e-mail.

1. Open Application Designer.
2. Select New Application Engine Program.

3. Create a New Step and Action and name it **Email**.
4. Change the default on the step to be PeopleCode.
5. Double-click PeopleCode.
6. Insert the following code, remembering to change the e-mail address to your own:

```
Local string &mail_text1, &to_emailid, &cc_name_list, &email_
subject, &mail_text2, &Mail_text3, &dbname;
&dbname = %DbName;
&RET = Char(13);
&mail_text2 = TC_JCEARN_AET.HR_NP_NOTE_TEXT;
&Mail_text3 = TC_JCEARN_AET.TC_PEN_NOTE_TEXT;

If &dbname = "TCPR1" Then
   &to_emailid = "test@test.com";
Else
   &to_emailid = "test2@test.com";
End-If;
&email_subject = &dbname | " " | "New earnings & job codes";
&mail_text1 = "This email is a system generated email, please do
not reply to this email." | &RET;
&mail_text1 = &mail_text1 | &RET | "The following are the
Earnings Codes in the last 31 days and Job Codes added in the
last 31 days: " | &RET;
&mail_text1 = &mail_text1 | &RET | "Earnings Codes: ";
&mail_text1 = &mail_text1 | &RET | "If the earnings code should
be pensionable or eligible for the 401k plans please contact the
Benefits Technical Liaison to have the new earnings code
updated" | &RET | &mail_text2 | &RET;
&mail_text1 = &mail_text1 | &RET | "Job Codes: ";
&mail_text1 = &mail_text1 | &RET | "If the jobcode has an
incorrect pension plan please contact compensation immediately
to have the jobcode updated" | &RET | &Mail_text3 | &RET;
SendMail(0, &to_emailid, &cc_name_list, "", &email_subject,
&mail_text1);
```

7. Save the code.
8. In the Main Section create an Action of type of Call and direct the Call to Email section.
9. Run it, and you should receive an e-mail.

Summary

In this chapter we looked at some of the tricks of the trade and how to do things more efficiently. We looked at where to place the code and what fires off before what. You saw in the exercises how to build a project that allows you to actually see messages from the various records, fields, and events. This becomes a nice tool that you can build to keep in case PeopleSoft decides to change any of the firing order. This chapter provided you with a start to your own bag of tricks, but remember that the Internet is an excellent place to expand your knowledge or to get tips provided by other developers—it is always fun to network with other developers at the User Group conferences. The list of web sites is just a starting point; you will find several to add to this list in your career as a PeopleSoft developer, plus new ones spring up every day when a new code guru is born. Enjoy and expand.

PART IV

Appendixes

This section it will take you through PL/SQL, COBOL, and the Reference material that were used in the creation of this book. PL/SQL allows you to modify the Oracle database on the database server. COBOL allows you to maintain legacy programs and to debug and modify delivered PeopleSoft. The ability to modify delivered PeopleSoft allows you to modify programs if you are behind in your patches. Both these languages and skills give you more flexibility in working with PeopleSoft and Oracle. The Reference section lists all the material that was used to write this book. Hopefully this section will provide you with additional skills and reference information to make you a better programmer. Enjoy.

APPENDIX A

PL/SQL in PeopleSoft

L/SQL can be a very useful tool within PeopleSoft. The main limitation, of course, is that, if you are not using the Oracle database, this tool is not an option for you. Because of this limitation, many shops are reluctant to rely on PL/SQL too heavily in case a change of platform is chosen by management. This is why the information about this tool is added to the book as an appendix: if you need to know how to use the tool, here is some helpful information; otherwise, you might need it for future reference.

PL/SQL

Why should you use PL/SQL in a PeopleSoft Environment when you have Application Engine and SQR? Performance! What are the syntax issues in putting PL/SQL in the PeopleSoft database? Now that another language is in the mix, how do you deal with what your DBA will say, what if PeopleSoft upgrade documents will not identify stored procedures, and how do you make certain that you are not causing more work for yourself and your DBA during a database upgrade? This appendix will provide examples of templates to embed PL/SQL into SQRs with defined and easy-to-follow standards. The syntax issues of Application Engine and how to embed PL/SQL will be covered. You'll also see how to create an external table to store the developer name, date, and PL/SQL code so that each time the database is upgraded, a SQL script call will be the only added process for the DBA. You'll learn how utilizing PL/SQL in your PeopleSoft environment will give you more flexibility and added processing speed.

PeopleSoft Available Options

When evaluating the available options, one of the easiest and fastest methods, PL/SQL, is often overlooked in favor of SQR, PeopleCode, or Application Engine. Because PL/SQL is stored in the database as a database object and is processed at the database server, several advantages can be realized. The following are the basics of PL/SQL and how to use the standard features to gain a large performance boast.

PL/SQL (Procedural Language SQL)

PL/SQL is a logical extension of SQL; it adds programming features to SQL statements. You are able to add conditional logic and process only the desired SQL code based on a true or false decision. The programming features give you the ability to cache results of SQL statements with cursors and loop through the results, allowing manipulation to take place on the cached data without ever affecting the underlying table. PL/SQL gives you unusual power to create complex 3GL-type programs. It also gives you the ability to write object-oriented programming with packages.

Compile Environment

When a PL/SQL block is submitted from a precompiler such as Pro*C, Pro*Cobol, iSQL*Plus, or Server Manager, the PL/SQL engine in the Oracle Server processes the block. It will strip off the SQL statements and handle them with the SQL statement executor, and it will process the PL/SQL with the Procedural Statement Executor. Anonymous blocks or unnamed PL/SQL blocks are executed from the client, whereas stored procedures, subprograms, or named blocks are handled on the Oracle Server. The difference is that the subprogram is stored with a name within the Oracle database.

SQL Statement Executor

There are three execution engines in the Oracle Server: SQL Statement Executor, Procedural Statement Executor, and Java Statement Executor. In Figure A-1 you can see the way the execution engines work together, including the SQL Statement Executor and the Procedural Statement Executor.

When PL/SQL runs blocks and subprograms, it parses off the SQL and runs it in the *SQL engine* while handling PL/SQL in the *PL/SQL engine.* Because of this parsing, each time SQL is called inside PL/SQL, a context switch occurs. To increase performance in PL/SQL, it is important to understand the fundamentals of this process and minimize the number of context switches within your code.

Precompiled

Remembering what is said in connection with Figure A-1 about the different engines for processing the code should help you understand that PL/SQL is an interpreted language because PL/SQL programs contain SQL statements. And we know that the

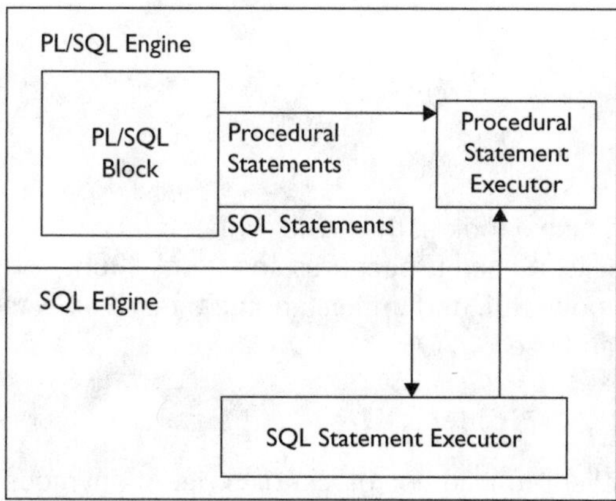

FIGURE A-1 *Execution engines*

SQL engine handles SQL statements and the PL/SQL engine handles PL/SQL. So, SQL statements must be identified and parsed off at runtime and handled by the SQL engine. The rest of the PL/SQL code need not be interpreted (it is essentially precompiled), but since the Oracle 9*i* release, you can compile PL/SQL packages, procedures, and functions into native code and have them reside in shared libraries. The process is similar to the native compilation of Java. PL/SQL blocks are interpreted into native C code and compiled by a C compiler; they then become linked into an Oracle process. The performance gains can vary. Usually native compilation is more efficient and can enhance performance.

Steven Feuerstein says in his book *Oracle PL/SQL Programming 3/e* (O'Reilly, 2005) that, "To enable compilation, you must first alter the value of your session or instance's PLSQL_COMPILER_FLAGS parameter to NATIVE (the default is INTERPRETED), then update the makefile supplied by Oracle with your specific environmental values, and finally compile your code."

You can also check the compiler status (NATIVE or INTERPRETED) with a query against the data dictionary

```
SELECT param_value
FROM user_stored_settings
WHERE param_name = 'PLSQL_COMPILER_FLAGS'
AND object_name = 'MY_PROC';
```

Errors

When you run your PL/SQL code, the only errors that will be displayed by the host environment are the syntax errors. Logic errors will only be shown through data checking. You can use bind variables to return the data results to SQL*Plus to see if the program is logically giving you the result that you desire. To see the syntax errors, you can use the SHOW ERRORS command from SQL*Plus.

```
SQL> show errors
No errors.
```

Syntax

In the following we will take a look at the basic syntax in PL/SQL. We will cover anonymous PL/SQL blocks, named procedures and blocks, functions, packages, and triggers. PL/SQL is very powerful, and understanding the syntax is the first step in allowing you to create and use PL/SQL.

Anonymous PL/SQL Blocks

Anonymous blocks are client-run, ad hoc blocks of code. Anonymous blocks are used for one-time program runs, for running blocks of PL/SQL from other programs such as SQR, within Oracle tools where you wish to have the PL/SQL code execute immediately, or as code attached directly within the tools environment. For example, when you place code directly into a form or report trigger, the tool will package this as an anonymous block within the form or report. Within the body of a trigger, although the trigger has a name and is stored on the server, the PL/SQL block is anonymous. SQL*Plus ad hoc programs and batch scripts are always anonymous. You can also embed PL/SQL blocks within other languages, including SQR, Application Engine, Visual Basic, and Pro* embedded languages.

Here is an example of the syntax of an anonymous PL/SQL block containing the three sections—declaration, execution, and exception:

```
DECLARE
   emp_name                emp.ename%TYPE;
   total_salary            NUMBER;
   invalid_emp             EXCEPTION;
BEGIN
   total_salary :=
      get_sal (emp_name, 'TOTAL');
   IF total_salary IS NULL
   THEN
      RAISE invalid_emp;
   ELSE
      DBMS_OUTPUT.PUT_LINE
          ('Annual Salary to date ' ||
           TO_CHAR (total_salary));
   END IF;
EXCEPTION
  WHEN invalid_employee
   THEN
      ...
END;
```

Note that an anonymous block must have a BEGIN and an END; the other sections, DECLARATION and EXCEPTION, are optional.

Named PL/SQL Blocks: Procedures and Functions

The named PL/SQL blocks of code become the server-side stored procedures and functions also known as subprograms. Because PL/SQL is a block-structured language, each of the blocks should be a logical unit of work. You can make your blocks modular, and it is best to create one block per solution within the program. By separating out the logical units of work into blocks, PL/SQL becomes a simple programming language to follow and understand.

Objects Stored at DB Server with Names That Can Be Shared

Procedures, functions, packages, and triggers are stored within the database server so that programmers and tools can share them. Storing them as objects within the database server allows for smooth and fast processing from within the database server itself. With the utilization of the server-side PL/SQL version, server-side processing is quick and convenient.

Procedures

A *procedure* is a named block of PL/SQL code that can be saved on the database server as a schema object that performs one or more tasks and is called from an executable PL/SQL statement. You can have parameters (also known as arguments) within the procedure that pass values into or out of the procedure via these parameters.

```
iSQL*Plus example of invoking a procedure:
SQL> EXECUTE emp_raise (176)
Invoking from within another procedure:
       emp_raise (176);
Invoking from within an Anonymous PL/SQL block
       DECLARE
            v_empid              emp.empno%type;
       BEGIN
            emp_raise (v_empid);
            COMMIT;
       ...
       END;
```

Functions

A *function* is a named PL/SQL block that accepts arguments, computes a value, and returns it in the name of the function; it must contain a return clause to return this value. Functions, just like procedures, can be saved at the database server as schema objects or created at the client-side application. Functions that are stored as schema objects are known as *stored* functions and are available for repeated use within multiple applications. A custom user-defined PL/SQL function can be called in SQL anywhere you can call an Oracle built-in function. You can invoke a user-defined function from a SELECT command, in the WHERE or HAVING clause, in the CONNECT BY, START WITH, ORDER BY, or GROUP BY clause, in the VALUES clause of an INSERT command, or in the SET clause of an UPDATE command. The restrictions to calling a function within SQL expressions are: the function must be a stored function, accept only IN parameters, have only valid SQL data types (not PL/SQL types as parameters), and return valid SQL data types; the function cannot contain DML statements; UPDATE/DELETE statements on a table cannot call DML on the same table or query the same table; and the function cannot call another subprogram that would violate one of the restrictions.

```
--Calling a function from SQL:
CREATE OR REPLACE FUNCTION tax_rate(p_amount in number)
RETURN NUMBER IS
BEGIN
  RETURN (p_amount * 0.675);
END tax_rate;
/
SELECT empno, name, sal, tax_rate(salary)
FROM emp
WHERE tax_rate(sal) > (SELECT MAX(tax_rate(sal)
                       FROM emp
                       WHERE deptno = 10)
ORDER BY tax_rate(sal) DESC;
```

Packages

The main focus today in programming is modularization, or object-oriented programming (OOP). *Packages* are the way you can bundle subprograms, items, and types into one location or module. For example, your business may have a human resource application, and within this application you may have many business processes. Adopting an OOP approach, you can break the application into logical units of work or business processes, within each business process you can have multiple tasks, and each task can be broken down into a package. An example of a task might be the calculation of the employee federal tax rate. You can create a package to store all of the subprograms that are called to calculate the employee's federal tax rate. Each package has a specification and a body. The specification is similar to a header; it contains all of the declarations, types, variables, cursors, constants, exceptions, subprograms, and PRAGMAs (directives to the compiler). The body completely defines the cursors and subprograms and uses the specifications for implementation. The package itself cannot be called—each of the subprograms within the package is called. The package simply acts as a container for the subprograms.

```
CREATE OR REPLACE PACKAGE ps_utl_pkg
AS
PROCEDURE log_new_line;
PROCEDURE Initialize _log ( p_pgm_name  IN VARCHAR2, p_log_file_output
IN   BOOLEAN);
PROCEDURE write_log (p_log_entry IN VARCHAR2);
PROCEDURE write_error (p_error_entry IN VARCHAR2);
END ps_utl_pkg;
/
```

```
CREATE OR REPLACE PACKAGE BODY ps_utl_pkg
AS
/************************************************************************
   NAME:       ps_utl_pkg

************************************************************************/
gv_output_type   VARCHAR2 (25)                      := 'LOG';
gv_pgm_name      tc_plsql_log.programname%TYPE;
PROCEDURE log_new_line
AS
BEGIN
      write_log (' ');
END;
PROCEDURE Initialize _log (p_pgm_name           IN   VARCHAR2,
p_log_file_output   IN   BOOLEAN)
AS
BEGIN
      gv_pgm_name := p_pgm_name;
IF p_log_file_output
THEN
   gv_output_type := 'LOG';
ELSE
   DBMS_OUTPUT.ENABLE (100000);
   gv_output_type := ' ';
    END IF;
    log_new_line;
    write_log (   'Log started for '|| gv_pgm_name|| ' at ' || TO_CHAR
(SYSDATE, 'YYYY-MM-DD HH24:MI:SS'));
    log_new_line;
END;
PROCEDURE close_log (p_pgm_name IN VARCHAR2)
AS
BEGIN
   log_new_line;
   write_log (   'End of log for '|| gv_pgm_name|| ' at '|| TO_CHAR
(SYSDATE, 'YYYY-MM-DD HH24:MI:SS'));
   log_new_line;
END;
PROCEDURE write_log (p_log_entry IN VARCHAR2)
AS
BEGIN
IF gv_output_type = 'LOG'
THEN
  INSERT INTO tc_plsql_msg_temp
```

```
  VALUES (SYSDATE, p_log_entry);
ELSE
  DBMS_OUTPUT.put_line (p_log_entry);
END IF;
END;
PROCEDURE write_error (p_error_entry IN VARCHAR2)
AS
  PRAGMA AUTONOMOUS_TRANSACTION;
BEGIN
IF gv_output_type = 'LOG'
THEN
   INSERT INTO tc_plsql_msg_temp
   VALUES (SYSDATE, p_error_entry);
   COMMIT;
ELSE
   DBMS_OUTPUT.put_line (p_error_entry);
   END IF;
END;
END ps_utl_pkg;
/
```

Built-in Packages

You can get most of the standard packages, also known as Oracle-supplied packages, by running the $ORACLE_HOME/rdbms/admin/catproc.sql script. These packages are supplied to give you access to certain SQL features or to extend the functionality of the database itself.

Database Trigger

Also known as a DML trigger, a database trigger has a few components that must be determined upon creation. The triggering statement should contain: trigger timing (for a table: BEFORE, AFTER; for a view: INSTEAD OF), a triggering event (INSERT, UPDATE, or DELETE), a table name, a trigger type (ROW or STATEMENT), a WHEN clause, and a trigger body (PL/SQL block).

Row A *row* trigger fires each time the table is affected by the event—if no rows are affected, then the trigger will not fire. These are useful when the trigger action depends on the data of rows that are affected or on data provided by the trigger.

Statement A *statement* trigger is fired once on behalf of the event, even if no rows are affected. These are useful when the trigger action does not depend on the data from the rows that are affected. An example is a security trigger that performs a complex security check on the user.

Executing PL/SQL

You can invoke PL/SQL anonymous blocks straight from SQL*PLUS, but remember to store them into a script and execute them from the SQL*Plus command line as @ scriptname.sql; this is how Oracle will parse the PL/SQL and the SQL and run the script from the client side. If you do not do this but paste the SQL into the SQL*Plus window and you have bind variables in the script, you will quickly see that Oracle has stripped these away in its parsing process. You can also run PL/SQL anonymous blocks by embedding them inside other programs, for instance, Visual Basic as a string variable, or inside BEGIN-SQL in SQR. If you have stored your PL/SQL as a stored procedure or function, you can call it in the following ways: SQL*PLUS or iSQL*Plus, Oracle Development tools (Oracle Forms Developer), or another procedure.

```
Anonymous  Block Example
@scriptname.sql
From SQL*Plus Example
EXECUTE      execution_one
Stored Procedure Example
execution_one;
From Another Procedure Example
CREATE OR REPLACE PROCEDURE emp_leave
(p_id IN emp.emp_id%TYPE)
IS
BEGIN
       DELETE FROM emp
       WHERE emp_id = p_id;
log_execution;
END
leave_emp;
```

SQR

Utilize the power of PL/SQL in SQR by embedding anonymous blocks inside of the SQR SQL sections. External procedures and functions can be called inside of SQRs to maximize the features of both languages.

```
--Example embedded anonymous block:
BEGIN-SQL on-error=Db_Error
  DECLARE
       V_ERR_CDE                      PS_UU_RPT_LDGR_ERR.UU_ERR_CODE%TYPE;;
       V_ERR_MSG                      PS_UU_RPT_LDGR_ERR.UU_ERR_MSG%TYPE;;
       V_BLOCK_NAME             PS_UU_RPT_LDGR_ERR.UU_BLOCK_NAME%TYPE;;
BEGIN
DBMS_STATS.GATHER_TABLE_STATS('FSPROD','PS_UU_RPT_LEDGER', NULL, NULL,
ALSE, 'FOR ALL COLUMNS SIZE 1', NULL, 'DEFAULT', TRUE, NULL, NULL, NULL);;
```

```
 EXCEPTION
     WHEN OTHERS THEN
         V_ERR_MSG := SUBSTR(SQLERRM,1,100);;
         V_ERR_CDE := SQLCODE;;
         V_BLOCK_NAME := 'ANALYZE STATS ';;
            INSERT INTO PS_UU_RPT_LDGR_ERR(UU_BLOCK_NAME
                                          ,UU_ERR_CODE
                                          ,UU_ERR_MSG
                                          ,UU_DATE)
             VALUES (V_BLOCK_NAME
                    ,V_ERR_CDE
                    ,V_ERR_MSG
                    ,SYSDATE);;
END;;
END-SQL
--Example calling a stored procedure:
BEGIN-SQL
BEGIN EXTCOPY.GW_DOWN_GET_STATUS_W_NUMS
                       ($project-num,
                        $task-num,
                        $v_ei_date,
                        $v_expend_type,
                        $v_non_labor_resource,
                        #v_emplid,
                        #v_quantity,
                        $status,
                        $status_desc);;
END;;
END-SQL
```

SQR Template

By creating standard SQR and SQC templates, you enable each person who needs to utilize PL/SQL in the organization to use this and have a standard output and error messaging platform. With the use of Oracle temp tables, you can write to the table, query it via SQR, and output the results in a report that can be e-mailed through the standard PeopleSoft system. This allows the programmer to utilize standard DBMS_OUTPUT type techniques to receive feedback from the SQR program.

SQR EXAMPLE

```
!* * * * * * * * * * * * * * * * * * * * * * * * * * * * * * * * * * * * *
!  PLSQL.SQC:  Department and Project/Task Codes
!* * * * * * * * * * * * * * * * * * * * * * * * * * * * * * * * * * * * *
!  Name:       PLSQL.SQC
!  Author:     Jason Follingstad
!  Date:         July 20, 2005
!  Description: PL/SQL TEMPLATE
```

```
!* * * * * * * * * * * * * * * * * * * * * * * * * * * * * * * * * * * *
#include 'setenv.sqc'   !Set environment
!* * * * * * * * * * * * * * * * * * * * * * * * * * * * * * * * * * * * *
!create a temporary table.  if exists, then skip
!* * * * * * * * * * * * * * * * * * * * * * * * * * * * * * * * * * * * *
begin-procedure Initialize -plsql-output
! create a temporary table to be used pl/sql for logging
begin-sql on-error=skip-error
create global temporary table sysadm.tc_plsql_msg_temp (tc_orig_timestamp
date,
   message_descr long varchar)
   on commit preserve rows
end-sql
! do grants on temp table
begin-sql on-error=skip-error
grant select, insert on tc_plsql_msg_temp to psuser, psdeveloper, workflow,
payroll
end-sql
end-procedure Initialize -plsql-output
!* * * * * * * * * * * * * * * * * * * * * * * * * * * * * * * * * * * * *
!SQL to extract and display output
!* * * * * * * * * * * * * * * * * * * * * * * * * * * * * * * * * * * * *
begin-procedure display-output
   let $sql-statement = 'select tc_plsql_msg_temp'
begin-select on-error=sql-error
a.message_descr
   print &a.message_descr   (+1,3,100)
from sysadm.tc_plsql_msg_temp a
order by tc_orig_timestamp
end-select
end-procedure display-output
!* * * * * * * * * * * * * * * * * * * * * * * * * * * * * * * * * * * * *
!error processing for pl/sql errors
!* * * * * * * * * * * * * * * * * * * * * * * * * * * * * * * * * * * * *
begin-procedure plsql-error
   display 'PL/SQL Error'
   display ' '
   display 'SQL Status = '       noline
   display #sql-status 99999     noline
   display ', SQL Error  = '     noline
   display $sql-error
   display ' '
   display ' - SQL Statement = ' noline
   display $sql-statement
   display ' '
   ! print log
   do display-output
   stop
end-procedure plsql-error
!* * * * * * * * * * * * * * * * * * * * * * * * * * * * * * * * * * * * *
!procedure to skip sql errors
```

```
!* * * * * * * * * * * * * * * * * * * * * * * * * * * * * * * * * * * * * * *
begin-procedure skip-error
! skip error and do nothing
end-procedure skip-errorSQR EXAMPLE
!*************************************************************************
! PLSQL_TEST:
#include 'setenv.sqc'     !Set environment
#include 'setup02.sqc'    !Printer and page-size initialization
!*************************************************************************
! Program Section
!*************************************************************************
begin-program
  do Init-Report
  display 'DEBUG: calling Initialize -plsql-output'
  do Initialize -plsql-output
  do Process-Main
  do End-Processing
end-program
!*************************************************************************
! Procedure Init-Report
!*************************************************************************
begin-procedure Init-Report
  move 'PL/SQL TEST' to $ReportID
  move 'PL/SQL TEST' to $ReportTitle
  display ' '
  display $ReportTitle
  display ' '
  do Init-DateTime
  do Init-Number
  do Get-Current-DateTime
  display 'Begin of Run'
  display $AsOfNow
  do Stdapi-Init
  do reset
! check if run through the process scheduler
  if  $prcs_process_instance = ''
  else
!      do Select-Parameters
  end-if
end-procedure Init-Report
!*************************************************************************
! Section Heading
!*************************************************************************
BEGIN-HEADING  6
#include 'stdhdg02.sqc'
  print 'Report output'     (+2)
  print '-'                 (+1,1,100) fill
END-HEADING
!*************************************************************************
! Process-Main
```

```
!*********************************************************************
begin-procedure Process-Main
  do process-ld-pa
  do select-log
end-procedure Process-Main
!*********************************************************************
! Invoke stored procedure created by DBA's.
!*********************************************************************
begin-procedure process-ld-pa
  let $sql-statement = 'Proc: PAY_FILE_AUDIT_PKG.AUDIT_LD_PA;'
BEGIN-SQL ON-ERROR=plsql-error
BEGIN
 SYSADM.PAY_FILE_AUDIT_PKG.AUDIT_LD_PA;;
END;;
END-SQL
end-procedure process-ld-pa
!**********************************************************************
! display log output
!*********************************************************************
begin-procedure select-log
   do display-output
end-procedure select-log
!*********************************************************************
begin-procedure END-PROCESSING
!*********************************************************************
   do reset
   do get-current-datetime
   display 'End of Run'
   display $AsOfNow
   do Stdapi-Term
   display 'Successful Completion'
end-procedure END-PROCESSING
!*************************************************************
!Included SQCs
!*************************************************************
#include 'stdapi.sqc'    !Routine to update run status
#include 'curdttim.sqc'  !Get-Current-DateTime procedure
#include 'datetime.sqc'  !Routines for date and time formatting
#Include 'askaod.sqc'    !Get desired 'as of' date
#include 'reset.sqc'     !Reset printer
#include 'datemath.sqc'  !Routines for date and time formatting
#include 'number.sqc'    !Number formatting routines
#include 'prcsdef.sqc'   !Process Definition
#include 'prcsapi.sqc'   !Process Scheduler API
#include 'pasrept.sqc'
#include 'pasrnctl.sqc'
#Include 'getcodta.sqc'  !Get-Company-Data procedure
#Include 'plsql.sqc'
```

SQC EXAMPLE

```
!* * * * * * * * * * * * * * * * * * * * * * * * * * * * * * * * * * * * * * *
!  PLSQL.SQC:  Department and Project/Task Codes
!* * * * * * * * * * * * * * * * * * * * * * * * * * * * * * * * * * * * * * *
!  Name:        PLSQL.SQC
*!***********************************************************************
#include 'setenv.sqc'   !Set environment
!* * * * * * * * * * * * * * * * * * * * * * * * * * * * * * * * * * * * * * *
!create a temporary table.  if exists, then skip
!* * * * * * * * * * * * * * * * * * * * * * * * * * * * * * * * * * * * * * *
begin-procedure Initialize -plsql-output
! create a temporary table to be used pl/sql for logging
begin-sql on-error=skip-error
create global temporary table sysadm.tc_plsql_msg_temp (tc_orig_timestamp
date,
   message_descr long varchar)
   on commit preserve rows
end-sql
! do grants on temp table
begin-sql on-error=skip-error
grant select, insert on tc_plsql_msg_temp to psuser, psdeveloper, workflow,
payroll
end-sql
end-procedure Initialize -plsql-output
!* * * * * * * * * * * * * * * * * * * * * * * * * * * * * * * * * * * * * * *
!SQL to extract and display output
!* * * * * * * * * * * * * * * * * * * * * * * * * * * * * * * * * * * * * * *
begin-procedure display-output
   let $sql-statement = 'select tc_plsql_msg_temp'
begin-select on-error=sql-error
a.message_descr
   print &a.message_descr   (+1,3,100)
from sysadm.tc_plsql_msg_temp a
order by tc_orig_timestamp
end-select
end-procedure display-output
!* * * * * * * * * * * * * * * * * * * * * * * * * * * * * * * * * * * * * * *
!error processing for pl/sql errors
!* * * * * * * * * * * * * * * * * * * * * * * * * * * * * * * * * * * * * * *
begin-procedure plsql-error
   display 'PL/SQL Error'
   display ' '
   display 'SQL Status = '       noline
   display #sql-status 99999     noline
   display ', SQL Error  = '     noline
   display $sql-error
   display ' '
   display ' - SQL Statement = ' noline
   display $sql-statement
```

```
   display ' '
   ! print log
   do display-output
   stop
end-procedure plsql-error
!* * * * * * * * * * * * * * * * * * * * * * * * * * * * * * * * * * * * *
!procedure to skip sql errors
!* * * * * * * * * * * * * * * * * * * * * * * * * * * * * * * * * * * * *
begin-procedure skip-error
! skip error and do nothing
end-procedure skip-error
```

PL/SQL Package Called in SQR Template Example

```
Package Header:
CREATE OR REPLACE PACKAGE pay_file_audit_pkg
AS
/*************************************************************************
   NAME:        pay_file_audit_pkg
   *************************************************************************/
   PROCEDURE audit_ld_pa;
END pay_file_audit_pkg;
/
```

Package Body

```
CREATE OR REPLACE PACKAGE BODY pay_file_audit_pkg
AS
   v_db_name    CONSTANT VARCHAR2 (15) := SYS_CONTEXT ('USERENV', 'DB_NAME');
   e_expected            exception;
   PROCEDURE audit_ld_pa
   AS
      v_file_name    VARCHAR2 (50)                          := 'ps_ld_pa.dat';
      v_file_dir     VARCHAR2 (50);
      v_file_data    VARCHAR2 (250);
      v_batch        sysadm.tc_ld_pa_stats.batch_run_id%TYPE;
      v_acctg_dt     sysadm.tc_ld_pa_stats.accounting_dt%TYPE;
      v_line_count   PLS_INTEGER;
      v_fh           UTL_FILE.file_type;
      TYPE t_ld_pa_rec IS RECORD (
         time_cd            VARCHAR (1),
         band_id            VARCHAR (2),
         batch_num          VARCHAR2 (10),
         acctg_dt           DATE,
         emplid             VARCHAR2 (9),
         proj_num           VARCHAR2 (25),
         task_num           VARCHAR2 (25),
         org                VARCHAR2 (8),
         expend_type        VARCHAR2 (30),
```

```
      wkend_dt              DATE,
      total_hrs             INTEGER,
      labor_chg             INTEGER,
      corr_num              VARCHAR2 (3),
      approve_id            VARCHAR2 (9),
      last_date_worked      DATE,
      filler                VARCHAR2 (100)
   );
   v_ld_pa_rec    t_ld_pa_rec                              := NULL;
   v_message      VARCHAR2 (1000);
   v_where_at     VARCHAR2 (500);
BEGIN
   v_file_dir := '/stage/' || LOWER (v_db_name) || '/data/load';
   sysadm.ps_utl_pkg. Initialize _log ('file_test', TRUE);
   v_fh := UTL_FILE.fopen (v_file_dir, v_file_name, 'r');
   v_line_count := 0;

   <<file_loop>>
   LOOP
      BEGIN
         UTL_FILE.get_line (v_fh, v_file_data);
         -- break out the record into fields
         v_ld_pa_rec.time_cd := SUBSTR (v_file_data, 1, 1);
         v_ld_pa_rec.band_id := SUBSTR (v_file_data, 2, 2);
         v_ld_pa_rec.batch_num := SUBSTR (v_file_data, 4, 10);
         v_ld_pa_rec.acctg_dt := SUBSTR (v_file_data, 14, 11);
         v_ld_pa_rec.emplid := SUBSTR (v_file_data, 25, 9);
         v_ld_pa_rec.proj_num := SUBSTR (v_file_data, 34, 25);
         v_ld_pa_rec.task_num := SUBSTR (v_file_data, 59, 25);
         v_ld_pa_rec.org := SUBSTR (v_file_data, 84, 8);
         v_ld_pa_rec.expend_type := SUBSTR (v_file_data, 92, 30);
         v_ld_pa_rec.wkend_dt := SUBSTR (v_file_data, 122, 11);
         v_ld_pa_rec.total_hrs := SUBSTR (v_file_data, 133, 15);
         v_ld_pa_rec.labor_chg := SUBSTR (v_file_data, 148, 15);
         v_ld_pa_rec.corr_num := SUBSTR (v_file_data, 163, 3);
         v_ld_pa_rec.approve_id := SUBSTR (v_file_data, 166, 9);
         v_ld_pa_rec.last_date_worked := SUBSTR (v_file_data, 175, 11);
         v_ld_pa_rec.filler := SUBSTR (v_file_data, 186, LENGTH (v_file_data));
         v_where_at :=
               ' insert into tc_pay_ld_pa_temp - '
            || v_ld_pa_rec.batch_num
            || '-'
            || v_ld_pa_rec.acctg_dt
            || '-'
            || v_ld_pa_rec.emplid
            || '-'
            || v_ld_pa_rec.proj_num
            || '-'
            || v_ld_pa_rec.task_num;
         INSERT INTO sysadm.tc_pay_ld_pa_temp
              VALUES (v_ld_pa_rec.time_cd, v_ld_pa_rec.band_id,
```

```
                 v_ld_pa_rec.batch_num, v_ld_pa_rec.acctg_dt,
                 v_ld_pa_rec.emplid, v_ld_pa_rec.proj_num,
                 v_ld_pa_rec.task_num, v_ld_pa_rec.org,
                 v_ld_pa_rec.expend_type, v_ld_pa_rec.wkend_dt,
                 v_ld_pa_rec.total_hrs, v_ld_pa_rec.labor_chg,
                 v_ld_pa_rec.corr_num, v_ld_pa_rec.approve_id,
                 v_ld_pa_rec.last_date_worked, v_ld_pa_rec.filler);
      v_line_count := v_line_count + 1;
      v_file_data := NULL;
   EXCEPTION
      WHEN NO_DATA_FOUND
      THEN
         EXIT;
   END;
END LOOP;
sysadm.ps_utl_pkg.log_new_line;
sysadm.ps_utl_pkg.write_log (   'Record read from file: '
                             || TO_CHAR (v_line_count, 99999)
                            );
sysadm.ps_utl_pkg.log_new_line;

v_where_at := ' sum data from tc_pay_ld_pa_temp';
FOR idx IN (SELECT   SUBSTR (batch_num, 1, 3) AS batch, acctg_dt,
                     SUM (total_hrs) AS total_hrs,
                     SUM (labor_chg) AS labor_chg
                FROM sysadm.tc_pay_ld_pa_temp
            GROUP BY SUBSTR (batch_num, 1, 3), acctg_dt)
LOOP
   BEGIN
      SELECT batch_run_id, accounting_dt
        INTO v_batch, v_acctg_dt
        FROM tc_ld_pa_stats
       WHERE batch_run_id = idx.batch OR accounting_dt = idx.acctg_dt;
      IF idx.batch = v_batch
      THEN
         v_message :=
            'Batch id has already been processed. Batch ID:' || v_batch;
         RAISE e_expected;
      ELSIF idx.acctg_dt = v_acctg_dt
      THEN
         v_message :=
               'Accounting date has already been processed. Accounting date:'
            || v_acctg_dt;
         RAISE e_expected;
      END IF;
   EXCEPTION
      WHEN NO_DATA_FOUND
      THEN
         v_batch := NULL;
         v_acctg_dt := NULL;
   END;
```

```
            v_where_at :=
                  ' insert into tc_ld_pa_stats -'
               || idx.batch
               || '-'
               || idx.acctg_dt
               || '-'
               || idx.total_hrs
               || '-'
               || idx.labor_chg;
            INSERT INTO tc_ld_pa_stats
                 VALUES (idx.batch, idx.acctg_dt, idx.total_hrs, idx.labor_chg,
                         SYSDATE);
         END LOOP;
         UTL_FILE.fclose (v_fh);
      EXCEPTION
         WHEN e_expected
         THEN
            sysadm.ps_utl_pkg.write_error (v_message);
            IF UTL_FILE.is_open (v_fh)
            THEN
               UTL_FILE.fclose (v_fh);
            END IF;
            raise_application_error (-20000, v_message);
         WHEN OTHERS
         THEN
            v_message := 'SQLERRM: ' || SUBSTR (SQLERRM, 1, 250) || v_where_at;
            sysadm.ps_utl_pkg.write_error (v_message);
            IF UTL_FILE.is_open (v_fh)
            THEN
               UTL_FILE.fclose (v_fh);
            END IF;
            raise_application_error (-20000, v_message);
      END;
   END pay_file_audit_pkg;
   /
```

Procedure

```
PROCEDURE audit_ld_pa
   AS
      v_file_name        VARCHAR2 (50)                            := 'ps_ld_pa.dat';
      v_file_dir               VARCHAR2 (50);
      v_file_data        VARCHAR2 (250);
      v_batch            sysadm.tc_ld_pa_stats.batch_run_id%TYPE;
      v_acctg_dt         sysadm.tc_ld_pa_stats.accounting_dt%TYPE;
      v_line_count        PLS_INTEGER;
      v_fh                     UTL_FILE.file_type;
                        TYPE t_ld_pa_rec IS RECORD (
                         time_cd              VARCHAR (1),
                         band_id              VARCHAR (2),
```

```
                    batch_num          VARCHAR2 (10),
                    acctg_dt           DATE,
                    emplid             VARCHAR2 (9),
                    proj_num           VARCHAR2 (25),
                    task_num           VARCHAR2 (25),
                    org                VARCHAR2 (8),
                    expend_type        VARCHAR2 (30),
                    wkend_dt           DATE,
                    total_hrs          INTEGER,
                    labor_chg          INTEGER,
                    corr_num           VARCHAR2 (3),
                    approve_id         VARCHAR2 (9),
                    last_date_worked   DATE,
                    filler             VARCHAR2 (100)
                );
   v_ld_pa_rec                t_ld_pa_rec                        := NULL;
   v_message                 VARCHAR2 (1000);
   v_where_at                VARCHAR2 (500);
BEGIN
   v_file_dir := '/stage/' || LOWER (v_db_name) || '/data/load';
   sysadm.ps_utl_pkg. Initialize _log ('file_test', TRUE);
   v_fh := UTL_FILE.fopen (v_file_dir, v_file_name, 'r');
   v_line_count := 0;
   <<file_loop>>
   LOOP
      BEGIN
         UTL_FILE.get_line (v_fh, v_file_data);
         -- break out the record into fields
         v_ld_pa_rec.time_cd := SUBSTR (v_file_data, 1, 1);
         v_ld_pa_rec.band_id := SUBSTR (v_file_data, 2, 2);
         v_ld_pa_rec.batch_num := SUBSTR (v_file_data, 4, 10);
         v_ld_pa_rec.acctg_dt := SUBSTR (v_file_data, 14, 11);
         v_ld_pa_rec.emplid := SUBSTR (v_file_data, 25, 9);
         v_ld_pa_rec.proj_num := SUBSTR (v_file_data, 34, 25);
         v_ld_pa_rec.task_num := SUBSTR (v_file_data, 59, 25);
         v_ld_pa_rec.org := SUBSTR (v_file_data, 84, 8);
         v_ld_pa_rec.expend_type := SUBSTR (v_file_data, 92, 30);
         v_ld_pa_rec.wkend_dt := SUBSTR (v_file_data, 122, 11);
         v_ld_pa_rec.total_hrs := SUBSTR (v_file_data, 133, 15);
         v_ld_pa_rec.labor_chg := SUBSTR (v_file_data, 148, 15);
         v_ld_pa_rec.corr_num := SUBSTR (v_file_data, 163, 3);
         v_ld_pa_rec.approve_id := SUBSTR (v_file_data, 166, 9);
         v_ld_pa_rec.last_date_worked := SUBSTR (v_file_data, 175, 11);
         v_ld_pa_rec.filler := SUBSTR (v_file_data, 186, LENGTH (v_file_data));
         v_where_at :=
               ' insert into tc_pay_ld_pa_temp - '
            || v_ld_pa_rec.batch_num
            || '-'
            || v_ld_pa_rec.acctg_dt
            || '-'
```

```
            || v_ld_pa_rec.emplid
            || '-'
            || v_ld_pa_rec.proj_num
            || '-'
            || v_ld_pa_rec.task_num;
         INSERT INTO sysadm.tc_pay_ld_pa_temp
              VALUES (v_ld_pa_rec.time_cd, v_ld_pa_rec.band_id,
                      v_ld_pa_rec.batch_num, v_ld_pa_rec.acctg_dt,
                      v_ld_pa_rec.emplid, v_ld_pa_rec.proj_num,
                      v_ld_pa_rec.task_num, v_ld_pa_rec.org,
                      v_ld_pa_rec.expend_type, v_ld_pa_rec.wkend_dt,
                      v_ld_pa_rec.total_hrs, v_ld_pa_rec.labor_chg,
                      v_ld_pa_rec.corr_num, v_ld_pa_rec.approve_id,
                      v_ld_pa_rec.last_date_worked, v_ld_pa_rec.filler);
         v_line_count := v_line_count + 1;
         v_file_data := NULL;
      EXCEPTION
         WHEN NO_DATA_FOUND
         THEN
            EXIT;
      END;
   END LOOP;
   sysadm.ps_utl_pkg.log_new_line;
   sysadm.ps_utl_pkg.write_log (   'Record read from file: '
                                || TO_CHAR (v_line_count, 99999)
                               );
   sysadm.ps_utl_pkg.log_new_line;

   v_where_at := ' sum data from tc_pay_ld_pa_temp';
   FOR idx IN (SELECT   SUBSTR (batch_num, 1, 3) AS batch, acctg_dt,
                        SUM (total_hrs) AS total_hrs,
                        SUM (labor_chg) AS labor_chg
                   FROM sysadm.tc_pay_ld_pa_temp
               GROUP BY SUBSTR (batch_num, 1, 3), acctg_dt)
   LOOP
      BEGIN
         SELECT batch_run_id, accounting_dt
           INTO v_batch, v_acctg_dt
           FROM tc_ld_pa_stats
          WHERE batch_run_id = idx.batch OR accounting_dt = idx.acctg_dt;
         IF idx.batch = v_batch
         THEN
            v_message :=
               'Batch id has already been processed. Batch ID:' || v_batch;
            RAISE e_expected;
         ELSIF idx.acctg_dt = v_acctg_dt
         THEN
            v_message :=
                  'Accounting date has already been processed. Accounting date:'
               || v_acctg_dt;
            RAISE e_expected;
```

```
            END IF;
         EXCEPTION
            WHEN NO_DATA_FOUND
            THEN
               v_batch := NULL;
               v_acctg_dt := NULL;
         END;

         v_where_at :=
               ' insert into tc_ld_pa_stats -'
            || idx.batch
            || '-'
            || idx.acctg_dt
            || '-'
            || idx.total_hrs
            || '-'
            || idx.labor_chg;
         INSERT INTO tc_ld_pa_stats
              VALUES (idx.batch, idx.acctg_dt, idx.total_hrs, idx.labor_chg,
                      SYSDATE);
      END LOOP;
      UTL_FILE.fclose (v_fh);
   EXCEPTION
      WHEN e_expected
      THEN
         sysadm.ps_utl_pkg.write_error (v_message);
         IF UTL_FILE.is_open (v_fh)
         THEN
            UTL_FILE.fclose (v_fh);
         END IF;
         raise_application_error (-20000, v_message);
      WHEN OTHERS
      THEN
         v_message := 'SQLERRM: ' || SUBSTR (SQLERRM, 1, 250) || v_where_at;
         sysadm.ps_utl_pkg.write_error (v_message);
         IF UTL_FILE.is_open (v_fh)
         THEN
            UTL_FILE.fclose (v_fh);
         END IF;
         raise_application_error (-20000, v_message);
   END;
END pay_file_audit_pkg;
/
```

PeopleSoft Upgrades

Organizational standards for PeopleSoft upgrades exist. Within one educational organization the standard is not to allow the creation of stored PL/SQL procedures. The justification for this standard is that PL/SQL stored elements, procedures, functions, packages, and triggers are not identified in the PeopleSoft upgrade plan and when the Database platform is upgraded, objects can be lost. Because of this standard, it is common in this organization to embed most PL/SQL via anonymous blocks inside of SQRs. This standard places a tremendous burden on the programmer and disallows the use of the dynamic features of PL/SQL. One possible solution is to query using the USER_SOURCE table and create a script that could easily regenerate all the stored objects quickly after a database upgrade. A table can be created to create version controlled database objects.

History Table

A History table can be created that will track all of your procedures, functions, packages, and package bodies that are created in USER_SOURCE and insert a row each time a new PL/SQL object is created. This table can be queried at PeopleSoft upgrade time to create a detailed report of each of the PL/SQL objects, date of creation, and change date. This will provide a nice, detailed upgrade plan for all of your PL/SQL objects in the PeopleSoft database.

```
--History table Creation
CREATE TABLE SOURCE_HIST AS SELECT SYSDATE CHANGE_DATE, USER_SOURCE.*
FROM USER_SOURCE WHERE 1=2;

--Trigger to Store and Maintain History
CREATE OR REPLACE TRIGGER CHANGE_HIST AFTER CREATE ON SCHEMA
BEGIN
       IF DICTIONARY_OBJ_TYPE in
            ('PROCEDURE', 'FUNCTION', 'PACKAGE', 'PACKAGE BODY', 'TYPE')
       THEN
            INSERT INTO SOURCE_HIST SELECT sysdate, user_source.* FROM
USER_SOURCE
            WHERE TYPE = DICTIONARY_OBJ_TYPE AND NAME = DICTIONARY_OBJ_NAME;
       END IF;
EXCEPTION
WHEN OTHERS THEN
       RAISE_APPLICAITON_ERROR(-20000, SQLERRM);
END;
--Metalink Note:258690.1
```

Util_file to Create an External File to Regenerate a PL/SQL Object after Upgrade

Before a database upgrade or a PeopleSoft software upgrade, the following PL/SQL anonymous block can be run to generate an external UTL_FILE. The external file will become a record of all of the PL/SQL objects in the database and will generate a script to re-create these objects after upgrades. A UTL_FILE that contains the procedures, functions, packages, and package bodies will need to be created as well as a UTL_FILE to hold the information to re-create the database triggers. The first example following will create from USER_SOURCE, and the second will create a script to re-create the database and table triggers. Note that both PL/SQL blocks need to be run prior to upgrade with a frozen point in time being determined and honored by developers. It would be useless to create a file to re-create all the PL/SQL objects if new objects were created after the documenting UTL_FILE is created. Be advised that timing of this is very important in capturing the correct PL/SQL objects.

```
--Example
DECLARE

v_file utl_file.file_type;
v_desc varchar2(4000);
v_host varchar2(40);

cursor c1 is select
name,
text
from user_source
order by line;
r1 c1%rowtype;

BEGIN
select host_name
into v_host
from v$instance;

v_file := utl_file.fopen('c:\oracle\admin\orcl\utl_file', 'plsql_exp
.utl', 'W');
utl_file.put_line(v_file, '/*');
utl_file.put_line(v_file, ' +-----------------------------+');
utl_file.put_line(v_file, ' UPDATED: '|| to_char(sysdate, 'MM-DD-YYYY
HH12:MIam'));
utl_file.put_line(v_file, ' SCHEMA: ' || lower(user));
utl_file.put_line(v_file, ' DB SERVER: ' || lower(v_host));
utl_file.put_line(v_file, ' +-----------------------------+');
utl_file.put_line(v_file, '*/');

open c1;
loop
fetch c1 into r1;
exit when c1%notfound;
utl_file.new_line(v_file,2);
v_desc := rtrim(rtrim(r1.name,chr(10) ));
--v_desc := rtrim(rtrim(substr(r1.name,10),chr(10) ));
utl_file.put_line(v_file, 'CREATE OR REPLACE PROCEDURE ' || v_desc);
utl_file.put_line(v_file, r1.text);
```

```
utl_file.put_line(v_file, '/');
end loop;
close c1;
utl_file.fclose(v_file);

END;
/
```

PeopleCode and Application Engine

We read this in the PeopleBooks Library for PeopleTools 8.14:

"The PeopleSoft ODBC driver will *not* support the minimum SQL conformance level even though it reports supporting extended syntax. Open Query will only support the ODBC extended SQL Grammar for stored procedures. The stored procedure syntax is:

```
{[? = ] call procedure_name [ (param, ...)]}
```

The stored procedure execution model was chosen because it supports the independent creation of an SQL statement. In our case, the independent creation is done through PeopleSoft Query. However, instead of a stored procedure, the result is a PeopleSoft Query object."

Because PeopleSoft is going to make your anonymous code a query object, any performance gain received by using PL/SQL will be negated because of the query object creation. Thus, if you wish to use PL/SQL objects in Application Engine or PeopleCode, be certain to store them in the Oracle database as a stored procedure that has a separate call. The benefit of calling a stored PL/SQL from inside of Application Engine is that you can use it anywhere PeopleCode can be called. This gives the flexibility of Pushbuttons and Process Scheduler. Imagine you have a procedure that does a weekly update to the database: you can embed the procedure call in Application Engine and schedule it to run nightly through PeopleSoft.

Here is an example of calling an anonymous block in a PeopleCode section in Application Engine:

```
%Execute(/)
DECLARE
      CURSOR c1 IS
      SELECT x.keyname
      , x.key1
      , x.key2
      , x.key3
      , x.key4
      , x.key5
      , x.key9
      , RANK () OVER (PARTITION BY x.keyname, x.key1
      ORDER BY x.keyname, x.key1, x.key9, x.key2) rk
```

```
        FROM recname x;
BEGIN
        FOR c1_rec IN c1 LOOP
                UPDATE recname y
                SET y.key3 = c1_rec.rk
                WHERE y.keyname = c1_rec.keyname
                AND y.key1 = c1_rec.key1
                AND y.key2 = c1_rec.key2
                AND y.key9 = c1_rec.key9;
        END LOOP;
END;
/
```

PeopleCode Example

To round out this appendix, here is an example quoted from the PeopleBooks Library, PeopleTools 8.14:

```
SQLExec("EXECUTE test1 'SMITH' ,'HEADQUARTERS','ATLANTA')");
```

Execution Models ODBC supports three execution models. Each accomplishes the same tasks, but each one differs with regard to when and where (on the client or on the server) each step is performed.

ExecDirect In this model, the SQL statement is specified, sent to the server, and executed, all in one step. This model is best suited for ad hoc SQL statements or SQL statements that will be executed only once. Parameters can be used, but they act merely as placeholders that the driver replaces with the parameter values before it sends the SQL statement to the server.

The DBMS discards the optimization information used to execute the SQL statement after execution is complete. If the same statement is specified again with SQLExecDirect, the entire process of parsing and optimizing happens again.

Prepare/Execute In this model, the SQL statement is "prepared" (sent to the server, parsed, and optimized) first and executed later. When the statement is executed, what flows to the server is not the SQL statement itself, but merely some way of referencing the statement so that the access plan can be executed immediately. Parameters are often used in these SQL statements, so the only items that flow to the server are the reference to the access plan and the parameter values, not the entire SQL statement.

The Prepare/Execute model should be used when repeated execution of the same SQL statement is needed and when the SQL statement must be constructed dynamically during runtime. To use this model, the application calls SQLPrepare, and then (presumably in a loop) calls SQLExecute.

Stored Procedures The stored procedure model is like the Prepare/Execute model except that with stored procedures, the preparation step can be done independently of the application and the stored procedure persists beyond the runtime of the application. To use stored procedures in ODBC, the application calls SQLExecDirect but uses the SQL statement to specify the stored procedure name:

```
SQLExecDirect(hstmt, "{call query.proc1(?,?,?)}", SQL_NTS);
```

References

- PeopleBooks Library PeopleTools 8.14
- Oracle Metalink
- *Oracle PL/SQL Programming, Third Edition* by Steven Feuerstein and Bill Pribyl, (O'Reilly, 2002)

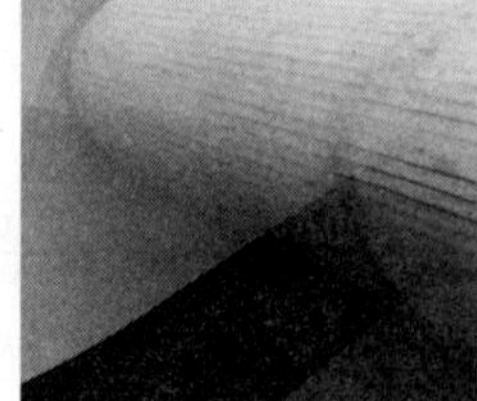

APPENDIX B

COBOL in Peoplesoft

eopleSoft has its roots firmly planted in the legacy code of COBOL because a lot of the early developers and or adopters of PeopleSoft came from the mainframe environment and it was an easy transition. I started working with PeopleSoft on version 8.0 and helped with an upgrade to 8.3. I came to this position from having been a DBA, and a developer before that, working with software such as Visual Basic, C++, and Java, so when I was asked to modify and work in COBOL I was truly like a deer in the headlights. Don't get me wrong—I took COBOL training, but that was in 1983. And if you have ever been in the same place as I was as that deer in the headlights, you know there isn't much out there in the way of documentation or books. You have to pick them up used, and you will pay a premium price to get them. So as you can imagine, I went about asking why PeopleSoft chose to do this to people, and the basic answer was it was the path of least resistance: they were just too busy getting PeopleTools working to find the time to develop a batch language. In this chapter we will look at what I learned as I scraped my knees and dusted off some 1983 brain cells and tried to relearn COBOL the PeopleSoft way.

COBOL

The first place I found that had real insight into the transition and why COBOL is still around was on the blog kept by Chris Heller and Larry Grey at Grey Sparling. The following is an excerpt from their web site blog, from an article titled "SQR vs Application Engine."

"One of the things that I've had in my list of things to do for a while now is to help out someone that I know answer the question of SQR vs. Application Engine. They have the challenge of having a staff that doesn't know much about SQR or Application Engine (they are just implementing PeopleSoft now), but they do have consultants available that do know SQR.

So, having set the stage of what we're trying to figure out, we're going to step way, way, way back from current day and look [at] how PeopleSoft even ended up with SQR and Application Engine. Brace yourself; this isn't going to be a short entry :-)

Going back to the early days of PeopleSoft, there were two main batch tools: COBOL and SQR. Both COBOL and SQR had the benefits of working well across the different platforms that PeopleSoft supported. COBOL also had the benefit of being something that most PeopleSoft developers understood, most of them having come from old mainframe players like M&D and Walker. SQR brought a simple, yet powerful, idea to the table: let people write conditional logic as well as output data as part of an SQL statement. Today that's not so strange, but back in the late 80s/early 90s, having your printing logic so tightly integrated (some might say "tied") to your SQL was powerful stuff.

The big unspoken question, of course, is why didn't PeopleSoft create some sort of batch/reporting tool as part of PeopleTools? The short answer is that, in the beginning, everyone was too busy just making PeopleTools work for online transactions to even think about some sort of batch/reporting tool.

PeopleSoft did add PS/Query and PS/nVision in the PeopleTools 2–3 timeframe, but they were only reporting tools. Batch was not even considered for a higher-level development tool at that point (although PeopleTools 3 also marked the delivery of the PeopleTools Process Scheduler). The only thing that PeopleTools provided was the concept of Meta-SQL, which helped smooth over some of the differences between database platforms.

As time went on, it wasn't even the PeopleTools team that came up with a good higher-level batch development tool. It was a lone coder on the PeopleSoft AR team, Owen O'Neill, who got sick of writing COBOL batch programs and decided to write a higher-level tool for developing batch programs. He called it Application Engine, and used PeopleTools for building the frontend, and (of all things) COBOL for the backend.

Application Engine was different than regular batch programs because it wasn't procedural. It focused on set-based SQL logic, and it had a much deeper understanding of the underlying application definitions that it was working [with]. Describing set-based logic is beyond the scope of this blog post, but suffice it to say that set-based logic is more in line with how SQL is supposed to work, but it's not as familiar to developers that have only worked with procedural logic.

To make an already long story short, Application Engine slowly won converts within PeopleSoft, and by the time that PeopleSoft 8 was being developed, Application Engine was adopted by the PeopleTools team. The frontend was converted to being a regular PeopleTool as part of Application Designer, and the backend was re-written in C++ and given the ability to run PeopleCode as well as SQL logic.

Although it took more than a decade for Application Engine to get developed and finally moved into PeopleTools, SQR and COBOL didn't really change that much during that time. PeopleSoft bought the source code for SQR, but that was really just to make our own lives easier for shipping new PeopleSoft versions—it was never made a full part of PeopleTools.

COBOL was even worse, since PeopleSoft never actually controlled the COBOL compilers in use. There were some real big headaches that happened because of that—catch me at a conference sometime and I'll tell you some stories that will make you laugh (or cry) about some of our dealings with the various vendors of COBOL compilers that we had to deal with. As for the COBOL language, well, it's COBOL. Nuf said.

Ultimately though, you could dig up an early PeopleSoft developer and they would still feel right at home with the versions of COBOL and SQR that are still in use with PeopleSoft today. On the other hand, Application Engine kept getting new features, both for development and runtime use, and there were big plans for adding something known as PeopleCode Print to App Engine for PeopleTools 9. That probably would have been the end for formal support for SQR within PeopleSoft.

An interesting thing happened on the way to PeopleTools 9, though. Although it was scoped on 3 separate occasions, for one reason or another, PeopleTools 9 never saw the light of day (other than a few PeopleTools 9 baseball hats that are collector's items now). But there are a number of PeopleTools developers that are working on the Fusion project, and I expect that you'll see something very similar to Application Engine in Fusion.

Why would Application Engine show up as part of Oracle Fusion? There are a couple of reasons: one is that Oracle really doesn't have a good tool for batch development. If you look at existing Oracle Applications, you'll notice that batch is done by writing raw PL/SQL or Pro*C code. Not the most straightforward thing for a typical application developer to do. The other thing about Application Engine that fits well within Oracle is that it is a set-based tool. Most of the processing is pushed to the database, and that plays well to Oracle's strengths. Oracle themselves list using Application Engine for batch as number 4 in their top 10 things for PeopleSoft Enterprise customers to do today to get ready for Fusion.

Coming back around to the original question of whether it makes sense to train people in SQR or Application Engine for current PeopleSoft customers, the answer is that both have pros and cons. For starters, there aren't many PeopleSoft applications that don't use both SQR and AppEngine, so you need to have some level of skills in both. I think that CRM is the exception here; I know that CRM has no COBOL, and I think that is true for SQR as well."

This blog entry was very insightful for understanding the roots of COBOL in PeopleSoft and a possible future path. Now that that is out of way, let's take a look at working with COBOL in PeopleSoft. All of the delivered COBOL comes with a section that is named "Before You Customize," and it cautions against customizing delivered PeopleSoft COBOL programs. Take it for what it is worth—which is very sound advice. But we all know in the real world there are times when you have to go against sound advice. If you ever cross this bridge, follow all of the excellent things you were taught in school, back up the original (I usually do this in a couple of places—but I get very nervous doing this sort of thing), never work from the backup, and always put the newly modified version in a new folder with a name that reflects that it is no longer a delivered COBOL. The last rule stated can be changed if the name is dependent on the process running and you have no way of changing the Component or Menu. Always make a note of all the important information about the modification in the comments section of the code.

With SOA (service-oriented architecture), legacy systems can be integrated over the Enterprise Service Bus. So while there might not be a surge of COBOL (currently ranked eighteenth by the TIOBE programming community ranking at www.tiobe.com/index.php/content/paperinfo/tpci/index.html), SOA does increase the chances of legacy COBOL programs not being replaced, and there is still a significant percentage of legacy COBOL code in production. It is a very valuable skill, looking at it from a practical standpoint: with the supply of programmers down and demand steady, this skill could very well equal opportunity. An important article about working with SOA in COBOL can be read at www.ddj.com/architect/20680032.

It is important to understand how the COBOL applications work in PeopleSoft. All database processing is passed through the PTPSQLRT module; it handles all of the SQL because no direct SQL execution exists within PeopleSoft; this is how PeopleSoft is able to have a standard SQL execution across different database platforms. The main difference between traditional COBOL programming and PeopleSoft COBOL is how the compiler accesses the database: it accesses the database using the PeopleSoft PTPSQLRT module. This means that the SQL statements are stored in the database in a table named PS_SQLSTMT_TBL. In this appendix we will look at how to code in this manner in COBOL.

Debugging in COBOL

One of the cool tricks that I learned from a coder is to create a variable called DISPLAY-DIAGNOSTICS, and then to set that value to Y when you are debugging and N when you roll into production. It is nice because you can leave the debugging code in place and just toggle it from Y or N, depending on whether you want to see the display values in the log. You can also add a variable at the table level so that you can see what you are returning in SQL and the values you are placing in your COBOL arrays is what you expect. The variable is named TABLE-VIEW, and you can see in the following code example that if both are set to Y, then you get a display of messages and data to determine where you may have a problem in the code.

```
01  NEW-FIELDS.
02  DISPLAY-DIAGNOSTICS          PIC X(01).
02  TABLE-VIEW                   PIC X(01).
/*****************************************************************
Place at start of Code section
*****************************************************************/
          MOVE 'Y' TO DISPLAY-DIAGNOSTICS.
          MOVE 'Y' TO TABLE-VIEW.
/*****************************************************************
Example of DISPLAY-DIAGNOSTICS to show statement for which section
you are in
*****************************************************************/
          IF DISPLAY-DIAGNOSTICS = 'Y'
             DISPLAY 'READING PERSONAL DATA...'
          END-IF.
```

```
/*****************************************************************
Example of showing the results of a SQL and what is being placed
in an array
*****************************************************************/
        IF DISPLAY-DIAGNOSTICS = 'Y' AND TABLE-VIEW = 'Y'
           DISPLAY SVC-NDX                                            ' '
                   EFFDT             OF SERVICE-TBL(SVC-NDX)  ' '
                   ESTABID           OF SERVICE-TBL(SVC-NDX)  ' '
                   RETPLN            OF SERVICE-TBL(SVC-NDX)  ' '
                   TST-BAND          OF SERVICE-TBL(SVC-NDX)  ' '
                   SERVICE-STATE     OF SERVICE-TBL(SVC-NDX)  ' '
                   SVC-APPLICABLE    OF SERVICE-TBL(SVC-NDX)  ' '
                   SEGMENT-CREDIT    OF SERVICE-TBL(SVC-NDX)  ' '
                   SEGMENT-LENGTH    OF SERVICE-TBL(SVC-NDX)
        END-IF.
```

SQL in COBOL

As was mentioned in the introduction to this chapter, there is no direct access to the database via PeopleSoft COBOL, so each time data must be brought back from the database, it has to be done with PS_SQLSTMT_TBL. The table has to be updated to store your SQL and define your SQL processing in PeopleSoft. Any number of ways can be used to put the SQL statement into the database; one way is with Data Mover, another would be to have your DBA update the table, using whichever method is the adopted standard. To understand what pieces of data are required in the table, let's take a look at the table structure and naming conventions. It is important to pay attention to some small things that exist in the setup. In the following illustration you can see the describe on the PS_SQLSTMT_TBL and which columns are required.

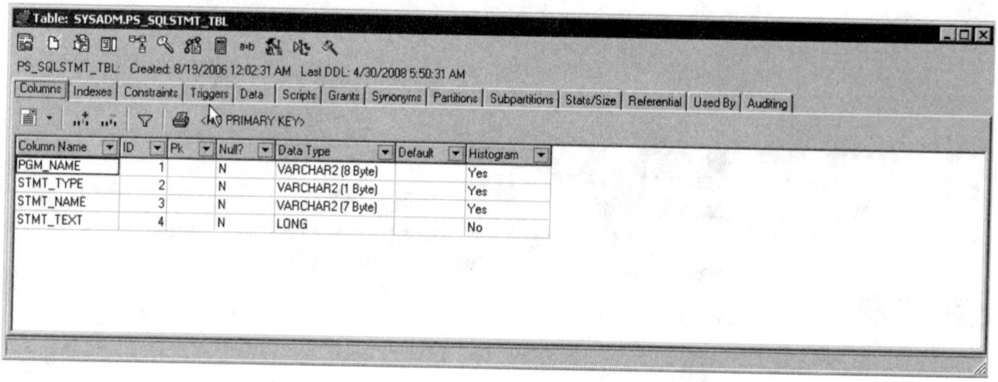

Table: SYSADM.PS_SQLSTMT_TBL

PS_SQLSTMT_TBL Created: 8/19/2006 12:02:31 AM Last DDL: 4/30/2008 5:50:31 AM

Columns | Indexes | Constraints | Triggers | Data | Scripts | Grants | Synonyms | Partitions | Subpartitions | Stats/Size | Referential | Used By | Auditing

<NO PRIMARY KEY>

Column Name	ID	Pk	Null?	Data Type	Default	Histogram
PGM_NAME	1		N	VARCHAR2 (8 Byte)		Yes
STMT_TYPE	2		N	VARCHAR2 (1 Byte)		Yes
STMT_NAME	3		N	VARCHAR2 (7 Byte)		Yes
STMT_TEXT	4		N	LONG		No

The PS_SQLSTMT_TBL table is constructed as follows:

PS_SQLSTMT_TBL Column	Description
PGM_NAME	Program Name
STMT_TYPE	Statement Type
STMT_NAME	Statement Name
STMT_TEXT	Statement Text—SQL statement

The following illustration is an SQL statement to pull the SQL associated with the example program that is used for this chapter; you can also see the result set.

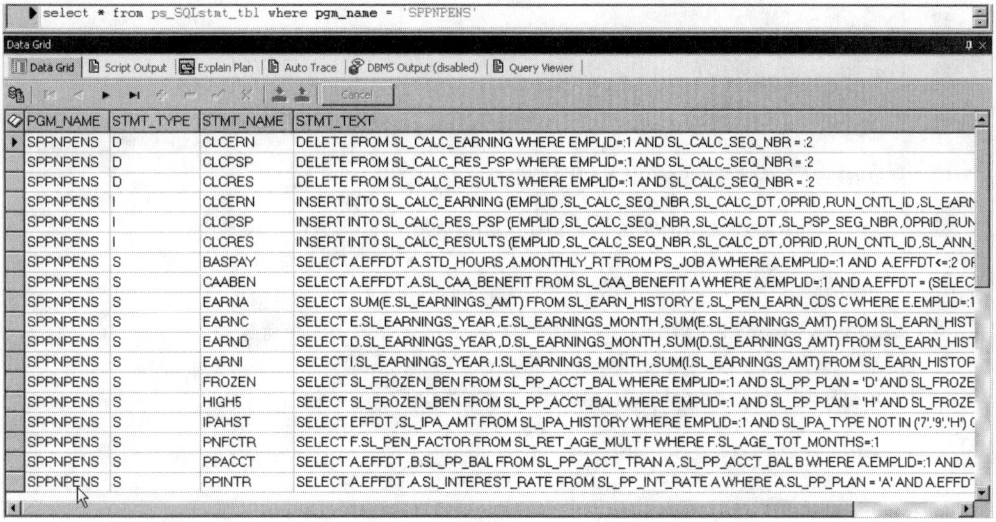

```
select * from ps_SQLstmt_tbl where pgm_name = 'SPPNPENS'
```

Data Grid | Script Output | Explain Plan | Auto Trace | DBMS Output (disabled) | Query Viewer

PGM_NAME	STMT_TYPE	STMT_NAME	STMT_TEXT
SPPNPENS	D	CLCERN	DELETE FROM SL_CALC_EARNING WHERE EMPLID=:1 AND SL_CALC_SEQ_NBR = :2
SPPNPENS	D	CLCPSP	DELETE FROM SL_CALC_RES_PSP WHERE EMPLID=:1 AND SL_CALC_SEQ_NBR = :2
SPPNPENS	D	CLCRES	DELETE FROM SL_CALC_RESULTS WHERE EMPLID=:1 AND SL_CALC_SEQ_NBR = :2
SPPNPENS	I	CLCERN	INSERT INTO SL_CALC_EARNING (EMPLID ,SL_CALC_SEQ_NBR ,SL_CALC_DT ,OPRID ,RUN_CNTL_ID ,SL_EAR
SPPNPENS	I	CLCPSP	INSERT INTO SL_CALC_RES_PSP (EMPLID ,SL_CALC_SEQ_NBR ,SL_CALC_DT ,SL_PSP_SEG_NBR ,OPRID ,RU
SPPNPENS	I	CLCRES	INSERT INTO SL_CALC_RESULTS (EMPLID ,SL_CALC_SEQ_NBR ,SL_CALC_DT ,OPRID ,RUN_CNTL_ID ,SL_ANN_
SPPNPENS	S	BASPAY	SELECT A.EFFDT ,A.STD_HOURS ,A.MONTHLY_RT FROM PS_JOB A WHERE A.EMPLID=:1 AND A.EFFDT<=:2 O
SPPNPENS	S	CAABEN	SELECT A.EFFDT ,A.SL_CAA_BENEFIT FROM SL_CAA_BENEFIT A WHERE A.EMPLID=:1 AND A.EFFDT = (SELEC
SPPNPENS	S	EARNA	SELECT SUM(E.SL_EARNINGS_AMT) FROM SL_EARN_HISTORY E ,SL_PEN_EARN_CDS C WHERE E.EMPLID=:1
SPPNPENS	S	EARNC	SELECT E.SL_EARNINGS_YEAR ,E.SL_EARNINGS_MONTH ,SUM(E.SL_EARNINGS_AMT) FROM SL_EARN_HIST
SPPNPENS	S	EARND	SELECT D.SL_EARNINGS_YEAR ,D.SL_EARNINGS_MONTH ,SUM(D.SL_EARNINGS_AMT) FROM SL_EARN_HIST
SPPNPENS	S	EARNI	SELECT I.SL_EARNINGS_YEAR ,I.SL_EARNINGS_MONTH ,SUM(I.SL_EARNINGS_AMT) FROM SL_EARN_HISTO
SPPNPENS	S	FROZEN	SELECT SL_FROZEN_BEN FROM SL_PP_ACCT_BAL WHERE EMPLID=:1 AND SL_PP_PLAN = 'D' AND SL_FROZE
SPPNPENS	S	HIGH5	SELECT SL_FROZEN_BEN FROM SL_PP_ACCT_BAL WHERE EMPLID=:1 AND SL_PP_PLAN = 'H' AND SL_FROZE
SPPNPENS	S	IPAHST	SELECT EFFDT ,SL_IPA_AMT FROM SL_IPA_HISTORY WHERE EMPLID=:1 AND SL_IPA_TYPE NOT IN ('7','9','H')
SPPNPENS	S	PNFCTR	SELECT F.SL_PEN_FACTOR FROM SL_RET_AGE_MULT F WHERE F.SL_AGE_TOT_MONTHS=:1
SPPNPENS	S	PPACCT	SELECT A.EFFDT ,B.SL_PP_BAL FROM SL_PP_ACCT_TRAN A ,SL_PP_ACCT_BAL B WHERE A.EMPLID=:1 AND A
SPPNPENS	S	PPINTR	SELECT A.EFFDT ,A.SL_INTEREST_RATE FROM SL_PP_INT_RATE A WHERE A.SL_PP_PLAN = 'A' AND A.EFFD

Note that the STMT_TEXT is the SQL, and when a block of COBOL code needs to be changed (maybe the data set isn't returning as expected), you change the statement in the STMT_TEXT, not the block of COBOL code. Using copy and paste pull out the text from the table, run it in SQL*Plus, and see if the result set is what is expected. In most cases the SQL can be slightly modified and very little if anything needs to be done to the COBOL program itself.

```
/*****************************************************************
*          DEFINES FOR SQL PROCESSING FOR PEOPLESOFT              *
*****************************************************************
      COPY SPCNPENS.
/*****************************************************************
*          SQL COMMUNICATION                                      *
*****************************************************************
       01  SQLRT.                         COPY PTCSQLRT.
```

```
/*****************************************************************
*           DATE WORK LINKAGE                                    *
******************************************************************
       01  DTWRK.                          COPY PTCDTWRK.
******************************************************************
*  END OF SQL DEFINES                                            *
******************************************************************
```

PTPSQLRT Module

The PTPSQLRT module handles the following in COBOL communication to the database:

- Executes SQL.
- Fetches result sets from the database.
- Processes DML statements Insert, Update, Delete.
- Handles COMMIT and ROLLBACK.
- Connects and disconnects from the database.
- Processes and disconnects cursors.
- Manages error handling.

Calling PTPSQLRT, the following format is used:

```
CALL 'PTPSQLRT' USING action,
            sqlrt,
            cursor,
            statement,
            bind-setup,
            bind-data,
            select-setup,
            select-data
```

Passing Parameters to PTPSQLRT

When passing parameters to PTPSQLRT, a single character code is used to specify the action. The single character codes are defined in the copybook PTCSQLRT.

```
02     ACTION-SELECT                PIC X              VALUE 'S'.
02     ACTION-FETCH                 PIC X              VALUE 'F'.
02     ACTION-UPDATE                PIC X              VALUE 'U'.
02     ACTION-COMMIT                PIC X              VALUE 'C'.
02     ACTION-ROLLBACK              PIC X              VALUE 'R'.
02     ACTION-DISCONNECT            PIC X              VALUE 'D'.
02     ACTION-DISCONNECT-ALL        PIC X              VALUE 'A'.
```

```
02    ACTION-CONNECT              PIC X          VALUE 'N'.
02    ACTION-ERROR                PIC X          VALUE 'E'.
02    ACTION-CLEAR-STMT           PIC X          VALUE 'L'.
02    ACTION-TRACE                PIC X          VALUE 'T'.
02    ACTION-START-BULK           PIC X          VALUE 'X'.
02    ACTION-STOP-BULK            PIC X          VALUE 'Y'.
02    ACTION-FLUSH-BULK           PIC X          VALUE 'Z'.
02    ACTION-DML-COUNT            PIC X          VALUE 'M'.
```

SQLRT

The SQLRT is the communications area of the PTPSQLRT; it stores information about the database, and the current run is stored there. All of the connectivity information is stored here: database platform, USERID, password, process instance, and job instance. A return code is passed back and should be evaluated to make certain connection and data retrieval with the PTCSQLRT copybook were successful.

The following code illustrates use of the parameters in a program:

```
/**************************************************************
Calling to retrieve the run control
**************************************************************/
CALL 'PTPSQLRT' USING   ACTION-SELECT OF SQLRT
                        SQLRT
                        SQL-CURSOR    OF S-RUNCTL
                        SQL-STMT      OF S-RUNCTL
                        BIND-SETUP    OF S-RUNCTL
                        BIND-DATA     OF S-RUNCTL
                        SELECT-SETUP  OF S-RUNCTL
                        SELECT-DATA   OF S-RUNCTL.
/**************************************************************
Error Handling
**************************************************************/
IF RTNCD-ERROR OF SQLRT
   MOVE 'GET-RUNCTL(SELECT)'  TO  ERR-SECTION OF SQLRT
   PERFORM ZZ000-SQL-ERROR
END-IF.
```

Calling to the SQLRT communications area:

```
/****************************************************************
B103-FETCH-RUNCTL-DATA.
   INITIALIZE SELECT-DATA OF S-RUNCTL.
   CALL 'PTPSQLRT' USING   ACTION-FETCH OF SQLRT
                           SQLRT
                           SQL-CURSOR OF S-RUNCTL.
B103-FETCH-RUNCTL-DATA-EXIT.
  EXIT.
/****************************************************************
B104-CHECK-FIRST-FETCH.
IF RTNCD-ERROR OF SQLRT
```

```
    IF RTNCD-END OF SQLRT
       DISPLAY 'Calculation Run Control Missing.'
       SET RTNCD-USER-ERROR OF SQLRT  TO  TRUE
       PERFORM ZZ000-SQL-ERROR
    ELSE
       MOVE 'GET-RUNCTL(FETCH)' TO  ERR-SECTION OF SQLRT
       PERFORM ZZ000-SQL-ERROR
    END-IF
  ELSE
    DISPLAY 'PROCESSING EMPLID: ' EMPLID OF S-RUNCTL ' '
    RECORD-COUNT
    ADD 1 TO RECORD-COUNT
  END-IF.
  B104-CHECK-FIRST-FETCH-EXIT.
  EXIT.
  /******************************************************************
  B105-CHECK-END-OF-CNTL.
    IF RTNCD-ERROR OF SQLRT
       IF RTNCD-END OF SQLRT
          DISPLAY 'END OF CONTROL RECORDS'
       ELSE
           MOVE 'GET-RUNCTL-DATA(FETCH)'
           TO  ERR-SECTION OF SQLRT
           PERFORM ZZ000-SQL-ERROR
           MOVE 'Y' TO ABORT-FLAG
        END-IF
  ELSE
     DISPLAY 'PROCESSING EMPLID...' EMPLID OF S-RUNCTL ' '
     RECORD-COUNT
     ADD 1 TO RECORD-COUNT
  END-IF.
  B105-CHECK-END-OF-CNTL-EXIT.
  EXIT.
```

Cursors

One of the nice programming features in COBOL, just as with PL/SQL, is the ability to use cursors, which provides the result set of an SQL statement you can then set the values returned in the cursor to be stored in memory with variables and use the variables throughout the program. When data retrieval is a one-time, one-row type of SELECT, SQL-CURSOR-COMMON can be reused and a cursor does not need to be declared. If multiple calls with multiple rows of data is the goal, then a cursor declaration is required. The following is an example:

```
/******************************************************************
B101-TEST-PRCSS-INSTANCE.
   CALL 'PTPSQLRT' USING ACTION-CONNECT OF SQLRT,
      SQLRT
      SQL-CURSOR-COMMON OF SQLRT.
```

```
   IF RTNCD-ERROR OF SQLRT
      MOVE 'SELECT-RUNCTL(CONNECT)' TO ERR-SECTION OF SQLRT
      PERFORM ZZ000-SQL-ERROR THRU ZZ000-SQL-ERROR
        MOVE 'Y' TO ABORT-FLAG
  END-IF.
  IF PROCESS-INSTANCE OF SQLRT NOT = ZEROS
       PERFORM B101-SET-RUN-STAT-PROCESS THRU
       B101-SET-RUN-STAT-PROCESS-EXIT
       MOVE PROCESS-INSTANCE OF SQLRT TO
       PROCESS-INSTANCE-ERRMSG OF W-PRC-INSTANCE
  ELSE
       CALL 'PTPRUNID' USING SQLRT
       PROCESS-INSTANCE-ERRMSG
       OF W-PRC-INSTANCE
  END-IF.
B101-TEST-PRCSS-INSTANCE-EXIT.
  EXIT.
```

SQL Statement Name

The SQL statement name is the name of the stored SQL statement. Remember earlier we discussed the names of the columns in PS_SQLSTMT_TBL, and how the SQL name is stored in the STMT_NAME column of the table. An example is S-RUNCNTL; this call may include Bind Setup/Data, Select Setup/Data, and SQL Cursor information. The code that follows is an example:

```
/******************************************************************
B102-SET-RUNCTL-CURSOR.
   DISPLAY 'Operator ID - SQLRT  ' OPRID OF SQLRT.
   DISPLAY 'Batch Run ID - SQLRT ' BATCH-RUN-ID OF SQLRT.
   MOVE OPRID        OF SQLRT  TO  OPRID        OF S-RUNCTL.
   MOVE BATCH-RUN-ID OF SQLRT  TO  BATCH-RUN-ID OF S-RUNCTL.
   DISPLAY 'Calculation Run Control:'.
   DISPLAY 'Operator ID  ' OPRID OF S-RUNCTL.
   DISPLAY 'Batch Run ID ' BATCH-RUN-ID OF S-RUNCTL.
   CALL 'PTPSQLRT' USING   ACTION-SELECT OF SQLRT
               SQLRT
   SQL-CURSOR    OF S-RUNCTL
                   SQL-STMT      OF S-RUNCTL
                   BIND-SETUP    OF S-RUNCTL
                   BIND-DATA     OF S-RUNCTL
                   SELECT-SETUP  OF S-RUNCTL
                   SELECT-DATA   OF S-RUNCTL.
IF RTNCD-ERROR OF SQLRT
   MOVE 'GET-RUNCTL(SELECT)'  TO  ERR-SECTION OF SQLRT
   PERFORM ZZ000-SQL-ERROR
END-IF.
B102-SET-RUNCTL-CURSOR-EXIT.
EXIT.
```

Bind

The sixth parameter in the call to PTPSQLRT given earlier is the Bind Data, which holds the bind variable values from the SQL statements. Each bind data value has a matching bind setup value; an example is when a bind variable is used in a WHERE clause of an SQL statement or in an INSERT statement. The following procedure is an example:

```
B210-GET-PERSONAL-DATA.
  IF DISPLAY-DIAGNOSTICS = 'Y'
     DISPLAY 'READING PERSONAL DATA...'
  END-IF.
  MOVE EMPLID OF S-RUNCTL TO EMPLID OF S-PERSONAL-DATA.
  CALL 'PTPSQLRT' USING   ACTION-SELECT OF SQLRT
                          SQLRT
                          SQL-CURSOR-COMMON OF SQLRT
                          SQL-STMT       OF S-PERSONAL-DATA
                          BIND-SETUP     OF S-PERSONAL-DATA
                          BIND-DATA      OF S-PERSONAL-DATA
                          SELECT-SETUP   OF S-PERSONAL-DATA
                          SELECT-DATA    OF S-PERSONAL-DATA.
  IF RTNCD-ERROR OF SQLRT
     MOVE 'GET-PERSONAL-DATA(SELECT)' TO ERR-SECTION OF SQLRT
     PERFORM ZZ000-SQL-ERROR
     MOVE 'Y' TO ABORT-FLAG
  END-IF.
  INITIALIZE SELECT-DATA OF S-PERSONAL-DATA.
  CALL 'PTPSQLRT' USING ACTION-FETCH OF SQLRT
                        SQLRT
                        SQL-CURSOR-COMMON OF SQLRT.
  IF RTNCD-ERROR OF SQLRT
  IF RTNCD-END OF SQLRT
                NEXT SENTENCE
  ELSE
     MOVE 'GET-PERSONAL-DATA(FETCH)'
     TO ERR-SECTION OF SQLRT
     MOVE 'Y' TO ABORT-FLAG
     PERFORM ZZ000-SQL-ERROR THRU
ZZ000-SQL-ERROR-EXIT
  END-IF
  END-IF.
  DISPLAY 'SELECT-DATA P ' SELECT-DATA   OF S-PERSONAL-DATA.
B210-GET-PERSONAL-DATA-EXIT.
  EXIT.
```

SELECT

The eighth parameter in our example call is the Select Data list; it retains the values that are returned from the FETCH. The return values in number and in data type correspond to the columns in the table that are returned with the select. The following is an example:

```
/***************************************************************
B220-GET-TOT-MO-AGE.
  IF DISPLAY-DIAGNOSTICS = 'Y'
      DISPLAY 'QUERYING/CALCULATING AGE IN MOS. AT RET...'
  END-IF.
      MOVE EMPLID OF S-RUNCTL TO EMPLID OF S-TOT-MO-AGE-AT-RET.
      CALL 'PTPSQLRT' USING   ACTION-SELECT OF SQLRT
                              SQLRT
                              SQL-CURSOR-COMMON OF SQLRT
                              SQL-STMT      OF S-TOT-MO-AGE-AT-RET
                              BIND-SETUP    OF S-TOT-MO-AGE-AT-RET
                              BIND-DATA     OF S-TOT-MO-AGE-AT-RET
                              SELECT-SETUP  OF S-TOT-MO-AGE-AT-RET
                              SELECT-DATA   OF S-TOT-MO-AGE-AT-RET.
   IF RTNCD-ERROR OF SQLRT
      MOVE 'GET-TOT-MO-AGE(SELECT)' TO ERR-SECTION OF SQLRT
PERFORM ZZ000-SQL-ERROR
       MOVE 'Y' TO ABORT-FLAG
  END-IF.
  INITIALIZE SELECT-DATA OF S-TOT-MO-AGE-AT-RET.
  CALL 'PTPSQLRT' USING ACTION-FETCH OF SQLRT
                        SQLRT
                        SQL-CURSOR-COMMON OF SQLRT.
  IF RTNCD-ERROR OF SQLRT
  IF RTNCD-END OF SQLRT
                  NEXT SENTENCE
  ELSE
     MOVE 'GET-TOT-MO-AGE(FETCH)'
     TO ERR-SECTION OF SQLRT
     MOVE 'Y' TO ABORT-FLAG
PERFORM ZZ000-SQL-ERROR THRU
      ZZ000-SQL-ERROR-EXIT
  END-IF
  END-IF.
B220-GET-TOT-MO-AGE-EXIT.
  EXIT.
```

Setup Lists

The Setup Lists are much more elaborate than we will explain here, but as a PeopleSoft developer where your primary role will be to maintain existing COBOL, not develop new programs, just note that the Setup List is an area for storage of the list of items that are declared and set up with a termination character of 'Z'. The following is an example of a simple Setup List:

```
01  S-CNT-MSG.
    02  SQL-STMT                PIC X(18)    VALUE 'PSPPYRUN_S_CNT_MSG'.
    02  BIND-SETUP.
        03  FILLER              PIC XXXX     VALUE ALL 'I'.
        03  FILLER              PIC X        VALUE 'Z'.
    02  BIND-DATA.
        03  PROCESS-INSTANCE    PIC S9(9)                COMP.
        03  FILLER              PIC X        VALUE 'Z'.
    02  SELECT-SETUP.
        03  FILLER              PIC X        VALUE ALL 'C'.
        03  FILLER              PIC X        VALUE 'Z'.
    02  SELECT-DATA.
        03  SELECT-X            PIC X.
        03  FILLER              PIC X        VALUE 'Z'.
```

Action

The basic actions in COBOL in PeopleSoft are as follows:

- CONNECT—Connects to the database

```
CALL 'PTPSQLRT' USING ACTION-CONNECT OR SQLRT
                        SQLRT
                        SQL-CURSOR-COMMON OF SQLRT
IF RTNCD-ERROR OF SQLRT
   MOVE 'TERM' TO ERR-SECTION OF SQLRT
   PERFORM ZZ000-SQL-ERROR THRU ZZ000-SQL-ERROR-EXIT
END-IF.
```

- DISCONNECT

```
CALL 'PTPSQLRT' USING ACTION-DISCONNECT OF SQLRT
                      SQLRT
IF RTNCD-ERROR OF SQLRT
   MOVE 'TERM' TO ERR-SECTION OF SQLRT
   PERFORM ZZ000-SQL-ERROR THRU ZZ000-SQL-ERROR-EXIT
END-IF.
```

- DISCONNECT ALL

```
CALL 'PTPSQLRT' USING ACTION-DISCONNECT-ALL OF SQLRT
                      SQLRT
```

```
IF RTNCD-ERROR OF SQLRT
   MOVE 'TERM' TO ERR-SECTION OF SQLRT
   PERFORM ZZ000-SQL-ERROR THRU ZZ000-SQL-ERROR-EXIT
END-IF.
```

■ ERROR and ACTION-ERROR

```
CALL 'PTPSQLRT' USING   ACTION-ERROR OF SQLRT
                        SQLRT.
 IF RUNNING-REMOTE-CALL OF NETRT
    IF RET-CODE-OK OF NETRT
       PERFORM ZZ050-NET-RESET THRU ZZ050-NET-RESET-EXIT
    END-IF
 PERFORM ZZ100-NET-TERMINATE THRU ZZ100-NET-TERMINATE-EXIT
 END-IF.
   COPY PSCRTNCD.
   .ACTION-ERROR
CALL 'PTPSQLRT' USING ACTION-DISCONNECT-ALL OF SQLRT
                      SQLRT
IF RTNCD-ERROR OF SQLRT
   MOVE 'TERM' TO ERR-SECTION OF SQLRT
   PERFORM ZZ000-SQL-ERROR THRU ZZ000-SQL-ERROR-EXIT
END-IF.
```

■ COMMIT and ACTION-COMMIT

```
/*****************************************************************
W121-COMMIT.
  CALL 'PTPSQLRT' USING ACTION-COMMIT OF SQLRT
                        SQLRT
                        SQL-CURSOR-COMMON OF SQLRT.
  IF RTNCD-ERROR OF SQLRT
     MOVE 'EARNINGS(COMMIT)' TO ERR-SECTION OF SQLRT
     PERFORM ZZ000-SQL-ERROR THRU ZZ000-SQL-ERROR-EXIT
     MOVE 'Y' TO ABORT-FLAG
  END-IF.
W121-COMMIT-EXIT.
  EXIT.
```

■ ROLLBACK and ACTION-ROLLBACK

```
CALL 'PTPSQLRT' USING ACTION-ROLLBACK OF SQLRT
                      SQLRT
IF RTNCD-ERROR OF SQLRT
   MOVE 'ROLLBACK' TO ERR-SECTION OF SQLRT
   PERFORM ZZ000-SQL-ERROR THRU ZZ000-SQL-ERROR-EXIT
END-IF.
```

- SELECT and ACTION-SELECT

```
/*****************************************************************
B102-SET-RUNCTL-CURSOR.
   DISPLAY 'Operator ID - SQLRT  ' OPRID OF SQLRT.
   DISPLAY 'Batch Run ID - SQLRT ' BATCH-RUN-ID OF SQLRT.
   MOVE OPRID        OF SQLRT  TO  OPRID        OF S-RUNCTL.
   MOVE BATCH-RUN-ID OF SQLRT  TO  BATCH-RUN-ID OF S-RUNCTL.
   DISPLAY 'Calculation Run Control:'.
   DISPLAY 'Operator ID  ' OPRID OF S-RUNCTL.
   DISPLAY 'Batch Run ID ' BATCH-RUN-ID OF S-RUNCTL.
   CALL 'PTPSQLRT' USING   ACTION-SELECT OF SQLRT
                           SQLRT
                           SQL-CURSOR    OF S-RUNCTL
                           SQL-STMT      OF S-RUNCTL
                           BIND-SETUP    OF S-RUNCTL
                           BIND-DATA     OF S-RUNCTL
                           SELECT-SETUP  OF S-RUNCTL
                           SELECT-DATA   OF S-RUNCTL.
   IF RTNCD-ERROR OF SQLRT
       MOVE 'GET-RUNCTL(SELECT)'  TO  ERR-SECTION OF SQLRT
   PERFORM ZZ000-SQL-ERROR
   END-IF.
   B102-SET-RUNCTL-CURSOR-EXIT.
   EXIT.
```

- FETCH and ACTION-FETCH

```
/*****************************************************************
B103-FETCH-RUNCTL-DATA.
   INITIALIZE SELECT-DATA OF S-RUNCTL.
   CALL 'PTPSQLRT' USING   ACTION-FETCH OF SQLRT
                            SQLRT
                            SQL-CURSOR OF S-RUNCTL.
B103-FETCH-RUNCTL-DATA-EXIT.
EXIT.
```

- UPDATE and ACTION-UPDATE

```
/*****************************************************************
W120-WRITE-ONE-EARN-REC.
     CALL 'PTPSQLRT' USING ACTION-UPDATE OF SQLRT
                           SQLRT
                           SQL-CURSOR OF I-CALCERN
                           SQL-STMT   OF I-CALCERN
                           BIND-SETUP OF I-CALCERN
                           BIND-DATA  OF I-CALCERN.
      IF RTNCD-ERROR OF SQLRT
         MOVE 'INSERT-EARNINGS'  TO  ERR-SECTION OF SQLRT
```

```
            PERFORM ZZ000-SQL-ERROR THRU ZZ000-SQL-ERROR-EXIT
            MOVE 'Y' TO ABORT-FLAG
         END-IF.
   W120-WRITE-ONE-EARN-REC-EXIT.
         EXIT.
```

Modifications

As stated earlier in this appendix, try to avoid modifications if you can, but from time to time they are a necessary evil. Take, for example, when PeopleSoft made the change in the COBOL file PSCLMTTB.cbl to allow for Roth 401(k) contributions and the recording of the limits for this type of contribution. Changes needed to be made in the COBOL; they were released in a bundle, but maybe your organization isn't as up on its bundles as it should be, and it is required that the changes be made manually. Let's take a look at the original copy of the program:

```
*****************************************************************
* PSCLMTTB - LIMIT (SECTION 415) RULES TABLE                    *
*****************************************************************
*               Confidentiality Information:                    *
* This module contains confidential and proprietary information *
* of PeopleSoft, Inc.; it is not to be copied, reproduced, or   *
* transmitted in any form, by any means, in whole or in part,   *
* nor is it to be used for any purpose other than that for      *
* which it is expressly provided under the applicable license   *
* agreement.                                                    *
* Copyright (c) 2004 PeopleSoft, Inc. All Rights Reserved.      *
*****************************************************************
*          $Date:  2004/08/10:12:54:20                          *
*       $Release:  HR89                                         *
*      $Revision:  101                                          *
*****************************************************************
* THE LIMIT RULES ARE LOADED AS THEY ARE USED.                  *
*****************************************************************
*****************************************************************
* MODIFIED FOR EDUCATION & GOVERNMENT                           *
* HP99999       RELEASE 8 TECHNICAL MERGE                       *
*****************************************************************
  02  LIMIT-TEST          PIC X       VALUE 'N'.
      88  LIMIT-TEST-NO               VALUE 'N'.
      88  LIMIT-TEST-YES              VALUE 'Y'.
  02  LIMIT-TYPE-COUNT    PIC 99      VALUE ZERO  COMP.
      88  LIMIT-TYPE-COUNT-MAX        VALUE 20.
  02  LIMIT-TYPE-TABLE                    OCCURS 20
                                          INDEXED BY
                                          LTTTB-IDX
                                          LTTTB-OTH-IDX.
```

```
03  LIMIT-TYPE          PIC X(4).
    88  LIMIT-401               VALUE '401'.
    88  LIMIT-402               VALUE '402'.
    88  LIMIT-403               VALUE '403'.
    88  LIMIT-415               VALUE '415'.
    88  LIMIT-415Z              VALUE '415Z'.
    88  LIMIT-457               VALUE '457'.
    88  REG-LIMIT               VALUE '401','402','403',
                                      '415','415Z','457'.
03  ERNCD-SPCL          PIC X(10).
03  PCT-OF-SALARY       PIC 999V9(5)        COMP-3.
03  MAX-BENEF-BASE      PIC 9(8)V99         COMP-3.
03  DED-YTD-MAX         PIC S9(8)V99        COMP-3.
03  ROLLOVER-ALLOWED    PIC X   VALUE 'N'.
    88  ROLLOVER-ALLOWED-YES    VALUE 'Y'.
    88  ROLLOVER-ALLOWED-NO     VALUE 'N' SPACE.
03  ALTA-SVC-YRS        PIC 999             COMP-3.
03  ALTB-ADDL-EXCL      PIC 9(8)V99         COMP-3.
03  ALTB-MAX-ADDL       PIC 9(8)V99         COMP-3.
03  PER-YEAR-EXPN       PIC 9(8)V99         COMP-3.
03  ANNL-CAP-EXPN       PIC 9(8)V99         COMP-3.
03  MAX-CAP-EXPN        PIC 9(8)V99         COMP-3.
03  ALT-402G-ELECTION   PIC X.
    88  ALT-402G-ELECTION-YES   VALUE 'Y'.
    88  ALT-402G-ELECTION-NO    VALUE 'N'.
    88  ALT-402G-ELECTION-AUTO  VALUE 'X'.
03  SERVICE-403B-PRORT  PIC X.
    88  SERVICE-403B-PRORT-FTE  VALUE 'F'.
    88  SERVICE-403B-PRORT-STD  VALUE 'S'.
03  MAX-457-CATCH-UP    PIC 9(8)V99         COMP-3.
03  EFFDT               PIC X(10).
03  IMPIN-COUNT         PIC 9999 VALUE ZERO COMP.
    88  IMPIN-COUNT-MAX         VALUE 50.
03  EXCLD-COUNT         PIC 9999 VALUE ZERO COMP.
    88  EXCLD-COUNT-MAX         VALUE 250.
03  INCLD-COUNT         PIC 9999 VALUE ZERO COMP.
   88  INCLD-COUNT-MAX         VALUE 250.
03  COORD-COUNT         PIC 99   VALUE ZERO COMP.
   88  COORD-COUNT-MAX         VALUE 10.
03  IMPIN-TABLE                         OCCURS 50
                                        INDEXED BY
                                        IMPIN-IDX.
04  PLAN-TYPE       PIC XX.
    88  PLAN-TYPE-DEDUCTION VALUE '00'.
04  BENEFIT-PLAN    PIC X(10).
04  DEDCD           PIC X(10).
04  DED-CLASS       PIC X.
03  EXCLD-TABLE                         OCCURS 250
                                        INDEXED BY
                                        EXCLD-IDX.
```

```
04  PLAN-TYPE        PIC XX.
    88  PLAN-TYPE-DEDUCTION VALUE '00'.
04  BENEFIT-PLAN     PIC X(10).
04  DEDCD            PIC X(10).
04  DED-CLASS        PIC X.
03  INCLD-TABLE                      OCCURS 250
                                     INDEXED BY
                                     INCLD-IDX.
04  PLAN-TYPE        PIC XX.
    88  PLAN-TYPE-DEDUCTION VALUE '00'.
04  BENEFIT-PLAN     PIC X(10).
04  DEDCD            PIC X(10).
04  DED-CLASS        PIC X.
03  COORD-TABLE                      OCCURS 10
                                     INDEXED BY
                                     COORD-IDX.
04  PLAN-TYPE        PIC XX.
    88  PLAN-TYPE-DEDUCTION VALUE '00'.
04  BENEFIT-PLAN     PIC X(10).
04  DEDCD            PIC X(10).
04  DED-CLASS        PIC X.
```

Here is the modified version of PSCLMTTB.cbl:

```
*****************************************************************
* PSCLMTTB - LIMIT (SECTION 415) RULES TABLE                    *
*****************************************************************
*               Confidentiality Information:                    *
* This module contains confidential and proprietary information *
* of Oracle; it is not to be copied, reproduced, or transmitted *
* in any form, by any means, in whole or in part, nor is it to  *
* be used for any purpose other than that for which it is       *
* expressly provided under the applicable license agreement.    *
* Copyright (C) 2007 Oracle. All Rights Reserved.               *
*****************************************************************
*          $Date:  2007/02/15:03:54:31                          *
*       $Release:  HR88SP1                                      *
*    $Resolution:  702297                                       *
*****************************************************************
* THE LIMIT RULES ARE LOADED AS THEY ARE USED.                  *
*****************************************************************
*****************************************************************
* MODIFIED FOR EDUCATION & GOVERNMENT                           *
* HP99999       RELEASE 8 TECHNICAL MERGE                       *
*****************************************************************
    02  LIMIT-TEST          PIC X        VALUE 'N'.
        88  LIMIT-TEST-NO                VALUE 'N'.
        88  LIMIT-TEST-YES               VALUE 'Y'.
    02  LIMIT-TYPE-COUNT    PIC 99       VALUE ZERO  COMP.
        88  LIMIT-TYPE-COUNT-MAX         VALUE 20.
```

```
02  LIMIT-TYPE-TABLE                      OCCURS 20
                                          INDEXED BY
                                          LTTTB-IDX
                                          LTTTB-OTH-IDX.
          03  LIMIT-TYPE          PIC X(4).
              88  LIMIT-401               VALUE '401'.
              88  LIMIT-401G              VALUE '401G'.
              88  LIMIT-402               VALUE '402'.
              88  LIMIT-403               VALUE '403'.
              88  LIMIT-415               VALUE '415'.
              88  LIMIT-415Z              VALUE '415Z'.
              88  LIMIT-457               VALUE '457'.
              88  REG-LIMIT               VALUE '401','401G',
                                   '402','403','415','415Z','457'.
          03  LIMIT-TYPE2         REDEFINES LIMIT-TYPE
                                  PIC X(2).
              88  LIMIT2-CHECK            VALUE 'CH'.
          03  ERNCD-SPCL          PIC X(10).
          03  PCT-OF-SALARY       PIC 999V9(5)         COMP-3.
          03  MAX-BENEF-BASE      PIC 9(8)V99          COMP-3.
          03  DED-YTD-MAX         PIC S9(8)V99         COMP-3.
          03  ROLLOVER-ALLOWED    PIC X   VALUE 'N'.
              88  ROLLOVER-ALLOWED-YES    VALUE 'Y'.
              88  ROLLOVER-ALLOWED-NO     VALUE 'N' SPACE.
          03  ALTA-SVC-YRS        PIC 999              COMP-3.
          03  ALTB-ADDL-EXCL      PIC 9(8)V99          COMP-3.
          03  ALTB-MAX-ADDL       PIC 9(8)V99          COMP-3.
          03  PER-YEAR-EXPN       PIC 9(8)V99          COMP-3.
          03  ANNL-CAP-EXPN       PIC 9(8)V99          COMP-3.
          03  MAX-CAP-EXPN        PIC 9(8)V99          COMP-3.
          03  ALT-402G-ELECTION   PIC X.
              88  ALT-402G-ELECTION-YES   VALUE 'Y'.
              88  ALT-402G-ELECTION-NO    VALUE 'N'.
              88  ALT-402G-ELECTION-AUTO  VALUE 'X'.
          03  SERVICE-403B-PRORT  PIC X.
              88  SERVICE-403B-PRORT-FTE  VALUE 'F'.
              88  SERVICE-403B-PRORT-STD  VALUE 'S'.
          03  MAX-457-CATCH-UP    PIC 9(8)V99          COMP-3.
          03  EFFDT               PIC X(10).
          03  IMPIN-COUNT         PIC 9999 VALUE ZERO COMP.
              88  IMPIN-COUNT-MAX         VALUE 50.
          03  EXCLD-COUNT         PIC 9999 VALUE ZERO COMP.
              88  EXCLD-COUNT-MAX         VALUE 250.
          03  INCLD-COUNT         PIC 9999 VALUE ZERO COMP.
              88  INCLD-COUNT-MAX         VALUE 250.
          03  COORD-COUNT         PIC 99   VALUE ZERO COMP.
              88  COORD-COUNT-MAX         VALUE 10.

          03  IMPIN-TABLE                       OCCURS 50
                                                INDEXED BY
                                                IMPIN-IDX.
```

```
        04  PLAN-TYPE        PIC XX.
            88  PLAN-TYPE-DEDUCTION VALUE '00'.

        04  BENEFIT-PLAN     PIC X(10).
        04  DEDCD            PIC X(10).
        04  DED-CLASS        PIC X.

    03  EXCLD-TABLE                        OCCURS 250
                                           INDEXED BY
                                           EXCLD-IDX.
        04  PLAN-TYPE        PIC XX.
            88  PLAN-TYPE-DEDUCTION VALUE '00'.

        04  BENEFIT-PLAN     PIC X(10).
        04  DEDCD            PIC X(10).
        04  DED-CLASS        PIC X.

    03  INCLD-TABLE                        OCCURS 250
                                           INDEXED BY
                                           INCLD-IDX.
        04  PLAN-TYPE        PIC XX.
            88  PLAN-TYPE-DEDUCTION VALUE '00'.

        04  BENEFIT-PLAN     PIC X(10).
        04  DEDCD            PIC X(10).
        04  DED-CLASS        PIC X.

    03  COORD-TABLE                        OCCURS 10
                                           INDEXED BY
                                           COORD-IDX.
        04  PLAN-TYPE        PIC XX.
            88  PLAN-TYPE-DEDUCTION VALUE '00'.

        04  BENEFIT-PLAN     PIC X(10).
        04  DEDCD            PIC X(10).
        04  DED-CLASS        PIC X.
```

Now let's take a look at the differences or the modification:

```
    03  LIMIT-TYPE           PIC X(4).
        88  LIMIT-401                VALUE '401'.
        88  LIMIT-401G               VALUE '401G'.
        88  LIMIT-402                VALUE '402'.
        88  LIMIT-403                VALUE '403'.
        88  LIMIT-415                VALUE '415'.
        88  LIMIT-415Z               VALUE '415Z'.
        88  LIMIT-457                VALUE '457'.
        88  REG-LIMIT                VALUE '401','401G',
                          '402','403','415','415Z','457'.
    03  LIMIT-TYPE2          REDEFINES LIMIT-TYPE
                             PIC X(2).
        88  LIMIT2-CHECK             VALUE 'CH'.
```

In the original version of this program, the LIMIT-401G did not exist; note it is added as a LIMIT-TYPE and as a REG-LIMIT Value. Also note that the original program did not have a LIMIT-TYPE2; these were added to allow for the contribution limit of the Roth 401(k) plan. No other modifications were required of this program, and it is important to learn to add and read these types of changes; they are very common in bundle releases.

Summary

This appendix includes an outline of the history of COBOL in PeopleSoft, along with an excellent history lesson, drawn from a blog from Grey Sparling. It explains the reason for no direct SQL from COBOL to the database and outlines the process of how to write SQL and store it in a table in the database. You've learned the importance of how to debug and look at the data that is in PS_SQLSTMT_TBL, and you learned about PTPSQLRT and the parameters that can be passed into this delivered module. And most important, the appendix reviews a modification from a delivered COBOL that was changed in a delivered module.

COBOL may be a legacy language, and very few organizations still develop new programs in the language, but its legacy remains with the maintenance and ability to debug existing COBOL programs. Let me add an important note provided by Steve Stein about speed performance: if your organization is running behind on updating to the next tools release, you can experience some performance issues. In one case that Steve experienced, the customer had a dramatic speed improvement in processing millions of transaction in a COBOL program for General Ledger allocations after upgrading to the later PeopleTools release. A PeopleSoft developer requires many skills, object-oriented programming as well as legacy structured COBOL coding skills. This appendix covers the basic skills to maintain and debug COBOL.

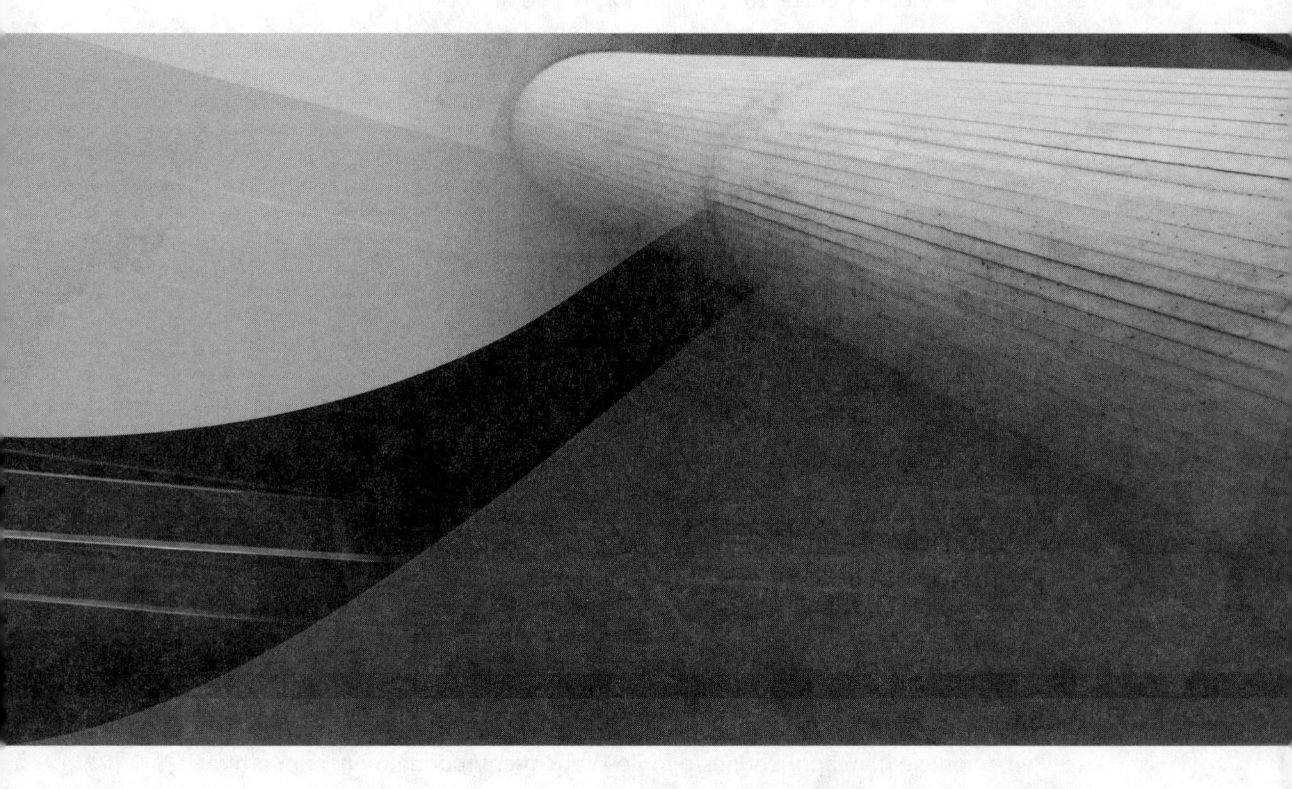

APPENDIX C

References

Chapter 1

- Enterprise PeopleTools 8.49 PeopleBooks
- **PeopleSoft from Wikipedia, the free encyclopedia**
  http://en.wikipedia.org/wiki/Peoplesoft
- **PeopleSoft HRMS** www.peoplesoft.com/corp/en/public_index.jsp
- **Enterprise PeopleTools 8.49 PeopleBooks** Appendix: Understanding Person Model Changes
- **PeopleSoft Enterprise Human Capital Management**
  www.oracle.com/applications/peoplesoft/hcm/ent/index.html
- **PeopleSoft Enterprise Absence Management**
  www.oracle.com/applications/peoplesoft/hcm/ent/module/absence_mgmt.html
- **PeopleSoft Enterprise Absence Management—Data Sheet**
  www.oracle.com/media/peoplesoft/en/pdf/datasheets/e_hcm_ds_absence_management.pdf
- **PeopleSoft Enterprise Benefits Administration**
  www.oracle.com/applications/peoplesoft/hcm/ent/module/ben_admin.html
- **PeopleSoft Enterprise eBenefits**
  www.oracle.com/applications/peoplesoft/hcm/ent/module/ebenefits.html
- **PeopleSoft Enterprise eCompensation**
  www.oracle.com/applications/peoplesoft/hcm/ent/module/ecomp.html
- **PeopleSoft Enterprise ePay**
  www.oracle.com/applications/peoplesoft/hcm/ent/module/epay.html
- **PeopleSoft Enterprise ePay—Data Sheet**
  www.oracle.com/media/peoplesoft/en/pdf/datasheets/enterprise-hcm-epay-data-sheet.pdf
- **PeopleSoft Enterprise eProfile**
  www.oracle.com/applications/peoplesoft/hcm/ent/module/eprofile.html
- **PeopleSoft Enterprise eProfile—Data Sheet**
  www.oracle.com/media/peoplesoft/en/pdf/datasheets/enterprise-hcm-eprofile-data-sheet.pdf
- **PeopleSoft Enterprise Payroll for North America**
  www.oracle.com/applications/peoplesoft/hcm/ent/module/payroll_na.html

- **PeopleSoft Enterprise Payroll for North America—Data Sheet**
  www.oracle.com/media/peoplesoft/en/pdf/datasheets/e_hcm_ds_payroll_na_0605.pdf
- **PeopleSoft Enterprise Pension Administration**
  www.oracle.com/applications/peoplesoft/hcm/ent/module/pen_admin.html
- **PeopleSoft Enterprise Stock Administration**
  www.oracle.com/applications/peoplesoft/hcm/ent/module/stock_admin.html
- **Stock Administration—Data Sheet**
  www.oracle.com/media/peoplesoft/en/pdf/datasheets/e_hcm_ds_stockadmin_04_05.pdf
- **Oracle PeopleSoft Enterprise Time and Labor**
  www.oracle.com/applications/peoplesoft/hcm/ent/module/time_labor.html
- **PeopleSoft Enterprise Talent Acquisition Manager**
  www.oracle.com/applications/peoplesoft/hcm/ent/module/erecruit_mgr.html
- **PeopleSoft Enterprise Candidate Gateway**
  www.oracle.com/applications/peoplesoft/hcm/ent/module/erecruit.html
- **PeopleSoft Enterprise Candidate Gateway—Data Sheet**
  www.oracle.com/media/peoplesoft/en/pdf/datasheets/enterprise-hcm-candidate-gateway-data-sheet.pdf
- **PeopleSoft Enterprise eDevelopment**
  www.oracle.com/applications/peoplesoft/hcm/ent/module/edev.html
- **PeopleSoft Enterprise eDevelopment—Data Sheet**
  www.oracle.com/media/peoplesoft/en/pdf/datasheets/e_hcm_ds_edevelopment_04_05.pdf
- **PeopleSoft Enterprise ePerformance**
  www.oracle.com/applications/peoplesoft/hcm/ent/module/eperformance.html
- **PeopleSoft Enterprise Learning Management**
  www.oracle.com/applications/peoplesoft/hcm/ent/module/learning_mgmt.html
- **PeopleSoft Enterprise Services Procurement**
  www.oracle.com/applications/peoplesoft/srm/ent/module/svc_procure.html
- **PeopleSoft Services Procurement**
  www.oracle.com/media/peoplesoft/en/pdf/datasheets/e_srm_ds_servicespro_05_05.pdf
- **PeopleSoft Enterprise Talent Acquisition Manager—Data Sheet**
  www.oracle.com/media/peoplesoft/en/pdf/datasheets/e_hcm_ds_talent_acquisition_manager.pdf

Chapter 2

- Enterprise PeopleTools 8.49 PeopleBook: PeopleCode API Reference
- Enterprise PeopleTools 8.49 PeopleBook: Internet Technology

Chapter 3

- Enterprise PeopleTools 8.49 PeopleBook: PeopleCode API Reference
- Enterprise PeopleTools 8.49 PeopleBook: Internet Technology

Chapter 4

- *Essential Guide to PeopleSoft Development and Customization* by Tony DeLia, Galina Landres, Isador Rivera, and Prakash Sankaran (Manning Publications Co., 2001)
- Enterprise PeopleTools 8.49 PeopleBooks: PeopleSoft Application Designer

Chapter 5

- *Essential Guide to PeopleSoft Development and Customization* by Tony DeLia, Galina Landres, Isador Rivera, and Prakash Sankaran (Manning Publications Co., 2001)
- Enterprise PeopleTools 8.49 PeopleBook: PeopleCode Developer's Guide

Chapter 6

- Enterprise PeopleTools 8.49 PeopleBook: PeopleCode Developer's Guide
- Enterprise PeopleTools 8.49 PeopleBook: PeopleCode Language Reference

Chapter 7

- Enterprise PeopleTools 8.49 PeopleBook: PeopleCode Developer's Guide
- Enterprise PeopleTools 8.49 PeopleBook: PeopleCode Language Reference
- **"Navigating the Component Buffer"** Kevin Reschenberg, 2006, www.sparkpath.com/techtalk-20061220.php

- **"Browse the App Server Filesystem via iScript"** Chris Heller and David Bain, 2007, www.erpassociates.com/peoplesoft-corner-weblog/peopletools/browse-the-app-server-filesystem-via-iscript.html
- **"Advanced PeopleTools Tips and Techniques"** Chris Heller, 2007, http://blog.greysparling.com/Alliance2007_AdvancedPeopleToolsTechniques_Posted.ppt

Chapter 8

- *Learn XML in a Weekend* by Erik Westermann (The Premier Press, 2002)
- **SOAP Standards** www.w3.org/TR/soap/
- **"XML Publisher within PeopleSoft"** http://peoplesofttipster.com/2007/05/24/xml-publisher-within-peoplesoft/
- **"Using PeopleSoft SOAP Classes"** www.zutshigroup.com/site/tech/peoplesoft_soap_example
- **XML Instructions and Template** www.oracle.com/technology/obe/obe_bi/xmlp_ps/index.html#t4
- **Report Templates** www.adobe.com/svg/viewer/install

Chapter 9

- Enterprise PeopleTools 8.49 PeopleBooks: PeopleSoft Query
- **"History of Tree Manager"** Larry Grey, 2007, http://blog.greysparling.com/labels/History.html

Chapter 10

- SQR I—Guide Title STU-430-812a
- *PeopleSoft Inc. PeopleTools 8.12* by Jim Gutenkauf (PeopleSoft, Inc., 2001) Contributors: Ed Kelly, Jeff Allen, Nancy Kenney, Andy Daugherty, Gail Alaska, Greg Ahearn, and Tim Burns
- Enterprise PeopleTools 8.49 PeopleBooks: SQR for PeopleSoft Developers
- Enterprise PeopleTools 8.49 PeopleBooks: SQR Language Reference for PeopleSoft

- *SQR in PeopleSoft and Other Applications* by Galina Landres and Vlad Landres (Manning Publications Co., 1999)
- **"SQR vs. Application Engine"** Chris Heller, 2007, http://blog.greysparling.com/2007/02/sqr-vs-application-engine.html

Chapter 11

- Application Engine—Guide Title STU-411-840
- *PeopleSoft Inc. PeopleTools 8.40* (PeopleSoft, Inc., 2000) Contributors: Cathy DeFeo, Adam Langley, Trudy How, Greg Salmon, Tom Spol, Randy Geyer, Harrison Kiai, Scott Sarris, Shyam Ranngaratham, Andy Daugherty, and Ed Kelly
- Enterprise PeopleTools 8.49 PeopleBooks: PeopleSoft Application Engine
- **"A Brief History of PeopleTools 9"** Larry Grey, 2007, http://blog.greysparling.com/labels/History.html

Chapter 12

- https://www.peoplesoft.com/corp/en/login.jsp
- http://jjmpsj.blogspot.com/
- http://blogs.oracle.com/jesper_andersen/
- http://oraclefusion.blogspot.com/
- http://blog.psftdba.com/
- http://peoplesoftexperts.blogspot.com/
- http://psguyblog.blogspot.com/index.html
- http://manalang.wordpress.com/2006/02/01/adding-live-search-to-peoplesoft-enterprise/
- http://blog.greysparling.com/
- www.searchpsoft.com/
- **"nVision with Query Prompts"** Brian Sparling, Chris Heller, and Larry Grey, 2007, http://blog.greysparling.com/2006/05/nvision-with-query-prompts.html
- www.oracle.com/technology/documentation/psftent.html

- www.questdirect.org/questdirect/
- www.ioug.org/networking/peoplesoft.cfm
- http://peoplesoft.ittoolbox.com/groups/#
- http://tech.groups.yahoo.com/group/peoplesoft-fans/

Appendix A

- *Oracle PL/SQL Programming, Third Edition* by Steven Feuerstein and Bill Pribyl (O'Reilly, 2002)

Appendix B

- *Essential Guide to PeopleSoft Development and Customization* by Tony DeLia, Galina Landres, Isador Rivera, and Prakash Sankaran (Manning Publications Co., 2001)
- *Advanced ANSI COBOL with Structured Programming for VS COBOL II and Microsoft/Micro Focus COBOL, Second Edition* by Gary DeWard Brown (John Wiley & Sons, Inc., 1992)
- *COBOL from Micro to Mainframe, Second Edition* by Robert T. Grauer and Carol Vazquez Villar (Prentice-Hall, Inc., 1994)
- *Fundamentals of Structured COBOL, Third Edition* by Robert C. Nickerson (HarperCollins Publishers Inc., 1991)

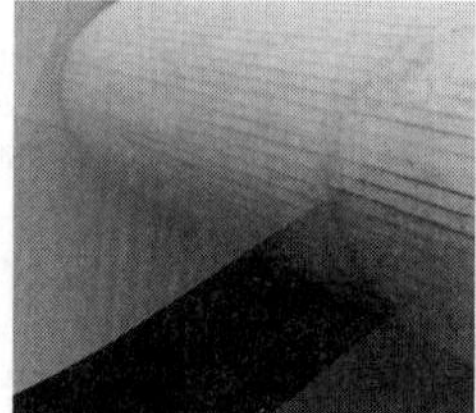

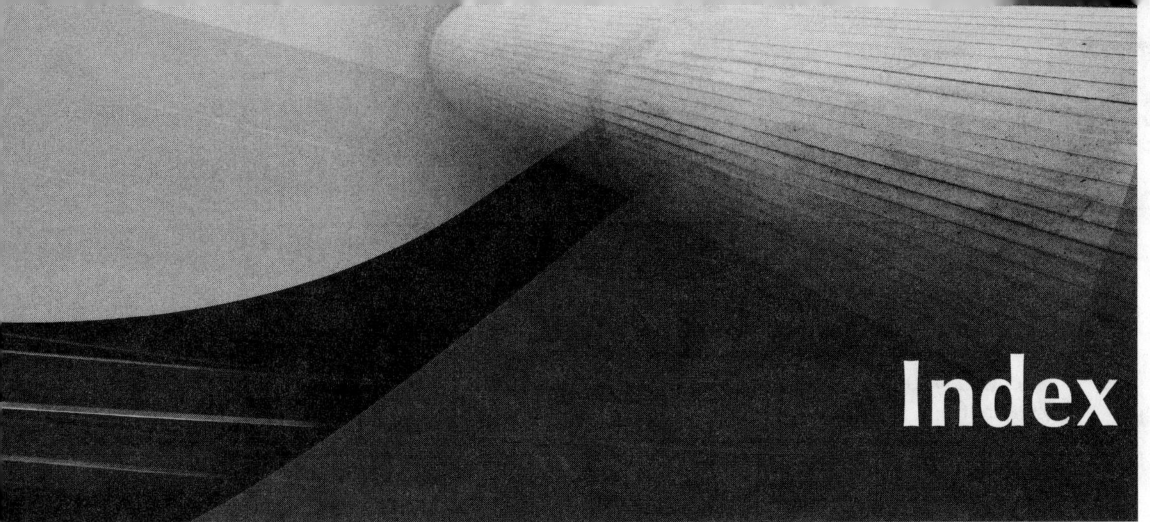

Index

References to figures are in italics.

A

D

E

F

G

H

I

J

L

M

N

O

P

Q

R

S